NON-DISCRIMINATION IN INTERNATIONAL TRADE IN SERVICES

The principle of non-discrimination is fundamental to the regulation of international trade in goods and services. In the context of trade in goods, the concept of 'like products' has become a key element of the legal analysis of whether a trade obstacle violates GATT non-discrimination obligations. The equivalent concept of 'like services and service suppliers' in GATS rules on non-discrimination has received little attention in WTO jurisprudence. In light of the remaining uncertainties, Nicolas Diebold analyses the legal problems of the GATS 'like services and services suppliers' concept using a contextual and comparative methodology. The 'likeness' element is not analysed in isolation, but in context with 'less favourable treatment' and regulatory purpose as additional elements of non-discrimination. The book also explores how far theories from non-discrimination rules in GATT, NAFTA, BITs and EU law, as well as market definition theories from competition law, may be applied to 'likeness' in GATS.

NICOLAS F. DIEBOLD is an attorney with Froriep Renggli, Zurich. He was formerly with the Department of Economic Law and the World Trade Institute, University of Bern.

CAMBRIDGE INTERNATIONAL TRADE AND ECONOMIC LAW

As the processes of regionalization and globalization have intensified, there have been accompanying increases in the regulations of international trade and economic law at the levels of international, regional and national laws.

The subject matter of this series is international economic law. Its core is the regulation of international trade, investment and cognate areas such as intellectual property and competition policy. The series publishes books on related regulatory areas, in particular human rights, labour, environment and culture, as well as sustainable development. These areas are vertically linked at the international, regional and national level, and the series extends to the implementation of these rules at these different levels. The series also includes works on governance, dealing with the structure and operation of related international organisations in the field of international economic law, and the way they interact with other subjects of international and national law.

Series Editors

Dr Lorand Bartels, *University of Cambridge*
Professor Thomas Cottier, *University of Bern*
Professor William Davey, *University of Illinois*

Books in the series

Trade Policy Flexibility and Enforcement in the WTO: A Law and Economics Analysis
Simon A.B. Schropp

The Multilaterization of International Investment Law
Stephan W. Schill

The Law, Economics and Politics of Retaliation in WTO Dispute Settlement
Edited by Chad P. Bown and Joost Pauwelyn

Non-Discrimination in International Trade in Services: 'Likeness' in WTO/GATS
Nicolas F. Diebold

NON-DISCRIMINATION IN INTERNATIONAL TRADE IN SERVICES

'Likeness' in WTO/GATS

NICOLAS F. DIEBOLD

CAMBRIDGE
UNIVERSITY PRESS

CAMBRIDGE UNIVERSITY PRESS
Cambridge, New York, Melbourne, Madrid, Cape Town, Singapore,
São Paulo, Delhi, Dubai, Tokyo, Mexico City

Cambridge University Press
The Edinburgh Building, Cambridge CB2 8RU, UK

Published in the United States of America by Cambridge University Press, New York

www.cambridge.org
Information on this title: www.cambridge.org/9780521191869

First published 2010

Printed in the United Kingdom at the University Press, Cambridge

A catalogue record for this publication is available from the British Library

Library of Congress Cataloguing in Publication data
Diebold, Nicolas F.
Non-discrimination in international trade in services : 'likeness' in
WTO/GATS / Nicolas F. Diebold.
p. cm. – (Cambridge international trade and economic law ; 4)
Includes bibliographical references and index.
ISBN 978-0-521-19186-9
1. General Agreement on Trade in Services (1994) 2. Service industries–Government
policy. 3. Trade regulation. I. Title. II. Series.
HD9980.6.D54 2010
382′.92–dc22
2010022111

ISBN 978-0-521-19186-9 Hardback

To my wife Valerie and our children

SUMMARY OF CONTENTS

CONTENTS

FOREWORD

The scope and definition of like products has always been at the heart of World Trade Organization (WTO) jurisprudence relating to Articles I and III of the General Agreement on Tariffs and Trade (GATT). It is the core of the fundamental principle of national treatment and its practical operation in international trade regulation. The General Agreement on Trade in Services (GATS) is built upon the same foundations, albeit, national treatment assumes a fundamentally different role of allowing for progressive liberalization. Accordingly, the role and function of likeness is not necessarily the same as in the field of goods. There are differences in the treaty texts. Moreover, and unlike GATT, dispute settlement has not brought about further clarification of the subject. The legal development in the field, some 15 years after the adoption of the new Agreement, is still in its infant stage.

The present book analyses the problem of likeness in the context of services in great depth, based upon the findings in GATT, and further developing the field in light of insights gained in the field of competition law. The different structure of services – short of physical properties and the absence of border measures – requires a new and fresh approach in addressing the goal of securing equal and fair conditions of competition for imported services. The author builds upon insights that the problem should, in the field of services, be addressed mainly in terms of substitution of demand, and that the analysis can be largely based on respective criteria developed in domestic competition law. The approach reflects an increasing transition in international trade regulation from border measures to domestic regulation. It may, in the future, also be of interest and relevant in the field of goods, with a view to achieve an overall coherent approach in the analysis of likeness, both in goods and services. The present thesis offers a substantial and in-depth contribution. It will greatly assist the development of an appropriate doctrine in case law and practice. The book is both highly relevant for theory as well as legal practice.

Research and the resulting book evolved while Nicolas Diebold was a research fellow at the Department of Economic Law and the World Trade Institute at the University of Bern, Switzerland, from 2007–2008. His PhD was completed during a subsequent one-year visit at Stanford University Law School, working with Professor Alan Sykes. Nicolas emerged as a meticulous and thoughtful researcher and writer, and discussions with him have been inspiring and a challenge. He was always far ahead in the subject matter and my contribution to debating underlying issues and philosophies was inherently limited to conceptual issues and to linking thoughts to other and comparable regulatory issues. It was a privilege to accompany him in this process. His work will mark a leading contribution to the subject of non-discrimination in the international regulation of services.

Prof. Thomas Cottier
Bern, January 2010

ACKNOWLEDGEMENTS

The writing of this doctoral thesis accompanied me over different stages of my professional life and it is my great pleasure to thank those who made this book possible. I owe my deepest gratitude to my supervisor and mentor in academic matters, Professor Thomas Cottier. His encouragement, guidance and support made the writing of this doctoral thesis and my time as research and teaching fellow at the University of Bern and the World Trade Institute a most enjoyable, motivating and rewarding experience. Moreover, I am thankful to Professor Markus Krajewski for the time-intense work of writing the second evaluation report and for contributing valuable comments.

This book greatly profited from the opportunity to conduct research as a visiting scholar at Stanford Law School. I would like to thank Professor Alan Sykes for acting as my faculty sponsor and for sharing his thoughts on a number of issues covered in this book. I am also thankful to Charles Koob, a great lecturer in US antitrust law, who inspired many of my ideas on market definition. My stay at Stanford would not have been possible without the generous fellowship for prospective researchers from the Swiss National Science Foundation.

My interest in international economic law was first awoken during my studies at Duke Law School. I am most grateful to Professor Joost Pauwelyn who taught me the principles of WTO law at Duke and who made his support for this book available in a number of ways. A very special thank you also goes to Professor Marion Panizzon for integrating my thesis in the research project on trade in services with the NCCR Trade Regulation. I am further indebted to many of my colleagues for supporting me during my time as a PhD student, in particular Professor Matthias Oesch and Rachel Liechti from the University of Bern as well as Pierre Sauvé, Professor Panagiotis Delimatsis and Martín Molinuevo from the NCCR Trade Regulation.

I am most thankful to my parents, Mechthild and Paul Diebold, who always approved of my undertakings and enabled me to pursue the studies in law at the University of Geneva. Most importantly, this book would not have been possible without the continuous and infinite love, encouragement and support from my wife Valerie. Her motivation and belief in my capabilities as well as her dedication to our family gave me the necessary determination and focus to complete this book. Lastly, our children have not only been a great source of inspiration, but they also provided the needed distraction and helped me to keep things in the right perspective.

Nicolas F. Diebold

January 2010

ABBREVIATIONS

AB	Appellate Body
ABA	American Bar Association
ACP	African, Caribbean and Pacific
AD Agreement	Agreement on Implementation of Article VI of the General Agreement on Tariffs and Trade 1994 (Anti-dumping Agreement)
aff'd	affirmed
AoA	Agreement on Agriculture
Art./Arts.	Article/Articles
ASEAN	Association of Southeast Asian Nations
ATC	Agreement on Textiles and Clothing (terminated on 1 January 2005)
BGH	Bundesgerichtshof
BIT/BITs	Bilateral investment treaty/treaties
cert.	certiorari
CETS	Council of Europe Treaty Series
Cir.	Circuit
CPC	Central product classification
CTFS	Committee on Trade in Financial Services
CTG	Council for Trade in Goods
CTS	Council for Trade in Services
CVA	Canadian value added
DCS	Directly competitive or substitutable
DSU	Understanding on Rules and Procedures Governing the Settlement of Disputes (Dispute Settlement Understanding)
EC	European Communities
ECJ	European Court of Justice
e-commerce	Electronic commerce
ECR	European Court Reports
ECSC	European Coal and Steel Community
EEC	European Economic Community
EU	European Union

Euratom	European Atomic Energy Community
FTA	Free trade agreement
FTC	Federal Trade Commission
GATS	General Agreement on Trade in Services
GATT	General Agreement on Tariffs and Trade
GNS	Group of Negotiations on Services (Uruguay Round)
HFCS	High-fructose corn syrup
ICSID	International Centre for Settlement of Investment Disputes
IIA	International investment agreement
ILM	International Legal Materials
LCIA	London Court of International Arbitration
Member	Member State of the World Trade Organization
MFN	Most-favoured-nation
MTN	Multilateral trade negotiations (Uruguay Round)
NAFTA	North American Free Trade Agreement
NGR	Negotiating Group on Rules
NT	National treatment
OECD	Organization for Economic Co-operation and Development
OJ	Official Journal of the European Communities
passim	here and there
PCB	Polychlorinated biphenyl
PPM/PPMs	Process and production method/methods
Prov.	Provisional
Rev'd	Reversed
SA	Agreement on Safeguards (Safeguards Agreement)
SCC	Stockholm Chamber of Commerce
SCM Agreement	Agreement on Subsidies and Countervailing Measures
SDMI	S.D. Myers, Inc.
SPF	Spruce–pine–fir (softwood lumber)
SPS Agreement	Agreement on the Application of Sanitary and Phytosanitary Measures
SR	Systematische Sammlung des Bundesrechts (Switzerland)
SSM	Service supply method
SSNDP	Small but significant non-transitory decrease in price
SSNIP	Small but significant non-transitory increase in price
SSRN	Social Science Research Network
Stat.	United States Statutes at Large
TBT Agreement	Agreement on Technical Barriers to Trade
TEC	Treaty establishing the European Community
TFEU	Treaty on the Functioning of the European Union (formerly TEC)
TNC	Trade Negotiations Committee (ministerial level overseeing Uruguay Round)

TRIMs Agreement	Agreement on Trade-Related Investment Measures
TRIPs Agreement	Agreement on Trade-Related Aspects of Intellectual Property Rights
U.S.C.	United States Code
UK	United Kingdom of Great Britain and Northern Ireland
UN	United Nations
UNCITRAL	United Nations Commission on International Trade Law
UNCTAD	United Nations Conference on Trade and Development
UNTS	United Nations Treaty Series
US/U.S./USA	United States of America
VAT	Value added tax
VCLT	Vienna Convention on the Law of Treaties
Ver.	Version
WGTCP	Working Group on the Interaction between Trade and Competition Policy
WPDR	Working Party on Domestic Regulation
WPGR	Working Party on GATS Rules
WTO	World Trade Organization
WuW/E BGH	Wirtschaft und Wettbewerb – Entscheidungssammlung des Bundesgerichtshofs

LIST OF CASES

List of full case names and references for short form citations used in the book.

WTO Panel and Appellate Body Reports

Argentina – Hides and Leather: Panel Report, Argentina – Measures Affecting the Export of Bovine Hides and Import of Finished Leather, WT/DS155/R and Corr.1, adopted 16 February 2001, DSR 2001:V, 1779

Australia – Salmon (Article 21.5 – Canada): Panel Report, Australia – Measures Affecting Importation of Salmon – Recourse to Article 21.5 of the DSU by Canada, WT/DS18/RW, adopted 20 March 2000, DSR 2000:IV, 2031

Australia – Salmon: Appellate Body Report, Australia – Measures Affecting Importation of Salmon, WT/DS18/AB/R, adopted 6 November 1998, DSR 1998:VIII, 3327

Brazil – Retreaded Tyres: Brazil – Measures Affecting Imports of Retreaded Tyres
Panel Report, WT/DS332/R, adopted 17 December 2007, as modified by Appellate Body Report
Appellate Body Report, WT/DS332/AB/R, adopted 17 December 2007

Canada – Aircraft: Appellate Body Report, Canada – Measures Affecting the Export of Civilian Aircraft, WT/DS70/AB/R, adopted 20 August 1999, DSR 1999:III, 1377

Canada – Autos: Canada – Certain Measures Affecting the Automotive Industry
Panel Report, WT/DS139/R, WT/DS142/R, adopted 19 June 2000, as modified by Appellate Body Report, DSR 2000:VII, 3043
Appellate Body Report, WT/DS139/AB/R, WT/DS142/AB/R, adopted 19 June 2000, DSR 2000:VI, 2985

Canada – Periodicals: Canada – Certain Measures Concerning Periodicals
Panel Report, WT/DS31/R and Corr.1, adopted 30 July 1997, as modified by Appellate Body Report, DSR 1997:I, 481
Appellate Body Report, WT/DS31/AB/R, adopted 30 July 1997, DSR 1997:I, 449

Canada – Wheat Exports and Grain Imports: Panel Report, Canada – Measures Relating to Exports of Wheat and Treatment of Imported Grain, WT/DS276/R,

21.5 of the DSU by Ecuador, WT/DS27/RW/ECU, adopted 6 May 1999, DSR 1999:II, 803

EC – Bananas III: European Communities – Regime for the Importation, Sale and Distribution of Bananas

Panel Report, *Complaint by the United States*, WT/DS27/R/USA, adopted 25 September 1997, as modified by Appellate Body Report, DSR 1997:II, 943

Appellate Body Report, WT/DS27/AB/R, adopted 25 September 1997, DSR 1997:II, 591

EC – Certain Measures Prohibiting the Importation and Marketing of Seal Products: DS 369, request for consultations, 25 September 2007.

EC – Hormones: European Communities – Measures Concerning Meat and Meat Products (Hormones)

Panel Report, Complaint by the United States, WT/DS26/R/USA, adopted 13 February 1998, as modified by Appellate Body Report, DSR 1998:III, 699

Appellate Body Report, WT/DS26/AB/R, WT/DS48/AB/R, adopted 13 February 1998, DSR 1998:I, 135

EC – Salmon (Norway): Panel Report, European Communities – Anti-Dumping Measure on Farmed Salmon from Norway, WT/DS337/R, adopted 15 January 2008, and Corr.1

EC – Tariff Preferences: Panel Report, European Communities – Conditions for the Granting of Tariff Preferences to Developing Countries, WT/DS246/R, adopted 20 April 2004, as modified by Appellate Body Report WT/DS/246/AB/R, DSR 2004:III, 1009

EC – Trademarks and Geographical Indications (Australia): Panel Report, European Communities – Protection of Trademarks and Geographical Indications for Agricultural Products and Foodstuffs, Complaint by Australia, WT/DS290/R, adopted 20 April 2005, DSR 2005:X, 4603

EC – Trademarks and Geographical Indications (US): Panel Report, European Communities – Protection of Trademarks and Geographical Indications for Agricultural Products and Foodstuffs, Complaint by the United States, WT/DS174/R, adopted 20 April 2005, DSR 2005:VIII, 3499

Indonesia – Autos: Panel Report, Indonesia – Certain Measures Affecting the Automobile Industry, WT/DS54/R, WT/DS55/R, WT/DS59/R, WT/DS64/R and Corr.1 and 2, adopted 23 July 1998, and Corr. 3 and 4, DSR 1998:VI, 2201

Japan – Alcoholic Beverages II: Japan – Taxes on Alcoholic Beverages

Panel Report, WT/DS8/R, WT/DS10/R, WT/DS11/R, adopted 1 November 1996

Appellate Body Report, WT/DS8/AB/R, WT/DS10/AB/R, WT/DS11/AB/R, adopted 1 November 1996, DSR 1996:I, 97

Korea – Alcoholic Beverages: Korea – Taxes on Alcoholic Beverages

Panel Report, WT/DS75/R, WT/DS84/R, adopted 17 February 1999, as modified by Appellate Body Report, DSR 1999:I, 44

Appellate Body Report, WT/DS75/AB/R, WT/DS84/AB/R, adopted 17 February 1999, DSR 1999:I, 3

Korea – Certain Paper: Panel Report, Korea – Anti-Dumping Duties on Imports of Certain Paper from Indonesia, WT/DS312/R, adopted 28 November 2005, DSR 2005:XXII, 10637

Korea – Commercial Vessel: Panel Report, Korea – Measures Affecting Trade in Commercial Vessels, WT/DS273/R, adopted 11 April 2005, DSR 2005:VII, 2749

Korea – Various Measures on Beef: Korea – Measures Affecting Imports of Fresh, Chilled and Frozen Beef

Panel Report, WT/DS161/R, WT/DS169/R, adopted 10 January 2001, as modified by Appellate Body Report, DSR 2001:I, 59

Appellate Body Report, WT/DS161/AB/R, WT/DS169/AB/R, adopted 10 January 2001, DSR 2001:I, 5

Mexico – Taxes on Soft Drinks: Panel Report, Mexico – Tax Measures on Soft Drinks and Other Beverages, WT/DS308/R, adopted 24 March 2006, as modified by Appellate Body Report WT/DS308/AB/R, DSR 2006:I, 43

Mexico – Telecoms: Panel Report, Mexico – Measures Affecting Telecommunications Services, WT/DS204/R, adopted 1 June 2004, DSR 2004:IV, 1537

Turkey – Rice: Panel Report, Turkey – Measures Affecting the Importation of Rice, WT/DS334/R, adopted 22 October 2007

US – Certain EC Products: Panel Report, United States – Import Measures on Certain Products from the European Communities, WT/DS165/R and Add.1, adopted 10 January 2001, as modified by Appellate Body Report WT/DS165/AB/R, DSR 2001:II, 413

US – Export Restraints: Panel Report, United States – Measures Treating Exports Restraints as Subsidies, WT/DS194/R and Corr.2, adopted 23 August 2001, DSR 2001:XI, 5767

US – FSC (Article 21.5 – EC): Panel Report, United States – Tax Treatment for 'Foreign Sales Corporations' – Recourse to Article 21.5 of the DSU by the European Communities, WT/DS108/RW, adopted 29 January 2002, as modified by Appellate Body Report WT/DS108/AB/RW, DSR 2002:I, 119

US – FSC: United States – Tax Treatment for 'Foreign Sales Corporations'

Panel Report, WT/DS108/R, adopted 20 March 2000, as modified by Appellate Body Report, DSR 2000:IV, 1675

Appellate Body Report, WT/DS108/AB/R, adopted 20 March 2000, DSR 2000:III, 1619

US – Gambling: United States – Measures Affecting the Cross-Border Supply of Gambling and Betting Services

Panel Report, WT/DS285/R, adopted 20 April 2005, as modified by Appellate Body Report, DSR 2005:XII, 5797

Appellate Body Report, WT/DS285/AB/R, adopted 20 April 2005, DSR 2005:XII, 5663 (Corr.1, DSR 2006:XII, 5475)

US – Gasoline: United States – Standards for Reformulated and Conventional Gasoline

Panel Report, WT/DS2/R, adopted 20 May 1996, as modified by Appellate Body Report, DSR 1996:I, 29

Appellate Body Report, WT/DS2/AB/R, adopted 20 May 1996, DSR 1996:I, 3

US – Section 211 Appropriations Act: Appellate Body Report, United States – Section 211 Omnibus Appropriations Act of 1998, WT/DS176/AB/R, adopted 1 February 2002, DSR 2002:II, 589

US – Shrimp: United States – Import Prohibition of Certain Shrimp and Shrimp Products

Panel Report, WT/DS58/R and Corr.1, adopted 6 November 1998, as modified by Appellate Body Report, DSR 1998:VII, 2821

Appellate Body Report, WT/DS58/AB/R, adopted 6 November 1998, DSR 1998:VII, 2755

US – Softwood Lumber IV: Appellate Body Report, United States – Final Countervailing Duty Determination with Respect to Certain Softwood Lumber from Canada, WT/DS257/AB/R, adopted 17 February 2004, DSR 2004:II, 571

US – Softwood Lumber V: United States – Final Dumping Determination on Softwood Lumber from Canada

Panel Report, WT/DS264/R, adopted 31 August 2004, as modified by Appellate Body Report, DSR 2004:V, 1937

Appellate Body Report, WT/DS264/AB/R, adopted 31 August 2004, DSR 2004:V, 1875

US – Upland Cotton: Panel Report, United States – Subsidies on Upland Cotton, WT/DS267/R, Corr.1, and Add.1 to Add.3, adopted 21 March 2005, as modified by Appellate Body Report WT/DS267/AB/R, DSR 2005:II, 299

US – Wool Shirts and Blouses: Appellate Body Report, United States – Measure Affecting Imports of Woven Wool Shirts and Blouses from India, WT/DS33/AB/R, adopted 23 May 1997, and Corr.1, DSR 1997:I, 323

GATT 1947 Reports and Rulings

Australia – Ammonium Sulphate: Working Party Report, *The Australian Subsidy on Ammonium Sulphate*, GATT/CP.4/39, adopted 3 April 1950, BISD II/188

Belgium – Family Allowances: GATT Panel Report, *Belgian Family Allowances*, G/32, adopted 7 November 1952, BISD 1S/59

Border Tax Adjustments: GATT Working Party Report, *Border Tax Adjustments*, L/3464, adopted 2 December 1970, BISD 18S/97

Brazil – Internal Taxes: Working Party Report, *Brazilian Internal Taxes*, GATT/CP.3/42 (First Report), adopted 30 June 1949, BISD II/181; GATT/CP.5/37 (Second Report), adopted 13 December 1950, BISD II/186

Canada – Gold Coins: GATT Panel Report, *Canada – Measures Affecting the Sale of Gold Coins*, L/5863, 17 September 1985, unadopted

Cuba – Consular Taxes: Ruling by the Chairman, *The Phrase 'Charges of any Kind' in Article I:1 in Relation to Consular Taxes*, 24 August 1948, BISD II/12

EEC – Animal Feed Proteins: GATT Panel Report, *EEC – Measures on Animal Feed Proteins*, L/4599, adopted 14 March 1978, BISD 25S/49

Germany – Sardines: GATT Panel Report, *Treatment by Germany of Imports of Sardines*, G/26, adopted 31 October 1952, BISD 1S/53

India – Tax Rebates: Ruling by the Chairman, *Application of Article I:1 to Rebates on Internal Taxes*, 24 August 1948, BISD II/12

Italy – Agricultural Machinery: GATT Panel Report, *Italian Discrimination Against Imported Agricultural Machinery*, L/833, adopted 23 October 1958, BISD 7S/60

Japan – Alcoholic Beverages I: GATT Panel Report, *Japan – Customs Duties, Taxes and Labelling Practices on Imported Wines and Alcoholic Beverages*, L/6216, adopted 10 November 1987, BISD 34S/83

Japan – SPF Dimension Lumber: GATT Panel Report, *Canada/Japan – Tariff on Imports of Spruce, Pine, Fir (SPF) Dimension Lumber*, L/6470, adopted 19 July 1989, BISD 36S/167

New Zealand – Finnish Transformers: GATT Panel Report, *New Zealand – Imports of Electrical Transformers from Finland*, L/5814, adopted 18 July 1985, BISD 32S/55

Spain – Soyabean Oil: GATT Panel Report, *Spain – Measures Concerning Domestic Sale of Soyabean Oil – Recourse to Article XXIII:2 by the United States*, L/5142, 17 June 1981, unadopted

Spain – Unroasted Coffee: GATT Panel Report, *Spain – Tariff Treatment of Unroasted Coffee*, L/5135, adopted 11 June 1981, BISD 28S/102

Thailand – Cigarettes: GATT Panel Report, *Thailand – Restrictions on Importation of and Internal Taxes on Cigarettes*, DS10/R, adopted 7 November 1990, BISD 37S/200

US – Customs User Fee: GATT Panel Report, *United States – Customs User Fee*, L/6264, adopted 2 February 1988, BISD 35S/245

US – Malt Beverages: GATT Panel Report, *United States – Measures Affecting Alcoholic and Malt Beverages*, DS23/R, adopted 19 June 1992, BISD 39S/206

US – Section 337 Tariff Act: GATT Panel Report, *United States Section 337 of the Tariff Act of 1930*, L/6439, adopted 7 November 1989, BISD 36S/345

US – Superfund: GATT Panel Report, *United States – Taxes on Petroleum and Certain Imported Substances*, L/6175, adopted 17 June 1987, BISD 34S/136

US – Taxes on Automobiles: GATT Panel Report, *United States – Taxes on Automobiles*, DS31/R, 11 October 1994, unadopted

US – Tuna (Mexico [1991]): GATT Panel Report, *United States – Restrictions on Imports of Tuna*, DS21/R, DS21/R, 3 September 1991, unadopted, BISD 39S/155

US – Tuna (EEC [1994]): GATT Panel Report, *United States – Restrictions on Imports of Tuna*, DS29/R, 16 June 1994, unadopted

Arbitral Awards Pertaining to NAFTA

ADM v. *Mexico*: ICSID/NAFTA Arbitral Tribunal, Final Award, Archer Daniels Midland Company and Tate & Lyle Ingredients Americas v. Mexico, Case No. ARB(AF)/04/05, 21 November 2007

Corn Products v. *Mexico*: ICSID/NAFTA Arbitral Tribunal, Decision on Responsibility, Corn Products International, Inc. v. the United Mexican States, Case No. ARB(AF)/04/01, 15 January 2008

Feldman v. *Mexico*: ICSID/NAFTA Arbitral Tribunal, Final Award, Marvin Feldmand v. Mexico, Case No. ARB(AF)/99/1, 16 December 2002

GAMI v. *Mexico*: UNCITRAL/NAFTA Arbitral Tribunal, Final Award, GAMI Investments v. Mexico, 15 November 2004

Grand River v. *US*: UNCITRAL/NAFTA Arbitration, Grand River Enterprises Six Nations *et al.* v. the United States; Claimants' Memorial Merits Phase, 10 July 2008 and Counter-Memorial of Respondent, 22 December 2008

Loewen v. *US*: ICSID/NAFTA Arbitral Tribunal, Final Award, The Loewen Group and Raymond L Loewen v. the United States, Case No. ARB(AF)/98/3, 26 June 2003

Methanex v. *US*: UNCITRAL/NAFTA Arbitral Tribunal, Final Award, Methanex Corporation v. the United States, 9 August 2005

Pope & Talbot v. *Canada*: UNCITRAL/NAFTA Arbitral Tribunal, Award on the Merits of Phase 2, Pope & Talbot v. Canada, 10 April 2001

S.D. Myers v. *Canada*: UNCITRAL/NAFTA Arbitral Tribunal, Partial Award on the Merits, S.D. Myers v. Canada, 13 November 2000

Thunderbird v. *Mexico*: UNCITRAL/NAFTA Arbitral Tribunal, Final Award, International Thunderbird Gaming Corporation v. Mexico, 26 January 2006

UPS v. *Canada*: UNCITRAL/NAFTA Arbitral Tribunal, Final Award, United Parcel Service of America v. Canada, 24 May 2007

US – Trucking Services: NAFTA Arbitral Panel, Final Report in the Matter of Cross-Border Trucking Services, USA-MEX-1998–2008–01, 6 February 2001

Other Arbitral Awards

Consortium RFCC v. *Morocco*: ICSID Arbitral Tribunal, Arbitral Award, Consortium RFCC v. Morocco, ICSID Case No. ARB/00/6, 22 December 2003 (Italy–Morocco BIT)

Nykomb Synergetics v. *Latvia*: SCC Arbitral Tribunal, Arbitral Award, Nykomb Synergetics Technology Holding AB v. Latvia, SCC Case No. 118/2001, 16 December 2003 (Energy Charter Treaty)

Occidental v. *Ecuador*: LCIA Arbitral Tribunal, Arbitral Award, Occidental Exploration and Production Company v. Ecuador, LCIA Case No. UN3467, 1 July 2004 (US–Ecuador BIT)

European Court of Human Rights

Case of *Fredin* v. *Sweden* [1991] ECHR 2, 18.02.1991

Case of *Salgueiro da Silva Mouta* v. *Portugal* [1999] ECHR 176, 21.12.1999

Case of *Thlimmenos* v. *Greece* [2000] ECHR 162, 6.04.2000

Case of *Edoardo Palumbo* v. *Italy* [2000] ECHR 649, 30.11.2000

Court of Justice of the European Communities

Joined cases 56 and 58/64 *Établissements Consten S.à.R.L. and Grundig-Verkaufs-GmbH* v. *Commission* [1966] ECR 299, [1966] CMLR 418
Case 6/72 *Europemballage Corporation and Continental Can* v. *Commission* [1973] ECR 215, [1973] CMLR 1999
Case 27/76 *United Brands* v. *Commission* [1978] ECR 207, [1978] 1 CMLR 429
Case 85/76 *Hoffmann-La Roche* v. *Commission* [1979] ECR 461, [1979] 3 CMLR 211
Case C-120/78 *Rewe-Zentral AG* v. *Bundesmonopolverwaltung für Branntwein* [1979] ECR 649, [1979] 3 CMLR 494
Case 168/78 *Commission* v. *French Republic* [1980] ECR 347, [1981] 2 CMLR 631
Case 170/78 *Commission* v. *United Kingdom* [1980] ECR 417, [1980] 1 CMLR 716
Case 171/78 *Commission* v. *Kingdom of Denmark* [1980] ECR 447, [1981] 2 CMLR 688
Case 31/80 *L'Oréal* v. *De Nieuwe AMCK* [1980] ECR 3775, [1981] 2 CMLR 235
Case 96/80 *Jenkins* v. *Kingsgate* [1981] ECR 911, [1981] 2 CMLR 24
Joined cases 62 and 63/81 *Seco et Desquenne & Giral* v. *Etablissement d'assurance contre la vieillesse et l'invalidité* [1982] ECR 223
Case 319/81 *Commission* v. *Italian Republic* [1983] ECR 601, [1983] 2 CMLR 517
Case 322/81 *Michelin* v. *Commission* [1983] ECR 3461, [1985] 1 CMLR 282
Joined cases 142 and 156/84, *British-American Tobacco Company Ltd and R. J. Reynolds Industries* v. *Commission* [1987] ECR 4487, [1987] 2 CMLR 551
Case 184/85 *Commission* v. *Italian Republic* [1987] ECR 2013
Case 356/85 *Commission* v. *Kingdom of Belgium* [1987] ECR 3299, [1988] 3 CMLR 277
Case C-62/86 *AKZO Chemie* v. *Commission* [1991] ECR I-3359, [1993] 5 CMLR 215
Case 66/86 *Ahmed Saeed Flugreisen and Others* v. *Zentrale zur Bekämpfung unlauteren Wettbewerbs* [1989] ECR 803, [1990] 4 CMLR 102
Case 230/89 *Commission* v. *Hellenic Republic* [1991] ECR I-1909, [1993] 1 CMLR 869
Case 234/89 *Stergios Delimitis* v. *Henninger Bräu AG* [1991] ECR I-935, [1992] 5 CMLR 210
Case C-76/90 *Säger* v. *Dennemeyer & Co. Ltd.* [1991] ECR I-4221, [1993] 3 CMLR 639
Case C-43/93 *Vander Elst* v. *Office des Migrations Internationales* [1994] ECR I-3803, [1995] 1 CMLR 513
Joined cases C-68/94 and 30/95 *French Republic* v. *Commission* [1998] ECR I-1375, [1998] 4 CMLR 829
Case C-333/94 *Tetra Pak International* v. *Commission* [1996] ECR I-5951, [1997] 4 CMLR 662
Case C-185/95 *Baustahlgewebe GmbH* v. *Commission* [1998] ECR I-8417, [1999] 4 CMLR 1203
Case C-7/97 *Oscar Bronner GmbH & Co KG* v. *Mediaprint Zeitungs- und Zeitschriftenverlag GmbH & Co KG* [1998] ECR I-7791, [1999] 4 CMLR 112
Case C-421/97 *Tarantik* v. *Direction des services fiscaux de Seine-et-Marne* [1999] ECR I-3633, [1999] 2 CMLR 1083
Case C-265/99 *Commission* v. *French Republic* [2001] ECR I-2305

Case C-462/99 *Connect Austria Gesellschaft für Telekommunikation* v. *Telekom-Control-Kommission, and Mobilkom Austria* [2003] ECR I-5197, [2005] 5 CMLR 6, 302
Case C-475/99 *Ambulanz Glöckner* v. *Landkreis Südwestpfalz* [2001] ECR I-8089, [2002] 4 CMLR 21, 726
Case C-17/00 *De Coster* v. *Collège des bourgmestre et échevins de Watermael-Boitsfort* [2001] ECR I-9445, [2002] 1 CMLR 12, 285
Case C-12/03 P *Commission* v. *Tetra Laval* [2005] ECR I-987, [2005] 4 CMLR 8, 573
Case C–49/07 *Motosykletistiki Omospondia Ellados* v. *Elliniko Dimosio* [2008] 5 CMLR 11, 790

European Court of First Instance

Case T-30/89 *Hilti AG* v. *Commission* [1991] ECR II-1439, [1992] 4 CMLR 16
Joined cases T-68, T-77 and T-78/89 *Società Italiana Vetro SpA* v. *Commission* [1992] ECR II-1403, [1992] 5 CMLR 302
Case T-7/93 *Langnese Iglo GmbH* v. *Commission* [1995] ECR II-1533, [1995] 5 CMLR 602
Case T-504/93 *Tiercé Ladbroke* v. *Commission* [1997] ECR II-923, [1997] 5 CMLR 309
Case T-229/94 *Deutsche Bahn* v. *Commission* [1997] ECR II-1689, [1998] 4 CMLR 220
Joined cases T-374, T-375, T-384 and T-388/94 *European Night Services Ltd.* v. *Commission* [1998] ECR II-3141, [1998] 5 CMLR 718
Case T-65/96 *Kish Glass* v. *Commission* [2000] ECR II-1885, [2000] 5 CMLR 229
Joined cases T-125 & T-127/97 *Coca-Cola* v. *Commission* [2000] ECR II-1733, [2000] 5 CMLR 467
Joined Cases T-191, T-212–14/98 *Atlantic Container Line* v. *Commission* [2003] ECR II-3275, [2005] 4 CMLR 20, 1283
Case T-25/99 *Roberts and Roberts* v. *Commission* [2001] ECR II-1881, [2001] 5 CMLR 21, 828
Case T-61/99 *Adriatica di Navigazione* v. *Commission* [2003] ECR II-5349, [2005] 5 CMLR 30
Case T-340/03, *France Télécom* v. *Commission* [2007] ECR II-107, [2007] 4 CMLR 21, 919
Case T-177/04 *easyJet Airline* v. *Commission* [2006] ECR II-1931, [2006] 5 CMLR 11, 663

European Commission Decisions

Case IV/33.384 and IV/33.378 *Distribution of Package Tours 1990 World Cup* OJ L326, 12.11.1992, pp. 31–42, [1994] 5 CMLR 253
Case IV/M.430 *Procter & Gamble/VP Schickedanz (II)* OJ L354, 13.12.1994, pp. 32–65
Case IV/M.619 *Gencor/Lonrho* OJ L11, 14.01.1997, pp. 30–72, [1999] 4 CMLR 1076
Case IV/M.938 *Guinness/Grand Metropolitan* OJ L288, 27.10.1998, pp. 24–54
Case IV/M.1225 *Enso/Stora* OJ L254, 29.9.1999, pp. 9–21, [2000] 4 CMLR 372
Case IV/M.1524 *Airtours/First Choice* OJ L93, 13.4.2000, pp. 1–33, [2000] 5 CMLR 494
Case COMP/36.653 *Opel* OJ L59, 28.02.2001, pp. 1–42, [2001] 4 CMLR 1441

Case COMP/M.1672 *Volvo/Scania* OJ L143, 29.05.2001, pp. 74–132, [2001] 5 CMLR 410
Case COMP/36.264 *Mercedes-Benz* OJ L257, 25.09.2002, pp. 1–47, [2003] 4 CMLR 2, 95
Case COMP/38.233 *Wanadoo Interactive* of 16.07.2003 [no OJ publication], [2005] 5 CMLR 5, 120
Case COMP/37.792 *Microsoft* of 24.03.2004 [no OJ publication], [2005] 4 CMLR 19, 965
Case COMP/38.096 *Clearstream* of 2.06.2004 [no OJ publication], [2005] 5 CMLR 22, 1302
Case COMP/36.623 *SEP/Automobiles Peugeot SA* OJ L173, 27.6.2006, pp. 20–4, [2006] 5 CMLR 12, 714

United States Supreme Court

United States v. *Trans-Missouri Freight Association*, 166 US 290 (1897)
Northern Securities Co. v. *United States*, 193 US 197 (1904)
United States v. *Columbia Steel Co.*, 334 US 495 (1948)
Times-Picayune Publishing Co. v. *United States*, 345 US 594 (1953)
United States v. *E. I. du Pont de Nemours & Co. (Cellophane)*, 351 US 377 (1956)
United States v. *E. I. du Pont de Nemours & Co.*, 353 US 586 (1957)
International Boxing Club v. *United States*, 358 US 242 (1959)
Brown Shoe Co. v. *United States*, 370 US 294 (1962)
United States v. *Philadelphia National Bank*, 374 US 321 (1963)
United States v. *Aluminum Co. of America*, 377 US 271 (1964)
United States v. *Continental Can Co.*, 378 US 441 (1964)
United States v. *Grinnell Corp.*, 384 US 563 (1966)
United States v. *Marine Bancorporation, Inc.*, 418 US 602 (1974)
Continental T.V., Inc. v. *GTE Sylvania, Inc.*, 433 US 36 (1977)
Broadcast Music, Inc. v. *CBS*, 441 US 1 (1979)
United States v. *Columbia Steel Co.*, 334 US 495 (1948)
Aspen Skiing Co. v. *Aspen Highlands Skiing Corp.*, 472 US 585 (1985)
Federal Trade Commission v. *Indiana Federation of Dentists*, 476 US 447 (1986)
Eastman Kodak Co. v. *Image Technical Services, Inc.*, 504 US 451 (1992)

United States Courts of Appeal

Twin City Sportservice, Inc. v. *Charles O. Finley & Co., Inc.*, 512 F 2d 1264 (9th Cir. 1975), cert. denied 459 US 1009 (1982)
Federal Trade Commission v. *Warner Communications, Inc.*, 742 F 2d 1156 (9th Cir. 1984)
Monfort of Colorado, Inc. v. *Cargill, Inc.*, 761 F 2d 570 (10th Cir. 1985), rev'd 479 US 104 (1986)
R.D. Imports Ryno Industries, Inc. v. Mazda Distributors (Gulf), 807 F 2d 1222 (5th Cir. 1987), cert. denied 484 US 818 (1987)
United States v. *Archer-Daniels-Midland Co.*, 866 F 2d 242 (8th Cir. 1988), cert. denied 493 US 809 (1989)

Murrow Furniture Galleries, Inc. v. *Thomasville Furniture Industries, Inc.*, 889 F 2d 524 (4th Cir. 1989)

Movie 1 & 2 v. *United Artists Communications, Inc.*, 909 F 2d 1245 (9th Cir. 1990), cert. denied 501 US 1230 (1991) and 502 US 1029 (1992)

Federal Trade Commission v. *University Health, Inc.*, 938 F 2d 1206 (11th Cir. 1991)

Fineman v. *Armstrong World Industries, Inc.*, 980 F 2d 171 (3rd Cir. 1992), cert. denied 507 US 921 (1993)

Rebel Oil Co., Inc. v. *Atlantic Richfield Co.*, 51 F 3d 1421 (9th Cir. 1995), cert. denied 516 US 987 (1995)

PepsiCo, Inc. v. *Coca-Cola Co.*, 315 F 3d 101 (2nd Cir. 2002)

Re/Max International, Inc. v. *Realty One, Inc.*, 173 F 3d 995 (6th Cir. 1999), cert. denied 535 US 987 (2002)

AD/SAT, A Division of Skylight, Inc. v. *Associated Press*, 181 F 3d 216 (2nd Cir. 1999)

United States v. *Microsoft Corp.*, 253 F 3d 34 (D.C.Cir. 2001), cert. denied 534 US 952 (2001)

United States v. *Dentsply Intern., Inc.*, 399 F 3d 181 (3rd Cir. 2005), cert. denied 546 US 1089 (2006)

Spirit Airlines, Inc. v. *Northwest Airlines, Inc.*, 431 F 3d 917 (6th Cir. 2005)

United States District Courts

United States v. *Mrs. Smith's Pie Co.*, 440 F Supp 220 (E.D.Pa. 1976)

United States v. *Archer-Daniels-Midland Co.*, 695 F Supp 1000 (S.D.Iowa 1987), rev'd 866 F 2d 242 (8th Cir. 1988), cert. denied 493 US 809 (1989)

America Online, Inc. v. *GreatDeals.Net*, 49 F Supp 2d 851 (E.D.Va. 1999)

PepsiCo, Inc. v. *Coca-Cola Co.*, 114 F Supp 2d 243 (S.D.N.Y. 2000), aff'd 315 F 3d 101 (2nd Cir. 2002)

Hamilton Chapter of Alpha Delta Phi, Inc. v. *Hamilton College*, 106 F Supp 2d 406 (N.D.N.Y. 2000)

United States v. *Oracle Corp.*, 331 F Supp 2d 1098 (N.D.Cal. 2004)

German Bundesgerichtshof

Beschluss des Bundesgerichtshofs vom 16.12.1976, KVR 2/76, WuW/E BGH 1445, at 1447 (*Valium*)

Swiss Bundesverwaltungsgericht

Urteil des Bundesverwaltungsgerichts, Abteilung III, of 8 April 2009, C-6900/2007

LIST OF LEGAL TEXTS

List of full names and references for legal texts used in the book.

International Treaties

Council of Europe, Convention for the Protection of Human Rights and Fundamental Freedoms, Rome, 4 November 1950, in force 3 September 1953, CETS No. 5; 213 UNTS 221; SR 0.101, as amended by Protocol No. 11, CETS No. 155.

Vienna Convention on the Law of Treaties, Vienna, 23 May 1969, in force 27 January 1980, 1155 UNTS 331; 8 ILM 679 (1969); SR 0.111.

Agreement on the establishment of the Association of South East Asian Nations Secretariat, Denpasar, 24 February 1976, 1331 UNTS 243.

North American Free Trade Agreement, 17 December 1992, US–Can.–Mex., in force 1 January 1994, 107 Stat. 2057; 32 ILM 605 (1993).

WTO, Final Act Embodying the Results of the Uruguay Round of Multilateral Trade Negotiations, Marrakesh, 15 April 1994, 1867 UNTS 14; 33 ILM 1143 (1994).

WTO, Marrakesh Agreement Establishing the World Trade Organization, 15 April 1994, 1867 UNTS 154; 33 ILM 1144 (1994).

WTO, General Agreement on Tariffs and Trade 1994, 15 April 1994, Marrakesh Agreement Establishing the World Trade Organization, Annex 1A, 1867 UNTS 187; 33 ILM 1153 (1994).

WTO, Agreement on Subsidies and Countervailing Measures, 15 April 1994, Marrakesh Agreement Establishing the World Trade Organization, Annex 1A, 1867 UNTS 14.

WTO, Agreement on Implementation of Article VI (Anti-dumping), 15 April 1994, Marrakesh Agreement Establishing the World Trade Organization, Annex 1A.

WTO, Agreement on Safeguards, 15 April 1994, Marrakesh Agreement Establishing the World Trade Organization, Annex 1A.

WTO, Agreement on Technical Barriers to Trade, 15 April 1994, Marrakesh Agreement Establishing the World Trade Organization, Annex 1A.

WTO, Agreement on Sanitary and Phytosanitary Measures, 15 April 1994, Marrakesh Agreement Establishing the World Trade Organization, Annex 1A.

WTO, Agreement on Trade-Related Aspects of Investment Measure, 15 April 1994, Marrakesh Agreement Establishing the World Trade Organization, Annex 1A, 1868 UNTS 186.

WTO, General Agreement on Trade in Services, 15 April 1994, Marrakesh Agreement Establishing the World Trade Organization, Annex 1B, 33 ILM 1168 (1994).

WTO, Agreement on Trade-Related Aspects of Intellectual Property Rights, 15 April 1994, Marrakesh Agreement Establishing the World Trade Organization, Annex 1C, 1869 UNTS 299, 33 ILM 1197 (1994).

WTO, Understanding on Rules and Procedures Governing the Settlement of Disputes, Marrakesh Agreement Establishing the World Trade Organization, Annex 2, 1869 UNTS 401; 33 ILM 1226 (1994).

Agreement between the European Community and its Member States, of the one part, and the Swiss Confederation, of the other, on the free movement of persons, 21 June 1999, in force 1 June 2002, OJ L114, 30.04.2002, pp. 6–72; SR 0.142.112.681.

Primary and Secondary Legislation of the European Union

Treaty on the Functioning of the European Union (Consolidated version, as amended by the Treaty of Lisbon), OJ C 115, 9.5.2008, pp. 47–199.

Treaty establishing the European Community (Consolidated version, as amended by the Treaty of Amsterdam), OJ C325, 24.12.2002, pp. 33–184.

Council Regulation (EC) No. 384/96 of 22 December 1995 on protection against dumped imports from countries not members of the European Community (as amended), OJ L56, 6.03.1996, p. 1.

Council Regulation (EC) No. 2026/97 of 6 October 1997 on protection against subsidised imports from countries not members of the European Community (as amended), OJ L288, 21.10.1997, p. 1.

EC Merger Regulation: Council Regulation (EC) No. 139/2004 of 20 January 2004 on the control of concentrations between undertakings, OJ L24, 29.01.2004, pp. 1–22.

Council Regulation (EC) No. 1095/2005 of 12 July 2005 imposing a definitive anti-dumping duty on imports of bicycles originating in Vietnam, and amending Regulation (EC) No. 1524/2000 imposing a definitive anti-dumping duty on imports of bicycles originating in the People's Republic of China, OJ L183, 14.07.2005, pp. 1–36.

Council Regulation (EC) No. 1890/2005 of 14 November 2005 imposing a definitive anti-dumping duty and collecting definitively the provisional duty imposed on imports of certain stainless steel fasteners and parts thereof originating in the People's Republic of China, Indonesia, Taiwan, Thailand and Vietnam and terminating the proceeding on imports of certain stainless steel fasteners and parts thereof originating in Malaysia and the Philippines, OJ L302, 19.11.2005, pp. 1–13.

Council Regulation (EC) No. 1184/2007 of 9 October 2007 imposing a definitive anti-dumping duty and collecting definitively the provisional duty imposed on imports of peroxosulphates (persulphates) originating in the United States of America, the People's Republic of China and Taiwan, OJ L265, 11.10.2007, pp. 1–19.

Council Regulation (EC) No. 261/2008 of 17 March 2008 imposing a definitive anti-dumping duty on imports of certain compressors originating in the People's Republic of China, OJ L81, 20.03.2008, pp. 1–20.

Directive 2006/123/EC of the European Parliament and of the Council of 12 December 2006 on services in the internal market, OJ L 376, 27.12.2006, pp. 36–68.

United States

Sherman Antitrust Act, July 2, 1890, ch. 647, 26 Stat. 209, 15 U.S.C. §§ 1–7.

Clayton Antitrust Act, October 15, 1914, ch. 323, 38 Stat. 730, 15 U.S.C. §§ 12–27, 29 U.S.C. §§ 52–53.

Celler-Kefauver Antimerger Act, December 29, 1950, ch. 1184, 64 Stat. 1125, 15 U.S.C. § 18.

Tariff Act, 17 June, 1930, ch. 497, 46 Stat. 590, as amended, 19 U.S.C. Ch. 4, Subt. 4 (§§ 1671–77), Countervailing and Antidumping Duties.

Switzerland

Federal Constitution of the Swiss Confederation of 18 April 1999, SR 101.

LIST OF DOCUMENTS

List of full document names and references for short form citations used in the book.

GATT/WTO Documents

Group of Negotiations on Services, Communication from Japan, MTN.GNS/W/18, 15 September 1987.

Group of Negotiations on Services, Note on the Meeting of 15–17 September 1987, MTN.GNS/10, 15 October 1987.

Group of Negotiations on Services, Note on the Meeting of 14–15 December 1987, MTN.GNS/12, 19 January 1988.

Group of Negotiations on Services, Note on the Meeting of 22–25 March 1988, MTN. GNS/14, 29 April 1988.

Group of Negotiations on Services, Report to the Trade Negotiations Committee meeting at Ministerial level, Montreal, December 1988, MTN.GNS/21, 25 November 1988.

Trade Negotiations Committee Meeting at Ministerial Level, Montreal, December 1988, MTN.TNC/7(MIN), 9 December 1988.

Group of Negotiations on Services, Reference List of Sectors, Note by the Secretariat, MTN.GNS/W/50, 13 April 1989.

Trade Negotiations Committee, Midterm Review in Montreal on 5–9 December 1988 and in Geneva on 5–8 April 1989, MTN.TNC/11, 21 April 1989.

Group of Negotiations on Services, Note on the Meeting of 23–25 October 1989, MTN. GNS/26, 17 November 1989, para. 119.

Group of Negotiations on Services, Draft – Multilateral Framework for Trade in Services, MTN.GNS/35, 23 July 1990.

Group of Negotiations on Services, Note on the Meeting of 12 and 22 November 1990, MTN.GNS/40, 28 November 1990, para. 14.

Trade Negotiations Committee, Draft Final Act Embodying the Results of the Uruguay Round of Multilateral Trade Negotiations, MTN.TNC/W/35-1/Rev.1, MTN. TNC/W/35-2/Rev.1, MTN.TNC/W/35-3/Rev.1, 3 December 1990.

Group of Negotiations on Services, Services Sectoral Classification List, Note by the Secretariat, MTN.GNS/W/120, 10 July 1991.

Group of Negotiations on Services, Scheduling of Initial Commitments in Trade in Services: Explanatory Note, MTN.GNS/W/164, 3 September 1993.

Group of Negotiations on Services, Scheduling of Initial Commitments in Trade in Services: Explanatory Note, Addendum, MTN.GNS/W/164/Add.1, 30 November 1993.

Working Party on GATS Rules, Subsidies and Trade in Services, Note by the Secretariat, S/WPGR/W/9, 6 March 1996.

Ministerial Conference (Singapore), Ministerial Declaration, WT/MIN(96)/DEC, 18 December 1996.

Council for Trade in Services, Health and Social Services, Background Note by the Secretariat, S/C/W/50, 18 September 1998.

Ministerial Conference (Geneva), Declaration on Global Electronic Commerce, WT/MIN(98)/DEC/2, 25 May 1998.

General Council, Work Programme on Electronic Commerce, WT/L/274, 30 September 1998.

Council for Trade in Services, The Work Programme on Electronic Commerce, Note by the Secretariat, S/C/W/68, 16 November 1998.

Council for Trade in Services, Presence of Natural Persons (Mode 4), Background Note by the Secretariat, S/C/W/75, 8 December 1998.

Council for Trade in Services, Disciplines on Domestic Regulation in the Accountancy Sector, S/L/64, 17 December 1998.

Council for Trade in Services, Work Programme on Electronic Commerce, Interim Report to the General Council, S/C/8, 31 March 1999.

Working Group on the Interaction between Trade and Competition Policy, The Fundamental WTO Principles of National Treatment, Most-Favoured-Nation Treatment and Transparency, Background Note by the Secretariat, WT/WGTCP/W/114, 14 April 1999.

Working Party on GATS Rules, Issues for Future Discussions on Emergency Safeguards, Note by the Secretariat, Revision, S/WPGR/W/27/Rev.1, 7 May 1999

Committee on Trade in Financial Services, Indicative Checklist of Issues for Discussion, Note by the Secretariat, S/FIN/W/14, 17 May 1999.

Council for Trade in Goods, Work Programm on Electronic Commerce, Information provided to the General Council, G/C/W/158, 26 July 1999.

Council for Trade in Services, Work Programme on Electronic Commerce, Progress Report to the General Council, S/L/74, 27 July 1999.

Council for Trade in Services, Special Session: Technical Review of GATS Provisions, Informal Note by the Secretariat, JOB(01)/17, 16 February 2001

Council for Trade in Services, Guidelines for the Scheduling of Specific Commitments under the General Agreement on Trade in Services (GATS), S/L/92, 28 March 2001.

Ministerial Conference (Doha), Ministerial Declaration, WT/MIN(01)/DEC/1, 20 November 2001.

Ministerial Conference, Accession of the People's Republic of China, Decision of 10 November 2001, WT/L/432, 23 November 2001.

Communication from Brazil, MFN, National Treatment and like circumstances, JOB(01)/165, 30 November 2001 (not publicly available, on file with author).

Council for Trade in Services, Report of the Meeting Held on 19 March 2002, Note by the Secretariat, S/C/M/59, 14 May 2002.

Canada, Draft Consolidated Schedule for Specific Commitments, S/DCS/W/CAN, 24 January 2003.

Cyprus, Draft Consolidated Schedule for Specific Commitments, S/DCS/W/CYP, 24 Janaury 2003.

Egypt, Draft Consolidated Schedule of Specific Commitments, S/DCS/W/EGY, 24 January 2003.

Fijy, Draft Converted Schedule of Specific Commitments, S/DCS/W/FIJ, 24 January 2003.

Kuwait, Draft Consolidated Schedule of Specific Commitments, S/DCS/W/KWT, 24 January 2003.

Qatar, Schedule of Specific Commitments, S/DCS/W/QAT, 24 January 2003.

Switzerland, Draft Consolidated Schedule of Specific Commitments, S/DCS/W/CHE, 24 January 2003.

The People's Republic of China, Draft Consolidated Schedule of Specific Commitments, S/DCS/W/CHN, 24 January 2003.

The Philippines, Draft Consolidated Schedule of Specific Commitments, S/DCS/W/PHL, 24 January 2003.

Working Party on Domestic Regulation, Report on the Meeting Held on 29 November 2001, Note by the Secretariat, S/WPDR/M/14, 29 January 2002.

Communication from the United States, United States' Schedule of Specific Commitments under the General Agreement on Trade in Services, S/DCS/W/USA, 27 February 2003.

Iceland, Draft Consolidated Schedule of Specific Commitments, S/DCS/W/ISL/Rev.1, 11 April 2003.

General Council, Doha Work Programme, WT/L/579, 1 August 2004.

Working Party on Domestic Regulation, Definitions of Qualification Requirements, Qualification Procedures, Licensing Requirements, Licensing Procedures and Technical Standards, Communication from the Separate Customs Territory of Taiwan, Penghu, Kinmen and Matsu, S/WPDR/W/37, 6 October 2005.

Negotiating Group on Rules, Draft Consolidated Chair Texts of the AD and SCM Agreements, TN/RL/W/213, 30 November 2007.

European Union Documents

European Commission, *XXVIIth Report on competition policy* (1997), para. 44, available at http://ec.europa.eu/comm/competition/annual_reports/rap97_en.html

Market Definition Notice: Commission Notice on the definition of relevant market for the purpose of Community competition law, OJ C372, 9.12.1997, pp. 5–13.

Commission Notice on agreements of minor importance which do not appreciably restrict competition under Article 81(1) of the Treaty establishing the European Community (de minimis)', OJ C368, 22.12.2001, pp. 13–15.

Commission Recommendation of 11 February 2003 on relevant product and service markets within the electronic communications sector susceptible to *ex ante* regulation in accordance with Directive 2002/21/EC of the European Parliament and of the Council on a common regulatory framework for electronic communication networks and services, OJ L114, 8.05.2003, pp. 45–49.

EU Merger Guidelines: Guidelines on the assessment of horizontal mergers under the Council Regulation on the control of concentrations between undertakings, OJ C31, 5.2.2004, pp. 5–18.

Commission Staff Working Paper 'Remote Gambling Services': Report to the Trade Barriers Regulations Committee, Examination Procedure Concerning an Obstacle to Trade, Within the Meaning of Council Regulation (EC) No. 3286/94, Consisting of Measures Adopted by the United States of America Affecting Trade in Remote Gambling Services, 10 June 2009, available at http://trade.ec.europa.eu/doclib/docs/2009/june/tradoc_143405.pdf.

United States Documents

Department of Justice, 1984 Merger Guidelines, available at www.usdoj.gov/atr/hmerger/11249.htm.

Department of Justice, 1992 Merger Guidelines, available at www.usdoj.gov/atr/hmerger/11250.htm.

US Merger Guidelines: Department of Justice, 1997 Merger Guidelines, available at www.usdoj.gov/atr/hmerger/11251.htm.

Merger Guidelines Commentary: Department of Justice/Federal Trade Commission, Commentary on the Horizontal Merger Guidelines (2006), available at www.usdoj.gov/atr/public/guidelines/215247.htm.

Competition and Monopoly Report: Department of Justice, Competition and Monopoly: Single-Firm Conduct Under Section 2 of the Sherman Act (2008), available at www.usdoj.gov/atr/public/reports/236681.htm.

Other Documents

League of Nations, Committee of Experts for the Progressive Codification of International Law, Report Adopted by the Committee at its Third Session, Held in March–April 1927, 'The Most-Favoured-Nation Clause', 22 The American Journal of International Law (1928) 133.

OECD, Process and Production Methods (PPMs): Conceptual Framework and Considerations on Use of PPM-Based Trade Measures, OECD Work Programme on

Trade and Environment, OCDE/GD(97)137 (1997), available at www.olis.oecd.org/olis/1997doc.nsf/LinkTo/ocde-gd(97)137.

OECD, The Multilateral Agreement on Investment: Commentary to the Consolidated Text, Negotiating Group on the Multilateral Agreement on Investment, DAFFE/MAI(98)8/REV1 (1998), available at www1.oecd.org/daf/mai/pdf/ng/ng988r1e.pdf.

UNCTAD, *National Treatment* (New York, NY/Geneva: United Nations Publication 1999), available at www.unctad.org/Templates/webflyer.asp?docid=191&intItemID=2322&lang=1.

UNCTAD, *International Investment Instruments: A Compendium*, vol. VII (New York, NY/Geneva: United Nations Publisher 2002), available at www.unctad.org/en/docs/dite3vol7_en.pdf.

UNCTAD, Recent Developments in International Investment Agreements (2007–June 2008), IIA Monitor No. 2 (2008), UNCTAD/WEB/DIAE/IA/2008/1, available at www.unctad.org/Templates/Page.asp?intItemID=3766&lang=1.

Introduction

Given the complexity of the subject-matter of trade in services, as well as the newness of the obligations under the GATS, we believe that claims made under the GATS deserve close attention and serious analysis. We leave [the] interpretation of Article II of the GATS to another case and another day.

WTO Appellate Body[1]

The General Agreement on Trade in Services (GATS) was concluded under the institutional framework of the World Trade Organization (WTO) resulting from the Uruguay Round in 1994. Even though the potential contribution of international trade in services to economic growth and development had long been recognized,[2] GATS was the first and only multilateral agreement aimed at the liberalization of international trade in services. In comparison to the General Agreement on Tariffs and Trade (GATT) from 1947 and other international agreements regulating trade in goods, it is still a relatively new agreement governing an economic sector which has not typically been subject to international trade regulations. The conclusion of GATS had thus been greeted as a new milestone in trade liberalization. Considering the potential of international trade in service and the fact that it is inhibited by many different types of trade obstacles, it is somewhat surprising that to date only five cases involving claims of GATS violations have arisen under WTO dispute settlement procedures.[3] This lack of substantial

[1] Appellate Body Report, *Canada – Autos*, para. 184.

[2] According to UNCTAD, 'services account for some 40% of employment in developing countries and up to 70% in the developed world. The liberalization of trade in services holds great potential for increasing global welfare', available at www.unctad.org/Templates/Page.asp?intItemID=3886&lang=1; see also e.g. Hoekman and Mattoo, 'Services Trade and Growth', p. 53; Sauvant, 'Tradability of Services', pp. 116 ff; Mattoo and Wunsch-Vincent, 'GATS and Outsourcing', 766 ff.

[3] Not including *Canada – Periodicals* where GATS was raised by the defendant, but not applied by the WTO adjudicating bodies, see Appellate Body Report, p. 20; for an overview

jurisprudence considerably contributes to the prevailing uncertainty among Members and trade practitioners with regard to the exact meaning of many obligations embodied in GATS.

It was in the year 2000 when the Appellate Body announced in *Canada – Autos* that it would leave the interpretation of Article II GATS 'to another case and another day', but this 'other case and other day' has yet to come. Following *EC – Bananas III* (1997), *Canada – Autos* was only the second time that the WTO adjudicating bodies were called upon to examine a claim under GATS. In both cases, the main issues were related to trade in goods and GATT. The GATS claims were mainly secondary and only concerned the distribution of the goods in question.[4] Since then, only three other major GATS cases arose under the WTO, namely *Mexico – Telecoms* (2004), *US – Gambling* (2005) and, most recently, *China – Publications and Audiovisual Products* (2009). While these decisions shed some additional light on certain obligations of the GATS framework, many provisions, in particular the non-discrimination obligations in Articles II and XVII, remain largely unexplored. Until currently pending and future GATS cases may bring further and much needed clarification to certain aspects of GATS,[5] this study seeks to make a contribution to the interpretation of the GATS obligations on non-discrimination embodied in Articles II and XVII, focusing in particular on the question of 'likeness'.[6]

I The quest for an appropriate standard of 'likeness' in GATS

A *'Likeness' linking trade liberalization and regulatory autonomy*

Whenever the WTO adjudicating bodies are called upon to examine a claim of discriminatory treatment, they need to assess whether the trade obstacle under scrutiny differentiates between 'like products' or between 'like services and service suppliers'. This mechanism of the 'likeness

of GATS disputes which did not lead to the establishment of a panel see Davey, 'Services Cases', pp. 280–86.

4 Matsushita, 'Jurisprudence on GATS and TRIPS', p. 461.

5 The dispute *China – Measures Affecting Financial Information Services and Foreign Financial Information Suppliers* (DS372, DS373, DS378) was resolved by a mutually agreed solution on 4 December 2008; an appeal was pending in *China – Publications and Audiovisual Products* by the time this book was completed.

6 Case law and scholarly writing is considered up to August 2009; all internet addresses have been last accessed in August 2009.

concept' in international economic law can be best illustrated with an example from WTO dispute settlement practice:

> In the case *Japan – Alcoholic Beverages II*, the US and the EU complained against Japan, arguing that the higher tax imposed on imported whisky as compared to domestically produced 'shochu' infringes with the principle of non-discrimination embodied in GATT. In order to find a violation of the non-discrimination principle, the Appellate Body was held to determine whether whisky is 'like' shochu for purposes of the GATT national treatment obligation.

As a general rule, it can be said that the broader the WTO adjudicating bodies construe the concept of 'likeness', the more intrusive the non-discrimination obligation becomes, which in turn intensifies the obligation's liberalizing effect. Under GATT 1947 and WTO jurisprudence, the element of 'like products' grew to be the decisive element in the legal analysis of non-discrimination cases. Respondents would generally try to defend a claim of non-discrimination violation with the argument that the measure under scrutiny legitimately differentiates between 'different products'. During GATT 1947 practice, 'like products' were primarily assessed on the basis of objective criteria, such as physical characteristics and tariff classifications of the concerned products. A later theory introduced a subjective element to the analysis of 'like products', allowing the regulatory purpose for differential treatment to be taken into account. The prevailing and most recent theory, finally, defines 'likeness' on the basis of economic considerations designed to assess the competitive relationship between the products under scrutiny. Considering this key function of 'like products' in GATT rules on non-discrimination, it is not surprising that the issue is receiving considerable attention in trade literature. An ongoing debate emerged among trade scholars and practitioners on various aspects of the 'like product' concept. However, while the specific problems have been identified and the different positions have been made clear, the WTO adjudicating bodies have yet to adopt a definite solution for many issues of 'likeness' and the law continues to evolve.

The concept of 'like products' has been matched by the GATS rules on non-discrimination which apply to the treatment of imported services. GATS non-discrimination obligations employ a concept of 'like services and service suppliers' which to date has only received very little attention in WTO jurisprudence. The Panels in *EC – Bananas III*, *Canada – Autos* and *China – Publications and Audiovisual Products* only marginally touched upon the issue of 'likeness' in GATS. By the same token, even though many scholars have recognized the importance and ambiguities of the GATS 'like services and service suppliers' concept,[7] it largely lacks a doctrinal analysis that is comparable to the one related to GATT 'like products'.[8]

The nature of services transactions as well as the particularities of the GATS framework considerably complicate the 'like services and service suppliers' concept in comparison to its 'like product' counterpart from GATT. Service transactions are intangible and thus cannot be compared on the basis of physical characteristics. Moreover, in contrast to trade in goods and tariffs, no detailed and internationally recognized nomenclature exists for service transactions. In addition, some services are highly individualized, while others are largely standardized. Many services are subject to different methods of supply, such as distance learning and class room teaching. Finally, given the intangible nature of service transactions, cross-border trade may require the supplier or the consumer to relocate. For all these reasons, the Working Party on GATS Rules recognized that 'the concept of likeness ... is more elusive in services than in goods'.[9]

In light of these considerations, the purpose of this study is to identify the interpretative problems that arise with regard to the concept of 'like services and services suppliers' under GATS and to develop possible methodologies for the 'likeness' analysis. The interpretation of 'likeness' in GATS has potentially far reaching consequences for the Members' autonomy to regulate the supply of services within their territory, which in turn may result in conflicts between domestic objectives of political, social and economic nature and the liberalization of international trade in services. Such conflicts are particularly sensitive in the context of

[7] See e.g. Abu-Akeel, 'MFN as it Applies to Service Trade', 110–14; Cottier and Oesch, *International Trade Regulation*, pp. 407–11; Davey and Pauwelyn, 'MFN Unconditionality', p. 36; Krajewski, 'Public Services and Trade Liberalization', 360–61; Drake and Nicolaidïs, 'Electronic Commerce and GATS', pp. 420–21; Krajewski, *National Regulation*, pp. 97–107; Krajewski and Engelke, 'Art. XVII GATS', pp. 406–9; Leroux, 'GATS Case Law', 779–80; Morrison, 'WTO Dispute Settlement in Services', p. 387; Mattoo, 'National Treatment in GATS', 122–33; Mattoo, 'MFN and GATS', pp. 73–80; Nicolaïdis and Trachtman, 'Policed Regulation', pp. 252–55; Wolfrum, 'Art. II GATS', pp. 82–85; Wunsch-Vincent, 'Lessons from US-Gambling', 329–35; Zdouc, '(1999) Dispute Settlement Practice', 331–34; Zdouc, *Comparative Analysis of GATS and GATT*, pp. 157–71; Zdouc, '(2004) Dispute Settlement Practice', pp. 397–403.

[8] As a notable exception Cossy, 'Thoughts on "Likeness" in GATS'; Cossy, 'Determining Likeness under GATS'.

[9] WPGR, Subsidies and Trade in Services, Note by the Secretariat, S/WPGR/W/9, 6 March 1996, para. 9.

services, where governments typically adopt regulations for reasons such as consumer protection, supply of public services, monopoly supply or limiting competition.[10]

B Linkage between 'likeness' and progressive liberalization

A key function attributable to the concept of 'likeness' relates to its role in the process of progressive liberalization for international trade in services. Under GATT, the principle of non-discrimination directly applies to *all* products which are traded internationally. Conversely, certain GATS non-discrimination obligations are limited to service sectors for which Members made explicit commitments. At the same time, the GATS framework allows for Members to further negotiate commitments in view of progressively facilitating international trade in more service sectors.[11] Yet, Members have so far been reluctant in making significant commitments for services trade, in particular with regard to the specific mode of service supply allowing the supplier to enter the importing country (mode 4) or with regard to public services.

One of the reasons for this reluctance may be that progressive liberalization can only be achieved to the extent that Members are able to assess the scope of their commitments,[12] which in turn presupposes that the mechanism of the GATS non-discrimination obligation is clear. Yet, due to the remaining open questions and uncertainties concerning the interpretation of GATS rules on non-discrimination – and in particular the concept of 'likeness' – Members are virtually left in the dark when formulating new commitments and limitations. Hence, more clarification is needed in order for Members to properly assess risks and benefits of future commitments.

C 'Likeness' linking trade with other policy and legal disciplines

Under GATT rules on non-discrimination, the 'like product' concept became the centre of attention with regard to the interaction between

[10] See e.g. Cass and Noam, 'Economics and Politics of Trade in Services', pp. 61 ff; Mattoo and Sauvé, 'Domestic Regulation', p. 2; Krommenacker, 'Multilateral Services Negotiations', p. 459; Francois and Wooton, 'Trade Liberalization and GATS', 392.

[11] Cottier, 'Progressive Liberalization to Progressive Regulation', 780; see also GATS Preamble, second recital: 'Wishing to establish a multilateral framework … a view to the expansion of such trade under conditions of transparency and progressive liberalization'.

[12] Similarly also Cossy, 'Thoughts on "Likeness" in GATS', p. 328; Ortino, 'Principle of Non-Discrimination', p. 173; Tietje, 'Stärken und Schwächen des GATS', p. 19; Howse and Tuerk, 'WTO Negotiations on Services', 3–4.

trade law and other legal disciplines, such as environmental law, labour law, human rights, animal welfare or consumer protection. The question of whether foreign goods or services produced to the detriment of human rights, labour standards or the environment are 'like' domestically produced goods or services of a 'higher standard' is crucial with regard to the regulatory autonomy of WTO Members to adopt regulations restricting the sale of such 'low standard' goods or services in order to protect its own societal values. Within this discussion, it is necessary to clearly distinguish the situation of a Member regulating the import and sale of a product for reasons pertaining to the way it was produced from the situation of a Member regulating the sale of a product for domestic policy reasons:[13]

- Regulations pertaining to the process and production method:

> For instance, in 2007 Canada requested consultations with the EU under WTO dispute settlement procedures for prohibiting the sale of Canadian seal fur which, in the view of the EU, is produced by Canadian hunters who catch and kill baby seals in a cruel way.[14] Similar trade restrictions may be considered by WTO Members to sanction environmentally damaging production methods, exploitation of workers, child labour, human rights violations etc. Such measures restricting trade in goods which are produced in a way that is inconsistent with domestic values could be found discriminatory and thus illegal under GATT to the extent that 'likeness' is affirmed between domestically produced 'high standard' products and imported 'low standard' products.

- Regulations pertaining to the product and domestic policies:

> This situation corresponds to the issue presented under section A above, which concerns the question whether Members retain the autonomy to pursue domestic non-economic policies – such as environment or consumer protection – by setting standards for the sale of goods and services. To the extent that such a regulation is subject to a non-discrimination claim, the question arises whether, for instance, environmentally harmful goods or services are 'like' environmentally friendly goods or services.

While the various legal problems related to these issues have been addressed by different WTO adjudicating bodies and extensively

[13] See e.g. Charnovitz, '*Alcoholic Beverages* Decision', 201; Brown Weiss and Jackson, 'Environment and Trade', pp. 28–9.

[14] *EC – Certain Measures Prohibiting the Importation and Marketing of Seal Products* (DS369).

discussed among trade scholars,[15] the corresponding problem with regard to trade in services has hardly received any attention. One of the reasons may be that the main GATS cases pertaining to non-discrimination, such as *EC – Bananas III* and *Canada – Autos*, did not concern the regulation of process and production methods or non-economic domestic policies. It is thus not surprising that in both cases the element of 'likeness' remained largely undisputed among the parties. Nonetheless, sooner or later the exact same issue is likely to arise under the GATS rules on non-discrimination, potentially even with much broader implications than under GATT. In fact, while the production of imported goods takes place in a foreign country, trade in services may require the foreign supplier to relocate to the country of the consumer. Consequently, a Member's autonomy to regulate the supply of a service within its own jurisdiction may be considerably restricted if 'likeness' is affirmed between services supplied by different methods or by differently qualified suppliers.

D 'Likeness' linking legal and economic analysis

To the extent that 'likeness' is subject to an economic interpretation and relates to the competitive relationship between the products or services under scrutiny, the question arises to what degree the legal analysis should be guided by economic theories. Other fields of law which have substantial experience in the application of economic theories could serve as a basis for a more refined analysis of 'likeness' in international trade law. In the 1950s, economists and lawyers developed the concept of a 'relevant market', which was designed to serve as a tool for the assessment of market power in US antitrust law. Lower federal courts implemented this concept in their antitrust jurisprudence, and eventually the US Supreme Court endorsed it in the famous *Cellophane* case on illegal monopolization.[16] The relevant market concept was originally based on a test of 'reasonable interchangeability by consumers'. While demand substitutability remains the main pillar of the relevant market analysis, US antitrust authorities

[15] From the many contributions on conflicts between international trade and other policy and legal disciplines see e.g. Bhagwati and Hudec (eds.), *Fair Trade*; Abbott, Breining-Kaufmann and Cottier (eds.), *Trade and Human Rights*; Cottier, Pauwelyn and Bürgi (eds.), *Human Rights and International Trade*; Cameron, Demaret and Geradin (eds.), *Trade & Environment*; Cottier and Oesch, *International Trade Regulation*, pp. 412–66, 513–42.

[16] *US v. E. I. du Pont de Nemours & Co. (Cellophane)*, 351 US 377 (1956), p. 395; Werden, 'History of Market Delineation', 130 ff.

and courts have further refined the methodologies, introducing *inter alia* considerations of supply substitutability, ease of entry as well as potential and future competition. The EU and other countries have relied on the relevant market concept from US antitrust law as a model and implemented the same or similar concepts in their own competition policies.

Against this background, it is manifest that the 'likeness' analysis could draw from economic theories developed under the 'relevant market' concept of competition law. A WTO panel soon recognized the overlaps between the two different fields of law, but noted that '[w]hile the specifics of the interaction between trade and competition law are still being developed, we concur that the market definitions need not be the same'.[17] Even though some panels subsequently acknowledged the relevance of price elasticity of demand,[18] – some even explicitly referring to market definitions of national competition authorities[19] – the vast majority of cases pertaining to 'likeness' completely ignore all economic theories under the 'like product' analysis. While a number of commentators from scholarly literature demand such an approach, only few contributions explore the comparative implications in more detail.[20] As the current analytical framework applied for the GATT 'like products' analysis – which in itself is not yet consolidated and continues to evolve – may not be sufficiently refined to resolve the specific issues raised by the 'like services and service suppliers' concept, this study analyses whether market definition in US and EU antitrust law could provide a basis for the 'likeness' test in GATS rules on non-discrimination.

II Methodology, scope and structure

All agreements concluded under the WTO framework constitute public international law[21] and are thus subject to customary international law on the law of treaty interpretation. Article 3.2 DSU even mandates WTO panels and the Appellate Body to construe the provisions of the WTO agreements in accordance with the customary rules of interpretation of

[17] Panel Report, *Korea – Alcoholic Beverages*, Para. 10.81.

[18] *Ibid.*, para. 10.44; Appellate Body Report, *Korea – Alcoholic Beverages*, para. 134.

[19] Panel Report, *Mexico – Taxes on Soft Drinks*, para. 8.77.

[20] Most notably Emch, 'What are "Like" Products?'; Goco, '"Likeness" and Market Definition'; Choi, '*Like Products*'; Neven, 'How Should "Protection" be Evaluated?'.

[21] Oesch, 'Commercial Treaties', n 1.

public international law. The Appellate Body recognized that Article 31 of the Vienna Convention on the Law of Treaties 'has attained the status of a rule of customary or general international law',[22] pursuant to which the provisions of international agreements must be analysed (i) in accordance with the ordinary meaning to be given to the terms (ii) in their context and (iii) in the light of their object and purpose. The WTO adjudicating bodies and other international tribunals called upon to rule on international economic law are thus compelled to justify their interpretations on the basis of the rules codified in Article 31 VCLT. For this reason, the WTO adjudicating bodies have a tendency to closely follow the text of the provisions, even referring to the dictionary definition of a certain term.[23] However, the Appellate Body also recognized that dictionary meanings leave many questions open and are not necessarily capable of resolving complex questions of interpretation.[24] The Appellate Body even adopted interpretations which may go against the mere text of the provisions:

> To state two examples, both of which are relevant for the present study, the terms 'like products' in Articles III:2, first sentence, and III:4 GATT were given different meanings and standards despite the identical text.[25] Similarly, all WTO non-discrimination clauses were found to apply to *de facto* discrimination, even though only Article XVII:2 GATS actually contains explicit text allowing for this conclusion.[26]

These developments in the interpretation of WTO agreements focusing more on context, object and purpose than text are to be welcomed. As the two examples on the interpretation of non-discrimination demonstrate, WTO agreements are frequently incomplete, incoherent and inconsistent from a textual and systemic point of view. Considering that the text of the agreements is a result of negotiations and compromises among governments of different countries – as opposed to a structured and systemic national legislative process – such textual shortcomings are not surprising. It follows that an interpretation of WTO agreements in the light of purpose and context is generally more conclusive – and provides superior

[22] Appellate Body Report, *US – Gasoline*, p. 16; the same is true for Art. 32 VCLT, see Appellate Body Report, *Japan – Alcoholic Beverages II*, p. 9; on treaty interpretation and Art. 31 VCLT see e.g. Brownlie, *Principles of Public International Law*, pp. 630 ff.

[23] See e.g. Appellate Body Report, *US – Gasoline*, p. 17, n 40; Panel Report, *US – Gambling*, paras. 6.20, 6.55 ff.

[24] Appellate Body Reports, *Canada – Aircraft*, para. 153; *US – Softwood Lumber IV*, para. 59; *US – FSC*, para. 129; *EC – Asbestos*, para. 92; *US – Gambling*, para. 164.

[25] See below, 5.I.

[26] See below, 3.I.A.2.

results – than a strict application of the text of the provisions in accordance with dictionary definitions.[27]

In light of these considerations, the aim of this book is not to strictly follow the rules of treaty interpretation in accordance with Article 31 VCLT, which would require mainly focusing on 'text', 'objects and purpose' and 'context'. The methodology applied in this research is predominantly a *comparative analysis*. While the primary aim is to explore the 'likeness' concept as it applies in GATS, the comparative analysis – by identifying different techniques applied to the same problems in related fields – also highlights potential issues for the adoption and modelling of future non-discrimination obligations in international economic law. When identifying the comparators to the 'likeness' concept in GATS rules on non-discrimination, the most obvious approach is to consider other non-discrimination obligations under the WTO framework. The rich jurisprudence and scholarly work pertaining to the 'like product' concept is particularly relevant. Hence, a main objective of this study is to analyse the extent to which the GATT theories can be transposed to the 'like services and service suppliers' concept of GATS. Such an approach requires discerning similarities and differences between GATT and GATS in general and between the applications of the 'likeness' concept in particular. In addition, it is also useful to look beyond GATT and GATS rules on non-discrimination. Such an extended comparative approach can basically be undertaken from two directions. The first and more obvious comparison is to examine the element of 'likeness' in other *non-discrimination clauses*. Many areas of law typically contain non-discrimination obligations, such as constitutional law or human and fundamental rights. Yet, the further away the comparative field is from international trade, the less relevant are the concepts for purposes of GATS. For this reason, this study limits the comparative approach to non-discrimination obligations in international economic law, such as NAFTA, BITs and EU law. A second comparative approach consists of looking beyond the principle of non-discrimination, by identifying other fields of law which require the determination of competitive relationships in legal analysis. Legal reasoning follows a process

[27] Ortino, 'Treaty Interpretation', 147: 'There is no doubt that the textual approach to treaty interpretation unanimously adopted by the Vienna Convention should be maintained … However, and this is the argument advanced in this paper, it must be a textuality which is qualified in a variety of important ways, for example, by giving meaning to the terms of the treaty in their context and in light of its object and purpose.' For an overview of reasons why Art. 31 VCLT is inadequate for the interpretation of WTO agreements see Qureshi, *Interpreting WTO Agreements*, pp. 4 ff.

of subsumption, which requires (i) to establish the relevant facts and the relevant legal rules and (ii) to apply the law to the facts. The concept of 'likeness' as part of the non-discrimination obligation constitutes a legal element, which – depending on its interpretation – requires determining the relevant facts by applying theories from economic science. This mechanism of linking legal and economic analyses can be found in other legal domains, particularly in the area of competition law. For the purpose of interpreting and defining 'likeness' in trade law, it may thus be useful to resort to experiences from competition law practice.

In addition to the comparative aspects, a second methodology applied in this research consists of a *contextual analysis*. It cannot be emphasized strongly enough that the concept of 'likeness' should not be analysed and interpreted in isolation, without paying attention to the other elements of non-discrimination, namely 'less favourable treatment' and 'regulatory purpose'. All of these closely connected elements form in their context the principle of non-discrimination. Consequently, a particular interpretation of one of the elements may require a specific interpretation of another element and vice versa.

In light of these two methodological approaches, the first part of this book is aimed at setting the foundations for the more specific analysis of 'likeness' in GATS non-discrimination obligations. Chapters 1 and 2 introduce the principle of non-discrimination in international trade law as well as the particularities related to the nature and regulatory framework of international trade in services. Chapter 3 breaks the non-discrimination principle down into its various elements of 'likeness', 'less favourable treatment' and 'regulatory purpose', using the GATT as a model, and analyses their meaning individually and in their context. On this basis, the concluding chapter 4 seeks to reconcile the different elements and to determine the appropriate standard for WTO non-discrimination, on the basis of which 'likeness' will be analysed in the subsequent parts II–IV.

Chapters 5 and 6 of part II define the conceptual breadth for 'likeness' in GATS rules on non-discrimination, analyzing each GATS non-discrimination obligation in the light of jurisprudence and scholarly theories developed under their respective counterparts in GATT. Chapter 7 extends this comparative analysis to 'likeness' in principles of non-discrimination outside the GATT and GATS framework and to 'likeness' as it applies in WTO law on trade remedies. The conclusions of part II are summarized in chapter 8.

Part III turns to GATS specific issues related to the 'likeness' concept. Chapter 9 explores the fact that GATS rules on non-discrimination not only apply to the treatment of services, but also to the treatment of service suppliers. This extension in scope of non-discrimination raises numerous issues with regard to the interpretation of 'likeness', which are discussed in chapter 10. Other GATS particularities addressed in chapter 11 are that identical services may be supplied by different means and that trade in services may require the movement of factors. Chapter 12 summarizes the conclusions of part III.

Finally, part IV seeks to develop a methodology for the analysis of the 'like services and service suppliers' element in GATS non-discrimination obligations. Chapter 13 explores to what extent the current GATT 'like product' approach may be transposed to the analysis of 'likeness' in GATS and chapter 14 consists of an in-depth comparative analysis between the concepts of 'relevant market' in competition policy and 'likeness' in trade law. Chapter 15 examines to what extent these 'likeness' methodologies are suitable to address measures differentiating between services or suppliers on the basis of 'process and production methods'. Part IV is concluded with chapter 16 which summarizes the different methodologies.

As a general remark, all examples appearing in this book are designed to illustrate theoretical concepts related to GATS without taking into account whether or not specific commitments have been made by the Members in their schedules. Unless stated otherwise, the examples are based on the assumption that the respective Member made full commitments to the services and modes of supply in question.

PART I

Foundations

Part I of this book provides the foundations for the analysis of non-discrimination in general and the concept of 'likeness' in particular. As this study focuses on non-discrimination in the context of international trade in services, chapters 1 and 2 set the stage by introducing the principle of non-discrimination in international trade law as well as the particularities of international trade in services and GATS as the main regulatory framework. The subsequent chapter 3 breaks the non-discrimination principle down into its legal elements of 'less favourable treatment', 'likeness' and 'regulatory purpose', analyzing their individual significance and their respective interdependencies. Part I closes with the summary and conclusions under chapter 4, highlighting in particular how the interpretation of each legal element affects the reach and substance of a non-discrimination obligation.

1

Objective and forms of non-discrimination

The obligation of non-discrimination constitutes a core principle in many different fields of domestic and international law, such as constitutional law, domestic trade law, human rights, public international law and international economic law.[1] The significance of non-discrimination within the WTO framework is highlighted by the fact that it is embodied in the Preamble to the 'Marrakesh Agreement Establishing the World Trade Organization', which names the 'elimination of discriminatory treatment in international trade relations' as one of the principal means to achieve the objectives related to trade liberalization.[2]

In general terms, the non-discrimination principle in international economic law serves a political as well as an economic purpose.[3] From a *political* perspective, discriminating actions in foreign affairs generally, and in trade relations particularly, provoke considerable tensions in international relations. Discriminating actions entail the unequal treatment of two subjects that are equal or in equal situations – either by granting an advantage or favour to one subject or by imposing a disadvantage or burden on the other subject – and are thus naturally perceived as strongly unfair. Such unfair treatment is likely to be answered with repercussions not necessarily limited to trade, and the situation may spiral into a serious quarrel that could ultimately lead to an armed conflict.[4] The best example

[1] For an overview of non-discrimination in different legal domains see e.g. Doebbler, *Non-Discrimination in International Law*, pp. 37–67; Schiek and Chege (eds.), *European Union Non-Discrimination Law*; Loenen and Rodrigues (eds.), *Non-Discrimination Law*; Rhoodie, *Discrimination in Constitutions*; Peters, 'Strukturähnlichkeit der Diskriminierungsverbote'.

[2] Preamble to the Marrakesh Agreement Establishing the World Trade Organization, para. 4; Stoll and Schorkopf, *WTO*, p. 48; Srinivasan, 'Nondiscrimination in GATT/WTO', 73.

[3] See e.g. Petersmann, 'Economic, Legal and Political Functions', 117–18; Trebilcock and Howse, *Regulation of International Trade*, p. 51; Jackson, *World Trading System*, pp. 158 ff; De Búrca, 'Concept of Discrimination', pp. 186–87; Newcombe and Paradell, *Law and Practice of Investment Treaties*, pp. 147–48.

[4] See e.g. Gardner, *Sterling-Dollar Diplomacy*, pp. 17–18: 'The First World War did much to stimulate American concern with the political importance of non-discrimination.

for illustrating the link between economic integration and political stabilization is the creation of the EU. In today's public debate about the role and purpose of the EU, it is often forgotten that in the aftermath of World War II, the core concern and motivation for the creation of the European Coal and Steel Community (ECSC) in 1951 was to bring stability, prosperity and peace to Europe.[5] The ECSC paved the way for the signature of the Treaties of Rome in 1957, creating the European Economic Community (EEC) and the European Atomic Energy Community (Euratom). Against this background, it is not surprising that the principle of non-discrimination played a fundamental role in the political integration of Europe by taking a prominent position in the treaty framework of the EU.[6]

In *economic* terms, the principle of non-discrimination as an instrument of trade liberalization seeks to prevent inefficiencies. According to the economic theories first developed by *Smith* in his work *Wealth of Nations* (1776) and *Ricardo* in *Principles of Political Economy and Taxation* (1817) on the efficient allocation of resources and comparative advantage, trade liberalization allows countries to specialize in the production and exportation of products and services for which they enjoy a comparative advantage and, in turn, import products and services which can be produced and supplied more efficiently in another country.[7] Following this rationale, the removal of trade obstacles benefits all parties to the agreement. Yet, trade relationships between countries are governed by legal rights and obligations that are negotiated bilaterally or multilaterally and embodied in trade agreements. Hence, it is necessary to implement economic trade theories, such as the protection of competitive advantages,

An influential body of literature developed which cited unequal opportunity as one of the major causes of the conflict'; Hull, *Memoirs of Cordell Hull*, pp. 81–84; Hudec, 'Discriminatory Trade Measures', p. 196.

[5] See speech by Winston Churchill, delivered in Zurich, 19 September 1946: 'Under and within that world concept, we must re-create the European family in a regional structure … The first step is to form a Council of Europe. If at first all the States of Europe are not willing or able to join the Union, we must nevertheless proceed to assemble and combine those who will and those who can.' Available at www.churchill-society-london.org.uk/astonish.html; Craig, 'Nature of the Community', p. 6.

[6] See Art. 18 of the TFEU (ex Art. 12 of the TEC): 'Within the scope of application of the Treaties, and without prejudice to any special provisions contained therein, any discrimination on grounds of nationality shall be prohibited'.

[7] On the theories of absolute and comparative advantage see e.g. Stoll and Schorkopf, *WTO*, pp. 33 ff; Kreinin and Plummer, 'Economic Principles of International Trade', pp. 4–5; with regard to services see e.g. Hindley and Smith, 'Comparative Advantage and Trade in Services', *passim*; Cass and Noam, 'Economics and Politics of Trade in Services', pp. 51 ff; Tietje, 'Stärken und Schwächen des GATS', pp. 11 ff.

into specific trade rules. The principle of non-discrimination constitutes one of the main instruments of international economic law designed to secure trade liberalization and guarantee trade commitments. It prevents discriminatory protection of the domestic industry or of specific trading partners, thereby averting inefficient allocation of resources and market distortions.[8] Thus, non-discrimination constitutes the core principle of international trade law and is embodied in virtually all trade agreements within and outside the WTO framework. This chapter provides an overview of the two principal forms of non-discrimination, namely national treatment (*below*, I.) and most-favoured-nation treatment (II.), and how they are implemented in the framework of the WTO, with particular focus on GATS and GATT.

I National treatment

The basic underlying principle of the national treatment obligation provides that a state must accord to imported goods and services the same treatment as to its domestic goods and services. Under the WTO, this principle applies, *inter alia*, to imported and locally produced goods, to foreign and domestic services as well as to foreign and local intellectual property rights, such as trademarks, copyrights and patents. National treatment is the form of non-discrimination with the deepest impact on national regulatory autonomy, requiring sovereign states to adopt regulations in a way so as not to treat its citizens more favourably than foreigners.

In the field of trade in services, GATS provides for a national treatment obligation in its Article XVII, according to which 'each Member shall accord to services and service suppliers of any other Member … treatment no less favourable than that it accords to its own like services and service suppliers'. This text is very closely related to the GATT 1947 national treatment provision on trade in goods, which served as a model when GATS was negotiated and drafted during the Uruguay Round.[9] National treatment for trade in goods is anchored in Article III GATT, of which paragraph 1 states the basic principle and provides a guide to the understanding and the interpretation of the specific obligations contained in other paragraphs of Article III.[10] It sets forth that taxes and

[8] Hudec, "Like Product", p. 108; De Búrca, 'Concept of Discrimination', p. 186; Jackson, *Jurisprudence of GATT and WTO*, p. 60.

[9] Eeckhout, 'Constitutional Concepts', p. 219.

[10] See Appellate Body Report, *Japan – Alcoholic Beverages II*, p. 16.

other regulations affecting internal sale of products as well as internal quantitative regulations 'should not be applied to imported or domestic products so as to afford protection to domestic production'. Article III:2 GATT provides for specific national treatment obligations on *internal taxes* and charges and Article III:4 GATT specifically applies to *regulatory measures* affecting the sale of products.

Under GATT 1947 the Contracting Parties undertook to bind their tariffs of specific goods at a certain level by making commitments in their individual schedules and in accordance with Article II GATT. The main purpose of GATT national treatment is to reinforce Members' commitments with regard to border measures (e.g. tariffs and quotas) by prohibiting the undermining of these commitments through discriminatory internal measures (e.g. taxes and regulatory measures).

> Consider, for instance, that a Member agreed under its schedule of commitments to bind the tariff on computers at 10 per cent. The Member could easily circumvent this maximum tariff (border measure) by imposing a sales tax (internal measure) of 10 per cent on imported computers and of only five per cent on domestically produced computers; with regard to the competitive relationship between imported and domestic computers, the disparate sales tax would have the same effects as an increase of the tariff by five per cent.[11] Similar results can be achieved with regulatory measures,[12] such as granting various types of advantages to domestic producers or to purchasers of domestic products or by placing a higher burden on imported goods and services, resulting in higher production costs and higher prices.

This main purpose of protecting tariff commitments with the national treatment obligation was reflected in the initial phase of GATT 1947 dispute resolution.[13] At that time, the primary focus of trade liberalization was to achieve a reduction of tariffs which, since the aftermath of World War I and the Great Depression, continued to be set at a very high level around the globe.[14]

Based on the rationale that the sole purpose of national treatment is to protect tariff commitments, some participants of the Uruguay Round

[11] Example from Jackson, Davey and Sykes, *International Economic Relations*, p. 358.

[12] Trebilcock and Howse, *Regulation of International Trade*, p. 83.

[13] See e.g. GATT Panel Reports, *Germany – Sardines*; *Spain – Unroasted Coffee*; *Japan – SPF Dimension Lumber*; on these cases see below, 6.I.

[14] See e.g. Irwin, Mavroidis and Sykes, *Genesis of the GATT*, pp. 5–8; Kenen, *The International Economy*, pp. 213–14; Jones, *Multinationals and Global Capitalism*, p. 28: 'By the end of the 1930s almost half of the world's trade was restricted by tariffs'; Oesch, 'Commercial Treaties', n 15.

supported the view that the scope of GATT national treatment should be strictly limited to those products for which Members have undertaken specific tariff commitments in their schedules.[15] Yet, this position succumbed to the opposing opinion that GATT national treatment goes further than simply protecting scheduled commitments. In this regard, the Appellate Body remarked that 'the statement … that "one of the main purposes of Article III is to guarantee that WTO Members will not undermine through internal measures their commitments under Article II" should not be overemphasized [and that] the sheltering scope of Article III is not limited to products that are the subject of tariff concessions under Article II'.[16] The Appellate Body summarized the purpose of GATT national treatment in the following terms:

> The broad and fundamental purpose of Article III is to avoid protectionism in the application of internal tax and regulatory measures. More specifically, the purpose of Article III 'is to ensure that internal measures "not be applied to imported or domestic products so as to afford protection to domestic production"'.[fn omitted] Toward this end, Article III obliges Members of the WTO to provide equality of competitive conditions for imported products in relation to domestic products.[fn omitted] '[T]he intention of the drafters of the Agreement was clearly to treat the imported products in the same way as the like domestic products once they had been cleared through customs. Otherwise indirect protection could be given[fn omitted].'[17]

This broader purpose became more and more important with the gradual reduction of tariffs and the more frequent occurrence of various forms of non-tariff barriers.[18] These developments resulted in a shift of GATT national treatment to a more general prohibition of discrimination, ensuring that imported and domestic products are treated the same way in the internal market. The measures falling under this second objective brought about a number of new challenges in the application of the national treatment obligations. First, more and more trade obstacles that were analysed under Article III GATT in the last 20 years tend to discriminate not directly on the basis of origin, but through indirect or *de facto* less favourable treatment of imported goods.[19] Second, many of these

[15] Jackson, *Law of GATT*, p. 277.

[16] Appellate Body Report, *Japan – Alcoholic Beverages II*, p. 15.

[17] Ibid., pp. 14 ff; see also Appellate Body Report, *Canada – Periodicals*, p. 18: 'The fundamental purpose of Article III of the GATT 1994 is to ensure equality of competitive conditions between imported and like domestic products'.

[18] Jackson, *Law of GATT*, p. 275.

[19] On *de facto* discrimination see below, 3.I.A.2.

measures are not designed as internal charges or taxes within the scope of Article III:2 GATT, but as regulations in terms of Article III:4 GATT.[20] Numerous of these regulations affect trade for reasons of environmental protection, animal welfare, or human rights. Trade obstacles such as the United States' ban on tuna and shrimp imports from countries not sufficiently protecting dolphins and turtles became notoriously famous.[21] The issue of WTO conformity of such measures resulted in very sensitive questions as to how permissive or intrusive national treatment should be interpreted in light of the regulatory autonomy and sovereign rights of WTO Members.

Against this background, the differences in structure between GATS national treatment and its counterpart from the goods sector become more apparent. The most important difference is that unlike in the case of trade in goods, services trade is generally not exposed to tariffs and other border measures. Instead, the supply of services is traditionally subject to domestic regulations. Given this high density of internal regulation and the absence of border measures, GATS national treatment only relates to one single and broad purpose of generally preventing discrimination in services trade. It strives to ensure the equality of competitive conditions between imported and like domestic services by prohibiting protectionism in the application of internal regulations. Hence, it was not necessary to provide for a mechanism comparable to Article III:2 GATT designed to specifically protect commitments on tariff bindings by prohibiting discriminatory internal charges. In consequence, Article XVII GATS does not contain two separate obligations differentiating between internal taxes and regulatory measures. The provision applies very broadly to 'all measures affecting the supply of services', including both internal charges and regulatory measures at the same time.

Next to GATT and GATS, other agreements of the WTO contain similar obligations on national treatment, for example regarding the equal protection of intellectual property rights (Article 3 of the TRIPs Agreement) or the application of trade-related investment measures (Article 2 of the TRIMs Agreement). Finally, the Agreement on Technical Barriers to Trade (TBT Agreement) and the Agreement on the Application of Sanitary and Phytosanitary Measures (SPS Agreement) contain more intrusive

[20] Observers of these developments include DiMascio and Pauwelyn, 'Nondiscrimination in Trade and Investment', 61; Howse and Tuerk, 'WTO Impact on Internal Regulations', p. 285; Jackson, 'National Treatment Obligations', 212.

[21] Appellate Body Report, *US – Shrimp*; GATT Panel Reports, *US – Tuna (Mexico [1991])*, unadopted, and *US – Tuna (EEC [1994])*, unadopted.

instruments of trade liberalization in the framework of the WTO. While both agreements provide for a basic national treatment obligation (Article 2.3 of the SPS Agreement and Article 2.1 of the TBT Agreement), they go beyond the mere prohibition of discriminatory obstacles to trade.[22]

Without relativizing the importance of non-discrimination and national treatment, it must be noted that it constitutes only one of many instruments of trade liberalization. Some instruments are less integrative than non-discrimination, such as the simple elimination of border measures. Other approaches go much further, such as the 'necessity' or 'proportionality' principle or the country of origin principle as expressed in the *Cassis-de-Dijon* jurisprudence in the European Communities.[23]

II Most-favoured-nation treatment

Whereas national treatment is concerned with the relation between the regulatory country and a specific trading partner, the most-favoured-nation (MFN) treatment provides that a state shall not discriminate between its different trading partners. In other words, favourable trading conditions with regard to goods, services or the protection of intellectual property rights granted to one trading partner must be accorded at the same time to all other Members of the WTO. The most-favoured-nation principle goes back to the eleventh century, when the Emperor of the Roman Holy Empire assured the city Mantua in Lombardy 'all customs privileges granted to whatsoever other town'.[24] The principle evolved from unilateral over bilateral to multilateral and from conditional to unconditional forms.[25] Following World War II, it has been perceived as a cornerstone of the multilateral trading system.

Next to the political rationale of inhibiting governments from implementing short-term *ad hoc* trade policies for political considerations, the principle of MFN treatment primarily serves economic goals. Against the background of the theories by *Smith* and *Ricardo* on the efficient allocation of resources and comparative advantage, discrimination between trading partners causes 'a misallocation of resources by inducing a shift of resources toward those relatively less efficient producers

[22] See below, 7.I.

[23] See below, 3.I.A.2; for a comparative analysis of the various instruments see e.g. Ortino, *Instruments for the Liberalisation of Trade, passim.*

[24] Trebilcock and Howse, *Regulation of International Trade*, p. 49, referring to Nolde, 'Clause de la Nation la Plus Favorisée', 25.

[25] For a comprehensive overview of the history, evolution and forms of MFN see Sauvignon, *Nation la Plus Favorisée.*

who are favoured and away from those more efficient producers who are disfavoured'.[26] In contrast, equal treatment of all trading partners with respect to tariffs and other measures 'ensures that imports are supplied by the countries that can produce them most cheaply'.[27] In addition to the economic purpose, the most-favoured-nation principle has a multiplier effect in negotiations on trade liberalization, in that concessions granted to one trading partner must be simultaneously granted to all other Members of the WTO.[28] In the words of the Appellate Body, the object and purpose of the obligation on MFN treatment is not only to prohibit discrimination between products originating from different countries, but it also 'serves as an incentive for concessions, negotiated reciprocally, to be extended to all other Members on an MFN basis'.[29]

Under the WTO framework, most-favoured-nation obligations are included as cornerstones of many agreements. In the field of services, GATS Article II:1 stipulates that 'each Member shall accord immediate and unconditionally to services and service suppliers of any other Member treatment no less favourable than that it accords to like services and service suppliers of any other country'. As is the case for national treatment, the GATS most-favoured-nation clause is also very closely related to – and apparently based on – the analogous provision in GATT. Article I GATT provides that with regard to customs, taxes and regulatory measures, 'any advantage, favour, privilege or immunity granted by any contracting party to any product originating in or destined for any other country shall be accorded immediately and unconditionally to the like product originating in or destined for the territories of all other contracting parties'.

Special provisions of MFN treatment apply with regard to sanitary and phytosanitary measures (Article 2.3 of the SPS Agreement) and technical regulations (Article 2.1 of the TBT Agreement). Finally, MFN treatment is provided for with regard to the protection of intellectual property rights (Article 4 of the TRIPs Agreement) and the application of trade-related investment measures (Article 2 of the TRIMs Agreement).

[26] Hudec, 'Discriminatory Trade Measures', p. 170; however, under certain circumstances, discrimination can also enhance efficiency (p 171); for a comprehensive discussion of MFN see e.g. Horn and Mavroidis, 'Economic and Legal Aspects of MFN', 244 ff; Schwartz and Sykes, 'Economics of MFN', *passim*.

[27] Sykes, 'Comparative Advantage', 78.

[28] Jackson, *World Trading System*, pp. 159–60; on the other hand, MFN creates a free-riding effect that may result in less trade liberalization as it prevents Members from agreeing on concessions, see Schwartz and Sykes, 'Economics of MFN', p. 59.

[29] Appellate Body Report, *Canada – Autos*, para. 84.

2

Particularities of trade in services and GATS

Even though international trade in services has been part of the multilateral trading system for over ten years, many uncertainties remain in the application of its trade rules. While the underlying economic theories as well as the legal instruments for liberalizing international trade in services are largely the same as for the liberalization of trade in goods,[1] numerous inherent differences between trade in services and trade in goods render the process of liberalization and the implementation of trade rules for services more difficult.[2] Thus, before venturing into the specific elements of non-discrimination and the concept of 'likeness', it is indispensable to present a brief overview of the main particularities of international trade in services in the GATS framework in general (*below*, I.) and of the main GATS obligations in particular (II.). It must be emphasized, however, that chapter 2 is limited to provide the basic information needed by the reader unfamiliar with GATS to understand this study on GATS non-discrimination rules and 'likeness'.[3]

I Modes and methods of service supply in GATS

A first and important difference between goods and services is that the latter are extremely heterogeneous and hence quasi impossible to conceptualize both in terms of substance and in terms of characteristics. From a substantive perspective, the Secretariat's revised Services Sectoral Classification List groups all services under the following 12 different sectors, which are divided into some 160 sub-sectors.[4]

[1] See e.g. Hindley and Smith, 'Comparative Advantage and Trade in Services', 374 ff; Adlung, 'Economic Effects of Services Liberalization', p. 2; Hoekman and Mattoo, 'Negotiations on Services', 286–87.

[2] Jackson, 'Constitution for Trade in Services', 187.

[3] GATS resources available at www.wto.org/english/tratop_e/serv_e/serv_e.htm; for a comprehensive GATS textbook introduction see e.g. Footer and George, 'The GATS'.

[4] GNS, Services Sectoral Classification List, Note by the Secretariat, MTN.GNS/W/120, 10 July 1991; see also below, 13.IV.

- *Business services*: e.g. professional services (legal, architectural, medical services), computer services (e.g. software, data processing, data base), research and development, marketing, consulting etc.
- *Communication services*: e.g. postal, courier, telecommunication and audiovisual (motion picture, radio, television, sound recording) services.
- *Construction and engineering services*: e.g. general construction, installation and building services.
- *Distribution services*: e.g. wholesale, retail and franchising.
- *Educational services*: e.g. primary, secondary and higher education.
- *Environmental services*: e.g. sewage, refuse disposal and sanitation services.
- *Financial services*: e.g. all insurance and banking services.
- *Health and social services*: e.g. hospital, ambulance, nursing, physiotherapeutic, acupuncture services etc.
- *Travel services*: e.g. hotels and restaurants, travel agent and tour guide services.
- *Recreational, cultural and sporting services*: e.g. entertainment (theatre, live music, circus), news agency, libraries, museums etc.
- *Transport services*: e.g. air, rail, road and water transportation.
- *Other services*: e.g. washing, cleaning, beauty, graphology, shoe shining, car parking, wedding planning, tattooist or body piercing services etc.

This categorization of services into 12 sectors provides for some structure under the framework of services trade regulation. However, next to the substantive classification of services, GATS omits to legally define the term 'service' for purposes of the agreement,[5] which makes it difficult to characterize the nature of services and trade in services. The main quality used to differentiate services from goods is the intangibility of service transactions. Other criteria frequently mentioned in economic literature are the inseparability between service and supplier, non-storability, non-durability, heterogeneity, as well as simultaneous production and consumption.[6] Yet, while some of these criteria are true for many service transactions, there are always numerous exceptions. With regard

[5] Abu-Akeel, 'Definition of Trade in Services', 191.

[6] On the nature of services and international trade in services see e.g. Messerlin and Sauvant (eds.), *Uruguay Round: Services*, *passim*; Sampson and Snape, 'Issues in Trade in Services', 172–73; Grubel, 'Traded Services', *passim*; Hoekman and Kostecki, *World Trading System*, pp. 238–39; Hoekman and Braga, 'Protection and Trade in Services', 2–3.

to the question of tradability of services, it appears thus appropriate to distinguish the following categories:

- *Services performed on a person or on a fixed object*: Many types of services are performed in relation to a person (e.g. medical and hairdressing services) or a fixed object (e.g. construction services) and meet the ideal type criteria of intangibility and non-storability. Due to non-storability, the service becomes inseparable from its supplier, which in turn entails that production and consumption occurs more or less simultaneously. The supply of such services characteristically requires close proximity between the supplier and the consumer. Consequently, international trade is only feasible if the supplier – in particular labour and capital – relocates to the country of the consumer. For this reason, these types of transactions are also referred to as factor-related trade in services.[7] Alternatively, for some services performed on persons it may be possible that the consumer relocates to the country of the supplier, thereby avoiding movement of factors. This is the case, for instance, for tourists travelling abroad or students attending a foreign university.
- *Intangible, non-storable services performed on a movable object*: A service performed on a movable object – such as maintenance and repair of products – also entails inseparability between the supplier and the service as well as simultaneous production and consumption. However, in contrast to the first category, tradability is facilitated by the fact that the product on which the service is performed may be moved between the consumer and the supplier.[8]
- *Communicated services*: Some services can be supplied without personal contact between the supplier and the consumer, even though they are not performed in relation to a movable object. This is the case for services which, despite their intangibility, are storable. For instance, an architect can draw and 'store' designs and plans on paper, a programmer can 'store' the software on a computer or education services can be 'stored' in books or digital media. Similarly, some services only require communication between the consumer and the supplier, such as many professional services (e.g. consulting, legal, accounting services) or

[7] Hindley, 'Factor-related Trade in Services', pp. 13 ff; Hoekman, 'Trade, and Factor Movements', pp. 39 ff.

[8] For services embodied in or related to goods it may be difficult to determine whether they are governed by rules on trade in goods or trade in services, see e.g. Zdouc, *Comparative Analysis of GATS and GATT*, p. 23; Trebilcock and Howse, *Regulation of International Trade*, p. 351.

financial services. However, even though close proximity between the supplier and the consumer is not strictly necessary, occasional physical meetings may facilitate and promote trade in these types of services.[9]

The nature of the service considerably affects its respective method of supply and hence its tradability. This particularity has been taken into account in GATS, in that Article I:2 defines four different modes of cross-border supply of services:[10]

- *Mode 1 (cross-border supply)* refers to the supply of a service 'from the territory of one Member into the territory of any other Member'. The two criteria are that the foreign supplier is located outside the importing Member's territory and the service is delivered within its territory.[11] In other words, a consumer located in the importing country receives the service from a foreign country by means of telecommunication or post. This mode excludes, by definition, on-site supply and always requires some form of remote supply,[12] such as 'consultancy or market research reports, tele-medical advice, distance training, or architectural drawings'.[13]
- *Mode 2 (consumption abroad)* refers to nationals of the importing country who move abroad in order to consume a service in another Member, for instance as tourist, student or patient. Modes 1 and 2 thus have in common that the service suppliers are located outside the territory of the importing Member and that no movement of factors is required.
- *Mode 3 (commercial presence)* refers to the foreign supplier who establishes and controls an affiliate, subsidiary or representative office within the territory of the importing Member. Common examples are hotel and bank groups or construction and transport companies operating across different countries. Considering that the establishment of a commercial presence in a foreign country usually requires investments and moving of capital, mode 3 is often compared with

[9] CTS, Presence of Natural Persons (Mode 4), Background Note by the Secretariat, S/C/W/75, 8 December 1998, para. 4(ii) and (iii).

[10] On the four modes see in general Zacharias, 'Art. I GATS', pp. 48–53.

[11] Gkoutzinis, 'Trade in Banking Services', 894.

[12] A purely theoretical exception would be that the supplier and consumer would meet right at the border, each staying in his/her country of origin, and performing the service across the border.

[13] See www.wto.org/english/tratop_e/serv_e/cbt_course_e/popup_animation_e.htm.

investment protection rules,[14] albeit limited to service sectors and at the exclusion of goods manufacturers.

- *Mode 4 (temporary movement of natural persons)* refers to a foreign individual who, in his or her capacity of an independent service supplier (e.g. lawyer, consultant, health worker) or employee of a foreign service company (e.g. law firm, consultancy firm, hospital), temporarily moves to the importing Member in order to provide the service. The 'Annex on Movement of Natural Persons Supplying Services Under the Agreement' further specifies the rules pertaining to mode 4. In particular, Article 2 Annex expressly exempts from mode 4 disciplines all measures affecting natural persons seeking access to the employment market as well as measures regarding citizenship, residence or permanent employment.[15]

In order to avoid confusion, the concept of 'modes of supply' must be clearly distinguished from the terms 'remote supply' and 'method of supply'. The four modes of supply in terms of GATS have one crucial element in common, namely that the service is supplied across borders and thus traded internationally. The term 'remote supply', in contrast, only indicates that the supplier and the consumer do not physically meet and, in consequence, that the service is offered through any means of distant communication.[16] Hence, remote supply is inherent to mode 1 supply, but it is not dependent on the cross-border element. In other words, domestic suppliers as well as foreign mode 3 and 4 suppliers can offer their services by means of distant communication *within* the borders of a country.

Finally, the term 'modes' of supply must not be confused with 'methods' of supply. Suppliers may choose a certain method to supply services in order to make it more attractive for consumers or to gain a competitive advantage. The differences in methods of supply are most obvious in cases of remote supply that require technical means, such as telephone, mail, or internet.[17] However, the method of supply can also differ significantly for on-site services, particularly if the service itself is defined very broadly. For instance, transportation services can be supplied by bus, train, or airplane. These are methods of supply distinguishing a very broadly defined

[14] See e.g. Zacharias, 'Art. I GATS', pp. 51–52, with references; Francois and Wooton, 'Trade Liberalization and GATS', 390.

[15] See in general on mode 4 e.g. CTS, Presence of Natural Persons (Mode 4), Background Note by the Secretariat, S/C/W/75, 8 December 1998; Mattoo and Carzaniga (eds.), *Moving People*.

[16] Panel Report, *US – Gambling*, para. 6.32.

[17] See ibid., referring to the term 'means of supply'.

category of transportation. If, in contrast, the service is defined more narrowly, such as for instance 'air travel service', then the methods of supply are less likely to substantially differ. In the given example, methods could be distinguished on the basis of different airplanes or routes, or different in-flight services in terms of comfort and entertainment. This example shows that the notion of method of supply largely overlaps with the nature of the service itself and that it is a pure definitional issue of whether a certain difference relates only to the method of supply or to the service itself.

While this classification of different methods and modes is a useful attempt to structure a legal framework for trade in services, it must be noted that many service transactions require simultaneous use of different methods and – if traded internationally – modes of supply.[18] In the context of the GATS rules on non-discrimination analysis, the concepts of 'modes', 'remote/on-site' and 'method' of supply lead to a number of thorny questions with regard to the legal element of 'likeness' (see Chapter 11).

II The main GATS obligations in a nutshell

The substantive provisions in GATS draw from the same legal principles which stood the test of time under the GATT 1947. However, GATS is equipped with numerous special rules designed to take account of the nature of international trade in services and which also reflect the strong domestic interests and objectives of individual Members. The following obligations are relevant for the present study.

A *Most-favoured-nation and national treatment*

The specific legal issues of the GATS rules on non-discrimination and their relation to the equivalent GATT non-discrimination rules are subject to a detailed discussion in the subsequent chapters. At this stage it suffices to address the scope of the non-discrimination obligations. While GATS most-favoured-nation (MFN) treatment applies, in principle, across all sectors of trade in services, Members were allowed to exempt certain existing measures or certain service sectors pursuant to Article II:2 GATS and the 'Annex on Article II Exemptions' at the time GATS was concluded. Many Members made use of the possibility to schedule exemptions on this so-called *negative* list of MFN treatment, in particular in areas such

[18] Comprehensively Chanda, 'Inter-modal Linkages'.

as audiovisual services, communication services, financial services and transport services. In contrast, the national treatment obligation only applies to those service sectors and modes of supply for which a Member scheduled specific commitments. Section C below illustrates the mechanism of this so-called *positive* list for national treatment.

B Market access

Similar to GATT Article XI, the GATS market access obligation of Article XVI:2 seeks to prevent quantitative import restrictions. Under GATS in particular, Members may not limit (a) the number of service suppliers; (b) the value of service transactions or assets; (c) the number of operations or quantity of output; (d) the number of natural persons supplying a service; (e) the type of legal entity or joint venture or, finally; (f) the participation of foreign capital. Such measures are prohibited even if they are not discriminatory. Yet, like national treatment, Members may individually schedule commitments and limitations with regard to each service sector and mode of supply to which the market access obligation should apply.

C Schedule of commitments for market access and national treatment

The GATS schedule of commitments introduced a new system of flexible and progressive trade liberalization in the WTO framework. It allows Members to designate individually for which sectors and for which modes of supply they intend to comply with the market access and national treatment obligations. Such a positive list bears the advantage that commitments are – similar to tariff concessions in the GATT context – subject to further negotiations and concessions (Article XIX GATS). At the same time, commitments may even be withdrawn against compensation (Article XXI GATS).

The scheduling technique is relatively complex. Members may schedule horizontal commitments and limitations which apply to all service sectors and all four modes of supply.

> For example, a common horizontal limitation concerning all service sectors is that subsidies may be limited to nationals or residents of a certain Member.[19]

[19] On subsidies see below, 3.I.C.5 and 7.III.A.2.

In addition, it is possible to schedule sector-specific commitments and limitations in regard to each mode of supply.[20]

> For instance, with regard to legal services (i.e. advice on home country and international law), Switzerland scheduled unlimited market access (Article XVI) commitments for modes of supply 1–3, but no commitments for mode 4; further, the Swiss schedule indicates full national treatment (Article XVII) commitments for modes of supply 1 and 2, mode 3 commitments which are limited to a nationality requirement for practice in the canton of St. Gall and no commitments for mode 4.[21]

This example illustrates that Members maintain a high degree of flexibility in deciding which service sectors should be subject to either market access or national treatment.

D *Domestic regulations*

The disciplines of Article VI GATS apply to measures of domestic regulations.[22] Most obligations contain procedural standards concerning the administration and application of domestic regulations (Article VI:1) as well as the review of administrative decisions by judicial or administrative tribunals (Article VI:2). Moreover, Members are obliged to provide for 'adequate procedures' to verify the competence of foreign professionals (Article VI:6). The current substantive obligations of Article VI, in contrast, are of very limited reach. The main provision of Article VI:4 mandates the Council for Trade in Services to develop new disciplines with regard to measures relating to qualification and licensing requirements as well as to technical standards. The most important aspect of such future disciplines is a necessity requirement (Article VI:4 lit. b), which entails that regulatory measures must not be 'more burdensome than necessary to ensure the quality of the service'. Consequently, future obligations to be adopted under Article VI:4 differ considerably from the principle of non-discrimination, in that they impose standards on domestic regulations

[20] See also CTS, Guidelines for the Scheduling of Specific Commitments under the General Agreement on Trade in Services (GATS), S/L/92, 28 March 2001; GNS, Scheduling of Initial Commitments in Trade in Services: Explanatory Note, MTN.GNS/W/164, 3 September 1993.

[21] Switzerland, Draft Consolidated Schedule of Specific Commitments, S/DCS/W/CHE, 24 January 2003, p. 8.

[22] For a comprehensive overview see e.g. Krajewski, 'Art. VI; Delimatsis, *Trade in Services and Domestic Regulations*, pp. 93 ff; Wouters and Coppens, 'GATS and Domestic Regulation', *passim*.

which do not differentiate between foreign and domestic services and suppliers. Such 'necessity test' obligations imposed on domestic regulations may potentially liberalize international trade in services much further than the current non-discrimination obligations, but at the same time they bear the risk to considerably interfere with the Members' regulatory autonomy. This potential threat to the sovereignty of the Members may be the main reason for which such new disciplines have so far only been concluded with regard to domestic regulations in the accountancy sector, and even these disciplines are not yet binding.

Finally, pending the adoption of new disciplines under Article VI:4, Article VI:5 aims to ensure that specific market access and national treatment commitments are not nullified or impaired through qualification and licensing requirements as well as technical standards which are not based on objective criteria or are more burdensome than necessary to ensure quality. Considering that this obligation is subject to the condition of 'nullification or impairment',[23] it is reduced to a variation of the non-violation complaint of Article XXIII:2 GATT and thus of limited practical significance.

E Further obligations

For the sake of completeness, it must be noted that GATS contains other obligations which, however, are not of further interest for the purpose of this study. The transparency obligation is frequently named as one of the fundamental principles of GATS. According to Article III:1 GATS, Members are required to publish all measures of general application 'which pertain to or affect the operation' of GATS. In addition, Article III:3 contains the obligation for all Members to notify the Council for Trade in Services 'of any new, or any changes to existing, laws, regulations or administrative guidelines which significantly affect trade in services'. Other obligations not further discussed at this stage concern monopolies (Article VIII), business practices (Article IX) and international money transfers and payments (Article XI) as well as specific sectors (e.g. Annex on Air Transport Services, on Financial Services and on Telecommunications).

[23] Trachtman, 'Lessons for GATS', p. 67.

3

Legal elements of non-discrimination obligations

The structure of any non-discrimination obligation, including national treatment and most-favoured-nation (MFN) treatment, consists of two principal elements that are comparative in nature. The first element of 'less favourable treatment' requires a comparison between the *treatments* accorded to the objects at issue (which are, in the case of trade, imported versus domestic goods and services) in order to assess whether one is treated less favourably than the other. The second element of 'likeness' calls for a comparison between the *objects* of the treatment.[1] The two elements of 'likeness' and 'less favourable treatment' are cumulative in nature.[2] An additional and third element that needs to be taken into account when speaking of non-discrimination relates to the regulatory purpose of the measure at issue.[3] In particular the question of whether and how the regulatory purpose of a discriminatory measure should be considered under the legal analysis of WTO law has led to considerable controversy among trade practitioners and scholars.

At the outset it must be noted that each of these three elements should never be examined in complete isolation, but always in context of their mutual relationship. An integral view is important because the interpretation of one element may have a certain effect on the interpretation of another element.[4] For instance, formulated in the abstract, a broad interpretation of the 'likeness' concept may require narrowly interpreting 'less favourable treatment' or taking into account the regulatory purpose in order to avoid an overly intrusive application of the non-discrimination

[1] See also Qin, 'Defining Nondiscrimination', 223.

[2] Appellate Body Report, *EC – Asbestos*, para. 100.

[3] For the sake of completeness, it must be noted that depending on the terms of the agreement and the specific provision in question, the complete legal test requires to analyse additional legal elements. For instance, GATT Art. III:4 only applies to measures which qualify as 'law, regulation or requirement'. Such other elements outside the core of non-discrimination are beyond the scope of this research.

[4] Also in favour of an integral approach is Ehring, 'De Facto Discrimination', 944; Fauchald, 'WTO Non-Discrimination Clauses', 446.

provisions. Hence, even though the present study primarily focuses on the concept of 'likeness', it is necessary to make references to the other elements of the non-discrimination obligations. The present chapter 3 presents a general overview of the elements' 'less favourable treatment' (*below*, I.), 'likeness' (II.), and 'regulatory purpose' (III.), taking into account the developments in GATT 1947 and WTO jurisprudence. Even though the following discussion is true for non-discrimination in both services and goods trade, this chapter primarily focuses on theories and concepts developed in relation to GATT on the one hand, as well as systemic questions and legal structure on the other hand. A deconstruction of non-discrimination into its various elements and a doctrinal analysis of each element not only provides a starting point for the concepts of 'like services' and 'like service suppliers' in GATS rules on non-discrimination, but is also important for the general understanding of non-discrimination obligations in international trade and future drafting of trade agreements.

I Less favourable treatment

The element of 'less favourable treatment' constitutes the basic discriminatory component and thus the essence of discrimination. Despite its importance, the term or standard is not generally defined in the WTO agreements. It is thus necessary to determine in what respect 'less favourable treatment' is illegal or, in other words, by what underlying principle the standard of 'less favourable' should be guided in the legal analysis. GATT 1947 and WTO jurisprudence has long acknowledged the *conditions of competition* as benchmark for the interpretation and application of 'less favourable treatment'. Surprisingly, however, this standard is only specifically phrased in one WTO provision. Article XVII:3 GATS states that 'different treatment shall be considered to be less favourable if it modifies the conditions of competition'. It appears that the wording of paragraph 3 was drafted on the basis of prior GATT 1947 panel reports which developed the principle of conditions of competition under the analogous provision of Article III GATT.[5] Even though Article III GATT does not provide for an explicit reference to the underlying principle of 'conditions of competition', it at least states that measures shall not be construed 'so as to afford protection

[5] The first report to adopt this standard was GATT Panel Report, *Italy – Agricultural Machinery*, para. 12; see also Zdouc, *Comparative Analysis of GATS and GATT*, pp. 172–73; Ortino, 'Principle of Non-Discrimination', p. 175.

to domestic production' (para 1).[6] The Appellate Body thus endorsed previous GATT 1947 jurisprudence on national treatment, confirming that 'less favourable treatment' requires an examination of 'whether a measure modifies the conditions of competition in the relevant market to the detriment of imported products'.[7] In contrast, neither GATT nor GATS provisions on MFN treatment make any reference to competition or protectionism. Nonetheless, GATT/WTO jurisprudence in both regards confirmed the relevance of competition as guiding principle for the standard of 'less favourable treatment' in regard to MFN treatment.[8]

In light of the above considerations, it can be concluded that 'less favourable treatment' requires a differential treatment of certain products or certain services that results in a competitive disadvantage for one group of the products or services. However, there are a number of interpretative issues that remain to be resolved. First, section A addresses the questions in respect to the *basis* of differential treatment, namely whether the measure differentiates directly or indirectly on the prohibited criterion and how this question relates to the subjective theory of 'less favourable treatment'. Second, 'less favourable treatment' of imported goods and services may result from all kinds of *measures*, the form and substance of which are only limited by one's imagination. Section B thus provides an outline of the most important types of 'less favourable treatment' in accordance with the classical GATT trade in goods categorization and, finally, section C examines to what extent the main *obstacles to services trade* qualify as treatment less favourable under the GATS.

A *Basis and standard of 'less favourable treatment'*

The principle of non-discrimination is not limited to international economic law, but applies in many different areas, such as constitutional law as well as fundamental rights and human rights. In abstract terms, a measure amounts to discrimination if there is some form of 'less favourable treatment' on the basis of a difference between two otherwise largely

[6] Englisch, *Wettbewerbsgleichheit*, pp. 414–15, linking the terms 'so as to afford protection' with the guiding principle 'conditions of competition'.

[7] Appellate Body Report, *Korea – Various Measures on Beef*, paras. 137–38.

[8] For GATS Art. II see e.g. Appellate Body Report, *Canada – Autos*, para. 174, where the Appellate Body criticized the Panel for not having examined 'the structure of competition in the wholesale trade services market for motor vehicles in Canada'; in great detail Englisch, *Wettbewerbsgleichheit*, pp. 410 ff.

identical 'objects', 'people' or 'situations'. Importantly, 'less favourable treatment' does not *per se* amount to undesired or even illegal discrimination. For instance, an employer who pays a lower salary to a woman who is less qualified than a man working on the same job treats the woman less favourably without, however, acting discriminatory. The problem in this simple hypothetical is that the two people subject to comparison differ in two ways, namely with regard to gender and qualification. Hence, as long as the differential treatment is based on *qualification* and not on *gender*, the measure does not amount to illegal discrimination. Depending on whether the discriminatory measure is based *directly* or *indirectly* on the illegal criterion, we speak of *de jure* or *de facto* discrimination. With regard to each area of law, the law-making body must make a policy choice by value judgment in order to determine the bases on which differential treatment is deemed illegal. In the case of fundamental and human rights, for instance, typical bases for differential treatment frowned upon are gender, race, age, language, religion, political or other opinion, national or social origin, association with a national minority, mental or physical condition, and so forth.[9]

1. *De jure* discrimination in trade

The first category of 'less favourable treatment', namely *de jure* discrimination, covers all measures that differentiate *directly* on the basis of the prohibited criterion.[10] A typical example falling under this category is the employer who pays a lower salary to all female employees compared to male employees, regardless of qualification and job requirements. This measure differentiates directly on the basis of gender and would thus be considered as an illegal *de jure* discrimination.

Unlike discrimination in other legal disciplines, such as fundamental and human rights, discrimination in trade law is only concerned with 'less favourable treatment' based on the difference in *origin* of the products or the services in question. In other words, origin is the only prohibited basis for differential treatment.[11] Thus, if for example only Swiss citizens or entities incorporated in Switzerland were allowed to supply banking and insurance services in Switzerland, this measure would amount to a

[9] See e.g. Article 14 of the European Convention of Human Rights (1950); Article 26 of the International Covenant on Civil and Political Rights (1966); for an overview of grounds for discrimination see e.g. Doebbler, *Non-Discrimination in International Law*, pp. 37–67.

[10] This form of discrimination is also referred to as direct, overt, formal, facial or explicit discrimination.

[11] Englisch, *Wettbewerbsgleichheit*, p. 412; Pauwelyn, 'Lightness of Likeness', p. 361.

straightforward *de jure* discrimination against foreign suppliers of such services. Similarly, a higher tariff or internal tax on computers imported from Taiwan compared to computers from China discriminates directly on the basis of origin and thus violates the obligation on MFN treatment under the GATT.

De jure discrimination is relatively easy to assess under WTO law as both elements of 'less favourable treatment' and 'likeness' are usually fulfilled. In fact, international economic law generally treats *de jure* discriminations as *prima facie* illegal or as creating a presumption of illegality.[12] In this regard, the Panel in *Korea – Various Measures on Beef* ruled in very resolute terms:

> 'Any regulatory distinction that is based exclusively on criteria relating to the nationality or the origin of the products is incompatible with Article III ... confirming that there is no need to demonstrate the actual and specific trade effects of a measure for it to be found in violation of Article III. The object of Article III:4 is, thus, to guarantee effective market access to imported products and to ensure that the latter are offered the same market opportunities as domestic products.' (para 627)

On appeal, the Appellate Body did not agree with the Panel's resolute interpretation and modified the latter's ruling in respect of the standard required for 'less favourable treatment' in *de jure* discrimination cases. It found that a formal difference in treatment is, by itself, not sufficient to show a violation of Article III:4, stating further that '[w]hether or not imported products are treated "less favourably" than like domestic products should be assessed ... by examining whether a measure modifies the *conditions of competition* in the relevant market to the detriment of imported products'.[13] Consequently, the complainant is always required to show under 'less favourable treatment' that the measure under scrutiny modifies the conditions of competition, regardless of the *de jure* or *de*

[12] Howse and Regan, 'Product/Process Distinction', 252, 270; Farber and Hudec, 'Domestic Environmental Regulations', p. 69; see also Hudec, 'Requiem for "Aim and Effects"', 621: 'Cases of explicit discrimination stand out because the explicitly different treatment is viewed as evidence that discrimination against foreign goods is a deliberate policy'; similarly on investment protection see Bjorklund, 'National Treatment', p. 38: 'In the case of a *de jure* measure, however, one need not show that a domestic entity has actually received any treatment if such is inherent in the terms of the measure'; on Art. 110 TFEU (ex Art. 90 TEC) see Ortino, *Instruments for the Liberalisation of Trade*, p. 146.

[13] Appellate Body Report, *Korea – Various Measures on Beef*, paras. 137–38: 'We conclude that the Panel erred in its general interpretation that "[a]ny regulatory distinction that is based exclusively on criteria relating to the nationality or the origin of the products is incompatible with Article III"'.

facto nature of the alleged discrimination. This conclusion also coincides with GATS Article XVII:3 which prescribes the same standard for both forms of less favourable treatment: '[f]ormally identical or formally different treatment shall be considered to be less favourable if it modifies the conditions of competition'. Consequently, a *prima facie* case always requires that the complainant shows how a measure results in a competitive disadvantage for its products or services.[14] In contrast, as will be demonstrated under section 3.II below, the analysis of 'likeness' as second element of non-discrimination differs considerably with regard to measures distinguishing on the basis of origin and measures distinguishing on the basis of other characteristics unrelated to origin.

2. *De facto* discrimination in trade

According to Article XVII:3 GATS, the requirements of 'less favourable treatment' are met not only by according formally different treatment to services and suppliers of any other Member, but also by *according formally identical* treatment. The 'formally identical' treatment referred to in this provision is aimed at forms of *de facto* discrimination, which are origin-neutral on their face. Again, the wording in paragraph 3 is based on prior GATT reports,[15] even though GATT non-discrimination obligations omit to expressly incorporate the concept to 'formally identical' treatment. Nonetheless, the WTO adjudicating bodies confirmed that the prohibition of *de facto* discrimination extends to all obligations of MFN and national treatment of both GATT and GATS.[16]

Discrimination falling under this second category is much more difficult to recognize as it concerns measures which appear facially or formally neutral. Such measures differentiate directly on the basis of

[14] EC submission in Panel Report, *Dominican Republic – Import and Sale of Cigarettes*, para. 5.161: 'in order to make a *prima facie* case, it is not sufficient to rely for the determination of a "less favourable treatment" solely on the relative market share of importers as a group and domestic producers as a group. Honduras would also have to show that the imposition of a specific, fixed-amount bond results in a higher burden and a competitive disadvantage for the group of imported goods, as compared to the group of domestic like products'.

[15] The first report referring to formally identical legal provision according less favourable treatment was GATT Panel Report, *US – Section 337 Tariff Act*, para. 5.11; see also Ortino, 'Principle of Non-Discrimination', p. 175.

[16] For de facto discrimination falling under Art. I GATT, see e.g. Appellate Body Report, *EC – Bananas III*, para. 232; with regard to Art. III GATT, see GATT Panel Report, *Japan – Alcoholic Beverages I*, paras. 3.5, 5.9 ff; with regard to Art. II GATS, see Appellate Body Report, *EC – Bananas III*, para. 233; with regard to Art. XVII GATS, see Panel Report, *EC – Bananas III (Article 21.5 – Ecuador)*, para. 6.149.

a permitted criterion, but at the same time *indirectly* treat one group defined by a prohibited criterion less favourably. Remaining in the area of gender equality in labour law, an employer who pays a lower salary to part-time employees differentiates in general on a permissible basis. However, one could make the argument that this measure constitutes a *de facto* discrimination of female employees, considering that women may more often work part-time jobs than men.[17] In this example, the discriminatory effect results from *factual circumstances*, namely that women are more likely to assume the role of primary caregiver than men.

In the trade context, all forms of non-tariff barriers can amount to *de facto* discrimination, but the most common forms are internal taxes and domestic regulations. Since formally neutral measures do not differentiate on the basis of origin, discrimination occurs only because of factual circumstances related to the producer/supplier, the production/supply method, the product/service or the market place, resulting in the effect of 'tilting the scales' against the imported products or services.[18] It is possible to distinguish different types of factual circumstances which may lead to a competitive disadvantage to foreign goods and services.

- *Factual impossibility*: A first factual setting leading to *de facto* less favourable treatment arises if the foreign producer or service supplier is neither theoretically nor practically in a position to comply with the regulation in an export market.

> Noting that the *Vaalserberg* is the highest point in the Netherlands rising to 322 metres above sea level, a mountainous country like Switzerland could adopt a measure providing that only milk produced by cows living at 330 metres above sea level could be imported and sold. Such a measure, even though applying to Swiss and foreign farmers alike, would *de facto* prohibit all milk imports from the Netherlands, while having almost no effect on Swiss farmers.[19] Such a scheme would clearly constitute a *de facto* discrimination against all milk produced in the Netherlands. In this example, Dutch farmers are neither theoretically nor practically in a position to meet the required standards.

[17] See e.g. in the EC context Case 96/80 *Jenkins* v. *Kingsgate* [1981] ECR 911.

[18] Jackson, 'National Treatment Obligations', 212.

[19] Example inspired by the German trade measure from 1904 allowing tariff reductions for 'large dappled mountain cattle or brown cattle reared at a spot at least 300 meters above sea level and which have at least one month's grazing each year at a spot at least 800 meters above sea level', see League of Nations, 'The Most-Favoured-Nation Clause', 145.

– *Higher transaction costs*: *De facto* discrimination occurs even if foreign producers or suppliers could theoretically comply with the regulation in question, but for reasons of higher transaction costs are not practically able to do so on a competitive basis.

Assume, for instance, that industrialized countries would wish to adopt certain environmental standards with regard to carbon emission, providing that only goods and services produced or supplied below a certain threshold of carbon emission could be sold on their territory. Even though enterprises located in developing countries could theoretically make their goods and services compliant with the environmental standard, they would most likely have more difficulties to meet these standards due to the lack of environmentally friendly infrastructure and lack of capital to build up such infrastructure.

In addition, even where producers and suppliers are able to change production and supply methods in order to meet the different regulatory standard or to qualify for a lower tax, such changes would still result in rising costs, making it more burdensome for foreign producers and suppliers to compete on the import market. Hence, origin-neutral regulations or taxes resulting in higher production costs for foreign producers and suppliers is one of the most important constellation of *de facto* discrimination.

– *Traditional practice*: Finally, a measure could be equally burdensome for domestic and foreign producers of goods or service suppliers allowing importing firms to comply both practically and theoretically, and still, for certain circumstances the measure negatively affects imports more frequently than domestic goods or services. The relevant factor leading to the asymmetric and thus discriminatory effect would in most cases stem from traditional practice.

For instance, a sales ban for beer containing more than 4.5 volume per cent alcohol is theoretically not more burdensome for some beer breweries than for others; however, if domestic breweries located in the regulatory country have been producing beer for decades below the threshold, the ban would most likely be discriminatory against, for instance, Belgian beer which is traditionally produced with a higher alcohol content. For factual circumstances, such as tradition or consumers' tastes and habits, that's the way beer is produced in either country for decades. Whereas the enterprises located in developing countries from the previous example would be factually unable to meet the required level of carbon emission due to lack of capital and infrastructure, Belgian breweries could comply with the required alcohol threshold; yet, it is unlikely for them to change their centuries old recipes, resulting in the removal of their products from the market of the regulatory country. Given the overall discriminatory effect, such measures would also qualify as *de facto* discrimination.

All of these examples refer to situations in which a measure imposes a disadvantage predominantly on imported goods or services, whereas domestically produced goods or supplied services remain predominantly unaffected. Accordingly, one possible interpretation of the non-discrimination provisions in WTO law is to say that *de facto* discrimination only occurs if a higher number or percentage of a certain group of imports is disfavoured by the measure in comparison to the same group of domestic goods or services. This interpretation has been referred to by *Ehring* as an 'asymmetric impact test',[20] whereas other commentators use the terminology of 'disparate impact view', 'discriminatory effect test', 'aggregate comparison approach' and 'narrow' standard of *de facto* discrimination.[21] The question of which type of measures amounts to 'less favourable treatment' or how this term should be defined is not further specified in GATT or GATS. The absence of any legal definition leads to considerable uncertainty with regard to the required impact intensity on foreign goods or services. In contrast to the above examples, the WTO provisions on most-favoured-nation and national treatment also allow an interpretation according to which *de facto* discrimination already exists if only very few – arguably even only potentially – imported products or services are treated less favourably than any of those from the domestic industry. *Ehring* referred to this approach as the 'diagonal test'.[22]

Assume for instance a theoretical model situation where 100 domestic producers/products stand vis-à-vis 100 imported 'like' products from foreign producers. Under the extreme *diagonal* test, a measure would already qualify as *de facto* discriminatory if it treats only one imported product less favourably in comparison to one domestic product, regardless of how the other 99 domestic and 99 imported products are affected by the measure. In consequence, there could be discrimination even if

20 Ehring, 'De Facto Discrimination', 924–25: under the 'asymmetric impact test' *de facto* discrimination occurs only 'if the burden arising from the measure is heavier for imports than for domestic goods'.

21 Regan, 'Regulatory Purpose and "Like Products"', 470; Regan, 'Further Thoughts on Regulatory Purpose', 756; Davey and Pauwelyn, 'MFN Unconditionality', pp. 38–41; Pauwelyn, 'GATT Phantoms Still Haunt the WTO', 583; Ortino, '*De Jure* and *De Facto* Discrimination', p. 260; Krajewski, *National Regulation*, pp. 108–9; Vranes, *Trade and the Environment*, pp. 235 ff; see also Eeckhout, 'Constitutional Concepts', pp. 233–34; Pauwelyn, 'Lightness of Likeness', p. 364.

22 Ehring, 'De Facto Discrimination', 924: under the 'diagonal test' *de facto* discrimination occurs if 'any imports receive less favorable treatment than any like domestic products'.

a large majority of imported products are treated more favourably than a large majority of domestic products, as long as 1 imported product receives less favourable treatment than 1 domestic product. In contrast, the extreme *asymmetric* test requires that at least a majority (i.e. 51) of foreign products are treated less favourably than a majority (i.e. 51) of domestic products. Alternatively, a less stringent application is to say that *de facto* discrimination occurs if more or a higher percentage of imported products are negatively affected compared to domestic products, regardless of the ratio. For instance, six imported products (=6 per cent) receiving less favourable treatment than three domestic products (=3%) would result in *de facto* discrimination just as 80 imports (=80%) compared to 10 domestic (=10 per cent).

The diagonal test could be paraphrased as an obligation to treat all foreign products or services equivalent to the 'best' treatment accorded to a 'like' domestic product or service. It has the effect that even measures with an extremely subtle element of discrimination fall under the WTO obligation of non-discrimination. In fact, under the diagonal test, the scope of the non-discrimination concept is construed in a broad way such that it is only a very small step away from the trade instrument generally referred to as principle of *non-restriction (Beschränkungsverbot)*. The legal concept of non-restriction goes much further in trade liberalization than the principle of non-discrimination. It is fundamental, for instance, to the freedom to provide services under EU law. According to the ECJ, Article 56 TFEU (ex Art. 49 TEC, formerly Art. 59 TEC)[23] 'requires not only the elimination of all discrimination against a person providing services on the ground of his nationality but also the abolition of any restriction, *even if it applies without distinction to national providers of services and to those of other Member States*, when it is liable to prohibit or otherwise impede the activities of a provider of services established in another Member State where he lawfully provides similar services.'[24] Under a non-restriction approach, the elements of 'less favourable treatment' and 'likeness' are replaced by a test of necessity and proportionality.[25] Similarly, the principle of 'mutual recognition' developed by the ECJ in the case

[23] Art. 56 TFEU reads: 'restrictions on freedom to provide services within the Union shall be prohibited in respect of nationals of Member States who are established in a Member State other than that of the person for whom the services are intended'.

[24] Case C-76/90 *Säger* v. *Dennemeyer & Co. Ltd.* [1991] ECR I-4221, para. 12 (emphasis added); Case C-17/00 *De Coster* v. *Collège des bourgmestre et échevins de Watermael-Boitsfort* [2001] ECR I-9445, para. 29; Case C-43/93 *Vander Elst* v. *Office des Migrations Internationales* [1994] ECR I-3803, para. 14; O'Leary, 'Free Movement of Persons', p. 402; Holoubek, 'EGV 49/50', pp. 726 ff.

[25] See e.g. Art. 16 of the EC Services Directive 2006/123/EC, OJ 2006 L376/36.

Cassis-de-Dijon for the rules on trade in goods is even more integrative than 'non-restriction'.[26]

In comparison, under an interpretation of *de facto* discrimination in accordance with an extreme diagonal test, 'less favourable treatment' of just one foreign producer or supplier who could potentially import into the domestic market compared to one domestic producer or supplier is discriminatory. Hence, the significance of the discriminatory element is reduced to an extent that almost any regulatory measure qualifies as *de facto* discrimination. In fact, any difference in technical standards or qualification requirements between the exporting and the importing country is in one way or another more burdensome to some producers and suppliers from the exporting country than to domestic firms.[27] Some commentators even make the final step towards non-restriction and necessity, suggesting that *de facto* discrimination in the case of GATS and GATT should be interpreted such that any measure which is more burdensome than necessary for foreign services and suppliers should qualify as discrimination in violation of Articles II or XVII GATS.[28]

[26] Case C-120/78 *Rewe-Zentral AG* v. *Bundesmonopolverwaltung für Branntwein* [1979] ECR 649, para. 14: On the basis of Art. 34 TFEU (ex Art. 28, formerly Art. 30 TEC) prohibiting quantitative restrictions and measures having equivalent effect, the ECJ introduced the principle of 'mutual recognition', requiring that any lawfully produced and marketed product of one Member State may be marketed in all other Member Sates; see e.g. Becker, 'EGV 28–30', p. 451; for a comparison between the WTO and EC trade instruments see e.g. De Búrca, 'Concept of Discrimination', pp. 183 ff; Nicolaïdis and Trachtman, 'Policed Regulation', p. 245; Eeckhout, 'Constitutional Concepts', *passim*; Eeckhout, 'Free Movement of Goods', p. 204; Wilsher, 'Non-Discrimination Principle within the European Single Market', 5 ff; Ortino, *Instruments for the Liberalisation of Trade*, pp. 388 ff; Ortino, '"Non-discrimination" to "Reasonableness"', *passim*; Weiler, 'Constitution of the Common Market Place', pp. 364 ff.

[27] Under the diagonal test, only few trade-restrictive measures would qualify as purely non-discriminatory, such as a quota: A measure allowing only 50 suppliers of banking services on a first-come-first-serve basis regardless of origin would not be captured by the diagonal test of Art. XVII GATS and would fall only under the market access obligation of Art. XVI GATS.

[28] Note that some commentators suggest 'necessity' as an independent substantive standard, while others see 'necessity' as an additional element to 'less favourable treatment' and 'likeness' within non-discrimination; see e.g. Mattoo, 'National Treatment in GATS', 131–3; Mattoo, 'MFN and GATS', pp. 77–79; Mattoo and Subramanian, 'Regulatory Autonomy and Multilateral Disciplines', 315–16; Mattoo, 'Future GATS Rules', 15; Verhoosel, *National Treatment*, pp. 51 ff; Cossy, 'Thoughts on "Likeness" in GATS', p. 349; on this issue in general but rejecting a 'necessity' approach see Krajewski, *National Regulation*, pp. 109–10; Krajewski and Engelke, 'Art. XVII GATS', p. 412; Trebilcock and Giri, 'National Treatment Principle', 59–60. This debate must not be confused with the GATS Art. VI mandate to negotiate a necessity test as new positive obligation (below, n 31), nor with necessity as part of the general exceptions clause.

The principles of non-restriction and mutual recognition require that the contracting parties maintain a certain level of confidence in one another's form of government and regulatory system, which is only possible if they share common or similar political systems, cultures and values. Such a common basis enables and justifies the deep economic integration of the EU Member States, but a comparable foundation is lacking among the Members of the WTO.[29] Moreover, the administration of such far-reaching trade instruments requires an institutional framework which is based on constitutional principles, such as legitimacy and good governance. Again, it is questionable whether the WTO meets such institutional standards. Consequently, WTO trade instruments are – aside from few exceptions[30] – limited to principles such as the prohibition of quantitative restrictions and discriminatory measures. In the GATS context, negotiators even explicitly refrained from incorporating a general non-restriction obligation on the basis of a necessity test.[31] Hence, it is very questionable whether an interpretation of WTO non-discrimination rules in accordance with the diagonal test and the principle of non-restriction is in line with the objective and purpose of the WTO framework.[32]

The WTO adjudicating bodies have not been entirely consistent in their findings on whether *de facto* discrimination applies in a broad sense to situations where only a very small number of imports is treated less favourably than any domestic goods or services, or whether a higher

[29] Oppermann, *Europarecht*, p. 417, referring to the 'Vertrauensprinzip' as a basis for the Cassis-de-Dijon approach; Wilsher, 'Non-Discrimination Principle within the European Single Market', 6–7; for a comparison between the WTO and EC principles see above, n 26.

[30] Notably the TBT/SPS Agreements, see below, 7.I; also CTS, Disciplines on Domestic Regulation in the Accountancy Sector, S/L/64, 17 December 1998.

[31] An earlier draft of GATS contained a necessity requirement for all domestic regulations, see GNS, Draft – Multilateral Framework for Trade in Services, MTN.GNS/35, 23 July 1990, draft Article VII on domestic regulation; see also comments by Pauwelyn, 'Distinguishing Domestic Regulation from Market Access', 138; on the mandate for a necessity test in Article VI:4 GATS see Delimatsis, *Trade in Services and Domestic Regulations*, pp. 166 ff.

[32] Cottier and Mavroidis, 'An Overview', p. 4: 'The WTO is not (and should not be interpreted as) an instrument for deregulation'; Mavroidis, '"Like Products": Some Thoughts', p. 125: '[the WTO] does not aim at establishing a unified market where all factors of production circulate without any restriction'; Englisch, *Wettbewerbsgleichheit*, p. 420; similarly also Puth, *Produkt-Prozess-Doktrin*, pp. 242–43; Krajewski, 'Adjudicating Necessity', p. 398.

percentage of all imports than of domestic goods or services have to be negatively affected by the measure.[33]

> In *EC – Asbestos*, the Panel omitted to examine the effect of the French asbestos ban on domestic products vis-à-vis 'like' imported products. It largely applied a diagonal test according to which it is sufficient that the ban disfavours some imported asbestos products and favours some 'like' domestic non-asbestos products (para 8.155).[34] Even though the Appellate Body reversed the Panel's ruling primarily on grounds of 'likeness', it also reversed the Panel's approach in regard to 'less favourable treatment' in an *obiter dictum*. It held that 'a complaining Member must ... establish that the measure accords to the group of "like" *imported* products less favourable treatment than it accords to the group of *domestic* products'. (para 100)

Despite this inconsistency among WTO adjudicating bodies in the interpretation of the standard for 'less favourable treatment', the Appellate Body's *obiter dictum* shows a strong tendency towards the narrower approach, requiring an asymmetric impact between the imported and domestic group of products or service. This approach is supported by most commentators.[35]

In comparison, in the case of Article 110 para. 2 TFEU (ex Art. 90 para. 2 TEC, formerly Art. 95 TEC) prohibiting tax discrimination – which is very similar to Article III:2 GATT on tax discrimination[36] – the ECJ also adopts the asymmetric impact test in order to demonstrate whether a tax is of protective nature:

> 'The protective nature of the tax system ... is clear. A characteristic of that system is in fact that an essential part of domestic production ... come[s] within the most favourable tax category whereas at least two types of product, almost all of which are imported from other Member States, are

33 See also regarding Art. 5.5 SPS Agreement Panel Report, *EC – Hormones*, para. 8.205, finding that the number of animals treated with hormones 'was significantly lower in the European Communities than in the United States'; for a comprehensive analysis of jurisprudence in regard to 'less favourable treatment' see Ehring, 'De Facto Discrimination', 931–48; Ortino, 'Principle of Non-Discrimination', pp. 180–86.

34 Panel Report, *EC – Asbestos*, para. 8.155.

35 Comprehensively Englisch, *Wettbewerbsgleichheit*, pp. 394, 428 ff; also Ehring, 'De Facto Discrimination', 942–46; Davey and Pauwelyn, 'MFN Unconditionality', pp. 38–41, discussing whether the 'discriminatory effect' should play a role in the analysis of Arts. III and I GATT; Ortino, '*De Jure* and *De Facto* Discrimination', pp. 258–62; Ortino, 'Principle of Non-Discrimination', pp. 179–85; DiMascio and Pauwelyn, 'Nondiscrimination in Trade and Investment', 66; Ortino, *Instruments for the Liberalisation of Trade*, pp. 336 ff; Puth, *Produkt-Prozess-Doktrin*, p. 251; Pauwelyn, 'Lightness of Likeness', p. 364.

36 See e.g. Slotboom, 'Different Treaty Purposes', 558–76.

> subject to higher taxation ... The fact that another domestic product ... is similarly placed at a disadvantage does not rule out the protective nature of the system'.[37]

From an interpretative point of view, the critical question is whether the asymmetric impact test can only be adopted if the non-discrimination provision requires protectionist effect as a legal element (see e.g. GATT III:1 and TFEU 110, para. 2) or whether the asymmetric impact test is inherent to *de facto* less favourable treatment and thus applicable for all non-discrimination clauses. In the light of the Appellate Body's findings in *EC – Asbestos* in regard to GATT III:4 – which according to WTO jurisprudence does not require a separate showing of a protectionist effect[38] – there is a strong tendency towards the second approach.

3. Subjective theory of 'less favourable treatment'

The standard of 'less favourable treatment' for *de facto* discriminations can be interpreted not only from an objective angle, but also so as to include a subjective component. The objective approach generally discussed above requires to limit the analysis to the actual or potential effects of *de facto* differential treatment on the competitive relationship in a given market. In other words, it is irrelevant whether the regulating Member takes advantage of the factual circumstances to hide a true protectionist objective or whether the differential treatment is based on a valid criterion. Under the subjective approach, in contrast, the anticompetitive effect of a measure is by itself not sufficient to qualify as 'less favourable treatment'. In addition, the measure must be adopted with the actual purpose to modify the conditions of competition in the domestic market. Consequently, if a measure is proven to pursue an objective unrelated to trade, such as the protection of policy goals related to environmental and consumer protection, human rights etc., it would not qualify as 'less favourable treatment' in terms of the trade non-discrimination obligation. In essence, the subjective theory incorporates the regulatory purpose into the analysis of *de facto* less favourable treatment. This approach is related to the subjective theory of 'likeness' and will thus be discussed in more detail under section 3.III.A.2 below.

[37] Case 168/78 *Commission* v. *French Republic* [1980] ECR 00347, para. 41; for an overview of ECJ jurisprudence see Ehring, 'De Facto Discrimination', 948–49.

[38] Appellate Body Report, *EC – Bananas III*, para. 216 (para 1 of Art. III applies only to para. 2, but not to para. 4); but see Appellate Body Report, *EC – Asbestos*, paras. 98, 100 (para 1 of Art. III 'informs' para. 4 of Art. III); see also Appellate Body Report, *Japan – Alcoholic Beverages II*, p. 17.

B *Typology of 'less favourable treatment' under GATT*

Under the GATT and international trade in goods, trade-restrictive measures are traditionally categorized in border measures imposed at the border and internal measures imposed once the goods have cleared customs.

1. 'Less favourable treatment' through border measures

The most obvious way to restrain international trade is to impose measures on imports at the border. Such border measures are generally categorized in two groups, namely tariffs on the one hand and quantitative restrictions on the other hand. A *tariff* is a duty imposed on a product at the moment it crosses the border. Tariffs usually apply to imports (import tariff), however, they can also be imposed on exports (export tariff). A quantitative restriction, commonly referred to as *quota*, is a limit with regard to the volume of imports or exports permitted over a certain period of time.[39]

In the context of non-discrimination, border measures are particularly relevant under the rules on MFN treatment. Setting higher tariffs or lower quotas for products originating from country A results in a straightforward competitive advantage for products imported from country B. This difference in treatment thus qualifies as 'less favourable' under the principle of MFN treatment and is, generally speaking, prohibited. It is important to note that any duty or charge imposed at the border – irrespective of whether it is formally applied as or called a tariff – can amount to less favourable treatment. GATT 1947 practice shows that the wide range of duties and charges includes, for instance, tax rebates,[40] merchandise processing fees[41] and consular fees.[42] Moreover, not only the tariff as such, but also the method of imposing or collecting the fee can result in less favourable treatment. For instance, the import licensing system for the administration of tariff quotas was found to violate the principle of MFN treatment.[43]

[39] On border measures see e.g. Trebilcock and Fishbein, 'Barriers to Trade', pp. 9 ff; Jackson, *World Trading System*, pp. 139 ff; on economic effects of discriminatory border measures e.g. Hudec, 'Discriminatory Trade Measures', p. 170.

[40] Ruling by the Chairman, *India – Tax Rebates*.

[41] GATT Panel Report, *US – Customs User Fee*, para. 7 (ad valorem charge imposed for the processing of commercial merchandise entering the US).

[42] Ruling by the Chairman, *Cuba – Consular Taxes*.

[43] Panel Report, *EC – Bananas III*, para. 7.195; Stoll and Schorkopf, *WTO*, p. 117.

In contrast, border measures are generally speaking not subject to Article III GATT. Tariffs and quotas do not apply to domestic products and, consequently, would always be inconsistent with national treatment. For this reason, such trade obstacles are addressed by other obligations, in particular straightforward prohibitions of quantitative restrictions (Article XI GATT) and mutually negotiated tariff bindings (Article II GATT). Yet, an internal measure (discussed under sub-section 2. below) which applies to imported as well as domestic products – such as a sales ban or a technical requirement –, but is, for administrative purposes, enforced at the border, remains subject to national treatment pursuant to *Ad* Article III GATT.[44]

2. 'Less favourable treatment' through internal measures

International trade is not only inhibited by measures imposed at the border, but also by measures applying to the goods once they have cleared customs and become available on the internal market. Following the continuous reduction of tariffs and other border measures over the last decades under the auspices of GATT, today's challenges in international trade regulation are to eliminate internal measures that result in a competitive advantage for domestically produced over imported products or discriminate between products originating from different trading partners. Internal measures are thus subject to both obligations of non-discrimination, namely national treatment and MFN treatment. Since internal measures can take any possible form and substance limited only by the government's creativity, it is difficult to develop an exhaustive categorization. However, the most common types of discriminatory measures imposed internally are taxes, regulatory requirements and subsidies.

There are many ways an *internal tax* scheme can be structured and applied such that it treats one group of products or services less favourably than another group. For instance, value added taxes can be set at different levels, tax refunds can be granted to some producers and suppliers but not to others,[45] or different consumption taxes may be imposed on certain products and services, such as taxes on alcohol and cigarettes.[46]

[44] See *Ad* Article III GATT; comprehensively Pauwelyn, 'Distinguishing Domestic Regulation from Market Access', 142 ff; Vranes, *Trade and the Environment*, pp. 251–55.

[45] See e.g. *China – Value-Added Tax on Integrated Circuits*, DS309, mutually agreed solution notified 6 October 2005.

[46] See e.g. Panel Report, *Dominican Republic – Import and Sale of Cigarettes*, paras. 7.317 ff; Panel Report, *Korea – Alcoholic Beverages*, para. 10.1.

Moreover, the measure does not have to be formally called or applied as a tax. Any form of internal charge is subject to the non-discrimination obligations.[47]

The second category of *internal regulations* encompasses a broad range of measures which generally provide for qualitative requirements, such as technical standards. While there is a direct correlation between a higher tax and its impact on the competitive relationship, this causal link is more difficult to establish with regard to regulatory measures. In most cases, the regulation in question leads to less favourable treatment because of higher transaction costs for foreign producers which in turn modifies the conditions of competition in a given market.[48] The following examples from WTO jurisprudence, by no means exhaustive, illustrate the kinds of regulations qualifying as less favourable treatment:

- *Import or sales bans* always create less favourable treatment of the concerned product. If the prohibition is aimed exclusively at imports in general or at imports from a certain origin, it creates a straightforward *de jure* discrimination. However, pursuant to *Ad* Article III GATT, bans imposed at the border and applying exclusively to imported products must be analysed under the prohibition of quantitative restrictions of Article XI GATT.[49] In contrast, origin-neutral bans which apply to a certain type of imported and domestic products are subject to Article III:4 GATT. Such measures create *de facto* less favourable treatment and – under the asymmetric impact test – violate national treatment to the extent the group of imported products is more heavily affected in comparison to the group of domestic products.
- *Administrative measures* resulting in burdens or disadvantages to imported goods can be adopted in unlimited ways and forms.

  In *China – Auto Parts*, for instance, the measure modified the conditions of competition to the detriment of imported auto parts by imposing certain administrative requirements – the review of which could take a couple of years – for car manufacturers using imported auto parts

[47] For a definition of internal charge and delimitation from customs duty see Panel Report, *China – Auto Parts*, paras. 7.102 ff, confirmed in Appellate Body Report, para. 181.

[48] Sykes, 'Regulatory Protectionism', 3–4.

[49] See e.g. Panel Report, *Brazil – Retreaded Tyres*, para. 7.34: 'the prohibition on granting of import licences … is an import prohibition inconsistent with the requirements under Article XI:1 of the GATT 1994' (finding not appealed).

(Panel Report, paras. 7.267 ff). In *Dominican Republic – Import and Sale of Cigarettes*, the Panel found that a tax stamp requirement applying to both imported and domestic cigarettes nonetheless 'imposes additional processes and costs on imported products' and 'leads to imported cigarettes being presented to final consumers in a less appealing manner' (paras 7.172 ff). In *EC – Trademarks*, the Panel found that a number of requirements in connection with the protection of geographical indications and designations of origin for agricultural products constitute 'less favourable treatment'.[50] As a final example, in *Mexico – Taxes on Soft Drinks* the Panel found that certain bookkeeping requirements for non-cane sugar sweeteners (predominantly imported) not applying to cane sugar (predominantly domestic) amount to 'less favourable treatment' (para 8.123).

– *Domestic purchase requirements* are frequently adopted in the form of obligations or incentives to induce buyers to favour the domestic production.

In *Turkey – Rice*, the Panel found that a requirement according to which importers must purchase domestic rice, in order to be allowed to import rice at reduced-tariff levels, constitutes less favourable treatment to imported rice than that accorded to like domestic rice (para 7.241). Similarly, in *India – Autos* the Panel condemned an indigenization requirement (i.e. domestic content requirement with the effect that a certain minimum of domestic parts and components are used for car production) as constituting 'less favourable treatment' (para 7.202).[51]

– *Various other regulations* that were found to constitute less favourable treatment are marketing prohibitions for imported products[52] or a requirement imposed on imported retreaded tyres to dispose of ten used tyres if domestic retreaded tyres need to dispose of just one used tyre.[53]

[50] Such requirements concerned, for instance, conditions of reciprocity and equivalence on the availability of protection for imported products (Panel Report, *EC – Trademarks and Geographical Indications [Australia]*, paras. 7.262 ff), application procedures (ibid., paras. 7.326 f), requirements of government participation in the inspection structures (Panel Report, *EC – Trademarks and Geographical Indications [US]*, paras. 7.440 f); for more examples on administrative burdens see e.g. Panel Reports, *Canada – Wheat Exports and Grain Imports*, paras. 6.174 ff, 6.269 ff; *Korea – Various Measures on Beef*, paras. 629 ff, 641 ff (as modified by Appellate Body Report, paras. 130 ff).

[51] Similarly also Panel Report, *Canada – Autos*, paras. 10.65 ff (concerning a Canadian value added requirement as a condition for receiving a duty exemption).

[52] Panel Report, *Brazil – Retreaded Tyres*, paras. 7.420 f.

[53] Ibid., paras. 7.434 ff.

C *Typology of 'less favourable treatment' under GATS*

In the context of international trade in services, the classical GATT characterization of discriminatory border measures and discriminatory internal measures is no longer adequate. The significance of border measures is much less pronounced in the context of services trade, given that cross-border transactions of intangible services cannot be inspected by customs officials. On the one hand, the import of services is thus not generally subject to tariffs.[54] On the other hand, trade in services is restrained predominantly by heavy internal regulations which, in contrast to GATT, may not only result in less favourable treatment of the service, but also of the supplier. The present section thus attempts to categorize a number of typical measures restricting trade in services and amounting to 'less favourable treatment' in terms of the GATS rules on non-discrimination. While it is obviously impossible to compile an exhaustive list, an indicative enumeration is developed on the basis of the schedule of commitments from different Members.[55] These individual limitations indicate what sort of measures are deemed as discriminatory by Members, bearing in mind however that the schedules are based on the Members' individual interpretation of 'less favourable treatment' and are thus not in any way binding for the WTO adjudicating bodies in regard to the interpretation of Article XVII GATS. At the outset it must be noted that according to Article XX:2 GATS, '[m]easures inconsistent with both Articles XVI and XVII shall be inscribed in the column relating to Article XVI. In this case the inscription will be considered to provide a condition or qualification to Article XVII as well'. It follows that not only limitations under national treatment must be taken into account, but also limitations under market access which oftentimes carve out discriminatory measures.

1. Spillovers from border measures applying to products

In general terms, tariffs only apply to the import of goods but not the cross-border supply of services. However, it may still be that tariff measures or quantitative restrictions on a certain product violate GATS national and MFN treatment, to the extent that the measure 'affects trade in services' and thus falls within the scope of application in terms of GATS Article I. For

[54] Copeland and Mattoo, 'Economics of Services Trade', p. 103; Hoekman and Braga, 'Protection and Trade in Services', 5; Snape, 'Principles in Trade in Services', p. 10.

[55] For individual schedules of commitments and schedules of MFN exemptions see the WTO Services Database available at http://tsdb.wto.org/default.aspx.

instance, a tariff quota differentiating between products from different origins or a higher tax on products delivered by mail may discriminate between suppliers of distribution services of that particular product.[56]

The Panel in *EC – Bananas III* found that the way *import licences* for bananas were granted under a tariff quota regime violated GATS national and most-favoured-nation treatment by creating less favourable conditions of competition for foreign suppliers of wholesale services (Article XVII) as well as among service suppliers from different origins (Article II) (paras 7.274 ff).

In *Canada – Autos* the Panel found that a measure allowing some wholesalers to import automobiles into Canada duty free, while wholesalers of automobiles from different origin were refused duty free importation, is in violation with GATS non-discrimination (paras 10.236–64). Even though this finding did not withhold the Appellate Body's scrutiny under appeal, it was overturned only because the Panel did not sufficiently substantiate the effect of the tax on manufacturers in their capacity as wholesale suppliers, and not because GATS does not apply to such a measure on products *per se* (paras 181 ff). According to the Appellate Body, a measure falls within the GATS scope of application only (i) if there *is* trade in services in the sense of Article I:2 and (ii) if the measure *affects* such trade in services within the meaning of Article I:1 (para 155).

Moreover, border measures applying to goods may also affect other sectors than distribution services, namely if the product is needed to supply a specific service. For instance, a prohibition for a foreign circus to 'import' animals into the country for its performance is discriminatory if domestic circuses are granted exceptional licences to import the same animals. Similarly, a restriction on the importation of research or construction equipment affects foreign suppliers of research or construction services.[57]

2. Quantitative restrictions

Measures restricting the quantity of certain services and types of suppliers or transactions are primarily subject to the market access obligation. Article XVI:2 GATS explicitly prohibits specific quantitative restrictions. Yet, quantitative restrictions may also fall under Article XVII GATS to the extent that they create a competitive advantage to domestic services and suppliers.

56 See also Mattoo, 'Distribution Services', pp. 204–8.

57 Kono, 'Construction and Related Service Industries', p. 185 (construction); Iceland, Draft Consolidated Schedule of Specific Commitments, S/DCS/W/ISL/Rev.1, 11 April 2003, p. 9 (research).

> For instance, a measure limiting the number of suppliers to 500 slots allocated to domestic and foreign suppliers on the basis of criteria unrelated to origin, constitutes a quantitative restriction which is not subject to national treatment. In contrast, if domestic suppliers are given preference over foreign suppliers, the measure would fall under Article XVII GATS.

This potential overlap creates numerous issues on the relationship between the two disciplines, in particular with regard to measures banning certain services or prohibiting certain methods of supply. The main question is whether such a ban should be treated as a *qualitative* requirement subject to national treatment (and rules on domestic regulation of Article VI GATS) or whether its *quantitative* effect essentially enforcing a zero quota should render the measure subject to market access. Under the GATT, *Ad* Article III provides some guidance on this problem by specifying that measures applying to both imported and domestic products are subject to national treatment, while only measures applying exclusively to imports are assessed under market access.[58] In comparison, GATS does not contain a similar guiding provision on the delimitation of Articles XVI and XVII. The Appellate Body ruled in *US – Gambling* that 'it is neither necessary nor appropriate for us to draw, in the abstract, the line between quantitative and qualitative measures' and analysed the quantitative effect (i.e. zero quota) of a qualitative domestic regulation (i.e. ban of online gambling) under Article XVI.[59] Even though the correctness of this legal analysis is at least questionable,[60] it suffices for the purpose of this study to conclude that import and supply bans as well as other qualitative regulations with quantitative effects are – even if discriminatory – likely to be subject to Article XVI.[61] Since market access obligations neither require 'less favourable treatment' nor 'likeness', future panels, as happened in *US – Gambling*, will most likely exercise judicial economy on a possible national treatment claim and limit their analysis to Article XVI.

[58] See above, n 44.

[59] Paras 221 ff, in particular 250.

[60] For detailed discussions see e.g. Pauwelyn, 'Distinguishing Domestic Regulation from Market Access', 148 ff; Ortino, 'Treaty Interpretation', 137 ff; Krajewski and Engelke, 'Art. XVII GATS', pp. 416–17; Delimatsis, 'Don't Gamble with GATS', 1061 ff; Mavroidis, 'Highway XVI re-visited', 9; Trebilcock and Howse, *Regulation of International Trade*, p. 371; Kaufmann and Weber, 'Financial Services and Domestic Regulation', pp. 420 ff.

[61] The Council for Trade in Services qualified GATS XVI as *lex specialis* to GATS XVII, see CTS, Special Session: Technical Review of GATS Provisions, Informal Note by the Secretariat, JOB(01)/17, 16 February 2001, para. 6.

3. Internal taxes, charges and fees

Both Articles I and III:2 GATT specifically prohibit discrimination through forms of internal taxes, duties, charges or other fees. Even though Articles II and XVII GATS do not specifically refer to taxes and charges, such measures fall within the scope of GATS provided that they affect trade in services. Consequently, internal taxes on services may amount to discriminatory barriers to trade under the same conditions as taxes on products. If the tax burden on imported services is *de jure* or *de facto* higher than on domestic services or if it differentiates between services originating from different Members, it violates GATS non-discrimination obligations.

> Under the US schedule of commitments, a higher excise tax may be imposed on insurance premiums covering US risks that are paid to companies not incorporated under US law. Similarly, a higher licence fee applies for non-residents providing brokerage or agency services in some US states.[62] Some EU Member States impose a higher tax on insurance policies issued by subsidiaries not established in the EU.[63]

Moreover, even if a tax applies to a certain product but not to a service, it could still fall within the scope of GATS disciplines to the extent that it affects the supply of a service. This is particularly the case for distribution services, the trade of which is strongly dependent on measures applying to the product to be distributed.

4. Domestic regulations

Domestic regulations are, generally speaking, subject to Article VI GATS and the mandate provided in paragraph 4 relating to 'qualification requirements and procedures, technical standards and licensing requirements'. Yet, if domestic regulations alter the conditions of competition to the detriment of foreign services and suppliers, they may also be subject to Article XVII. Hence, Article VI applies to non-discriminatory and Article XVII to discriminatory domestic regulations, but the relationship between the two provisions remains unclear. From a conceptual point of view, the creation of a non-restriction principle on the basis of a necessity test in Article VI:4 would render any national treatment obligation superfluous. As

[62] Communication from the United States, United States' Schedule of Specific Commitments under the General Agreement on Trade in Services, S/DCS/W/USA, 27 February 2003, pp. 51 (excise tax), 59 (license fee).

[63] Communication from the European Communities and its Member States, Certification, Draft Consolidated GATS Schedule, S/C/W/273, 9 October 2006, p. 180.

illustrated by Article 56 TFEU, the principle of non-restriction prohibits all unnecessary or non-proportional trade obstacles, regardless of whether they differentiate between foreign and domestic services.[64] Consequently, the development of a horizontal necessity test would wash out all Member-specific commitments and limitations in regard to Article XVII. One way of preventing the undermining of the schedule of commitments is to interpret the scope of Article XVII and future disciplines of Article VI as mutually exclusive. In other words, domestic regulations qualifying as discriminatory in terms of Article XVII would be excluded from current and future disciplines of Article VI.[65]

For the purpose of this analysis, the question of delineation may be left open, considering that – regardless of the interpretative approach – discriminatory domestic regulations remain subject to Articles XVII and II. Moreover, since Article VI lacks meaningful substantive obligations and since GATS is far form incorporating a non-restriction obligation on the basis of necessity and proportionality, domestic regulations continue to be assessed primarily under Articles XVI on market access as well as XVII and II on non-discrimination. Accordingly, the question arises what kind of domestic regulations and under what conditions they qualify as *de jure* or *de facto* 'less favourable treatment'.[66]

a. Nationality, residency and ownership requirements Residency or citizenship requirements affect in particular modes 1, 2 and 4. The same is true if the supply of a certain service is conditioned upon the establishment of a local subsidiary.[67] These types of requirements modify *de facto* – or even *de jure* – the conditions of competition to the detriment of foreign service suppliers.[68] The Scheduling Guidelines state that 'whether

[64] See above, 3.I.A.2.

[65] See WPDR, Report on the Meeting Held on 29 November 2001, Note by the Secretariat, S/WPDR/M/14, 29 January 2002, para. 18; CTS, Guidelines for the Scheduling of Specific Commitments under the General Agreement on Trade in Services (GATS), S/L/92, 28 March 2001, Attachment 4, para. 2; Krajewski, *National Regulation*, p. 112; Krajewski and Engelke, 'Art. XVII GATS', p. 420: future 'disciplines under Art. VI:4 should explicitly exempt discriminatory measures from their scope' (emphasis omitted); Wouters and Coppens, 'GATS and Domestic Regulation', p. 230.

[66] On discriminatory domestic regulations see also Mattoo, 'MFN and GATS', pp. 69–73.

[67] Carter, 'Insurance', p. 65.

[68] CTS, Guidelines for the Scheduling of Specific Commitments under the General Agreement on Trade in Services (GATS), S/L/92, 28 March 2001, para. 13; Krajewski, *National Regulation*, p. 108; for an overview of cases pertaining to Art. 56 TFEU (ex Art. 49 TEC) see Holoubek, 'EGV 49/50', p. 730.

residency requirements constitute national treatment limitations has to be determined on a case-by-case basis'.[69]

> The US scheduled residency or even citizenship requirements in respect to some states in the case of, for instance, lawyers, accountants, engineers, real estate services, private detectives, radio licences etc.[70] Also common are residency requirements for managers and members of the board of directors.[71] According to the EU schedule, residency or citizenship is required in some Member States in sectors such as auditing/bookkeeping/taxation, real estate, agronomist, security, publishing, education.[72] Switzerland requires citizenship for independent suppliers of medical and dental services.[73]

Ownership requirements in respect to legal entities are the mode 3 counterpart to nationality and residency requirements for natural persons. They require certain services to be only provided by legal entities that are wholly or partially owned by citizens or residents of the respective country. Even though this type of measure is specifically addressed by market access Article XIV:2(e) and (f), it could also fall under Article XVII. Nonetheless, similarly to the above reasoning in respect of import and supply bans, it is unlikely that such a measure would be analysed under national treatment, considering that a claim under Article XIV is easier to sustain. Accordingly, limitations are generally listed under the column on market access. The relevance of non-discrimination for this type of measure is thus limited to cases where a Member has undertaken different commitments under Articles XVI and XVII respectively, or to cases pertaining to MFN treatment.

b. Registration/authorization and qualification/licensing requirements In many countries, the permission to supply certain services is subject to prior approval by a government agency or a professional

[69] CTS, Guidelines for the Scheduling of Specific Commitments under the General Agreement on Trade in Services (GATS), S/L/92, 28 March 2001, Attachment 1 para. 2.

[70] US Schedule of Commitments (above n 62), pp. 14 f (lawyer), 33 (accountant), 34 (engineer), 35 (real estate), 38 (private detectives), 43 f (radio and television license).

[71] Ibid., pp. 53 (insurance companies), 63 (banks).

[72] EC Schedule of Commitments (above n 63), pp. 52 ff (auditing/bookkeeping/taxation), 105 (real estate), 123 (agronomist), 134 (security), 138 (publishing), 161 ff (education).

[73] Switzerland, Draft Consolidated Schedule of Specific Commitments, S/DCS/W/CHE, 24 January 2003, p. 10.

association.[74] Depending on what the conditions for prior approval are, one would generally speak of registration or authorization requirements versus qualification or licensing requirements, even though the terms are not always used consistently.[75] In general terms, registration and authorization requirements are *quantitative* restrictions. Governments require registration or authorization either for administrative purposes, such as controlling, or to limit the number of service suppliers for policy reasons or due to technical feasibility.[76] Qualification and licensing requirements, in contrast, are *qualitative* restrictions. They generally require that the applicant meets certain standards of qualification or passes an exam in order to protect consumers. Most accredited professional services are subject to such requirements.[77] With regard to the validity of such requirements, the Scheduling Guidelines state that:

> 'licensing and qualification requirements, registration requirements and authorization requirements will constitute national treatment limitations subject to scheduling only where they discriminate in favour of services and service suppliers of national origin. In the absence of discrimination, these type[s] of requirements will not constitute measures subject to scheduling under Article XVII and would possibly fall under Article VI GATS.'[78]

These types of requirements qualify as *de jure* less favourable treatment if they are tied with a nationality requirement, such that different standards apply depending on the origin of the supplier. Origin-based measures are, for instance, if only nationals of country A receive an authorization to work as teachers or if only nationals of A had the possibility to receive the required education for a licence to practise law.

> The US Schedule of Commitments provides, for instance, that foreign banks are required to register (including record maintenance, inspections, submission of reports and payment of a fee), whereas domestic

[74] Hoekman and Braga, 'Protection and Trade in Services', 9–10.

[75] See also WPDR, Definitions of Qualification Requirements, Qualification Procedures, Licensing Requirements, Licensing Procedures and Technical Standards, Communication from the Separate Customs Territory of Taiwan, Penghu, Kinmen and Matsu, S/WPDR/W/37, 6 October 2005.

[76] For examples see Krajewski, *National Regulation*, p. 30.

[77] Mallampally, 'Professional Services', p. 102; Kono, 'Architectural and Engineering Services', pp. 120–21.

[78] CTS, Guidelines for the Scheduling of Specific Commitments under the General Agreement on Trade in Services (GATS), S/L/92, 28 March 2001, Attachment 1 para. 2.

banks are exempt from registration. The EU requires authorization for public translators for some Member States.[79]

In contrast, the question of whether an origin-neutral requirement qualifies as *de facto* 'less favourable treatment', is much more difficult to answer and strongly depends on how *de facto* 'less favourable' is interpreted. Quantitative *authorization and registration* requirements designed only to enforce a maximum number of suppliers irrespective of origin do not amount to less favourable treatment and thus have to be assessed under Article XVI GATS. Conversely, the authorization requirement would be discriminatory if foreign nationals are disadvantaged in the registration process.

The situation becomes even more complex for *qualification* require ments. Many Members require a licence to provide an accredited professional service, such as law or medicine. Similarly, the supply of architectural, engineering and teaching services, requires a degree from an educational institution of the country where the licence is sought.[80] Even though access to these educational institutions is, in most cases, not dependent on origin, it is evident that the qualification requirement places a heavier burden on foreigners because (i) there is a higher administrative hurdle for foreign students to receive the required degree in comparison to local professionals (admission requirements, visa, language etc.) and (ii) an applicant may already be trained in, or even admitted to practise the same profession in another country.[81] Hence, the argument that such qualification requirements qualify as 'less favourable treatment' in terms of GATS – certainly under the diagonal test, but also under the asymmetric impact test – is not unfounded. For this reason, most Members did not undertake commitments for this type of requirement or scheduled stringent limitations.

The US' commitments for legal services is conditioned upon prior licensing in the State where the service is supplied.[82] Similarly, the EU did not make many commitments for the practice of domestic law and mode 4 medical services.[83] In addition, the EU more generally states

[79] US Schedule of Commitments (above n 62), p. 63; EC Schedule of Commitments (above n 63), p. 141.

[80] See e.g. Canada, Draft Consolidated Schedule for Specific Commitments, S/DCS/W/CAN, 24 January 2003, requiring domestic training as condition for accreditation for geological services (p 29).

[81] Similarly but rejecting such a broad interpretation Wouters and Coppens, 'GATS and Domestic Regulation', p. 235.

[82] US Schedule of Commitments (above n 62), pp. 14 ff.

[83] EC Schedule of Commitments (above n 63), pp. 41 ff (law), 79 ff (medical).

> that the 'EC directives on mutual recognition of diplomas do not apply to nationals of third countries. Recognition of the diplomas which are required in order to practise regulated professional services by non-Community nationals remains within the competence of each Member State, unless Community law provides otherwise'.[84] China did not make any commitments for the practice of Chinese law; it requires certain qualifications for the supply of, for instance, IT, translation and educational services.[85]

The delicate question remains whether such licensing and qualification requirements really should violate national treatment in case of full commitments, or whether they – even if *de facto* modifying the conditions of competition – should be exclusively dealt with under Article VI.[86] The WTO Handbook on GATS notes with regard to domestic regulations that '[g]overnments remain free under the GATS to pursue such policy objectives [e.g. equitable access, consumer protection, job creation etc.] even in sectors where they have undertaken full commitments on market access and national treatment'.[87] Similarly, a WTO explanatory note regarding the scheduling for initial commitments states:

> 'The requirement to obtain an approval or a licence is not in itself a trade restriction and therefore does not need to be scheduled. However, if the criteria for granting licenses or approval contain a market access restriction (e.g. economic needs test) or discriminatory treatment, the relevant measures would need to be scheduled if a Member wishes to maintain

[84] Ibid., pp. 29 f.

[85] China, Draft Consolidated Schedule of Specific Commitments, S/DCS/W/CHN, 24 January 2003, pp. 5 (law), 9 ff (IT), 15 (translation), 27 (education).

[86] To date, no such claim has been raised under GATS; see e.g. CTS, Presence of Natural Persons (Mode 4), Background Note by the Secretariat, S/C/W/75, 8 December 1998, para. 34: 'Although frequently referred to in Schedules, licensing requirements and procedures are not as such captured by Articles XVI and XVII of the GATS, but by the disciplines governing domestic regulation under Article VI'; in comparison see e.g. Urteil des Bundesverwaltungsgerichts, Abteilung III, 8 April 2009, C-6900/2007, where the Swiss Federal Administrative Tribunal ruled that the requirement for a German national to pass a Swiss examination for the authorization to work as food chemist and the non-recognition of the German diploma does not violate the non-discrimination principle in Art. 2 of the Agreement between the EC and Switzerland on the free movement of persons (OJ 2002 L114/6); but see in scholarship Krajewski, *National Regulation*, p. 108 (the requirement to graduate from a national university is discriminatory); Mattoo, 'MFN and GATS', p. 70 (distinguishing between educations with high country-specific components and educations with high universal components).

[87] WTO-Secretariat, *Handbook on GATS*, p. 21; interestingly, the objectives listed in the Handbook are not stated in the exceptions clause of GATS Article XIV; it follows that the

> them as limitations under Article XVI or XVII. It has been pointed out that in some offers the granting of licences is subject to review, meaning they are granted on a discretionary basis. In such a case the right to supply the service is unbound.'[88]

Unfortunately, neither of these guidelines substantiate the statement with a legal analysis. To be more specific, the outcome of a national treatment analysis strongly depends on the interpretation adopted in regard to the standard of 'less favourable treatment' (i.e. asymmetric impact or diagonal test, or even equal to non-restriction), the concept of 'likeness' (i.e. relevance of qualification and quality for differentiating between services)[89] and 'regulatory purpose and context' (i.e. relevance of purpose such as consumer protection in the analysis of non-discrimination or only as justification).[90] A clarification of the uncertainty in respect to the standard of the GATS non-discrimination obligations would greatly enhance the Member's' readiness to schedule more substantial commitments.

c. **Restrictions on the purchase, lease and use of real estate** Restrictions related to ownership, lease and use of real estate heavily impedes services trade, in particular with regard to mode 3 commercial presence.[91] Such restrictions related to real estate distinguish on the basis of origin and thus qualify as *de jure* 'less favourable treatment'.

d. **Supplier and employment-related measures** Considering that independent service suppliers or employees need to relocate in order to supply services under modes 3 and 4, all types of labour market regulations in a broad sense may potentially result in 'less favourable treatment' of foreign service suppliers. While measures regarding immigration and permanent employment are excluded from the scope of GATS, all other employment-related measures are in principle subject to commitments

Handbook espouses the theory that such domestic regulations are not in violation with national treatment in the first place.

88 GNS, Scheduling of Initial Commitments in Trade in Services: Explanatory Note, Addendum, MTN.GNS/W/164/Add.1, 30 November 1993, para. 1; similarly CTS, Guidelines for the Scheduling of Specific Commitments under the General Agreement on Trade in Services (GATS), S/L/92, 28 March 2001, para. 10.

89 On a methodology for the 'likeness' analysis see below, part IV.

90 On regulatory purpose see below, 3.III.

91 For instance, the US Schedule of Commitments (above n 62) contains a horizontal limitation providing that the federal government may restrict initial sale of federally owned

on market access and national treatment, as well as other GATS obligations.[92] There are innumerable ways to design employment conditions – including also social security conditions[93] – such that foreign employees suffer a competitive disadvantage. Employee-related restrictions may also affect mode 3 supply, for instance if a foreign company is restricted in the employment of expatriate staff.[94]

e. Other horizontal and sector-specific requirements Next to the most common types of 'less favourable treatment' discussed above, there are countless other possibilities of horizontal or sector-specific discriminations. The following list illustrates a few forms which appear in the Members' schedule of commitments and respective literature:

- *Language requirements*: A very efficient origin-neutral measure designed to exclude foreign service suppliers from the domestic market is to require proficiency in the national language as a pre-requisite to supply a certain service. The EU Schedule provides, for instance, that all medical personnel in Lithuania must communicate in Lithuanian language. The Icelandic Schedule provides that knowledge of the Icelandic language is required to supply veterinary services under modes 3 and 4.[95]
- *Domestic purchase requirements*: All measures that are designed to induce consumers to purchase local services modify the conditions of competition in favour of domestic service suppliers. The US Schedule restricts mode 2 supply of health services by limiting reimbursement of medical expenses to services purchased from licensed, certified

lands to US citizens, p. 8; similarly EC Schedule of Commitments (above n 63), pp. 22 ff; see also CTS, Guidelines for the Scheduling of Specific Commitments under the General Agreement on Trade in Services (GATS), S/L/92, 28 March 2001, para. 17.

92 CTS, Presence of Natural Persons (Mode 4), Background Note by the Secretariat, S/C/W/75, 8 December 1998, para. 31; also Kono, 'Construction and Related Service Industries', p. 186.

93 See e.g. Joined cases 62 and 63/81 *Seco et Desquenne & Giral* v. *Etablissement d'assurance contre la vieillesse et l'invalidité* [1982] ECR 223 on Art. 56 TFEU (ex Art. 49 TEC) (foreign employee has to pay employer share).

94 Carter, 'Insurance', p. 65.

95 EC Schedule of Commitments (above n 63), p. 78; Iceland, Draft Consolidated Schedule of Specific Commitments, S/DCS/W/ISL/Rev.1, 11 April 2003, p. 7; see also CTS, Health and Social Services, Background Note by the Secretariat, S/C/W/50, 18 September 1998, para. 62.

facilities in the US or in a specific US state.[96] In *Canada – Autos*, the Panel struck down a measure providing for tax benefits to car manufacturers which obtained services related to the production and repair of motor vehicles from suppliers within Canada.[97] Domestic purchase requirements are common also in the insurance services sector, in that many Members typically require its citizens to purchase a mandatory insurance from a domestic supplier.[98] Domestic content and buy-national programs are also common for construction services.[99]

- *Training requirements*: Specific requirements for foreign mode 3 and 4 suppliers to provide training to local staff constitutes 'less favourable treatment' of foreign suppliers to the extent that the same conditions do not apply to domestic suppliers. For instance, Cyprus scheduled an economic needs test as horizontal limitation for mode 3 supply, which provides that the granting of a permission depends *inter alia* on the 'creation of new job opportunities for scientists, qualitative improvement and training of local staff'. Similarly, Egypt limits mode 3 commitments by the requirement that training should be provided to Egyptian employees.[100]
- *Technology transfer requirements*: Similar to training requirements, an economic needs test may require the foreign supplier to transfer technological knowledge to the exporting Member. For example, Kuwait requires that '[f]oreign commercial presence, must add some economic interests to the country, like high technology transfer, research and development programs, technical or marketing assistance'.[101]
- *Banking services*: Origin-based and thus *de jure* differential treatment may consist of limiting source of funds (restricting deposits from certain business sectors; depositing public funds exclusively on domestic banks; restricting access to central bank marginal lending or discount rate); limiting authorization to deposit-taking and lending services;

96 US Schedule of Commitments (above n 62), p. 71; see also Adlung, 'Health and Social Services', p. 379.

97 On this case see below, 10.I.A.2.

98 Carter, 'Insurance', p. 66.

99 See Lee, 'Construction', p. 74.

100 Kono, 'Construction and Related Service Industries', p. 186; Cyprus, Draft Consolidated Schedule for Specific Commitments, S/DCS/W/CYP, 24 January 2003, p. 3; Egypt, Draft Consolidated Schedule of Specific Commitments, S/DCS/W/EGY, 24 January 2003, pp. 7 (travel services), 15 (banking services); see also Fiji, Draft Converted Schedule of Specific Commitments, S/DCS/W/FIJ, 24 January 2003, p. 2.

101 Kuwait, Draft Consolidated Schedule of Specific Commitments, S/DCS/W/KWT, 24 January 2003, p. 3; similarly The Philippines, Draft Consolidated Schedule of Specific Commitments, S/DCS/W/PHL, 24 January 2003, p. 8; Qatar, Schedule of Specific Commitments, S/DCS/W/QAT, 24 January 2003, p. 3.

limiting repatriation of profits, differential capital requirements etc. Even origin-neutral capital requirements may constitute a competitive disadvantage if the foreign subsidiary – which holds only a fraction of the bank's home capital – is required to comply individually.[102]
- *Audiovisual services*: Origin-based discrimination is possible if preference is given to domestic suppliers of audiovisual services in the allocation of frequencies for transmission within the national territory, or if time frames for the broadcasting of foreign productions are limited.[103]
- *Legal Services*: In addition to the licensing and residency requirements, measures such as restrictions on firm names, legal forms and multidisciplinary practices as well as different ethical standards may potentially result in 'less favourable treatment' of foreign suppliers of legal services.[104]

5. Subsidies

All forms of financial contributions to the domestic industry generally result in a competitive advantage over imported goods and services not benefiting from the subsidy. Such measures thus qualify as straight forward 'less favourable treatment' in terms of non-discrimination. Nonetheless, in the context of trade in goods, subsidies are explicitly excluded from the national treatment obligation pursuant to Article III:8(b) GATT,[105] but they remain subject to the more specific disciplines set forth in Article XVI GATT and the separate SCM Agreement. Conversely, financial contributions and subsidies granted to domestic service suppliers must respect the national treatment obligation of Article XVII GATS.[106] For this reason, most Members scheduled subsidy-specific horizontal limitations, reserving eligibility for subsidies to citizens or permanent residents.

> The US scheduled various horizontal limitation on national treatment with regard to, *inter alia*, subsidies from the Trade and Development

[102] Gelb and Sagari, 'Banking', pp. 56–57.

[103] CTS, Guidelines for the Scheduling of Specific Commitments under the General Agreement on Trade in Services (GATS), S/L/92, 28 March 2001, para. 13; Honeck, 'Audiovisual Services', p. 141.

[104] See in general Chapman and Tauber, 'International Trade in Legal Services', 963 ff; Nnona, 'Multidisciplinary Practice', 82–83; Terry, 'Applying GATS to Legal Services', 103 ff; Gamberale, 'Legal Services', pp. 408–18.

[105] Cottier and Oesch, *International Trade Regulation*, p. 990; on subsidies see also below, 7.III.A.2.

[106] CTS, Guidelines for the Scheduling of Specific Commitments under the General Agreement on Trade in Services (GATS), S/L/92, 28 March 2001, para. 16; Poretti, 'Subsidy Disciplines in Services Trade', pp. 468–70.

Agency,[107] support for members of socially or economically disadvantaged groups, educational scholarships or in the area of audiovisual services.[108] The EU limits mode 4 subsidies to its nationals and mode 3 to juridical persons established within the territory; subsidies for research and development and subsidies in the public sector are unbound.[109] China limits subsidies in the audiovisual sector to domestic suppliers.[110]

6. Exception: disadvantages inherent to foreign character

Footnote 10 to the national treatment provision of Article XVII:1 limits the reach of the obligation by stating that it 'shall not be construed to require any Member to compensate for any inherent competitive disadvantages which result from the foreign character of the relevant services or service suppliers'. The only aspect which is truly 'inherent' to the foreign character is the geographical distance between the origin of the service and the place of consumption. This aspect may lead to a competitive disadvantage due to the costs associated with making the service available in the country of consumption. Consequently, Members have no obligation under Article XVII to compensate foreign suppliers for their costs of 'transportation'. However, the absence of such an obligation is self-evident for all national treatment obligations, given that the 'competitive disadvantage inherent to the foreign character' results from factual circumstances (i.e. geographical distance), and not from measures or 'treatment' by a Member. Yet, it seems unlikely that the negotiators intended to simply spell out an already evident aspect of national treatment. Consequently, footnote 10 must be interpreted as a standard for 'less favourable treatment', such that origin-neutral measures should not be deemed to violate national treatment if the competitive disadvantage merely results from geographic distance.

In dispute settlement procedures, respondents attempted to invoke footnote 10 in order to exempt measures restricting modes 1 and 2 of supply. In *Canada – Autos*, Canada essentially argued that a measure granting advantages to suppliers within the Canadian territory (i.e. domestic

[107] 'The U.S. Trade and Development Agency (USTDA) advances economic development and U.S. commercial interests in developing and middle income countries. The agency funds various forms of technical assistance, early investment analysis, training, orientation visits and business workshops that support the development of a modern infrastructure and a fair and open trading environment', available at www.ustda.gov.

[108] US Schedule of Commitments (above n 62), pp. 10 ff, 44 (audiovisual), 48 (scholarships).

[109] EC Schedule of Commitments (above n 63), pp. 15 f.

[110] China, Draft Consolidated Schedule of Specific Commitments, S/DCS/W/CHN, 24 January 2003, p. 2.

suppliers and foreign mode 3 and 4 suppliers) does not violate national treatment. The Panel rejected this argument. It noted that certain consulting and advisory services which could be supplied through modes 1 and 2 suffer a competitive disadvantage in view of the advantages granted to suppliers within Canada. The Panel ruled that footnote 10 'does not provide cover for actions which might modify the conditions of competition against services and service suppliers which are already disadvantaged due to their foreign character'.[111] While this interpretation only identifies what footnote 10 is apparently not designed to mean, it does not shed any light into the positive meaning of footnote 10.

The US invoked a similar argument in *US – Gambling*. It claimed that an origin-neutral prohibition of remote supply of gambling services does not breach national treatment in combination with footnote 10, considering that foreign suppliers may still resort to non-remote supply. More specifically, the US argued that it is 'under no obligation to make up for the fact that Antiguan services and their suppliers are from somewhere other than Nevada, New Jersey, etc., and by reason of that fact may find it inherently more difficult to offer non-remote gambling services in the United States than would be the case for some domestic suppliers'.[112] The WTO adjudicating bodies exercised judicial economy on the national treatment claim and thus refrained from interpreting footnote 10. The argument made by the US raises the fundamental question whether national treatment – and possibly also MFN treatment – is intended to protect competitive opportunities within each *individual* mode of supply, or whether GATS non-discrimination rules protect only *overall* competitive opportunities between all competing services in a certain sector, regardless of modes of supply. As will be discussed in detail under section 11.I.D.2, this study submits that footnote 10 as well as cross-mode and policy considerations are strong indications against a mode-specific application of non-discrimination under GATS.

On a side note it is worth mentioning that some commentators interpreted footnote 10 as a basis to incorporate the regulatory purpose and a necessity test in the analysis of GATS national treatment.[113]

111 Panel Report, *Canada – Autos*, paras. 6.1088 f (Canada) and 10.300 (Panel).

112 Panel Report, *US – Gambling*, para. 3.231.

113 See e.g. Zdouc, *Comparative Analysis of GATS and GATT*, p. 185; Zdouc, '(2004) Dispute Settlement Practice', pp. 412–13; Verhoosel, *National Treatment*, p. 90; Cossy, 'Thoughts on "Likeness" in GATS', p. 349; on fn 10 as basis for consideration of the regulatory purpose already Farber and Hudec, 'Domestic Environmental Regulations', p. 77; on fn 10 as issue of causation Ortino, 'Principle of Non-Discrimination', p. 180.

II Likeness

While the element of less favourable treatment constitutes the essence of discrimination, it is by itself insufficient to conclude that there is a violation of WTO law. As the term *less* favourable and the language of WTO non-discrimination provisions indicate, a comparison must take place not only between the different treatments, but also between the two 'objects' or 'situations' (the comparators) to which differential treatment is accorded. A violation of a non-discrimination obligation only occurs if these products or services are alike, with the exception of the one difference that provides for the (direct or indirect) basis of the discrimination, i.e. origin in the case of international trade.

This section provides an introduction to the role of 'likeness' in WTO law (*below*, A.) and summarizes the interpretative approach *in abstracto* as well as the possible theories on how the concept could be interpreted and how it has been applied by the WTO adjudicating bodies *in concreto* (B.).

A Introduction to the concept of 'likeness'

The concept of 'likeness' plays a crucial role in the scrutiny of discrimination because the outcome of the analysis depends strongly on how broad or how narrow the comparative group of like 'objects' or 'situations' is defined. The comparative element is equally important in all non-discrimination analyses, regardless whether it is in trade, constitutional law or human rights.[114] With regard to non-discrimination obligations in human rights, the European Court of Human Rights, for instance, requires that a complainant is in a 'similar', 'comparable' or 'analogous' situation to the person from which it is treated differently.[115] The function of 'likeness' can be best illustrated with an example from the area of fundamental rights: In his theory on justice, *Aristotle* developed the principle that all equal people or situations are to be treated equally, whereas

[114] In general Heinze, *Logic of Equality*, pp. 57 ff; Cottier, 'Progressive Liberalization to Progressive Regulation', 796: 'It similarly follows from the principle of equality that like should be treated like, and unlike should be treated unlike in and before the law'; for constitutional law see e.g. Waldmann, *Diskriminierungsverbot von Art. 8 Abs. 2 BV*, pp. 307 ff; Oesch, *Differenzierung und Typisierung*, pp. 33–38; for a comparison between trade and human rights see e.g. Peters, 'Strukturähnlichkeit der Diskriminierungsverbote', p. 572.

[115] See e.g. *Fredin* v. *Sweden*, 18.02.1991, para. 60; *Salgueiro da Silva Mouta* v. *Portugal*, 21.12.1999, para. 26; *Edoardo Palumbo* v. *Italy*, 30.11.2000, paras. 51 f; *Thlimmenos* v. *Greece*, 6.04.2000, para. 44; on this issue e.g. Arnardóttir, *Equality and Non-*

unequal people or situations may be treated unequally.[116] As the ancient world distinguished between people who are naturally free and those who are naturally slaves,[117] this principle of relative equality justified the institutions of slavery and servitude on the basis of 'unlikeness'. In contrast, according to the prevailing understanding of modern times that all human beings are equal or 'like', it is evident that any 'less favourable treatment' on the basis of gender or race is discriminatory and thus prohibited by fundamental rights. It follows that the breadth of the term 'like' has a strong impact on the scope of the non-discrimination clause. In fact, the wider the term 'likeness' and the comparative group is defined, the wider in scope and thus more restrictive the non-discrimination obligation becomes. For the non-discrimination analysis in trade in goods it is necessary to define categories of comparative products which can be either narrow or wider based on the interpretation of 'likeness' in the respective provision.[118]

> Referring to the examples stated in the previous section 3.I.A.2, a violation of the non-discrimination obligation would not only require 'less favourable treatment', but also that Dutch milk is *like* Swiss milk, that carbon-neutral goods are *like* goods not meetings the standard, or that Belgian beer containing a high alcohol content is *like* domestic beer below 4.5 volume per cent alcohol content.

In the context of WTO law, the concept of 'likeness' is embodied in all non-discrimination provisions. Under GATS, it is expressed in Articles II and XVII, which provide that a Member shall accord to services and service

discrimination, pp. 10–13; Dijk *et al.* (eds.), *European Convention on Human Rights*, pp. 1036 ff.

116 Aristotle, 'Nicomachean Ethics', 1131a: 'For if the persons are not equal, they will not receive equal shares; in fact quarrels and complaints arise either when equals receive unequal shares in an allocation, or unequals receive equal shares'; see also Westen, *Speaking of Equality*, p. 185, who interprets Aristotle, Politics Book III, 1280a(8–15) as meaning '(1) It is just to treat people who are equal equally. (2) It is also just to treat people who are unequal unequally. (3) The foregoing propositions are self-evident, being universally accepted even without the support of an argument'.

117 Aristotle, 'Politics I & II', *Book I*, 1254a(14–15): 'anyone who, though human, belongs by nature not to himself but to another is by nature a slave'.

118 Appellate Body Report, *Korea – Alcoholic Beverages*, para. 142: 'Some grouping is almost always necessary … since generic categories commonly include products with *some* variation in composition, quality, function and price, and thus commonly give rise to sub-categories.[fn omitted] From a slightly different perspective, we note that "grouping" of products involves at least a preliminary characterization by the treaty interpreter that certain products are sufficiently similar as to, for instance, composition, quality, function and price, to warrant treating them as a group for convenience in analysis. But, the use of such "analytical tools" does not relieve a panel of its duty to make an objective

suppliers of any other Member treatment no less favourable than that it accords to its own *like services and services suppliers* (national treatment) or to those of any other Member (MFN treatment). Similarly, the provision on national and MFN treatment in the GATT apply the terms 'like products',[119] meaning that imported products shall be accorded treatment no less favourable than that accorded to *like products* of national origin (national treatment) or those from other WTO Members (MFN treatment). It must be noted that unlike GATS, GATT national treatment provides for two different standards of product relationship, namely 'likeness' and 'directly competitive or substitutable'. These two different standards, their inconsistent use in the GATT legal text as well as the absence of a legal definition in the agreements has led to some confusion and uncertainty which the WTO adjudicating bodies could not yet completely clarify.[120]

At the outset it must be recalled that *de jure* discriminations are considered *prima facie* illegal under Article III GATT.[121] More particularly, in order to establish a *prima facie* illegality of origin-based differential treatment, the complainant does not need to prove the *actual existence* of a 'like' domestic or imported product, but only that such 'like' products *could exist* or *could be traded*. For instance, the Panel in *Canada – Wheat Exports and Grain Imports* held that '[g]iven the existence of an origin-based distinction ... the United States need only demonstrate that there can or will be domestic and imported products that are like'.[122] Other reports go even further, noting that in cases of *de jure* discrimination the complainant does not even have to show that a 'like' domestic or imported product *could* exist. In other words, proof by the complainant that the measure at issue differentiates on the basis of origin entails the *presumption* that the 'likeness' requirement is fulfilled.[123] It is unclear from WTO

assessment of whether the components of a group of imported products are directly competitive or substitutable with the domestic products' (emphasis original).

[119] See e.g. GATT Articles I:1, III:2, III:4.

[120] See below, 5.I; see also Matheny, '"Like Products" and Cultural Products', 250–51.

[121] See above, 3.I.A.1, n 12.

[122] Paras 6.164, 6.262; see also Panel Reports, *China – Publications and Audiovisual Products*, paras. 7.975, 7.1284 (Art. XVII GATS), 7.1446 (Art. III:4 GATT); *China – Auto Parts*, para. 7.216; *US – FSC (Article 21.5 – EC)*, paras. 8.132–34; *Argentina – Hides and Leather*, para. 11.169: 'the quantum and nature of the evidence required for a complaining party to discharge its burden of establishing a violation is dependant, above all, on the structure and design of the measure in issue'.

[123] See on this issue e.g. McGovern, *International Trade Regulation*, § 8.121 *in fine*, issue 23; Ortino, 'Principle of Non-Discrimination', p. 198; Ortino, '*De Jure* and *De Facto* Discrimination', p. 221, n 17; Regan, 'Regulatory Purpose and "Like Products"', 455–56; with regard to national treatment in BITs see Bjorklund, 'National Treatment', p. 38.

jurisprudence whether this presumption is rebuttable, but at least some panel reports strongly indicate that it is in fact a non-rebuttable presumption. The Panel in *Indonesia – Autos* noted that '[i]n our view, such an origin-based distinction in respect of internal taxes suffices in itself to violate Article III:2, without the need to demonstrate the existence of actually traded like products'.[124] Similarly, the Panel in *Argentina – Hides and Leather* found that '[i]n circumstances such as those confronting us in this case [i.e. higher tax applying to imported products] no comparison of specific products is required'.[125] For the purpose of this study, the question may be left open whether in cases of *de jure* discrimination the complainant has to demonstrate that a 'like' product could potentially exist, or whether there is a rebuttable or non-rebuttable presumption of 'likeness'. Regardless of which solution is adopted, the relevance of 'likeness' will be marginal. In contrast, 'likeness' constitutes the core element of the legal analysis for most dispute settlement proceedings under the GATT 1947 and the WTO where the breach of a non-discrimination obligation was claimed on a *de facto* basis.

GATT 1947 practice developed a theory according to which 'likeness' must be determined on a case-by-case analysis.[126] This approach was endorsed by the Appellate Body under the GATT/WTO jurisprudence[127] and has ever since been constantly emphasized by the WTO adjudicating

[124] Para 14.113.

[125] Para 11.168; see also Panel Report, *Korea – Various Measures on Beef*, para. 627: 'Any regulatory distinction that is based exclusively on criteria relating to the nationality or the origin of the products is incompatible with Article III and this conclusion can be reached even in the absence of any imports (as hypothetical imports can be used to reach this conclusion)', as modified by Appellate Body Report, paras. 137 f; Panel Report, *Turkey – Rice*, para. 7.214: 'where a difference in treatment between domestic and imported products is based exclusively on the products' origin, it is correct to treat products as "alike" within the meaning of Article III:4 … there is no need to establish the likeness between imported and domestic products in terms of the traditional criteria – that is, their physical properties, end-uses and consumers' tastes and habits'; Panel Report, *US – Certain EC Products*, para. 6.54: 'We find that the 3 March additional bonding requirements violated the most-favoured-nation clause of Article I of GATT, as it was applicable only to imports from the European Communities, although identical products from other WTO Members were not the subject of such an additional bonding requirement. The regulatory distinction (whether an additional bonding requirement is needed) was not based on any characteristic of the product but depended exclusively on the origin of the product and targeted exclusively some imports from the European Communities'. On the concept of presumption in WTO law see e.g. Appellate Body Report, *US – Wool Shirts and Blouses*, p. 14.

[126] Working Party Report, *Border Tax Adjustments*, para. 18.

[127] Appellate Body Report, *Japan – Alcoholic Beverages II*, p. 20.

bodies as an introduction to every single analysis of 'likeness'. This case-by-case approach is also true in the analysis of 'like services and service suppliers' under GATS. However, while it is certainly true that the determination of 'likeness' depends strongly on the facts and circumstances of a given case, it does not mean that it is impossible to establish a consistent approach to the issue of like products or services. Consistency is indispensable to guarantee a certain legal security, predictability and to avoid arbitrary decisions.

B *Tertium comparationis for 'likeness' in trade*

From a doctrinal point of view, the crucial element for the comparative analysis of non-discrimination – regardless of whether it is in trade, constitutional law or human rights – is the identification of the *tertium comparationis*. The *tertium comparationis* is the quality or element two 'situations' or 'objects' should have in common allowing for the conclusion that they are 'alike' for the purpose of the comparison.[128] A proper interpretation of the element of 'likeness' and the identification of the *tertium comparationis* requires a two-step approach. It is first necessary to clearly determine the general purpose of the comparison in order to then identify specific factors or criteria of comparison in light of the overall purpose in a second step.[129]

The main starting point for any attempt to identify the *tertium comparationis* of 'likeness' is to determine the *purpose* for which the products or the services are compared with one another. It is impossible to make any generally valid or abstract statements as to the breadth of 'likeness' or the relevant criteria without knowing for what purposes the comparison is undertaken.

> Assume, for instance, one were asked whether apples and pineapples are alike. This question can only be answered on the basis of the purpose of the comparison. If the goal were the production of apple juice, the breadth of 'likeness' could be defined as extremely narrow so as to include only apples or even apples of a certain species; the *tertium comparationis* would be 'apple'. In contrast, if the purpose were the production of exotic fruit juice, the breadth of 'likeness' could be defined somewhat broader, including a

[128] On the *tertium comparationis* for non-discrimination in trade law see Englisch, *Wettbewerbsgleichheit*, pp. 293, 412 ff; in constitutional law see Oesch, *Differenzierung und Typisierung*, pp. 34–38, with references.

[129] Similarly Qin, 'Defining Nondiscrimination', 223–24, 234–35.

> range of different fruits comprehending both apples and pineapples; in this case the *tertium comparationis* would be 'fruit'. Finally, for the purpose of running a grocery store, the breadth of 'likeness' would be defined very broadly, leading to a *tertium comparationis* of all sorts of foodstuffs.[130]

Moving from this general example to international trade, it may be recalled that the overall economic purpose of non-discrimination is to ensure equal opportunities in a given market. Only if the 'playing field is levelled' can the producers and service providers make use of their individual competitive advantage which they gain through the more efficient use of resources. For this reason, differential treatment only qualifies as 'less favourable' under WTO law if it modifies the conditions of competition in a given market.[131] Against this background it becomes apparent that the most relevant *tertium comparationis* for 'likeness' in trade law is the *competitive relationship* between certain products or certain services in a given market.[132] In fact, the competitive advantage only plays a role to the extent that the products or services in question actually compete with one another. Accordingly, the Appellate Body clearly stated on various occasions that 'likeness' is, 'fundamentally, a determination about the nature and extent of a competitive relationship between and among products'.[133]

Having recognized the competitive relationship as the general *tertium comparationis* in the analysis of 'likeness' in trade non-discrimination rules, it is then possible to identify criteria and factors that are applied in the specific case in order to show the existence or non-existence of a competitive relationship. As the discussion of these criteria constitutes the main component of parts II and IV in this book, the present introduction is limited to a brief overview of the factors and standards in GATT jurisprudence.

The origin of all WTO jurisprudence on 'likeness' relates back to the early Working Party Report on *Border Tax Adjustments*, adopted by the contracting parties in 1970, which stated:

> 'With regard to the interpretation of the term "like or similar products", which occurs some sixteen times throughout the General Agreement,

[130] Similarly Roessler, 'Domestic Policies and Multilateral Trade', p. 29: 'Whether two products that are not identical are nevertheless considered to be like products depends on the perspective from which they are viewed: A fox and an eagle are like animals to a hare but not to a furrier'.

[131] See above, 3.I.

[132] For an extensive analysis see below, part II.

[133] Appellate Body Report, *EC – Asbestos*, para. 99, in respect to Art. III:4 GATT; for a discussion of whether this is true also for other provisions, in particular the GATS, see below, part II.

> it was recalled that considerable discussion had taken place … but that no further improvement of the term had been achieved. The Working Party concluded that problems arising from the interpretation of the terms should be examined on a case-by-case basis. This would allow a fair assessment in each case of the different elements that constitute a 'similar' product. Some criteria were suggested for determining, on a case-by-case basis, whether a product is "similar": the product's end-uses in a given market; consumers' tastes and habits, which change from country to country; the product's properties, nature and quality.'[134]

In addition to the three criteria of physical characteristics, end-uses and consumers' tastes and habits, GATT 1947 practice recognized the uniform classification in tariff nomenclatures as a fourth criterion. Subsequently, these criteria had been applied by different GATT 1947 panels, until they were endorsed under WTO jurisprudence by the Appellate Body in *Japan – Alcoholic Beverages II*.[135] The so-called *Border Tax Adjustments* framework still constitutes the core element of every 'likeness' analysis. However, different theories have been developed as to the applicable standard of 'likeness' depending on the specific provision in question.

1. Economic standard of 'likeness'

Under the economic standard, the *tertium comparationis* is defined as the competitive relationship between products or between services.[136] While there can be an unlimited number of different degrees of competitive relationships, previous interpretations of 'likeness' distinguished broadly between a marketplace approach and a narrower characteristics approach.

a. Broad marketplace standard of 'likeness' The marketplace standard is applicable to most WTO non-discrimination obligations.[137] It requires assessment of the competitive relationship and substitutability of certain products or services in a given marketplace. Starting point

[134] Working Party Report, *Border Tax Adjustments*, para. 18.

[135] Appellate Body Report, *Japan – Alcoholic Beverages II*, p. 23.

[136] Also Wilsher, 'Non-Discrimination Principle within the European Single Market', 5 (market equivalence); Horn and Mavroidis, 'Economic and Legal Aspects of MFN', 242 (sophisticated market test).

[137] As will be shown under part II below, the marketplace standard applies, *inter alia*, to GATT national treatment Articles III:4 and III:2, second sentence, as well as most forms of GATT MFN treatment under Art. I GATT; moreover, it is the appropriate standard for all GATS non-discrimination obligations.

of the analysis are the four criteria from the *Border Tax Adjustments* framework; however, WTO jurisprudence varies considerably in respect to the elaborateness of the analysis. In some instances, all four criteria are discussed in one single paragraph, whereas other cases extensively discuss each criterion separately. Yet again, other panel and Appellate Body reports consider additional factors, such as marketing studies, price differences, channels of distribution, points of sale, statements by national authorities, evidence from third markets and health risks. Only few panels resorted to economic tools of market analysis, such as cross-price elasticity.[138] The Appellate Body meanwhile clarified that 'all pertinent evidence' must be examined under the four criteria from *Border Tax Adjustments*.[139]

b. Narrow physical characteristics standard of 'likeness' Under the narrower economic standard, competitiveness and substitutability is by itself not sufficient to conclude 'likeness', but the products in question must additionally share most physical characteristics. The physical characteristics standard is a sub-set of the broader marketplace standard. It follows that all products meeting this narrow test at the same time qualify for the broader marketplace standard.[140] In consequence, it is possible that physically identical products are not 'like products' in a narrow sense if they are not in a competitive relationship. As will be discussed in section 5.I.A below, the application of the economic physical characteristics test is limited to a specific form of GATT national treatment for tax discrimination (Article III:2, first sentence, GATT).

138 Panel Report, *Japan – Alcoholic Beverages II*, para. 6.22: 'In the Panel's view, the decisive criterion in order to determine whether two products are directly competitive or substitutable is whether they have common end-uses, *inter alia*, as shown by elasticity of substitution', confirmed in Appellate Body Reports, *Japan – Alcoholic Beverages II*, p. 26 and *Canada – Periodicals*, pp. 27 ff.

139 Appellate Body Report, *EC – Asbestos*, para. 102: 'the adoption of a particular framework to aid in the examination of evidence does not dissolve the duty or the need to examine, in each case, *all* of the pertinent evidence. In addition, although each criterion addresses, in principle, a different aspect of the products involved, which should be examined separately, the different criteria are interrelated. For instance, the physical properties of a product shape and limit the end-uses to which the products can be devoted. Consumer perceptions may similarly influence – modify or even render obsolete – traditional uses of the products. Tariff classification clearly reflects the physical properties of a product' (emphasis original).

140 Appellate Body Report, *Korea – Alcoholic Beverages*, para. 118; confirmed in Panel Report, *Chile – Alcoholic Beverages*, para. 7.51; also Horn and Mavroidis, 'Interpretation of National Treatment', 45.

2. Objective standard of 'likeness'

The objective standard of 'likeness' follows a similarly narrow approach as the preceding physical characteristics test without, however, requiring a competitive relationship between the products or services. The main *tertium comparationis* generally is tariff classification with some focus also on physical characteristics. The elements of end-uses and consumers' tastes and habits, in contrast, are less relevant. In consequence, two physically identical products would be considered 'alike' even if they are not in a competitive relationship. It will be shown in chapters 5 and 6 that the objective standard of 'likeness' has been applied particularly by GATT 1947 panels in the analysis of MFN treatment (Article I GATT) and of regulatory measures under national treatment (Article III:4 GATT).

3. Subjective standard of 'likeness'

Both preceding standards require an objective analysis of 'likeness', according to which the competitive relationship or an identical tariff classification is a necessary and sufficient condition to conclude that certain products or certain services are alike. In contrast, the subjective theory of 'likeness' requires, in addition to the competitive relationship between the products or services, that there is no legitimate public policy purpose in support of the differential treatment. In other words, if there is a valid regulatory purpose of the measure that clarifies the differential treatment of the products or services at stake, then such products or services are considered unlike.[141] Accordingly, there can be no violation of the WTO non-discrimination obligation. The subjective theory of 'likeness' overlaps with the third element of regulatory purpose and is part of the discussion whether and to what extent the latter should be considered in the legal analysis of non-discrimination under section 3.III.A.1 below.

III Protectionist regulatory purpose

It is evident that the main objective of non-discrimination obligations in international trade is to outlaw measures with a protectionist purpose, meaning in particular measures directly aimed at the protection of the domestic market or at favouring one trading partner over another.[142]

[141] Also referred to as 'regulatory equivalence', see Wilsher, 'Non-Discrimination Principle within the European Single Market', 6.

[142] De Búrca, 'Concept of Discrimination', p. 188.

Oftentimes, however, measures may pursue a legitimate non-trade policy objective but nonetheless have a protectionist effect. For instance, if a Member wishes to impose certain standards related to health, environment, labour or human rights, it would have to ban the import and sale of foreign products and services which fail to comply with the required standard. Against this background, the question arises whether and how the regulatory purpose of a trade-restrictive measure should flow into the analysis of the non-discrimination obligation. While trade scholars and practitioners agree on the fact that the regulatory purpose *should* be considered, the opinions vary greatly with regard to the question of *how* or at which analytical step it should be taken into account.

The two fundamentally different schools of thought require either assessment of the regulatory purpose under the non-discrimination obligation (*below*, A.), or resorting to the regulatory purpose only as an element to justify GATT/GATS-inconsistent measures (B.).[143] These possibilities will each be outlined separately by referring in particular to the various developments in GATT 1947 and WTO jurisprudence, followed by a discussion of the main difficulties in the application of the regulatory purpose in a legal analysis (C.).

A Regulatory purpose under non-discrimination

At the outset it must be noted that WTO jurisprudence does not recognize the regulatory purpose as part of the non-discrimination analysis. Nonetheless, some considerations of regulatory purpose found their way into non-discrimination cases through the wording of the GATT national treatment obligation, which in Article III:1 outlaws the application of trade-restrictive measures 'so as to afford protection' to domestic production.[144] Based on this wording of Article III:1 GATT, different theories were developed over the time of how the regulatory purpose could be placed in the systematic structure of Article III GATT. First, the regulatory purpose could be seen as a self-standing substantive element of the non-discrimination obligation. Second, it could be considered as part of the 'likeness' analysis or, third, as part of the 'less favourable treatment' test.

Before going into the analysis of these three possibilities, it must be noted that GATT Article III is the only provision in WTO law that contains the terms 'so as to afford protection'; neither Article I GATT nor

[143] Ibid., p. 191 speaks of 'definitional stage' and 'justificatory stage'.

[144] On Art. III GATT see below, 5.I.

Articles II and XVII GATS embody a similar reference. The following discussion thus relates predominantly to jurisprudence on GATT national treatment. This leads to the contextual problem that if the regulatory purpose is interpreted into the analysis of Article III GATT based on the specific wording, it is questionable whether the same could be done for GATS national treatment or for MFN treatment in GATT and GATS. Yet – in comparison – it is widely recognized that all non-discrimination provisions apply to *de facto* less favourable treatment, even though only Article XVII:2 GATS contains explicit text.[145] Accordingly, since there is no reasonable ground to take a different approach to GATT national treatment in relation to other WTO non-discrimination obligations with regard to regulatory purpose, the absence of similar text in the latter provisions does not in principle preclude the adjudicating bodies from adopting a coherent interpretation.

1. Regulatory purpose under 'likeness': aim and effects test

In order to understand the subjective approach to the concept of 'likeness', it is important to place the question of regulatory purpose and non-discrimination in the context of the developments in trade relations and how they reflect in WTO jurisprudence. The changing interpretation of GATT national treatment over the last decades illustrates best the issues at stake.[146] As outlined under section I.1 above, national treatment as applied in the initial GATT 1947 phase of tariff reductions was concerned primarily with *de jure* discriminations and the protection of tariff commitments. The function of national treatment was similar to a safety net that prevents circumvention of tariff concessions and the obligation was thus applied in a relatively permissive way. Moreover, *de jure* discriminations are considered *prima facie* illegal,[147] leading to the presumption of the existence of a 'like' product or service.[148] However, the shift from discriminatory taxes to discriminatory regulatory measures, such as technical standards, led to the more frequent occurrence of *de facto* discriminations that require a thorough analysis of 'likeness'. In order to meet this

[145] See above, 3.I.A.2.

[146] DiMascio and Pauwelyn, 'Nondiscrimination in Trade and Investment', 62 ff.

[147] See above, n 12.

[148] See above, n 122; due to the presumption of likeness, there remains no leeway for an argument of 'unlikeness' due to the regulatory purpose of the measure. Hence, *de jure* discriminations are only in conformity with WTO law if the regulatory purpose falls within the scope of any grounds for justification listed exhaustively under Art. XIV GATS or Art. XX GATT (on the general exceptions clause see below, 3.III.B).

new challenge, GATT panels began to apply the national treatment obligation more strictly, primarily by focusing on an objective and economic interpretation of the 'like product' concept. This more intrusive application of national treatment led to considerable tension between trade liberalization and the Members' autonomy to pursue non-economic goals, such as the protection of the environment or of fundamental rights.

The first theory which emerged in GATT jurisprudence attempting to find a way of balancing the values at stake by incorporating the regulatory purpose into the analysis of non-discrimination focused on the element of 'likeness'. According to this school of thought, the element of 'likeness' is not only analysed in light of objective and economic factors indicating the existence of a competitive relationship between two products (competitive 'likeness'), but also in consideration of the subjective question whether the purpose of the national regulation is to distinguish the products for legitimate reasons (regulatory 'likeness').[149] Importantly, the difference between these two theories lies in the fact that the subjective theory of 'likeness' allows for a distinction between two products that are in a full competitive relationship; in other words, taking into account the regulatory purpose leads to the result that the competitive relationship is a necessary, but not by itself a sufficient condition for 'likeness'.[150]

In order to implement the subjective theory of 'likeness', GATT 1947 jurisprudence developed the so-called 'aim and effects' test as part of the 'like product' analysis,[151] which it based on the legal text 'so as to afford protection' in Article III:1 GATT. This test requires that the 'likeness' analysis takes into account whether a measure 'aims' at the protection of the domestic market and/or has a protectionist 'effect'. The theory was

[149] From numerous scholarly contributions see e.g. Porges and Trachtman, 'Resurrection of Aim and Effects', 785, who appropriately speak of 'competitive likeness' and 'regulatory likeness'; see also Puth, *Produkt-Prozess-Doktrin*, pp. 239 ff and Choi, 'Aim and Effect Theory', 114, referring to objective and subjective determination of like products; Mattoo and Subramanian, 'Regulatory Autonomy and Multilateral Disciplines', 305 speak of a textual and a contextual approach; see also WGTCP, The Fundamental WTO Principles of National Treatment, Most-Favoured-Nation Treatment and Transparency, Background Note by the Secretariat, WT/WGTCP/W/114, 14 April 1999, para. 35.

[150] See in this regard also Regan, 'Further Thoughts on Regulatory Purpose', 750.

[151] Note that some commentators understand the aim and effects test as a self-standing substantive element within non-discrimination (below, 3.III.A.3), as opposed to a variation of the 'likeness' element as suggested here, see e.g. Krajewski, *National Regulation*, p. 100.

developed by the GATT 1947 Panel Reports on *US – Malt Beverages* in 1992 and *US – Taxes on Automobiles* (unadopted) in 1994.[152]

> In *US – Malt Beverages*, Canada complained against US taxes on certain alcoholic beverages, arguing that these measures violate the GATT national treatment obligation. One of the measures addressed in this case was a Mississippi tax system applying different tax rates on wines made from different grapes, having the effect that mainly Mississippi vintners benefited from lower taxes. In its 'like product' analysis, the Panel mainly considered that the US was unable to provide any public policy purpose in support of its product distinction and on this basis concluded the products at issue to be alike (paras 5.23–26). Another measure in this case concerned the restrictions on points of sale, distribution and labelling based on the alcohol content of beer imposed by some States. When analysing the issue of 'likeness' in relation to high and low alcohol content beer, the Panel strongly focused on the policy goals of the measures. Reasons such as the aim to encourage the consumption of low alcohol beer and the absence of a protectionist purpose led the Panel to conclude that low and high alcohol content beers are not 'like' for the purpose of Article III:4 GATT (paras 5.70–77).

These rulings provided the foundations for the Panel in *US – Taxes on Automobiles* to establish the aim and effects test. It based its theory on the interpretation of the notion 'so as to' under Article III:1 GATT which it found to refer to both aim and effects:

> '[T]he phrase "so as to afford protection" called for an analysis of elements including the aim of the measure and the resulting effects. A measure could be said to have the *aim* of affording protection if an analysis of the circumstances in which it was adopted, in particular an analysis of the instruments available to the contracting party to achieve the declared domestic policy goal, demonstrated that a change in competitive opportunities in favour of domestic products was a desired outcome and not merely an incidental consequence of the pursuit of a legitimate policy goal. A measure could be said to have the *effect* of affording protection to domestic production if it accorded greater competitive opportunities to domestic products than to imported products.' (para 5.10, emphasis original)

While these reports attempt to find a textual interpretative justification to include the regulatory purpose into the analysis, they failed to identify and analyse the doctrinal legal issues in respect to the link between 'purpose' and 'likeness'. In fact, from a legal systemic point of view, the

[152] Both cases commented by Hudec, 'Requiem for "Aim and Effects"', 627; Tsai, 'GATT Article III's "Like Product"', 32–36.

subjective 'likeness' approach is nothing else than an effort to identify the adequate *tertium comparationis*.[153] The theory of competitive or economic 'likeness' follows the argument that the competitive relationship is the only valid *tertium comparationis* under the 'likeness' element, resulting in a purely economic analysis of the market situation. The subjective or regulatory theory of 'likeness', in contrast, requires evaluating whether the competitive relationship really is the adequate *tertium comparationis*, or whether 'something else' should serve as basis for the comparison.[154] This 'something else' is usually provided by the purpose and regulatory context of the measure in question.

> For instance, a measure prohibiting the sale of cars with a carbon emission above a certain threshold is aimed at the protection of the environment; accordingly, the subjective theory of 'likeness' requires a choice between either 'competitive relationship' or 'environment' as *tertium comparationis*. If the cars are compared on the basis of competitive relationship, they will likely be considered to be alike. In contrast, if the cars are compared on the basis of environmental impact, they are clearly unlike.

The theory of the aim and effects test is one of the issues that received most of the attention in trade law scholarship.[155] The example above illustrates that the subjective theory of 'likeness' always requires a value judgment between the economic argument and a different policy objective. Hence, the opponents of the aim and effects test argue that it unduly entrusts the WTO adjudicating bodies with the difficult task to determine which purposes are legitimate.[156] Moreover, the test requires identifing the true regulatory purpose of a trade-restrictive measure, which is particularly difficult in view of the fact that most measures simultaneously pursue different policy objectives.[157] Another main argument against aim and effects is that the analysis of the regulatory purpose under the non-discrimination obligation compromises the general exceptions clauses of Articles XX GATT and XIV GATS. These provisions list exhaustively which public interests can be pursued in contradiction with WTO trade obligations.[158] The argument goes to say that the aim and effects test

[153] On the *tertium comparationis* see above, 3.II.B.

[154] Similarly Horn and Weiler, 'EC – Asbestos', 140.

[155] For an overview see e.g. Berrisch, 'Allgemeines Zoll- und Handelsabkommen', pp. 86–87; Cottier and Oesch, *International Trade Regulation*, pp. 403–7; Hudec, 'Requiem for "Aim and Effects"'.

[156] Davey and Pauwelyn, 'MFN Unconditionality', p. 38.

[157] Cottier and Oesch, *International Trade Regulation*, p. 407.

[158] On the general exceptions clause see below, 3.III.B.

would, on the one hand, render the general exceptions clause inutile,[159] and, on the other hand, allow the pursuit of other public interests to the detriment of free trade, which could undermine the effectiveness of the WTO non-discrimination principle and contradict the will of the GATT negotiators.[160] Moreover, one could argue that the test lacks a sound legal basis and results from an over-interpretation of the phrase 'so as to afford protection'. Similarly, given the absence of an analogous wording under the GATT most-favoured-nation obligation and GATS non-discrimination clauses, the test would potentially remain limited to certain forms of GATT national treatment.[161] An application of an aim and effects test under Article III:2 GATT, while at the same time disregarding the regulatory purpose under other WTO non-discrimination obligations, would constitute an unreasonable inconsistency. For all these reasons,[162] the aim and effects test did not prevail in WTO jurisprudence. The Panel Report *US – Taxes on Automobiles* was never adopted by the GATT Contracting Parties, mainly because the EU was opposed to the aim and effects test.[163] Subsequently, on the first occasion the issue was raised under the WTO dispute settlement procedure in the case *Japan – Alcoholic Beverages II*, both the Panel and Appellate Body rejected the aim and effects approach under the GATT 'like product' analysis.[164] In addition, the first time the issue arose under GATS non-discrimination in *EC – Bananas III*, the Appellate Body made clear that aim and effects are also inappropriate for the interpretation of the concept 'like services and service suppliers'.[165]

These developments are much to the regret of the proponents of the aim and effects test. They argue that the limited number of public interests listed in Articles XX GATT and XIV GATS are insufficient to truly respect the Members' regulatory autonomy in the pursuit of internal policy objectives unrelated to trade.[166] This deference to Members is particularly necessary in light of the institutional and substantive developments

159 Panel Report, *Japan – Alcoholic Beverages II*, para. 6.17.

160 Mavroidis, '"Like Products": Some Thoughts', p. 130: 'The principals (WTO Members) are constantly opposed to any sort of judicial activism'; also opposing a subjective interpretation of 'likeness' Puth, *Produkt-Prozess-Doktrin*, pp. 243 ff.

161 But see above, 3.III.A.

162 For an overview also Trebilcock and Howse, *Regulation of International Trade*, p. 92.

163 Matsushita, Schoenbaum and Mavroidis, *World Trade Organization*, p. 240.

164 Panel Report, *Japan – Alcoholic Beverages II*, para. 6.16; Appellate Body Report, *Japan – Alcoholic Beverages II*, p. 18.

165 Appellate Body Report, *EC – Bananas III*, para. 241.

166 See e.g. Roessler, 'Domestic Policies and Multilateral Trade', p. 30; Roessler, 'Beyond the Ostensible', 779–80; also favouring the subjective interpretation of 'likeness' e.g. Hudec, 'Requiem for "Aim and Effects"', 626 ff; Howse and Regan, 'Product/Process Distinction', 260–61; Regan, 'Regulatory Purpose and "Like Products"', 454.

from the GATT 1947 as a mere trade agreement to the WTO as an international organization assuming constitutional functions in a globalized economy.[167] Moreover, a subjective interpretation of 'likeness' does not render the general exceptions clauses inutile, as they remain applicable in cases of *de jure* discrimination as well as violations of other WTO obligations.[168] Finally, some commentators claim that, in any event, all criteria from *Border Tax Adjustments* serving as a basis for the analysis of 'likeness' are always determined on the basis of a value judgment which, in the case of Article III, includes the protectionist purpose set out in para. 1.[169]

2. Regulatory purpose under 'less favourable treatment'

Following the rejection of the 'aim and effects' test and, consequently, the option to consider the regulatory purpose under 'likeness', a new theory is emerging which allows for an analysis of the purpose under the element of 'less favourable treatment'.[170] Under section 3.I.A.3 above, this approach has been introduced as the subjective theory of 'less favourable treatment', which has so far not received much attention in trade scholarship and has not yet been acknowledged by WTO jurisprudence.

While the subjective theory of 'likeness' centres around the question of the true *tertium comparationis*, the systemic rationale behind the subjective theory of 'less favourable treatment' recognized primarily by *Pauwelyn* is to focus on the true *basis* of differential treatment.[171] Measures pursuing an objective unrelated to trade – but nonetheless modifying the conditions of competition – do not differentiate between goods or services on the prohibited basis of *origin*, but on other distinguishing criteria such as the product's or service's effect on environment, consumers, labour etc. The critical question thus is whether an importing country distinguishing between certain products on the basis of a permitted criterion truly pursues an objective related to that criterion, or whether the true purpose of the measure is to discriminate indirectly on the basis of origin.

> Assume an imported 'yellow' product from the foreign country F is identical to the domestic 'blue' product from country D except for its

[167] Cottier, 'WTO and Environmental Law', pp. 58–59; Cottier and Caplazi, 'Labour Standards and World Trade', pp. 489–90.

[168] See e.g. Howse and Regan, 'Product/Process Distinction', 266; Pauwelyn, 'Lightness of Likeness', pp. 367–68; Regan, 'Regulatory Purpose and "Like Products"', 454–55.

[169] Tietje, *Behandlung nichttarifärer Handelshemmnisse*, pp. 237–38.

[170] See e.g. Trachtman, 'Lessons for GATS', p. 64; see already Farber and Hudec, 'Domestic Environmental Regulations', pp. 76–77.

[171] Pauwelyn, 'Lightness of Likeness', *passim*.

colour. If country D prohibits the sale of such products from country F, it differentiates on the basis of origin and thus commits a *de jure* discrimination under both the objective and the subjective theory. If country D prohibits the sale of 'yellow' products, it differentiates not on the prohibited basis of origin, but on a permitted basis of – in this example – colour. Under the objective approach, this measure constitutes a straightforward *de facto* discrimination against imported products originating from country F. The analysis under the subjective theory, in contrast, requires determining whether the true regulatory purpose of the measure is indeed related to the criterion of colour, or whether the true intent is simply to create a competitive advantage for the domestic product by discriminating on the basis of origin.

From this hypothetical it is possible to derivate the following abstract rule. Under the objective theory, the link from the permitted (e.g. colour) to the prohibited (i.e. origin) basis of differential treatment is created *ipso facto*, resulting in a violation of the non-discrimination obligation. Under the subjective theory, the link is only established under the condition that there are no reasons that support differential treatment on the basis of the permitted criterion. Accordingly, the subjective theory of 'less favourable treatment' – as the aim and effects test of 'likeness' – is only relevant in cases of *de facto* discrimination. Given that *de jure* discrimination always differentiates directly on the prohibited criterion of origin, it is systemically not possible to argue that due to the regulatory purpose, origin suddenly becomes a permitted criterion for differential treatment.

In order to avoid confusion between subjective 'likeness' and subjective 'less favourable treatment', it may be helpful to highlight the substantial systemic difference: Under subjective 'likeness' – focusing on the *tertium comparationis* – the question is whether the products should be compared in light of their *competitive relationship* or 'something else'; under subjective 'less favourable treatment' – focusing on the *basis* of differential treatment – the question is whether differential treatment is truly based on the permitted criterion of 'something else' or on the prohibited criterion of *origin*. In both cases, 'something else' is identical and provided by the regulatory purpose of the measure, such as environment, consumer protection, labour standards etc. Also, the value judgment and legal conclusion remain the same under both theories; however, the legal reasoning in one case leads to 'unlikeness' and in the other case to a lack of differential treatment.

Moreover, the subjective theory must be clearly distinguished from the question of asymmetric impact and diagonal standard. The latter is only concerned with the objective effect of the measure on imports in comparison to domestic products, whereas the former looks at the aim or purpose of the measure. For instance, some commentators view the Appellate Body's *obiter dictum* in *EC – Asbestos* (para 100) as the return of the aim and effects test under the element of 'less favourable treatment'.[172] This interpretation is not entirely accurate, as the Appellate Body in the said paragraph only discussed the effect of a measure – endorsing the asymmetric impact view[173] – without, however, addressing the issue of aim or purpose.[174] Other statements by the WTO adjudicating bodies leave more room for interpreting the 'purpose' element into the 'less favourable treatment' test. For instance, the Appellate Body in *Dominican Republic – Import and Sale of Cigarettes* found that a measure's detrimental effect on imports may be explained by factors other than origin:

> 'the existence of a detrimental effect on a given imported product resulting from a measure does not necessarily imply that this measure accords less favourable treatment to imports if the detrimental effect *is explained by factors or circumstances unrelated to the foreign origin of the product, such as the market share of the importer in this case*. In this specific case, the mere demonstration that the per-unit cost of the bond requirement for imported cigarettes was higher than for some domestic cigarettes during a particular period is not, in our view, *sufficient* to establish "less favourable treatment" under Article III:4 of the GATT 1994.' (para 96, first emphasis added)[175]

Yet, the factors other than origin were not related to the measure's aim or purpose, but related to economic factors of market share. The Panel in *EC – Approval and Marketing of Biotech Products* is closer to the consideration of purpose:

> 'Argentina is not alleging that the treatment of products has differed depending on their origin. In these circumstances, it is not self-evident that the alleged less favourable treatment of imported biotech products *is explained by the foreign origin of these products rather than, for instance, a perceived difference between biotech products and non-biotech products in terms of their safety, etc*. In our view, Argentina has not adduced

[172] Howse and Tuerk, 'WTO Impact on Internal Regulations', p. 299; Howse, 'Shrimp/Turtle Case', 515; Porges and Trachtman, 'Resurrection of Aim and Effects', 796; Trebilcock and Howse, *Regulation of International Trade*, p. 103; Horn and Weiler, 'EC – Asbestos', 147; Lang, 'GATS and Regulatory Autonomy', 831; see also Ortino, '*De Jure* and *De Facto* Discrimination', p. 261.

[173] See above, 3.I.A.2.

[174] Also rejecting this interpretation Ehring, 'De Facto Discrimination', 945–46.

[175] See on this ruling Leroux, 'GATS Case Law', 782; Pauwelyn, 'Lightness of Likeness', p. 365.

argument and evidence sufficient to raise a presumption that the alleged less favourable treatment *is explained by the foreign origin* of the relevant biotech products.' (para 7.2514, emphasis added)

In this case, it seems that the Panel does not *ipso facto* infer origin-based discrimination from differential treatment on the basis of a permitted criterion (biotech vs. non-biotech products). To the contrary, the Panel requires the complainant to submit evidence showing that the differential treatment is explained by the origin, and not by a permitted criterion such as safety. In sum, even though WTO jurisprudence has neither explicitly recognized the subjective theory of less favourable treatment nor has it been approved or rejected, there are some indications showing the adjudicating bodies' tendency to shift into this direction.

3. Regulatory purpose as a self-standing and substantive element

Alternatively to the subjective theory of 'likeness' and the subjective theory of 'less favourable treatment', the regulatory purpose could be considered as a self-standing and third substantive legal element in the analysis of non-discrimination. In contrast to the previous two theories where the regulatory purpose would only be relevant in cases of *de facto* discrimination, this approach allows consideration of the regulatory purpose as a distinct element for both *de facto* and *de jure* cases.

This third approach to regulatory purpose has not yet been explicitly documented by GATT 1947 and WTO jurisprudence, mainly because the WTO non-discrimination obligations lack a textual basis for such an interpretation. The only provision allowing for some flexibility in this regard is – once again – Article III:1, stating that measures 'should not be applied to imported or domestic products so as to afford protection to domestic production'.[176] The interpretation of this wording has proven to be one of the most controversial issues in GATT law and has led to considerable confusion. As outlined above, this phrase has served as a basis for the aim and effects test (likeness) and for the asymmetric impact test (less favourable treatment).[177] Moreover, at one point of time it was found

[176] According to WTO jurisprudence on GATT Art. III:2, second sentence, the element 'applied so as to afford protection' is incorporated in the legal test by reference to paragraph 1 of Article III and must thus be separately analysed, Appellate Body Report, *Japan – Alcoholic Beverages II*, pp. 25 f; on the legal structure of Art. III:2 GATT see below, 5.I.A.

[177] See above, 3.III.A (in general), 3.III.A.1 (likeness/aim and effect) and 3.I.A.2 (asymmetric impact test).

to apply exclusively to GATT Article III:2, second sentence, but according to more recent jurisprudence it serves as an informative principle for the entire Article III.[178] This section thus analyses the substantive meaning of the 'so as to afford protection' element in order to determine whether this phrase could serve as a basis to incorporate the regulatory purpose as a distinct, substantive element under non-discrimination.[179]

The Appellate Body developed the test for 'so as to afford protection' in *Japan – Alcoholic Beverages II* on the basis of the earlier GATT Panel Report *Japan – Alcoholic Beverages I*, emphasizing that the test is about protective *application*, not about protective *intent*.[180] The Appellate Body held that the 'protective application can most often be discerned from the design, the architecture, and the revealing structure of a measure'.[181] Various commentators have critically questioned the Appellate Body's reasoning, finding that, in reality, the Appellate Body did nothing else under this test than covertly looking at the intent and purpose of the regulation as a substitute for the rejected aim and effects test.[182] Indeed, it seems that subjective elements always flow into the analysis of 'so as to afford protection'.

> Panel Report, *Mexico – Taxes on Soft Drinks*, para. 8.91: 'the declared intention of legislators and regulators of the Member adopting the measure should not be totally disregarded'; Appellate Body Report, *Chile – Alcoholic Beverages*, para. 71: 'The conclusion of protective application reached by the Panel becomes very difficult to resist, in the absence of countervailing explanations by Chile'; Panel Report, *Indonesia – Autos*, para. 14.115: 'the nature of the discrimination, which is to promote a national industry by giving it advantages vis-à-vis imported products,

178 See above, n 38.

179 See e.g. Mattoo and Subramanian, 'Regulatory Autonomy and Multilateral Disciplines', 315–16; Choi, 'Aim and Effect Theory', 122: 'The consideration of aim and effect can be fully given at the next step of examining the existence of discrimination or whether the measure was taken "so as to afford protection"'.

180 See p. 29: 'It is irrelevant that protectionism was not an intended objective if the particular tax measure in question is nevertheless, to echo Article III:1, "applied to imported or domestic products so as to afford protection to domestic production". This is an issue of how the measure in question is applied'; confirmed in Appellate Body Reports, *Chile – Alcoholic Beverages*, paras. 61 f, 71; *Korea – Alcoholic Beverages*, para. 149.

181 p. 31.

182 Hudec, 'Requiem for "Aim and Effects"', 633–34; Verhoosel, *National Treatment*, p. 55; see also on this issue Horn and Mavroidis, 'Interpretation of National Treatment', 48–49; Roessler, 'Beyond the Ostensible', 781; Regan, 'Further Thoughts on Regulatory Purpose', 739–40; Regan, 'Regulatory Purpose and "Like Products"', 443, referring to Appellate Body Report, *Chile – Alcoholic Beverages*, para. 62.

is clearly designed so as to afford protection to domestic production', where it is unclear what the real difference between 'nature' and 'purpose' should be; Appellate Body Report, *Canada – Periodicals*, p. 30 ff, referring to statements by the Canadian government about the protectionist purpose of the measure.

To the extent that the element 'so as to afford protection' should purely be limited to an objective test, it may be observed that it has become largely irrelevant with the Appellate Body's endorsement of the asymmetric impact test under 'less favourable treatment'. In fact, the main – if not the only – objective element discussed under 'so as to afford protection' is whether the tax affects imports as a group more heavily than domestic products as a group.

On 'so as to afford protection' see Panel Report, *Mexico – Taxes on Soft Drinks*, para. 8.86: 'this means that the challenged measures mostly affect imported sweeteners as opposed to domestic like products'; Appellate Body Report, *Chile – Alcoholic Beverages*, para. 66: 'the first applying a rate of 27 per cent *ad valorem* which ends at the point at which most domestic beverages, by volume, are found, and the second applying a rate of 47 per cent *ad valorem* which begins at the point at which most imports, by volume, are found'; Appellate Body Report, *Korea – Alcoholic Beverages*, para. 150: 'the tax operates in such a way that the lower tax brackets cover almost exclusively domestic production, whereas the higher tax brackets embrace almost exclusively imported products'; Panel Report, *Indonesia – Autos*, para. 14.115, arguably not analysing any objective elements at all.

This analysis of disparate effects is exactly what the asymmetric impact test stands for; and this test has now been endorsed by the Appellate Body not only for GATT Article III:2, second sentence, but for the entire Article III and WTO non-discrimination in general.[183]

Finally, even if 'so as to afford protection' were interpreted as a distinct, substantive element of regulatory purpose, it would be difficult to transpose the same reasoning to other WTO non-discrimination obligations – in particular Articles I GATT, II GATS and XVII GATS – which lack an analogous wording. As it would be systemically inconsistent to apply a regulatory purpose test under national treatment in GATT but not in GATS – or vice versa –,[184] a coherent solution would only be possible

[183] See above, 3.I.A.2; Appellate Body Report, *EC – Asbestos*, para. 100; see in this regard also Ortino, '"Non-discrimination" to "Reasonableness"', 21–22.

[184] Also Pauwelyn, 'Lightness of Likeness', p. 363: 'if aims-and-effects is to return, in whatever guise, it should return in both GATS and GATT'.

by interpreting the regulatory purpose into non-discrimination on a non-textual basis, either by analogy from GATT III:1 or by accepting the principle as inherent to non-discrimination.[185]

B Regulatory purpose as justification

The second school of thought is fundamentally different from the first, in that it allows for a consideration of the regulatory purpose only in a second step, that is as justification following the finding of a breach of non-discrimination. This approach corresponds to the current Appellate Body jurisprudence, officially refusing to consider the regulatory purpose under any elements of non-discrimination. Both GATT and GATS embody a so-called 'general exceptions' clause, providing an exhaustive list of public interests that allow Members to deviate from their WTO obligations. According to Article XX GATT, a measure may be justified for reasons of (a) public morals; (b) human, animal or plant life or health; (c) gold and silver trade; (d) securing compliance with WTO-consistent regulations; (e) prison labour; (f) protecting national treasures; (g) conserving exhaustible natural resources; (h) pursuing obligations under intergovernmental commodity agreements; (i) restricting domestic materials necessary for domestic industry; and (j) distributing products in cases of short supply. GATS Article XIV contains a similar but much shorter list of public interests serving as grounds for justification, namely (a) public morals and public order; (b) human, animal or plant life or health; (c) the securing of compliance with GATS-consistent laws or regulations; (d) the imposition or collection of direct taxes; and (e) agreements of double taxation.[186]

In order to justify a measure violating a WTO non-discrimination provision – or any other substantive obligation – the respondent must show that (i) the policy objective (as synonym to regulatory purpose) falls within the scope of one of the exhaustively listed public interests; (ii) the nexus between the measure and the policy objective meets the required level (generally the necessity test); and (iii) the measure neither arbitrarily and unjustifiably discriminates between countries where like conditions prevail nor constitutes a disguised restriction on trade (good faith

[185] In comparison, it is well recognized that Articles I, III GATT and II, XVII GATS all apply to *de facto* discrimination, even though only GATS XVII contains specific text, see above, 3.I.A.2.

[186] For a comparison of the GATT and GATS general exceptions clauses see Diebold, 'Morals and Order Exceptions', 44 ff.

requirements of the *chapeau*).[187] Each one of these legal elements poses a number of interpretative issues, a discussion of which is beyond the scope of this study.[188] For the purpose of this study it is sufficient to retain that both GATT and GATS provide an exhaustive list of regulatory purposes that may be invoked to justify a measure violating a non-discrimination obligation. The main and very important difference between the consideration of regulatory purposes as justification in contrast to a substantive element of non-discrimination consists in the burden of proof. In case of the latter, it is up to the complaining Member – who bears the burden to establish its case – to show that a measure is adopted for protectionist purposes. In contrast, the justification has to be invoked and proven by the respondent after the claimant has established a violation.[189]

C *The legal challenges of regulatory purpose*

Having established the doctrinal possibilities of how the purpose of a measure could be considered in the legal analysis of non-discrimination, this section now turns to a discussion of the multiple challenges and difficulties the application of a subjective element raises in the context of a legal analysis.

1. Determining the legitimacy of a purpose

Once it is concluded that the regulatory purpose should matter in the analysis – be it as substantive element of non-discrimination, be it as justification – the question becomes which purposes are legitimate.[190] The fundamental issue of this question is whether preference should be given to the value protected by the measure at stake or the interests of free trade and economic development pursued by the prohibition of discriminatory trade restrictions. One approach is to say that this policy choice lies exclusively in the power of the Members. Only the Members determine the legitimate public interests for which one may deviate from its obligations by agreeing upon an exhaustive list at the time the agreement is adopted or by subsequently revising the agreement. The main disadvantage of this approach lies in its inflexibility to swiftly adapt to new challenges that may not have been apparent at the time the agreement was adopted, such as climate change. The second, more flexible solution is to empower the

187 Ibid., 47–48.

188 On the general exceptions clause see e.g. Cottier, Delimatsis and Diebold, 'Art. XIV GATS', *passim*.

189 On burden of proof see below, 3.III.C.3.a.

190 Mattoo and Subramanian, 'Regulatory Autonomy and Multilateral Disciplines', 321.

adjudicating bodies to identify new public interests to be given preference over free trade in the course of time by judicial construction. While this approach raises issues of legitimacy[191] and the risk of undermining the WTO system, Members could at least theoretically correct far-reaching jurisprudence by revising the agreements.

The solution incorporated in the framework of the WTO was to establish a list of public interests which to date has been consistently interpreted as exhaustive in nature.[192] Hence, to the extent that the WTO adjudicating bodies are unwilling to interpret the general exceptions clauses as illustrative, the inclusion of new legitimate public interests in the WTO framework – such as consumer protection or an explicit protection of the environment – would require a revision of the respective agreement within the competence of the Members. Alternatively, the WTO adjudicating bodies have some flexibility to take account of new policy concerns by broadly interpreting public morals and public order (Article XX(a) GATT, XIV(a) GATS).[193]

In comparison, the ECJ transformed the analogous general exceptions clause of Article 36 TFEU (ex Art. 30 TEC) from an exhaustive to an illustrative list of public interests serving as grounds for justification.[194] This development has to be viewed against the background of the ECJ's creation of the principle of 'mutual recognition' on the basis of Article 34 TFEU (ex Art. 28 TEC), which goes much further in trade liberalization than non-discrimination.[195] On the one hand, the ECJ considerably restricted the Member States' regulatory autonomy by imposing a mutual recognition of technical standards and regulations. On the other hand, the ECJ counterbalanced this intrusive approach by creating an open list of exceptions, such as 'relating in particular to the effectiveness of fiscal supervision, the protection of public health, the fairness of commercial transactions and the defence of the consumer.'[196] Contrasting these EU developments with the WTO, it may be concluded that the question of an exhaustive or illustrative list of exceptions strongly depends on the interpretation of 'less favourable treatment' (diagonal or asymmetric impact test), of 'likeness' (broad or narrow standard) and thus on the overall intrusiveness of non-discrimination.

[191] See for a comprehensive discussion e.g. Cottier and Mavroidis (eds.), *Role of the Judge*.

[192] See e.g. Mavroidis, *GATT Commentary*, p. 184; CTS, Work Programme on Electronic Commerce, Progress Report to the General Council, S/L/74, 27 July 1999, para. 14.

[193] Diebold, 'Morals and Order Exceptions', 48 ff.

[194] Cottier, Delimatsis and Diebold, 'Art. XIV GATS', pp. 297–98.

[195] See above, 3.I.A.2, n 26.

[196] Case C-120/78 *Rewe-Zentral AG* v. *Bundesmonopolverwaltung für Branntwein* [1979] ECR 649, para. 8; the Cassis-de-Dijon principle stands for both the principle of mutual recognition and the principle for an open list of exceptions.

In case the WTO adjudicating bodies would assume the authority to consider an open list of public interests as legitimate justifications, the question becomes how much deference should be given to the various regulatory purposes claimed by the Members. This is essentially a question of what standard of review, in a broad sense, should be applied.[197] In order to avoid an undermining of the non-discrimination obligation by having to accept any purpose asserted by a Member, the WTO adjudicating bodies need to have the authority to determine whether an alleged purpose is sufficiently important to override the free trade obligation.

2. Means of proof and evidence

Once the legitimate purposes have been determined, the difficulty then becomes to identify the true purpose and objective of the measure in question, which essentially depends on the actual intent of the government and the legislator.

a. Subjective determination with direct proof The identification of the subjective intent is generally a thorny exercise due to lack of evidence, even more so in case the intent of state organs is at stake. The difficulty relates on the one hand to the numerous governmental actors and interest groups involved in the decision-making process and, on the other hand, to the sensitivity of foreign politics and international relations when it comes to imputing bad faith to a government.[198] Nonetheless, it may be possible to discern intent in those countries where the legislative process is open and transparent. In Switzerland, for instance, direct democracy and the possibility to take referendums against a new legislation require the government to circulate each draft of a new law among political parties and interested groups and explain reasons and motives of the regulatory project.[199] These documents are publicly available and could be easily accessed by other Members in preparation for WTO dispute settlement procedures. Such transparent processes would make it very difficult for the government to

[197] Standard of review in a broad sense refers to a general adjudicating body's approach towards the assessment of a Members' compliance with WTO law, including criteria such as 'judicial activism', 'judicial restraint' or 'deference', see Oesch, *Standards of Review*, p. 14; for standard of review in a narrow, procedural sense see below, 3.III.C.3.b.

[198] But see Regan, 'Regulatory Purpose and "Like Products"', 461, arguing convincingly that there is nothing wrong with the 'accusation' of protectionist purpose by the WTO adjudicating bodies.

[199] See Arts. 141 (referendum) and 147 (consultation procedure) of the Federal Constitution of the Swiss Confederation.

conceal a protectionist purpose. Even though the Appellate Body categorically refuses to acknowledge any reference to subjective intent, previous cases have indeed considered the declared intent of legislators and governments in the analysis of non-discrimination.

However, direct proof of subjective intent may not always be available. In the legislative process some Members may allow for more possibilities to hide a true protectionist motive behind alleged legitimate policy objectives. If the preparatory work behind a trade-restrictive measure is not publicly available, it would be almost impossible for a complaining Member to produce evidence about a government's true motive and intent. Hence, a *subjective* determination of the regulatory purpose would impose an undue burden of proof on the complaining party and would unacceptably favour Members that allow intransparent adoption of legislation and other measures.

b. Objective determination with circumstantial evidence Alternatively, an objective determination does not require proof of the subjective intent of the authority that adopted the measure, but focuses on circumstantial evidence indicating a protective intent. The most important type of circumstantial evidence is the effect of the measure. This is the solution generally applied by the Appellate Body under the 'so as to afford protection' test pursuant to Article III:2, second sentence, GATT and which it now endorsed as a standard for 'less favourable treatment' with the asymmetric impact test.[200]

In addition to effect, circumstantial evidence could relate to the design, structure and application of a measure.[201] Elements to be considered are, for instance, the purpose and objective of the government and legislature 'to the extent that they are given objective expression in the statute itself',[202] unexplained changes in drafts during the legislative history[203] or the application of differential standards.[204]

[200] See above, 3.III.A.3.

[201] See Howse and Regan, 'Product/Process Distinction', 265, who argue that objective evidence by itself may be sufficient, but that *all* evidence – subjective and objective – must be 'carefully evaluated'.

[202] Appellate Body Report, *Chile – Alcoholic Beverages*, para. 62; commented by Horn and Mavroidis, 'Interpretation of National Treatment', 49; on objective assessment of intent also Cossy, 'Thoughts on "Likeness" in GATS', p. 348.

[203] Appellate Body Report, *Australia – Salmon*, para. 170.

[204] Ibid., para. 176: 'The Panel merely stated its doubts on whether Australia applies similarly strict sanitary standards on the internal movement of salmon products within Australia as it does on the importation of salmon products and considered that as a factor which can be taken into account in the examination under the third element of Article 5.5'.

3. Allocating the burden of proof and setting a standard of review

Both burden of proof and standard of review are procedural concepts. The burden of proof corresponds to the duty of a party to support its allegations with evidence sufficient to prove the existence of a fact.[205] Standard of review, in contrast, refers to the level of judicial deference towards the parties' factual allegations and legal interpretations.[206]

a. Burden of proof As a general rule, the complainant bears the burden of proving the violation of an obligation by showing that all the legal elements are fulfilled. Once the violation is established, the respondent bears the burden of proving that the measure is justified.[207] Depending on the allocation of 'regulatory purpose' as a substantive element of the obligation or as a justification, the burden bears on the complainant or the respondent. The allocation of burden of proof thus has considerable impact on the intrusiveness of non-discrimination. Imposing on the complainant a burden to prove the protectionist intent constitutes a very high hurdle and thus leads to a lenient form of non-discrimination. In contrast, burdening the respondent with the proof of showing a legitimate purpose may considerably infringe with its regulatory autonomy.

One way of striking a balance between the two extreme solutions is to apply the procedural concept of presumption. Under this approach, the complainant would bear a low burden of showing a protectionist intent of the respondent with circumstantial evidence, such as effect, design, structure and application of the measure in question. In case the circumstantial evidence indicates the existence of a protectionist intent, the burden shifts to the respondent to prove that its measure pursues a legitimate objective. The respondent's proof could be required either within the analysis of the non-discrimination obligation or in a second step within the justifications.

The traditional and classical approach within the WTO framework is to consider the regulatory purpose only as a justification and thus allocate the burden of proof with the respondent. However, a gradual shift can be noticed in WTO jurisprudence to a more restrictive application

205 Pauwelyn, 'Who Bears the Burden?', 229–30.

206 Oesch, *Standards of Review*, p. 15; for a delimitation of the two concepts, see p. 169.

207 See e.g. Appellate Body Report, *US – Wool Shirts and Blouses*, pp. 12 ff; Pauwelyn, 'Who Bears the Burden?', 235 ff; comprehensively on burden of proof Ishikawa, 'Burden of Proof', *passim*.

of non-discrimination. The Appellate Body in *EC – Asbestos* adopted the asymmetric impact test of 'less favourable treatment', requiring the complainant to establish that the measure affects imports as a group more heavily than domestic products as a group.[208] Similarly, the element 'so as to afford protection' requires the complainant to show circumstantial evidence of protective intent, at the same time allowing the respondent to provide evidence of legitimate intent. In *Chile – Alcoholic Beverages*, for instance, the Appellate Body found that '[t]he conclusion of protective application reached by the Panel becomes very difficult to resist, in the absence of countervailing explanations by Chile'.[209]

b. Standard of review The concept of standard of review in essence addresses the issue of how much deference the adjudicating bodies should give to the respondent's evidence and conclusions concerning the purpose of its measure. In other words, what standard or review should a panel apply if circumstantial evidence indicates a protectionist intent, but the respondent submits evidence demonstrating the pursuance of a legitimate purpose?[210] As observed by *Oesch*, a panel is held to 'thoroughly and critically examine a domestic authority's explanation of how the "raw" evidence supports its overall factual conclusions', which is close to a standard of *de novo* review.[211] However, Members have some margins of appreciation when it comes to the review of economic and scientific data.[212] Considering that regulatory purpose – to the extent that it becomes accepted as part of the legal test – constitutes the core element of the analysis, it seems appropriate that the WTO adjudicating bodies apply a *de novo* review of the evidence on purpose submitted by the respondent. Any other approach would entail the risk that Members could easily deviate from their WTO obligations by providing insufficient, inconclusive or even constructed evidence of a legitimate purpose.

4. Delimiting regulatory purpose with necessity or proportionality

Finally, even if the regulatory purpose of a measure could be identified, sufficiently proven and qualified as legitimate, there still remains a risk

[208] Para 100; see above, 3.I.A.2.

[209] Para 71.

[210] This issue must be distinguished from the question of whether the submitted purposes are sufficiently important to qualify as legitimate, see above 3.III.C.1.

[211] Oesch, *Standards of Review*, p. 136.

[212] Ibid., pp. 137 ff.

that the measure in question is overly restrictive in view of achieving the pursued objective. For instance, a total import ban of cigarettes may not be necessary to achieve certain objectives related to ensuring the quality or to reducing consumption of cigarettes.[213] For this reason, an analysis of the regulatory purpose is generally combined with a necessity or proportionality test.

In the WTO context, a necessity test is incorporated in the general exceptions clauses of Articles XX GATT and XIV GATS. Accordingly, a respondent must not only show that its measure pursues a policy objective falling within the scope of the listed public interests, but also that the measure is necessary to attain the pursued objective. According to Appellate Body jurisprudence, necessity is assessed through a 'weighing and balancing' process by considering (i) the relative importance of the interests or values pursued; (ii) the contribution of the measure to the realization of the objective; (iii) the restrictive impact of the measure in international commerce; and (iv) the existence of reasonably available alternative measures.[214] Similarly, the proportionality test in EU law is fundamental for the exceptions clause of Article 36 TFEU (ex Art. 30 TEC) as well as for the *Cassis-de-Dijon* principle.[215]

[213] See e.g. GATT Panel Report, *Thailand – Cigarettes*, para. 81.

[214] See e.g. Appellate Body Reports, *Brazil – Retreaded Tyres*, para. 178; *Korea – Various Measures on Beef*, para. 166; Cottier, Delimatsis and Diebold, 'Art. XIV GATS', pp. 313–20.

[215] Becker, 'EGV 28–30', pp. 491 ff; Desmedt, 'Proportionality in WTO Law', 462 ff; for a comparison between necessity and proportionality see e.g. Andenas and Zleptnig, 'Proportionality and Balancing', *passim*; Hilf and Puth, 'Proportionality on its Way into WTO/GATT', pp. 211 ff.

4

Concluding summary: reconciling the three elements

Part I analysed how each of the legal elements – 'less favourable treatment', 'likeness' and 'regulatory purpose' – can be interpreted differently and how each interpretation affects the scope and intrusiveness of the non-discrimination principle. It would thus be wrong to assume that non-discrimination in international economic law has a firmly defined meaning.[1] Depending on how each element is interpreted and combined with the respective interpretation of another element, the *de facto* non-discrimination obligation turns out to be extremely intrusive or very lenient.[2] Table 4.1 attempts to illustrate the different combinations and to develop seven indicative levels of non-discrimination:

- *Level 7*: The diagonal test captures any situation in which an imported product or service receives less favourable treatment than any 'like' domestic product or service. At the same time, 'likeness' is defined on the basis of market factors, meaning that all products and services that are in a competitive relationship are covered. The broad definition of 'likeness' in combination with the diagonal test results in an *extremely* intrusive interpretation of national or MFN treatment. Almost any differential treatment of products or services that are in a competitive relationship results in a violation of the non-discrimination obligation. Such an interpretation of non-discrimination is close to the EU principle of non-restriction, which, however, also incorporates the regulatory purpose and proportionality.
- *Level 6*: The very broad standard of 'less favourable treatment' combined with a very narrow definition of 'likeness' is still intrusive. In contrast to level 7, however, only differential treatment among products that share most physical characteristics or among very similar services results in a violation of the non-discrimination obligation.

[1] De Búrca, 'Concept of Discrimination', p. 182.

[2] For a different categorization see e.g. Horn and Weiler, 'EC – Asbestos', 131 ff; Ortino, '"Non-discrimination" to "Reasonableness"', 14.

Table 4.1

		De facto Less Favourable Treatment			
		diagonal test	asymmetric impact test	subjective theory of 'less favourable treatment'**	regulatory purpose as separate element (+ necessity)
Likeness	market-based competitive relationship (broad economic standard)	7	5	2b	2ab
Likeness	physical characteristics (narrow objective standard)	6	4	1b	1c
Likeness	subjective theory of 'likeness'* (aim and effects test)	3a	2a	n/a	n/a
	regulatory purpose as separate element (+ necessity)	3b	2ab	n/a	n/a

* For the purpose of Table 4.1, the aim and effects test is combined with a market-based standard of 'likeness'. However, it would also be possible to combine aim and effects with a narrow objective standard of 'likeness' grouping only identical products or services. The result would match the standard of 1b and 1c of the Table.
** For the purpose of Table 4.1, the subjective theory of less favourable treatment is combined with the asymmetric impact test. A combination of the diagonal test and the regulatory purpose would be equivalent to 3a and 3b of the Table.

– *Level 5*: A measure only amounts to 'less favourable treatment' if a higher number or percentage of a certain group of imports is disfavoured by the measure in comparison to the same group of domestic goods or services (national treatment). The group is defined on the basis of market conditions and competitive relationship. This approach was adopted by the Appellate Body in *EC – Asbestos*, focusing on the competitive relationship for 'likeness' and, in its *obiter dictum*, adopting an asymmetric impact test for 'less favourable treatment'.[3] To the extent that the test 'so as to afford protection' is met merely by showing asymmetric impact, this level also applies to GATT Article III:2, second

[3] Horn and Weiler, 'EC – Asbestos', 133 ff, refer to an 'objective' methodology.

sentence, which requires different taxation of directly competitive or substitutable products so as to afford protection.

- *Level 4*: In contrast to level 5, the group is defined narrower so that only largely identical products and identical services meet the standard of 'likeness'. This level generally applies to GATT Article III:2, first sentence, which requires that physically identical (and at the same time competing) products are taxed differently.
- *Level 3*: In the case of *3a*, the very broad diagonal test capturing any differential treatment is counterbalanced with the possibility of considering the purpose of the differential treatment as part of the 'likeness' test. Consequently, if the differential treatment occurs for a legitimate purpose, then the products or services are considered unlike. The two cases *US – Malt Beverages* and *US – Taxes on Automobiles* followed this approach.[4] *3b* provides the same standard and result as 3a with the systemic difference, however, that the regulatory purpose is considered as its own element and not as part of the 'likeness' test.
- *Level 2*: This level combines the asymmetric impact test and a market-based standard of 'likeness' with the regulatory purpose. Different systemic structures are possible: The purpose of the regulation can be considered as part of the 'likeness' analysis (*2a*), as part of the 'less favourable treatment' standard (*2b*) or, finally, as a separate substantive element (*2ab*). Accordingly, the complainant needs to prove that its industry is affected more heavily than the industry of the regulating country, that there is a competitive relationship between the industries and, finally, that the measure does not make a distinction for valid policy objectives other than trade.[5] To the extent that the test 'so as to afford protection' is interpreted subjectively, level *2ab* applies to GATT Article III:2, second sentence.
- *Level 1*: In comparison to level 2, the non-discrimination obligation is attenuated by the fact that the goods or services need not only be in a competitive relationship, but largely identical. The regulatory purpose can be considered either under the element of 'less favourable treatment' (*1b*) or as a distinct substantive element (*1c*).
- *n/a*: These situations are not applicable due to multiple considerations of the regulatory purpose.

[4] Ehring, 'De Facto Discrimination', 939–40.

[5] Horn and Weiler, 'EC – Asbestos', 137 ff, refer to an 'effect and purpose' methodology (subjective purpose as separate element) and an 'alternative comparators' methodology (subjective analysis of 'likeness'); on the blurred distinction between non-discrimination and other tests Trachtman, 'Agency Model', pp. 136 ff.

As this analysis illustrates, the non-discrimination principle can be construed in various different forms. In addition to a change in the substantive elements, the obligation can be further altered by varying the allocation of the burden of proof among the parties or by incorporating the concept of *prima facie* and presumptions. It is submitted that among the many possibilities, there are three main combinations that reflect the different approaches most pertinently:

- *A pure necessity approach (not reflected in the above Table 4.1)*: An equation of non-discrimination with necessity basically transforms the non-discrimination obligation into a *non-restriction* obligation. Under this approach, any measure inhibiting trade in goods or services could be regarded as illegal, even if it applies to domestic and imported goods and services alike and has no discriminatory effect on imports. However, Members could justify the measure with policy objectives not limited to an exhaustive list, under the condition that the measure is necessary or proportionate to achieve the pursued objective. The legal analysis turns around the issue of 'purpose' and 'necessity', whereas the elements of 'less favourable treatment' and 'likeness' become largely irrelevant. This difference in the analysis shows that non-restriction constitutes an instrument that goes far beyond non-discrimination. Its integrative character is enforced by the fact that the respondent needs to prove the legitimacy of its objective and the necessity of the measure by which it is pursued. This approach largely corresponds to the trade instruments embodied in Articles 34 and 56 TFEU (ex Arts. 28 and 49 TEC), namely the principle of non-restriction and mutual recognition.
- *A diagonal test with regulatory purpose as part of the obligation*: Under this approach, there is technically speaking a requirement of differential treatment, albeit a very limited one. The element of 'less favourable treatment' is met even if very few imports are negatively affected in comparison to very few domestic products of the same group, regardless of how the remaining imported and domestic products of the same group are affected. Consequently, non-discrimination requires treating all foreign products or services equivalent to the 'best' treatment accorded to a 'like' domestic product or service. In order to avoid an overly intrusive application, the broad interpretation of 'less favourable treatment' would need to be counterbalanced by requiring proof of a protectionist purpose or at least the absence of a legitimate purpose. For reasons of transparency, the 'purpose' requirement should

constitute a distinct substantive element independent from 'likeness' or 'less favourable treatment'. Thus, in contrast to the necessity approach, the burden of proving a protectionist purpose lies with the complainant. Yet, the burden could be lessened by incorporating the concept of *prima facie*.

- *An asymmetric impact test with regulatory purpose as justification*: According to this theory, the standard for 'less favourable treatment' is higher in that the complainant needs to demonstrate how the measure affects its products as a group more heavily than domestic products as a group. In exchange for the effect-based interpretation, the complainant does not need to prove a protectionist purpose. The requirement of 'likeness' is assessed on the basis of competitive relationships in the marketplace. Finally, the respondent may justify a measure found to violate non-discrimination to the extent that it is necessary to pursue an objective which falls within the scope of a limited number of legitimate public interests.

The GATT/WTO adjudicating bodies have struggled to incorporate a consistent theory of non-discrimination into the agreements. The interpretation of GATT 1947 and WTO non-discrimination obligations has been subject to a constant evolution, changing between different levels of intrusiveness. The main difficulties lie in the fact that the non-discrimination provisions not only lack in defining a standard for each legal element, but the text also varies from one non-discrimination obligation to another. Due to the adjudicating bodies' obedience to a textual interpretation, this has lead to an inconsistent application between the various non-discrimination obligations.

Recent developments in the Appellate Body's jurisprudence suggest that the current interpretation of Article III:4 GATT follows quite closely the asymmetric impact test with a market-based interpretation of 'likeness' and regulatory purpose as justification. While the number of legitimate interests is limited, the general exceptions clauses allow some flexibility with the public morals and public order exceptions. It is submitted that this interpretation suits the current WTO framework best. In contrast to the WTO, the EU has developed a constitutional structure with the necessary institutions and legitimacy to apply and enforce integrative principles such as non-restriction and mutual recognition which strongly impede the Member States' sovereignty. The WTO, in comparison, is a Member-driven international organization. Given the absence of specific non-restriction obligations in the agreements, the adjudicating bodies lack the legitimacy to adopt an interpretation of non-discrimination that transforms it into an obligation of non-restriction and necessity.

On a final note it is interesting to point out an alternative theory of de facto discrimination suggested most recently by Pauwelyn, which consists of viewing the different elements as flexible criteria rather than cumulative legal conditions in a strict sense. Under this approach, the WTO adjudicating bodies would balance the relevant criteria, such as 'structure, design and architecture of the regulation; the way the regulation is applied; the effect of the group of imports as opposed to the group of like domestic products; evidence of a protectionist purpose' etc.[6] Depending on how each of the criteria plays out, the adjudicating bodies would then come to an overall conclusion of whether or not there is discrimination. The theory of a factor-based obligation of non-discrimination deserves close attention in view of the drafting of future trade and investment agreements. For reasons of legal security, such an approach requires that the agreement not only lists the elements to be taken into account, but also states explicitly that the elements are weighed and balanced as flexible criteria. Consequently, it seems difficult to interpret such an approach into the non-discrimination provisions as they are currently framed in the WTO agreements.

[6] Pauwelyn, 'Lightness of Likeness', pp. 366–67, see also Diebold, 'Non-discrimination', pp. 17ff.

PART II

Framing the conceptual breadth of 'likeness' in GATS

Having established the asymmetric impact test as an appropriate standard for 'less favourable treatment', the question becomes whether 'likeness' should be interpreted on the basis of an economic, objective or subjective standard and how it should be analysed in a specific case. While part I concluded that, in the abstract and on the example of GATT, an economic framework is appropriate with regard to 'likeness' in WTO non-discrimination rules, part II seeks to confirm this conclusion by analyzing the concept of 'like services and service suppliers' in the specific GATS provisions and its interpretation in relevant GATT/WTO jurisprudence. Once the appropriate standard and conceptual breadth has been established, it will then be possible in parts III and IV to derive from these conceptual considerations concrete criteria that can be applied in a specific case. For an interpretation and discussion of 'like services and service suppliers', it is indispensable to take into account the WTO adjudicating bodies' interpretation of 'like products' in GATT MFN and national treatment. In *EC – Bananas III* the Appellate Body held that it is correct to interpret the GATS most-favoured-nation obligation on the basis of previous GATT practice relating to the interpretation of GATT MFN treatment.[1] Accordingly, the following analysis of 'likeness' in GATS national treatment in chapter 5 and MFN treatment in chapter 6 is each preceded by a detailed overview of how the same problem in the respective GATT provision has

[1] Appellate Body Report, *EC – Bananas III*, para 231: 'provisions elsewhere in the GATS relating to national treatment obligations, and previous GATT practice relating to the interpretation of the national treatment obligation of Article III of the GATT 1994 are not necessarily relevant to the interpretation of Article II of the GATS. The Panel would have been on safer ground had it compared the MFN obligation in Article II of the GATS with the MFN and MFN-type obligations in the GATT 1994'; for a comparative interpretation of national treatment in different WTO agreements also Appellate Body Report, *US – Section 211 Appropriations Act*, para. 242 (TRIPs Agreement and GATT III:4); Panel Report, *EC – Approval and Marketing of Biotech Products*, para. 7.2406 (Annex C[1] to the SPS Agreement and GATT III:1).

been interpreted by the adjudicating bodies. The focus lies primarily on the WTO jurisprudence and less on the many opinions that have been voiced by scholars in the 'like product' context. Yet, some of these ideas are introduced to the extent that they are relevant for the concept of 'like services and service suppliers' under GATS. Moreover, the subjective theory of 'likeness' analysed under section 3.III.A.1 was rejected in the concluding chapter 4 of part I and will thus not be discussed extensively under part II. The landmark case by which the Appellate Body set the standard for the interpretation of 'likeness' in GATT national treatment was *Japan – Alcoholic Beverages II*. This decision contained findings that go beyond GATT national treatment, clarifying the Appellate Body's general approach to the concept of 'likeness' in all WTO non-discrimination clauses, including GATS. The Appellate Body illustrated its theory by means of a colourful metaphor, which became one of the most quoted holdings in WTO jurisprudence and literature:

> 'The concept of "likeness" is a relative one that evokes the image of an accordion. The accordion of 'likeness' stretches and squeezes in different places as different provisions of the *WTO Agreement* are applied. The width of the accordion in any one of those places must be determined by the particular provision in which the term "like" is encountered as well as by the context and the circumstances that prevail in any given case to which that provision may apply.'[2]

This differentiated approach by the Appellate Body deserves support in view of the fact that the determination of 'likeness' depends primarily on the *purpose* for which the products or the services are compared which, in turn, depends on the purpose of the respective non-discrimination clause. Even though all non-discrimination obligations serve the overall purpose of protecting competitive opportunities by ensuring equal conditions for competitors in a given market, the specific provisions of MFN and national treatment may well serve an additional, more specific purpose. In fact, even within the provision on national treatment the purpose may vary from one national treatment obligation to another.[3] Following the interpretation of GATS MFN and national treatment, the comparative analysis in chapter 7 looks at 'likeness' in other WTO agreements as well as the concept of 'like circumstances' as it applies in NAFTA and BITs. Finally, part II closes with chapter 8, summarizing and concluding the guiding principles for the 'likeness' interpretation in GATS.

[2] Appellate Body Report, *Japan – Alcoholic Beverages II*, pp. 21 ff.
[3] Qin, 'Defining Nondiscrimination', 241.

5

'Likeness' in national treatment

During the Uruguay Round, the negotiators specifically pointed out that Article III GATT 'had been set up for products, *not for producers (or activities)*, and it was therefore difficult to see how it could be applied to services, the imports of which were not covered by customs duties at the border as was the case with trade in goods'.[1] Due to the potentially very broad implications of a national treatment obligation for services, the negotiators even argued that '[i]n the context of trade in services, national treatment should thus be seen only as a yardstick and not as a basic obligation'.[2] Despite these prior reservations, the negotiators recognized the importance of including basic GATT principles into GATS, including the national treatment obligation.[3] Under GATS, the national treatment obligation is set forth in Article XVII, which states as follows:

> '1. In the sectors inscribed in its Schedule, and subject to any conditions and qualifications set out therein, each Member shall accord to services and service suppliers of any other Member, in respect of all measures affecting the supply of services, treatment no less favourable than that it accords to its own like services and service suppliers.'

Even though the GATT and GATS provisions on national treatment embody the same basic principle of non-discrimination, there are a number of differences between the two agreements that must be taken into consideration in a comparative analysis. To date, only two cases have been

[1] GNS, Note on the Meeting of 15–17 September 1987, MTN.GNS/10, 15 October 1987, para. 12 (emphasis added).

[2] Ibid., para. 13; see also Jackson, 'Constitution for Trade in Services', 188: 'it seems dangerous and probably impractical to try to develop sweeping rules, such as a broad national-treatment obligation, which would apply to all "services", regardless of industry', see also at 197; Mestmäcker, 'Free Trade in Services', p. 20: 'The principle of national treatment ... would, however, have a much more profound impact in its application to services'; moreover Jackson, *World Trading System*, p. 307; Jackson, *Competition in Services*, pp. 28–29.

[3] TNC, Midterm Review in Montreal on 5–9 December 1988 and in Geneva on 5–8 April 1989, MTN.TNC/11, 21 April 1989, part II, para. 7(c).

decided on the basis of Article XVII GATS, both of which lack any conceptual scrutiny of the 'likeness' element. For this reason, the methodological approach for this chapter is to first outline the WTO jurisprudence with regard to 'like products' in terms of Article III GATT (*below*, I.), followed by a comparative interpretation of the 'likeness' concept in Article XVII GATS (II.). Aware of the fact that GATT national treatment and its 'like products' concept have been subject to countless contributions from trade scholars, this chapter aims to take a slightly different angle to this topic, namely developing a conceptual structure that is suitable for an analogical application in the context of services trade and GATS.

I GATT national treatment

The national treatment obligation with regard to fiscal measures was meticulously interpreted by the Appellate Body in *Japan – Alcoholic Beverages II*. In this case the US, Canada and the EU complained against a Japanese measure which taxed locally produced shochu at a lower rate than imported whisky, brandy, rum, gin, vodka and liqueurs. When interpreting Article III GATT, the Appellate Body first turned to its paragraph 1, which embodies the general principles of GATT national treatment:

> '1. The contracting parties recognize that internal taxes and other internal charges, and laws, regulations and requirements affecting the internal sale, offering for sale, purchase, transportation, distribution or use of products, and internal quantitative regulations requiring the mixture, processing or use of products in specified amounts or proportions, should not be applied to imported or domestic products so as to afford protection to domestic production.'

The Appellate Body found that this 'general principle informs the rest of Article III' and that it serves 'as a guide to understanding the specific obligations contained in Article III:2 and in other paragraphs of Article III'.[4] Accordingly, paragraph 1 does not constitute a basis for an individual claim. It is only relevant for interpreting the GATT national treatment obligations with regard to taxes (Article III:2) and with regard to internal regulatory measures (Article III:4).[5]

[4] Appellate Body Report, *Japan – Alcoholic Beverages II*, p. 17.

[5] Ibid.; Choi, '*Like Products*', p. 106.

A Tax measures, Article III:2 GATT

After having established the purpose of paragraph 1, the Appellate Body in *Japan – Alcoholic Beverages II* then turned to the analysis of paragraph 2 on tax measures, which states:

> '2. The products of the territory of any contracting party imported into the territory of any other contracting party shall not be subject, directly or indirectly, to internal taxes or other internal charges of any kind in excess of those applied, directly or indirectly, to *like domestic products*. Moreover, no contracting party shall otherwise apply internal taxes or other internal charges to imported or domestic products in a manner *contrary to the principles set forth in paragraph 1*.' (emphasis added)

This provision must be read in conjunction with *Ad* Article III, paragraph 2 of the GATT Annex I on 'Notes and Supplementary Provisions', according to which

> '[a] tax conforming to the requirements of the first sentence of paragraph 2 would be considered to be inconsistent with the provisions of the *second sentence* only in cases where competition was involved between, on the one hand, the taxed product and, on the other hand, a *directly competitive or substitutable* product which was not similarly taxed'. (emphasis added)

In this context it becomes apparent that Article III:2 contains two separate obligations of national treatment. The first sentence of paragraph 2 concerns taxes that are imposed on 'like products', whereas the second sentence read in connection with *Ad* Article III applies to taxes imposed on 'directly competitive or substitutable products'.[6] In interpreting the relationship between these two sentences, the Appellate Body noted that the first sentence, in contrast to the second sentence, does not specifically refer to paragraph 1 of Article III. It concluded from this omission that the notion 'so as to afford protection' contained in paragraph 1 has no separate and substantive meaning for paragraph 2, first sentence.[7] In other words, it suffices under Article III:2, first sentence, to demonstrate that (i) the imported and the domestic products are 'like' and (ii) the taxes imposed on the imported product are 'in excess of' the taxes applied to domestic products.[8] Conversely, the substantive elements for a breach of Article III:2, second sentence, require that (i) the imported and domestic

[6] For an overview of the negotiating history of Art. III and *Ad* Art. III, see ibid., pp. 107 ff.

[7] Appellate Body Report, *Japan – Alcoholic Beverages II*, p. 17.

[8] Ibid.; Jackson, Davey and Sykes, *International Economic Relations*, p. 554.

products are 'directly competitive or substitutable'; (ii) the imported and domestic products 'are not similarly taxed'; and (iii) the dissimilar taxation is 'applied so as to afford protection'.[9]

Against this background the Appellate Body concluded, *inter alia*, that 'like' products in terms of the first sentence require a much narrower product relationship than the concept of 'directly competitive or substitutable products' set forth in the second sentence.[10] Consequently, 'all like products are, by definition, directly competitive or substitutable products, whereas not all directly competitive or substitutable products are like'.[11] In *Canada – Periodicals*, the Appellate Body further clarified the applicable benchmarks, ruling that 'like products' requires a standard of 'perfect substitutability', implying at the same time that 'imperfect substitutability' is a sufficiently strong relationship for the broader prohibition of the second sentence.[12]

The rationale behind these two different levels of product relationship is to protect 'like' imported products more strongly than imported products which are only 'competitive or substitutable'. If the products are 'like' in terms of the first sentence (i.e. competing and physically similar), even very small differential taxation to the detriment of imported products meets the 'in excess of' requirement and thus constitutes a breach of Article III:2, first sentence; no *de minimis* exception is granted.[13] In contrast, if the products in question are not 'like', but nevertheless in direct competition or substitutable (i.e. competing regardless of physical differences), the requirements on the difference in taxation are more strict. In these cases, a supplemental *de minimis* tax on imported products is not sufficient to find a breach of Article III:2, second sentence, and, unlike in the case of the first sentence, the taxation must be construed so as to afford protection.[14] In other words, the broad standard of 'directly competitive

[9] Appellate Body Report, *Japan – Alcoholic Beverages II*, p. 25.

[10] Ibid., pp. 19, 26; confirmed in Appellate Body Report, *Canada – Periodicals*, p. 23.

[11] Appellate Body Report, *Korea – Alcoholic Beverages*, para. 118; confirmed in Panel Report, *Chile – Alcoholic Beverages*, para. 7.51; also Horn and Mavroidis, 'Interpretation of National Treatment', 45.

[12] Appellate Body Report, *Canada – Periodicals*, p. 31: 'A case of "perfect substitutability" would fall within Article III:2, first sentence, while we are examining the broader prohibition of the second sentence'.

[13] In case of *de facto* discrimination, it could even be argued that the standard of 'less favourable treatment' for Art. III:2, first sentence, follows the diagonal test, meaning that the tax violates GATT even if only one imported product is taxed more heavily. This broad interpretation of 'less favourable treatment' is counterbalanced with a very narrow interpretation of 'likeness'.

[14] Appellate Body Report, *Japan – Alcoholic Beverages II*, p. 28.

or substitutable' product relationship expanding the scope of the national treatment obligation is counterbalanced with the more stringent requirement for the intensity of the discrimination and the additional step to show the element 'so as to afford protection'.[15]

Having established the theoretical and systemic functioning of Article III:2, the Appellate Body found that the analysis of whether the product relationship meets the required standard must be done on a case-by-case basis.[16] The analysis is based on a number of criteria designed to establish the existence of 'like products' or of 'directly competitive or substitutable products' in terms of Article III:2 GATT. Most of these criteria were first developed by the Working Party on *Border Tax Adjustments*, adopted by the GATT Contracting Parties in 1970, which stated:

> '[T]he interpretation of the term should be examined on a case-by-case basis. This would allow a fair assessment in each case of the different elements that constitute a "similar" product. Some criteria were suggested for determining, on a case-by-case basis, whether a product is "similar": the product's end-uses in a given market; consumers' tastes and habits, which change from country to country; the product's properties, nature and quality.'[17]

In addition to the three criteria of physical characteristics, end-uses and consumers' tastes and habits, GATT 1947 practice recognized the uniform classification in tariff nomenclatures as a fourth factor. Subsequently, these criteria had been applied by different GATT 1947 panels, until they were endorsed under WTO jurisprudence by the Appellate Body in *Japan – Alcoholic Beverages II*.[18]

In view of the two different standards contained in Article III:2 GATT, the criterion of physical characteristics plays a crucial role in order to demonstrate 'perfect substitutability' between products, which is the benchmark required for Article III:2, first sentence.[19] With regard to the

15 Similarly Fauchald, 'WTO Non-Discrimination Clauses', 445; see also Howse and Regan, 'Product/Process Distinction', 266–68; Horn and Weiler, 'EC – Asbestos', 136–37; Quick and Lau, 'Environmentally Motivated Tax Distinctions', 435; critically Neven, 'How Should "Protection" be Evaluated?', 427.

16 Appellate Body Report, *Japan – Alcoholic Beverages II*, pp. 21, 26.

17 Working Party Report, *Border Tax Adjustments*, para. 18.

18 Appellate Body Report, *Japan – Alcoholic Beverages II*, p. 23.

19 See Panel Report, *Korea – Alcoholic Beverages*, para. 10.66: 'The determination of whether two products are "like" has traditionally turned to a greater extent (although not exclusively), on the physical characteristics of products'; Panel Report, *Chile – Alcoholic Beverages*, para. 7.51; for this reason, this standard has also been referred to as 'physical characteristics test', see Matsushita, Schoenbaum and Mavroidis, *World Trade Organization*, p. 237.

broader standard, the Appellate Body confirmed the Panel's finding that in order to determine whether two products are 'directly competitive or substitutable', it is necessary to look additionally at the 'marketplace' and to consider the elasticity of substitution as one means to determine the relevant markets. For this standard, the question of substitutability from the consumers' perspectives is given considerably more weight than the factors of physical characteristics and tariff classifications.[20] Importantly, 'like products' and 'directly competitive or substitutable' in Article III:2 are *both economic* standards of comparison.[21] While a competitive relationship is sufficient to meet the latter standard,[22] the former requires *in addition* that the products share most physical characteristics.[23] In most cases, this approach has the effect that the standard of 'like products' reflects a stronger competitive relationship than the standard of 'directly competitive or substitutable'.

Despite the relatively clear distinction between these two groups of product relationship, there remains considerable discretion in the analysis

[20] Panel Report, *Japan – Alcoholic Beverages II*, para. 6.22: 'In the Panel's view, the decisive criterion in order to determine whether two products are directly competitive or substitutable is whether they have common end-uses, *inter alia*, as shown by elasticity of substitution', confirmed in the Appellate Body Reports, *Japan – Alcoholic Beverages II*, p. 26 and *Canada – Periodicals*, pp. 27 ff; see also Panel Report, *Korea – Alcoholic Beverages*, para. 10.40: 'an assessment of whether there is a direct competitive relationship between two products or groups of products requires evidence that consumers consider or could consider the two products or groups of products as alternative ways of satisfying a particular need or taste'; see also Choi, '*Like Products*', p. 109: 'the national treatment obligation finally reaches even those product relationships, in which the two products in question share absolutely no physical similarity with each other, as long as they appeal to the consumers as "directly competitive or substitutable"'.

[21] Also Vranes, *Trade and the Environment*, pp. 197–99; note that this approach is different from the '*objective* standard' which requires strong physical similarities irrespective of a competitive relationship, see above 3.II.B.1 and 3.II.B.2. In contrast to 'like products' in terms of Art. III:4 and I GATT (see below, 5.I.B and 6.I), 'like products' in Art. III:2 GATT appear to have never been subject to a purely objective interpretation, not even in GATT 1947 practice, see e.g. GATT Panel Reports, *US – Superfund*, para. 5.11 and *Japan – Alcoholic Beverages I*, para. 5.5(d), both referring also to end-uses; but see also GATT Panel Report, *Canada – Gold Coins*, unadopted, para. 14, referring mainly to objective criteria.

[22] See Panel Report, *Japan – Alcoholic Beverages II*, para. 6.22: 'the wording of the term "directly competitive or substitutable" does not suggest at all that physical resemblance is required in order to establish whether two products fall under this category'.

[23] Ibid.: 'The wording of the term "like products" [in terms of Article III:2, first sentence, GATT] however, suggests that commonality of end-uses is a necessary but not a sufficient criterion to define likeness. In the view of the Panel, the term "like products" suggests that for two products to fall under this category they must share, apart from commonality of end-uses, essentially the same physical characteristics'.

to the extent that it is almost impossible to fully explain why two products are directly competitive or substitutable, but not 'like'. As the following overview of WTO jurisprudence on Article III:2 shows, panels are usually content to analyse the product relationship under only one of the two obligations of Article III:2 GATT, thereby avoiding to clearly delimit 'like' from 'directly competitive or substitutable'. Moreover, the approaches lack systemic consistency in regard to the question of which standard or obligation should be examined first:

– *'Directly competitive or substitutable' but not 'like'*:

> The leading case *Japan – Alcoholic Beverages II* is one of the few cases where the Panel clearly analysed the facts in light of the two obligations contained in Article III:2 GATT, finding that only shochu and vodka share sufficient physical characteristics to qualify as 'like products' in terms of the first sentence (para 6.23). Imported whisky, brandy, rum, gin, genever, liqueurs and domestic shochu, in contrast, were found to be 'directly competitive or substitutable' based on marketplace factors (paras 6.28 ff).

– *Both 'directly competitive or substitutable' and 'like'*:

> The Panel in *Mexico – Taxes on Soft Drinks* examined the relationship between imported soft drinks containing beet sugar and domestic soft drinks containing cane sugar with regard to paragraph 2, first sentence, and high-fructose corn syrup (HFCS) vs. cane sugar under the second sentence of paragraph 2. Under the 'likeness' analysis of the first sentence, the Panel strictly applied the four factors without looking at the market place (paras 8.27 ff). In contrast, for the 'directly competitive or substitutable' standard of the second sentence, the Panel specifically referred to the competition in a marketplace (para 8.68). Hence, the Panel elaborated considerably more on the consumers' perceptions and behaviours and introduced evidence related to the determination of the product relationship by authorities of the respondent (paras 8.72, 8.76). Similarly, the required product relationship was affirmed under both sentences of Article III:2 GATT in *Indonesia – Autos* with regard to at least some of the imported cars and domestic cars (paras 14.110, 14.115), even though the Panel only specifically analysed 'likeness' with regard to the first sentence. It noted that the measure under scrutiny differentiates based on nationality and thus constitutes a *de jure* discrimination; accordingly, even 100 per cent identical products would be taxed differently, reason for which Article III:2 GATT is necessarily breached (paras 14.112 ff).

– *Only 'like'*:

> In *Dominican Republic – Import and Sale of Cigarettes*, the Panel found that the two cigarette brands in question are 'like products' and

concluded a violation of GATT III:2, first sentence (paras 7.329 ff), without analysing the standard of the second sentence. For the 'like product' analysis, the Panel referred to the traditional four factors[24] and noted in addition that the narrow approach does not hinder cigarettes distinguished by brands from qualifying as 'like products' in terms of paragraph 2, first sentence. Similarly, the Panel in *China – Auto Parts* also limited its analysis to the first sentence of Article III:2 GATT (para 7.226).

– *Only 'directly competitive or substitutable'*:

The approach was different in *Korea – Alcoholic Beverages*, where the Panel first concluded that vodka and soju are 'directly competitive or substitutable', followed by the ruling that there is insufficient evidence in order to determine whether the narrow standard of 'like products' is met. Among the traditional factors, the Panel also took into account cross-price elasticity, evidence from outside the Korean market, and potential competition in order to establish the directly competitive or substitutable standard.[25] Similarly, the Panel in *Chile – Alcoholic Beverages* also analysed the relationship between imported whisky and domestic pisco only in relation to the broad standard of the second sentence, given that the EU did not claim a violation of GATT III:2, first sentence. The Panel explicitly noted the Appellate Body's ruling from *Japan – Alcoholic Beverages II* requiring to consider the marketplace characteristics and found that it will thus consider 'the channels of distribution, price relationships (including cross-price elasticities), and other relevant characteristics'.[26] Another case which was found by scholars to reflect the marketplace approach was *Canada – Periodicals*, where the Appellate Body established a directly competitive or substitutable relationship between domestic non-split-run periodicals and imported split-run periodicals 'in so far as they are part of the same segment of

[24] Para 7.330: '[T]he available evidence demonstrates that both imported and domestic cigarettes have similar physical properties; they are made from similar materials; have a similar presentation; they have the same end-use (i.e. they are smoked by consumers); and they are classified under the same tariff heading'.

[25] Panel Report, *Korea – Alcoholic Beverages*, paras. 10.34 ff, 10.103 ff; confirmed by Appellate Body Report, *Korea – Alcoholic Beverages*, para. 124: 'We, therefore, conclude that the term "directly competitive or substitutable" does not prevent a panel from taking account of evidence of latent consumer demand as one of a range of factors to be considered when assessing the competitive relationship between imported and domestic products under Article III:2, second sentence, of the GATT 1994. In this case, the Panel committed no error of law in buttressing its finding of "present direct competition" by referring to a "strong potentially direct competitive relationship"'.

[26] Panel Report, *Chile – Alcoholic Beverages*, paras. 7.12, 7.30. The Panel found that the products at issue are directly competitive or substitutable; the issue of product relationship remained unappealed.

> the Canadian market for periodicals'.[27] On the other hand, the Appellate Body reversed the Panel's conclusion affirming 'like products' due to 'lack of proper legal reasoning based on inadequate factual analysis'.[28] Due to the flawed determination of the facts, the Appellate Body was unable to rule on the issue of 'like products'.

This overview of WTO case law on Article III:2 GATT allows the observation that next to *Japan – Alcoholic Beverages II* there is no other case in which the adjudicating bodies found that for clear reasons two products are in a 'directly competitive or substitutable' relationship, but not sufficiently close to meet the 'like' standard. Hence, while the distinction between the narrow conceptual breadth of 'like products' and the broad marketplace 'directly competitive or substitutable' approach is well established in theory, it remains difficult in practice to draw a line between the two categories.

B Regulatory measures, Article III:4 GATT

Next to the Article III:2 GATT prohibition of internal taxes, paragraph 4 of the same provision addresses regulatory measures:

> '4. The products of the territory of any contracting party imported into the territory of any other contracting party shall be accorded treatment no less favourable than that accorded to like products of national origin in respect of all laws, regulations and requirements affecting their internal sale, offering for sale, purchase, transportation, distribution or use. The provisions of this paragraph shall not prevent the application of differential internal transportation charges which are based exclusively on the economic operation of the means of transport and not on the nationality of the product.'

In contrast to paragraph 2 on taxes, the provision on regulatory measures does not distinguish between different standards of product relationships. It only applies the notion 'like products', without specifically referring to paragraph 1 and without applying the 'directly competitive and substitutable' standard. Hence, the question arises of how wide or

[27] Appellate Body Report, *Canada – Periodicals*, p. 32; Ortino, '*De Jure* and *De Facto* Discrimination', p. 236; on this case also Matheny, '"Like Products" and Cultural Products', 260–68.

[28] Appellate Body Report, *Canada – Periodicals*, p. 25; the Panel found 'that imported "split-run" periodicals and domestic non "split-run" periodicals are like products' and subsequently did not analyse whether they are also directly competitive or substitutable (para 5.27).

narrow the breadth of 'like products' should be interpreted under Article III:4 GATT.

While the notion of 'like products' in terms of Article III:2, first sentence, GATT has always been interpreted in view of physical characteristics *and* competitive relationship, early GATT 1947 jurisprudence interpreted 'like products' in Article III:4 purely objectively, in a similar way to 'like products' in Article I GATT:[29]

> In *Australia – Ammonium Sulphate* the Panel concluded purely on the basis of differences in tariff classifications that ammonium sulphate fertilizer is not 'like' nitrate fertilizer for purposes of Article III:4 GATT (para 9, referring to the analysis of Article I 'like products' in para 8).[30]

Under the WTO, panels started to adopt a more economic interpretation of Article III:4 GATT by applying the *Border Tax Adjustments* criteria.

> The Panel in *US – Gasoline* noted that previous panels applied the *Border Tax Adjustments* criteria under Article III:2 and 'considered that those criteria were also applicable to the examination of like products under Article III:4' (para 6.8). On this basis it found that 'chemically-identical imported and domestic gasoline by definition have exactly the same physical characteristics, end-uses, tariff classification, and are perfectly substitutable' (para 6.9).[31] Yet, in this case as well as the following cases on Article III:4, namely *EC – Bananas III*, *Indonesia – Autos*, *Canada – Autos* and *Korea – Beef*, 'likeness' was not a central issue in the dispute.

Following the introduction of the *Border Tax Adjustments* framework to Article III:4 GATT, the Appellate Body in *EC – Asbestos* specifically interpreted the breadth of 'like products' in Article III:4 in relation to 'like products' and 'directly competitive or substitutable' in Article III:2 GATT. The EU as defendant supported a textual interpretation, according to which 'like products' in Article III:4 should have a narrower meaning than 'directly competitive or substitutable'.[32] However, this approach would considerably limit the scope of paragraph 4 to products which are practically identical. Such a narrow interpretation is justified under

[29] On 'like products' in GATT Art. I MFN see below, 6.I.

[30] Similarly also GATT Panel Reports, *EEC – Animal Feed Proteins*, paras. 4.11 and 4.3; *Spain – Soyabean Oil*, unadopted, para. 4.6.

[31] Similar approach also in Panel Report, *EC – Bananas III*, para. 7.62.

[32] Panel Report, *EC – Asbestos*, para. 3.442: 'The European Communities emphasized that it follows clearly from a textual analysis of Article III:4 that the "like products" provision therein does not cover "directly competitive or substitutable" products' (emphasis omitted).

paragraph 2, first sentence, because there the discriminatory element of tax treatment is applied very strictly, such that even a *de minimis* tax difference results in a breach of the national treatment obligation. The discriminatory standard of 'less favourable treatment' in paragraph 4, on the other hand, is closer related to the 'not similarly taxed' standard in paragraph 2, second sentence. From this point of view it appears more appropriate to interpret the breadth of 'like products' in paragraph 4 in line with 'directly competitive or substitutable products' of paragraph 2, second sentence.

The Appellate Body rightfully rejected the Article III:2 narrow interpretation of 'like products' with regard to Article III:4 GATT, even though it applied a slightly different reasoning.[33] The Appellate Body recognized that paragraph 2 contains two distinct obligations, while paragraph 4 applies only to like products. Accordingly, the general principle set forth in paragraph 1 'is expressed in Article III:4, not through two distinct obligations, as in the two sentences in Article III:2, but instead through a single obligation that applies solely to "like products"'.[34] Therefore the Appellate Body concluded that 'given the textual difference between Articles III:2 and III:4, the "accordion" of "likeness" stretches in a different way in Article III:4'.[35] In light of the general principle articulated in paragraph 1, the Appellate Body went on to find that paragraph 4 aims to ensure 'equality of competitive conditions' and 'seeks to prevent Members from applying … regulations in a manner which affects the competitive relationship, in the marketplace, between the domestic and imported products involved'.[36] Thus, the Appellate Body found that 'a determination of "likeness" under Article III:4 is, fundamentally, a determination about the nature and extent of a competitive relationship between and among products'.[37] It is noteworthy that as for Article III:2, second sentence, the Appellate Body specifically referred to the marketplace and thus pursued a similar approach as for the 'directly competitive or substitutable' standard of Article III:2, second sentence.

However, when the Appellate Body then turned to an abstract analysis of the conceptual breadth of 'like products' in terms of Article III:4,

33 The Appellate Body thus clearly rejected a strict reading of 'like products' in Article III:4 GATT as it was proposed by the early GATT Panel Report, *EEC – Animal Feed Proteins*, paras. 4.2 f.

34 Appellate Body Report, *EC – Asbestos*, para. 96.

35 Ibid.

36 Ibid., para. 98 (emphasis omitted).

37 Ibid., para. 99.

taking into consideration the general principle of paragraph 1 and its findings from *Japan – Alcoholic Beverages II* with regard to paragraph 2, it cautiously avoided making a concrete ruling. It is illustrative to reproduce the respective paragraph of the decision *in extensu*, as it nicely shows how the Appellate Body navigates through this issue:

> 'As products that are in a competitive relationship in the marketplace could be affected through treatment of *imports* "less favourable" than the treatment accorded to *domestic* products, it follows that the word "like" in Article III:4 is to be interpreted to apply to products that are in such a competitive relationship. Thus, a determination of "likeness" under Article III:4 is, fundamentally, a determination about the nature and extent of a competitive relationship between and among products. In saying this, we are mindful that there is a spectrum of degrees of "competitiveness" or "substitutability" of products in the marketplace, and that it is difficult, if not impossible, in the abstract, to indicate precisely where on this spectrum the word "like" in Article III:4 of the GATT 1994 falls. We are not saying that *all* products which are in *some* competitive relationship are "like products" under Article III:4. In ruling on the measure at issue, we also do not attempt to define the precise scope of the word "like" in Article III:4. Nor do we wish to decide if the scope of "like products" in Article III:4 is co-extensive with the combined scope of "like" and "directly competitive or substitutable" products in Article III:2. However, we recognize that the relationship between these two provisions is important, because there is no sharp distinction between fiscal regulation, covered by Article III:2, and non-fiscal regulation, covered by Article III:4. Both forms of regulation can often be used to achieve the same ends. It would be incongruous if, due to a significant difference in the product scope of these two provisions, Members were prevented from using one form of regulation – for instance, fiscal – to protect domestic production of certain products, but were able to use another form of regulation – for instance, non-fiscal – to achieve those ends. This would frustrate a consistent application of the "general principle" in Article III:1. For these reasons, we conclude that the scope of "like" in Article III:4 is broader than the scope of "like" in Article III:2, first sentence. Nonetheless, we note, once more, that Article III:2 extends not only to "like products", but also to products which are "directly competitive or substitutable", and that Article III:4 extends only to "like products". In view of this different language, and although we need not rule, and do not rule, on the precise product scope of Article III:4, we do conclude that the product scope of Article III:4, although broader than the *first* sentence of Article III:2, is certainly *not* broader than the *combined* product scope of the *two* sentences of Article III:2 of the GATT 1994.' (emphasis original)[38]

[38] Appellate Body Report, *EC – Asbestos*, para. 99; see also Appellate Body Report, *Korea – Various Measures on Beef*, para. 137: 'Whether or not imported products are treated "less

The impression that the Appellate Body struggled with its interpretation is reinforced by the fact that one Member stated a concurring opinion, essentially rejecting an economic interpretation of 'like products'.[39] In any event, even though refraining from making explicit rulings as to the breadth of 'like products' in Article III:4, it is argued here that the Appellate Body implicitly confirmed that it should be essentially identical to the breadth of 'directly competitive or substitutable products' articulated in Article III:2 GATT.[40] The Appellate Body not only referred explicitly to the marketplace factors, it also stated that 'like products' of paragraph 4 cannot be broader than the 'directly competitive or substitutable' standard of paragraph 2.[41] While it defined in the abstract a common ceiling of the two comparative standards, it left the question open if there is also a common floor.

Against the background of the Appellate Body's holding, it is highly improbable that two products would be 'directly competitive or substitutable' in terms of Article III:2 (second sentence), but not 'like' in terms of Article III:4 GATT; or vice versa. Arguing that paragraph 4 sets forth a narrower product scope than paragraph 2, second sentence, would in fact lead to the inconsequent result that a Member could, for instance, protect domestically produced whisky with regulations – such as maximum alcohol content requirements – from imported alcoholic beverages (III:4), while at the same time a protectionist tax on the exact same imported alcoholic beverages would be inconsistent with GATT national treatment

favourably" than like domestic products should be assessed … by examining whether a measure modifies the *conditions of competition* in the relevant market to the detriment of imported products' (emphasis original).

39 Para 154: 'My second point is that the necessity or appropriateness of adopting a "fundamentally" economic interpretation of the "likeness" of products under Article III:4 of the GATT 1994 does not appear to me to be free from substantial doubt'.

40 Same opinion Bronckers and McNelis, '"Like Product" Definition', p. 373: 'it seems fair to assume that the market-based approach adopted in Japanese Liquor Taxes II could also apply in relation to Article III:4'; similarly also Mavroidis, '"Like Products": Some Thoughts', pp. 133–34; McGovern, *International Trade Regulation*, § 8.123, issue 20; Quick and Lau, 'Environmentally Motivated Tax Distinctions', 428–29; Ortino, *Instruments for the Liberalisation of Trade*, p. 330; Vranes, *Trade and the Environment*, pp. 199–200; but see Choi, '*Like Products*', pp. 111–14; differentiated also Berrisch, 'Allgemeines Zoll- und Handelsabkommen', p. 89.

41 Appellate Body Report, *EC – Asbestos*, para. 100: 'We recognize that, by interpreting the term "like products" in Article III:4 in this way, we give that provision a relatively broad product scope – although no broader than the product scope of Article III:2'. It is not apparent why the Appellate Body in para. 99 speaks of 'the *combined* product scope of the *two* sentences of Article III:2', considering that the broad standard of the second sentence comprehends the narrow scope of the first sentence, see above, n 11.

(III:2). The reason for this unsatisfying result would be due to the fact that domestic whisky and imported alcoholic beverages could be considered as not related closely enough to be 'like' in terms of paragraph 4 but nevertheless as 'directly competitive or substitutable' in terms of paragraph 2.[42] In the above cited excerpt from the decision, the Appellate Body explicitly referred to this problem, stating that such an outcome would frustrate a consistent application of the general principle in paragraph 1. The only possible solution to avoid such results is that the standards of comparative relationship are interpreted in an identically broad way for Articles III:2 (second sentence) and III:4 GATT.

The practically important conclusion from these considerations is that Article III:4 GATT requires a 'likeness' analysis based on the same market-based test and factors as they apply to the 'directly competitive or substitutable' standard of Article III:2, second sentence. In *EC – Asbestos*, the Appellate Body referred to criteria from *Border Tax Adjustments* which it had already confirmed to be relevant for the scrutiny of Article III:2, namely (i) the properties, nature and quality of the products; (ii) the end-uses of the products; (iii) consumers' tastes and habits; and (iv) the tariff classification of the products.[43] However, the Appellate Body further ruled that 'all pertinent evidence' needs to be examined under the four traditional factors.[44] This slight modification in the test should not, however, have any impact on the outcome. Accordingly, in *Mexico – Taxes on Soft Drinks*, the only case where a breach of GATT Article III:2, second sentence, and Article III:4 was claimed simultaneously with regard to the same products, the Panel confirmed the existence of the required product relationship under both provisions on the basis of an identical test:

> 'As regards the likeness of cane sugar and HFCS [under Art. III:4], the factors to be taken into account … are *the same* as those examined by the

[42] See also Choi, '*Like Products*', p. 110; Berrisch, 'Allgemeines Zoll- und Handelsabkommen', pp. 88–89.

[43] Appellate Body Report, *EC – Asbestos*, para. 101.

[44] Ibid., para. 102: 'the adoption of a particular framework to aid in the examination of evidence does not dissolve the duty or the need to examine, in each case, *all* of the pertinent evidence. In addition, although each criterion addresses, in principle, a different aspect of the products involved, which should be examined separately, the different criteria are interrelated. For instance, the physical properties of a product shape and limit the end-uses to which the products can be devoted. Consumer perceptions may similarly influence – modify or even render obsolete – traditional uses of the products. Tariff classification clearly reflects the physical properties of a product' (emphasis original).

> Panel when considering whether the two products were "directly competitive or substitutable" under Article III:2, second sentence.'[45]

Attributing to Articles III:4 and III:2, second sentence, the same standard for 'likeness' requires considering the systemic differences between the two provisions. In fact, under Article III:2, second sentence, the broad product relationship is counterbalanced with the additional requirement provided by the element 'so as to afford protection'. The absence of an equivalent requirement for Article III:4 could potentially lead to an overbroad restriction on regulatory measures in comparison to tax measures.[46] Yet, since the Appellate Body endorsed the asymmetric impact test as a standard for 'less favourable treatment' under Article III:4,[47] there remains no significant difference between Articles III:2 and III:4 in terms of their overall standard of non-discrimination. In consequence, an identical interpretation of 'directly competitive or substitutable products' and 'like products' is not only feasible, but it is even required in order to maintain a balanced standard of non-discrimination for tax and regulatory measures respectively.

II GATS national treatment

Having established the conceptual breadth of 'like products' as applied by the WTO adjudicating bodies under GATT national treatment, section II now turns to the question of whether these considerations can help for the interpretation of the 'like services and service suppliers' concept in GATS national treatment. Given the absence of clear-cut 'likeness' categories under GATT national treatment jurisprudence, the main question is whether the concept of 'likeness' in GATS is to be interpreted as narrowly as 'like products' under Article III:2 (first sentence), or more broadly along the lines of 'directly competitive or substitutable' (Article III:2, second sentence) and 'like products' in Article III:4 GATT. In view of determining whether an analogous interpretation is justified, a comparative

[45] Panel Report, *Mexico – Taxes on Soft Drinks*, para. 8.106 (emphasis added). For other cases on 'like products' in Art. III:4 GATT, see Panel Reports, *Turkey – Rice*, paras. 7.213–216; *Brazil – Retreaded Tyres*, paras. 7.414–16; *EC – Trademarks and Geographical Indications (US)*, paras. 7.255–73; *Dominican Republic – Import and Sale of Cigarettes*, paras. 7.164–66; *Canada – Wheat Exports and Grain Imports*, paras. 6.260–64; *India – Autos*, paras. 7.173–76; *US – FSC*, paras. 8.130–135; *Korea – Various Measures on Beef*, para. 618; *Canada – Autos*, para. 10.74; *EC – Bananas III*, paras. 7.62–63; *US – Gasoline*, paras. 6.7–9.

[46] Jackson, Davey and Sykes, *International Economic Relations*, p. 579.

[47] See above, 3.I.A.2.

interpretation requires identifing similarities and differences between the national treatment obligation in GATT and GATS respectively.

A Comparing national treatment in GATT and GATS

While GATS and GATT national treatment serve the same overall economic purpose of preventing misallocation of resources through discriminatory measures, there are a number of differences in the more specific goals as well as in the legal structure of the provisions.[48] As outlined under section 1.I above, one of the prime goals of GATT national treatment is to protect tariff concessions by prohibiting discriminatory internal measures. In contrast, services are in general not subject to border measures, such as tariffs and quotas. Hence, GATS national treatment primarily serves as a broad and general prohibition of discriminatory regulations, similar to the GATT national treatment obligations with regard to unbound products. Still, national treatment was recognized by the negotiators as a principle of paramount importance in the area of trade in services,[49] considering that the supply of many types of services is subject to heavy internal regulations, monopolized, or state controlled. The WTO Secretariat describes GATS national treatment as implying 'the absence of all discriminatory measures that may modify the conditions of competition to the detriment of foreign services or service suppliers'.[50]

Second, GATT national treatment applies to all products, regardless of whether or not they are subject to tariff bindings under the schedules to Article II GATT.[51] In contrast, GATS national treatment only applies to services for which Members undertook explicit concession in their schedules of commitments. Each Member has the possibility to individually determine which service supplied under which mode is subject to the national treatment obligation. At the same time, Members have the right to deviate from their commitments by scheduling specific

[48] See also Cossy, 'Thoughts on "Likeness" in GATS', pp. 328–29; Weiss, 'GATS', 1204–208; Mattoo, 'National Treatment in GATS', 112–14, 123; Zdouc, '(2004) Dispute Settlement Practice', pp. 383–86; Ahnlid, 'Comparing GATT and GATS', 79–81.

[49] Reyna, 'Services', pp. 2356, 2376–77, 2386–87.

[50] WTO-Secretariat, *Handbook on GATS* .

[51] Appellate Body Report, *Japan – Alcoholic Beverages II*, pp. 16–17; see already GATT Working Party Report, *Brazil – Internal Taxes*, para. 4: 'The working party agreed that a contracting party was bound by the provisions of Article III whether or not the contracting party in question had undertaken tariff commitments in respect of the goods concerned'.

limitations.[52] Accordingly, the GATS national treatment system of positive listing of commitments with negative listing of limitations provides for a framework of progressive liberalization.[53] However, Members are only able to properly assess the impact of a commitment on their regulatory autonomy if the scope and interpretation of GATS national treatment is clear. The breadth of the 'like services and service suppliers' concept considerably affects the dimension of an individual commitment. In this regard there is significant uncertainty among WTO Members. In a background note from the Council for Trade in Services on health and social services, for instance, the question arose whether GATS national treatment applies to language requirements and, consequently, whether such requirements would need to be scheduled.[54] The answer to this question depends, *inter alia*, on whether the factor of language could have an impact on the 'likeness' analysis between the service and the supplier.

A third difference between GATT and GATS national treatment lies in the fact that Article XVII GATS stipulates only one single standard of service/supplier relationship, namely the one of 'likeness'; the provision contains no reference similar to the term 'directly competitive or substitutable' in *Ad* Article III:2 GATT. At the same time, GATS national treatment differs from Article III GATT because it neither distinguishes between different measures, such as taxes and regulatory measures, nor does it provide for different intensities of less favourable treatment, such as '*de minimis* taxes' and 'not similar taxes'. To the contrary, paragraph 1 of Article XVII defines the scope of application very broadly as 'all measures affecting the supply of services', including both taxes and regulations as well as other instruments not covered by GATT national treatment, such as subsidies.

Fourth, GATS national treatment specifically applies to the service and the service supplier. GATT national treatment, in contrast, only applies to the product, but not to the producer. Finally, intangible services are not suitable for a comparison on the basis of physical characteristics the way products are compared for purposes of a narrow interpretation of 'likeness' under GATT Article III:2, first sentence.

52 Ahnlid, 'Comparing GATT and GATS', 80.

53 See Cottier, 'Progressive Liberalization to Progressive Regulation', 780; Weiss, 'GATS', 1205; WTO-Secretariat, *Handbook on GATS,* p. 3.

54 CTS, Health and Social Services, Background Note by the Secretariat, S/C/W/50, 18 September 1998, para. 62; see also above, 3.I.C.4.e.

B Interpreting 'likeness' in GATS national treatment

To date, no WTO case law exists on the issue of whether 'likeness' should be construed narrowly, along the lines of 'like products' in terms of GATT Article III:2, first sentence, or in a broad sense, similar to the 'directly competitive or substitutable' standard of GATT Article III:2, second sentence. Hence, an interpretation needs yet to be adopted, taking into account the negotiating history as well as the text, purpose and context of Article XVII:1 GATS.

A look at the negotiating history reveals that an earlier draft of the GATS national treatment concept from 1988 contained a specific reference to the marketplace, which would support a broad economic comparative relationship between services and suppliers:

> '[National treatment means that [the services exports of any signatory] [foreign services and foreign service suppliers] that are granted access to the market of any other signatory will be accorded, in respect of all laws, regulations and administrative practices, treatment "no less favourable" than that accorded domestic services [or service suppliers] *in the same market* ...'[55]

Instead of 'likeness', the draft applies the term 'in the same market'. This reference to the 'same market' is very remarkable in that it directly requires an analysis of the market conditions without resorting to the concept of 'likeness' in the first place. However, it is not apparent from the negotiating protocols why the 'same market' notion had been abandoned. The question thus arises whether this change from 'marketplace' in the draft to 'likeness' in the final text supports a narrow or broad interpretation of 'likeness' in Article XVII:1 GATS. On the one hand, one could argue that the change from 'same market' to 'like' indicates that market conditions should not be emphasized in the analysis. On the other hand, the fact that already earlier drafts acknowledge the importance of market conditions in the context of GATS national treatment could speak in favour of a broad economic interpretation of 'likeness' in Article XVII:1 GATS. The latter argument deserves support, given that the change from 'same market' to 'like' occurred without explicit discussion on this very issue in the TNC and GNS. One could expect that a conscious change in concept from a *broad economic* 'marketplace' to *narrow and objective* 'likeness' would have left traces in the protocols, which in turn is not necessarily

[55] GNS, Report to the Trade Negotiations Committee meeting at Ministerial level, Montreal, December 1988, MTN.GNS/21, 25 November 1988, para. 11 (emphasis added).

the case for a change from a *broad economic* 'marketplace' wording to a *broad economic* 'likeness' notion. Hence, the absence of such traces from the negotiating protocols indicates that the change in wording does not reflect a renunciation of the marketplace approach. The main reason may simply have been that the negotiators strived to achieve some consistency with the text of GATT national treatment.

In July 1990, the draft text released by the Chairman of the GNS[56] departed from the concept of 'same markets'. Instead it introduced the concepts of 'likeness' and 'like circumstances'. The draft Article XVII:1 reads as follows:

> 'In conformity with other relevant provisions of the framework, and as set out in their appropriate schedules, parties shall grant to services and service providers of other parties, in the application of all laws, regulations, administrative practices, and decisions of general application, treatment no less favourable than that accorded to *like domestic services* <u>or</u> *service providers in like circumstances*.'[57]

This draft provision very clearly distinguishes between treatment accorded to the service itself and treatment accorded to the supplier. Unlike the final version of GATS national treatment, the July 1990 draft separated services from suppliers with the term 'or' and made them subject to different standards of 'likeness'. The relationship required for the services was one of 'likeness', which is equivalent to the GATS final version. In contrast, the providers were subject to a standard of 'like circumstances'. Interestingly, the non-discrimination provision in NAFTA on trade in services and investment protection applies the notion of 'like circumstances'. While this concept will be discussed in more detailed under section 7.II below, it can be noted at this stage that 'like circumstances' appears to be broader than the 'same market' concept, as it allows for considerations of 'regulatory situations' in addition to 'market situations'. Yet, the December 1990 draft already abandoned the 'like circumstances' concept:[58]

> '1. In conformity with other relevant provisions of this Agreement, and in accordance with the conditions and qualifications set out in its schedule, each Party shall accord to services and service providers of other Parties, in respect of all measures affecting the supply of services, treatment no

[56] For background information on the July 1990 draft see Reyna, 'Services', p. 2382.

[57] GNS, Draft – Multilateral Framework for Trade in Services, MTN.GNS/35, 23 July 1990, draft Article XVII on national treatment (emphasis added).

[58] For background information on the December 1990 draft, see Reyna, 'Services', p. 2394.

> less favourable than that accorded to *like domestic services* or *providers of like services*.'[59]

This December 1990 draft is close to the final version of GATS Article XVII in that they both apply the concept of 'likeness'. One interesting difference to be discussed in more detailed under section 10.I.B.1 below relates to the fact that under the December 1990 draft, the providers are compared exclusively on the basis of the services they provide.

Against the background of this negotiating history it becomes apparent that the wording for Article XVII GATS changed from 'same market' to 'like circumstances' to 'like services and service suppliers', which seems to indicate a constant departure from a market-specific analysis. The prevailing concept of 'likeness' is the least specific, leaving the most room for interpretation and choice of the applicable *tertia comparationis*. However, such a conclusion based only on the negotiating history would be premature. Other interpretative elements must be considered, in particular the analogous wording of 'likeness' in GATS and GATT national treatment as well as the entirety of Article XVII GATS. In fact, the specific reference to the marketplace and the competitive relationship nevertheless found its way into the final text of GATS national treatment, albeit at a slightly different position and in a different context than in the draft versions. Paragraphs 2 and 3 of Article XVII GATS read as follows:

> '2. A Member may meet the requirement of paragraph 1 by according to services and service suppliers of any other Member, either formally identical treatment or formally different treatment to that it accords to its own like services and service suppliers.
> 3. Formally identical or formally different treatment shall be considered to be less favourable if it modifies the conditions of competition in favour of services or service suppliers of the Member compared to like services or service suppliers of any other Member.'

These two paragraphs set the standard and purpose in the light of which GATS national treatment must be interpreted and applied. They essentially codify previous jurisprudence on the interpretation of GATT national treatment.[60] The purpose of paragraph 2 is to specify that the *form* of differential treatment is not the decisive criterion in determining

[59] TNC, Draft Final Act Embodying the Results of the Uruguay Round of Multilateral Trade Negotiations, MTN.TNC/W/35-3/Rev.1, 3 December 1990, draft Article XVII (emphasis added).

[60] See above, 3.I; GATT Panel Reports, *Italy – Agricultural Machinery*, para. 12; *US – Section 337 Tariff Act*, para. 5.11.

whether there is a breach of the national treatment obligation. In other words, national treatment applies to measures that explicitly differentiate on the basis of origin as well as to measures that facially treat services/suppliers of different origins alike, but due to factual circumstances still result in differential treatment. Paragraph 2 thus expressly extends the obligation to both *de jure* and *de facto* discriminations. This specific inclusion of *de facto* discrimination is as such not revolutionary, considering that previous GATT 1947 jurisprudence and subsequently the Appellate Body recognized the coverage of *de facto* situations with regard to GATT MFN and national treatment as well as GATS MFN treatment.[61] However, it is remarkable that WTO jurisprudence extends *all* non-discrimination provisions to *de facto* differential treatment without further ado, even though Article XVII GATS is in fact the only provision that expressly incorporates this standard into the legal text. This situation very nicely illustrates that a comprehensive interpretation of WTO provisions requires going beyond the mere text of the agreement and focusing more on purpose and context of the provisions.

Paragraph 3, in turn, sets the *standard* or guiding principle for the examination of 'less favourable treatment'. The reference to 'conditions of competition' in paragraph 3 is designed to define further the meaning of 'formally identical' treatment (*de facto* discrimination) and 'formally different' treatment (*de jure* discrimination). According to a combined reading of the two paragraphs, formally different treatment based on origin does not amount to a violation of national treatment if it does not modify the conditions of competition. By the same token, formally identical treatment (i.e. differentiation not based on origin) could very well be inconsistent with the national treatment obligation, provided that it modifies the conditions of competition. In sum, paragraphs 2 and 3 specify that the scope of national treatment not only covers *de jure*, but also *de facto* discrimination and that 'less favourable treatment' must be interpreted in the light of competition.[62]

> This approach to Article XVII has also been confirmed by WTO jurisprudence. The Panel in *EC – Bananas III* found that the standard of Article XVII GATS follows Article III GATT, 'which has been consistently interpreted by past panel reports to be concerned with conditions of competition between like domestic and imported products on internal markets'.[63]

[61] See above, 3.I.A.2, n 16.

[62] Mattoo, 'National Treatment in GATS', 110; Weiss, 'GATS', 1211; Weiler, 'Non-Discrimination in International Investment Law', p. 563.

[63] Para 7.302.

The Appellate Body confirmed that GATS national treatment is designed to protect equal condition of competition between domestic and foreign services and suppliers.[64]

By setting a standard for the element of 'less favourable treatment' on the basis of competition, the GATS negotiators at the same time provided for the underlying principle according to which the element of 'like services and service suppliers' of paragraph 1 must be interpreted. Even though the text is not explicitly directed at the relationship between domestic and foreign services and suppliers as is the case in the GATT *Ad* Article III:2 'directly competitive or substitutable' standard, it nonetheless provides for a very similar reference to the marketplace. In fact, the conditions of competition can only be unduly modified through discriminatory measures if the services or suppliers to be compared are in a competitive relationship in the first place. It follows that the 'likeness' analysis must primarily answer the question of whether the domestic and foreign services and suppliers compete in a given marketplace.[65] Against this background it becomes apparent that the *market-based standard* is applicable with regard to the relationship between services and suppliers under Article XVII:1 GATS. Consequently, this approach rules out any consideration of the regulatory purpose and the 'necessity' of the measure in light of the purpose,[66] as well as purely objective differences between

[64] Paras 244, 246.

[65] Also supporting an economic interpretation of 'likeness' in GATS Art. XVII, Englisch, *Wettbewerbsgleichheit*, p. 414; Mavroidis, '"Like Products": Some Thoughts', pp. 126–27; Matsushita, Schoenbaum and Mavroidis, *World Trade Organization*, p. 663; Pitschas, 'Subventionen', pp. 123–24; Marchetti and Mavroidis, 'Challenges for GATS', 533; Bhala, *International Trade Law*, p. 1589; Lang, 'GATS and Regulatory Autonomy', 822–23; EC submission in Panel Report, *US – Gambling*, para. 4.40; in principle also Krajewski, *National Regulation*, pp. 98–100, but leaving the door open for the introduction of an 'aim and effect' test outside of 'likeness' (p 100); Mattoo, 'National Treatment in GATS', 128, but at the same time proposing a necessity test (p 132).

[66] Appellate Body Report, *EC – Bananas III*, para. 241: 'We see no specific authority either in Article II or in Article XVII of the GATS for the proposition that the "aims and effects" of a measure are in any way relevant in determining whether that measure is inconsistent with those provisions'; also EC submission in Panel Report, *US – Gambling*, para. 4.39; but see Trachtman, 'Lessons for GATS', p. 62: 'this [economic] test is relatively ignorant of factors that motivate regulation. The economic theory of regulation suggests that regulation is necessary precisely where consumers cannot adequately distinguish relevant goods – where the goods are in close competitive relation'; also favouring regulatory purpose as part of GATS non-discrimination e.g. Hudec, 'Requiem for "Aim and Effects"', 641; Cottier and Oesch, *International Trade Regulation*, p. 411; Cossy, 'Thoughts on "Likeness" in GATS', pp. 346–49; Eeckhout, 'Constitutional Concepts', p. 235; Zdouc, '(1999) Dispute Settlement Practice', 341–42; Mattoo, 'National Treatment in GATS', 131–33; Japan submission in Panel Report, *US – Gambling*, para. 4.44 f.

the services or the suppliers. As set out in the previous section, 'like products' in a narrow sense are primarily determined based on objective factors, in particular physical characteristics. While the applicability of the 'like product' criteria from *Border Tax Adjustments* to services will be discussed in great detail under chapter 13, it is possible already at this stage to retain that intangible services do not have any physical appearance and are thus not comparable on the basis of physical characteristics. Hence, a narrow approach on the basis of prior GATT practice is not suitable for a narrow determination of 'like services and like suppliers'.

Having established the appropriate standard for 'likeness' in GATS national treatment, it is now useful to undertake a comparative interpretation in light of the jurisprudence pertaining to GATT national treatment. The preceding section A concluded that both the 'directly competitive or substitutable' concept in *Ad* Article III as well as the 'like product' concept in Article III:4 GATT follows a market-based standard. Hence, the Appellate Body's interpretation of 'directly competitive or substitutable products' according to which competition in the relevant market is one among a number of means of identifying the broader category of products[67] is also relevant for 'likeness' under GATS Article XVII:1.[68] By the same token, the Appellate Body's finding that 'a determination of "likeness" under Article III:4 is, fundamentally, a determination about the nature and extent of a competitive relationship between and among products'[69] can also be transposed *mutatis mutandis* to GATS national treatment. Moreover, the narrow economic interpretation of 'like products' in terms of GATT Article III:2, first sentence, is justified, *inter alia*, by the fact that the element of 'less favourable treatment' relating to taxes is applied very strictly, allowing no *de minimis* exceptions. GATS national treatment, on the other hand, uses the same language as Article III:4 GATT with regard to the discriminatory element, namely the one of 'less favourable treatment'. Accordingly, given the similarities between Articles XVII:1 GATS and III:4 GATT, the 'like services and suppliers' standard should be at least as broad as 'like products' in terms of

[67] Appellate Body Report, *Japan – Alcoholic Beverages II*, p. 26.

[68] Mattoo, 'National Treatment in GATS', 127: 'If GATS Article XVII is not to be more limited in scope than GATT Article III:2, then clearly the term "like" must be interpreted widely to also include "directly competitive or substitutable" services. In any case, it will be necessary to deviate in the GATS from the more literal GATT interpretations of "likeness" to arrive at an economically meaningful interpretation which would necessarily incorporate the notion of substitutability' (but Mattoo also suggests a necessity test approach, see p. 132); see also Footer and George, 'The GATS', p. 852.

[69] See above, n 37.

Article III:4 GATT on regulatory measures. Even though the Appellate Body refused to rule on the exact breadth of 'like products' in relation to regulatory measures on products,[70] it has been argued above that it should include market-based considerations and thus correspond to 'directly competitive or substitutable products' with regard to not similar taxation. However, – similar to the comparison between GATT Article III paragraph 2, second sentence, and paragraph 4 – there is one valid argument that could be made against an application of the 'directly competitive or substitutable' standard to Article XVII GATS. Under GATT Article III:2, second sentence, the broad comparative standard is somewhat counterbalanced by the additional substantive requirements that the discriminatory tax must be of a certain importance (not only *de minimis*) and that it must have been adopted so as to afford protection. These more stringent requirements provide for a certain compensation to the broad notion of directly competitive or substitutable. In contrast, Article XVII GATS not only applies to *de minimis* discriminatory measures, but also lacks the explicit requirement that the discriminatory measure has been adopted 'so as to afford protection'. Hence, a broad market-based interpretation of 'likeness' bears a certain risk that the regulatory autonomy of the Members could be considerably impaired. Yet, as it is the case of Article III:4 GATT, a balance can be achieved by interpreting the standard of 'less favourable treatment' of Article XVII GATS in accordance with the asymmetric impact test. In addition to GATT, the GATS framework allows Members to individually define and limit their commitments with regard to each service sector and mode of service supply. Moreover, the general exceptions clause of Article XIV GATS provides an additional ground for justification with regard to 'public order' which is unknown to GATT.[71] These mechanisms are sufficient to counterbalance a broad interpretation of 'likeness' and to prevent an overly broad application of the GATS national treatment obligation.

In sum, this chapter submits the thesis that the breadth of 'like services and service suppliers' in GATS national treatment should be determined analogous to the 'directly competitive and substitutable' standard of Article III:2 (second sentence) GATT.

[70] See above, n 38.

[71] Diebold, 'Morals and Order Exceptions', *passim*.

6

'Likeness' in MFN treatment

Even though some Members expressed critical remarks with regard to a transposition of the MFN principle from GATT to GATS, it appears from the overall negotiating history that there were in general less concerns than with regard to national treatment. One of the main disagreements arose over the issue of whether the obligation should apply to all services or whether some sectors should be excluded from its scope of application.[1] Moreover, some negotiators opted for an optional MFN obligation,[2] while others viewed MFN as a key in progressive liberalization of trade in services, as it entails that bi- and plurilaterally negotiated concessions are automatically extended to all other Members.[3] Switzerland, for instance, argued that MFN 'would have to be the corner-stone of the future agreement and [that] it was crucial for small countries'.[4] Yet, while the automatic extension of bi- and plurilateral concessions has proven very effective under GATT for the reduction of tariffs, it is more difficult to identify measures in national regulations on the supply of services which favour one country over another.[5] In spite of these reservations, the negotiators agreed that the multilateral framework on trade in services shall contain a MFN provision.[6] This obligation is implemented in Article II:1 GATS, which states as follows:

[1] Reyna, 'Services', p. 2393; Ahnlid, 'Comparing GATT and GATS', 79; see also Jackson, *Competition in Services*, p. 27.

[2] GNS, Note on the Meeting of 14–15 December 1987, MTN.GNS/12, 19 January 1988, para 4.

[3] GNS, Note on the Meeting of 22–25 March 1988, MTN.GNS/14, 29 April 1988, para. 54; GNS, Note on the Meeting of 23–25 October 1989, MTN.GNS/26, 17 November 1989, para 119.

[4] GNS, Note on the Meeting of 12 and 22 November 1990, MTN.GNS/40, 28 November 1990, para. 14.

[5] Mestmäcker, 'Free Trade in Services', pp. 17–18; Hoekman and Messerlin, 'Liberalizing Trade in Services', pp. 492 ff.

[6] TNC, Midterm Review in Montreal on 5–9 December 1988 and in Geneva on 5–8 April 1989, MTN.TNC/11, 21 April 1989, part II para. 7(d).

> 'With respect to any measure covered by this Agreement, each Member shall accord immediately and unconditionally to services and service suppliers of any other Member treatment no less favourable than that it accords to like services and service suppliers of any other country.'

Given that no case law exists for a conceptual interpretation of 'likeness' in Article II GATS, the interpretative approach is again to first outline the previous experiences with the concept of 'like products' in GATT MFN treatment (*below*, I.), followed by an interpretation of the conceptual breadth of 'likeness' in Article II GATS (II.).

I GATT most-favoured-nation treatment

Article I:1 GATT applies to a very broad range of trade-restrictive measures, including both border measures and internal regulations. The provision reads as follows:

> '1. With respect to customs duties and charges of any kind imposed on or in connection with importation or exportation or imposed on the international transfer of payments for imports or exports, and with respect to the method of levying such duties and charges, and with respect to all rules and formalities in connection with importation and exportation, and with respect to all matters referred to in paragraphs 2 and 4 of Article III, any advantage, favour, privilege or immunity granted by any contracting party to any product originating in or destined for any other country shall be accorded immediately and unconditionally to the like product originating in or destined for the territories of all other contracting parties.'

The principle of MFN treatment simultaneously serves a substantive and a trade policy goal. First, as is the case with regard to national treatment, it strives to prevent discriminatory measures which distort the competitive relationship between products originating from different countries. Second, the MFN principle has the effect of fostering trade liberalization by automatically extending reciprocally negotiated tariff concessions to all other Members.[7]

The primary importance of the MFN provision in the GATT 1947 originally was to ensure equal treatment of products at the border. The same tariffs had to be imposed on like products originating from different Contracting Parties in order to ensure equal opportunities in the market of the importing country. In this sense, many of the GATT 1947 cases

[7] See above, 1.II.

turned around the question whether two types of products originating from different countries and subject to different tariffs could be qualified as 'like' in terms of Article I:1 GATT. In the affirmative, the preferential tariff had to be accorded to both products. In order to avoid triggering the MFN obligation, Members were tempted to make very fine product distinctions in their national tariff classifications.[8] The following three GATT 1947 cases are the most illustrative on the issue of 'likeness' in Article I GATT with regard to tariff measures:

> In *Germany – Sardines* the Panel examined a German tariff scheme differentiating between three types of sardines, namely pilchard, herring and sprat. The import of pilchard was favoured over herring and sprat with regard to tariff rates and quantitative limitations. The measure negatively affected Norway as an exporter of herring and sprat in comparison to those countries – in particular Portugal – exporting primarily pilchard. The Panel noted that Article I GATT does not distinguish between 'like products' and 'directly competitive or substitutable products' (para 12). The Panel was not prepared to qualify the three types of sardines as 'alike', relying predominantly on different tariff classifications (para 13). The Panel thus found no violation of Article I GATT, but it struck down the German measure by upholding Norway's non-violation complaint pursuant to Article XXIII GATT.
>
> The approach in *Spain – Unroasted Coffee* differs from the previous case in that the Panel was not prepared to rely exclusively on the factors of physical characteristics and tariff classification, and at least implicitly considered marketplace factors.[9] Spain sub-divided imports of unroasted coffee into five tariff lines with different tariff rates, resulting in higher tariffs for coffee exported mainly from Brazil in comparison to coffee exported from Spain's former colonies. The Panel noted that organoleptic differences resulting from geographical factors, cultivation methods, the processing of the beans, and the genetic factor are not sufficient to allow for different tariff treatment. It considered the different types of unroasted coffee as 'like products', primarily on the basis that it was 'sold in the form of blends, combining various types of coffee, and that coffee in its end-use, was universally regarded as a well-defined and single product intended for drinking' (para 4.7).
>
> Eight years later, *Japan – SPF Dimension Lumber* returned to a narrow interpretation of 'likeness' in Article I GATT. In this case, Canada complained against Japan's tariff scheme for the importation of softwood

[8] Jackson, Davey and Sykes, *International Economic Relations*, p. 481; Hudec, 'Discriminatory Trade Measures', p. 175: 'The MFN obligation of GATT Article I:1 does prohibit differences in tariff treatment based on national origin. But it does not prohibit governments from establishing different tariff levels for different *kinds* of goods' (emphasis original).

[9] See also Hudec, '"Like Product"', p. 114.

> lumber, which differentiated between dimension lumber produced from different tree species, such as spruce–pine–fir (SPF) and hemlock-fir. SPF dimension lumber originating mainly from Canada was subject to a higher tariff rate than hemlock-fir lumber originating mainly from the US. For the 'likeness' analysis, the Panel recognized tariff differentiations as a legitimate means for domestic trade policies. It placed a high burden of proof on the complainant to show that 'such tariff arrangement has been diverted from its normal purpose so as to become a means of discrimination in international trade' (para 5.10). Against this background it rejected Canada's complaint on the basis that not all types of dimension lumber are alike (paras 5.13 ff).

In spite of *Spain – Unroasted Coffee*, these cases illustrate a tendency that GATT 1947 practice concerning tariff measures under Article I mainly applied a narrow, objective interpretation of the 'like product' concept.[10] The main criterion in the analysis was not the extent of competitive relationship, but physical characteristics and the harmonized system for classification.[11] More recent Article I GATT cases on tariff and border measures under the WTO framework did not engage in a detailed analysis of 'likeness', which is mainly due to the fact that 'likeness' remained either uncontested by the respondent or did not arise because the measure discriminated directly on the basis of origin.

> The case *EC – Tariff Preferences* concerned a measure applying different tariff rates on a *de jure* basis and 'likeness' was generally uncontested: 'As the Panel understands it, the following facts are not in dispute: (i) the Drug Arrangements, as prescribed in the current Council Regulation (EC) No. 2501/2001, provide lower tariff rates than the MFN bound rates on certain products; and (ii) the treatment of lower tariff rates is only accorded to products originating in 12 beneficiary Members, not to like products originating in other Members' (Panel Report, para. 7.57, fn omitted).
>
> In the case *Canada – Autos*, it was 'not in dispute that there are imported products which do not benefit from this exemption which are like imported products which benefit from the exemption' (Panel Report, para. 10.16).
>
> Similarly, in *EC – Bananas III* the EU did not contest that bananas from different origins constituted 'like products' for purposes of GATT Article I and III (Panel Report *[US]*, para. 7.62).

In addition to tariff measures, the MFN obligation also applies to *internal measures* by specifically referring to paragraphs 2 and 4 of

[10] On objective interpretation of 'likeness' see above, 3.II.B.2.

[11] Trebilcock and Howse, *Regulation of International Trade*, p. 65; Englisch, *Wettbewerbsgleichheit*, p. 403.

Article III GATT. Following decades of negotiations on tariff reductions, border measures no longer constitute today's primary obstacles to trade; they have been largely succeeded by internal tax and regulatory measures. Consequently, the importance of MFN treatment is shifting away from border measures and tariffs to internal measures, which is most likely to reflect in future WTO dispute settlement proceedings.

The two GATT 1947 cases engaging in an analysis of 'like products' of Article I with regard to internal measures focused primarily on an objective interpretation, similar to the cases on tariff measures:

> In the case *Australia – Ammonium Sulphate* the Panel was held to determine 'likeness' between two types of fertilizers. Australia maintained a domestic consumption subsidy on imported ammonium sulphate fertilizer while discontinuing the subsidy on imported sodium nitrate fertilizer. Chile, an exporter of sodium nitrate fertilizer, claimed a violation of Article I GATT. The Panel noted that Article I GATT does not distinguish between 'like products' and 'directly competitive or substitutable products' and explicitly refused to examine the competitive relationship of the two fertilizers. It found the two products to be 'unlike', primarily on the basis that Australia and other countries listed the two products in different tariff classifications subject to different tariff rates (para 8).
>
> The case *EEC – Animal Feed Proteins* concerned a compulsory purchase programme of skimmed powder milk adopted by the EEC. Under these measures, EEC domestic producers or importers of feeding stuff had an obligation to purchase a certain quantity of skimmed milk powder and to have it denatured for use as feed for animals. The Panel was held to analyse whether all products used for the purpose of adding protein to animal feeds should be considered as 'like products'. Based on different tariff classifications as well as physical differences relating to varying protein content and different vegetable, animal and synthetic origins, the Panel found the products to be 'unlike' (para 4.2).

The more recent WTO cases do not contribute to the interpretation of 'likeness' under Article I GATT with regard to regulatory measures. Again, either the measures under scrutiny discriminated on a *de jure* basis or the parties agreed on the existence of 'like products':

> The case *US – Certain EC Products* concerned a US retaliation measure against the EU following the dispute *EC – Bananas III*. The measure discriminated on the basis of origin, as it only applied to imports from the EU but not to 'like' imports from other countries. Hence, the issue of 'like products' was not analysed (paras 6.53 f).

Similarly, in *EC – Trademarks and Geographical Indications (US)* the regulation discriminated on its face and the EU did not contest the existence of 'like' products (para 7.714, see also below, n 20).

The case *Indonesia – Autos* concerned both internal taxes and customs duties. Given that the measures discriminated on the basis of origin, the Panel was not obliged to thoroughly examine the question of 'likeness' (para 14.113).[12] Nonetheless, to the extent that the Panel decided to analyse 'likeness', it resolved the question of Article I GATT by simply referring to its previous findings concerning 'likeness' under Article III:2, first sentence, GATT:

> 'We have found in our discussion of like products under Article III:2 that certain imported motor vehicles are like the National Car.[fn 714] The same considerations justify a finding that such imported vehicles can be considered like National Cars imported from Korea for the purpose of Article I.
>
> [fn 714] We refer to our discussions in paragraphs 14.110 and 14.111 where we found that given that the Timor, Escort, 306, Optima and Corolla models are in the same market segments, there would not appear to be any relevant differences in respect of consumers' tastes and habits sufficient to render these products unlike. In our view, this evidence is also sufficient to establish a presumption of likeness between the Timor, Corolla, Escort, 306 and Optima for purposes of Article I of GATT. Since Indonesia has submitted no evidence or argument to rebut the presumption of likeness for purposes of Article I of GATT, we find that at least these imported motor vehicles are like the National Car for purposes of Article I of GATT.' [13]

[12] On *de jure* discrimination and 'likeness' see above, 3.I.A.1 and 3.II.A.

[13] Panel Report, *Indonesia – Autos*, para. 14.141; para. 14.110 referred to in fn 714 reads in relevant part: 'it appears to us that these models of cars have the same end uses and the same basic properties, nature and quality. Given that these models are in the same market segments, there would not appear to be any relevant differences in respect of consumers' tastes and habits sufficient to render these products unlike'; a similar technique was applied by the Panel Report, *EC – Trademarks and Geographical Indications (US)*, para. 7.714: 'The Panel also recalls its finding at paragraph 7.229 that the Regulation discriminates on its face among products and that the European Communities does not contest that there are, among this group, "like products" among the imported products and products of European Communities origin, for the purposes of Article III:4 of GATT 1994. Protection under the Regulation is provided against use of a name in respect of products "comparable to the products registered under that name". In the Panel's view, this is sufficient basis to conclude that there are "like products" among the imported products of other countries including WTO Members for the purposes of Article I:1 of GATT 1994'; see also Panel Report, *EC – Bananas III*, para. 7.62, where the Panel reiterated the applicable factors for the 'likeness' analysis without, however, making a difference between Articles I and III GATT.

While this approach by the Panel does not shed much light in the conceptual interpretation of 'likeness' in Article I GATT, it at least confirms implicitly that the same criteria which are applied in regard to Article III:2, first sentence, are also relevant for Article I GATT.[14] Still, to date neither the WTO panels nor the Appellate Body adopted an explicit interpretation of 'like products' in Article I:1 GATT in relation to the same concept set forth in paragraphs 2 and 4 of Article III GATT.[15] Commentators regarded GATT 1947 panel reports on MFN treatment as applying a rather narrow, non-economic interpretation of 'like products'.[16] However, the question remains open whether this narrow interpretation focusing on physical characteristics and tariff classification still is valid under the WTO regime and, more importantly, whether such a narrow approach is justified not only in relation to border measures, but also to internal regulations. As the applicable *tertium comparationis* and the conceptual breadth of 'likeness' in Article I GATT have not yet been defined by WTO jurisprudence, it is helpful to resort to the scholarly discussions on this subject.

Most prominently, *Hudec* argues convincingly that the breadth of 'likeness' under Article I GATT must be differentiated based on whether the measure at issue relates to tariff measures or to internal taxes and internal regulations. The author bases his argument on the fact that both Articles III and I follow the same policy goals when it comes to the regulation of internal measures, namely to eliminate market distortions. However, when it comes to the issue of tariffs covered by Article I, *Hudec* claims that there is 'no overall "no-distortions" policy' but the goal is 'the orderly management of protection in order to contain its effects and remove its unnecessary evils'.[17] In fact, a broad interpretation of 'likeness' in this context would lead to the result that mutually negotiated tariff concessions

[14] Similarly Trebilcock and Howse, *Regulation of International Trade*, p. 72.

[15] In the two cases the Appellate Body was confronted with a claim under the GATT MFN provision, the issue of 'likeness' was not appealed and thus not specifically examined by the Appellate Body, see Appellate Body Report, *EC – Bananas III*, paras. 205–7; Appellate Body Report, *Canada – Autos*, paras. 64–86.

[16] Hudec, '"Like Product"', pp. 113–19; Cottier and Oesch, *International Trade Regulation*, p. 364; Matsushita, Schoenbaum and Mavroidis, *World Trade Organization*, p. 211; Tietje, *Behandlung nichttarifärer Handelshemmnisse*, p. 211; Zedalis, '"Like" Product', 77–86; but see Jackson, Davey and Sykes, *International Economic Relations*, p. 480: 'Since both Articles I and III are basic non-discrimination provisions … it can be argued that the term [i.e. likeness] should be construed broadly in those articles, so as to strike down discriminatory measures wherever possible'.

[17] Hudec, '"Like Product"', p. 108; see also Hudec, 'Discriminatory Trade Measures', p. 175.

with regard to a certain product between some Members would have to be extended to a variety of products of other Members, without any corresponding concessions from the latter.[18] It follows that governments may have a justified need to make fine product distinctions in order to pursue a certain policy of tariff protection, which is only possible under Article I GATT if 'likeness' is construed narrowly. With regard to internal measures, on the other hand, the breadth of 'likeness' should reflect the competitive relationship of the products in the marketplace, as has been recognized by the Appellate Body with regard to Article III:2, second sentence, and Article III:4 GATT.[19]

Even though the differentiation in the 'likeness' concept in view of the measure at issue is not yet confirmed by WTO jurisprudence, it is questionable whether the GATT 1947 panel reports pursuing a very narrow standard are still authoritative. For instance, in *EEC – Animal Feed Proteins* the Panel applied the narrow, non-economic interpretation of 'likeness' not only to Article I, but also to Article III:4 GATT (para 4.11), conducting a pure textual differentiation between 'likeness' and 'substitutable'. Consequently, since it is widely recognized today that Article III:4 GATT follows a broad marketplace interpretation of 'likeness', the same should be true for Article I GATT,[20] at least with regard to internal taxes and regulations. An additional argument in support of such an approach can be drawn from the text of Article I GATT. The provision reads in relevant part that it applies 'with respect to all matters referred to in paragraphs 2 and 4 of Article III'. This explicit reference does not simply enlarge the scope of application of Article I to internal measures, but at the same time incorporates the relevant Article III interpretations. In other words, the Appellate Body's conceptual findings as to the breadth of 'likeness' in paragraphs 2 and 4 of Article III should also be relevant for the interpretation of 'likeness' under Article I GATT with regard to internal measures.[21] It follows that a *de minimis* difference in the taxation (in analogy to Article

[18] Choi, '*Like Products*', p. 95.

[19] Hudec, "Like Product", pp. 108–9.

[20] In Panel Report, *EC – Trademarks and Geographical Indications (US)*, para. 7.714, the Panel at least confirmed that a finding of 'likeness' under Art. III:4 GATT due to non-contradiction allows for a finding of 'likeness' for purposes of Art. I GATT.

[21] Davey and Pauwelyn, 'MFN Unconditionality', p. 35; Jackson, Davey and Sykes, *International Economic Relations*, p. 489 *in fine*; Vranes, *Trade and the Environment*, pp. 215–16; similarly Fauchald, *Environmental Taxes and Trade Discrimination*, p. 144; Zedalis, '"Like" Product', 59, 68–70; more nuanced Trebilcock and Howse, *Regulation of International Trade*, pp. 66–67; Choi, '*Like Products*', p. 97; sceptical also Charnovitz, 'GATT and Environmental Trade Measures', 323: 'The term "like product" in Article

III:2, first sentence) of products originating from different trading partners only amounts to a breach of the MFN obligation if the products are 'like' in a narrow sense (i.e. competitive relationship and physically similar). In case of 'non-similar taxation' (in analogy to Article III:2, second sentence) and other internal regulatory measures (in analogy to Article III:4), on the other hand, the breadth of 'likeness' in terms of Article I GATT should be extended to the standard of 'directly competitive or substitutable' or 'likeness' in a broad economic sense. Similar to Article III:4 GATT, an overly broad application of Article I GATT is prevented by the asymmetric impact test as a standard for 'less favourable treatment'. In the context of MFN treatment this test requires that the products from one Member are more heavily affected as a group than the group of like products originating from another Member.

II GATS most-favoured-nation treatment

This section follows the same approach as the interpretation of GATS national treatment above, first pointing out differences and similarities between GATT and GATS MFN treatment and secondly interpreting the breadth of 'likeness' under Article II GATS in the light of its negotiating history, context, jurisprudence and of a comparative analysis with Article I GATT.

A Comparing most-favoured-nation treatment in GATT and GATS

The underlying purpose and objective of the MFN principle is the same for trade in goods and trade in services. From a political point of view, equal treatment of services and suppliers of different origins prevents political tensions in international relations. In economic terms, the principle of MFN treatment fosters an efficient allocation of resources in the supply of services and its multiplier effect accelerates the liberalization of trade in services.[22]

III:4 does not necessarily mean the same as the term "like product" in Article I:1, but the case law has not diverged significantly'; Qin, 'Defining Nondiscrimination', 241: 'differences in policy objectives between the MFN and NT provisions may warrant a narrower definition of "like products" under Article I:1 than that under Article III'.

22 Abu-Akeel, 'MFN in Service Trade', 107; Lowenfeld, *International Economic Law*, p. 120; Jackson, 'Constitution for Trade in Services', 196.

Next to this convergence on a broad scale, there are a number of technical and systemic differences between Articles I GATT and II GATS.[23] While MFN treatment in GATT differentiates between various kinds of measures and incorporates internal taxes and regulations only by reference to the GATT national treatment provision, GATS Article II is applicable very broadly to any measure that affects trade in services. Consequently, GATS Article II does not need to refer to the GATS national treatment provision in order to extend its scope to internal taxes and regulations. With regard to the element of differential treatment, GATT Article I contains an obligation to extend any *advantage, favour, privilege or immunity* granted to one Member to all other Members. In contrast, GATS Article II uses the language comparable to the national treatment provisions, obliging Members to accord to all Members *treatment* no less favourable than that it accords to one Member. Even though the term 'treatment' appears wider than 'advantage, favour, privilege or immunity', a broad interpretation of the latter leads to the result that there is no significant difference in practice.[24] Another difference which has already been observed in the national treatment comparison is that the scope of GATS MFN treatment extends to service suppliers, whereas Article I GATT only applies to products. Finally, while Article I GATT applies to *all* goods, Article II:2 GATS allowed Members to schedule horizontal exemptions for certain services at the time of the acceptance of the Agreement, in principle not exceeding the duration of ten years.

B *Interpreting 'likeness' in GATS most-favoured-nation treatment*

An interpretation of Article II GATS in the light of its negotiating history allows for similar observations regarding the 'likeness' concept as with regard to the GATS national treatment provision. The draft from 1988 only described the mechanisms of the principle:

> '[MFN means that signatories grant all other signatories *[under the same conditions]* any advantage granted to another country unilaterally or as a result of trade negotiations. Non-discrimination means that signatories accord to each other treatment no less favourable than that accorded to any country.]

[23] See also Mattoo, 'MFN and GATS', pp. 53–56.

[24] Zdouc, '(2004) Dispute Settlement Practice', pp. 382–83; see also Wang, 'MFN under GATS', 97.

> [The agreement shall provide that signatories to the agreement shall receive the same benefits granted by one signatory to another.]'[25]

The proposed comparative standard of 'same conditions' refers more to the prevailing conditions in the respective Member than the characteristics of the service or service supplier. The later draft from July 1990 was more specific in that it contained a first attempt to formulate an explicit obligation:

> 'With respect to any measure covered by this framework, each party shall accord to services and service providers of another party, treatment no less favourable than that it accords *in like circumstances* to services and service providers of any other [country] [party].'[26]

Similar to the national treatment provision in the same draft, the MFN obligation suggests the concept of 'like circumstances'. The same wording was in principle retained for the December 1990 draft which, however, also contained an alternative text proposing already the concept of 'like services and like service providers'.[27] This overview of the negotiating history does not clarify whether the Members intended to adopt a broad marketplace or a narrow definition of the 'likeness' concept. Moreover, in contrast to Article XVII:3 GATS, the MFN obligation in Article II omits to specify a standard for 'less favourable treatment' that would allow to draw any conclusions for the conceptual breadth of 'likeness'.

Absent any interpretative guidance in the GATS framework, it is helpful to undertake a comparative approach with GATT MFN treatment.[28] With regard to Article I GATT, it has been suggested above to apply two different standards of 'like products', depending on whether the measure at issue relates to border measures, in particular tariffs, or to internal regulations in terms of Article III GATT. In case of the latter, 'likeness'

[25] GNS, Report to the Trade Negotiations Committee meeting at Ministerial level, Montreal, December 1988, MTN.GNS/21, 25 November 1988, para. 11 (emphasis added).

[26] GNS, Draft – Multilateral Framework for Trade in Services, MTN.GNS/35, 23 July 1990, draft Article III on MFN treatment (emphasis added).

[27] TNC, Draft Final Act Embodying the Results of the Uruguay Round of Multilateral Trade Negotiations, MTN.TNC/W/35–3/Rev.1, 3 December 1990, draft Article II; the alternative text reads as follows: '[In applying the provisions of this Agreement, including the commitments in its schedule, a Party shall accord to the services and service providers of another Party treatment no less favourable than the treatment it accords to like services and like service providers of any other Party.]'.

[28] Comparative MFN interpretation confirmed by Appellate Body, *EC – Bananas III*, para. 231; see also Weiss, 'GATS', 1195.

is to be interpreted broadly based on the competitive relationship of the products in the marketplace. With regard to tariffs, a more narrow interpretation may be justified in order to balance mutually negotiated tariff concessions. A transposition of this theory to the MFN concept in services trade supports a broad market-specific interpretation of 'likeness'. Since services are not subject to tariffs, the GATS framework does not provide for a GATT-like structure of tariff schedules. In consequence, there is no apparent reason that would justify a narrow interpretation of GATS Article II 'likeness' along the lines of *Germany – Sardines* and *Japan – SPF Dimension Lumber*. The very little Appellate Body jurisprudence on Article II GATS also appears to reject the narrow interpretation of MFN treatment the way it was applied in these two cases on tariffs as well as in *Australia – Ammonium Sulphate* and *EEC – Animal Feed Proteins* on internal regulations:

> In *Canada – Autos*, the Appellate Body explicitly criticized the Panel's application of Article II GATS because the latter omitted to examine 'the structure of competition in the wholesale trade services market for motor vehicles in Canada'.

This finding by the Appellate Body confirms an economically oriented interpretation of MFN treatment on the basis of competitive opportunities, which presupposes that the conceptual breadth of 'likeness' reflects competitive relationships in a marketplace rather than a narrow relationship based on specific characteristics.[29] Likewise, this approach rules out any consideration of the regulatory purpose or the necessity of the measure in light of its purpose.[30] In consequence, the standard of 'likeness' in Article II GATS is identical to the one in Article I GATT pertaining to internal regulations, which in turn corresponds to the 'directly competitive or substitutable' standard of Article III:2 GATT as well as the 'likeness' standard of Articles III:4 GATT and XVII GATS.

One could argue that an identical standard for 'likeness' in GATS MFN and national treatment is flawed due to the fact that Article II lacks a specific reference to the 'conditions of competition' contained in Article XVII:3. While this position certainly deserves some merit from a purely textual point of view, it can be countered with the argument that

[29] Also in favour of an economic interpretation of 'likeness' in GATS Art. II, Lang, 'GATS and Regulatory Autonomy', 822–23; Pitschas, 'GATS', p. 514; similarly Gkoutzinis, 'Trade in Banking Services', 898–99; but see also Mattoo, 'MFN and GATS', pp. 77–79, suggesting an economic interpretation of 'likeness' in combination with a necessity test.

[30] Appellate Body Report, *EC – Bananas III*, para. 241.

the Appellate Body has previously interpreted incomplete and imprecise provisions on the basis of their object and purpose rather than text. For instance, as outlined previously, the Appellate Body gave a different meaning to the notion of 'like products' under Article III:2, first sentence, as compared to the identical term under Article III:4 GATT. Similarly, it found that Article II GATS on MFN treatment also covers *de facto* discrimination despite the absence of a specific text comparable to paragraphs 2 and 3 of GATS Article XVII.

In *EC – Bananas III*, the Panel found that 'the "treatment no less favourable" standard of Article XVII:1 is clarified and reinforced in the language of paragraphs 2 and 3. The absence of similar language in Article II is not, in our view, a justification for giving a different ordinary meaning in terms of Article 31(1) of the Vienna Convention to the words "treatment no less favourable", which are identical in both Articles II:1 and XVII:1' (para 7.301). The Panel mainly followed the comparative analysis argued by the US (para IV.643). The Appellate Body was overly harsh in its criticism of the Panel's comparative analysis between Articles II and XVII GATS (para 231), but confirmed the Panel's result primarily on a comparative analysis between Articles I GATT and II GATS (paras 232 f). The Appellate Body's approach is remarkable, considering that Article I GATT does not even use the terms 'treatment no less favourable'.

Accordingly, it is viable to argue that due to the similar object and purpose of GATS MFN and national treatment – which is to generally prevent discriminatory measures leading to market distortions – the notion of 'likeness' in the two provisions should have an identical breadth. A coherent approach for the 'likeness' question of both MFN and national treatment is further justified in the context of services trade, considering that the more specific GATT purpose of protecting tariff concessions is irrelevant.[31]

[31] Also supporting an identical breadth of 'likeness' in Articles II and XVII GATS, Matsushita, Schoenbaum and Mavroidis, *World Trade Organization*, p. 620; in *EC – Bananas III*, the Panel analysed the element of 'likeness' in Art. II GATS (para 7.346) by simply referring to its previous analysis of 'likeness' under Art. XVII GATS (para 7.322); see also Wolfrum, 'Art. II GATS', p. 83, supporting recourse to the *Border Tax Adjustments* framework as applied in Art. III GATT for purposes of Art. II GATS.

7

Comparative analysis of 'likeness'

Following the interpretation of 'likeness' in GATS in the light of GATT non-discrimination rules, chapter 7 extends this comparative analysis to other disciplines within and outside the WTO framework. Section I looks at 'likeness' the way it applies in non-discrimination obligations in the TBT and SPS Agreements, whereas section II turns to non-discrimination obligations of international economic law outside the WTO agreements, focusing in particular on NAFTA and BIT provisions. Section III returns to the WTO framework, but analyses the element of 'likeness' as it applies under trade remedies law outside the non-discrimination principle.

I 'Likeness' in the TBT and SPS Agreements

Both the TBT and the SPS Agreement provide for more specific obligations in their respective field of regulation than the basic obligations set forth in GATT. The TBT Agreement prevents unnecessary trade obstacles being created by technical regulations, such as standards and certification procedures. The SPS Agreement seeks to prevent the creation of trade obstacles through the application of sanitary and phytosanitary measures, such as food safety and health regulations. Both agreements contain basic non-discrimination obligations similar to the ones in GATT and GATS. Pursuant to Article 2.1 TBT Agreement:

> 'Members shall ensure that in respect of technical regulations, products imported from the territory of any Member shall be accorded treatment no less favourable than that accorded to like products of national origin and to like products originating in any other country.'

This non-discrimination obligation combines both MFN and national treatment in one provision. It is composed of the two basic elements of 'less favourable treatment' and 'like products'. The main difference to Articles I and III GATT relates to the fact that its scope is limited to technical regulations, as opposed to the more broad notion of 'laws, regulations and requirements'. In view of these close similarities, the considerations under chapters 5 and 6 can be transposed *mutatis mutandis* to Article 2.1 TBT Agreement. Consequently, the concept of 'like products' follows the same broad market-based standard which is proposed for GATS Articles II and XVII as well as most GATT non-discrimination provisions.[1] At the same time it must be noted, however, that the TBT Agreement lacks a general exceptions clause comparable to Articles XX GATT and XIV GATS. Consequently, some authors suggest a very narrow or subjective interpretation of the 'likeness' concept in Article 2.1 TBT Agreement.[2] Alternatively, the preferred solution is to view Article 2.1 in relation to Article 2.2 TBT Agreement. Pursuant to Article 2.2 TBT Agreement 'technical regulations shall not be more trade-restrictive than necessary to fulfil a legitimate objective'. This type of obligation applies to measures which do not differentiate – *de jure* or *de facto* – between foreign and domestic products and thus constitutes a form of the more integrative 'non-restriction' principle.[3] The potentially far-reaching consequences of Article 2.2 TBT Agreement are counterbalanced with an open list of legitimate objectives which the Members may pursue by adopting trade-restrictive measures.[4] Considering that a discriminatory measure in terms of Article 2.1 always constitutes at the same time an obstacle to trade in terms of Article 2.2,[5] it appears inconsistent that the measure could be justified under Article 2.2 but not under Article 2.1 TBT Agreement. Hence, the exceptions from Article 2.2 should in principle also apply to discriminatory measures in terms of Article 2.1 TBT Agreement. A third and final approach to resolve the lack of a general exceptions clause is to rely on the relationship between GATT and the TBT Agreement. The Appellate Body found that in comparison to GATT, the TBT Agreement

[1] Appleton, 'TBT Agreement', p. 390: 'Given however that the like product provisions of the TBT Agreement appear to be a logical extension of the non-discrimination obligations … it is probable that GATT non-discrimination disputes, in particular those dealing with GATT Article III:4, will provide guidance in the interpretation of the term "like products" which appears in various places in the TBT Agreement'; Tamiotti, 'Art. 2 TBT', p. 216.

[2] Tamiotti, 'Art. 2 TBT', p. 217.

[3] Above, 3.I.A.2; see in general Ortino, *Instruments for the Liberalisation of Trade*, pp. 434 ff; Desmedt, 'Proportionality in WTO Law', 453 ff.

[4] Such legitimate objectives are, inter alia: national security requirements; the prevention of deceptive practices; protection of human health or safety, animal or plant life or health, or the environment.

[5] Note that the opposite is not the case, i.e. an unnecessary obstacle to trade is not necessarily discriminatory.

constitutes a specialized legal regime which imposes additional obligations.[6] Due to the cumulative nature of the two agreements, a discriminatory technical regulation falls within the scope of Article III:4 GATT as well as Articles 2.1 and 2.2 TBT Agreement. Again it appears inconsistent if such a measure could be justified under Article XX GATT and Article 2.2 TBT Agreement, but not under Article 2.1 TBT Agreement. Considering the *lex specialis* character of the TBT Agreement, one could argue that in the absence of a general exceptions clause in the more specialized regime, Article XX of the more general regime becomes applicable. The main difference between the two here-preferred solutions is that Article XX GATT contains an exhaustive list of legitimate policy objectives, whereas the enumerative list of Article 2.2 TBT Agreement leaves more room to justify a trade-restrictive measure. The open list in Article 2.2 TBT Agreement may be explained by the fact that the non-restriction principle is more integrative than the non-discrimination obligation, thus requiring a broader form of exceptions. However, since both Articles 2.1 TBT Agreement and III GATT are limited to the principle of non-discrimination, it appears appropriate to apply the exhaustive list of general exceptions from Article XX GATT to Article 2.1 TBT Agreement.[7]

In comparison, the general non-discrimination obligation in the SPS Agreement differs considerably from the respective provisions in the TBT Agreement, GATT and GATS. Article 2.3 SPS Agreement reads as follows:

> 'Members shall ensure that their sanitary and phytosanitary measures do not arbitrarily or unjustifiably discriminate between Members where identical or similar conditions prevail, including between their own territory and that of other Members.'[8]

By referencing to 'arbitrarily or unjustifiably' discrimination, Article 2.3 SPS Agreement basically incorporates the *chapeaux* of Articles XX GATT and XIV GATS into the non-discrimination obligation itself.[9]

[6] Appellate Body Report, *EC – Asbestos*, para. 80.

[7] See also Vranes, *Trade and the Environment*, p. 305 who prefers to apply the exceptions of Article 2.2 to Article 2.1 TBT Agreement.

[8] Similarly also Art. 5.5 SPS Agreement; on the relationship between Art. 2.3 and 5.5 see Appellate Body Reports, *Australia – Salmon*, para. 252 and *EC – Hormones*, para. 212; see further Qin, 'Defining Nondiscrimination', 277–81; Pauwelyn, 'The First Three SPS Disputes', 653.

[9] Appellate Body Report, *Australia – Salmon*, para. 251: 'This provision takes up obligations similar to those arising under Article I:1 and Article III:4 of the GATT 1994 and incorporates part of the "chapeau" to Article XX of the GATT 1994'.

This structure allows the *e contrario* interpretation that justifiable discriminations are not in violation of Article 2.3 SPS Agreement, which consequently means that the regulatory context becomes an element of the non-discrimination obligation itself,[10] as opposed to a mere justification-type analysis as is the case in GATT and GATS. This conclusion is enforced by the fact that Article 2.3 SPS Agreement employs a concept of 'identical or similar conditions', which requires not only to compare the products at issue, but also their situation in the light of the regulatory context.[11] The comparative clause in Article 2.3 SPS Agreement thus follows a subjective interpretation and is not limited to an assessment of the competitive relationship between the products under scrutiny. This solution is comparable to the interpretation of the 'like circumstances' concept discussed under the subsequent section 7.II. Finally, it is noteworthy that – similar to the TBT Agreement – the SPS Agreement also contains the more stringent trade obligation of non-restriction. Article 5.6 SPS Agreement requires Members to 'ensure that such measures are not more trade-restrictive than required to achieve their appropriate level of sanitary or phytosanitary protection'.

II 'Like circumstances' in NAFTA rules on non-discrimination

The WTO agreements are not the only body of international economic law which embody non-discrimination obligations. Numerous regional trade agreements and investment protection treaties incorporate MFN and national treatment provisions similar to those of the WTO. Despite this fragmentation of non-discrimination obligations in international economic law, there is a tendency of more convergence in the application of analogous treaty obligations. Arbitral tribunals interpreting a specific principle in one area of international economic law (such as investment) frequently take into account the legal developments in another area (such as trade).[12] The WTO panel and Appellate Body decisions appear to take a lead function in the application and interpretation of international economic law, in particular with regard to fundamental principles such as MFN and national treatment. NAFTA and BIT tribunals frequently feel

[10] See above, 3.III.A.

[11] Panel Report, *Australia – Salmon (Article 21.5 – Canada)*, para. 7.113: 'we also harbour doubts as to whether "identical or similar conditions" in the sense of the third element of Article 2.3, first sentence, prevail in the territories of both Canada and Australia in respect of the *situations compared*' (emphasis added); Seibert-Fohr, 'Art. 2 SPS', p. 408.

[12] Weiler, 'Non-Discrimination in International Investment Law', p. 559.

compelled to justify their own interpretations as either concordant with or diverging from WTO practice.[13] While it is certainly reasonable to consider WTO jurisprudence to inspire the interpretation of NAFTA and BIT principles – and vice versa – in case the provisions are truly analogous, it is at the same time necessary to exercise great caution with regard to differences in the object and purpose as well as legal structure and context of the specific provisions. Most prominently, investment treaties are designed to protect the value of a specific foreign investment whereas international trade law protects a more abstract value of equal conditions of competition, not the actual value of the exported goods and services. This main difference in the object and purpose is explained by the fact that the investment in a foreign market is a more substantial and binding commitment to participate in the foreign market than merely exporting goods and services. A new regulation – for instance an environmental standard – may have severe consequences for the foreign investor who, in case he is unable to comply with the standard, may have to disinvest and suffer actual damages. Conversely, a foreign producer unable to meet the new standard may simply cease to export without incurring actual damages, but only loss of potential gains. However, this circumstance is taken care of in that investment treaties accord to the foreign investor an individual right to claim damages, whereas trade agreements are only enforceable by the governments of the contracting parties who can only claim the abolition of the measure but not damages. It is however not entirely apparent why these conceptual differences between trade and investment should explain different substantive standards of non-discrimination. The circumstances may very well justify a 'best treatment' or similar standard in a trade case, whereas the 'best treatment' approach may just as well lead to absurd results in investment protection law. Against this background, a comparative analysis of 'likeness' between WTO and NAFTA appears to be an informative exercise for the interpretation of both areas.[14]

NAFTA was adopted in 1994 and pursues the main objective of removing tariff barriers between the US, Canada and Mexico. In addition to the rules on trade in goods, NAFTA contains obligations on cross-border trade in services (chapter 12) as well as rules on investment protection (chapter 13). Both chapters provide for non-discrimination obligations

[13] See e.g. *Corn Products* v. *Mexico*, para. 122: 'the Tribunal does not accept that the fact that HFCS and sugar are like products for the purposes of GATT is irrelevant to the application of the Article 1102 test'.

[14] See also Communication from Brazil, MFN, National Treatment and like circumstances, JOB(01)/165, 30 November 2001, paras. 6 ff.

which use the concept of 'like circumstances'. With regard to trade in services, the national treatment obligation is phrased as follows:[15]

> 'Each Party shall accord to service providers of another Party treatment no less favorable than that it accords, in like circumstances, to its own service providers.' (Article 1202)

In addition, chapter 12 contains a provision on MFN treatment for service providers:

> 'Each Party shall accord to service providers of another Party treatment no less favorable than that it accords, in like circumstances, to service providers of any other Party or of a non-Party.' (Article 1203)

In comparison, chapter 11 on investment protection embodies the following non-discrimination obligations:

> 'Article 1102: National Treatment
>
> 1. Each Party shall accord to *investors* of another Party treatment no less favorable than that it accords, in like circumstances, to its own investors with respect to the establishment, acquisition, expansion, management, conduct, operation, and sale or other disposition of investments.
> 2. Each Party shall accord to *investments* of investors of another Party treatment no less favorable than that it accords, in like circumstances, to investments of its own investors with respect to the establishment, acquisition, expansion, management, conduct, operation, and sale or other disposition of investments.'
>
> Article 1103: Most-Favored-Nation Treatment
>
> 1. Each Party shall accord to *investors* of another Party treatment no less favorable than that it accords, in like circumstances, to investors of any other Party or of a non-Party with respect to the establishment, acquisition, expansion, management, conduct, operation, and sale or other disposition of investments.
> 2. Each Party shall accord to *investments* of investors of another Party treatment no less favorable than that it accords, in like circumstances, to investments of investors of any other Party or of a non-Party with respect to the establishment, acquisition, expansion, management, conduct, operation, and sale or other disposition of investments.'

The concept of 'like circumstances' used in NAFTA differs in one fundamental point from the simple concept of 'likeness' in WTO law. The wording 'like products' and 'like services and service suppliers' indicates clearly that the comparison only takes place between the *subjects*, i.e. the

[15] See also the non-discrimination provisions for financial services in particular, Arts. 1405 and 1406 NAFTA; Schefer, *Financial Services*.

products, services or suppliers. In contrast, the NAFTA concept of 'like circumstances' is open as to whether the analysis requires comparing the *subjects*, and/or whether the analysis focuses on the question of whether the differential *treatment* occurs in like or different circumstances.[16] This difference in the 'likeness' clauses translates into a modification of the legal analysis. With regard to chapter 11 rules on non-discrimination, the structure of the legal test was established early in *Pope & Talbot* v. *Canada* and subsequently confirmed by other NAFTA tribunals. Accordingly, the determination of an alleged national treatment breach under Article 1102 can be summarized in three analytical steps:[17]

– identifying domestic investors and/or investments in a comparable position with the claimant (like-circumstanced suppliers, investors or investments);
– determining whether more-favourable treatment has been provided to the domestic investor/investment; and
– determining whether the circumstances of the application of the measure justify the difference in treatment (like-circumstanced treatment).

The same structure was in principle followed by the arbitral panel in the case *US – Cross-Border Trucking Services* with regard to Articles 1202 and 1203 NAFTA, even though the report does not explicitly spell out such a test.[18] It must be noted, however, that not all cases under chapters 11 and 12 follow this ideal-type legal structure. Oftentimes the three steps are not clearly separated. Moreover, arbitral tribunals in NAFTA and other investor-state proceedings do not feel themselves bound by prior decisions, which in turn renders the development of a coherent test more difficult.

A 'Like-circumstanced' investors or suppliers: an economic standard

At the outset it must be recalled that the existence of a 'like comparator' is presumed in WTO non-discrimination cases concerning measures which discriminate directly on the basis of nationality, and hence the issue of 'likeness' only arises in cases of *de facto* discrimination.[19]

16 Bjorklund, 'National Treatment', p. 39.

17 *Pope & Talbot* v. *Canada*, paras. 31–81, in particular para. 78; Grierson-Weiler and Laird, 'Standards of Treatment', p. 291; Weiler, 'Non-Discrimination in International Investment Law', p. 567; Bjorklund, 'National Treatment', p. 37; Dolzer and Schreuer, *International Investment Law*, pp. 180–81.

18 *US – Cross-Border Trucking Services*, paras. 246–78.

19 See above, 3.II.A, n 122.

This study submits that this reasoning is inherent to the principle of non-discrimination in international economic law and should thus also apply to NAFTA and BITs.[20]

The NAFTA non-discrimination analysis is similar to WTO law, in that the first step requires determining whether the foreign investor, investment or supplier is in 'like circumstances' compared to the domestic or another foreign investor, investment or supplier. The question thus arises whether the concept of 'like circumstances' also follows a pure economic standard with the competitive relationship as *tertium comparationis*, or whether 'like circumstances' should be interpreted in accordance with the subjective or objective standard. As already noted in the introductory chapter above, it must be emphasized that an isolated comparison of the 'likeness' element would be a misleading approach. It is important to consider the 'likeness' element as part of the entire non-discrimination structure, including also the elements of 'less favourable treatment' and 'justifying regulatory purpose'.

1. Chapter 11 on investment

In the case *S.D. Myers* v. *Canada* involving an export ban of PCB waste from Canada to remediation facilities in the US, the arbitral tribunal explicitly referred to the Appellate Body's famous quote in *Japan – Alcoholic Beverages II* according to which '[t]he accordion of "likeness" stretches and squeezes in different places'.[21] At the same time the tribunal referred to a 1993 OECD analysis on 'National Treatment for Foreign-Controlled Enterprises' as well as the jurisprudence of the Canadian Supreme Court on the prohibition of discrimination between 'similarly situated' individuals. On this basis the tribunal concluded that '[t]he concept of "like circumstances" invites an examination of whether a non-national investor complaining of less favourable treatment is in the same "sector" as the national investor', noting 'that the word "sector" has a wide connotation that includes the concepts of "economic sector" and "business sector"'.[22] Following these considerations, the tribunal concluded:

> 'From the business perspective, it is clear that SDMI and Myers Canada were in "like circumstances" with Canadian operators such as

[20] Similarly Bjorklund, 'National Treatment', p. 38: 'In the case of a *de jure* measure, however, one need not show that a domestic entity has actually received any treatment if such is inherent in the terms of the measure'. Note that also in NAFTA (and BITs) *de jure* discrimination is subject to justification on the basis of 'like circumstances', see below 7.II.B.

[21] *S.D. Myers* v. *Canada*, para. 244.

[22] Ibid., para. 250.

> Chem-Security and Cintec. They all were engaged in providing PCB waste remediation services. SDMI was in a position to attract customers that might otherwise have gone to the Canadian operators because it could offer more favourable prices and because it had extensive experience and credibility. It was precisely because SDMI was in a position to take business away from its Canadian competitors that Chem-Security and Cintec lobbied the Minister of the Environment to ban exports when the U.S. authorities opened the border.' (para 251)

Even though the tribunal omits to explicitly identify the competitive relationship as the decisive factor to delimit a 'sector', it supports its conclusion with the main argument that the waste remediation companies are substitutable from the consumers' perspective. Hence, the competitive relationship appears to be the underlying rationale of the analysis. The finding that the concept of 'like circumstances' under chapter 11 includes investors and investments 'in the same business or economic sector' was subsequently confirmed by numerous arbitral tribunals:

> In *Pope & Talbot* v. *Canada* the arbitral tribunal confirmed the 'same business or economic sector' test as the first step of the like circumstances analysis (para 78). The tribunal in *Feldman* v. *Mexico* stated that 'the "universe" of firms in like circumstances are those foreign-owned and domestic-owned firms that are in the business of reselling/exporting cigarettes' (para 171), at the same time excluding Mexican cigarette producers that might also export cigarettes. In the more recent case *ADM* v. *Mexico* the tribunal specifically recognized that Article 1102 is designed to protect competitive opportunities; it confirmed the 'business or economic sector' test and found that fructose and cane sugar producers are in 'like circumstances' on the basis of a competitive relationship (paras 198 ff). Finally, *Corn Products* v. *Mexico* explicitly found that there is direct competition between Mexican sugar and HFCS (paras 120, 126), referring also to the Appellate Body Report, *Mexico – Taxes on Soft Drinks* (paras 121 f).[23]

In spite of this strong jurisprudence, chapter 11 non-discrimination provisions are not interpreted consistently among different arbitral tribunals.[24] In *UPS* v. *Canada* the tribunal rejected the investors' arguments

[23] See also the very recent case *Grand River* v. *US* where the claimant clearly interpreted the underlying purpose of the national treatment provision in chapter 11 as ensuring the equality of competitive opportunities between foreign and domestic investors and investments and, consequently, identified the competitive relationship as the decisive standard for 'like circumstances', see Claimants' Memorial, para. 246; for a detailed discussion of national treatment objectives in trade and investment see DiMascio and Pauwelyn, 'Nondiscrimination in Trade and Investment', *passim*.

[24] See also Grierson-Weiler and Laird, 'Standards of Treatment', pp. 292–93 regarding *Loewen* v. *US*.

on the existence of a competitive relationship and instead analysed directly whether the treatment occurs in like circumstances in the light of the regulatory purpose.[25] Similarly, the *Methanex* v. *US* tribunal explicitly noted the difference between the concept of 'like circumstances' in chapter 11 on the one hand, and the GATT concept of 'like products' and the NAFTA Article 301(2) notion of 'like, directly competitive or substitutable goods' on the other hand. Against this background the tribunal held 'that Article 1102 is to be read on its own terms and not as if the words "any like, directly competitive or substitutable goods" appeared in it'.[26] In consequence, the tribunal found that methanol and ethanol producers are not in 'like circumstances', but it omitted to specify a basis or standard for its own comparison.

This study submits that the *Methanex* tribunal was correct in pointing out the differences between the 'like circumstances' concept as it applies in chapter 11 (and chapter 12) and the mere 'likeness' concept of GATT and GATS. However, in contrast to the *UPS* approach it is argued here that NAFTA 'like circumstances' contains two elements, namely an economic standard needed to demonstrate discrimination, and a subjective standard serving as justification.[27] The second element will be addressed under section B following below.

2. Chapter 12 on cross-border services trade

Chapter 12 non-discrimination provisions are largely identical to the ones in chapter 11, reason for which the same interpretation applies. To date, Article 1202 NAFTA has only been subject to the one dispute, *US – Trucking Services*, which concerned a US moratorium on the processing of any applications by Mexican-owned trucking firms for permission to operate in the US. Considering that this measure discriminates directly on the basis of nationality (*de jure*), the complainant did not have to establish a competitive relationship between the trucking companies.[28] The Panel thus only interpreted and analysed the justificational element of 'like circumstances'. However, in analogy to chapter 11 NAFTA it is submitted

[25] *UPS* v. *Canada*, para. 102 (customs measure) and paras. 173 ff (Publications Assistance Program); less clear, but probably also following this approach *GAMI* v. *Mexico*, para. 114; *Thunderbird* v. *Mexico*, para. 183; possibly also *Loewen* v. *US*, para. 140.

[26] *Methanex* v. *US*, part IV(B), paras. 30 ff, in particular para. 37.

[27] See also Ortino, '"Non-discrimination" to "Reasonableness"', 24–25.

[28] Para 257; it is however not apparent whether the Panel made a connection between *de jure* discrimination and the presumption of a competitive relationship.

that for the analysis of measures differentiating on grounds other than origin, the 'like circumstances' test would first require establishing the competitive relationship between the services and suppliers.[29]

Interestingly, the Panel also established a link between chapter 12 'like circumstances' and GATS 'like services and service suppliers', noting that '[t]he Parties do not dispute that the use of the phrase "in like circumstances" was intended to have a meaning that was *similar* to the phrase "like services and service providers," as proposed by Canada and Mexico during NAFTA negotiations'.[30] While it remains open what the Panel meant by using the word 'similar', it is argued here that the similarity only relates to the first step of the 'like circumstances' analysis that requires – in case of *de facto* discrimination – to determine the competitive relationship between the suppliers. However, the similarity cannot go as far as to adopt a subjective interpretation or to incorporate a justification clause into the narrower GATS 'likeness' concept. Such an approach was resolutely rejected by the Appellate Body.[31]

B 'Like-circumstanced' treatment: a subjective exception

As explained under section 3.III.B above, the general exceptions clauses in Articles XX GATT and XIV GATS embody a list of public interests which allow the respondent to justify an otherwise discriminatory measure. Similarly, NAFTA chapter 21 also provides for exceptions. Article 2101(1) NAFTA explicitly incorporates Article XX GATT by reference for purposes of trade in goods. In contrast, Article 2101(2) NAFTA does not incorporate the general exceptions clause of GATS Article XIV for purposes of trade in services under chapter 12, but spells out its own substantive exception. Accordingly, no obligation in chapter 12 'shall be construed to prevent the adoption or enforcement by any Party of measures necessary to secure compliance with laws or regulations that are not inconsistent with the provisions of this Agreement, including those relating to health and safety and consumer protection'. This justification

[29] The same economic analysis is required for 'like circumstances' in Art. 1405 NAFTA; Schefer, *Financial Services*, p. 172.

[30] Para 249 (emphasis added).

[31] See above chapters 5 and 6, *passim*; in particular Appellate Body Report, *EC – Bananas III*, para. 241: 'We see no specific authority either in Article II or in Article XVII of the GATS for the proposition that the "aims and effects" of a measure are in any way relevant in determining whether that measure is inconsistent with those provisions'; but see also below, n 58.

of so-called compliance measures corresponds to Article XIV(c) GATS[32] and has so far not been of much relevance in WTO and NAFTA dispute settlement. Interestingly, NAFTA omits to incorporate the more important exceptions, such as for measures necessary to protect public morals or public order (Article XIV(a) GATS) and life or health (Article XVI(b) GATS). Finally, NAFTA does not set out any general exceptions for purposes of chapter 11 on investment protection at all.

This study submits that the development of a general 'like circumstances' exception under NAFTA chapters 11 and 12 must be understood in light of the lack of a substantive general exceptions clause. The tribunal in *Pope & Talbot* v. *Canada* very accurately stated the applicable test:[33]

> 'the treatment accorded a foreign owned investment … should be compared with that accorded domestic investments in the same business or economic sector. However, that first step is not the last one. Differences in treatment will presumptively violate Article 1102(2), unless they have a reasonable nexus to rational government policies that (1) do not distinguish, on their face or de facto, between foreign-owned and domestic companies, and (2) do not otherwise unduly undermine the investment liberalizing objectives of NAFTA'. (para 78, fns omitted)

Quite similarly, the arbitral tribunal in *S.D. Myers* v. *Canada* quoted an OECD analysis on the concept of 'like situations' according to which 'the policy objectives of Member countries could be taken into account to define the circumstances in which comparison between foreign-controlled and domestic enterprises is permissible inasmuch as those objectives are not contrary to the principle of national treatment' (para 248). The tribunal went on to consider legitimate policy objectives, but it omitted to state 'like circumstances' as the legal basis for its considerations on intent and effect (paras 252 ff). In *Feldman* v. *Mexico* the tribunal also considered whether the differential treatment is based on reasons other than nationality without, however, basing this analysis directly on 'like circumstances' (paras 181 ff). Finally, *Corn Products* v. *Mexico* explicitly noted under the 'like circumstances' analysis that the purpose of the measure was to affect competition between different types of sugar (paras 120, 136).

Importantly, the 'like circumstances' justification must be limited with a nexus requirement – such as 'necessity' similar to the *chapeaux* of

32 On Art. XIV(c) GATS see e.g. Cottier, Delimatsis and Diebold, 'Art. XIV GATS', p. 307.

33 See also Weiler, 'Discrimination in NAFTA Chapter 11', pp. 37–39, referring to a 'like circumstances exception'.

Articles XX GATT and XIV GATS or the 'proportionality' principle in EU law – in order to avoid the undermining of the non-discrimination obligations.[34] A 'reasonable' nexus standard suggested in *Pope & Talbot* v. *Canada* does not seem sufficiently restrictive. More appropriately, the arbitral panel in *US – Trucking Services* regarding chapter 12 rules on non-discrimination interpreted a general exceptions clause including a necessity test into the 'like circumstances' concept. The panel noted, together with the parties to the dispute, that Article 1402 of the FTA between the US and Canada constitutes 'the "immediate source" of the "in like circumstances" language in Articles 1202 and 1203 of NAFTA'.[35] The US–Canada FTA non-discrimination provision allows the justification of discriminatory measures if they are necessary for prudential, fiduciary, health and safety, or consumer protection reasons. The panel thus concluded 'that the phrase "like circumstances" may properly include differential treatment under the conditions specified in the FTA Article 1402', which includes a necessity requirement.[36] This study submits that the justification under 'like circumstances' is not limited to the public interests listed in FTA Article 1402, but allows the pursuance of additional policy objectives to the extent that the measure is necessary.[37]

Against the background of these considerations, the NAFTA structure can be summarized as follows:

- Chapter 3 *on trade in goods*: Article 301 NAFTA on national treatment applies to like, directly competitive or substitutable goods. This standard is comparable to 'like and DCS products' in Article III GATT which allow for no incorporated exceptions (such as an 'aim and effects' test). Instead, Article 2101(1) NAFTA incorporates the entire GATT general exceptions clause of Article XX by reference.
- Chapter 12 *on trade in services*: Articles 1202 and 1203 NAFTA incorporate the 'like circumstances' concept. In contrast to GATS 'like services and service suppliers', it requires a comparison of the suppliers (economic standard) as well as an analysis of whether the treatment occurs in like circumstances (subjective standard). Unlike Article XIV GATS, Article 2101(2) NAFTA only contains the very limited justification of

[34] See on this issue generally Grierson-Weiler and Laird, 'Standards of Treatment', pp. 296–99.

[35] Para 249.

[36] Para 258.

[37] But see Leroux, 'GATS Case Law', 784 and DiMascio and Pauwelyn, 'Nondiscrimination in Trade and Investment', 88, both rejecting a 'necessity' standard for NAFTA chapter 11.

compliance measures. As a counterbalance, however, the 'like circumstances' concept allows the justification of differential treatment in light of the circumstances – i.e. purpose – of the measure.
- Chapter 11 *on investment*: The reasoning is similar to chapter 12. NAFTA does not set forth any general exceptions for measures in violation with the substantive rules on investment protection. Instead, the concept of 'like circumstances' allows the justification of differential treatment due to the circumstances of the measure.

Finally, one could question whether it makes any difference to divide the concept of 'like circumstances' into an economic and a subjective element as opposed to analysing 'like circumstances' directly in the light of the regulatory context. The practically relevant difference relates to the issue of whether the claimant or the respondent bears the burden to prove the main regulatory purpose of the measure.[38] In *UPS* v. *Canada*, one arbitrator very accurately criticized the majority's reasoning in a separate statement and outlined how the correct approach should be:

> 'A showing that there is a competitive relationship ... establishes a *prima facie* case of like circumstances. Once the investor has established the competitive relationship between two investors or investments, the burden shifts to the respondent Party to explain why two competing enterprises are not in like circumstances.'[39]

This approach is appropriate, considering that the proof of a measure's non-legitimate or protectionist purpose would constitute an unduly high burden for the complainant.[40] Once the complainant demonstrates a competitive relationship between the comparators and the applicable standard of 'less favourable treatment', it must be up to the respondent to

[38] See also above, 3.III.C.a.

[39] Separate Statement by Dean Ronald A. Cass, *UPS* v. *Canada*, para. 17; same opinion *Feldman* v. *Mexico*, paras. 183 f; *Pope & Talbot* v. *Canada*, para. 78; Separate Statement by Thomas W. Wälde, *Thunderbird* v. *Mexico*, para. 2; probably also *S.D. Myers* v. *Canada*, paras. 243 ff, 246 and *ADM* v. *Mexico*, para. 212; with regard to chapter 12 see *US – Trucking Services*, para. 257; similarly also Grierson-Weiler and Laird, 'Standards of Treatment', p. 295: 'Once a prima facie breach of a non-discrimination provision has been established, the burden shifts to the respondent government to explain why the difference in treatment is justified'; Weiler, 'Non-Discrimination in International Investment Law', pp. 568–89, 573; Weiler, 'Discrimination in NAFTA Chapter 11', p. 37.

[40] But see Newcombe and Paradell, *Law and Practice of Investment Treaties*, p. 163: 'the claimant must identify the relevant subjects for comparison, demonstrate how it is in comparable circumstances in light of the purpose of the measure at issue', see also pp. 165, 176; DiMascio and Pauwelyn, 'Nondiscrimination in Trade and Investment', 86: 'the *Pope & Talbot* and *Feldman* tribunals, in our view, wrongly imposed a presumption of

justify its measure by showing that it is linked – by the applicable 'nexus' – to legitimate objectives.

C *The 'less favourable treatment' standard*

Having outlined the NAFTA structure with regard to 'like circumstances' and 'justificational regulatory purpose', this section now turns to the issue of the applicable standard with regard to the element of 'less favourable treatment'. To be recalled, the basic question is whether 'less favourable treatment' follows the asymmetric impact test according to which the overall treatment of foreign investors should be compared to the overall treatment of domestic investors who are in 'like circumstances' (i.e. in a competitive relationship). Or, alternatively, whether under the diagonal test 'less favourable treatment' implies an obligation to treat all foreign investors equivalent to the 'best' treatment accorded to a domestic investor in 'like circumstances'.

The arbitral tribunal in *Feldman* v. *Mexico* found that 'NAFTA is on its face unclear as to whether the foreign investor must be treated in the most favorable manner provided for *any* domestic investor, or only with regard to the treatment generally accorded to domestic investors, or even the least favorably treated domestic investor'.[41] Since in this case the tribunal only identified one domestic and one foreign investor in 'like circumstances', it left the issue undecided.[42] The *Feldman* tribunal seemed to have neglected paragraph 3 of Article 1102, which states that the 'treatment accorded by a Party under paragraphs 1 and 2 means, with respect to a state or province, treatment no less favorable than the *most* favorable treatment accorded,

"like circumstances" for investments in the same business and economic sector. In particular, they were wrong to shift the burden of proof from complainant to defendant'; Bjorklund, 'National Treatment', p. 58; dissenting opinion by Jorge Covarrubias Bravo, *Feldman* v. *Mexico*, pp. 9 f; probably also *Thunderbird* v. *Mexico*, paras. 176 ff and *GAMI* v. *Mexico*, para. 114.

[41] Para 185 (emphasis original).

[42] Para 186: 'the Tribunal need not decide whether Article 1102 requires treatment equivalent to the best treatment provided to any domestic investors. Presumably, if there was evidence that another domestic investor had been treated in a manner equivalent to the Claimant, in terms of export registration, audit, and granting or withholding of rebates, the Respondent would have provided that evidence to the Tribunal. In this case, the known "universe" of investors is only two, or at the most three, one foreign (the Claimant) and one domestic (the Poblano Group companies), and the Tribunal must make its decision on the evidence before it. Thus, the only relevant domestic investor is the Poblano Group and the comparison must be between the Poblano Group and Claimant'.

in like circumstances'. The tribunal in *Pope & Talbot* v. *Canada* was very explicit in how this language should be interpreted:

> 'The Tribunal also interprets both standards to mean the right to treatment equivalent to the "best" treatment accorded to domestic investors or investments in like circumstances. The Tribunal thus concludes that "no less favorable" means equivalent to, not better or worse than, the best treatment accorded to the comparator.' (para 42, also paras. 43–72)

This analysis clearly suggests a diagonal test for the element of 'less favourable treatment'.[43] The main argument in support of such an approach is that NAFTA chapter 11 and BIT national treatment protects not only an abstract value of competitive opportunities, but more specifically the individual foreign investor.[44] As opposed to WTO law, investment protection treaties empower the concerned individual to request the establishment of an arbitral tribunal. Moreover, since Article 1202(2) NAFTA contains an equivalent standard to Article 1102(3), the same interpretation also applies with regard to cross-border services trade. The very intrusive nature of the diagonal test additionally justifies that the concept of 'like circumstances' in non-discrimination of chapters 11 and 12 includes not only an economic standard, but also a general exceptions clause.

Yet again, NAFTA jurisprudence is inconsistent on this issue. While most NAFTA cases interpreted national treatment as an obligation to treat foreign investors equivalent to the 'best' treatment accorded to domestic investors in like circumstances,[45] the tribunal in *S.D. Myers* v. *Canada*

[43] Same opinion Ortino, '"Non-discrimination" to "Reasonableness"', 22–24; Grierson-Weiler and Laird, 'Standards of Treatment', p. 293; DiMascio and Pauwelyn, 'Nondiscrimination in Trade and Investment', 77; Bjorklund, 'National Treatment', pp. 54–56.

[44] *Pope & Talbot* v. *Canada*, para. 79; DiMascio and Pauwelyn, 'Nondiscrimination in Trade and Investment', 78.

[45] See also *ADM* v. *Mexico*, para. 205: 'Claimants and their investment are entitled to the best level of treatment available to any other domestic investor or investment operating in like circumstances'; *Loewen* v. *US*, para. 140: 'What Article 1102(3) requires is a comparison between the standard of treatment accorded to a claimant and the most favourable standard of treatment accorded to a person in like situation to that claimant'; *Methanex* v. *US*, part IV(B), para. 21: 'the investor or investment of another party is entitled to the most favourable treatment accorded to some members of the domestic class'; less clear *Thunderbird* v. *Mexico*, para. 177, but see Separate Statement by Thomas W. Wälde, *Thunderbird* v. *Mexico*, para. 105.

followed the GATT and GATS approach requiring an asymmetric impact on the group of foreign investors:[46]

> 'The Tribunal takes the view that, in assessing whether a measure is contrary to a national treatment norm, the following factors should be taken into account: – whether the practical effect of the measure is to create a disproportionate benefit for nationals over non nationals.' (para 252)

The difference between the two theories has become clearly apparent once more in the parties' submissions of the currently pending case *Grand River* v. *US*:

> The investor as claimant contends that '[t]here is simply no room in the language of these provisions for reading-in the requirement for an investor … to demonstrate that the impact of the measures fell disproportionately on investors of his or her nationality as opposed to those of the host state or another'.[47] It is not surprising that the US as respondent supports the opposing view, noting that 'as found by the *S.D. Myers* v. *Canada* tribunal, analysis under Article 1102 involves considerations of "whether the practical effect of the measure is to create a disproportionate benefit for nationals over non nationals"'.[48]

In sum, while there is a strong tendency by NAFTA tribunals to apply a diagonal test as a standard for 'less favourable treatment', it is not certain whether this approach is going to prevail in future cases in view of the developments under WTO law.

D *Excursus: like 'circumstances' and 'situations' in BITs*

Considering that over 2,600 BITs existed worldwide already in 2007[49] and that they contain different forms and structures of non-discrimination clauses which are then applied by arbitral tribunals of different institutions, it is not surprising that the jurisprudence is highly fragmented. As a detailed analysis of all the various forms of BIT non-discrimination provisions and the resulting jurisprudence is beyond the scope of this research, the present section is limited to a general overview of the main issues in light of designated examples.

[46] Similarly *Corn Products* v. *Mexico*, para. 138, which looked at both effect and intent of the measure.

[47] Claimants' Memorial Merits Phase, *Grand River* v. *US*, para. 239, see also para. 254.

[48] Counter-Memorial of Respondent, ibid., p. 80.

[49] UNCTAD, Recent Developments in International Investment Agreements, IIA Monito No. 2 (2008), UNCTAD/WEB/DIAE/IA/2008/1, p. 2.

With regard to the 'likeness' element,[50] many BITs use the concept of 'like circumstances'[51] or 'same circumstances',[52] but some also contain the language of 'like situations',[53] 'comparable situations'[54] or 'similar situations'.[55] Other investment agreements use the 'likeness' concept, similar to the non-discrimination provisions in GATT and GATS.[56] This study submits that it is neither possible nor appropriate to establish an abstract graduation of various breadths by a simple dictionary definition of the different terms. At the same time, it would be oversimplifying to say that all concepts have the exact same meaning and comparative standard.[57] In particular the frequently expressed view that 'like circumstances' in BITs entails the same substantive meaning as 'like services and service suppliers' in GATS may – in view of a possible inbuilt exceptions clause requiring to consider the regulatory purpose and necessity – in many cases not be accurate.[58] It is important that every single BIT non-discrimination provision is interpreted in the light of its text and structure as well as its context in the entire agreement. In general terms, the comparative clause is subject to the following three interpretations:

- The comparative clause follows a pure *economic* standard, requiring the complainant to demonstrate a competitive relationship between the comparators; possible legitimate policy objectives of the measure are irrelevant for the non-discrimination analysis, but the BIT may provide for a distinct general exceptions clause;

[50] For an overview of comparator clauses in BITs see e.g. Molinuevo, 'International Disputes'; Newcombe and Paradell, *Law and Practice of Investment Treaties*, p. 160; UNCTAD, 'National Treatment', pp. 28 ff.

[51] US model-BIT (2004), Art. 3 and 4, available at www.state.gov/documents/organization/117601.pdf.

[52] UK–Belize BIT (1982), Art. 3(1).

[53] US–Honduras BIT (1995), Art. II(1); US–Senegal BIT (1983), Art. II(2).

[54] China–Iran BIT (2000), Art. 4(1).

[55] Ethiopia–Turkey BIT (2000), Art. 3(1).

[56] Framework Agreement on the ASEAN Investment Area (1998), Art. 7(1)(b).

[57] But see Newcombe and Paradell, *Law and Practice of Investment Treaties*, p. 161: 'These words are interchangeable with no substantive differences in their usage or meaning'.

[58] See above, n 31; but note that in the view of the US, the terms 'like circumstances' featured in BITs and the concept of 'likeness' in GATS does not entail any difference in scope, see CTS, Report of the Meeting Held on 19 March 2002, Note by the Secretariat, S/C/M/59, 14 May 2002, para. 29, but more sceptically Canada, para. 32; see also Molinuevo, 'International Disputes'; for an identical interpretation also *Tietje*, contra *Zdouc* in: Ehlers, Wolffgang and Lechleitner (eds.), *Rechtsfragen des Dienstleistungsverkehrs*, p. 151.

- The comparative clause follows a *subjective* standard, requiring the complainant to demonstrate not only that there is a competitive relationship between the comparators, but also that the measure does not pursue a legitimate policy objective and/or differentiates purely on the basis of nationality and/or is motivated by protectionism;
- The comparative clause contains an *economic* element and a *built-in general exceptions* clause. Following the claimant's proof of a competitive relationship between the comparators and the applicable standard of 'less favourable treatment', the respondent may justify the measure by showing that the measure bears a certain nexus (e.g. necessity, proportionality) to a legitimate policy objective. This interpretation is particularly appropriate where the agreement lacks a general exceptions clause and/or applies 'less favourable treatment' as an obligation to treat all foreign investors equivalent to the 'best' treatment accorded to a domestic investor.

While different solutions may apply to different BITs, it is important that the tribunal interpreting the non-discrimination provision is aware of the existing options and consciously makes a decision as to the appropriate standards; otherwise the result risks being arbitrary. For instance, NAFTA non-discrimination rules in chapters 11 and 12 allow for a 'like circumstances' exception because, on the one hand, the concept refers to the circumstances of both the comparators and the treatment:

> 'each Party shall accord to service providers of another Party treatment no less favorable than that it accords, *in like circumstances*, to its own service providers [investments, investors'.[59]

On the other hand, NAFTA lacks general exceptions for chapter 11 and 12, which are needed to counter balance the very intrusive diagonal standard for the element of 'less favourable treatment'. In comparison, the same result is likely to prevail, for instance, with regard to the former Norwegian model-BIT, where a footnote specifies the applicable standard:[60]

> '1. Each Party shall accord to investors of the other Party and to their investments, treatment no less favourable than the treatment it accords in

[59] The interpretation would presumably be different for a provision stating 'treatment no less favourable than that accorded [~~in like circumstances~~] to like domestic services or service providers *in like circumstances*'; this text was suggested during the GATS negotiations, see above, 5.II.B, n 57.

[60] Norway withdrew its model-BIT in June 2009 (see Investment Treaty News, June 2009, available at www.investmenttreatynews.org/documents/p/158/download.aspx); former draft version available at www.regjeringen.no/upload/NHD/Vedlegg/hoeringer/Utkast%20til%20modellavtale2.doc.

like circumstances[fn 2] to its own investors and their investments, in relation to the establishment, acquisition, expansion, management, conduct, operation and disposal of investments.

[fn 2] The Parties agree/ are of the understanding that a measure applied by a government in pursuance of legitimate policy objectives of public interest such as the protection of public health, safety and the environment, although having a different effect on an investment or investor of another Party, is not inconsistent with national treatment and most favoured nation treatment when justified by showing that it bears a reasonable relationship to rational policies not motivated by preference of domestic over foreign owned investment.'

Finally, it is noteworthy that some BIT non-discrimination obligations entirely lack a comparator clause.[61] To date, it is not settled whether the absence of a comparator clause entails that no less favourable treatment must be granted even across economic sectors,[62] or whether a comparative element should be viewed as inherent to the logic and structure of the non-discrimination principle in international economic law.[63] Considering that the existence of a 'like' comparator is presumed in cases of *de jure* discrimination, the absence of a comparator clause is only – if at all – relevant with regard to *de facto* discriminations as well as the question of an inbuilt exceptions clause.

In this context it is illustrative to point out the notoriously famous interpretation of the 'like situations' concept in the award *Occidental* v. *Ecuador*. In this case, the US oil exporter Occidental claimed that the denial of VAT reimbursements to domestic and foreign oil exporters while granting the reimbursement to domestic and foreign exporters of other

[61] See e.g. Art. 3 of the German model-BIT (1998), reproduced in UNCTAD, 'International Investment Instruments', p. 298; also Switzerland–India BIT (1997), Art. 4.

[62] In this sense Adlung and Molinuevo, 'Bilateralism in Services', 383–84; Stadler, *Liberalisierung des Dienstleistungshandels*, p. 141; Molinuevo, 'International Disputes'; UNCTAD, 'National Treatment', p. 34.

[63] In this sense see e.g. *Nykomb Synergetics* v. *Latvia* [on Art. 10(1) of the Energy Charter Treaty], p. 34: 'in evaluating whether there is discrimination in the sense of the Treaty one should only "compare like with like"'; *Consortium RFCC* v. *Morocco* [on Italy–Morocco BIT (1990)], para. 53; also Newcombe and Paradell, *Law and Practice of Investment Treaties*, p. 160; OECD, The Multilateral Agreement on Investment, Negotiating Group on the Multilateral Agreement on Investment (1998), DAFFE/MAI(98)8/REV1, p. 11: 'National treatment and MFN treatment are comparative terms. Some delegations believed that the terms for national treatment and MFN treatment implicitly provide the comparative context for determining whether a measure discriminates against foreign investors and their investments; they considered that the words "in like circumstances" were unnecessary and open to abuse. Other delegations believed that the comparative context should be spelled out and thus inclusion of the phrase "in like circumstances"'.

> goods constituted a breach of the non-discrimination obligation. The claim was based mainly on the argument that 'in like situations' refers not to companies in the same business sector, but to all companies engaged in exports, even across sectors. The tribunal distinguished 'like situations' from GATT 'like products' and upheld the claimant's argument (paras 168, 173 and 176 ff). In consequence, the oil exporter Occidental was considered 'in like situations' with domestic exporters of flowers, mining and seafood products as well as lumber and bananas (paras 79 and 168).[64]

It is important to emphasize that *Occidental* is about an alleged *de facto* discrimination. While 'likeness' is presumed in cases of *de jure* discrimination, this study submits that the non-discrimination principle in international economic law only prohibits *de facto* differential treatment between competitors. In other words, the existence of a competitive relationship between the foreign and domestic entities – or the two foreign entities in case of MFN – is a necessary condition in cases of *de facto* discrimination.[65] This is true regardless of whether the obligation contains an explicit comparator clause or of how it is phrased. At the same time, this theory does not prevent that legitimate policy objectives are taken into account as justifications on the basis of the comparator clause to the extent that the structure of the provision and the agreement is open to such an interpretation.

In contrast, the *Occidental* tribunal essentially strips all substantive content from the 'likeness' element and, in its result, turns the non-discrimination provision into a non-restriction obligation.[66] The non-restriction principle prohibits trade obstacles even if they apply without distinction between domestic and foreign investors. Hence, a violation may occur even if 'likeness' (and 'less favourable treatment') is not established – or if 'likeness' is found to exist across all economic sectors. Such an extensive interpretation does not seem appropriate for non-discrimination in BITs, even in the absence of a comparator clause. A non-restriction approach

[64] The *Occidental* award has been subject to substantial criticism, see e.g. McLachlan, Shore and Weiniger, *International Investment Arbitration*, p. 252; Newcombe and Paradell, *Law and Practice of Investment Treaties*, pp. 169–70; Franck, 'Occidental v. Ecuador', 679; but see in defense of the tribunal's reasoning DiMascio and Pauwelyn, 'Nondiscrimination in Trade and Investment', 85.

[65] But see Bjorklund, 'National Treatment', p. 39: 'the existence of a competitive relationship between the comparator and the claimant is not essential to a finding of like circumstances, but it helps'.

[66] See Art. 56 TFEU (ex Art. 49 TEC) and respective ECJ jurisprudence, above 3.I.A.2, n 24.

would require that the parties directly incorporate a respective obligation into the agreement.

III 'Likeness' in WTO trade remedies

WTO law on trade remedies allows Members to *unilaterally* adopt import restrictions against foreign products, provided that certain conditions are met. The WTO agreements on trade remedies are rather complex and most technical, reason for which a comprehensive discussion would go beyond the scope of this research.[67] This section is thus limited to an analysis focusing solely on the interpretation and application of the 'like products' element, with the purpose of highlighting similarities and divergences in relation to the non-discrimination principle.

A 'Like products' in trade remedy provisions

The WTO framework provides for three categories of trade remedies, namely anti-dumping (*below*, 1.) and countervailing measures (2.) as well as safeguards (3.). Each area of trade remedies makes use of the 'like products' concept in a similar way.

1. Anti-dumping measures

Article VI:1 and 2 GATT allows Members to impose anti-dumping duties on imported products which are sold on the domestic market below their 'normal value', provided such imports cause injury to a domestic industry. An anti-dumping measure is thus subject to two main requirements, namely 'dumping' and 'injury'. The specific rules governing the implementation of such anti-dumping measures are set out in the Anti-dumping (AD) Agreement, which was concluded at the end of the Tokyo Round in 1979 and slightly revised during the Uruguay Round. The imprecise term 'less than normal value' is legally defined in Article 2.1 AD Agreement (and Article VI:1(a) GATT), which states that a product is being dumped 'if the export price of the product exported from one country to another is less than the comparable price … for the like product when destined for consumption in the exporting country.' At the same time Article 3

[67] On trade remedies law see e.g. Cottier and Oesch, *International Trade Regulation*, pp. 486 ff, 990 ff; Wolfrum, Stoll and Feinäugle (eds.), *WTO – Trade Remedies*; Sykes, 'Trade Remedies'; Macrory, Appleton and Plummer (eds.), *World Trade Organization*, pp. 485 ff, 679 ff, 749 ff; with regard to 'likeness' also Choi, '*Like Products*', pp. 126 ff; Zedalis, '"Like" Product', 94–103.

AD Agreement states that injury is determined by evaluating the dumped products' impact on domestic producers in the light of the products' volume and price effect on domestic like products. Unlike GATT, Article 2.6 AD Agreement provides for a definition of the term 'like product':

> '2.6 Throughout this Agreement the term "like product" ("produit similaire") shall be interpreted to mean a product which is identical, i.e. alike in all respects to the product under consideration, or in the absence of such a product, another product which, although not alike in all respects, has characteristics closely resembling those of the product under consideration.'

The concept of 'like products' is thus fundamental in anti-dumping practice, both for determining 'dumping' and 'injury' as well as other elements such as the scope of the 'domestic industry' and the 'margin of dumping'.[68] The 'like products' analysis begins with the description of the allegedly dumped product under investigation. In a second step, the price of the allegedly dumped product designed for exportation is compared to 'like' products that are sold in the country of origin in order to determine whether there is dumping. In a third step, all domestic products that are 'like' the product under investigation must be identified in order to determine the scope of the domestic industry and to assess injury. Once the respective scope of the foreign 'like' products and the domestic 'like' products is determined, it must remain unchanged during the entire anti-dumping analysis.[69]

2. Countervailing measures and subsidies

When speaking of countervailing measures and subsidies, it is important to clearly distinguish between the situation where a Member takes action against the import of subsidized products (countervailing measures) and the situation where a Member takes action in order to protect its exports from having to compete against subsidized products in a foreign market. Strictly speaking, only countervailing measures form part of trade remedies law (*below*, a.), whereas the latter situation is governed by substantive trade law obligations on subsidies (b.).

a. Countervailing measures Members may unilaterally impose countervailing duties on imported products that are unfairly subsidized by the state of origin. Part V of the SCM Agreement specifies the rules

[68] Bronckers and McNelis, '"Like Product" Definition', p. 349.

[69] Appellate Body Report, *US – Softwood Lumber V*, para. 99; see also Stewart and Mueller, 'Art. 2 ADA', pp. 19 ff.

and procedures that must be followed before levying a countervailing duty. In broad terms, the requirements are again twofold, namely that there is a 'subsidy' in terms of Article 1 SCM Agreement and material 'injury' to the domestic industry. Similar to the AD Agreement, Article 15.1 SCM Agreement provides that 'injury' is determined by evaluating the impact of the subsidized products on domestic producers in the light of the volume and price effect on domestic like products. The concept of 'like products' is thus vital for the assessment of 'injury'. The footnote in Article 15.1 SCM Agreement defines the 'like product' concept as follows:

> '[fn 46] Throughout this Agreement the term "like product" ("produit similaire") shall be interpreted to mean a product which is identical, i.e. alike in all respects to the product under consideration, or in the absence of such a product, another product which, although not alike in all respects, has characteristics closely resembling those of the product under consideration.'

This definition of 'like products' is identical to the one provided in Article 2.6 AD Agreement discussed above.

b. Excursus: substantive rules on subsidies As noted previously, subsidies on the production of goods are subject to the more specific regulations set forth in Article XVI GATT and the SCM Agreement which was negotiated during the Uruguay Round.[70] The SCM Agreement establishes three categories of subsidies, namely prohibited subsidies (part II), actionable subsidies (part III) and non-actionable subsidies (part IV). While subsidies contingent upon export and use of domestic goods are prohibited, subsidies that cause injury or serious prejudice to another Member are merely actionable. The consequences of this distinction are mainly of procedural nature. For purposes of this study, the focus lies on the element of 'serious prejudice',[71] which according to Article 6.3 SCM Agreement requires an analysis of 'like products'. For instance, according to paragraph (a), serious prejudice arises in cases where 'the effect of the subsidy is to displace or impede the imports of a like product of another Member into the market of the subsidizing Member'. The structure and substance of this provision is very different from trade remedies (such as part V on unilateral

[70] See above, 3.I.C.5.

[71] For a discussion of 'injury' see previous sub-section a.

countervailing duties),[72] and resembles the GATT/GATS general national treatment obligations which prohibit 'less favourable treatment' between 'like products'. The main difference relates to the fact that the obligations under part III of the SCM Agreement set out more stringent requirements with regard to the prohibited differential treatment (i.e. existence of a subsidy to a domestic product, effect of such subsidy and causation) than GATT/GATS national treatment. The basic underlying rationale of protecting competitive opportunities, however, remains the same.

In the light of this parallelism, it appears that the same economic interpretation of 'likeness' in GATT and GATS non-discrimination rules should apply to 'like products' under part III of the SCM Agreement. Yet, footnote 46 to Article 15.1 SCM Agreement defines 'like products' 'throughout this agreement' and not only for purposes of trade remedies law under part V.[73] Thus, it appears at first sight that 'like products' under Article 6.3 SCM Agreement is limited to a purely objective interpretation.[74]

> In *Indonesia – Autos*, the EU and US argued that an Indonesian subsidy for the locally produced Timor car caused serious prejudice to 'like' passenger cars imported from the US and EU (para 14.163). Following an extensive analysis of 'like products' in Article 6.3 SCM Agreement, the Panel concluded that certain types of imported cars (Optima, Escort, 306 and Neon) are 'like' the Indonesian Timor (para 14.193).

It is important to highlight the Panel's finding that the term 'characteristics closely resembling' is not limited to an analysis of physical characteristics.[75] Based on this wide interpretation of the term 'characteristics', the Panel rightfully opened the door for including economic considerations

[72] On differences and similarities between part V and parts II & III SCM Agreement see Panel Report, *US – Upland Cotton*, paras. 7.1166 ff; on interpretative consequences, para. 7.1167: 'while they [i.e. rules under part V] may provide contextual – and general conceptual – guidance, the more precise quantitative concepts and methodologies found in Part V of the *SCM Agreement* are not directly applicable in our examination of ... actionable subsidy claims under Part III'.

[73] Panel Report, *Korea – Commercial Vessel*, para. 7.544.

[74] On objective interpretation of 'likeness' see above, 3.II.B.2.

[75] Panel Report, *Indonesia – Autos*, para. 14.173: 'the term "characteristics closely resembling" in its ordinary meaning includes but is not limited to physical characteristics, and we see nothing in the context or object and purpose of the SCM Agreement that would dictate a different conclusion'; for an interesting 'like product' discussion in context of Art. 6.3(c) SCM Agreement see Panel Report, *Korea – Commercial Vessel*, paras. 7.538 ff.

into the analysis.[76] It linked the 'likeness' standard in part III of the SCM Agreement with the economic interpretation developed by the Appellate Body in relation to GATT Article III 'like products':

> 'Although we are required in this dispute to interpret the term "like product" in conformity with the specific definition provided in the SCM Agreement, we believe that useful guidance can nevertheless be derived from prior analysis of "like product" issues under other provisions of the WTO Agreement. Thus, we note the statement of the Appellate Body in *Alcoholic Beverages (1996)* that, in this context as in any other, the issue of "like product" must be considered on a case-by-case basis, that in applying relevant criteria panels can only use their best judgment regarding whether in fact products are like, and that this will always involve an unavoidable element of individual, discretionary judgement.' (para 14.174)

Considering the similarities between the concept of 'likeness' in regard to 'actionable subsidy' and national treatment, as well as its differences in relation to trade remedies where 'like product' is part of the injury analysis, one could even argue that the definition in footnote 46 should be limited to the exercise of injury determination within part V of the SCM Agreement.

3. Safeguards

As a third category of trade remedies, the safeguard mechanism set forth in Article XIX GATT and the Safeguards Agreement (SA) allows Members to restrict market access in order to protect a specific domestic industry from an increase of imports.[77] Safeguards differ from anti-dumping and countervailing measures in that they are directed against legitimate imports and not against unfair trade practices of a foreign private or public entity.[78] Safeguard measures are subject to three general requirements, namely an 'increase' in imports due to 'unforeseen developments', which causes or threatens to cause 'serious injury' to a domestic industry. Article 2.1 SA specifies that the injury must occur to the domestic industry which produces 'like' or 'directly competitive' products in relation to the imported products under scrutiny.

[76] Panel Report, *Indonesia – Autos*, para. 14.173: 'the extent to which products are substitutable may also be determined in substantial part by their physical characteristics. Price differences also may (but will not necessarily) reflect physical differences in products'.

[77] Specific safeguard provisions are found in Article 5 AoA, Article 6 ATC (agreement terminated on 1 January 2005) and Article X GATS (criteria left to future negotiations, see e.g. WPGR, Issues for Future Discussions on Emergency Safeguards, Note by the Secretariat, Revision, S/WPGR/W/27/Rev.1, 7 May 1999).

[78] Diebold and Oesch, 'Durchsetzung von WTO-Recht', 1532.

B A variable interpretation of 'like products' for trade remedies

As outlined above, the element of 'likeness' in non-discrimination is designed to set the scope and boundaries for the protection of competitive opportunities for imported goods and services. In contrast, the element of 'likeness' in trade remedy law primarily serves to assess whether the domestic industry suffers injuries from imported products. While a broad definition of 'likeness' results in a more restrictive application of non-discrimination, the opposite may be the case for trade remedies. In fact, the more products that are included in the analysis, the more difficult it becomes to show injury to the domestic industry.[79]

Despite this difference in objectives and analytical structure, the competitive relationship appears, in principle, to be the appropriate underlying rationale for purposes of both non-discrimination and trade remedies. The domestic industry only suffers injury if demand decreases to a certain degree as a direct result of the dumped or subsidized imports. Hence, products should be viewed as 'like' for purposes of trade remedies if they are viewed as substitutable from a consumer's perspective.[80] Yet, only the SA specifically provides that injury is assessed on the basis of 'directly competitive' products. Both the AD and SCM Agreements seem to define 'like products' as a purely objective concept, providing that the products must be either 'identical' or, in the absence of a domestic identical product, have 'closely resembling characteristics'.[81] Considering that products are rarely ever 'identical', the second standard becomes of more importance.[82] Hence, the *tertium comparationis* are the 'characteristics' of the products for purposes of anti-dumping and countervailing measures.

[79] Bronckers and McNelis, '"Like Product" Definition', p. 350; Vermulst and Waer, *E.C. Anti-Dumping Law*, p. 283.

[80] Sykes, 'Trade Remedies', p. 91: injury test is required to determine the domestic producers who compete with the imports under investigation, which 'is an exercise somewhat akin to (though imperfectly) the task of defining the relevant market in antitrust cases'.

[81] On objective interpretation of 'likeness' see above, 3.II.B.2; see also the similar definitions of 'like products' in US trade remedies law 19 U.S.C. § 1677(10) as well as in the EC Art. 1(4) Anti-dumping Regulation No. 384/96, OJ 1996 L56/1 and Art. 1(5) Anti-subsidy Regulation No. 2026/, OJ 1997 L288/1.

[82] See in general Panel Report, *EC – Salmon (Norway)*, para. 7.56: 'Article 2.6 first refers to whether goods are identical in assessing likeness. Since every article is identical to itself, each such article would have to be considered separately. There would never be occasion to move on to consideration of whether another article has "characteristics closely resembling" it. Thus, a product under consideration could not consist of any grouping of non-identical product categories. This would, in our view, be an absurd result'.

As shown by the Panel in *Indonesia – Autos*, a wide interpretation of this term allows the inclusion of economic considerations.[83]

Importantly, more recent WTO anti-dumping cases show that the 'like products' concept for purposes of injury (and dumping) assessment consists of two aspects that must be clearly separated. Any investigation firstly requires describing the product under scrutiny. In most cases, the investigation is targeted at a whole range of products, such as softwood lumber products, various products of farmed salmon, different types of paper or transformers with different power capacities.[84] The first 'like product' issue thus becomes whether the products under investigation have to be 'like' in terms of the applicable standard.[85] A number of WTO anti-dumping panels decided that this is not the case. Neither Article 2.1 nor Article 2.6 AD Agreement provide any obligation or guidance on how the initial product under investigation should be determined.[86] Hence, following consistent panel jurisprudence, if the investigation is directed against categories of products, there is no requirement that all products of these different categories have to be 'alike' in terms of Article 2.6 AD Agreement.[87] Consequently, even though these products usually have one or more *tertium comparationis*, there is no guarantee that it is

[83] See above, n 76.

[84] Panel Reports, *EC – Salmon (Norway)*; *US – Softwood Lumber V*; *Korea – Certain Paper*; GATT Panel Report, *New Zealand – Finnish Transformers*.

[85] For the identical issue in domestic EC anti-dumping law, e.g. Vermulst and Waer, *E.C. Anti-Dumping Law*, pp. 282–83: 'The definition of the like product is in first instance in the hands of the E.C. industry because it mostly depends on the scope of the complaint'.

[86] Panel Report, *US – Softwood Lumber V*, para. 7.153: 'Article 2.6 therefore defines the basis on which the product to be compared to the "product under consideration" is to be determined, that is, a product which is either identical to the product under consideration, or in the absence of such a product, another product which has characteristics closely resembling those of the product under consideration. As the definition of "like product" implies a comparison with another product, it seems clear to us that the starting point can only be the "other product", being the allegedly dumped product. Therefore, once the product under consideration is defined, the "like product" to the product under consideration has to be determined on the basis of Article 2.6. However, in our analysis of the AD Agreement, we could not find any guidance on the way in which the "product under consideration" should be determined'; confirmed in Panel Report, *EC – Salmon (Norway)*, paras. 7.43, 7.57; see also Panel Report, *Korea – Certain Paper*, paras. 7.219 ff.

[87] Very informative *EC – Salmon (Norway)*, paras. 7.43 ff, in particular para. 7.76 (farmed salmon filleted, fresh, chilled or frozen): 'we do not accept Norway's view that Articles 2.1 and 2.6 must be interpreted to require the EC to have defined the product under consideration to include only products that are all "like"'; also *US – Softwood Lumber V*, paras. 7.139 ff (softwood lumber products, including bed frame components, finger-jointed flangestock, Eastern White Pine and Western Red Cedar).

the competitive relationship; the *tertium comparationis* may also be an objective element, such as identical material (softwood lumber), resource (farmed salmon), end-use (different types of paper or transformers) etc.

Once the initial products are defined, the second 'like product' aspect is to assess whether there is injury to domestic producers of like products. Anti-dumping in addition requires determining whether there is dumping in comparison to like products sold in the country of origin. Considering that the products under investigation are not necessarily in a competitive relationship, it would lead to absurd results if, for purposes of dumping and injury assessment, only products were considered which compete with the products under investigation.

> For instance, in *EC – Salmon (Norway)*, the EU defined 'farmed salmon' as the product under consideration, ranging from 'whole head-on gutted salmon' to fillets. Yet, the EU excluded domestic filleting-only companies for defining the domestic industry. The Panel noted that the domestic industry consists of producers of 'like products'. Since fillets are 'like' the product under consideration identified by the EU, producers of fillets must be considered as part of the domestic industry (paras 7.115, 7.124).

This example illustrates that if the products under investigation are defined by a *tertium comparationis* such as a common resource (farmed salmon), the same *tertium comparationis* must be applied to determine 'like products' and, in consequence, to analyse dumping, domestic industry and injury.[88] Against this background it becomes apparent that the key for the entire 'like product' analysis is the description of the product(s) under investigation. The more abstract the *tertium comparationis*, the broader the product under investigation, the broader the range of 'like products', which in turn affects, *inter alia*, the assessment of dumping, injury and domestic industry.[89]

[88] Similarly Stewart and Mueller, 'Art. 2 ADA', p. 19: 'once the scope of the product under consideration is set, the scope of both the product under consideration as well as the like product must remain consistent'.

[89] See e.g. Panel Report, *EC – Salmon (Norway)*, para. 7.110: 'the like product perforce included the specified "farmed (other than wild) salmon, whether or not filleted, fresh, chilled or frozen". In our view, the plain language of Article 4.1 establishes that the domestic industry in this case was therefore to be defined as producers "as a whole" of *this* product'; and para. 7.620: 'we noted that whether the EC defined the domestic industry in a proper manner may well be decisive in the consideration of other claims in dispute, *i.e.*, subsidiary claims regarding initiation, as well as claims regarding injury and causation'.

In light of the above considerations it becomes apparent that the concept of 'like products' in Articles 2.6 AD Agreement, 15.1 SCM Agreement and 2.1 SA cannot be meaningfully interpreted without defining first the 'likeness' element in relation to the products under consideration. Despite the lack of any guidance on this issue, there must be some limitation as to the possible differences between the products under investigation.[90] During the Doha Round negotiations, the following draft text was developed attempting to close the gap in the AD Agreement:[91]

> 'The term "product under consideration" shall be interpreted to mean the imported product subject to investigation or review. The product under consideration shall be limited to imported products that share the same basic physical characteristics. The existence of differences with respect to factors such as models, types, grades and quality shall not prevent imported products from being part of the same product under consideration if they share the same basic physical characteristics. Whether such differences are so significant as to preclude inclusion of imported products within a single product under consideration shall be determined on the basis of relevant factors, which may include similarity in use, interchangeability, competition in the same market and distribution through the same channels.'[92]

At first sight, the draft Article appears to propose an objective analysis of 'likeness' on the basis of physical characteristics only. However, the last sentence notes that differences in physical characteristics must be evaluated in the light of 'similarity in use, interchangeability, competition in the same market and distribution through the same channels'. Considering that these are all economic factors, the proposed solution is in fact a 'hidden' economic assessment of 'likeness'. Only products competing in the same market may be subject to a single investigation. While the draft text focuses on demand-side factors, it may also be

[90] See e.g. ibid., para. 7.58, where Norway made the example of an investigation against cars and bicycles, noting that 'if products that are not "like" are treated as the product under consideration in a single investigation, a dumping determination cannot reveal whether some or all of those products are dumped'.

[91] With regard to countervailing measures, the products under consideration are determined in that they are subject to a subsidy; the question could still be whether subsidized cars and bicycles are subject to one or two investigations, but such a case is unlikely to arise.

[92] NGR, Draft Consolidated Chair Texts of the AD and SCM Agreements, TN/RL/W/213, 30 November 2007, draft Article 2.6(a) AD Agreement.

appropriate to take into account supply substitutability considerations.[93] In sum, such a test combining physical characteristics with economic factors deserves support,[94] but it is important that the same test extends to the analysis of 'like products' in terms of Articles 2.6 AD Agreement, 15.1 SCM Agreement and 2.1 SA.

[93] On supply substitutability see below, 14.III.B.

[94] It appears that the European Commission applies a similar test when it determines the product concerned and like products in anti-dumping investigations, see e.g. anti-dumping duties on bicycles (Regulation No. 1095/2005), OJ 2005 L183/1, para. 22: 'The investigations confirmed that all types of bicycles as defined above have the same basic physical and technical characteristics. Furthermore, they are sold through similar distribution channels such as specialised retailers, sport chains and mass merchandisers on the Community market. The basic application and use of bicycles being identical, they are largely interchangeable and models from different categories therefore compete with each other. On this basis, it was concluded that all the categories form one single product'; see also compressor and compressor pumps (Regulation No. 261/2008), OJ 2008 L81/1, para. 18; peroxosulphates (Regulation No. 1184/2007), OJ 2007 L265/1, paras. 8 ff; nuts and bolts (Regulation No. 1890/2005), OJ 2005 L302/1, paras. 10 ff; for a discussion of relevant case law see Bronckers and McNelis, '"Like Product" Definition', pp. 352–57; Vermulst and Waer, *E.C. Anti-Dumping Law*, pp. 282 ff; for US trade law see Jackson, Davey and Sykes, *International Economic Relations*, pp. 817 ff.

8

Concluding summary: economic standard

Part II of this book attempted to determine the *tertium comparationis* and the conceptual breadth of 'likeness' in Articles II and XVII GATS. It must be emphasized that this is a very abstract and theoretical exercise, which is not designed to yield a result of different and clearly defined breadths of 'likeness' as suggested by some commentators. *Choi*, for instance, proposes various standards, including 'identical', 'closely similar', 'remotely similar', 'directly competitive or substitutable' and 'indirectly competitive or substitutable'.[1] Such a fine classification of the 'likeness' concept allows consideration to be given to the particularities of the 'likeness' element in the various WTO provisions and thus certainly deserves merit from a doctrinal and systemic point of view. However, it is doubtful whether these classifications are in fact practically feasible, such as to demonstrate convincingly in a specific case why two products are, for instance, 'remotely similar' but not 'closely similar'. Such a finding could only be validly justified if different *factors* underlie the various categories or if different weight is given to the same factors. Otherwise the classifications remain purely theoretical and cannot be applied to a specific set of facts. *Choi* excellently identifies a number of relevant factors, distinguishing between objective characteristics, demand and supply substitutability as well as potential or future competition;[2] however, the exercise to attribute the various factors to the different classifications of 'likeness' proves more difficult. To a certain degree, *Choi* resolves this problem by giving the conceptual classifications of 'likeness' a *procedural* as opposed to a *substantive* effect.[3] In other words, the factors could be the same across all breadth classifications, but the burden of proving specific factors shifts between

[1] Choi, '*Like Products*', pp. 12–21 (figure II.1), 151 (figure III.2); similarly also Goco, '"Likeness", and Market Definition', 335.

[2] Choi, '*Like Products*', *chapter II*.

[3] Ibid., pp. 100–4, 118–20; see also Mavroidis, '"Like Products": Some Thoughts', p. 128, who opines that the distinction between 'like' and 'DCS' '(in a post- exchanges of concessions world) is essentially mandated by procedural concerns (burden and quantum of proof)'.

the parties. He argues, for instance, that in case of narrow 'likeness' in the sense of 'identical', demonstration of the objective factors should create a presumption of 'likeness', which could in turn be rebutted with demand substitutability factors.[4] Even though theoretically interesting, the WTO adjudicating bodies refrain from adopting such a highly nuanced approach with regard to 'like products'.[5] The usual analytical approach is to simply reiterate the four criteria from *Border Tax Adjustments* and apply them to the facts. In doing so, the Appellate Body even consciously omits to make clear-cut findings as to the conceptual breadth of 'likeness' when comparing the different GATT non-discrimination provisions with one another.[6] The reason for this may well be that such a highly nuanced mechanism of 'likeness' would, on the one hand, not be practicable and eventually become too complex. On the other hand, the Appellate Body may want to preserve some flexibility in the 'likeness' analysis, which it would lose by committing to strictly defined degrees of 'likeness'. In addition to the issue of practicability, it is questionable whether an interpretation providing for very highly nuanced classifications of 'likeness' and procedural consequences could still be justified in light of the text of the respective provisions which, after all, only apply the simple terms of 'likeness' or 'directly competitive or substitutable'.

Following these considerations it must be emphasized that the goal of this part II is not to define multiple clear-cut categories for 'like services and service suppliers'. The first issue to be decided in the 'likeness' analysis is the fundamental question of whether 'like services or service suppliers' follows an economic standard, or whether a different approach – such as an objective or even subjective interpretation – is more appropriate. Previous GATT practice shows that an economic standard of 'likeness' is not self-evident. In particular Articles I and III:4 GATT have been frequently interpreted in disregard of economic considerations, which resulted in an objective analysis of 'like products' primarily on the basis of tariff classifications and physical characteristics. Under Article III, two GATT panels suggested a subjective interpretation of 'likeness' and even

[4] Choi, '*Like Products*', p. 119.

[5] See e.g. Panel Report, *Mexico – Taxes on Soft Drinks*, paras. 8.24–36, where the Panel only applied the 'traditional' factors without the procedural presumption/rebuttal system.

[6] See e.g. Appellate Body Report, *EC – Asbestos*, para. 99; similarly Appellate Body Report, *Japan – Alcoholic Beverages II*, p. 26: 'How much broader that category of "directly competitive or substitutable products" may be in a given case is a matter for the panel to determine based on all the relevant facts in that case'.

a Member of the Appellate Body in *EC – Asbestos* rejected an economic interpretation in its concurring opinion.[7]

Against the background of the analyses in part II, this study submits the theory that the element of 'likeness' in both GATS MFN and national treatment is to be interpreted purely on the basis of economic considerations. Article XVII GATS indirectly mandates an economic interpretation of 'likeness' by defining differential treatment as the modification of competitive conditions. Article II GATS lacks a similar definition of 'less favourable treatment'; however, a comparative analysis with Article I GATT shows that there is no justification for a narrow, objective interpretation in the context of GATS where no tariffs apply. Additional arguments for an economic interpretation of 'likeness' can be found in the negotiating history as well as developments in WTO jurisprudence. Moreover, a consistent interpretation of WTO non-discrimination provisions greatly enhances legal certainty, predictability and transparency. Finally, an economic interpretation of 'likeness' must also be placed in context of the applicable standard for 'less favourable treatment' and the existence of a general exceptions clause. As concluded under part I, less favourable treatment is analysed by virtue of an asymmetric impact test, posing a higher hurdle for the complainant than a diagonal test. In consequence, an overly intrusive application of national treatment is prevented by a higher standard of 'less favourable treatment', reason for which it is not necessary to adopt a subjective interpretation of 'likeness' by including the regulatory purpose in the analysis.

Once an economic standard of 'likeness' in GATS is accepted, the question becomes about what degree of breadth should be attributed to 'likeness' which, from an economic perspective, essentially corresponds to the question of degree of competitive relationship. The Appellate Body stated that 'there is a spectrum of degrees of "competitiveness" or "substitutability" of products in the marketplace, and that it is difficult, if not impossible, in the abstract, to indicate precisely where on this spectrum the word "like" in Article III:4 of the GATT 1994 falls'.[8] While the same finding is true with regard to 'likeness' in Articles II and XVII GATS, there are two caveats to the Appellate Body's account. First, it is possible to define 'likeness' of one non-discrimination provision in relation to the same concept as it applies in another provision of the same or another WTO agreement. Second, legal certainty requires using a coherent methodology for the

[7] Para 154.

[8] Appellate Body Report, *EC – Asbestos*, para. 99.

analysis of 'likeness' across different non-discrimination provisions to the extent they apply a similar concept of 'likeness'. While the question of methodology is examined more in detail under part IV, the conclusion of the present part II is that the conceptual breadth of 'likeness' in Articles II and XVII GATS is to be construed broadly. Article III:2 illustrates two different economic categories of 'likeness'. One standard is very narrow, requiring identical or 'perfectly substitutable' products (Article III:2, first sentence, GATT). A second standard based on the notion of 'directly competitive or substitutable' is more broad and focuses on the conditions of a specific marketplace (Article III:2, second sentence, GATT). Chapters 5 and 6 conclude that it is this second marketplace standard that should be applied *mutatis mutandis* to Articles II and XVII GATS.

Finally, the comparative analysis of chapter 7 shows that the form and interpretation of 'likeness' varies between non-discrimination obligations in different fields of international economic law. In particular, the concept of 'like circumstances' in NAFTA non-discrimination is usually interpreted as including both an economic and a subjective standard. The subjective standard can be largely explained by the absence of a meaningful general exceptions clause under chapters 11 and 12 NAFTA. Conversely, 'likeness' in non-discrimination under the TBT and SPS Agreements as well as 'likeness' in WTO trade remedies law also follows an economic standard.

PART III

GATS specific 'likeness' issues

Whereas GATT rules on non-discrimination only apply to products and not to producers, non-discrimination obligations in GATS extend not only to the service itself, but also to the person or entity supplying the service. This particularity gives rise to a number of systemic and interpretative questions which are addressed in part III of the book. Chapter 9 first addresses the issues of why it is necessary in the services trade context to extend non-discrimination obligations to the supplier and how the supplier is defined under GATS. On this basis, chapter 10 identifies the interpretative consequences which the service–supplier correlation entails and determines the different interpretations which can be developed under the GATS 'likeness' analysis of Articles II and XVII. Chapter 11 analyses how different modes of supply and different methods of supply affect the 'likeness' analysis. Finally, chapter 12 summarizes part III and draws the relevant conclusions.

9

The scope of GATS rules on non-discrimination

The GATS negotiating history shows how some Members specifically pointed out that GATT rules on non-discrimination 'had been set up for products, *not for producers (or activities)*, and it was therefore difficult to see how it could be applied to services, the imports of which were not covered by customs duties at the border as was the case with trade in goods'.[1] In spite of these concerns, the principle of non-discrimination has been included in the GATS framework both as MFN and national treatment, with the innovative feature that it applies not only to the service, but also extends to the supplier. This chapter presents a general overview of the various issues arising from the inclusion of service suppliers in GATS rules on non-discrimination. It discusses the different reasons for which non-discrimination in services trade is only effective if it applies to the service and its supplier (*below*, I.), followed by a legal definition of the term 'service supplier' (II.).

I Reasons for including 'suppliers' in GATS rules on non-discrimination

The inseparability between the service and its supplier constitutes the main reason for which the regulation of international trade in services requires the expansion of obligations such that they apply to natural persons and companies.[2] This inseparability entails not only consequences for the way Members regulate services domestically, but also for how services are traded internationally.

In the goods sector, domestic policy objectives are pursued best by adopting regulations which apply directly to the product, for instance ensuring consumer protection by setting minimum technical standards.

[1] GNS, Note on the Meeting of 15–17 September 1987, MTN.GNS/10, 15 October 1987, para. 12 (emphasis added).

[2] Cossy, 'Determining Likeness under GATS', 6; Wyss, *Bankdienstleistungen*, p. 63.

In contrast, the regulation of intangible services proves more difficult. Instead of adopting regulations governing the service itself, it is mostly easier to regulate the supplier instead. For instance, in the area of health and legal services, consumer interests are protected not with regulations as to the minimum standard of the service, but with licence requirements applying to the supplier. With regard to international trade, the inseparability between the service and the supplier frequently requires that the supplier enters the territory of the importing Member in order to supply the service locally. For example, a supplier of construction services concerning the maintenance and repair of a plant can provide the service only on-site.

The need for some suppliers to cross the border in order to internationally trade a particular service, combined with the fact that services regulations frequently apply to the supplier, provides the key for the understanding of why treatment of the 'supplier' is part of the GATS non-discrimination obligation. In fact, by entering the territorial jurisdiction of the consumer's country, the supplier itself – and not only its service – becomes subject to the laws and regulations of the importing Member.[3] Consequently, discrimination occurs not only through measures governing the service, but also through measures applying to the supplier. For instance, a Member could effectively hinder the import of services supplied through modes 3 and 4 by discriminating against the foreign supplier,[4] thereby creating a competitive advantage for domestic suppliers. Supplier-based discrimination is particularly effective regarding service that cannot possibly be supplied through modes 1 and 2, such as construction or repair services. The same reasoning applies *mutatis mutandis* to the MFN treatment of Article II GATS, in that service suppliers originating from two different Members may have to enter the importing country under modes 3 or 4 in order to supply the service on-site. For these reasons, the negotiators in the GNS recognized early the need to take account of the service suppliers. Japan, for instance, submitted the following suggestion:

[3] See also Krajewski, *National Regulation*, p. 103; Nicolaïdis and Trachtman, 'Policed Regulation', p. 253; Wyss, *Bankdienstleistungen*, p. 60; Morrison, 'WTO Dispute Settlement in Services', pp. 385–87; Weiss, 'GATS', 1205: 'The primary objective of national treatment is to prevent discrimination against *foreign service providers* as compared with their national counterparts' (emphasis added).

[4] For example by setting discriminating qualification requirements for foreign suppliers or by simply preventing them from entering into the country.

> 'Given these transactions in trade in services, the national treatment for trade in services could be defined, for example, that imported services, foreign service *enterprises or sellers delivering the service, and agents thereof* shall be accorded treatment no less favourable than that accorded to like domestic services, domestic service enterprises or sellers.'[5]

Similar statements can be found in the meeting protocols:

> 'One participant drew attention to the fact that some services could only be provided with a commercial presence, either for the purpose of commercial facilitation or for the production of the service itself. All such services required a different concept of national treatment to that normally considered within the context of GATT. He suggested that the concept of national treatment in relation to trade in services should *recognize the inseparability between the provider of a service and the service itself.* Since national laws and regulations often limited the competitive position and market access *of the foreign service provider*, it would seem necessary to examine regulatory needs for such limitations and their implications.'[6]

The Montreal Ministerial Declaration of 1988 thus explicitly recognized that the service suppliers must be part of the scope of a national treatment provision in services trade:

> 'When accorded in conformity with other provisions of the multilateral framework, it is understood that national treatment means that the services exports *and/or exporters* of any signatory are accorded in the market of any other signatory, in respect of all laws, regulations and administrative practices, treatment "no less favourable" than that accorded domestic services or services providers in the same market.'[7]

The acknowledgement that service suppliers need to be protected from discriminatory measures already reflected in early drafts of the GATS national treatment clause, which foresaw the inclusion of suppliers in brackets as possible alternatives:

> '[National treatment means that [the services exports of any signatory] [foreign services and foreign service suppliers] that are granted access to

[5] GNS, Communication from Japan, MTN.GNS/W/18, 15 September 1987, para. 2 (emphasis added).

[6] GNS, Note on the Meeting of 15–17 September 1987, MTN.GNS/10, 15 October 1987, para 16.

[7] TNC Meeting at Ministerial Level, Montreal, December 1988, MTN.TNC/7(MIN), 9 December 1988, Part II, para. 7(c) (emphasis added); also TNC, Midterm Review in Montreal on 5–9 December 1988 and in Geneva on 5–8 April 1989, MTN.TNC/11, 21 April 1989, part II para. 7(c); on the 'supplier' in the negotiating history see also Marconini, 'Uruguay Round Negotiations on Services', p. 23.

> the market of any other signatory will be accorded, in respect of all laws, regulations and administrative practices, treatment "no less favourable" than that accorded domestic services [*or service suppliers*] in the same market. ...]'[8]

In contrast, the early MFN draft clause did not refer to services or service suppliers at all, but stated as follows:

> '[MFN means that signatories grant all other signatories [under the same conditions] any advantage granted to another country unilaterally or as a result of trade negotiations. Non-discrimination means that signatories accord to each other treatment no less favourable than that accorded to any country.]'[9]

Assume *arguendo* that GATS had been adopted without including the 'service supplier' in the MFN and national treatment provisions, prohibiting only the discriminatory treatment of 'services'. Under this assumption, the importing Member could simply prevent a foreign supplier from entering into its territory in order to protect like domestic suppliers or to favour like foreign suppliers from another Member. Similarly, the importing Member could impose disadvantageous supply conditions on foreign suppliers, for example requiring mountain guides from certain countries to pass an examination that is more difficult than the examination administered for local mountain guides or those from other Members. Or, finally, the importing Member could favour its domestic suppliers through subsidies, free training and the like. Even though such measures would, without doubt, 'affect' trade in services and thus fall within the *scope of application* of GATS in terms of Article I:1,[10] they would not necessarily constitute a *breach* of MFN or national treatment. In fact, under the assumption that the GATS non-discrimination clauses would only prohibit less favourable treatment of the *service*, differential treatment of the *supplier* would not constitute a breach of MFN or national treatment.[11] This discussion shows that without the explicit mentioning of the supplier, the legal situation would be highly ambiguous, reason for which the drafters of GATS chose

[8] GNS, Report to the Trade Negotiations Committee meeting at Ministerial level, Montreal, December 1988, MTN.GNS/21, 25 November 1988, para. 11 (emphasis added).

[9] Ibid.

[10] According to Art. I:1, GATS 'applies to measures by Members affecting trade in services'.

[11] In comparison, a similar problem could not arise for trade in goods under GATT, considering that the producer is not required to travel into the territory of another Member in order to export its products.

wisely to explicitly mention the suppliers as beneficiaries in Articles II and XVII.[12]

As a comparative excursus, it is interesting to note that there is one exception to the GATT's limitation of non-discrimination to products. In its accession protocol, China specifically agreed to extend its non-discrimination obligations and rights to producers. For instance, China committed to treat 'foreign individuals and enterprises and foreign-funded enterprises … no less favourable than … other individuals and enterprises in respect of (a) the procurement of inputs and goods and services necessary for production and the conditions under which their goods are produced, marketed or sold, in the domestic market and for export'.[13] Similarly, 'all foreign individuals and enterprises, including those not invested or registered in China, shall be accorded treatment no less favourable than that accorded to enterprises in China with respect to the right to trade'.[14] Yet, the accession protocol omits to specify a standard for comparison. It thus remains unclear whether China's obligation relates to 'like' producers, to producers of 'like products', or to producers and products that are in a competitive relationship.

It is also noteworthy that TRIP rules on non-discrimination apply to individuals as holders of the intellectual property right, and not to the right itself. Article 3(1) TRIPs on national treatment states in relevant part that '[e]ach Member shall accord to the *nationals* of other Members treatment no less favourable than that it accords to its own *nationals* with regard to the protection of intellectual property'. Similarly, Article 4(1) TRIPs on MFN treatment provides that '[w]ith regard to the protection of intellectual property, any advantage, favour, privilege or immunity granted by a Member to the *nationals* of any other country shall be accorded immediately and unconditionally to the *nationals* of all other Members'. Article 1(3) TRIPs defines 'nationals of other Members' as 'natural or legal persons'. Yet, the structure of TRIPs non-discrimination rules is different to the one in GATT and GATS in that they lack the 'likeness' element. Consequently, TRIPs non-discrimination does not require a comparison between the 'nationals of other Members' and local entities. All natural and legal persons are deemed equal in their capacity as holders

[12] See Morrison, 'WTO Dispute Settlement in Services', pp. 386–87, who argues that the inclusion of the 'supplier' may have been to ensure 'greater certainty' and to protect the 'choice of modes' for service suppliers.

[13] Ministerial Conference, Accession of the People's Republic of China, Decision of 10 November 2001, WT/L/432, 23 November 2001, para. 3.

[14] Ibid., para. 5.

of intellectual property rights for the purpose of non-discrimination, regardless of whether or not they are in a direct competitive relationship. For this reason, a comparative analysis between TRIPs and GATS rules on non-discrimination is not appropriate.

On a final comparative note, it is interesting to point out that under the NAFTA rules on trade in services, MFN and national treatment only apply to the 'service provider', but not to the 'service' (Articles 1202 and 1203).[15] Arguably, this limited scope entails that non-discrimination does not protect services supplied under modes 1 and 2, considering that measures affecting these modes do not apply to the service provider.[16] In comparison, NAFTA rules on investment protection provide for separate non-discrimination obligations applying to the treatment of 'investments' and the treatment of 'investors' respectively (see paragraphs 1 and 2 of Articles 1102 and 1103).

II Definition of 'service suppliers'

The term 'service supplier' is legally defined in GATS with a rather perplexing system of nested definitions. Article XXVIII(g) states that a '"service supplier" means any person that supplies a service'. This definition has no meaning by itself and must be read in context with Article XXVIII(b), according to which the '"supply of a service" includes the production, distribution, marketing, sale and delivery of a service'. Moreover, according to letter (j) of that same Article, a '"person" means either a natural person or a juridical person', both of which are defined further in letters (k) and (l).[17] Finally, footnote 12 to Article XXVIII(g) clarifies that service suppliers also include forms of commercial presence[18] without legal status of a juridical person, such as branches or representative offices, which are

[15] See above, 7.II.

[16] Wang, 'MFN under GATS', 105.

[17] Art. XXVIII(k): '"natural person of another Member" means a natural person who resides in the territory of that other Member or any other Member, and who under the law of that other Member: (i) is a national of that other Member; or (ii) has the right of permanent residence in that other Member, in the case of a Member which: …'; Art. XXVIII(l): '"juridical person" means any legal entity duly constituted or otherwise organized under applicable law, whether for profit or otherwise, and whether privately-owned or governmentally-owned, including any corporation, trust, partnership, joint venture, sole proprietorship or association'.

[18] Art. XXVIII(d) '"commercial presence" means any type of business or professional establishment, including through (i) the constitution, acquisition or maintenance of a juridical person, or (ii) the creation or maintenance of a branch or a representative office, within the territory of a Member for the purpose of supplying a service'.

not organized as legal entities. Consequently, Members do not have the discretion to exclude certain entities from the scope of GATS by virtue of their national law that may not grant legal personality to certain entities or that may not recognize certain foreign juridical persons, such as trust or associations.[19]

Against the background of these definitions, it becomes apparent that an entity must meet a formal and a substantive requirement to qualify as service supplier in terms of GATS. From a formal perspective, the definition is very broad, such that virtually any entity or person could be a service supplier. The critical question thus becomes whether the entity or person engages in an activity that falls within the legal definition of 'service supply'. The term 'supply' is again circumscribed broadly as 'production, distribution, marketing, sale and delivery'. The final element remaining for defining 'service suppliers' is the term 'service' which, however, is not defined in the entire GATS. With regard to national treatment and market access, the definition of what constitutes a 'service' is found in the positive list of the Members' schedule of commitments. The 1993 Scheduling Guidelines requested Members to use the Secretariat's revised Services Sectoral Classification List[20] and the corresponding CPC description for drawing up their schedule of commitments.[21] Even though these documents do not provide an authoritative interpretation of the substantive scope and content of the commitments, they constitute supplementary means of interpretation in accordance with Article 32 VCLT.[22]

In *EC – Bananas III*, for instance, the EU's commitments on wholesale trade services referred to CPC 622,[23] according to which wholesale

[19] On the notion of service supplier see also Zdouc, '(1999) Dispute Settlement Practice', 324–25.

[20] GNS, Services Sectoral Classification List, Note by the Secretariat, MTN.GNS/W/120, 10 July 1991.

[21] See GNS, Scheduling of Initial Commitments in Trade in Services: Explanatory Note, MTN.GNS/W/164, 3 September 1993, para. 16: 'In general the classification of sectors and sub-sectors should be based on the Secretariat's revised Services Sectoral Classification List. Each sector contained in the Secretariat list is identified by the corresponding Central Product Classification (CPC) number. Where it is necessary to refine further a sectoral classification, this should be done on the basis of the CPC or other internationally recognised classification (e.g. Financial Services Annex). The most recent breakdown of the CPC, including explanatory notes for each sub-sector, is contained in the UN Provisional Central Product Classification' (fns omitted).

[22] Appellate Body Report, *US – Gambling*, para. 197; on the legal status of these documents, see also Leroux, 'GATS Case Law', 759–67.

[23] Referring to the UN product classification version CPCprov, available at http://unstats.un.org/unsd/cr/registry/regcst.asp?Cl=9&Lg=1.

consists of 'selling merchandise to retailers, to industrial, commercial, institutional or other professional business users, or to other wholesalers, or acting as agent or broker'.[24] Moreover, the main activity of 'reselling merchandise' may be accompanied by related subordinated activities, such as maintaining inventories of goods, physically assembling, sorting and grading goods in large lots, breaking bulk and redistribution in smaller lots, refrigeration services or sales promotion services. Such activities are within the scope of wholesale trade service commitments 'when they accompany the reselling of merchandise and are not performed as a separate service in their own right'.[25] Thus, when these activities are performed by individual firms, each one would qualify as a supplier of wholesale services.[26] Additionally, in *EC – Bananas III* the question arose whether vertically integrated companies capable of executing all activities related to wholesaling of bananas could be regarded as 'service suppliers', considering that the activities form part of a production chain, eventually resulting in the sale of bananas as a good. The Panel decided this issue in the affirmative:

> 'Where operators form part of vertically integrated companies, they have the capability and opportunity to enter the wholesale service market. They could at any time decide to re-sell bananas which they have imported or acquired from EC producers, or cleared in customs, or ripened instead of further transferring or processing bananas within an integrated company.'[27]

This ruling has been interpreted and mostly criticized by commentators to signify that trade-restrictive measures may be subject to GATS obligations even if they affect a service that is not actually, but could potentially be supplied by foreign suppliers with the necessary capabilities.[28] As will be argued under section 14.III.B.2.a below, the reach of 'potential suppliers' should be limited to those who can immediately and effectively supply the service in question. In *Canada – Autos*, the Appellate Body attempted to limit the consequences of its previous interpretation on 'potential

[24] Ibid., explanatory note to section 6; Panel Report, *EC – Bananas III*, para. 7.290.

[25] Panel Report, *EC – Bananas III*, para. 7.291.

[26] Ibid., para. 7.320: 'When operators provide wholesale services with respect to bananas which they have imported or acquired for marketing, cleared in customs or ripened, they are actual wholesale service suppliers'.

[27] Ibid.; confirmed in Appellate Body Report, *EC – Bananas III*, paras. 227 f.

[28] See e.g. Zdouc, '(1999) Dispute Settlement Practice', 327; Zdouc, *Comparative Analysis of GATS and GATT*, pp. 133–35; Feinäugle, 'Art. XXVIII GATS', pp. 553–54; Krajewski, *National Regulation*, p. 103; Krajewski and Engelke, 'Art. XVII GATS', p. 406.

suppliers' by adopting a narrow interpretation of the scope of GATS. Pursuant to Article I:1, GATS applies to measures affecting trade in services. The Appellate Body reversed the Panel on the issue of scope, stating that the Panel omitted to satisfactorily analyse how the duty exemptions for certain cars affect the vertically integrated car manufacturers in their capacity as suppliers of distribution services.[29] According to the Appellate Body, GATS only applies if there is trade in services and if the measure affects a person in its capacity as a service supplier.[30]

Consequently, the two findings from *EC – Bananas III* and *Canada – Autos* may lead to a contradictory result. In fact, a 'potential supplier' qualifies as 'service supplier' in terms of Article XVII GATS and thus benefits from national treatment as 'like service supplier' (*EC – Bananas III*), but the measure affecting a 'potential supplier' may fall outside the scope of GATS because it does not 'affect the supply of services' in terms of Article I:2 GATS (*Canada – Autos*). Leaving aside this contradiction, the Appellate Body's findings entail that the 'service supplier' is relevant with regard to three different aspects of the non-discrimination analysis, namely whether (i) the measure is within the scope of GATS by affecting trade in services or a person in its capacity as service supplier; (ii) foreign suppliers engage – possibly potentially – in the supply of this service; and (iii) whether they are 'like' domestic suppliers.

[29] Appellate Body Report, *Canada – Autos*, para. 165.

[30] Zdouc, *Comparative Analysis of GATS and GATT*, pp. 155–56; Smith and Woods, 'Boundary Between Goods and Services', 13 ff.

10

'Likeness' across 'services' and 'suppliers'

Scholars addressing the issue of 'suppliers' in GATS rules on non-discrimination argued that the reference to services and suppliers in GATS MFN treatment does not have any practical significance because 'any treatment of services is also, in effect, a treatment of the suppliers thereof and vice versa'.[1] This denial of practical significance is overly broad for two reasons. First, as demonstrated above, the reference to the supplier is an important precondition in order to ensure equal treatment of suppliers who trade under modes 3 and 4. Second, the argument omits to differentiate between the two elements of the non-discrimination principle, namely 'less favourable treatment' and 'likeness'. In fact, each element is affected differently by the inclusion of the supplier in the non-discrimination obligation. The observation that 'any measure applying to the service applies indirectly to the supplier and vice versa' is only true for the element of 'less favourable treatment'. It essentially means that a complainant only needs to demonstrate 'less favourable treatment' of *either* its service *or* its supplier, as the treatment of one indirectly affects the treatment of the other.

However, prior to the scrutiny of 'less favourable treatment', it is necessary to determine whether 'likeness' exists between the two comparators. In other words, even if a measure treats the supplier and, consequently, the service less favourably, the non-discrimination obligation is only breached if the element of 'likeness' is met. Hence, the practical interpretative relevance of the 'supplier' in the text of GATS rules on non-discrimination relates to the relationship between the service and the supplier with regard to 'likeness', i.e. whether the services, the suppliers, or both need to be alike in order to find a violation of non-discrimination.[2] Consequently,

[1] Abu-Akeel, 'MFN in Service Trade', 109–10.

[2] However, *Abu-Akeel* later presents factors designed to compare services and suppliers, see p. 115: 'the terms can be interpreted by the two parties to have diametrically opposite meanings … Thus, at one extreme, the beneficiary may claim that likeness should only mean that the service be in the same sector or sub-sector and that service suppliers

the 'likeness' analysis may not only require the comparison of 'services', but also of persons or companies as 'service suppliers'.[3]

The text used in the GATS MFN and national treatment clauses allows for different systemic interpretations. Aware of this fact, the Panel in *US – Gambling* submitted to the parties the question whether in their view there is always a need 'to assess likeness for both "services" and "service suppliers" under Article XVII of the GATS'.[4] The diametrically different responses from the parties illustrates the great uncertainty in this regard. The US opined that 'Article XVII requires likeness of both services and service suppliers'.[5] The EU took the exact opposite stance, arguing that 'it is e.g. sufficient, for a violation of Article XVII to occur, that discrimination is made between foreign and domestic services'.[6] Antigua sided with the EU, noting that a different approach would considerably limit the scope of GATS non-discrimination obligations. The opinions voiced by the parties need to be taken with a pinch of salt, as they primarily reflect the parties' respective positions in the dispute rather than a systematic interpretation of the legal text.

> As a respondent, the US was interested in requiring 'likeness' of both services and suppliers, considering that this would have made the case more difficult for the complainant. The complainant Antigua, on the other hand, was interested to argue that it only had to prove 'likeness' between either the services or the suppliers. Given that the case was ultimately decided based on the market access obligation of Article XVI GATS, the Panel exercised judicial economy with regard to Antigua's claim under Article XVII and refrained from adopting an interpretation.[7]

Against the background of this confusion, the present chapter is devoted to an in-depth interpretation of the 'supplier'–'service' correlation as it is

be those authorized/licensed in their home country to supply the service. At the other extreme, the granting State may claim that likeness should extend to all relevant aspects such as the content of the services, their duration, place of delivery, method of supply, capacity of suppliers, scope of their activities and length of their experience'.

3 Morrison, 'WTO Dispute Settlement in Services', p. 385.

4 Panel Report, *US – Gambling*, p. C-44, question 18(a); see also Cossy, 'Determining Likeness under GATS', 8.

5 Panel Report, *US – Gambling*, p. C-45.

6 Ibid.; the answer provided by the EC, however, lacks precision and it appears that it did not sufficiently distinguish between the question of discrimination or 'less favourable treatment' and the question of 'likeness'. As explained above, less favourable treatment between services always affects the suppliers and vice versa; but the question here is whether, in a previous step, 'likeness' must be established between both suppliers and services or only one of the two.

7 Ibid., para. 6.426.

phrased in the GATS non-discrimination provisions, focusing on the following issues: Can 'likeness' of the services and 'likeness' of the suppliers be determined *individually* or does 'likeness' of one automatically entail 'likeness' of the other (*below*, I.)? In case of an individual determination of 'likeness', how do the conditions of 'like services' and 'like suppliers' correlate with one another? In this regard, the text of GATS non-discrimination provisions allows for three different interpretations, namely a cumulative (II.), alternative (III.) and merged test (IV.).

I Are suppliers of 'like' services 'like' suppliers?

A differentiation between 'likeness' of services and 'likeness' of suppliers is only of any practical relevance to the extent that the GATS non-discrimination obligations are interpreted in a way that actually allows to determine 'likeness' individually and separately between the two *services* and between the two *suppliers*. In other words if – in case of a dependent determination – a finding of 'likeness' of the services necessarily entails 'likeness' of the suppliers (or vice versa), then there would be no need to distinguish between the two.

A *Mutually dependent determination in panel jurisprudence*

To date, only *EC – Bananas III*, *Canada – Autos* and *China – Publications and Audiovisual Products* contain rulings on GATS non-discrimination obligations, all of which superficially address the issue of 'like services and service suppliers'. In *US – Gambling* the WTO adjudicating bodies refrained from ruling on the non-discrimination claim for reasons of judicial economy, after having found that the measures violate the GATS market access obligation.

1. EC – Bananas III

The dispute *EC – Bananas III* concerned the EC Council Regulation (EEC) 404/93 on the importation, distribution and sale of bananas, which was challenged by a number of WTO Members, including the US, Ecuador, Guatemala, Honduras and Mexico. Title IV of the regulation distinguished between three categories of imports, namely (i) traditional imports from 12 African, Caribbean, and Pacific (ACP) countries (i.e. bananas *within quantitative limits* established for each ACP country); (ii) non-traditional imports from ACP countries (i.e. imports *above the quantitative limits*); and (iii) imports from third or non-ACP countries.[8] Each of the three categories was subject to individual trade regulations with regard to tariffs, quantitative restrictions and import licences. This rather complex regime for the importation of bananas was challenged by the complainants under GATT, TRIMs and GATS. For the purpose of this analysis, it suffices to outline the import licensing system as the only measure of the regime that was subject to GATS, without going into the very details of the EC Regulation as a whole.[9]

With regard to categories (ii) and (iii), the EC Regulation provided for a 'basic tariff quota' of 2.2 million tonnes in 1995. This quota of 2.2 million tonnes was subject to an import licensing system that allocated licences based on 'operator categories' and 'activity functions'. The operator categories were defined as follows, dividing the operators established in the EC into three categories:[10]

- Category A receiving 65 per cent of the quota: operators who marketed third-country (so called 'dollar' bananas[11]) and/or non-traditional ACP bananas (mainly US multinationals).
- Category B receiving 30 per cent of the quota: operators who marketed EC and/or traditional ACP bananas (mainly European-based companies).
- Category C receiving 3.5 per cent of the quota: operators who started marketing bananas other than EC and/or traditional ACP bananas as from 1992 or thereafter ('newcomer category').

Import licences were distributed to importers among these categories based on quantities of bananas marketed during the latest three-year period for which data were available. Within the operator categories A and B, import licences were allocated to the following economic activity groups:

- Primary importers receiving 57 per cent: this activity includes purchasing or producing green bananas in country of origin, transportation and entry into the EC (mainly US multinationals).
- Secondary importers receiving 15 per cent: this activity includes further supply and release for free circulation and sale of green bananas

8 Panel Report, *EC – Bananas III*, para. III.7.

9 For a comprehensive presentation of the EC banana regime, see Thagesen and Matthews, 'Banana Regime', *passim*.

10 Panel Report, *EC – Bananas III*, para. III.21.

11 Dollar bananas refer to bananas produced by Latin American producers.

within the EU, carrying the commercial risk for the product during the period of legal ownership (mainly European-based transport companies).

– Ripeners receiving 28 per cent: this activity includes ripening of green bananas and sale within the EC (mainly independent companies).

The overall effect of this regime was that the generally more expensive bananas from the EC/ACP were cross-subsidized by the more lucrative dollar bananas.[12] Hence, the complainants argued that the EC regime for the importation, sale and distribution of bananas violates GATS MFN as well as national treatment 'in that it discriminates against distributors of Latin American and non-traditional ACP bananas in favour of distributors of EC and traditional ACP bananas'.[13] According to the complainants, the banana distributors are suppliers of wholesale services and thus subject to GATS. They argue further that Latin American and ACP banana distributors are 'like' distributors of EC and traditional ACP bananas.[14] The Panel followed the complainants' arguments, stating that:

> 'the nature and the characteristics of wholesale transactions as such, as well as of each of the different subordinated services mentioned in the headnote to section 6 of the CPC, are "like" when supplied in connection with wholesale services, irrespective of whether these services are supplied with respect to bananas of EC and traditional ACP origin, on the one hand, or with respect to bananas of third-country or non-traditional ACP origin, on the other. Indeed, it seems that each of the different service activities taken individually is virtually the same and can only be distinguished by referring to the origin of the bananas in respect of which the service activity is being performed. Similarly, in our view, to the extent that entities provide these like services, they are like service suppliers.' (para 7.322, see also para. 7.346)

The Panel firstly established 'likeness' between 'wholesale transactions'. It relied on the nature and characteristics as well as the relevant CPC classification for wholesale and subordinated services. It seems obvious that the origin of the bananas is irrelevant for purposes of the 'likeness' analysis. The Panel then concluded that all entities providing 'like' services – that is wholesale and subordinated services – are 'like' service suppliers. According to this reasoning, the question of 'likeness' of suppliers has no

[12] Thagesen and Matthews, 'Banana Regime', 618.

[13] Panel Report, *EC – Bananas III*, para. 7.274, see also US argument at para. IV.678.

[14] Ibid., para. 7.274.

individual and separate meaning as it is directly dependent on the analysis of 'likeness' of services. In its conclusions, the Panel only referred to 'less favourable treatment' of service *suppliers*, holding that the operator categories and the activity functions create 'less favourable conditions for like service suppliers of Complainants' origin'.[15]

The Appellate Body confirmed the Panel's analysis with regard to the GATS non-discrimination provisions without, however, specifically addressing the issue of 'likeness'.[16] At the same time the Appellate Body rejected the EC's argument that the 'design or effect' of the measures should be taken into account. It specifically pointed out that the GATS non-discrimination provisions do not provide any basis for an 'aim and effects' test.[17]

2. Canada – Autos

In *Canada – Autos*, Japan and the EU challenged Canada's measures allowing a limited number of motor vehicle manufacturers to import vehicles into Canada duty free and to distribute the motor vehicles in Canada at the wholesale and retail distribution levels. The duty exemption was contingent upon three factors, one of which required manufacturers to achieve a certain amount of 'Canadian value added' (CVA) through, for instance, the use of parts produced in Canada, use of Canadian labour or the consumption of services supplied by Canadian enterprises (e.g. repair, engineering, or insurance services). While a large part of the case concerned issues related to GATT and the SCM Agreement, a violation of GATS was claimed by the complainant because the duty exemption and the CVA requirement allegedly affected trade in distribution services of motor vehicles.

a. Import duty exemption and GATS MFN With regard to GATS *MFN treatment*, the complainants argued that the import duty exemption *de facto* grants more-favourable treatment to suppliers of wholesale services from the US, such as Ford Canada, General Motors Canada and Chrysler Canada, than to wholesale service suppliers from other Members, such as Honda Canada and Toyota Canada.[18] With regard to the issue of 'likeness' in Article II, the EU claimed that 'beneficiaries [of

[15] Ibid., paras. 7.341, 7.353, 7.368, 7.380, 7.385.

[16] The Panel's holding regarding 'likeness' between these two groups of wholesale suppliers remained unchallenged by the disputing parties, reason for which the Appellate Body did not rule explicitly on this issue.

[17] Appellate Body Report, *EC – Bananas III*, para. 241.

[18] Panel Report, *Canada – Autos*, paras. 6.834 ff (Japan), 6.855 ff (EC), 10.236 ff (Panel).

the duty exemption] supply the same type of distribution services as the other firms established in Canada which are engaged in the purchase, importation and re-sale of automobiles to local dealers'.[19] Referring to the Panel Report *EC – Bananas III*, Japan alleged that the manufacturers benefiting from the duty exemption and those who do not 'are rendering "like" services "in connection with wholesale trade services", "irrespective of whether these services are supplied with respect to automobiles imported by the Auto Pact Manufacturers [benefiting from duty exemptions] or their related companies on the one hand or with respect to automobiles imported by the Non-Auto Pact Manufacturers [not benefiting from duty exemptions] on the other hand"'.[20]

The Panel, in considering the complainants' arguments and taking note that Canada did not contest 'likeness', found that 'manufacturer beneficiaries and non-manufacturer-beneficiaries provide "like" services and are "like" service suppliers, irrespective of whether their services are supplied with respect to motor vehicles imported by the manufacturer beneficiaries or with respect to motor vehicles imported by non-manufacturer-beneficiaries, and regardless of whether or not they have production facilities in Canada'. The Panel further adopted the same approach as in *EC – Bananas III*, holding that 'to the extent that the service suppliers concerned supply the same services, they should be considered "like" for the purpose of this case'. [21]

Under appeal, the Appellate Body reversed the Panel's finding of an MFN violation. It based its reversal not on substantive grounds, but by pointing out that the Panel failed to properly analyse that the import duty exemption 'affects' trade in services and thus falls within the scope of GATS Articles I and II.[22]

> 'the Panel is confusing the *application* of the import duty exemption to *manufacturers* with its possible *effect* on *wholesalers*. In our view, the Panel has conducted a "goods" analysis of this measure, and has simply extrapolated its analysis of how the import duty exemption affects manufacturers to wholesale trade service suppliers of motor vehicles. The Panel surmised, without analyzing the effect of the measure on wholesalers *as service suppliers*, that the import duty exemption, granted to a limited number of manufacturers, *ipso facto* affects conditions of competition among wholesalers *in their capacity as service suppliers* … In reaching

[19] Ibid., para. 6.860.

[20] Ibid., para. 6.843, quoting Panel Report, *EC – Bananas III*, para. 7.346.

[21] Ibid., para. 10.247 f.

[22] Appellate Body Report, *Canada – Autos*, paras. 170 ff.

its conclusions under Article II:1 of the GATS, the Panel has neither assessed the relevant facts – we see no analysis of any evidence relating to the supply of *wholesale trade services* of motor vehicles – nor has it interpreted Article II of the GATS and applied that interpretation to the facts it found.'[23]

According to the Appellate Body, for a measure to fall under GATS, the Panel would have had to show 'that the measure at issue affects wholesale trade services of motor vehicles, as services, or wholesale trade service suppliers of motor vehicles, in their *capacity as service suppliers*'.[24]

b. Import duty exemption and GATS national treatment Japan also claimed that the import duty exemption violates Article XVII GATS 'in that it constitutes more favourable treatment accorded to Canadian services and service suppliers, which have the right to import vehicles duty free, than to Japanese ones who do not'.[25] The Panel rejected this claim mainly on the basis that Japan could not prove the existence of any 'like' Canadian suppliers of wholesale services. It found that 'there is no clear evidence before the Panel that the Canadian manufacturers of buses and specified commercial vehicles, which benefit from the import duty exemption, also supply wholesale trade services of motor vehicles as defined in the CPC'.[26] Importantly, the issue was not whether Japanese and Canadian service suppliers were alike, but whether Canadian beneficiaries of the measure qualify as suppliers of a service.

c. CVA requirements and GATS national treatment The complainants contended further that the CVA requirement is inconsistent with the GATS obligation on *national treatment*, given that it provides an incentive to manufacturers to obtain services related to the production and repair of motor vehicles from suppliers within Canada. As a consequence, the complainants argued, 'services supplied under mode 1 (cross-border supply) and mode 2 (consumption abroad) by service suppliers of other Members are accorded treatment less favourable than the treatment

[23] Ibid., para. 181.

[24] Ibid., para. 167 (emphasis original).

[25] Panel Report, *Canada – Autos*, para. 10.273.

[26] Ibid., para. 10.289, see also Canadian argument at para. 7.367: 'In any event, there are two fundamental reasons why Intermeccanica is not "like" other suppliers of wholesale trade services for automobiles. In the first place, it is not a supplier of wholesale trade services at all. As the European Communities acknowledged, it is a producer of automobiles. It is not a wholesaler and is irrelevant for the purposes of a GATS analysis. It does not import automobiles for resale or distribute them at all'.

accorded to like services supplied by Canadian service suppliers located in Canada'.[27] Japan, referring again to the Panel Report *EC – Bananas III*, claimed that 'the nature and characteristics of services are "like" irrespective of where they are supplied'.[28] Similarly, the EU pointed out that the 'distinctions drawn by the CVA requirements are based exclusively on the territory where the service is supplied, and not on the nature and characteristics of the services themselves'.[29]

Following the arguments of the complainants and given that Canada did not claim 'unlikeness' of services and suppliers, the Panel found that services supplied locally in Canada and those 'supplied from the territory of other Members through modes 1 and 2 are "like" services'.[30] The CVA requirements in conjunction with the import duty exemption was thus found to be inconsistent with GATS Article XVII. This finding was not subject to the appeal and thus remained unaddressed by the Appellate Body.

3. China – Publications and audiovisual products

In this very recent case, the US claimed, *inter alia*, that China restricted foreign-invested companies in the wholesale-, electronic- and sub-distribution of imported reading materials, electronic publications as well as sound and video recordings. The Panel found that the measures governing the electronic distribution of sound recordings were in conformity with the GATS national treatment obligation, but it also ruled that foreign-invested enterprises and foreign suppliers were prohibited 'from engaging in the wholesale of imported reading materials subject to subscription, while like domestic service suppliers are not similarly prohibited'.[31] These measures thus violated Article XVII GATS.

Concerning the issue of 'likeness' the Panel noted that '[s]ince the United States focuses its claim on the treatment of suppliers rather than services,

[27] Ibid., paras. 6.997, 6.1012 ff (Japan), 6.1041 ff (EC), and 10.291: 'Canadian value-added means the part of the following costs that is reasonably attributable to the production of motor vehicles: (i) the cost of maintenance and repair work executed in Canada on buildings, machinery and equipment used for production purposes; (ii) the cost of engineering services, experimental work and product development work executed in Canada; (iii) administrative and general expenses incurred in Canada. The European Communities notes that CVA also includes (iv) "fire and insurance premiums, in respect of production inventories and the production plant and equipment, paid to a company authorised by federal or provincial law to carry on business in Canada or a province"'.

[28] Ibid., para. 6.1028, referring to Panel Report, *EC – Bananas III*, para. 7.322.

[29] Ibid., para. 6.1054.

[30] Ibid., para. 10.307.

[31] Paras 7.1428–440.

we will likewise centre our analysis on the likeness of the suppliers of the services at issue'.[32] It thus appears that the Panel departed from earlier jurisprudence on the relationship between 'likeness' of services and 'likeness' of suppliers, attributing to the latter its own substantive meaning. However, since the measures under scrutiny differentiated directly and exclusively on the basis of origin, they qualified as *de jure* discrimination. As a result, the Panel did not have to undertake a substantive analysis of 'likeness'. It found that in cases of *de jure* discrimination 'the "like service suppliers" requirement is met, provided there will, or can, be domestic and foreign suppliers that under the measure are the same in all material respects except for origin'.[33] Consequently, the question of whether 'likeness' should be assessed between the suppliers only, the services only or both was irrelevant to the outcome of the analysis, as in any case the existence of a 'like' comparator could be presumed.

B Critical appraisal of the jurisprudence

In all GATS non-discrimination cases, the issue of 'likeness' was not the critical element of the analysis. The decisive questions were whether the measures at stake fell within the scope of GATS, whether the entities subject to the measures qualify as service suppliers in terms of Articles II and XII GATS and, finally, whether there was 'less favourable treatment' of foreign service suppliers. Nonetheless, three interpretative findings were made with regard to 'likeness' in GATS:

- The *EC – Bananas III* and *Canada – Autos* Panels adopted a dependent determination of 'like services' and 'like suppliers' in that they only analysed 'likeness' of the services, inferring from this analysis 'likeness' of the suppliers.[34] The Panel in *China – Publications and Audiovisual Products* appears to depart from this theory, even though its holding needs to be relativized in view of the fact that the measure differentiated directly on the basis of origin.
- The Appellate Body in *EC – Bananas III* explicitly rejected the aim and effects test.
- The Panel in *Canada – Autos* found that services supplied from a foreign country by virtue of modes 1 and 2 can be 'like' services supplied domestically.

[32] Ibid., para. 7.1283.

[33] Ibid., paras. 7.975, 7.1284.

[34] Antigua also used this argumentation in Panel Report, *US – Gambling*, para. 3.151 *in fine*; see also Gkoutzinis, 'Trade in Banking Services', 898–99.

The two last points will be addressed later in this book,[35] but a number of comments must be made with regard to this theory of a mutually dependent determination of 'likeness'. First, it is noteworthy that in both cases the panels as well as the Appellate Body refrained from undertaking a thorough analysis of the 'likeness concept' in the GATS rules on non-discrimination.[36] The scrutiny is by no means comparable to previous GATT practice, where the Appellate Body undertook great efforts to develop a coherent interpretation of the 'like products' concept. The main reason for the absence of a comparable analysis under GATS probably lies in the fact that neither in *EC – Bananas III* nor in *Canada – Autos* did the respondent claim that the services and suppliers at issue are not 'like'. Moreover, in both cases that lead the panels to reject the practical significance of supplier-based distinctions, the measure under scrutiny did in fact not discriminate on the basis of the type of supplier,[37] but on the basis of service-related issues. More specifically, in both proceedings the basis for the differential treatment was the underlying object of the distribution service, namely the origin of the Bananas or the CVA amount of car parts. Similar types of discriminatory bases can be imagined in other services sectors. For instance, differential treatment could occur based on the object of repair with regard to the sector of construction and related services, or on the origin or type of client in the case of professional services.

The stakes of these cases were thus entirely different from, for instance, *Japan – Alcoholic Beverages II*, where 'likeness' was in fact *the* decisive element of the case. Moreover, the regulation in both GATS cases concerned exclusively economic issues; the absence of any regulatory purpose aimed at the protection of non-economic values – such as health, environment and morals – saved the adjudicating bodies from having to analyse in depth the sensitive issue of subjective 'likeness' and the aim and effects test.[38] Yet, it is very likely that future measures subject to GATS dispute settlement will not provide for differential treatment based on the service or its underlying object, but precisely on the basis of the type of supplier.

Second, the panels did not bring forward any interpretative argument in support of their interpretation. In *EC – Bananas III* the Panel simply stated

[35] See below, section 15.II (rejection of aim and effect test in GATS) and chapter 11 ('likeness' across modes of supply).

[36] Eeckhout, 'Constitutional Concepts', p. 232; Zdouc, '(1999) Dispute Settlement Practice', 331.

[37] Davey and Pauwelyn, 'MFN Unconditionality', p. 36.

[38] In *EC – Bananas III*, para. 241, the Appellate Body rejected the aim and effect test for Art. II and XVII GATS without expanding on the issue, see below, chapter 15, n 27.

that 'in our view, to the extent that entities provide these like services, they are like service suppliers'[39] and the *Canada – Autos* Panel justified its interpretation with a mere reference to the previous ruling in *EC – Bananas III*.[40] Considering these circumstances and in particular the absence of an Appellate Body ruling on this issue, the authoritative weight of the panel jurisprudence on the interpretation of 'like suppliers' is very limited.[41]

1. Text and negotiating history

The panel jurisprudence on 'like suppliers' is supported neither by the text of the provision nor by the negotiating history of GATS. The December 1990 draft of the GATS non-discrimination obligations submitted by the GNS to the TNC in 1990 stated as follows:[42]

> Most-Favoured-Nation Treatment
> 'With respect to any measure covered by this Agreement, each Party shall accord immediately and unconditionally to services and service providers of any other Party, treatment no less favourable than that it accords to like services and *providers of like services* of any other country [in like circumstances] [with respect to the same mode of delivery].'
>
> National Treatment
> '1. In conformity with other relevant provisions of this Agreement, and in accordance with the conditions and qualifications set out in its schedule, each Party shall accord to services and service providers of other Parties, in respect of all measures affecting the supply of services, treatment no less favourable than that accorded to like domestic services or *providers of like services*.'

This draft does not use the term 'like suppliers', but instead refers to 'suppliers of like services'. The panel jurisprudence on 'like suppliers' is precisely in line with the December 1990 draft text which, however, was changed in the course of the negotiations. Unfortunately, the negotiating protocols are silent on the reason for this change and it remains unclear whether it occurred simply due to stylistic or due to substantive considerations. In cither case, the difference between the draft and the final provision demonstrates that the panel jurisprudence is not supported by the specific text of Articles II and XVII GATS.[43]

39 Para 7.322, see also para. 7.346.

40 Para 10.248.

41 Similarly Verhoosel, *National Treatment*, pp. 34, 61.

42 TNC, Draft Final Act Embodying the Results of the Uruguay Round of Multilateral Trade Negotiations, MTN.TNC/W/35-3/Rev.1, 3 December 1990, draft Articles II and XVII (emphasis added).

43 See e.g. Krajewski, *National Regulation*, p. 104: 'If only the likeness of the service should be considered, Article XVII would have been worded differently. For example, it could

2. Deficiencies of a mutually dependent determination of 'likeness'

Having established that the panel jurisprudence on 'like suppliers' lacks not only any interpretative arguments but also any support from negotiating history, the next step is to demonstrate that it may in fact be important for WTO adjudicating bodies to distinguish between suppliers in GATS rules on non-discrimination.

a. 'Different' suppliers of like services The main flaw of the dependent interpretation is that it outlaws measures which make a valid distinction between two completely 'different' suppliers, simply because they provide 'like' services in one area. Consequently, Members would be unduly restrained in their regulatory autonomy.[44] For instance, one of the main services provided by banks is the offering of loans. At the same time, many entities completely 'different' from banks may offer loans to their customers. For instance, department stores issue customer cards allowing customers to purchase for credit. Similarly, many stores, car dealers and other sellers offer financing plans for the purchase of their products. It is very likely that domestic regulation provides for different terms for the issuance of credits by banks and other entities, such as capital, advertising and disclosure requirements. To the extent predominantly foreign suppliers are among the disadvantaged group, such measures would constitute a breach of GATS non-discrimination obligations, given that in the logic of the panel a bank and a department store would be 'alike' on the basis that they provide like services. It is argued here that it should be possible to find such measures as GATS compliant, without having to resort to the exceptions of Article XIV GATS.

b. 'Similar' suppliers of like services Moreover, even if different suppliers are more closely related than banks and department stores, there may be valid reasons for Members to treat the suppliers differently. For instance, it may be necessary to distinguish between suppliers for reasons of qualification and experience. The supply of many professional services, such as legal services, are subject to qualification and licensing requirements.[45] Similarly, many professional services are subject to rules

have obliged members to non-discrimination concerning "like services and their suppliers"'; Krajewski and Engelke, 'Art. XVII GATS', p. 408.

[44] Similarly Krajewski, *National Regulation*, p. 104; Verhoosel, *National Treatment*, p. 61; Zdouc, *Comparative Analysis of GATS and GATT*, pp. 163–64.

[45] Chapman and Tauber, 'International Trade in Legal Services', 970: 'Because substantial differences in education, training, and experience requirements exist between lawyers

of conduct and ethics which may require a different standard than the equivalent rules in force in a different country applying to foreign suppliers.[46] Other supplier characteristics that may justify differential regulation relate to the legal form, the size or the financial state of the company.[47] According to the panels' theory, 'likeness' would have to be affirmed in all of the above examples despite the significant differences between the suppliers. This approach ignores the fact that such supplier-related differences may very well affect the competitive relationship between service transactions and must thus be taken into account under the 'likeness' analysis.

c. **Regulation of public services** A particular area where an analysis of 'likeness' between suppliers may potentially become very important concerns the supply of public services. Public services are traditionally subject to different forms of regulations, most of which would be considered discriminatory in terms of GATS. Some public services are dependent on intense infrastructure, such as rail transportation, airport services or the supply of gas, water and electricity. In these cases, countries may create monopolies by designating authorities or a limited number of private or public entities to supply a certain public service. Alternatively, a public interest may supersede the advantages of subjecting the service to the free market economy, prompting a government to subsidize, regulate prices or demand universal distribution of a public service. For instance, it may be necessary to regulate prices for train tickets, postal services or necessities such as water supply in order to ensure the supply of such services in remote areas at affordable prices.[48] Similarly, a government may want to subsidize education and health services in order to guarantee access for all

of different countries, Members might argue that domestic and foreign lawyers do not provide "like services" and should not be considered "like service suppliers"' (emphasis omitted); see also Verhoosel, *National Treatment*, p. 62; Krajewski, *National Regulation*, p. 105: 'It could be argued that a nurse who received a university education is not like a nurse who received "only" a vocational training'.

[46] Nnona, 'Multidisciplinary Practice', 83: 'the issue arises whether legal services provided by domestic U.S. lawyers practicing independently of other professionals in the context of stricter ethical rules and constraints of the legal profession are alike to legal services offered by professionals (be they U.S. or foreign) working collaboratively in the MDP context under manifestly different ethical rules and cultures'.

[47] Bossche, *Law and Policy of WTO*, pp. 340, 394: 'two service suppliers that supply a like service are not necessarily "like service suppliers". Factors such as the size of the companies, their assets, their use of technology and the nature and extent of their expertise must all be taken into account'; Krajewski, *National Regulation*, p. 105.

[48] With regard to water services see Lang, 'GATS and Regulatory Autonomy', 823–24.

social stratums. As a final example, a government may provide favourable conditions to public broadcasting services and film producers to promote audiovisual services reflecting domestic culture and values that may not be sufficiently competitive in a free market. The question thus becomes whether such regulations of 'public services' are subject to the rules and obligations of GATS.

As a general rule, GATS does not apply to measures affecting trade in 'services supplied in the exercise of governmental authority'. This phrase is defined by Article I:3(b)(c) GATS as 'any service which is supplied neither on a commercial basis, nor in competition with one or more service suppliers'. There remains a great amount of uncertainty with regard to the meaning of this definition.[49] Consequently, it is not clear which public services are outside the scope of GATS and which public services may in fact be subject to the GATS obligations. *Krajewski* arrives at the conclusion that 'most services commonly understood as public services are not "supplied in exercise of governmental authority" and are hence not exempt from the sectoral scope of GATS'.[50] To the extent a Member omitted to schedule a specific limitation in its schedule of commitments, the regulations of public services must respect the national treatment obligation. In many cases, such regulations are explicitly designed to provide more-favourable conditions of competition to the domestic supplier and thus regularly meet the element of 'less favourable treatment'. The legality of such regulations thus depends on the element of 'likeness'. Considering that the domestic 'services' benefiting from the regulation would be 'like' the foreign service, the panel jurisprudence implementing a dependent determination results in 'likeness' of the suppliers. Supplier-related characteristics such as public ownership, monopoly supply or supplier-related infrastructure could not be taken into consideration. Consequently, many regulations of public services potentially violate national treatment and would have to be either scheduled under a limitation or justified under Article XIV GATS.

This approach to national treatment potentially interferes considerably with the Members' autonomy to regulate public services. It is submitted that the WTO adjudicating bodies should have the flexibility to consider supplier-related characteristics in the 'likeness' analysis in order to find regulations of public services to be consistent with GATS national treatment.[51]

[49] See e.g. Adlung, 'Public Services and GATS', 462 ff.
[50] Krajewski, 'Public Services and Trade Liberalization', 358.
[51] Ibid., 360–61; Krajewski, *National Regulation*, p. 105.

However, the practical significance of this issue is somewhat mitigated by the fact that Members may be hesitant to actually bring a claim against domestic regulations of public services due to fear of a boomerang effect on their own regulatory system.

d. Method of service supply Another area for which supplier-based distinctions are of crucial importance concerns the issue known under GATT terminology as 'process and production methods' (PPMs). While the legality of PPM-regulations under GATS rules on non-discrimination will be addressed in more detail under chapter 15 below, it is necessary already at this stage to point out how the panel jurisprudence on 'like suppliers' affects the regulation of PPMs.

The types of PPMs commonly mentioned in the trade context concern production standards related to labour regulations, human rights, animal welfare or environmental protection. Domestic measures inhibiting trade in goods for reasons of low PPM-standards in the country of origin are, according to WTO jurisprudence on *Ad* Article III GATT, not subject to GATT national treatment, but must be analysed under the market access obligation of Article XI GATT. The main argument for this so-called product–process doctrine is that GATT national treatment only applies to the product, but not to the producer.[52] Following this line of reasoning, PPM-measures generally relate to the producer and are thus outside the scope of Article III GATT. However, it is questionable whether this rigid interpretation of *Ad* Article III GATT would still be followed by the WTO adjudicating bodies today, considering that it has become largely accepted that many forms of PPM-measures should clearly fall within the scope of GATT national treatment.[53] To the extent that Article III GATT is applicable, the crucial question becomes whether or not PPM-related factors may be considered in the analysis of 'like products'. The prevailing

[52] GATT Panel Reports, *US – Tuna (Mexico [1991])*, unadopted, paras. 5.14 and 5.18; *US – Tuna (EEC [1994])*, unadopted, paras. 5.6 ff, according to which PPM-measures fall outside the scope of Art. III if they do not affect the *product* as such; also Panel Report, *US – Gasoline*, para. 6.11; similarly, in Panel Report, *US – Shrimp*, paras. 7.11 ff, the complainants only raised Art. XI GATT claims in the first place; see also e.g. Charnovitz, 'Environmental "PPMs"', 86 ff; Marceau and Trachtman, 'Domestic Regulations of Goods', 856 ff; Read, 'Interpretation of PPMs', 128–33.

[53] See e.g. Hudec, 'Product-Process Doctrine', p. 198: 'The suggestion that Article III does not apply to ("cover") process-based regulations is just plain wrong'; Howse and Regan, 'Product/Process Distinction', 252: 'process-based measures are within the scope of Article III, and are not remitted to Article XI'; Charnovitz, 'GATT and Environmental Trade Measures', 319–22; Potts, *Legality of PPMs*, pp. 11–12; Puth, *Produkt-Prozess-Doktrin*, pp. 75–76; Cho, *Free Markets and Social Regulation*, pp. 31–32.

understanding is that only characteristics of the products themselves may be considered, thereby generally excluding PPM- or producer-related factors from the determination of 'like products'. In other words, two products may be considered as 'alike' despite differences in the way they have been produced.[54] Consequently, many PPM-measures either violate Article XI or Article III GATT and can only be maintained to the extent they are justifiable under Article XX GATT.

In the context of service transactions, the term 'process and production method' or PPM is not suitable, given that services are neither processed nor produced, but simply supplied. However, this does not mean that a PPM-type problem may not occur in relation to trade in services.[55] The way goods can be produced in an environmentally damaging manner or in violation of basic labour rights, services can be supplied by excessively polluting transport vehicles, energy-wasting infrastructure or in violation with the prohibition of child labour; and as is the case in the goods context, a low standard of service supply methods may grant a competitive advantage to foreign suppliers, while at the same time impairing domestic standards of supply methods. Yet, given the intangible nature of services, it is more appropriate to speak of 'service supply methods' or 'SSM' instead of 'process and production methods'.

Under GATS, foreign suppliers are explicitly stated as direct beneficiaries of non-discrimination. As noted above, this extension of non-discrimination is required because the foreign supplier of services traded by modes 3 and 4 becomes subject to the rules and regulations of the importing Member. The flip side of the coin is, however, that Members must be able to differentiate between suppliers if they are considered 'unlike' without having to resort to the general exceptions of Article XIV GATS.[56] In comparison, there is no need for foreign producers to be direct beneficiaries of GATT non-discrimination obligations, as they are located outside the territory of the importing Member and are thus not subject to the latter's rules and regulations. Consequently, it also makes sense that Members may not, in principle, differentiate between competing products on the basis of different producers without violating national treatment. Such producer or PPM-based discriminations are only allowed to the extent that they are justifiable under the general exceptions of Article XX GATT.

[54] See below, 15.I, n 14 f.

[55] See already Diebold, 'Morals and Order Exceptions', 70.

[56] Implicitly Nicolaïdis and Trachtman, 'Policed Regulation', pp. 252–53.

e. Inseparability of supplier and service The panels' jurisprudence implies that only service-based factors are permitted for the 'likeness' analysis of domestic and foreign service transactions. Measures differentiating between 'unlike' services are GATS consistent, whereas measures differentiating between 'unlike' suppliers of 'like' services are inconsistent with GATS. Consequently, the question of whether a certain factor is related to the service or the supplier becomes crucial in the 'likeness' analysis. In case of the former, the measure is more likely to be in compliance with GATS than in case of the latter. Yet, many characteristics cannot be clearly attributed to either the service or the supplier. For instance, qualification is arguably a characteristic of the supplier, not the service. Under this assumption, a qualification requirement would be differentiating between suppliers of 'like' services and thus violate GATS national treatment. However, the qualification of the supplier directly affects the quality of the service, reason for which it could also be regarded as a characteristic of the service itself. Under this assumption, the qualification requirement would differentiate between 'unlike' services and, consequently, 'unlike' suppliers, reason for which it could not possibly violate GATS national treatment. The impossibility to clearly attribute a certain characteristic to either the supplier or the service shows that the panels' test is impracticable and may yield arbitrary results.

C *Conclusion: individual determination*

A dependent determination of 'likeness' has the main advantage of avoiding the issues (i) of whether GATS rules on non-discrimination contain two distinct obligations – one for services and one for suppliers – and how they interrelate with one another; and (ii) of which supplier-related criteria are relevant for the analysis of 'like suppliers'. The panels chose a simple, pragmatic approach and, for purposes of the two cases, it may even have been sufficient. However, it is certain that sooner or later a case will arise under GATS where a Member differentiates between different types of suppliers. For instance, had the case *US – Gambling* not been decided under Article XVI, the Appellate Body would have had to rule on the question of 'likeness' between suppliers of casino gambling and suppliers of online gambling. The panels' interpretation of 'like suppliers' should thus not be viewed as binding or authoritative for future cases.[57]

[57] The Panel Report *Canada – Autos* specifically limited the reach of a dependent determination to this specific case, para. 10.248: 'to the extent that the service suppliers concerned

On the one hand, as shown by the foregoing analysis, the panels' dependent determination of 'likeness' broadens the scope of non-discrimination and greatly enhances the liberalization of trade in services. On the other hand, the main concern is that this approach may prove overly restrictive of the Members' regulatory autonomy. This concern is reinforced by the fact that, according to the Appellate Body, natural and judicial persons actually and *potentially* supplying a certain service qualify as 'service suppliers' in terms of GATS.[58] *Zdouc* points out that virtually any foreign 'person' may claim the benefits of non-discrimination even if it only potentially supplies a service that is 'like' a domestic service.[59] Against this background it is submitted that GATS rules on non-discrimination should be interpreted such that 'likeness' is assessed individually and separately for the 'services' on the one hand, and for the 'suppliers' on the other hand.[60]

Having established that 'likeness' between the services and the suppliers needs to be assessed individually, the question arises of how the correlation between the two conditions is interpreted. The text of Articles II and XVII GATS allows for three different interpretations, namely that the 'suppliers' and 'services' as the two beneficiaries of non-discrimination can be interpreted as cumulative, alternative or merged conditions with regard to 'likeness' and 'less favourable treatment'.

II Cumulative test: two separate and cumulative elements

A first approach of a textual interpretation is to focus on the connecting term 'and', arguing that 'services' and 'suppliers' constitute two separate elements of the respective provision and that discrimination only occurs if a measure meets both elements cumulatively. In order to assess the effects of this interpretation, it is necessary to carefully distinguish between the two elements of 'less favourable treatment' and 'likeness'.

With regard to the first element, the cumulative test requires – in the case of national treatment – that one and the same measure treats a foreign

supply the same services, they should be considered "like" *for the purpose of this case*' (emphasis added).

58 See above, 9.II, n 27 f.

59 Zdouc, '(1999) Dispute Settlement Practice', 327.

60 Similarly Verhoosel, *National Treatment*, pp. 34, 61; Nicolaïdis and Trachtman, 'Policed Regulation', p. 254; Zdouc, '(1999) Dispute Settlement Practice', 332–34; Krajewski and Engelke, 'Art. XVII GATS', pp. 407–8; also on this issue Mattoo, 'National Treatment in GATS', 133; Cossy, 'Determining Likeness under GATS', 10–12; Davey and Pauwelyn, 'MFN Unconditionality', p. 36.

service *and* a foreign supplier less favourably than a like domestic service *and* a like domestic supplier. Or, in the case of MFN treatment, a service and a supplier originating from country A are both treated less favourably than a like service and a like supplier from country B. In order for the cumulative test to work, it is necessary to assume that a measure which – directly – treats a service less favourably at the same time – indirectly – treats the supplier less favourably, and vice versa; otherwise it would be practically impossible to find a violation of MFN or national treatment as domestic regulations usually only apply directly to either the service or the supplier. Yet, the idea that any less favourable treatment of the service is also a less favourable treatment of the supplier (and vice versa) is well-founded and received support from scholars.[61]

> Assume, for example, two banks located in countries A and B respectively desire to supply exactly the same financial services in country X, but the latter refuses to issue the required licences to the suppliers originating from country B. Even though the measure primarily applies to the suppliers, it treats not only the suppliers but also the services originating from B less favourably.

As this example illustrates, the cumulative test has no practical significance with regard to the element of 'less favourable treatment'. However, a breach of Articles II and XVII GATS not only requires 'less favourable treatment', but presupposes also 'likeness' between the comparators. In consequence, the cumulative test requires determining for each case 'likeness' of *both* the domestic and imported services as well as the domestic and foreign suppliers.[62] Referring to the above example, the MFN obligation would only be violated if 'likeness' could be established not only between the banking services, but also between the banks. If the 'likeness' test leads to the conclusion that either the services or the suppliers are not 'alike', there can consequently be no less favourable treatment and thus no violation of the national treatment or the MFN treatment obligation. Figure 10.1 illustrates the mechanism of the cumulative test.

A cumulative test, requiring 'likeness' of both the services and the suppliers, considerably narrows the scope of national and most-favoured-treatment in GATS. Under this approach, it would be more difficult for a complaining Member to demonstrate discrimination under GATS than

[61] See e.g. Abu-Akeel, 'MFN in Service Trade', 109.

[62] See also Krajewski and Engelke, 'Art. XVII GATS', pp. 408–9, referring in this context to a 'narrow cumulative test'.

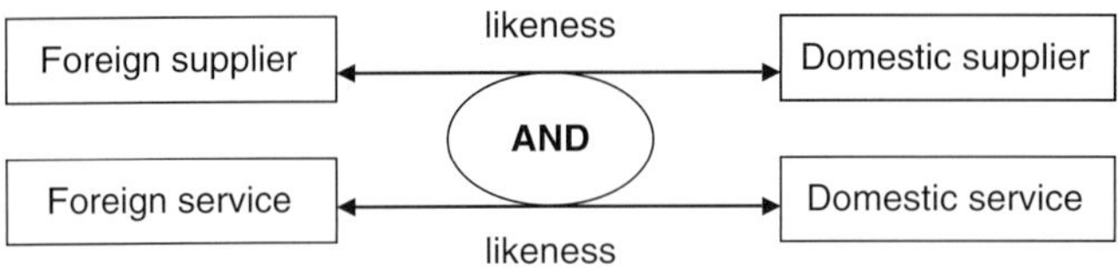

Figure 10.1 Cumulative test

under the respective provisions of GATT. It is highly doubtful whether the cumulative test is in fact in line with the actual intent of the GATS negotiators. As explained in chapter 9 above, the purpose of extending GATS rules on non-discrimination to 'suppliers' was to expand the scope of application in order to meet the particularities of international trade in services. Yet, under the cumulative test, the scope of MFN and national treatment would even be narrower under GATS than under GATT, the latter only requiring 'like products' but not 'like producers'. For these reasons, the cumulative test is contradictory to the object and purpose of the non-discrimination principle in GATS.

In addition, one could argue that a cumulative test is contrary to the language of the GATS non-discrimination provisions. If the negotiators had intended to include the cumulative test, they would have had to use a different wording. For instance, prohibiting less favourable treatment of 'like services supplied by like service suppliers' would have clearly expressed the intent of the GATS negotiators to mandate a cumulative test and to restrict the scope of the GATS non-discrimination obligations.[63]

Finally, it is questionable whether a cumulative test is appropriate for measures affecting modes of supply 1 and 2. Both modes are characterized by the fact that the supplier is located within the territory of a foreign country. Similarly to the producer in the trade in goods context, the foreign supplier cannot be directly subject to the regulation due to lack of jurisdiction. Consequently, mode 1 and 2 suppliers are not direct beneficiaries of GATS national treatment. As specified by the GATS Scheduling Guidelines, 'the national treatment obligation in Article XVII does not require a Member to extend such treatment to a service *supplier* located in the territory of another Member'.[64] Nonetheless, the cumulative test would require separate 'likeness' of the services (e.g. legal advice) and of the suppliers (e.g. lawyer). Even though supplier-related characteristics may be relevant, such

[63] See answer provided by Antigua in Panel Report, *US – Gambling*, p. C-44.

[64] CTS, Guidelines for the Scheduling of Specific Commitments under the General Agreement on Trade in Services (GATS), S/L/92, 28 March 2001, para. 15 (emphasis added).

an approach is not sufficiently flexible to allow for an overall conclusion of 'likeness' in cases where the suppliers differ in a certain way.

III Alternative test: two separate and alternative elements

A second way of interpreting Articles II and XVII GATS is to say that services and suppliers constitute two separate and alternative elements. According to this approach, GATS national treatment is breached already if the measure *either* treats imported services less favourably than like domestic services *or* if it treats foreign suppliers less favourably than like domestic suppliers.[65] Conversely, under the cumulative test a measure only qualifies as discriminatory if it simultaneously treats 'like' services *and* its 'like' suppliers less favourably.

Distinguishing again between the elements of 'less favourable treatment' and 'likeness', it can be noted that with regard to the former, there is no practical difference between the cumulative and the alternative test. As the treatment of either the service or the supplier inevitably affects the other, there is no difference for the complainant if it has to show 'less favourable treatment' of only one (alternative test) or of both (cumulative test). However, concerning the element of 'likeness', the two tests vary considerably:

> Assume a foreign insurance company would like to supply the same services in country A as the local bank A. If country A treats the foreign service less favourably than the 'like' domestic service, the alternative test allows the adjudicating bodies, in principle, to find a violation of the GATS national treatment obligation purely on the basis that the services are 'like' and that the imported service is treated less favourably. In contrast, to the extent the foreign insurance company and the domestic bank are not considered as 'like', the measure adopted by country A would not be in breach with GATS national treatment if a cumulative test is applied.

The mechanism of the alternative test is illustrated in figure, 10.2.

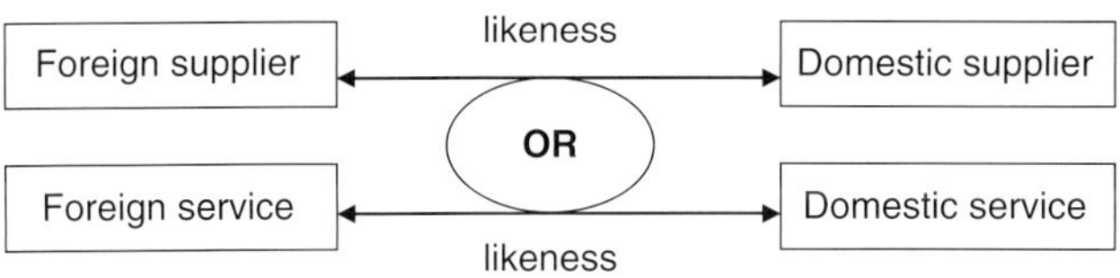

Figure 10.2 Alternative test

[65] This is the approach in NAFTA chapter 11, where the investment and the investor are subject to two different national treatment and MFN obligations, above 7.II.

Against this background it becomes apparent that the alternative test broadens scope of the GATS non-discrimination provisions in comparison to their GATT counterparts. Yet, the question whether such an approach is in line with the actual text of the provision deserves closer attention. In fact, considering that both Articles II and XVII GATS apply the connective term 'and' instead of 'or', a first intuition would be to say that the alternative test is contrary to the actual text of the provisions. Interestingly, earlier drafts of GATS suggest that the negotiators initially considered using the connective term 'or' to determine the relationship between services and suppliers in GATS rules on non-discrimination:

> '[National treatment means that [the services exports of any signatory] [foreign services and foreign service suppliers] that are granted access to the market of any other signatory will be accorded, in respect of all laws, regulations and administrative practices, treatment 'no less favourable' than that accorded domestic services [*or* service suppliers] in the same market. ...]'[66]

Even though the connective term 'and' prevailed in the final text, a close reading of the GATS non-discrimination provisions reveals that the text does not contradict the alternative test. For instance, GATS national treatment provides in relevant part that 'each Member shall accord to services and service suppliers of any other Member ... treatment no less favourable than that it accords to its own like services and service suppliers'. Instead of reading the phrase 'services and service suppliers' as cumulative elements, it is feasible to read that Members bear two distinct and alternative obligations, that is (i) to treat foreign services no less favourably; and (ii) to treat foreign suppliers no less favourably. Indeed, nothing in this provision prescribes that a measure is discriminatory only if it amounts – at the same time – to less favourable treatment of the service *and* its supplier.[67]

Importantly, the GATS non-discrimination clauses would have been inconclusive had the connective term 'and' been replaced with the term 'or'. In this case the obligation would have read that 'each Member shall accord to services *or* service suppliers of any other Member treatment no less favourable than that it accords to its own like services *or* service suppliers'. Such a

[66] GNS, Report to the Trade Negotiations Committee meeting at Ministerial level, Montreal, December 1988, MTN.GNS/21, 25 November 1988, para. 11 (emphasis added).

[67] See also Antigua in the Panel Report, *US – Gambling*, p. C-44: 'Thus Article XVII mandates treatment "no less favourable" for "like services" *and* "like service suppliers", without limiting that obligation to situations in which both the services and the services suppliers are "like"' (emphasis original).

wording would have opened the door to the argument that a Member could actually choose whether it wants to treat services or its suppliers no less favourably, meaning that it could treat foreign suppliers less favourably as long as the services itself are treated equally, or vice versa.

> Under this assumption there would arguably be no breach of the GATS national treatment obligation in case a Member treats all banking services supplied within its territory equally, but discriminates against foreign banks wanting to establish a subsidiary. Obviously, this would have been contrary to the purpose and objective of the national treatment provision.

In contrast to the cumulative test, the alternative test raises an additional interpretative question: Would the WTO adjudicating bodies in a specific case be allowed to scrutinize 'likeness' of both the supplier and the service, finding violation in case only one of the two is 'like' and 'treated less favourably'?[68] Or would the scrutiny of 'likeness' be limited to either the service or the supplier? Previously, commentators referred to these approaches as the 'cumulative' and the 'disjunctive' test.[69] However, in order to avoid confusion with the cumulative test discussed above, the following sections use a different terminology, namely the 'combined' and the 'disjunctive' approach as two sub-categories of the alternative test.

A Combined approach

Under the combined approach, the WTO adjudicating bodies would analyse first whether there is no less favourable treatment between like services and, secondly, whether there is no less favourable treatment between like suppliers. Accordingly, a positive answer to either of the two questions would lead to the conclusion that the GATS non-discrimination obligation has been violated. The analysis would hence be similar to the one under the cumulative test, with the crucial difference, however, that 'likeness' between – and less favourable treatment of – *either* the supplier *or* the service results in a breach of the non-discrimination obligation. In contrast, the cumulative test requires 'less favourable treatment' and 'likeness' between services *and* suppliers for a violation to occur.

[68] The difference to the 'cumulative' interpretation lies in the fact that under the latter 'likeness' and 'less favourable treatment' must exist between both the supplier and the service.

[69] Nicolaïdis and Trachtman, 'Policed Regulation', pp. 253–54; Krajewski, *National Regulation*, pp. 106–7; Krajewski and Engelke, 'Art. XVII GATS', p. 408; compare n 62 above.

The combined approach leads to somewhat unsatisfactory results. Similarly to the mutually dependent analysis of 'likeness' discussed above, a measure could amount to a breach of the non-discrimination obligation if it discriminates between like services, even if the suppliers are unlike, and vice versa.

> Consider, for instance, a measure would require higher qualifications for lawyers than for notary public in order to provide a legal advice or to draft a legal instrument, thereby treating foreign lawyers less favourably as compared to domestic notary public. This measure could arguably not amount to discrimination between the suppliers, given the probable lack of 'likeness' between lawyers and notary publics. However, the measure could still be invalidated because it treats – indirectly – foreign services less favourably than like domestic services. A similar example was proposed by *Nicolaïdis* and *Trachtman* who mention the invalidation of a measure 'that requires a bank to maintain reserves different from those maintained by an insurance company before making a loan' based on the 'likeness' of the services and despite the unlikeness of the suppliers.[70]

The unsatisfactory aspect of these results is that a measure may treat suppliers differently for valid reasons and nonetheless violate the non-discrimination obligation due to the fact that the services are alike. In comparison, under the very narrow scope of the cumulative test, such unsatisfactory results are not possible, considering that 'likeness' and 'less favourable treatment' of solely the service or solely the supplier is not sufficient by itself, but both elements must be met cumulatively. However, even under the alternative test such flawed results can be avoided by applying a disjunctive approach.

B Disjunctive approach and determination of the comparators

The disjunctive approach requires the WTO adjudicating bodies to limit the scrutiny to either the service or the supplier. In other words, if the adjudicating bodies analyse whether there is less favourable treatment between like services, they have no possibility to additionally look at the situation of the suppliers, and vice versa. Accordingly, it suffices that 'likeness' exists either between the foreign and domestic suppliers or between the foreign and domestic services. The main advantage of this approach is that a measure treating 'unlike suppliers' differently for valid reasons could not be invalidated based on the sole fact that they supply like

[70] Nicolaïdis and Trachtman, 'Policed Regulation', p. 254.

services. However, the disjunctive approach raises the difficult question of how it should be determined whether, in a specific case, the services or the suppliers should be subject to the 'likeness' (and 'less favourable treatment') analysis.

1. At the discretion of the complainant

A first application of the disjunctive approach is to say that the complainant may freely decide whether to bring a claim for 'less favourable treatment' of its suppliers or of its services. Depending on how the claim is formulated, 'likeness' would either have to exist between the suppliers or between the services. It appears that this solution was adopted by the Panel in *China – Publications and Audiovisual Products*.[71] However, considering that the complainant is certain to direct its claim against the treatment of its services or the suppliers depending on which of the two is more likely to be 'like' a comparator of the importing Member, the result will not be much different from the 'combined approach' where the WTO adjudicating bodies analyse *ex officio* the treatment of both the service and the supplier.

2. Based on the subject matter of the measure

The most intuitive solution for a determination of the comparators under the disjunctive approach is to look at whether the measure in question applies directly to the supplier or whether it governs the supply of the service. If the measure directly affects the treatment of suppliers, the non-discrimination analysis requires that the foreign and domestic suppliers are 'alike'. Conversely, if the measure directly governs the service, only foreign and domestic services need to be 'alike'. Hence, under this approach it is necessary to determine the regulatory subject or object of the measure, i.e. whether it applies directly to the supplier or directly to the service.[72]

> Referring to the above example, the qualification requirements for lawyers apply to the suppliers and thus only discrimination between the suppliers could be scrutinized.

Yet, such an interpretation is only feasible to the extent the identification of the comparators is indeed possible; in fact, the disjunctive

[71] Para 7.1283: 'Since the United States focuses its claim on the treatment of suppliers rather than services, we will likewise centre our analysis on the likeness of the suppliers of the services at issue'.

[72] This solution has been suggested by a number of commentators, see e.g. Krajewski and Engelke, 'Art. XVII GATS', p. 409: 'If [the measure] applied to services, the likeness

approach would be inconclusive if a measure governing neither the treatment of the supplier nor of the service would fall within the scope of GATS and, more precisely, the scope of either of the two non-discrimination clauses.

a. Measures applying neither to the service nor to the supplier (Mode 2) Article I:2 states a very broad scope of application of GATS, providing that it 'applies to measures by Members affecting trade in services'. Based on this provision, the Panel in *EC – Bananas III* found that 'in principle, no measures are excluded a priori from the scope of the GATS as defined by its provisions. The scope of the GATS encompasses any measure of a Member to the extent it affects the supply of a service regardless of whether such measure directly governs the supply of a service or whether it regulates other matters but nevertheless affects trade in services.'[73] In other words, GATS not only applies to measures governing explicitly the service or the supplier, but to all measures affecting trade in services more generally.

Against this background it becomes apparent that it is very well possible that a measure applying neither to a service nor to its supplier, but nevertheless affecting trade in services, would fall under GATS and, more particularly, would have to be analysed under the MFN or national treatment obligations. For instance, a restriction on mode 2 trade in services would generally have to apply to the consumer, considering that the service is consumed abroad and that the supplier is located outside the jurisdiction of the importing Member.[74]

> Measures could be designed such that the purchase of foreign services results in sanctions or refusal of advantages. For example, a state health insurance could provide that health expenses of the insured are only reimbursed if the medical treatment is obtained domestically. Or, given

of services would have to be demonstrated. Conversely, if it applied to service suppliers, the existence of like service suppliers would have to be established'; Nicolaïdis and Trachtman, 'Policed Regulation', p. 254: 'Laws regulating the service, as such, would only be evaluated to determine whether like services are treated alike, while those regulating the service provider, as such, would only be evaluated to determine whether like service providers are treated alike'; see also Krajewski, *National Regulation*, p. 106; Trachtman, 'Lessons for GATS', p. 63.

73 Panel Report, *EC – Bananas III*, para. 7.285.

74 Mode 2 obligations and commitments for national treatment 'relate to consumers insofar as services or service suppliers of *other* Members are affected', see CTS, Guidelines for the Scheduling of Specific Commitments under the General Agreement on Trade in Services (GATS), S/L/92, 28 March 2001, para. 30 (emphasis added).

that mode 2 includes not only the movement of the consumer but also of property, a tax levied on car repairs abroad would also fall under mode 2 national treatment obligation. Finally, mode 2 services trade could be restricted with measures designed not to recognize foreign permits (e.g. driving permit, paragliding permit) or diplomas in order to prevent own citizens from consuming the respective educational and qualification services abroad.

In such a case, the disjunctive approach is inconclusive as to whether 'likeness' would need to be established between the services or between the suppliers.

b. Measures applying to the supplier (Modes 3 and 4) Trade-restrictive measures applying to the supplier can intervene at two different stages, namely (i) at the stage the supplier enters the importing country or establishes himself on the territory of the importing country; or (ii) at the stage of service supply.[75] In simple terms, the former are aimed at preventing the supplier from *entering or staying* on the territory and the latter try to prevent the supplier from *providing the service* on the territory of the importing country. Measures governing the supplier could not generally affect trade in services by modes 1 and 2, considering that under these modes the foreign supplier is located abroad and thus not subject to the rules and regulations of the importing Member.

Concerning the mode of supply through commercial presence (mode 3), a measure on *entering and establishing* could take the form of more burdensome capital requirements, limitation of foreign capital, allowing only specific legal entities or joint ventures or an outright prohibition for foreign suppliers to set up an office, or any other legal entity. At the stage of *supply*, the restriction could occur, for example, in the refusal of a licence that is required to provide the service or by imposing unfavourable or additional supply conditions.

Measures applying to natural persons (mode 4) with regard to *entering and establishing* could take various trade-restrictive forms, such as the refusal of an entry visa, limitation of duration of stay, imposing inadequate living conditions, unjustified criminal prosecution, and so forth. Yet, pursuant to the 'Annex on Movement of Natural Persons Supplying Services Under the Agreement', measures affecting natural persons seeking access to the employment market as well as measures regarding citizenship, residence or permanent employment are outside the scope of

[75] See also Deardorff and Stern, 'Empirical Analysis of Barriers', pp. 178–79.

GATS mode 4 commitments. With regard to trade-restrictive measures intervening at the stage of *supply*, the possible measures are identical to those applying to legal persons, such as the refusal of an authorization, requiring foreigners to pass an examination that is more difficult than for national citizens in order to obtain a licence, or imposing unfavourable supply conditions to foreign suppliers.

> For example, a foreign nurse could be refused a working permit or a regulation could impose less-favourable working conditions (e.g. more working hours, lower salary, less holiday) for foreign nurses employed by a public hospital compared to national nurses.

In all of these cases, the measure targets the supplier as a person, either with regard to their right to enter the country or their right to supply the service; the service itself, in contrast, is not directly affected by the regulation, but only indirectly. However, there is not always a clear-cut line between measures affecting the right to enter the country and the right to supply the service. For instance, a measure on working permits could be linked with entry visas; depending on the perspective, such a measure could be attributed to either of the two categories. The same is true for a law imposing intolerable working conditions on foreign suppliers, which may result in the foreign supplier not being able to supply the service or having to leave the country.

c. Measures applying to the service (Modes 1, 3 and 4) Measures applying to the service could require a certain standard of the service or proscribe a specific way in which a certain service must be supplied. Such measures could apply to foreign services traded by modes 1, 3 and 4. For instance, a Member may impose that educational services must be supplied in the national language. Such a regulation would at the same time effectively prevent distance learning courses in a foreign language (mode 1), the establishment of international schools (mode 3) as well as foreign suppliers from teaching in that particular country (mode 4).

d. Conclusions: deficiencies of the subject matter approach While a subject matter approach may in most cases allow a selection to be made between the services and the suppliers, a number of situations remain where such an approach is inconclusive. First, some measures subject to GATS non-discrimination disciplines apply neither to the service nor the supplier, making it impossible to select the comparator. Moreover, it may in many cases be arguable whether a measure regulates an aspect of a service transaction which is more directly attributable to the supplier or to the service.[76] Finally, under modes 3 and 4, where the Members have the ability to regulate both the foreign supplier and the foreign service, the distinction becomes arbitrary in that a Member may in some instances circumvent its non-discrimination obligation by shaping the trade obstacle accordingly. This risk for abuse exists in particular for situations where 'unlike' suppliers supply 'like' services, and vice versa. In such cases, a Member could adopt a valid regulation differentiating between unlike foreign and domestic suppliers in order to achieve a competitive advantage for the domestic service over the foreign 'like' service.

3. Based on modes of service supply

Alternatively to the subject matter approach, another possible solution is to say that the comparators are the suppliers in case the service is supplied through modes 3 or 4, whereas 'likeness' needs to exist between the services in the case of modes 1 or 2.[77] As specified by the GATS Scheduling Guidelines, 'the national treatment obligation in Article XVII does not require a Member to extend such treatment to a service *supplier* located in the territory of another Member'.[78] Considering that the suppliers do not benefit from GATS non-discrimination obligations to the extent that they trade services by modes 1 and 2, it is indeed questionable whether their 'likeness' should be of any relevance. Following a mode-based determination of the comparators, mode 1 would always require 'likeness' and 'less favourable treatment' to be analysed with regard to the service, which is essentially the same result as if the comparators are determined on the basis of the regulatory subject. A measure restricting trade in mode 2 service supply would also be assessed on the basis of the services. With regard to mode 2, this solution is preferable over an inconclusive determination of the comparators based on the regulatory subject.

Based on the fact that the specific reference to 'suppliers' had been included in the non-discrimination clauses of GATS so as to protect foreign suppliers supplying within the jurisdiction of the importing Member under modes 3 and 4, the argument is feasible that the focus of differential treatment and 'likeness' lies on the suppliers. In *US – Gambling*, the Panel

[76] See also above, 10.I.B.2.e.

[77] Cossy, 'Determining Likeness under GATS', 10–11.

[78] CTS, Guidelines for the Scheduling of Specific Commitments under the General Agreement on Trade in Services (GATS), S/L/92, 28 March 2001, para. 15 (emphasis added).

contemplated a mode-based determination of the comparators, in that it submitted the following question to the parties:[79]

> 'Is there a difference in the relevance of the "likeness" of service suppliers for modes 1 and 2 as compared to for modes 3 and 4? In other words, should the "likeness" of *service suppliers* as well as the "likeness" of *services* be considered in the case of modes 1 and 2?'

The complainant Antigua seemed to argue that more importance should be attributed to the suppliers in the case of modes 3 and 4:

> 'In modes 3 and 4, arguably the *identity* of the service supplier might be more relevant, given that both modes involve the actual, physical presence of businesses or natural persons located in the territory of the Member. In such circumstances it is perhaps more likely that denial of national treatment may occur on the basis of the identity of the service supplier without regard to the actual services being provided. Further, the actual presence of businesses or natural persons may invoke the many concerns that may arise in that context, such as immigration, use of public resources and services and a host of other issues raised by actual physical presence.'

The EU favouring the 'combined' over the 'disjunctive' approach noted that a differentiation on the basis of modes of supply is moot. Finally, the US as the respondent pointed out that the complainant 'bears the burden of proving likeness of service suppliers regardless of the mode of supply concerned'. This position is in line with the US' support of the cumulative test.

In the case *EC – Bananas III* on wholesale service supply through commercial presence (mode 3), both the Panel and the Appellate Body only referred to differential treatment of the service suppliers. The question of 'like suppliers' was resolved on the basis that they supply 'like services'. The fact that the treatment of the services remained unattended indicates that the mode 1 supply was not an issue of the case, 'since in case of supply across borders (mode 1) only foreign "services" are direct beneficiaries of GATS rights'.[80] However, even though the identity of the supplier may be of particular importance for modes of supply 3 and 4, it seems arbitrary to consider treatment and 'likeness' only of the suppliers. In fact, not only the suppliers, but also the services benefit from non-discrimination if traded under modes 3 and 4.

[79] Panel Report, *US – Gambling*, p. C-44, question 18(b).

[80] Zdouc, '(1999) Dispute Settlement Practice', 324.

4. Conclusion: a combined subject matter and modes of supply approach

The alternative test in combination with a disjunctive approach bears the difficulty to determine whether in a given case 'likeness' should exist between either the suppliers or the services. A selection on the basis of the subject matter of the regulation is unsatisfactory because it is inconclusive with regard to regulations applying neither to the service nor to the supplier, such as measures affecting trade in mode 2. A mode-based selection is insufficient because it allows for no flexibility for a differentiation between services and suppliers traded under modes 3 and 4. In order to reach a feasible solution for the disjunctive approach, it is necessary to combine the two options for selecting the comparators. With regard to modes 1 and 2 it is appropriate to apply a purely mode-based test. Considering that suppliers do not benefit from GATS non-discrimination obligations for services traded under modes 1 and 2, it is safe to say that under a disjunctive approach only the services should be considered. With regard to modes 3 and 4, in contrast, a more nuanced approach is required allowing the WTO adjudicating bodies to either consider direct treatment and 'likeness' of the services *or* the suppliers, depending on how the measure is structured. Yet, the difficulty remains to determine whether a measure applies to the service or the supplier. Moreover, Members could theoretically abuse the possibility to differentiate between 'unlike' suppliers that supply 'like' services, and vice versa.

IV Merged test: one merged element

In addition to the cumulative and the alternative test, the text of the GATS non-discrimination provisions allows for a third reading, which in a way leads to a combination of the previous two interpretations. Instead of separating the service from the supplier in two cumulative or alternative elements, they could be considered as one united element. In fact, the phrase 'each Member shall accord to services and service suppliers of any other Member ... treatment no less favourable than that it accords to its own like services and service suppliers' allows the notion of 'services and service suppliers' to be read *en bloc*. Accordingly, the domestic 'service-supplier' situation is compared against the imported 'service–supplier' situation.

By analysing the effects of this test in relation to the two elements of the non-discrimination principle, it can be noted that, as for the cumulative and the alternative tests, there is no practical significance regarding the element of 'less favourable treatment'. But of all three possible interpretations the merged test takes best into account the inseparability between the supplier and the service and that any measure disturbing trade in services affects both the service and the supplier.

On the side of the 'likeness' element, the merged test requires looking at the supplier/service situation as a whole. Accordingly, the test allows a 'likeness' analysis to be conducted based on factors relating to both the service and the supplier. For instance, in the case of a bank and an insurance company supplying the same service, the adjudicating bodies would have to take into account service-related factors – which support 'likeness' – as well as supplier-based factors – which indicate 'unlikeness'. The next step would be to weigh and balance these factors in light of the measure at stake in order to determine whether the domestic service/supplier situation as a whole is 'like' – or 'unlike' – the foreign service/supplier situation. Figure 10.3 illustrates the test.

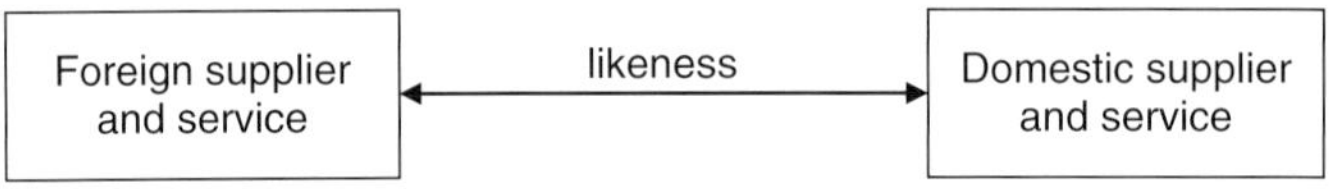

Figure 10.3 Merged test

The merged test entails numerous advantages in contrast to the cumulative and alternative tests. First, unlike the cumulative test, it does not narrow the scope of GATS non-discrimination obligations because there is no need to establish 'likeness' between both the services and the suppliers. Second, in contrast to the combined approach of the alternative test, it allows measures to be upheld that make a supplier-based distinction for valid reasons, even though the suppliers provide like services. In case of the example where a bank and an insurance company supply the same service, the merged test allows more weight to be given to the different suppliers, negating 'likeness' of the supplier/service situation as a whole. Finally, unlike the disjunctive approach of the alternative test, the adjudicating bodies are released from the difficult task to make a choice between the suppliers and the services, given that both can be taken into consideration. The merged test thus takes account of the inseparability between services and suppliers.[81] Yet, even though no explicit choice must be

[81] As suggested by a participant of the Uruguay Round negotiations, 'the concept of national treatment in relation to trade in services should recognize the inseparability between the provider of a service and the service itself', see GNS, Note on the Meeting of 15–17 September 1987, MTN.GNS/10, 15 October 1987, para. 16.

made between the comparators, the Appellate Body and panels must still undertake a weighing and balancing of the service-based against the supplier-based factors in order to determine which ones prevail. Despite – or because of – this discretion, it may be helpful for the adjudicating bodies to have some guidance on the question of whether service- or supplier-related factors should be given more weight. In this regard, the subject matter of the measure as well as the mode of supply discussed under the disjunctive test above indicate whether more consideration should be given to the supplier or the service.

11

'Likeness' across 'methods' and 'modes' of supply

The concept of 'like services and service suppliers' entails specific problems unknown to its GATT 'like product' counterpart. As explained under section 2.I above, services can be supplied by different 'methods' of supply and some GATS obligations only apply in relation to different 'modes' of supply. Failure to clearly distinguish modes from methods in relation to MFN and national treatment leads to confusion and incorrect conclusions, in particular with regard to the analysis of 'likeness'. The two main questions are whether 'likeness' can exist across modes of service supply and/or across methods of service supply. Whereas the MFN cross-mode issue may entail supply by different *methods* and *modes* (*below*, III.), the only crossover issue arising under national treatment obligation concerns the supply by different *methods* (I.). A different issue resulting from a *mode-based fragmentation* of national treatment concerns the fact that certain foreign suppliers may benefit from a national treatment claim even though they use a mode of supply which is not subject to a commitment (II.)

I Cross-method 'likeness' in national treatment

A national treatment analysis is based on the comparison between a foreign service that is supplied under one of the four modes of supply set forth in Article I:2 GATS and a service that is supplied domestically. Modes 1 to 4 define 'trade in services' as including a cross-border element, be it the service, the supplier or the consumer that crosses the border. Domestic services, in contrast, are per definition not traded internationally and thus cannot be supplied through any of the four modes of supply. The Panel in *Canada – Autos* failed to recognize this difference in that it compared domestic services 'supplied through modes 3 and 4' with foreign services supplied through modes 1 and 2.[1]

[1] Para 10.307; also incorrect Antigua's argument in Panel Report, *US – Gambling*, para. 3.150: 'The fact that services of Antiguan gaming operators are supplied via a different

However, even though domestic services cannot be supplied through modes 1 to 4 within the technical meaning of Article I:2, they can nevertheless take a form or method of supply similar to the GATS modes. Foreign mode 3 and 4 suppliers each face a domestic counterpart, namely company suppliers and natural person suppliers. From a consumer's perspective there is generally no difference whether the service is supplied by a foreign-owned or domestic company, or by a foreign or domestic natural person. In contrast, it is more difficult to determine a domestic counterpart with regard to modes 1 and 2. The decisive criteria for these modes are not the characteristics of the supplier, but the supplier's location within the territory of another Member. Since mode 1 is limited to remote supply, it is frequently associated with a particular method of supply. For example, a consumer of a service supplied by mail or telephone will not experience any difference between a domestic and a foreign supplier. The Panel in *US – Gambling* was correct in distinguishing clearly between mode 1 cross-border supply and remote supply of gambling services, the latter referring to 'any situation where the supplier, *whether domestic or foreign*, and the consumer of gambling and betting services are not physically together'.[2]

In sum, even though domestic service suppliers cannot make use of any cross-border supply mode in terms of GATS, there is a potential issue regarding the comparison between a foreign and domestic service supplier using different methods. The term 'method' is used very broadly so as to include characteristics related to the supplier.

A *Natural person suppliers vs. company suppliers*

Largely identical services may be supplied by different suppliers. A domestic supplier may act as an individual (domestic natural person supply) similar to the foreign mode 4 supplier. Likewise, a domestic company (domestic company supply) is in a similar situation to a foreign mode 3 supplier.

"mode of supply" than services of suppliers of United States origin (cross-border as opposed to commercial presence) does not make these "unlike"'; also Commission Staff Working Paper, 'Remote Gambling Services', pp. 70 ff; for a correct approach see Krajewski and Engelke, 'Art. XVII GATS', p. 405; Cossy, 'Determining Likeness under GATS', 14–15.

[2] Para 6.32 (emphasis original).

> For instance, education services may be provided by a domestic school (domestic company supply) or an international school (foreign mode 3 supply) as well as an individual national teacher (domestic natural person supply) or foreign teacher (foreign mode 4 supply).

Many Members are likely to implement a different regulatory framework for natural person suppliers as compared to company suppliers, even though they supply identical services. In other words, domestic companies and mode 3 suppliers are treated the same way, and so are domestic natural person suppliers and mode 4 suppliers. However, a complainant could theoretically argue that its mode 3 suppliers are treated less favourably than domestic natural person suppliers of 'like' services.[3] Considering that origin-neutral differential treatment between natural person and company supply may be perfectly legitimate, the GATS non-discrimination obligation should not strike down such measures unless they are designed or intended to protect the domestic industry in a specific service sector.

B *Domestic suppliers vs. mode 1 and 2 suppliers*

While domestic natural person and company suppliers are comparable to mode 3 and 4 suppliers, there is no domestic analogous counterpart for mode 1 and 2 suppliers. Hence, the problem discussed under the previous sub-section is unlikely to arise in the mode 1 and 2 context. The more basic question here is which domestic suppliers are comparable to mode 1 and 2 suppliers for the purpose of national treatment in the first place.

The situation where domestic suppliers are treated more favourably than foreign mode 1 and 2 suppliers was subject to the case *Canada – Autos*. The Canadian CVA requirement allowed for a duty exemption for the importation of cars contingent upon the consumption of car production-related services within Canada.[4] Hence, the measure created an incentive for car manufacturers to procure certain services within Canada – either from domestic natural person or company suppliers or from foreign mode 3 and 4 suppliers –, to the detriment of foreign mode 1 and 2 suppliers. The question thus arose whether foreign mode 1 and 2 suppliers of services related to car production could be 'like' the services provided by domestic natural person and company suppliers.

[3] This situation is also discussed by Zdouc, *Comparative Analysis of GATS and GATT*, pp. 168–69; Zdouc, '(2004) Dispute Settlement Practice', pp. 401–2.

[4] On this case above, 10.I.A.2.

As a preliminary remark it must be noted that the CVA requirement differentiates on the basis of origin and nationality to the detriment of modes 1 and 2. Consequently, it would not have been necessary to analyse the issue of 'likeness', considering that the existence of a foreign 'like service and supplier' is presumed in the case of *de jure* discrimination. Nonetheless, the Panel addressed the issue as follows:

> '... it is reasonable to consider for the purposes of this case that services supplied in Canada through modes 3 and 4 and those supplied from the territory of other Members through modes 1 and 2 are "like" services. In turn, this leads to the conclusion that the CVA requirements provide an incentive for the beneficiaries of the import duty exemption to use services supplied within the Canadian territory over "like" services supplied in or from the territory of other Members through modes 1 and 2, thus modifying the conditions of competition in favour of services supplied within Canada. Although this requirement does not distinguish between services supplied by service suppliers of Canada and those supplied by service suppliers of other Members present in Canada, it is bound to have a discriminatory effect against services supplied through modes 1 and 2, which are services of other Members.' (para 10.307)

Even though the Panel erroneously referred to '*domestic* mode 3 and 4 suppliers', it is significant to note that it compared foreign mode 1 and 2 suppliers with domestic company and natural person suppliers while not taking into account foreign mode 3 and 4 suppliers. This methodology is more important with regard to 'less favourable treatment' than 'likeness'. In fact, by excluding foreign mode 3 and 4 suppliers which are not negatively affected by the measure from the analysis of 'less favourable treatment', it is easier to conclude that foreign suppliers are, as a group, affected more heavily than the group of all domestic suppliers.

C *On-site supply vs. remote and electronic supply*

Another difficult issue of 'likeness' in GATS arises due to the fact that a service may be supplied either on-site (i.e. the supplier and consumer meet physically) or remotely. This problem has received most attention in the context of e-commerce,[5] for instance if a foreign service supplied

[5] E-Commerce in the WTO context 'is understood to mean the production, distribution, marketing, sale or delivery of goods and services by electronic means', see General Council, Work Programme on Electronic Commerce, WT/L/274, 30 September 1998, para. 1.3.

electronically under mode 1 (or 2) competes with a service supplied on-site domestically.

Recognizing the increasing significance of e-commerce in international trade, the WTO General Council established the Work Programme on Electronic Commerce during the Second Ministerial Conference in 1998.[6] The Work Programme mandated the GATT, GATS and TRIPs Councils to explore all trade-related issues to global e-commerce and to examine how they should be dealt with under the WTO framework. The Council for Trade in Services addressed a number of issues relating to e-commerce and GATS,[7] the results of which are summarized in the e-Commerce Interim and Progress Reports of 1999.[8] Without going into a detailed discussion, this sub-section summarizes the main conclusions with regard to scope and classification issues, as both are relevant for the 'likeness' analysis.

- *Scope*: Most Members agreed that the GATS is technologically neutral and that its obligations apply to services supplied by electronic means.[9] With regard to national treatment and market access, the principle of 'intra-modal technological neutrality' signifies that mode 1 commitments apply to the electronic supply of services.[10] In contrast, GATS does in principle not apply to an electronic order of goods which are delivered physically,[11] unless transportation or internet services constitutes a major part of the transaction. It still remains open whether GATT and/or GATS applies to transactions

[6] Ministerial Conference (Geneva), Declaration on Global Electronic Commerce, WT/MIN(98)/DEC/2, 25 May 1998; confirmed during Ministerial Conference (Doha), Ministerial Declaration, WT/MIN(01)/DEC/1, 20 November 2001, para. 34.

[7] General Council, Work Programme on Electronic Commerce, WT/L/274, 30 September 1998, para. 2.1.

[8] CTS, Work Programme on Electronic Commerce, Interim Report to the General Council, S/C/8, 31 March 1999, and Progress Report to the General Council, S/L/74, 27 July 1999.

[9] Ibid. (Interim Report, para. 4 and Progress Report, para. 4); Panel and Appellate Body Reports, *US – Gambling*.

[10] Interim Report (above n 8), p. 3; recognized in Panel Report, *US – Gambling*, paras. 6.285, 6.355; see on this issue Wunsch-Vincent, 'Trade Rules for the Digital Age', p. 503; Wunsch-Vincent, 'Lessons from US-Gambling', 329–30.

[11] CTG, Work Programme on Electronic Commerce, Information provided to the General Council, G/C/W/158, 26 July 1999, para. 4.2: 'There seemed to be agreement by delegations that goods that were sold or marketed by electronic means, but still delivered physically across borders, would be subject to the existing WTO commitments and provisions related to trade in goods, e.g. customs duties'.

concerning the electronic delivery of digital products, such as software, music and videos.[12]

- *Classification*: Members were unable to come to an agreement on the issue of whether services transmitted electronically should be classified under mode 1 or mode 2.[13] The same issue has received considerable attention in the context of financial services.[14] According to the GATS Scheduling Guidelines, the essential criterion for mode 2 is 'that the service is delivered outside the territory of the Member making the commitment'; this requires that either the consumer or its property moves abroad.[15] In the context of e-commerce, the distinction between modes 1 and 2 appears somewhat artificial. A proper classification may depend less on the service at stake than on the question of whether the measure under scrutiny restricts either the foreign supplier to electronically deliver its service or the consumer to electronically purchase the service – or both.[16] Depending on the answer, the measure is analysed in the light of the respective commitments. In *US – Gambling*, all parties to the dispute and the WTO adjudicating bodies implicitly agreed that mode 1 is applicable.[17]

Having concluded that GATS applies to electronic service transactions, the question thus becomes whether the electronic or remote supply of a service can be 'like' a physically supplied service for purposes of the non-discrimination obligations. In the context of national treatment, an origin-neutral restriction of online service supply – such as prohibiting online gambling, restricting online medical advice or taxing the online purchase of education services – may discriminate against foreign mode 1 or 2 suppliers in comparison to domestic suppliers who are able to physically meet with their consumers. While such measures also affect mode 3 and 4 suppliers,

[12] Progress Report (above n 8), para. 6; for a comprehensive discussion see Wunsch-Vincent, *Trade in Digital Products*, pp. 48 ff; Baker *et al.*, 'E-Products and WTO', 7 ff; Mitchell, 'Towards Compatibility', 703–5.

[13] Progress Report (above n 8), para. 5; see also Weber, 'International E-Trade', 856 ff; Mitchell, 'Towards Compatibility', 690–92; Hoekman and Kostecki, *World Trading System*, p. 265.

[14] CTFS, Indicative Checklist of Issues for Discussion, Note by the Secretariat, S/FIN/W/14, 17 May 1999, Annex I; see also Gkoutzinis, 'Trade in Banking Services', 894; Low and Mattoo, 'Alternative Approaches', p. 452.

[15] CTS, Guidelines for the Scheduling of Specific Commitments under the General Agreement on Trade in Services (GATS), S/L/92, 28 March 2001, paras. 29 f.

[16] Similarly CTS, The Work Programme on Electronic Commerce, Note by the Secretariat, S/C/W/68, 16 November 1998, paras. 7 ff.

[17] Wunsch-Vincent, 'Lessons from US-Gambling', 324–27.

they are less concerned in that they are able to perform on-site supply just as domestic suppliers. Hence, this situation is in essence a variation of the 'domestic suppliers vs. mode 1 and 2 suppliers' analysis in *Canada – Autos* discussed above, with the difference that the methods are defined as foreign modes 1 and 2 electronic and domestic non-electronic supply.

The Work Programme on Electronic Commerce recognized that 'likeness' is the key issue when applying GATS non-discrimination obligations to measures restricting electronic transactions.[18]

> 'Members noted that the issue of likeness is central to the application of MFN and that the main question to be addressed in this regard is whether electronically delivered services and those delivered by other methods should be considered "like services".'[19]

Even though the Members concluded that more work needs to be devoted to this particular issue, there seems to be a tendency that the principle of technological neutrality also applies to the issue of 'likeness'.[20] This view supporting 'likeness' between services supplied by traditional and electronic means received strong support from commentators.[21]

D Legal analysis

Measures evoking cross-method issues must be analysed under the common structure of GATS national treatment, namely the elements of 'likeness', 'less favourable treatment' and justification.

1. Likeness

According to current panel jurisprudence, suppliers which supply 'like' services are 'like suppliers' for purposes of GATS non-discrimination rules. Hence, supplier-related characteristics are not taken into consideration, irrespective of whether 'likeness' is analysed within the *Border Tax*

[18] Progress Report (above n 8), paras. 8, 18; Interim Report (above n 8), *passim*.

[19] Progress Report (above n 8), para. 7.

[20] Interim Report (above n 8), p. 8, also p. 6; CTS, The Work Programme on Electronic Commerce, Note by the Secretariat, S/C/W/68, 16 November 1998, paras. 10, 33.

[21] Wunsch-Vincent, *Trade in Digital Products*, p. 65: 'a positive reaffirmation that the electronic delivery does not change the nature of a particular service or service supplier is warranted'; Wunsch-Vincent, 'Lessons from US-Gambling', 335; also Weber, 'International E-Trade', 860; Leroux, 'GATS Case Law', 780; implicitly Pauletto, 'Digital Trade', p. 531; less pronounced Drake and Nicolaidïs, 'Electronic Commerce and GATS', pp. 420–21; Mitchell, 'Towards Compatibility', 694–95; undecided Zleptnig, 'GATS and Internet', pp. 395–96; but see critically towards cross-method 'likeness' Krajewski and Engelke, 'Art. XVII GATS', p. 406; Krajewski, *National Regulation*, p. 102.

Adjustments or the substitutability framework.[22] Consequently, domestic companies would be 'like' mode 4 suppliers and domestic natural persons would be 'like' mode 3 suppliers. Depending on whether the method of supply is attributed to the service or the supplier, it would also be difficult to find 'unlikeness' between remote and on-site supply or e-commerce and traditional supply. Accordingly, chapter 10 above argues that a differentiation between service and supplier for purposes of 'likeness' analysis is inappropriate. The following discussion of cross-method issues in the light of different 'likeness' theories is thus based on the merged test which requires weighing and balancing supplier- and service-related characteristics.

Both the *subjective* and the *objective* theory of 'likeness' would allow differentiation between services supplied by different methods. A finding of 'unlikeness' under the subjective theory would depend on whether the measure is primarily designed to protect domestic services and suppliers, or whether it is aimed at a legitimate policy objective. The objective theory would allow finding 'unlikeness' on the basis of different supply methods, without the need to further elaborate on the underlying reasoning for which method-related characteristics are relevant in the 'likeness' analysis.

Under the current *Border Tax Adjustments* framework discussed in detail in chapter 13, the four elements of 'properties, nature and quality', 'end-uses', 'consumer tastes and habits' as well as 'classification' each have an independent meaning and are equally important. Hence, even if consumer tastes and habits indicate that the services supplied by different methods are substitutable, the first two criteria of the framework could support a conclusion of 'unlikeness'. The main criticism against this approach is that the analysis will always be implicitly influenced by the objective of the regulation under scrutiny, even though the regulatory purpose is not an explicit element of the framework.

Under the here-favoured *economic interpretation*, the 'likeness' analysis depends on whether consumers view the service supplied by the natural person as substitutable with the service supplied by the company. The differences in method of supply (e.g. natural person vs. company; remote vs. on-site supply) are only relevant if they are perceived by consumers as affecting substitutability. The mere difference by itself is insufficient to conclude 'unlikeness'. Hence, depending on the specific service under scrutiny and the circumstances, there may or may not be a competitive

[22] On these methods see below, chapters 13 and 14.

relationship between a natural person supplier and a company supplier. Similarly, consumers may or may not view physical on-site and electronic remote supply as substitutable.[23] However, many situations would presumably allow the conclusion that the different suppliers and methods of supply are in a competitive relationship and thus 'alike' for purposes of national treatment.[24] This conclusion is best illustrated with a case from US antitrust law pertaining to an alleged monopolization in the advertisement sector:[25]

> The e-mail services provider AOL blocked all unsolicited bulk e-mails with the result that advertising e-mails from GreatDeals.Net could not reach AOL e-mail account holders. GreatDeals.Net claimed that this behaviour violates § 2 Sherman Act, arguing that 'e-mail advertisement' constitutes a distinct relevant market. The court rejected such a narrow market, finding that there are 'numerous substitutes for e-mail advertising, some of which are less expensive, including use of the World Wide Web, direct mail, billboards, television, newspapers, radio, and leaflets'.[26]

2. Less favourable treatment and asymmetric impact test

The affirmation of 'likeness' does by itself not lead to an automatic violation of the national treatment obligation. Under the asymmetric impact test, the complainant needs to show additionally that its suppliers – as a group – are affected more negatively than the group of 'like' domestic suppliers. The impact assessment is rendered more complex in GATS due to the fact that the national treatment obligation is fragmented into four modes of supply which can be subject to individual commitments. The crucial question is whether GATS national treatment indeed protects competitive opportunities of foreign suppliers with respect to each individual mode of supply for which commitments are undertaken;[27] due

[23] See also Leroux, 'GATS Case Law', 780.

[24] Similarly with regard to the term 'competition' in Art. I:3(c) GATS, Zacharias, 'Art. I GATS', p. 67 (albeit referring to 'modes' instead of 'methods'); also in favour of cross-method 'likeness' Zdouc, 'Streitigkeiten über den Dienstleistungsverkehr', p. 134; but see Krajewski and Engelke, 'Art. XVII GATS', pp. 405–6: 'there is usually no full competitive relationship between services supplied through different means of supply because they may have different end-uses. Therefore, services supplied through different methods of supply should generally be considered unlike'.

[25] On market definition in competition law see below, chapter 14.

[26] *America Online* v. *GreatDeals.Net*, 49 F Supp 2d 851 (E.D.Va. 1999), p. 858.

[27] See e.g. Weiss, 'GATS', 1206: '[n]ational treatment … means treating all service providers – *in a given* sector and *mode of supply* – located within the territory of a Member in a non-discriminatory manner, irrespective of their nationality or ownership' (emphasis added).

to the fact that domestic services are not supplied under any of the four modes, a mode-specific national treatment obligation would be difficult to implement for lack of a criterion to define the domestic comparators. Alternatively, GATS national treatment can be interpreted such that it protects only competitive opportunities of all foreign suppliers as a group, irrespective of the mode of supply. The relevant issues can be illustrated as follows: The asymmetric impact test requires comparing a group of foreign services and suppliers (foreign comparators) with a group of 'like' domestic services and suppliers (domestic comparators). Each group is individually defined by a *tertium comparationis*.

- *Group of foreign comparators*: The group of foreign comparators can be limited to competing suppliers and services within the specific modes which are affected by the measure under scrutiny. Alternatively, the group could even be narrowed down to suppliers which use a certain method within a mode of supply. In contrast, the group could consist of all competing suppliers under all modes for which commitments are undertaken or even suppliers under all four modes regardless of commitments.

  For instance, assume a Member with full commitments for education services under modes 1–3 and none for mode 4 adopts an origin-neutral tax for online language courses; assume further that distance learning competes both with language schools in the exporting country (mode 2) and the importing country (mode 3). If national treatment is designed to protect the competitive opportunities of mode 1 suppliers individually, then the group of the foreign comparators would consist only of mode 1 suppliers. National treatment could even be narrowed down to the specific method, such that only mode 1 suppliers using electronic supply form part of the group of comparators. In contrast, if national treatment protects competitive opportunities of foreign suppliers of language courses as a whole, then all mode 1–3 suppliers would be part of the group of comparators for purposes of the asymmetric impact test.

- *Group of domestic comparators*: While the group of domestic comparators cannot be defined by modes of supply, it would be possible to narrow the group to either natural persons or companies in case of measures affecting modes 3 or 4. In case the measure affects a certain method of supply, the group of domestic comparators could be defined as competing suppliers using that same method.

  Using the same example, the group of domestic comparators can consist of all competing domestic suppliers of language courses. Alternatively, the group could be defined as including suppliers of distance learning or only suppliers of distance learning using the method of electronic supply.

Against this background it becomes apparent that depending on how narrowly or widely the respective groups are defined, the easier or the more difficult it is to find an asymmetric impact. While GATS national treatment specifies that the criterion linking the two groups is 'likeness' (i.e. defined here as competitive relationship), it is silent with regard to the criteria that should be used to define the respective groups (e.g. competitive relationship, mode of supply, method of supply, natural person or company etc).[28] Theoretically, it would even be possible to define the respective groups by a different *tertium comparationis*. For instance, if the foreign group consists only of suppliers using the mode that is affected by the measure (e.g. mode 1 language course suppliers), then there will almost always be an asymmetric impact if the domestic comparative group consists of all competing services and suppliers (e.g. language schools, language teachers, distance learning suppliers).

> This seems to be the approach taken by the Panel in *Canada – Autos*. Here the Panel limited the group of foreign comparators to mode 1 and 2 suppliers which were affected by the measure; at the same time it excluded mode 3 and 4 suppliers which were not treated less favourably. Under this approach, an asymmetric impact on foreign suppliers is inevitable if the domestic group consists of all competitors.

In contrast, if both the foreign and domestic groups are limited to a specific method, then there is basically never an asymmetric impact on the foreign group.

> This would be the case if foreign suppliers of electronic language courses were compared to domestic suppliers of electronic language courses; obviously, they are equally affected.

As both of these approaches are not satisfying, this study suggests that GATS national treatment must be interpreted such that it protects the competitive opportunities of *all* foreign services and suppliers – regardless of the respective mode or method of supply – which as a group compete with *all* domestic services and suppliers. Such an interpretation does not contradict the text of GATS national treatment. Article XVII:1 GATS states that the national treatment obligation is subject to the schedules, commitments and limitations, but it does not stipulate that the obligation applies to each mode of supply individually.

Hence, under the proposed method the group of foreign comparators is defined by all competing services and suppliers using modes of supply

[28] This method is similar to the analysis of injury in trade remedies law, see above, 7.III.

for which the respondent has undertaken commitments and which are technically feasible. In some circumstances it would make sense to include services and suppliers of a mode for which no commitments are scheduled. In fact, the absence of a commitment does not necessarily entail that foreign suppliers are actually unable to trade and compete under this mode; it simply means that Members retain the right to adopt discriminatory measures with respect to the specific mode. Depending on whether foreign suppliers and services have the actual ability to compete under a non-committed mode, they need to be added to the group of foreign comparators. In comparison, the group of domestic comparators consists of all competing services and suppliers, regardless of any method of supply or legal personality.

The main advantage of the proposed method is that the criterion of competitive relationship is used consistently to define the respective group of comparators as well as the element of 'likeness' used to compare the two groups. Most importantly, this method reflects the true objective of GATS national treatment, which is to protect competitive opportunities. In other words, an origin-neutral measure restricting a particular method of supply (e.g. electronic supply) – which in turn leads to a restriction of a particular mode of supply (e.g. mode 1) – only breaches national treatment if the foreign suppliers are unable to resort to other modes of supply. At the same time, such a method prevents that breaches of national treatment are constructed by defining a narrow group of foreign comparators and comparing it to a broad group of domestic comparators.

> For example, the suggested method would not allow comparing only foreign mode 1 suppliers using electronic means with all competing domestic suppliers. Similarly, it is not possible to simply compare foreign mode 3 suppliers with domestic natural person suppliers (above, 11.I.A). Such a measure differentiating between natural person suppliers and competing company suppliers only violates national treatment if mode 4 and 3 suppliers (possibly also mode 1 and 2 suppliers) are – as a group – affected more heavily than domestic suppliers. Finally, no national treatment violation occurs if there is no competitive relationship between the comparators (e.g. if natural person suppliers do not compete with company suppliers; if electronic supply does not compete with on-site supply etc).

Moreover, composing the group of comparators with foreign suppliers and services using modes that are affected by the measure and those using modes that are unaffected does not undermine mode-specific commitments. If, from the perspective of the regulating Member, its measure affects a mode of supply for which no commitment is scheduled, then no issue of national treatment arises in the first place.

> For instance, there is no national treatment violation if a Member restricts modes 3 and 4 which are not subject to commitments, even if full commitments are scheduled under modes 1 and 2.

Conversely, from the perspective of the exporting Member, a commitment does *not* grant a right to non-restriction which would prohibit unnecessary trade obstacles;[29] in other words, a Member may still restrict a specific mode of supply which is subject to full commitments, provided that the measure does not modify the overall conditions of competition in favour of its own services and suppliers compared to 'like' (i.e. competing, regardless under which mode of supply) services and suppliers of another Member (see Article XVII:3 GATS).

> For instance, mode 1 commitments are not washed out if, in case of mode 1 restrictions, mode 2–4 suppliers are included in the group of foreign comparators for purposes of asymmetric impact assessment; in fact, mode 1 commitments do not give mode 1 suppliers a right to *unrestricted* mode 1 market access, but only a right not to be deprived of their competitive opportunities; such competitive opportunities continue to exist if they can feasibly resort to other modes of supply.

In this context it is also worth mentioning footnote 10 to Article XVII GATS, according to which '[s]pecific commitments assumed under this Article shall not be construed to require any Member to compensate for any inherent competitive disadvantages which result from the foreign character of the relevant services or service suppliers'. In other words, limiting the analysis of competitive opportunities to mode 1 and 2 suppliers would place considerable emphasis on the competitive disadvantage resulting from the foreign character (i.e. competing from a distant geographical location), in disregard to the possibility to compete domestically via modes 3 and 4.[30]

3. Justification

In particular the restriction of mode 1 supply – or of any method inherent to mode 1 supply – will oftentimes still lead to an overall asymmetric impact on foreign suppliers and services. In such cases the respondent may be able to justify its measure under the general exceptions clause.

[29] On non-restriction see above, 3.I.A.2.
[30] On footnote 10 to Art. XVII GATS see above, 3.I.C.6.

As mentioned above, Article XIV GATS is broader than its GATT counterpart in that it allows the justification of measures that are necessary to protect public order. Moreover, GATS provides for additional sector-specific exceptions.

II Mode-overreaching commitments in national treatment

While there is technically speaking no cross-mode issue in national treatment, the mode-based fragmentation of national treatment could undermine mode-specific limitations if a measure simultaneously affects two or more modes of supply which are subject to different commitments.[31] For instance, a Member could schedule full commitments for mode 1 and none for modes 2–4. If the government of a mode 1 supplier successfully challenges a measure under Article XVII GATS as constituting less favourable treatment, the abolition of such a measure may at the same time benefit mode 2–4 suppliers, albeit the lack of any commitments. The mode-overreaching extension of commitments is regularly a problem in case 'less favourable treatment' consists of an advantage granted to domestic suppliers, rather than a restriction imposed on foreign suppliers. The situation can best be illustrated with the example of subsidies.[32] Assume a Member subsidizes domestic suppliers of a sector under which only mode 1 commitments are scheduled. If the government of a mode 1 supplier successfully challenges the subsidy as violating GATS national treatment, the respondent would either have to extend the subsidy to foreign mode 1 suppliers or cease to subsidize domestic suppliers. In case of the latter, mode 2–4 suppliers would indirectly benefit from the mode 1 commitment. The consequences are even more striking with regard to subsidies which are not directed at a service sector, but at specific suppliers of a certain service. For instance, a subsidy could be designed to benefit certain national citizens in their capacity as service suppliers. In the absence of a mode 3 commitment, a complainant could challenge the subsidy as discriminating against mode 1 suppliers. In order to achieve compliance, the

[31] This issue received some attention from commentators, most of whom did not pay sufficient attention to the fact that domestic services are not supplied through 'modes of supply': Mattoo, 'National Treatment in GATS', 119–21; Low and Mattoo, 'Alternative Approaches', pp. 452–53; Cossy, 'Determining Likeness under GATS', 13; Verhoosel, *National Treatment*, p. 60.

[32] See also WPGR, Subsidies and Trade in Services, Note by the Secretariat, S/WPGR/W/9, 6 March 1996, paras. 28 ff.

regulating Member would either have to cease the subsidy – from which foreign mode 3 suppliers would also profit in spite of the lack of mode 3 commitments – or extend the subsidy to foreign mode 1 suppliers. Both solutions are not satisfying.

These examples illustrate that a mode-fragmented national treatment obligation does not lead to satisfying results in cases where 'less favourable treatment' consists of an advantage granted to domestic suppliers, such as subsidies. The Scheduling Guidelines specify that GATS national treatment does not contain an obligation which requires a Member to take measures outside its territorial jurisdiction. Consequently, 'the national treatment obligation in Article XVII does not require a Member to extend such treatment to a service supplier located in the territory of another Member'.[33] Despite this limitation of mode 1 and 2 commitments, it is unclear whether a complainant could, on the basis of mode 1 and 2 commitments only, request that the subsidy is ceased. In fact, one way of preventing mode-overreaching commitments is to interpret mode 1 and 2 commitments as limiting the scope of national treatment to measures governing the *service*, at the exclusion of measures concerning domestic *suppliers*. In other words, not only do national treatment mode 1 and 2 commitments not entail an obligation to extend treatment to a *foreign supplier* located abroad, such commitments also give no claim with regard to measures granting an advantage to *domestic suppliers*.[34] In the absence of such an interpretation, Members need to be aware of the possible mode-overreaching effect with regard to subsidies and other advantages granted to domestic suppliers.

III Cross-mode and cross-method 'likeness' in MFN

The crossover issue in the MFN context differs from national treatment in that it entails not only the question of 'likeness' across methods, but also across modes of supply. Also in difference to national treatment, the MFN obligation applies across all service sectors and is not fragmented by mode-specific commitments.

[33] CTS, Guidelines for the Scheduling of Specific Commitments under the General Agreement on Trade in Services (GATS), S/L/92, 28 March 2001, para. 15.

[34] This interpretation could be supported with footnote 10 to Article XVII GATS, according to which '[s]pecific commitments assumed under this Article shall not be construed to require any Member to compensate for any inherent competitive disadvantages which result from the foreign character of the relevant services or service suppliers'.

A Symmetric modes: cross-method 'likeness' within identical modes

The question whether services supplied by different methods within identical modes can be 'alike' for purposes of Article II GATS concerns in particular modes 1 and 2. In case of mode 1, there are different means of service supply given the intangibility of services, such as by phone, regular mail, e-mail and internet more generally. However, even mode 3 and 4 suppliers may use different methods to supply their respective services. There appears to be a large consensus among Members that such differences in methods of supply do not automatically exclude intra-modal 'likeness' under Article II GATS:

> 'Some Members suggested that within the limits of individual sectors and modes of supply, it should be possible to agree that likeness would not depend on whether a service was delivered electronically or otherwise.'[35]

It is appropriate that intra-modal 'likeness' is not only limited to technological differences in supply, but applies also to different non-electronic methods of supply.

B Asymmetric modes: cross-mode 'likeness'

Since Article II GATS does not allow for mode-specific individual commitments and since the comparison takes place exclusively between internationally traded services, the question arises whether 'likeness' could exist across different modes of supply. A prerequisite for an asymmetric-mode situation to arise is that the service in question can be supplied through different modes in the first place.

> For example, a Dutch and a Belgian skiing instructor could not feasibly supply their service through mode 1 (contact with the clients required), mode 2 (no snow mountains in the Netherlands and Belgium), or mode 3 (most likely not economically feasible); in this case, a cross-mode situation is *per se* excluded as both skiing instructors would have to resort to mode 4. In contrast, legal or education services could easily be supplied through any of the four modes.

In most cases, the cross-mode question at the same time entails a cross-method issue.

> For example, a mode 1 supplier by electronic means could be treated differently to an on-site mode 4 supplier. Yet, a mode 4 supplier could also use electronic means comparable to the mode 1 supplier.

[35] Progress Report (above n 8), para. 7.

Measures that favour some modes over others may potentially have a significant impact on trade, given that the cost of supply varies considerably across different modes and that some Members may have a competitive advantage in different modes of supply.[36] The negotiating history shows that GATS negotiators were aware of the problem, as an earlier draft proposed a mode-specific MFN obligation:

> 'With respect to any measure covered by this Agreement, each Party shall accord immediately and unconditionally to services and service providers of any other Party, treatment no less favourable than that it accords to like services and providers of like services of any other country [in like circumstances] [with respect to the same mode of delivery]'[37]

The fact that GATS negotiators contemplated but decided against a mode-specific limitation of MFN treatment is a strong indication that 'likeness' should be independent of supply modes. This corresponds with the here-preferred economic interpretation, according to which 'likeness' should exist across modes if the different modes (and possibly also different methods) do not negate demand substitutability.[38] However, as suggested for the national treatment analysis above, *all* competing services and suppliers must be taken into consideration for the analysis of 'less favourable treatment'. In other words, incase mode 1 suppliers from Member A are 'like' (and thus competing with) mode 3 suppliers from Member B, it would not be appropriate to limit the asymmetric impact test to mode 1 suppliers from A and mode 3 suppliers from B. Since MFN treatment protects overall – as opposed to mode-specific – competitive opportunities, all factually available modes must be included both for Member A and Member B.

It is theoretically possible to distinguish between the situation where the suppliers from two different exporting Members A and B are factually able to supply their service through the same modes, and the situation where suppliers from one exporting Member are factually prevented from supplying through some of the four.

> For instance, travel agents located in countries A and B can provide tourism services through all four modes to consumers located in country Z. Assume the importing Member Z requires travel agents working on its territory by virtue of modes 3 and 4 to be licensed. Theoretically, travel

[36] Copeland and Mattoo, 'Economics of Services Trade', p. 99.

[37] TNC, Draft Final Act Embodying the Results of the Uruguay Round of Multilateral Trade Negotiations, MTN.TNC/W/35–3/Rev.1, 3 December 1990, draft Article II.

[38] Also in favour of cross-mode 'likeness' Hoekman and Mattoo, 'Trade in Services', p. 135.

agents originating from A working in Z (modes 3 or 4) could argue that they are treated less favourably compared to travel agents originating from B who provide their services to consumers in Z through modes 1 and 2, and are thus not subject to the licensing requirement.

In such cases, the asymmetric impact test would require considering all competing mode 1–4 suppliers from one Member with those of another Member. The measure under scrutiny only breaches Article II GATS if the suppliers and services of the complaining Member are, all modes considered, affected more heavily than mode 1–4 suppliers and services of another Member.

In contrast, the situation is somewhat different in case the suppliers from an exporting Member A are, due to factual circumstances or high transaction costs, prevented from supplying their services through some of the modes, while their competitors from another exporting Member B are able to resort to all modes of service supply. If the importing country restricts exactly those supply modes which are factually available to country A, then these suppliers and their services are treated less favourably than their counterparts from country B which can still resort to other modes of supply.[39]

For example, the importing country allows the supply of construction services through commercial presence mode 3, but not through presence of natural persons mode 4. Assume suppliers from country A have the capabilities to supply the service through both modes 3 and 4, whereas suppliers from country B are limited to the prohibited mode 4 because, for instance, a large majority of its population lacks the capital to establish a commercial presence in the importing country. Against this background, suppliers from country B may argue that they, or their services supplied through mode 4, are treated less favourably than the service and suppliers originating from country A supplied through mode 3.

Even though such a situation could theoretically occur, it must be noted that the construction is somewhat hypothetical and it is questionable whether it has any concrete practical relevance.

[39] In contrast, no asymmetric or cross-mode situation arises if *all* modes of supply are restricted by laws or regulations instead of factual circumstances. Assume the importing country prohibits the entry of suppliers from A and B through modes 3 and 4 (measure 1) and, at the same time, adopts a different measure restricting modes 1 and 2 from suppliers B without, however, affecting modes 1 and 2 originating from A (measure 2). In this case, measure 2 treats service suppliers through modes 1 and 2 from B less favourably than suppliers through modes 1 and 2 from A (symmetric modes). If, however, modes 1 and 2 are barred for suppliers from B due to factual circumstances, then measure 1 treats services supplied through modes 3 and 4 from B less favourably than services supplied through modes 1 and 2 from A (asymmetric modes).

12

Concluding summary: merged test and crossover 'likeness'

Chapters 9 and 10 of part III first analysed the rationale and consequences for extending the rules of non-discrimination in GATS to the service supplier as a natural or legal person. The main reason lies in the fact that the service is oftentimes inseparable from the supplier and requires instant consumption. Consequently, Members have the possibility to distort trade in services either by putting the supply of the foreign service to a disadvantage or by discriminating directly against the foreign supplier in its capacity as an individual or enterprise. It was thus necessary to include the 'supplier' as beneficiary of non-discrimination, which in turn raises a number of interpretative difficulties. According to the language used in GATS, Members are obliged to treat 'foreign services and service suppliers' no less favourably than domestic services and suppliers as well as those from other Members. For an analysis of this obligation, it is necessary to clearly distinguish between the two elements of 'treatment' and 'likeness'. Chapter 10 submits that with regard to the element of 'treatment', the distinction between the service and the supplier has no consequences. Any treatment of the service inevitably affects the supplier, and vice versa. Thus, the question whether the GATS non-discrimination obligations require 'less favourable treatment' of the service *and* the supplier or just one of the two becomes moot. However, since a violation of non-discrimination requires that the differential treatment occurs between 'like' comparators, it is highly relevant to determine whether GATS rules on non-discrimination are interpreted as setting forth a cumulative, an alternative or a merged test with regard to 'likeness'. Following the analysis under chapter 10, the benefits and drawbacks of each of the various different interpretations and tests can be summarized as follows.

The main advantage of the *cumulative test* is that it operates the same way for Articles II and XVII GATS. It is easy to apply even in asymmetric cross-mode constellations and thus enhances legal security and predictability. However, this test results in the least invasive interpretation of the GATS non-discrimination obligations and significantly raises the burden for a complaining Member to demonstrate a violation. Members retain the right to differentiate between 'like' services that are supplied by 'unlike' suppliers, even though the services might be in a perfect competitive relationship. Finally, it seems particularly unreasonable to require 'likeness' of the suppliers for services traded under modes 1 and 2. In these cases, the foreign suppliers are neither direct beneficiaries of the GATS non-discrimination obligations, nor are they directly subject to the importing Member's jurisdiction.

The *alternative test* in connection with a *combined* approach results in the most intrusive application of the GATS non-discrimination obligations with a high liberalizing effect. The test applies easily and consistently under both Articles II and XVII GATS, as well as to symmetric and asymmetric constellations. However, such an approach may lead to the absurd result that Members are not allowed to differentiate between entirely 'unlike' services if the suppliers are found to be 'alike'; and vice versa. Such a result may be particularly disturbing in the case of services traded under modes 1 and 2, where the foreign supplier is not even located within the jurisdiction of the importing Member.

The *alternative test* in connection with a *disjunctive* approach is highly flexible and is best suitable to adapt to the circumstances of a specific case. It allows the invasiveness of GATS rules on non-discrimination to be balanced. However, the main drawback of such an interpretation is that it requires a method allowing to predictably select between a comparison of either the services or the suppliers. A selection of the comparators according to the subject matter of the regulation or the mode of supply is in certain situations inconclusive and a selection at the discretion of the complaining Member is arbitrary.

In comparison, the panels previously abstained from differentiating between 'likeness' of the services and the suppliers. Even though the panels addressed both 'likeness' of services and 'likeness' of suppliers, they analysed 'like suppliers' solely on the basis of whether they supply like services.[1] In other words, 'services' is the only factor considered in the analysis of 'like suppliers'.[2] As a result, the panels *de facto* only required 'likeness' of the suppliers, refusing to consider any supplier-related factors.

[1] It must be noted that the Panel's approach could also be viewed as a form of the cumulative test, requiring 'likeness' of both the services and the suppliers; however, since 'likeness' of the suppliers is determined solely on the basis of the services, the Panel essentially requires 'likeness' of the services only; also Zdouc, *Comparative Analysis of GATS and GATT*, pp. 162–63.

[2] See also Krajewski and Engelke, 'Art. XVII GATS', p. 407.

Such an approach had been considered in earlier drafts of GATS which stated 'like services and providers of like services'. Not only is the panels' approach thus not supported by the final text of GATS, it also leads to overly intrusive results in that Members could not differentiate between different suppliers if they happen to supply 'like' services.

Against the background of this overview, it is submitted that the relationship between 'likeness' of services and of suppliers in GATS non-discrimination rules should be interpreted in accordance with the *merged test*.[3] The merged test combines the advantages of all other possibilities in that it is applicable to Articles II and XVII in the same way and also works for asymmetric cross-mode situations. At the same time it leaves sufficient flexibility in balancing the intrusiveness of GATS rules on non-discrimination without having to develop a method for selecting the comparators. The application of the test requires a weighing and balancing of service-related and supplier-related factors. In order to ensure legal security, consistency and predictability, there are a number of guiding principles that should be respected in the application of the merged test.

- First, in light of the conclusions drawn under part II, the merged test should be applied in view of determining the *competitive relationship* between the foreign service and supplier and the domestic service and supplier. Consequently, only service- and supplier-related factors that affect the competitive relationship should be considered.
- From a consumer's perspective, the *characteristics of the services* are of predominant importance. Accordingly, the question of 'like services' must be the starting point of the analysis. The WTO adjudicating bodies thus have to examine the extent to which the services compete with one another in accordance with the methodologies discussed under part IV of this book.
- In a second step, the extent of *'likeness' between the suppliers* must be determined. This process is best viewed as a corrective exercise designed to overturn, if appropriate, the result from the comparison of the services. If the services are found to be 'alike', a difference between the suppliers may lead to an overall conclusion of 'unlikeness' to the extent it negates or considerably diminishes the competitive relationship as a whole.

[3] This opinion is shared by Zdouc, *Comparative Analysis of GATS and GATT*, p. 167: 'the determination of which service suppliers are "like" should be based on a *combination of service-related and supplier-related factors*' (emphasis original); Zdouc, '(2004) Dispute Settlement Practice', p. 401.

For instance, to a Swiss consumer a medical doctor located in Germany may not compete with a medical doctor located in Australia for purposes of mode 2 supply due to high travel costs and time efforts. Yet, the analysis may be different if the medical doctor is one among very few specialists in a certain field. Similarly, a very highly trained and qualified supplier may not compete with an unqualified supplier from a consumer's perspective even though the service performed is identical.

If, in contrast, the services are found to be 'unlike', a strong competitive relationship between the suppliers could theoretically lead to an overall conclusion of 'likeness'. Even though such situations would presumably arise very rarely under GATS non-discrimination rules, a high degree of supply substitutability may result in the conclusion that the suppliers compete with one another.[4]

- The *weight and importance* to be attributed to supplier characteristics depends on the circumstances of the case. Only very little weight should be given to a comparison between the suppliers with regard to measures affecting the modes of supply 1 and 2. In these cases, the suppliers are not direct beneficiaries of non-discrimination. More weight should be given to the supplier comparison in cases regarding modes 3 and 4 and, finally, much of the attention should focus on supplier characteristics if the subject matter of the measure under scrutiny directly relates to the supplier who is supplying a service under modes 3 and 4.

The second technical issue arising under the concept of GATS 'likeness' addressed in chapter 11 is whether 'likeness' can exist across modes and/or methods of service supply. Noting that domestic suppliers never resort to a 'mode of supply' in terms of GATS, the cross-mode issue does not arise under national treatment. However, the national treatment obligation raises sensitive issues of Members' ability to regulate certain methods of supply, such as electronic supply and the supply by natural persons or by companies. In contrast to national treatment, GATS MFN treatment raises both the cross-mode and cross-method issue. To the extent that cross-method 'likeness' is affirmed, an exporting Member could, for instance, claim that a restriction of electronic supply discriminates against its mode 1 suppliers in comparison to domestic on-site suppliers. Similarly, a Member could claim under MFN treatment that a regulation affecting mode 1 is discriminatory to its mode 1 suppliers in comparison to mode 4 suppliers of another Member.

Chapter 11 submits that these types of claims need to be assessed pursuant to an economic interpretation of 'likeness' in combination with the

[4] On the relevance of supply substitutability see below, 14.III.B.2.

asymmetric impact test and footnote 10 to Article XVII GATS. Moreover, GATS rules on non-discrimination should be construed such that they protect overall and not mode- or method-specific competitive opportunities. Under an analytical framework following this approach, the first step is to determine whether the service supplied by different methods compete with one another in the same relevant market; in the absence of a competitive relationship, national treatment is not breached due to 'unlikeness'. In the affirmative, the effect of the measure needs to be assessed on the basis of a relevant market comprising *all* competing foreign and domestic services and suppliers, even if the measure only affects a specific mode or a specific method of supply. This approach entails the advantage that a measure restricting a specific method of supply (e.g. electronic supply) does not automatically violate GATS non-discrimination obligations, even if electronic supply competes with on-site supply and is thus considered 'alike'. In fact, the competitive conditions remain intact if there are other means or modes available to foreign suppliers, which allow them to compete on a level playing field with domestic suppliers. Finally, such an approach does not undermine the individual commitments as they remain important in order to determine whether a measure is subject to GATS national treatment in the first place.

A final technical issue arising under national treatment due to the scheduling system is that mode-specific commitments may automatically extend to other modes if the differential treatment consists of an advantage granted to domestic suppliers, such as in the case of subsidies. One way of resolving this problem is to interpret the scope of mode 1 and 2 commitments as limited to treatment of the service, at the exclusion of measures related to the supplier. Consequently, a subsidy granted to domestic suppliers would give no claim for violation of mode 1 and 2 commitments, but only for mode 3 and 4 commitments.

PART IV

Methodology for the 'likeness' analysis in GATS

Having established the conceptual breadth of the GATS 'likeness' concept in part II and examined the relationship between the 'service' and the 'supplier' as well as between 'modes' and 'methods' of supply in the light of 'likeness' in part III, part IV turns to the actual analysis of 'likeness' in GATS with the aim of developing a methodology and criteria according to which the relationship of services and suppliers should be assessed. Chapter 13 analyses the obvious starting point, which is to consider the tests and criteria which have been developed under the jurisprudence of GATT 'like products' and determine whether this approach can be transposed to the assessment of 'likeness' in GATS. Subsequently, part IV looks beyond the WTO framework in order to assess whether similar concepts from other legal domains could provide for new methods to resolve 'likeness' in WTO law in general, and 'likeness' in GATS in particular. Consequently, chapter 14 draws a comparison between the concept of market definition in EU and US competition law and WTO 'likeness', arguing that the competition law approach would be particularly useful for the analysis of competitive relationships in service sectors under GATS. Chapter 15 examines to what extent the specific 'like product'-related problem of PPM-measures may arise under GATS and whether the proposed methodologies are suitable to address this problem. Finally, chapter 16 draws the conclusions from part IV.

13

The border tax adjustments framework

The most intuitive approach to the 'likeness' issue in GATS is to apply the *Border Tax Adjustments* framework developed by GATT/WTO jurisprudence for purposes of the GATT 'like products' concept.[1] This framework received its name from the Working Party Report on *Border Tax Adjustments*, adopted by the contracting parties in 1970, which developed three of the four criteria for the determination of 'like products':

> 'With regard to the interpretation of the term "like or similar products", which occurs some sixteen times throughout the General Agreement, it was recalled that considerable discussion had taken place ... but that no further improvement of the term had been achieved. The Working Party concluded that problems arising from the interpretation of the terms should be examined on a case-by-case basis. This would allow a fair assessment in each case of the different elements that constitute a "similar" product. Some criteria were suggested for determining, on a case-by-case basis, whether a product is "similar": the product's end-uses in a given market; consumers' tastes and habits, which change from country to country; the product's properties, nature and quality.'[2]

In addition to the three factors of physical characteristics, end-uses and consumers' tastes and habits, GATT 1947 practice recognized – *nota bene* already prior to the *Border Tax Adjustments* report[3] – the uniform classification in tariff nomenclatures as a factor in the 'likeness' analysis. Subsequently, the four criteria had been applied by different GATT 1947 panels, until they were endorsed under WTO jurisprudence by the Appellate Body in *Japan – Alcoholic Beverages II*.[4] The adjudicating bodies'

[1] Pitschas, 'GATS', pp. 512–13; Ortino, 'Principle of Non-Discrimination', p. 198; Wyss, *Bankdienstleistungen*, p. 65; Michaelis, 'Dienstleistungshandel', p. 398; implicitly Horn and Mavroidis, 'Economic and Legal Aspects of MFN', 243.

[2] Working Party Report, *Border Tax Adjustments*, para. 18.

[3] See e.g. GATT Panel Report, *Australia – Ammonium Sulphate*, para. 8: 'In the Australian tariff the two products are listed as separate items and enjoy different treatment'.

[4] Appellate Body Report, *Japan – Alcoholic Beverages II*, p. 23.

fixation with the factors from *Border Tax Adjustments* received numerous critical comments from scholars, pointing out that the Working Party referred very generally to the concept of 'like or similar products' which it counted 16 times to occur in the GATT, and not to the specific 'like product' concept in a particular provision, such as non-discrimination.[5] However, GATT and WTO practice following the *Border Tax Adjustments* report resorted to these factors as a core part of the analysis for *all* 'like product' elements in GATT. It is thus safe to say that they can be attributed authoritative value.[6]

Yet, the framework from *Border Tax Adjustments* is only practicable to the extent that the underlying purpose of the comparison is clearly determined. For instance, it is only possible to assess whether or not a different colour or taste of certain products is relevant under the *Border Tax Adjustments* framework with regard to 'likeness' or 'unlikeness' under the condition that the purpose of 'likeness' is clearly defined. With regard to Article III:4, the Appellate Body confirmed that the criteria from *Border Tax Adjustments* must be applied in view of assessing the existence of a *competitive relationship*:

> 'We have noted that, under Article III:4 of the GATT 1994, the term "like products" is concerned with competitive relationships between and among products. Accordingly, whether the *Border Tax Adjustments* framework is adopted or not, it is important under Article III:4 to take account of evidence which indicates whether, and to what extent, the products involved are – or could be – in a competitive relationship in the marketplace.'[7]

This very important finding by the Appellate Body should not be limited to Article III:4 GATT, but should apply to all WTO non-discrimination clauses. With regard to GATT Article III, the finding is supported by the text of paragraph 1 referring to protectionism as well as *Ad* Article III:2 referring to 'directly competitive or substitutable'. Moreover, even the narrow standard of 'likeness' under Article III:2, first sentence – referred

[5] Hudec, '"Like Product"', p. 113; Emch, 'What are "Like" Products?', 395.

[6] Different Emch, 'What are "Like" Products?', 395: 'It should be recalled, however, that this report [i.e. Border Tax Adjustments] should only be seen as persuasive, never as authoritative text ... nor is it likely to be considered as binding "subsequent practice".' While it is true that the *Border Tax Adjustments* report has no authoritative value, the subsequent Appellate Body jurisprudence largely endorsing the *Border Tax Adjustments* criteria certainly does.

[7] Appellate Body Report, *EC – Asbestos*, para. 103; for a comprehensive discussion of the AB's rulings on 'likeness' in *Asbestos* see Trebilcock and Howse, *Regulation of International Trade*, pp. 101 ff.

to as the 'physical characteristics' test – is essentially about competitive relationships. The different standards merely express different degrees of competitiveness.[8] Hence, the different breadths of the 'like product' concept across different non-discrimination provisions does not require different factors – as these remain the same for all provisions – but the evidence considered under the four factors would vary.[9] For instance, a case concerning the broad 'like products' concept of Article III:4 GATT requires including marketplace evidence in the analysis.[10] Consequently, the following comparative analysis draws from 'like product' jurisprudence in general, without distinguishing between particular GATT provisions and the different standards of 'directly competitive or substitutable' and 'like products'.

I Properties, nature and quality

The first criterion under the *Border Tax Adjustments* report was referred to as the 'properties, nature and quality of the product', but the WTO adjudicating bodies generally use the term 'physical characteristics'. In accordance with the considerations above, such characteristics should only be considered as relevant to the extent they affect consumer behaviour and, consequently, the competitive relationship between goods or services.[11] Hence, even physically identical products can theoretically be found 'unlike' and vice versa.[12] However, it must be noted that in the case of GATT Article III:2, first sentence, physical characteristics have their own substantive meaning, in that 'like products' require not only a competitive relationship between the products, but also that they share most physical characteristics.[13]

[8] See above, part II.

[9] Appellate Body Report, *EC – Asbestos*, para. 103: 'The kind of evidence to be examined in assessing the "likeness" of products will, necessarily, depend upon the particular products and the legal provision at issue. When all the relevant evidence has been examined, panels must determine whether that evidence, as a whole, indicates that the products in question are "like" in terms of the legal provision at issue'.

[10] Ibid.: 'We have noted that, under Article III:4 of the GATT 1994, the term "like products" is concerned with competitive relationships between and among products. Accordingly, whether the *Border Tax Adjustments* framework is adopted or not, it is important under Article III:4 to take account of evidence which indicates whether, and to what extent, the products involved are – or could be – in a competitive relationship in the marketplace'.

[11] Also Emch, 'What are "Like" Products?', 398.

[12] See also Ortino, '*De Jure* and *De Facto* Discrimination', pp. 256–57.

[13] On the narrow economic interpretation of 'likeness' see above, 3.II.B.1.b.

A *WTO/GATT jurisprudence*

While the criterion of physical characteristics has been consistently applied in all cases involving the question of 'like products', its significance and weight varies considerably between the different cases. For instance, prior GATT, 1947 and WTO jurisprudence has not always followed a clear approach focusing on competitiveness, thereby lacking a clear objective of the comparison and omitting the appropriate conclusions from the test. In particular, many GATT 1947 cases applied a purely objective or abstract test:[14]

> For instance, in *EEC – Animal Feed Proteins*, the 'varying protein contents and the different vegetable, animal and synthetic origins of the protein products' led the Panel to conclude that the various protein products are not "like products" for purposes of Article I and III (para 4.2), but the protein products are directly competitive or substitutable in terms of Article III:2, second sentence (para 4.3).

In other cases, particularly with regard to GATT Article III:2, second sentence, the WTO adjudicating bodies were more explicit in linking the physical characteristics with the question of substitutability and competitive relationship:

> The Panel in *Korea – Alcoholic Beverages*, a case on 'directly competitive or substitutable' products in terms of Article III:2, second sentence, GATT, noted that 'if two products are physically identical or nearly so, then it obviously means that there is a greater potential for a direct competitive relationship' (para 10.64). The Panel went on to find that all products at issue are distilled alcoholic beverages produced on the basis of ethyl alcohol. The physical differences due to filtration, aging process, colour and flavour were found to be insufficiently important to render the products non-substitutable (para 10.67).

Even though the *Alcoholic Beverages* cases take a correct approach, they all omit to clearly separate the analysis of physical characteristics from the third criterion of consumers' tastes and habits.[15] Such an application of the *Border Tax Adjustments* framework is problematic as the analysis lacks a clear structure, which in turn makes it more difficult to balance the

[14] For an overview see also Melloni, *National Treatment in GATT*, pp. 122–25.

[15] See Panel Report, *Japan – Alcoholic Beverages II*, paras. 6.21 ff; Panel Report, *Chile – Alcoholic Beverages*, para. 7.54, not specifically addressing consumers' tastes and habits; also not distinguishing between the criteria, Panel Report, *Canada – Periodicals*, paras. 5.22 ff ('like products') and Appellate Body Report, *Canada – Periodicals*, pp. 25 ff ('DCS'); Panel Report, *EC – Asbestos*, paras. 8.145 ff.

various factors in view of an overall conclusion on 'likeness'. It is mainly for this reason that the Appellate Body in *EC – Asbestos* saw itself compelled to set new and clear guidelines for the application of the *Border Tax Adjustments* framework. In its report, it very heavily criticized the Panel for blending the examination of physical characteristics with considerations on end-uses and consumers' tastes and habits. The Appellate Body held that 'the Panel should have examined the evidence relating to *each* of those four criteria' separately.[16] Accordingly, the first criterion should analyse whether the products physically differ or resemble one another, whereas the third criterion examines how such differences and similarities affect the products' competitive relationship from the consumers' perspective.[17]

An exemplary illustration for a correct examination of the physical characteristics within the *Border Tax Adjustments* framework is provided by the Panel in *Mexico – Taxes on Soft Drinks*:

> In respect to the claim under Articles III:2, second sentence, GATT, the Panel found that high-fructose corn syrup (HFCS) and cane sugar share similar characteristics in that they are both a combination of glucose and fructose, albeit of different proportions (para 8.70). Only under the third criterion of consumers' tastes and habits, the Panel noted that 'taste, colour and other physical characteristics of soft drinks and syrups sweetened with HFCS and cane sugar are indistinguishable' (para 8.17). The same exemplary analysis was conducted for the claims under the first sentence of GATT Article III as well as under GATT Article III:4.

With regard to the type of evidence, the Appellate Body further clarified in *EC – Asbestos* that *all* relevant evidence must be considered, noting in particular that 'evidence relating to the health risks associated with a product may be pertinent in an examination of "likeness"'.[18] Such evidence could be taken into account either under the first criterion of properties, nature and quality or under the third criterion of consumers' tastes and habits. Finally, it is also worth mentioning the Panel Report on *Dominican Republic – Import and Sale of Cigarettes*, which stated that '[t]he Panel agrees with the Dominican Republic that quality is an

[16] Para 109 (emphasis original).

[17] Para 118: 'In such cases [i.e. if products are physically different], in order to overcome this indication that products are *not* "like", a higher burden is placed on complaining Members to establish that, despite the pronounced physical differences, there is a competitive relationship between the products such that *all* of the evidence, taken together, demonstrates that the products are "like" under Article III:4 of the GATT 1994.' (emphasis original).

[18] Para 113.

important factor in the determination of the likeness of products'.[19] Yet, in this case the Panel did not find any relevant difference in quality that would support the conclusion of 'unlikeness'.

B Application to GATS

In the GATS context, it is at first sight impossible to apply the 'physical characteristics' test as it is referred to in WTO/GATT jurisprudence, considering that services are intangible and thus lack any physical characteristics. Some scholars argue that for this reason, the physical characteristics test cannot be transposed to the GATS context at all.[20] Others suggest that 'intrinsic' characteristics could distinguish services from one another.[21] Alternatively, it is proposed here that the criterion should be applied in its original terms from *Border Tax Adjustments* that referred to 'properties, nature and quality' rather than 'physical characteristics'.

Following the conclusions from part III, both *suppliers* and their *services* must be compared with respect to properties, nature and quality in order to assess how overall differences and similarities affect consumer behaviour in regard to the question of substitutability. The test under GATS thus provides for an additional step, in that it must be determined whether a substantial difference between the suppliers outweighs the fact that they supply exactly identical services – or vice versa – resulting in an overall conclusion of 'unlikeness' in terms of the GATS.

> For instance, two hairdressers could have exactly the same education and experience, but one offers services exclusively to women and the other exclusively to men. In this case, the substantial difference in the nature of the service outweighs all similarities of the suppliers in light of demand substitutability. In contrast, two men's hairdressers could be considered unlike from a consumer's perspective if one has proper education and 20 years of experience while the other has his first day at work.

[19] Para 7.333 (issue not appealed).

[20] Davey and Pauwelyn, 'MFN Unconditionality', p. 49, n 114: 'It would seem to be difficult to transpose this approach to the GATS. Since most, if not all, features of services and service suppliers are intangible, none of them can really be said to be objectively linked to the service or service supplier itself'; similarly also Zdouc, 'Streitigkeiten über den Dienstleistungsverkehr', p. 134; Pitschas, 'GATS', p. 513; Zdouc, '(2004) Dispute Settlement Practice', p. 396; Zdouc, *Comparative Analysis of GATS and GATT*, p. 159; Footer and George, 'The GATS', p. 851; Leroux, 'GATS Case Law', 780, n 118; Michaelis, 'Dienstleistungshandel', p. 398; Cottier and Oesch, *International Trade Regulation*, p. 407.

[21] Cossy, 'Thoughts on "Likeness" in GATS', pp. 335–36; see also EC submission in Panel Report, *US – Gambling*, para. 4.37.

This example shows that properties, nature and quality of both suppliers and services must be balanced in order to come to an overall conclusion whether this factor supports or negates substitutability. While it is impossible to determine in advance and in the abstract all relevant suppliers' and services' characteristics – many of which are sector specific –, it is possible to at least indicate some of the characteristics that are likely to be significant in the view of consumers regardless of the sector in question.

1. Properties and nature of services

From the few cases pertaining to GATS rules on non-discrimination, we have some limited indications as to what kind of characteristics could be taken into account under the heading of 'properties and nature'. In *EC – Bananas III*, for instance, the Panel ruled that the 'nature' and 'characteristics' of wholesale transactions are all alike when supplied in connection with wholesale services, without, however, illustrating what these characteristics are. The only difference the Panel noted between the wholesale services for bananas related to the *origin* of the distributed bananas. Quite obviously, the origin of the bananas does not affect the nature and characteristics of the wholesale service with respect to bananas.[22] Likewise, in *Canada – Autos* the wholesale services were found to be alike by the Panel, regardless of the autos' origin and of whether the suppliers were so-called 'manufacturer beneficiaries' or 'non-manufacturer-beneficiaries', and irrespective of whether or not they had production facilities in Canada.[23]

A more appropriate characteristic to consider under the heading of 'properties and nature' would have been to look at the *method of supply* and whether such methods could influence consumer behaviour. It is likely that in the case of wholesale services for identical products, the method of distribution does not differ significantly from one distributor

[22] Panel Report, *EC – Bananas III*, para. 7.322: 'the nature and the characteristics of wholesale transactions as such, as well as of each of the different subordinated services mentioned in the headnote to section 6 of the CPC, are "like" when supplied in connection with wholesale services, irrespective of whether these services are supplied with respect to bananas of EC and traditional ACP origin, on the one hand, or with respect to bananas of third-country or non-traditional ACP origin, on the other. Indeed, it seems that each of the different service activities taken individually is virtually the same and can only be distinguished by referring to the origin of the bananas in respect of which the service activity is being performed'.

[23] Panel Report, *Canada – Autos*, para. 10.247, as modified by the Appellate Body on the Panel's analysis regarding the applicability of the GATS, see Appellate Body Report, paras. 168 ff; for an outline of the case see above, 10.I.A.2.

to another. However, in other cases, the method of supply can be of critical importance in the 'likeness' analysis. For instance, in *US – Gambling* the parties extensively discussed how the cross-border supply of gambling services via remote communication would compare to domestically supplied gambling services.[24] The complainant Antigua was of the view that, by definition, cross-border supply requires the use of remote communication. In consequence, this difference in method of supply could not lead to a conclusion of 'unlikeness', as such a result would undermine the Members' commitments on mode 1 national treatment in GATS.[25] The US, in contrast, argued that in virtual casinos, the result is generated by a software algorithm of some random number that is visualized through cards, dice, wheels, or gambling boards similar to what one would find in a casino. Accordingly, the online casino reflects a virtual reality providing for odds manipulated by a software simulation, not necessarily corresponding with the outcome of physical gambling in a real casino. In addition, the US argued that the physical surroundings of a real casino, such as layout, amenities and real-world stimuli, differ considerably from online casinos where a lone gambler sits at home in front of a terminal.[26]

As the Panel exercised judicial economy on the national treatment claim, there is up until today no jurisprudence on how such characteristics on the method of supply should be evaluated. The unwillingness of the Panel to tackle this issue is unfortunate, considering that these questions essentially go to the heart of the issue of whether mode 1 cross-border supply via remote communication can be 'like' a domestic service supplied on-site. This particular question has already been discussed in detail under section 11.I above. To be recalled, the critical question that should be asked in the *Gambling* case is how the differences in method of supply are perceived by consumers in terms of substitutability. In this regard, the US' arguments tend to show convincingly that people who visit casinos for its atmosphere would not necessarily be the typical consumer of online gambling services and that thus demand substitutability is low for this type of gambler.

Next to the method of supply, adjudicating bodies should examine the *nature of the service itself*, which includes intrinsic characteristics of the service.[27] The types of characteristics to be considered depend largely on the nature of the service under scrutiny. In the *Gambling* case, for

[24] See also Wunsch-Vincent, 'Lessons from US-Gambling', 329–35.

[25] Panel Report, *US – Gambling*, para. 3.161.

[26] Ibid., para. 3.155.

[27] Cossy, 'Thoughts on "Likeness" in GATS', p. 335.

instance, Antigua points out that the types of gambling games are essentially the same, as they all 'involve the placing of wagers and the winning or losing sums of money'.[28] This argument relating to the nature of the service, rather than the supply method, demonstrates that demand substitutability is much higher for those people who gamble because of the excitement and the motivation of actually winning money. Such players are more likely to switch to online gambling if, for instance, online providers structure the games such that there are higher odds of winning, higher jackpots or lower costs of play. The US, in contrast, referred to a study of the National Research Council which 'has found that "[t]he characteristics of game technologies, such as the number of gambles offered per time period, the physical and informational environment of games, game rules, speed of play, probabilistic structure, cost per play, and jackpot size, appear to affect gambling preferences and habits"'.[29]

In consequence, for a complete legal analysis the Panel would have needed more relevant facts submitted by the parties – in particular by the complainant bearing the burden of proof – that show the real market situation on the various types of gamblers and the substitutability of online and on-site casinos. Arguably, it would have been necessary to distinguish between the different gambling games, as consumers may, for instance, not view lottery games, black jack and horse-race betting as interchangeable. Yet, the purpose of these illustrations is to show that in all non-discrimination cases on trade in services, the *properties and nature* of the service itself and the method of supply are highly relevant under the first factor from *Border Tax Adjustments*.

2. Properties and nature of suppliers

Due to the panel jurisprudence finding that suppliers are alike if they supply 'like' services, there is currently no case law on the issue of which supplier-based characteristics could or should be considered under this test. As discussed under chapter 10 above, the panels' limitation to service-related characteristics is unfounded. To the extent properties and nature of suppliers affect consumer behaviour, they must be included in the analysis under the merged test. A first starting point in determining what supplier-related characteristics could be relevant is to look at the arguments brought forward by the parties in support of their claims of 'likeness' or 'unlikeness' in specific cases. For instance, Canada argued that even if the auto manufacturer

[28] Panel Report, *US – Gambling*, para. 3.151.
[29] Ibid., para. 3.153.

Intermeccanica were a wholesale distribution service supplier, it would be utterly 'unlike' the foreign service suppliers listed by Japan:

> '... even if it were a wholesale distribution supplier, which it clearly is not, its size and sales volumes, and the vehicles it "distributes", are vastly different from those of any of the commercial presences identified by Japan as wholesale distribution service suppliers. Intermeccanica has 8 employees. It has never produced more than 22 vehicles in a year. The vehicles it does produce are hand-built replicas of famous automobiles. It is simply preposterous to contend that it is a potential competitor for the wholesale distribution business of companies like Toyota or Honda, which import tens of thousands of cars each year.'[30]

Canada essentially names three supplier characteristics in support of its claim of 'unlikeness', namely size, sales volumes and the underlying product of the service. The latter seems to be a factor that should be considered for the comparison of the *services*, similar to wholesale services of bananas. While the origin of the bananas is irrelevant for purposes of 'likeness',[31] a substantial difference in the types of cars to be distributed may well support the argument for 'unlikeness' of the services, but not the suppliers. In contrast, differences in the size and sales volumes of suppliers are likely to affect the competitive relationship and may thus be relevant as 'properties and nature' of the suppliers. Similar characteristics that could be considered are the legal form and structure of the companies as well as assets and number of employees. In *EC – Bananas III*, the US used such characteristics to demonstrate the existence of a competitive relationship between the wholesalers.[32] In many instances, however, it will be difficult to demonstrate how such characteristics negatively affect the competitive relationship.

An entirely different approach is to determine the relevant supplier-related characteristics in the light of the policy objective of the measure.[33] For instance, in *US – Gambling* the US claimed that:

> 'Antigua also ignores potentially relevant differences in service suppliers. For example, Antigua states that US state lotteries are supplied exclusively

[30] Panel Report, *Canada – Autos*, para. 7.368; for an outline of the case see above, 10.I.A.2.

[31] Panel Report, *EC – Bananas III*, para. 7.322; for an outline of the case see above, 10.I.A.1.

[32] Panel Report, *EC – Bananas III*, para. IV.677: 'firms that supplied distribution services for EC/ACP bananas were "like" those firms that supplied the same services for Latin American bananas. Their respective activities, equipment, types of personnel employed and marketing stages were either identical or virtually so and the extent to which they had competed directly with each other in the EC market had been limited only by the restrictive regulatory regimes established by certain member States (e.g. United Kingdom, France) and by traditional marketing relationships built up over time'.

[33] Cossy, 'Thoughts on "Likeness" in GATS', p. 338.

> through state monopolies, but nowhere does it attempt to say what, if anything, makes its (presumably private, non-state) service suppliers "like" state lottery monopolies in any sense. Nor does it try to explain how its suppliers are "like" the associations that control pari-mutuel wagering services on horseracing in the United States, or any other special type of supplier in the US market.'[34]

The US essentially argues that suppliers should – or could – be considered 'unlike' on the basis of ownership. The question thus is whether state-owned or state-created monopoly suppliers could be 'like' a foreign supplier of like services for purposes of GATS rules on non-discrimination. From a purely competition-based consumer perspective, the question of ownership and monopoly supply appears to be less relevant.[35] In order to distinguish suppliers on such a basis, it would be necessary to take into account the policy objective of the regulation. In other words, the policy objective – for instance for creating a state monopoly – would justify the consideration of certain supplier-related characteristics – such as public or private ownership. One could be inclined to introduce an 'aims test' in the comparison of suppliers, simply because in many instances supplier-related regulations differentiate for reasons other than protectionism. The US adopted this position in the Gambling case:

> 'Regulatory distinctions are directly relevant under GATS Article XVII, and should be considered in their own right – not solely through the lens of consumer perceptions ... Thus one must consider not only the different competitive characteristics of a service or supplier as such, but also the existence of regulatory distinctions between services in interpreting and applying the likeness analysis under Article XVII ... As previously discussed, the United States maintains and applies a regulatory distinction between remotely supplied gambling services and other gambling services, with the former subject to even tighter restrictions than the latter. This distinction arises from the numerous distinguishing law enforcement, consumer protection, and health concerns associated with the remote supply of gambling.'[36]

In the *Bananas III* case, the EU made a similar argument, albeit not directly related to differences between the suppliers. It claimed that in general terms, the measures pursue entirely legitimate policies and are not inherently discriminatory in design or effect. Yet, the Appellate Body

[34] Panel Report, *US – Gambling*, para. 3.154.
[35] But see Marchetti and Mavroidis, 'Challenges for GATS', 534.
[36] Panel Report, *US – Gambling*, para. 3.188.

clearly rejected any consideration of a measure's 'aims and effects' under Articles II and XVII GATS.[37]

Hence, it is submitted that the 'likeness' analysis is not the right place in the non-discrimination framework to take account of such policy considerations. This approach is inevitably linked with the questions (i) which objectives are more important than trade liberalization and (ii) whether the measure is necessary to pursue the ends sought.[38] Both issues should be dealt with either under Article XIV or under Article VI GATS. According to the here-preferred theory, 'likeness' should follow a pure economic interpretation, counter-balanced with an asymmetric impact test of 'less favourable treatment'. The effect-based interpretation of 'less favourable treatment' – requiring that foreign services and suppliers as a group are more heavily disadvantaged than 'like' domestic services and suppliers as a group – allows the keeping in place of many non-protectionist measures that differentiate for reasons unrelated to trade. If, however, the effect of the measure turns out to be protectionist between competing services and suppliers, a Member may still schedule a limitation of its commitments or resort to the justifications of Article XIV GATS.

If, *arguendo*, one would want to introduce the policy objective in the non-discrimination analysis, it should be done with a subjective interpretation of 'less favourable treatment', rather than a subjective interpretation of 'likeness'.[39] Accordingly, the policy objective could be used to demonstrate that the differentiation is not based on origin. The US used this argument in the *Gambling* case:

> 'According to the United States, even if it were to be assumed that likeness could be established between some remotely supplied gambling and betting services and service suppliers and non-remote gambling and betting service and service suppliers, the United States may, nonetheless, maintain a regulatory distinction between remote and non-remote supply of such services given that such a distinction does not afford less favourable treatment to foreign suppliers *on the basis of national origin*.'[40]

Conversely, should a more lenient standard of 'less favourable treatment' be favoured – such as the diagonal test – then it would indeed become appropriate to determine supplier-related factors not only on the basis of competitive relationships, but also in the light of the policy objective

[37] Para 241.

[38] See above, 3.III.C; but see Cossy, 'Thoughts on "Likeness" in GATS', pp. 346–53.

[39] On the subjective interpretation of 'less favourable treatment' see above, 3.III.A.2.

[40] Panel Report, *US – Gambling*, para. 6.423 (emphasis added).

of the regulation. Whichever approach will be adopted by the Appellate Body in the future, it should be done consistently for non-discrimination of both GATS and GATT. Moreover, it is important for the WTO adjudicating bodies to clearly justify the consideration of certain supplier-related characteristics by demonstrating their effect on the competitive relationship or – should the alternative approach prevail – by the policy objective of the measure.[41] Otherwise the selection of the criteria, and at the same time the scope of non-discrimination, would be purely abstract and arbitrary similar to early GATT 1947 cases,[42] and it would most likely result in a hidden consideration of the policy objective.

3. Quality of services and qualification of suppliers

In addition to nature and properties, the first factor requires consideration of the quality, which again should be analysed with regard to the service itself and the method of supply.[43] The quality of the service is in many cases, but not necessarily always, directly linked to the qualification of the supplier. One of the advantages of the merged test is that the result is not affected by the selection on whether quality and qualification are considered as service-related or supplier-related factors.

The quality and qualification criteria should be examined with caution, given that it is one of the main elements – next to price – that suppliers use to gain a competitive advantage in the market. In GATT jurisprudence, a difference in quality of the products has never led to the conclusion of 'unlikeness'.[44] In the context of services trade, however, the issue of quality and qualification is potentially a very important element in the 'likeness' analysis,[45] considering that many licensing requirements pursue the objective of ensuring a minimum standard and consumer protection. Again, the main issue is whether quality of the service and qualification

[41] Some commentators omit to state a reason for possibly relevant supplier-related characteristics, see e.g. Krajewski, *National Regulation*, p. 105; Bossche, *Law and Policy of WTO*, pp. 340, 394.

[42] Also Cossy, 'Thoughts on "Likeness" in GATS', p. 338, quoting *[recte]* Zdouc, *Comparative Analysis of GATS and GATT*, p. 166.

[43] The differentiation between 'service' and 'supply method' is, however, less relevant with regard to the criterion of quality, given that the quality of supply directly affects the quality of the service itself.

[44] For a consideration of quality see e.g. Panel Report, *Dominican Republic – Import and Sale of Cigarettes*, para. 7.333: 'The Panel agrees with the Dominican Republic that quality is an important factor in the determination of the likeness of products. However, it does not think that values declared by importers for customs purposes can be the only factor used in order to determine the quality of a product'.

[45] In favour of a quality-based distinction also Michaelis, 'Dienstleistungshandel', p. 399.

of the supplier is applied as a factor assessing strictly the competitive relationship, or whether it reflects the policy objective of the measure. Under the here-preferred economic interpretation of 'likeness', quality and qualification would only be relevant to the extent that consumers view the respective services or suppliers not as substitutable due to the different standard in supply or education of the supplier. Without doubt, such a difference would have to be very substantial for a fully informed consumer to consider the service as non-substitutable.

> For instance, a consumer with a problem related to Swiss law is unlikely to view an attorney admitted in the State of California as a substitute to a lawyer admitted to a bar in Switzerland. Similarly, a patient who needs complicated brain surgery would not view any medical doctor as a substitute to a neurosurgeon.

However, in order to avoid having to justify a licensing requirement for reasons of, for instance, public order under Article XIV(a) GATS, Members are recommended to provide for a respective limitation in their schedule of commitments. In contrast, a subjective interpretation of 'likeness' would allow the consideration of any regulatory distinction between quality of services or qualification of suppliers,[46] leaving open the question whether the objective of the regulation is 'legitimate' and whether the measure is indeed necessary.

II End-uses

The Appellate Body defines end-uses as 'the extent to which products are capable of performing the same, or similar, functions'.[47] However, prior to this definition by the Appellate Body, the methodology for the analysis of end-uses was inconsistent and frequently overlapped with the criterion of consumers' tastes and habits.

A WTO/GATT jurisprudence

Since some GATT 1947 panels took an objective approach to 'like products' which is limited to physical similarities and tariff classifications,[48] there was technically no need to analyse the products' end-uses. This

[46] Krajewski and Engelke, 'Art. XVII GATS', p. 407 consider the qualification of the supplier as relevant without, however, stating the reason for its relevancy.

[47] Appellate Body Report, *EC – Asbestos*, para. 117.

[48] See above, chapters 5 and 6.

criterion was only relevant for the concept of 'directly competitive or substitutable' in Article III:2, second sentence, GATT:

> In *EEC – Animal Feed Proteins* on Article III:2, second sentence, GATT, the Panel noted that 'vegetable proteins and skimmed milk powder were technically substitutable in terms of their final use' of adding proteins to feeding stuffs (para 4.3).

Yet, despite the prevailing objective interpretation of 'likeness', some panels considered 'end-uses' also in the 'like product' analysis:

> The Panel in *Spain – Unroasted Coffee*, one of the few to interpret 'like products' in Article I GATT economically, found that 'coffee in its end-use, was universally regarded as a well-defined and single product intended for drinking' (para 4.7). In *US – Superfund* on Article III:2, second sentence, GATT, the Panel noted that liquid hydrocarbon products are 'like' certain types of crude oil because they serve substantially identical end-uses and an '[o]verlap in end-use determines to a great extent direct competitiveness' (para 5.1.1).

These cases have in common that 'end-uses' of products are determined objectively.[49] If the different products under scrutiny were found to have common objective end-uses, it was inferred that they compete with one another. This reasoning neglects that in spite of common end-uses, consumers in a given market may not perceive the products as substitutable. In other words, the consumers' tastes and habits are not sufficiently taken into account in the analysis. The Panel in *Japan – Alcoholic Beverages II* changed this approach in that it referred to end-uses not from an objective, but strictly from a consumer's perspective:

> 'In the Panel's view, the decisive criterion in order to determine whether two products are directly competitive or substitutable is whether they have common end-uses, *inter alia*, as shown by elasticity of substitution.' (para 6.33)

Even though the Panel does not specifically say so, it essentially merged the criteria of end-uses and consumers' tastes and habits into one element of 'substitutability'. The same reasoning was essentially applied by the subsequent Panel Reports *Korea – Alcoholic Beverages*[50] and *Chile – Alcoholic Beverages*.[51]

49 Melloni, *National Treatment in GATT*, p. 125 speaks of 'abstract end-uses'.

50 Para 10.78: 'End-uses constitute one factor which is particularly relevant to the issue of *potential* competition or substitutability. If there are common end-uses, then two products may very well be competitive, either immediately or in the near and reasonably predictable future'.

51 Para 7.32: 'the overall inquiry focuses on whether there are common end-uses by examining a number of factors which can include elasticity of substitution'.

In *EC – Asbestos*, the Appellate Body changed this approach in that it clearly required an analysis of end-uses that is separate from consumers' tastes and habits.[52] It defined end-uses as 'the extent to which products are capable of performing the same, or similar, functions'.[53] Similar to the GATT 1947 jurisprudence, this definition requires an objective determination of the products' end-uses. Consumers' tastes and habits, in contrast, is defined as 'the extent to which consumers are willing to use the products to perform these functions'.[54] In other words, consumers' tastes and habits analyse whether the objectively determined common end-uses are perceived by the consumers in a given market such that the products are regarded as interchangeable.[55] The Appellate Body emphasized the importance of both end-uses and consumers' tastes and habits, as they are highly relevant in order to determine whether the products are substitutable and thus in a competitive relationship.[56]

This new approach introduced by the Appellate Body was followed by the Panel in *Mexico – Taxes on Soft Drinks*, where it objectively determined the end-uses of cane sugar and HFCS and subsequently analysed the consumers' perceptions and behaviour in regard to the common end-use.[57]

B Application to GATS

In the GATT context, end-uses refers to the different functions that can be performed by a certain product. While consumer goods generally serve only one function, most raw materials can be used to perform many different tasks. Services, in contrast, require instant consumption and are generally supplied directly to the end-consumer. Hence, most services only perform one or a very limited number of functions. As noted by *Zdouc*, the criterion end-uses is particularly useful with regard to 'intangible service transactions that bring about a change in the condition or are embodied in a good'.[58] In other words, if the result of a service trans-

[52] Appellate Body Report, *EC – Asbestos*, para. 109: 'the Panel should have examined the evidence relating to *each* of those four criteria' (emphasis original), also paras. 117 ff.

[53] Ibid., para. 117.

[54] Ibid. [55] Emch, 'What are "Like" Products?', 409–12.

[56] Appellate Body Report, *EC – Asbestos*, para. 117.

[57] Paras 8.71 f (issue not appealed).

[58] Zdouc, '(2004) Dispute Settlement Practice', p. 395; see also Mattoo, 'MFN and GATS', p. 73: 'the conventional criteria … need to be replaced by a consideration of the end-

action takes a 'materialized' form, it will be easier to determine common end-uses of services on the basis of the materialized result.

> Compare, for instance, the service supplied by McDonald's and a French cuisine restaurant with 3 Michelin stars. The service materializes either as a Big Mac with fries in a cardboard box or as a filet mignon with potato gratin on a golden plate. Both the filet and the burger, and thus the restaurateur services, have a common end-use of satisfying hunger – whether they are viewed as substitutes, however, depends on the consumers' tastes and habits analysed under the following step. Similarly, the artwork of a painter, a photographer and a sculptor are all displayed in museums, but consumers may not view the different expositions as substitutable.

As illustrated by these examples, the question whether two or more groups of suppliers and their services have common end-uses strongly depends on the level of abstraction that is applied.[59] The purpose of the end-uses analysis could be best described as finding the lowest common denominator. The more specific the denominator is, the higher the probability that the suppliers and their services will be viewed as substitutable under the subsequent analysis of consumers' tastes and habits. It is submitted that this approach works also for purely intangible services, even though the term 'end-use' is not entirely accurate:

> Compare, for instance, an opera, a movie theatre, a live concert and a movie rental. The lowest common denominator between these services is the very abstract notion of 'entertainment'. A movie theatre and a movie rental, in contrast, have a more specific common end-use of 'motion picture entertainment'. The closest common end-use of an opera and a live concert could be described as 'live music entertainment', whereas in comparison to a circus performance, the common end-use would only be 'live entertainment'.

In addition, if the focus of the analysis lies more on the supplier than on the service – which would be particularly the case for measures applying to foreign suppliers under modes 3 and 4 – the skills of the very specific suppliers in question may play an important role in determining the various end-uses.

> For instance, an actor may be able to perform not only in cinema movies, but also in television shows, live theatre or musical shows. Similarly, a

uses of services'; Mattoo, 'National Treatment in GATS', 128; Footer and George, 'The GATS', p. 852.

59 Similarly Horn and Mavroidis, 'Interpretation of National Treatment', 63.

bank provides a variety of different financial services or a highly trained chef could also work in a fast-food chain.

Finally, in the services context it may be difficult to find common end-uses if the service is highly individualized and designed to the consumer's specific needs. In these cases, it will always be necessary to search for common end-uses at a high level of abstraction.

For instance, if a software company writes software to control the very specific performance of an automated robot, there would be no other software company supplying exactly the same service designed for the same end-use. However, there would be a number of software companies supplying programming services that are capable of developing the same software.

In sum, if the analysis shows that there are common end-uses of certain suppliers and their services – even on a high degree of abstraction – the next step will be to determine whether they are viewed as substitutable in accordance with the consumers' tastes and habits in a given market. In contrast, if no common end-use can be found even at the highest degree of abstraction – for instance in the case of entertainment and construction services – it would be possible to conclude 'unlikeness' without analyzing the remaining criteria.

III Consumers' tastes and habits

At the outset it must be noted that the criterion of consumers' tastes and habits does not apply any differently in the services context than it does with regard to trade in goods. Accordingly, there is no need to separate the WTO/GATT discussion of consumers' tastes and habits from its application to GATS non-discrimination rules. As noted in the preceding section, WTO/GATT jurisprudence considered the criterion of consumers' tastes and habits at times only implicitly as part of end-uses, and at times it was not taken into account at all, in particular when a panel did not undertake an economic analysis of 'likeness'. It was only in *EC – Asbestos* where the Appellate Body specifically emphasized the significance of an independent analysis of consumers' tastes and habits.[60] Many commentators suggest that the consumer's view is particularly important for the 'likeness' analysis in GATS non-discrimination.[61]

[60] Para 139.

[61] Cossy, 'Thoughts on "Likeness" in GATS', pp. 338–39; Krajewski and Engelke, 'Art. XVII GATS', p. 403; Krajewski, *National Regulation*, p. 99; Zdouc, '(2004) Dispute Settlement Practice', p. 395; Zdouc, 'Streitigkeiten über den Dienstleistungsverkehr', p. 134.

It is submitted that a correct analysis of this criterion should focus on whether consumers view the products or services as interchangeable, examining *in particular* how the similarities and differences in 'properties, nature and quality' as well as 'end-uses' affect consumer choice in a given market. Moreover, consumers' tastes and habits allow additional evidence that has not yet been considered under the previous two criteria to be taken into consideration. In other words, the *Border Tax Adjustments* framework should be shaped such that the evidence analysed under the first two criteria, plus all additional relevant evidence, are altogether evaluated and balanced under the umbrella of consumers' tastes and habits in order to determine the overall competitive relationship between the products or services from a consumer's perspective.

The Appellate Body seemed to propose a similar, although not entirely identical and consistent, methodology in *EC – Asbestos*. On the one hand, it recognized the importance of consumers' tastes and habits as well as the linkages with the other criteria:

> 'in a case such as this one, where the physical properties of the fibres are very different, an examination of the evidence relating to consumers' tastes and habits is an indispensable – although not, on its own, sufficient – aspect of any determination that products are "like"'. (para 139)

On the other hand, the Appellate Body emphasized that consumers' tastes and habits are not, on their own, sufficient and that the criteria of physical characteristics and end-uses have their own and independent significance.[62] However, it is important to note that the analysis of physical characteristics and end-uses *in the abstract* has no value in determining the competitive relationship of the products or services. Hence, under the Appellate Body's approach it remains unclear why and what kind of physical characteristics should be relevant for the assessment of 'likeness'.[63]

Given that 'likeness' is about competitive relationship, it is argued here that contrary to the Appellate Body's methodology, consumers' tastes and habits should indeed be the decisive element.[64] The question thus is not whether consumers' tastes and habits is a sufficient criterion, but whether *all* the relevant evidence has been considered under this criterion to

[62] Ortino, *Instruments for the Liberalisation of Trade*, p. 333: 'it appears that, except for the criterion of tariff classification, all other criteria are *equally* relevant' (emphasis added).

[63] Also recognizing the AB's inconsistency e.g. Howse and Tuerk, 'WTO Impact on Internal Regulations', pp. 302–3; Trebilcock and Howse, *Regulation of International Trade*, pp. 105–6.

[64] Also Emch, 'What are "Like" Products?', 371–2; Vranes, *Trade and the Environment*, pp. 194–95.

properly assess whether consumers view the products or services as interchangeable. While the criteria of 'nature, properties and quality' as well as 'end-uses' will always be an important aspect, there is a whole range of other evidence that should be taken into account. Among such evidence, the WTO adjudicating bodies have already considered marketing studies, price differences, channels of distribution, points of sale, statements by national authorities, evidence from third markets and health risks;[65] this type of evidence is discussed in detail under section 14.III.A.3 below.

The entire argument can be taken even one step further. Considering that the *Border Tax Adjustments* framework focusing on consumers' tastes and habits is essentially nothing else than an analysis of demand substitutability, it is suggested that the entire analysis of 'likeness' should focus on substitutability of demand in the first place.[66] Consequently, the analysis of 'likeness' should take into account all evidence relevant to affect demand substitutability. While the three criteria from *Border Tax Adjustments* would preserve their significance, they would be merely a tool helping to guarantee that no relevant evidence is neglected in the analysis. Such an approach shows strong resemblances to the concept of market definition to be analysed in detail in chapter 14.

IV Tariff and service classification

The criterion of tariff classifications was not originally part of the *Border Tax Adjustments* report, but it had already been applied by earlier decisions and it was subsequently confirmed by WTO jurisprudence.[67] The classification of products is necessary for tariff purposes because tariff levels vary considerably from one product to another. The applicable tariff rate thus depends on the category to which a specific product is attributed. Since the negotiations of tariff concessions and tariff bindings would be very difficult if each Member used its own classification system, Members have been relying on the internationally Harmonized Commodity Description and Coding System (Harmonized System). The Harmonized System Convention was developed by the Customs

[65] Critically on the AB's analysis of health risks Cone, 'Asbestos Case', 125.

[66] *Emch* argues that 'the only reliable method to ascertain "consumers' tastes and habits" is to measure their purchases. As a result, the criterion of "consumers' tastes and habits" responds directly to the two aforementioned requirements – that the relationship between products be *economic* and that it be determined by *demand*' (emphasis original), Emch, 'What are "Like" Products?', 379.

[67] Forrester QC and Kaul, 'Tariff Classification', pp. 1587 ff.

Cooperation Council (today World Customs Organization) and came into force in 1988.[68]

In the services context, the equivalent criterion is the classification of service transactions. During the GATS negotiations, the Montreal Ministerial Declaration requested the WTO Secretariat to compile a reference list of service sectors in order to assess the 'implications and applicability of concepts, principles and rules for particular sectors and specific transactions'.[69] Following this mandate, the Secretariat submitted a draft to the negotiators, discussing the different sectoral classification systems, in particular the activity-, transaction- and product-based classification.[70] Preference was given to the latter, relying on the example of the United Nations Central Product Classification (CPC).[71] Subsequently, the Secretariat compiled the Service Sectoral Classification List.[72] This classification of services is particularly useful for the negotiations of commitments under Articles XVI and XVII GATS, as it allows Members to schedule their commitments and limitations with regard to specific service sectors. Both the Guidelines on Scheduling of Initial Commitments of 1993 and the Scheduling Guidelines of 2001 recommend Members explicitly to base their schedule on the Service Sectoral Classification List in order to ensure greater clarity in the description of the sectors.[73] WTO jurisprudence already resorted to the classification lists for the analysis of 'likeness' under Articles II and XVII GATS.

> In *EC – Bananas III*, the Panel relied on the CPC in order to qualify the distribution of bananas as 'wholesale trade services' (para 7.289 ff) and subsequently noted that 'wholesale transactions as such, as well as of each of the different subordinated services mentioned in the headnote to section 6 of the CPC, are "like" when supplied in connection with wholesale services' (para 7.322).

[68] See e.g. Cottier and Oesch, *International Trade Regulation*, p. 596; Trebilcock and Howse, *Regulation of International Trade*, p. 188.

[69] TNC Meeting at Ministerial Level, Montreal, December 1988, MTN.TNC/7(MIN), 9 December 1988, Part II, para. 10.

[70] GNS, Reference List of Sectors, Note by the Secretariat, MTN.GNS/W/50, 13 April 1989.

[71] For the most recent CPC Ver.2 completed on 31 December 2008 see http://unstats.un.org/unsd/cr/registry/cpc-2.asp.

[72] GNS, Services Sectoral Classification List, Note by the Secretariat, MTN.GNS/W/120, 10 July 1991.

[73] GNS, Scheduling of Initial Commitments in Trade in Services: Explanatory Note, MTN.GNS/W/164, 3 September 1993, para. 16; CTS, Guidelines for the Scheduling of Specific Commitments under the General Agreement on Trade in Services (GATS), S/L/92, 28 March 2001, para. 23.

> Antigua also referred to the CPC in its argument on 'likeness' among gambling services: 'Finally, the international classification of services used in the WTO context, the CPC Prov., provides only one category for gambling and betting services. The more recent versions of the CPC classification, CPC 1.0 and CPC 1.1 also provide for just one category for gambling and betting services.'[74]

Next to WTO jurisprudence, some commentators also suggest that the service classification lists are useful in the 'likeness' context.[75] In a 'like product' comparative analysis, it is noteworthy that under GATT 1947 jurisprudence the importance of tariff classifications was particularly high in the context of an objective interpretation of 'like products' for purposes of MFN treatment. As, in accordance with the current interpretation of 'like products', the objective approach is – if at all – only appropriate with regard to differential tariff treatment under Article I GATT, the overall significance of tariff classifications is very limited. Under an economic interpretation of 'likeness', it is unlikely that a difference in the tariff classification would overturn a finding of 'likeness' if all the relevant evidence indicates the existence of a competitive relationship, and vice versa. Tariff classifications are only a limited reflection of the competition taking place in a given marketplace. This is particularly true with regard to the Service Sectoral Classification List, given that it is based on the CPC which has been adopted by the UN primarily for statistical and not for trade purposes. Hence, this criterion could be used at best as a first starting point to circumscribe a group of potentially competitive products or in order to confirm – but not overturn – the results from the previous three criteria.[76]

> The Appellate Body in *Japan – Alcoholic Beverages II* for instance stated: 'It is true that there are numerous tariff bindings which are in fact extremely precise with regard to product description and which, therefore, can provide significant guidance as to the identification of "like products". Clearly enough, these determinations need to be made on a case-by-case basis. However, tariff bindings that include a wide range of products are

[74] Antigua's argument in Panel Report, *US – Gambling*, para. 3.151; see also EC argument, para. 4.37.

[75] Zdouc, '(2004) Dispute Settlement Practice', pp. 396–97; Wang, 'MFN under GATS', 98–99; Leroux, 'GATS Case Law', 780, n 118; Pitschas, 'GATS', p. 513; but see sceptically Cossy, 'Thoughts on "Likeness" in GATS', pp. 333–34; Mattoo, 'National Treatment in GATS', 128; Krajewski and Engelke, 'Art. XVII GATS', p. 404; Krajewski, *National Regulation*, pp 101–2; see also Abu-Akeel, 'MFN in Service Trade', 111–13, arguing that the individual schedules of commitments should serve as a benchmark for the "likeness"' analysis.

[76] Similarly Cossy, 'Thoughts on "Likeness" in GATS', p. 334.

> not a reliable criterion for determining or confirming product "likeness" under Article III:2.' (p 23)

This statement needs to be relativized. On the one hand it is certainly true that very precise tariff bindings indicate the existence of a competitive relationship if the products fall within the same classification. On the other hand, however, the value of extremely narrow tariff bindings or service classifications is very limited for determining a competitive relationship if the products or services are within different categories. In this case, a broader classification may even reflect the market situation more accurately. In sum, the criterion of tariff or service classifications should be considered cautiously and its significance should not be overestimated.

V Conclusions

The very limited jurisprudence and scholarly work on 'likeness' in GATS largely suggests that the *Border Tax Adjustments* framework should be applied, but some commentators also recognize the shortcomings of such an approach. One of the main difficulties lies in the fact that the *Border Tax Adjustments* framework has been subject to continuous substantial developments. Early versions of the framework relied heavily on objective criteria. Some later decisions only applied one or two of the four criteria and others added new criteria to the analysis. In consequence, the types of evidence considered in the 'likeness' analysis vary considerably between the different cases. In sum, the *Border Tax Adjustments* framework has been applied very inconsistently and its methodology is still not entirely clear. Yet, the application of an unsettled *Border Tax Adjustments* framework to GATS is likely to concede to the temptation to conclude 'unlikeness' on the basis of abstract differences between the suppliers without sufficiently taking into consideration the consumers' perspective.

In *EC – Asbestos*, the Appellate Body attempted to bring much needed structure into the *Border Tax Adjustments* framework, albeit limiting its findings to Article III:4 GATT. The most important findings were that the framework must be applied strictly to assess the competitive relationship, that each criterion requires an individual analysis and that all relevant evidence must be considered. It is argued here that the *Border Tax Adjustments* framework should be designed such that consumers' tastes and habits take a key role in the analysis; the conclusions on the differences and similarities from the first two criteria, namely properties, nature and quality as well as end-uses, should be assessed – together with all other relevant evidence – in the light of the consumers' perspective in a given market. Tariff and service classifications, in contrast, are only of minor importance. Only such an approach lives up to the overall purpose of the comparison, which is to determine the competitive relationship between the products or services.

Considering the clear developments towards a market analysis, the time seems to be ripe to pose the fundamental question whether the historically grown *Border Tax Adjustments* framework is still appropriate and sufficiently elaborate to meet the needs of a modern 'like product' and, even more predominantly, 'like services and service suppliers' analysis. It appears that in *EC – Asbestos*, the Appellate Body opened the door for the development of a new test:

> 'These criteria are, it is well to bear in mind, simply tools to assist in the task of sorting and examining the relevant evidence. They are neither a treaty-mandated nor a closed list of criteria that will determine the legal characterization of products.' (para 102) 'Accordingly, whether the *Border Tax Adjustments* framework is adopted or not, it is important under Article III:4 to take account of evidence which indicates whether, and to what extent, the products involved are – or could be – in a competitive relationship in the marketplace.' (para 103)

Despite this invitation by the Appellate Body and sporadic alternative proposals by commentators, subsequent panels all were – and continue to be – clutching to the familiar *Border Tax Adjustments* framework. It is submitted that the concept of 'likeness' in GATS as well as the current understanding of the same concept in GATT requires a new approach, focusing more specifically on a market analysis than the conventional framework. The central element of a new methodology is *substitutability*. An analysis of market conditions and substitutability is not new in the science of law, as competition authorities around the globe define relevant product and service markets on a daily basis. The following chapter thus takes a comparative approach to market definition in competition law and 'likeness' in trade.

14

Applying market definition theories to 'likeness'

The policy of international trade is undoubtedly linked very closely to competition policy, as both areas strive to ensure equal conditions of competition by eliminating market distortions. The main broad difference between the two areas lies in the fact that trade law addresses market limitations that are created by governments, whereas competition law prohibits market distortions created by non-state actors, in particular private enterprises.[1] Despite the complementary character of the two legal and economic fields, competition law is still largely a matter of national domain. Unlike in the area of trade, international cooperation in rule making and enforcement of competition policy is very limited.[2]

The WTO initiated numerous attempts to explore the interactions between trade and competition policy. At the Singapore Ministerial Meeting of 1996, the WTO established the Working Group on the Interaction of Trade and Competition (WGTCP).[3] During the Doha Ministerial Meeting in 2002, it was decided to include the interaction of trade and competition in the Doha Declaration in order to conduct further studies and negotiations on this subject. The mandate was formulated very broadly, directing the Working Group to focus on the clarification of 'core principles, including transparency, non-discrimination and procedural fairness, and provisions on hard core cartels; modalities for voluntary cooperation; and support for progressive reinforcement

[1] Trebilcock, 'Competition Policy and Trade Policy', 73–74; Lowenfeld, *International Economic Law*, p. 453; Gifford and Matsushita, 'Competition Laws in Trading Context', pp. 269–70; but see Bellis, 'Anti-competitive Practices and WTO', p. 366 (no strong link between antitrust practices and market access).

[2] For an overview of international cooperation in competition policy see Lowenfeld, *International Economic Law*, pp. 453–64; Fox, 'Antitrust Law on a Global Scale', *passim*; Guzman, 'International Competition Law', pp. 423 ff.

[3] Ministerial Conference (Singapore), Ministerial Declaration, WT/MIN(96)/DEC, 18 December 1996, para.20.

of competition institutions in developing countries through capacity-building'.[4] However, already in August 2004 the issue had been dropped from the Doha agenda. Primarily developing countries refused further negotiations on competition policy, partly because it was construed as part of the Singapore issues including also investment, government procurement and trade facilitation.[5] Accordingly, the WTO General Council decided that the subject of competition policy 'will not form part of the Work Programme set out in that Declaration and therefore no work towards negotiations on any of these issues will take place within the WTO during the Doha Round'.[6] Hence, the Working Group is currently inactive.

Despite this absence of a comprehensive competition policy under the WTO, the two fields overlap in various ways and WTO law even contains some elements of competition-related principles with regard to certain sectors, in particular in the area of services.[7] For instance, GATS Article VIII requires monopoly service suppliers to respect the MFN obligation and Member governments to ensure that monopoly suppliers do not abuse their monopoly position in a way that would frustrate their specific GATS commitments. Even more pertinent, the Reference Paper on Basic Telecommunications[8] provides for principles known from competition policy, namely the prohibition for domestic suppliers to engage in anticompetitive practices or to abuse their dominant market position.[9] Finally, even non-competition principles such as non-discrimination in GATT and GATS apply to internal regulations and as such require national competition policy to be adopted and, in principle, enforced on a non-discriminatory basis.[10]

[4] Ministerial Conference (Doha), Ministerial Declaration, WT/MIN(01)/DEC/1, 20 November 2001, paras. 23–25.

[5] Stewart, 'Competition Policy in Cancun', 7 ff.

[6] General Council, Doha Work Programme, WT/L/579, 1 August 2004, para.1(g).

[7] Warner, 'Trade and Competition Policy Rule-Making', 311–13, 334–51; Wyss, *Bankdienstleistungen*, pp. 60–61.

[8] Many Members incorporated the Reference Paper on Basic Telecommunications as additional commitments in their schedule of commitments; for an overview see www.wto.org/english/tratop_e/serv_e/telecom_e/tel10_e.htm.

[9] See e.g. Bobjoseph, *WTO Agreements on Telecommunications*, pp. 124 ff; Mavroidis and Neven, 'WTO Agreement on Telecommunications', pp. 311–13; Bronckers, 'Reference Paper on Telecommunications', p. 372; Fischer, *Entbündelung der letzten Meile*, p. 123.

[10] On compliance of competition policy with non-discrimination see e.g. Ehlermann and Ehring, 'WTO Dispute Settlement and Competition Law', 1520, 1527; Marsden, *Competition Policy for the WTO*, pp. 148 ff; Kearns, 'Competition Policy and GATS', p. 658; Trebilcock, 'Competition Policy and Trade Policy', 96.

In terms of substance, the question of 'likeness' under the principle of non-discrimination is very closely related to the concept of 'market definition', a fundamental element of competition law.[11] In *Korea – Alcoholic Beverages* the issue was raised whether the same criteria should be used for defining 'likeness' under Article III:2 GATT as for market definition in competition law. The Panel noted in this regard that '[w]hile the specifics of the interaction between trade and competition law are still being developed, we concur that the market definitions need not be the same'.[12] The linkage is particularly significant with regard to the broader standard of 'directly competitive or substitutable' products or services, which – as argued in chapters 5 and 6 above – is not only relevant for GATT Article III:2, second sentence, but also applies to Article III:4 GATT and Articles II and XVII GATS. Moreover, it is worth emphasizing that GATS explicitly applies the concept of relevant market in Article VIII:1, according to which monopoly suppliers *in the relevant market* must comply with Article II GATS.[13] Similarly, Article 1.1 of the Reference Paper on Basic Telecommunications contains obligations for Members to adopt appropriate measures in order to prevent major suppliers from engaging in anticompetitive practices. The legal term 'major supplier' is defined on the basis of the relevant market concept from competition law.[14] Finally, some commentators suggest that the term 'competition' in Article I:3(c) GATS must also be interpreted on the basis of a relevant market.[15]

Considering the close similarities and underlying theories of the 'relevant market' and 'likeness' even within the WTO framework, a comparative analysis is useful to determine whether the interpretation of 'likeness'

[11] Janow, 'Trade and Competition Policy', p. 500.

[12] Para 10.81.

[13] The term 'monopoly supplier of a service' is defined in Art. XXVIII(h) GATS as 'any person, public or private, which in the *relevant market* of the territory of a Member is authorized or established formally or in effect by that Member as the sole supplier of that service'; also linking 'relevant market' and 'likeness' in trade and competition law Bigdeli and Rechsteiner, 'Art. VIII GATS', p. 213.

[14] Definition in the Reference Paper on Basic Telecommunications; Panel Report, *Mexico – Telecoms*, para.7.152; Bronckers and Larouche, 'Telecommunications Services', p. 1002: 'The use of "relevant market" must be taken as a reference to competition law where the concept is well known'; also Bronckers and Larouche, 'Review Telecommunications Services', p. 333; Gao, 'Telecommunications Services: Reference Paper', p. 729.

[15] Zacharias, 'Art. I GATS', p. 66; Krajewski, *National Regulation*, p. 70; Krajewski, 'Public Services and Trade Liberalization', 352.

in WTO law could draw from experiences related to the concept of market definition in competition law.[16]

Due to the lack of a substantive international agreement on competition policy, competition law is applied and interpreted by national authorities and judiciary. This chapter firstly introduces in section I the concept of market definition as it applies in EU and US competition law. The second section focuses on similarities and differences between competition and trade policy specifically in view of the application of 'market definition' and 'likeness'. Section III of this chapter illustrates how markets are defined in EU and US competition law in the light of relevant statutes, guidelines and jurisprudence and analyses how the respective methodology could inform the 'likeness' analysis in trade non-discrimination. While the conclusions in section IV are equally relevant for the concepts of 'like products' in GATT as well as 'like services/suppliers' in GATS, the focus lies more on the services sector, specifically with regard to the analysis of relevant case law.

I 'Market definition' in competition law

A The concept of market definition in EU competition law

The main pillars of EU competition policy are antitrust law as well as merger and state aid control. For the purpose of this study, the former two are of particular interest. Antitrust law in general prohibits cartelistic behaviour as well as the abuse of dominant positions. The law on merger control, in contrast, aims at preventing adverse impacts on competition as a result of merging firms in the same sector, which could occur for instance because of a reduced choice for consumers at higher prices. Both

[16] This view is shared by numerous commentators, see e.g. Mavroidis, '"Like Products": Some Thoughts', p. 131; Choi, '*Like Products*', p. 33; Goco, '"Likeness", and Market Definition', 329–35; Horn and Mavroidis, 'Interpretation of National Treatment', 66; Marchetti and Mavroidis, 'Challenges for GATS', 532–33; Neven, 'How Should "Protection" be Evaluated?', 437; Neven, 'Economic Evaluation of Protection', p. 332; Trebilcock and Giri, 'National Treatment Principle', 60; Quick and Lau, 'Environmentally Motivated Tax Distinctions', 433; for 'like products' in anti-dumping see Bronckers and McNelis, '"Like Product" Definition', p. 358; for 'like circumstances' in NAFTA/BIT see Grierson-Weiler and Laird, 'Standards of Treatment', p. 291 *in fine*; for 'like product' in US trade law see Berg, 'Economic Interpretation of "Like-Product"', 197; for 'like product' in the EC law see Wilsher, 'Non-Discrimination Principle within the European Single Market', 5–6; Englisch, *Wettbewerbsgleichheit*, pp. 293–94.

principles require determining the position of the firms in a given market, either in regard to their dominance or in regard to the competitive effect of the merger.[17]

1. Cartelistic behaviour (Art. 101 TFEU)

Article 101 TFEU (ex Art. 81 TEC) prohibits all agreements and concerted practices which may affect trade between Member States and which prevents, restricts or distorts competition within the common market. The provision further specifies prohibited cartel behaviour, such as price fixing, limitation of markets, discrimination between trading partners and conditioning the conclusion of a contract with supplementary conditions that are unrelated to the subject of the contract. Market definition only plays a very limited role for the legal assessment of cartels. The Commission may in most cases make a finding of a violation of Article 101 without defining precisely what the relevant market is.[18] The decisive questions arise with regard to other legal elements of Article 101, namely the qualification of 'agreements' and 'concerted practices' as well as the substantive definition of 'restriction of competition'.

Nonetheless, it may be necessary to define the market in order to determine whether an agreement has an appreciable impact on competition under the *de minimis* doctrine.[19] Yet, this doctrine only has a corrective and subordinate function in the analysis of prohibited cartel behaviour. Similarly, the relevant market may be of interest to analyse the effect of an agreement on *trade between Member States.*

> For example, the Court of First instance stated with regard to the legitimacy of beer supply agreements that the 'delimitation of the relevant market is essential in order to analyse the effects on competition of beer supply agreements with an exclusive purchasing obligation, and in particular to analyse the opportunities available to new domestic and foreign competitors to establish themselves in the market of the consumption of beer or to increase their market shares'.[20]

[17] For a comprehensive overview see e.g. Lindsay and Scola, 'Market Definition', pp. 242 ff; also Golz, *Relevante Markt bei Verlagserzeugnissen*, pp. 4–5.

[18] See e.g. Lindsay and Scola, 'Market Definition', p. 242, referring to Joined cases T-374/94, T-375/94, T-384/94 and T-388/94 *European Night Services* v. *Commission* [1998] ECR II-3141; also Cárdenas Tomažič, *Marktabgrenzung*, p. 78.

[19] See 'Commission Notice on agreements of minor importance which do not appreciably restrict competition under Article 81(1) of the Treaty establishing the European Community (de minimis)', OJ 2001 C368/13.

[20] Case T-25/99 *Roberts* v. *Commission* [2001] ECR II-1881, para.26; see already Case 234/89 *Stergios Delimitis* v. *Henninger Bräu AG* [1991] ECR I-935, paras. 15–16.

Finally, the concept of market definition may become relevant under Article 101 TFEU in order to assess specific aspects of a cartel, such as its scope or the extent of individual participation.[21]

2. Abuse of dominant positions (Art. 102 TFEU)

In addition to cartel behaviour, antitrust law of the EU prohibits in Article 102 TFEU (ex Art. 82 TEC) any abuse by one or more undertakings of a dominant position within the common market in so far as it may affect trade between Member States. The provision contains an exemplary list of typical forms of abusive conduct, such as unfair prices or trading conditions, limitation of production, discrimination between trading partners and conditioning the conclusion of contracts with supplementary obligations unconnected to the subject of the contract. Accordingly, Article 102 does not prohibit market power of monopolies *per se*, but only the abuse of such power. The essence is the control of market behaviour. However, Article 102 requires that the firm is in a dominant position before the prohibition of abusive conduct becomes applicable.

The concept of dominance is not legally defined in the treaty provision. The ECJ interpreted it as 'a position of economic strength enjoyed by an undertaking which enables it to prevent effective competition being maintained on the relevant market by affording it the power to behave to an appreciable extent independently of its competitors, its customers and ultimately of the consumers'.[22] As this definition suggests, the application of the dominance concept depends strongly on an economic analysis of the market. More specifically, dominance of a firm can only exist with regard to the supply of certain products or services and thus requires the definition of the relevant product or service market. As a general rule, the narrower a product market is defined, the fewer competitors will be taken into consideration and the more likely the firm under scrutiny will be found to be in a dominant position. In contrast, a broad product market in general leads to less market shares of the individual competitors and thus to weaker market positions. Accordingly, the question of a relevant

[21] Case T-61/99 *Adriatica di Navigazione* v. *Commission* [2003] ECR II-5349, para.30: 'objections to the Commission's definition of the relevant market may impinge upon other factors which have a bearing upon the application of Article 85(1) of the Treaty, such as the scope of the cartel in question, the question whether it is a specific or general cartel, or the extent of the individual participation of each of the undertakings concerned'.

[22] Case 85/76 *Hoffmann-La Roche* v. *Commission* [1979] ECR 461, para.38.

product market constitutes a key issue in the analysis of all Article 102 cases.[23]

3. Merger regulation

While the control of abusive conduct focuses on market behaviour, the control of mergers addresses the issue of market structures. The aim of merger control is to prohibit concentration of market power that would allow the merged firm to obstruct effective competition. The TFEU does not provide any specific rules on mergers. The ECJ tried to fill this gap by applying Article 102 to control the merger of firms in a dominant position, and later the court also considered the relevance of Article 101 in the context of merger control.[24] These legal uncertainties led to the adoption of the first EU Merger Regulation in 1989 which was replaced in 2004 by a revised Regulation.[25]

Even though the EU Merger Regulation constitutes the main legislative text for the assessment of concentrations, numerous guidelines and notices play a very important role in its interpretation. The *Guidelines on the assessment of horizontal mergers under the Council Regulation on the control of concentrations between undertakings* specify the analytical steps which the Commission's assessment of mergers normally entail, namely the (a) definition of the relevant product and geographic markets; and (b) competitive assessment of the merger.[26] According to para.10, the main purpose of market definition is to 'identify in a systematic way the immediate competitive constraints facing the merged entity'. Accordingly, the ECJ emphasized that – as for the application of Article 102 – 'a proper

[23] See e.g. Case T-61/99 *Adriatica di Navigazione* v. *Commission* [2003] ECR II-5349, para.27: 'For the purposes of Article 86, the appropriate definition of the relevant market is a necessary precondition for any judgment concerning allegedly anti-competitive behaviour ... since, before an abuse of a dominant position is ascertained, it is necessary to establish the existence of a dominant position in a given market, which presupposes that such a market has already been defined'; also Joined cases T-68/89, T-77/89 and T-78/89 *Società Italiana Vetro SpA* v. *Commission* [1992] ECR II-1403.

[24] For Art. 82 see Case 6/72 *Europemballage Corporation and Continental Can* v. *Commission* [1973] ECR 215; for Art. 81 see Joined cases 142 and 156/84, *British-American Tobacco Company Ltd and R. J. Reynolds Industries* v. *Commission* [1987] ECR 4487; for a comprehensive overview of the relationship between Art. 81, 82 and merger control, see Mestmäcker and Schweitzer, *Europäisches Wettbewerbsrecht*, pp. 529 ff.

[25] Council Regulation (EC) No. 139/2004 of 20 January 2004 on the control of concentrations between undertakings, OJ 2004 L24/1.

[26] OJ 2004 C31/5.

definition of the relevant market is a necessary precondition for any assessment of the effect of a concentration on competition'.[27]

B *The concept of market definition in US antitrust law*

The Sherman Antitrust Act (Sherman Act) of 1890 was the first US federal statute on antitrust law adopted to prohibit agreements 'in restraint of trade' as well as monopolization and attempts to monopolize. It is interesting to note that the first courts applying the Sherman Act faced similar interpretative issues as the panels in the first GATT 1947 cases. As outlined above, GATT 1947 panels had to define 'conditions of competition' as the underlying principle of non-discrimination, given that the treaty provisions are silent in this regard. Similarly, the Sherman Act does not contain any relevant language on competition, reason for which it was originally not undisputed whether the text 'in restraint of trade or commerce' should in fact be guided by the principle of competition and competitive relationships. In the Supreme Court case *Northern Securities*, for instance, the majority of the court found that 'the natural effect of competition is to increase commerce, and an agreement whose direct effect is to prevent this play of competition restrains instead of promotes trade and commerce'.[28] In contrast, Justice *Holmes* declared in his dissenting opinion that the majority 'argued as if maintaining competition were the expressed object of the act. The act says nothing about competition. I stick to the exact words used.'[29]

1. Cartels (Sherman Act § 1)

In a similar way to Article 101 TFEU, section 1 of the Sherman Act outlaws all forms of cartelistic behaviour, stating that '[e]very contract, combination in the form of trust or otherwise, or conspiracy, in restraint of trade or commerce among the several States, or with foreign nations, is declared to be illegal'.[30] The principal legal elements are thus the existence of some form of an 'agreement' and the 'restraint of trade'. Similarly to the corresponding principle of Article 101 TFEU, market definition is only of limited relevance under section 1 Sherman Act and does not constitute a

[27] Joined cases C-68/94 and 30/95 *French Republic* v. *Commission* [1998] ECR I-1375, para.143; see comprehensively Neveling, *Marktabgrenzung bei der Fusionskontrolle*, pp. 140–44.

[28] *Northern Securities* v. *US*, 193 US 197 (1904), p. 331.

[29] Ibid., p. 403.

[30] 15 U.S.C. § 1.

precondition for finding a violation. Courts traditionally analyse restraints of trade either under the rule of *per se* illegality or the rule of reason. On the one hand, the *per se* rule declares certain types of conducts that are manifestly anticompetitive – first and foremost price-fixing agreements – as illegal as a matter of law, not requiring the courts to conduct an analysis of the actual market consequences.[31] Agreements that are not found to be *per se* illegal, on the other hand, are analysed under the rule of reason, which entails an examination of the agreements' anticompetitive impact in a relevant market. Such an examination of the anticompetitive effect generally requires the definition of a relevant market.[32] Hence, US courts analyse market structures and market power in section 1 cases only in view of the likely consequences of the allegedly unlawful agreement.[33]

2. Single firm conduct (Sherman Act § 2)

The Sherman Act not only prohibits cartels, but also restrains unilateral conduct under certain circumstances. It states in section 2 that '[e]very person who shall monopolize, or attempt to monopolize, or combine or conspire with any other person or persons, to monopolize any part of the trade or commerce among the several States, or with foreign nations, shall be deemed guilty of a felony'.[34] In 2008, the US Department of Justice issued an extensive Competition and Monopoly Report explaining how it analyses single firm conduct under Section 2 of the Sherman Act.[35]

It is important to note the similarities and differences of section 2 Sherman Act in comparison to Article 102 TFEU. In a similar way to Article 102, the Sherman Act sets forth a two-step test consisting of a structural and a conduct element. As held by the US Supreme Court, it is first necessary to examine whether the firm possesses monopoly power (structure) and, second, whether the firm engages in the illegal conduct of 'monopolizing' (conduct).[36] The first step requires defining the relevant market in order to determine whether the firm has a monopoly. The

[31] See e.g. *Broadcast Music* v. *CBS*, 441 US 1 (1979), pp. 19–20.

[32] See e.g. *Continental T.V.* v. *GTE Sylvania*, 433 US 36 (1977); but see *FTC* v. *Indiana Federation of Dentists*, 476 US 447 (1986), p. 460: 'the Commission's failure to engage in detailed market analysis is not fatal to its finding of a violation of the Rule of Reason'.

[33] For an overview of market power in § 1 Sherman Act see e.g. ABA Section of Antitrust Law, *Market Power Handbook*, pp. 11–17.

[34] 15 U.S.C. § 2; for further reading e.g. Elhauge, 'Defining Better Monopolization Standards'; Piraino, 'Exclusionary Conduct'.

[35] US Dep't of Justice, Competition and Monopoly: Single-Firm Conduct Under Section 2 of the Sherman Act (2008).

[36] *US* v. *Grinnell Corp.*, 384 US 563 (1966), pp. 570 f.

analysis thus far is similar to Article 102 TFEU, according to which it is necessary to determine whether a firm is in a domination position. The important difference between the two systems relates to the second element of conduct, in that the EU prohibits abusive behaviour, whereas the US outlaws the conduct of monopolizing.[37] Unlike EU law, section 2 of the Sherman Act does not provide an indicative list of behaviour falling under the prohibited conduct of 'monopolizing'. The US Court of Appeals for the Third Circuit summarized the principles from a century of case law on this term and clarified its meaning in the *Microsoft* case by developing the following test:[38] First, the monopoly's behaviour must have an 'anticompetitive effect' by harming not only competitors, but in particular consumers. Second, the plaintiff must show that 'its injury is of the type that the statute was intended to forestall'. A positive answer to these elements establishes a *prima facie* case that can be rebutted by the respondent in a third step, showing procompetitive justifications for its behaviour. Finally, the last step requires the plaintiff to demonstrate that the anticompetitive effect outweighs the procompetitive justifications.

3. Merger control (Clayton Act § 7)

The regulation of mergers was not originally part of the Sherman Act and was introduced in US antitrust law by the Clayton Act of 1914. Section 7 of the Clayton Act prohibits mergers and acquisitions where the effect 'may be substantially to lessen competition, or to tend to create a monopoly'.[39] Accordingly, market structure plays an important role in the analysis of section 7 Clayton Act. In order to make the analysis of merger cases more transparent, the US Department of Justice released its first merger guidelines already in 1968, which were significantly revised in 1982 and again in 1984. These guidelines were replaced by the 1992 Horizontal Merger Guidelines issued jointly by the Department of Justice and the Federal Trade Commission. The 1992 Merger Guidelines provide for more refined tools for the market analysis. The 1997 version of these guidelines and the corresponding Merger Guidelines Commentary 2006 are still effective today and provide the basis for this chapter's comparative analysis.[40] However, while these guidelines constitute an important element in the

[37] For a comprehensive discussion Hawk, 'Abuse and Monopolizing Conduct'.

[38] *US* v. *Microsoft Corp.*, 253 F 3d 34 (D.C.Cir. 2001), p. 58.

[39] 15 U.S.C. § 18.

[40] 1997 US Merger Guidelines; US Dep't of Justice/Federal Trade Commission, Commentary on the Horizontal Merger Guidelines (2006).

interpretation of merger law, the only authoritative source remains to be case law.

The first time the US Supreme Court referred to the concept of 'relevant market' in the context of a merger case – albeit under section 2 of the Sherman Act – was in its decision *Columbia Steel* in 1948, where it recognized 'the difficulty of laying down a rule as to what areas or products are competitive, one with another' and ultimately omitted to develop a test for market definition.[41] In 1950 Congress amended section 7 of the Clayton Act with the Celler-Kefauver Act, prohibiting mergers 'where in any line of commerce or in any activity affecting commerce in any section of the country, the effect of such acquisition may be substantially to lessen competition'. The courts equated the new phrase 'in any line of commerce' with the concept of 'relevant market', which introduced the exercise of 'market definition' into the legal analysis.[42] Another important milestone in the application of section 7 of the Clayton Act came with the case *Philadelphia National Bank*, where the Supreme Court announced a simplified test of *prima facie* illegality in cases where a 'merger produces a firm controlling an undue percentage share of the relevant market'.[43] US merger control strictly distinguishes between two theories of competitive harm, namely coordinated and unilateral effects.[44] Under the coordinated effects approach, a merger is prohibited if it leads to a high risk of coordinated behaviour among the small number of remaining competitors. The unilateral effects theory, in contrast, is concerned with the increased market power of the merged entities.

II 'Likeness' and market definition compared

From a consumer perspective, the degree of competitive relationship and substitutability does not change on the basis of whether the relevant market is defined for purposes of non-discrimination, trade remedies, merger control or single firm conduct; competitive relationship remains the basic rationale underlying all forms of 'market definition' and 'likeness'. Nonetheless, the circumstances of the specific case as well as the purpose of the applied principle may justify different results with regard to the

41 *US* v. *Columbia Steel Co.*, 334 US 495 (1948), pp. 508 ff.

42 See Werden, 'History of Market Delineation', 129–30; also *US* v. *Philadelphia Nat'l Bank*, 374 US 321 (1963), p. 356.

43 *US* v. *Philadelphia Nat'l Bank*, 374 US 321 (1963), p. 363.

44 *US* v. *Oracle Corp.*, 331 F Supp 2d 1098 (N.D.Cal. 2004), pp. 1112 ff; Merger Guidelines Commentary, pp. 17 ff.

relevant market. It is widely recognized, for instance, that the market definition analysis may lead to different results depending on the legal principle of competition law for which it is conducted.[45] Similarly, the Appellate Body found that the accordion of 'likeness' stretches in different ways under the various GATT and GATS provisions. At the outset it is thus important to emphasize that the expected outcome of a comparative analysis is not that a market defined for purposes of, for instance, merger control should be identical in a case on trade non-discrimination. Much rather, the argument is that all domains should follow a similar methodology in market analysis, considering that the underlying principle is identical, namely competitive relationship. The following considerations illustrate the policy and legal reasons for why different markets are relevant in different domains.[46] Even though it will be referred predominantly to 'product markets', it must be noted that both EU and US competition law apply the same principles to define a relevant market for services.[47]

A *Protection of competitors vs. protection of consumer welfare*

The original policy reasons behind competition law are manifold and vary considerably between countries, which can best be illustrated by the example of the US and the EU. Even though there are diverging opinions about the origins of the Sherman Act, one of the predominant views is that Congress pursued the objective to put in place instruments against monopolies and trusts emerging from rapid industrialization that were getting overly powerful, for instance in the railroad and tobacco industries.[48] Such a concentration of power was considered a threat both economically

[45] For the EC see Market Definition Notice, para.12; Joined cases T-125/97 & T-127/97 *Coca-Cola* v. *Commission* [2000] ECR II-1733, paras. 81–85: The Commission's finding about the existence of a dominant position in a merger control case does not provide a binding market analysis for a case on the abuse of a dominant position (Art. 102 TFEU, ex Art. 82 TEC); for the US see e.g. *US* v. *Mrs. Smith's Pie Co.*, 440 F Supp 220 (E.D.Pa. 1976), p. 230: 'Although Sherman Act cases certainly are relevant and are entitled to some weight in defining a "line of commerce" under the Clayton Act, we believe that cases decided under the Clayton Act, are stronger precedents, since the test may differ somewhat under each act'.

[46] Also recognizing the importance of this comparison, Krajewski, 'Review: Choi, Like Products', 201.

[47] For the EC see Market Definition Notice, para.7; for the US see e.g. *Spirit Airlines* v. *Northwest Airlines*, 431 F 3d 917 (6th Cir. 2005), p. 933, finding that the test of 'reasonable interchangeability' also applies for service markets.

[48] For an overview see e.g. Sullivan (ed.), *Political Economy of the Sherman Act,* part I; Peritz, *Competition Policy in America*, pp. 13 ff; Hylton, *Antitrust Law*, pp. 38 ff; Sullivan and Grimes, *Law of Antitrust*, pp. 4–8.

and politically. When the US Supreme Court was confronted with the Sherman Act for the first time in 1897, it found that the prohibition of 'contracts in restraint of trade' was primarily designed to maintain a competitive market structure in which numerous small businesses compete.[49]

In the EU, in contrast, competition law provisions were originally introduced in the Treaty of Rome of 1957 as a means to reinforce the four freedoms of the common market.[50] Under the common market, Member States must not impede the free movement of goods, services, capital and persons. In order to avoid that state trade barriers removed by the four freedoms are replaced by private party conduct, the EU put in place competition law instruments, outlawing anticompetitive cartels and abusive conduct of dominant firms.[51] In spite of the originally different policy objectives, judicial construction as well as the interpretation by antitrust and competition authorities have been resulting in a new focus of modern US and – arguably to a slightly lesser extent – EU competition law towards total and consumer welfare.[52] Among such welfare goals are the efficient allocation of goods and services, lower prices by preventing price fixing and monopoly pricing while maintaining high consumer choice and promotion of innovation and technology.[53] This shift in policy objectives at the same time affects the interpretation and application of competition law, including the concept of market definition. Albeit at the risk of oversimplification, we shall thus accept, for the purpose of this study, 'welfare' as the main guiding principle of modern competition law, and contrast this objective with international trade law.

[49] *US* v. *Trans-Missouri Freight Ass'n*, 166 US 290 (1897), *passim*.

[50] Note that US antitrust law also contains an element of interstate commerce; while this element was applied strictly in the beginning, the Supreme Court expanded its meaning in the mid-30s, see Sullivan and Grimes, *Law of Antitrust*, p. 8.

[51] Joined cases 56 and 58/64 *Établissements Consten S.à.R.L. and Grundig-Verkaufs-GmbH* v. *Commission* [1966] ECR 299, *passim*; Motta, *Competition Policy*, pp. 13 ff, 23; Rose and Roth, 'Territorial Reach', p. 41; Oppermann, *Europarecht*, p. 310.

[52] In the EC, the element of consumer protection is expressed in Art. 101(3) TFEU (ex Art. 81(3) TEC) (exemption only applies if the gains from the cartelistic agreement are passed on to the consumers) and Art. 2.1 Merger Regulation; see Weitbrecht, '50 Years of European Competition Law', 85: 'a process of Americanisation began and the Commission gradually adopted its own version of the consumer welfare approach'; for the US see e.g. *Continental T.V.* v. *GTE Sylvania*, 433 US 36 (1977), *passim*; Rule and Meyer, 'Wealth of all Consumers', p. 212: 'Whether the critics like it or not, consumer welfare is today the guiding principle of antitrust law and policy'.

[53] For a comprehensive discussion of welfare economics and competition policy see e.g. Cseres, *Competition Law and Consumer Protection*, pp. 241 ff; Motta, *Competition Policy*, pp. 18 ff; Sullivan and Grimes, *Law of Antitrust*, pp. 12–16.

The governments of sovereign states enter into trade agreements by offering market access to foreign exporters in exchange for access to foreign markets for their own exporting industries.[54] Even though the underlying economic theory maintains that the liberalization of international trade will enhance global welfare, it would be overly idealistic to accept welfare as the guiding principle. International trade essentially consists of agreements between countries guaranteeing mutual access to their respective markets under equal competitive conditions. Accordingly, the guiding principle in the interpretation and application of trade law, including the concept of 'likeness', is 'equal conditions of competition' or 'competitive opportunities'. Against this background it appears that competition law is more aimed at the benefit of consumers, whereas international trade law primarily protects foreign competitors. Even though no clearly defined dichotomy exists between the objectives of the two domains, the general tendency still constitutes an important interpretative element to consider in the definition of the respective markets.

B *Competitive opportunities vs. market power*

Having thus broadly defined the policy objectives of international trade and competition law, this section now turns to the more specific regulatory objectives and their implications for the concept of market definition. Competition law primarily regulates market power, which is generally defined as the ability to profitably raise prices above competitive levels. Consequently, market definition is neither a legal element, nor does it have its own significance in the relevant provisions; it is simply a factual instrument for determining whether concentration of power exists in a relevant market.[55] Conversely, international trade law is not primarily concerned with private market power, but with trade-restrictive measures adopted by governments and other public authorities. Non-discrimination is thus designed to regulate and protect competitive opportunities for foreign products and services. In contrast to market definition, 'likeness'

[54] Stoll and Schorkopf, *WTO*, p. 38: 'the world trade order counts on the mutual interest of the Members in access to foreign markets and on the mechanism for negotiating and regulating this reciprocal market access in detail', and p. 44: 'governments ... do not strictly follow the rational recommendations inherent in free trade theory and do not exclusively aim at maximizing overall national economic welfare'.

[55] See e.g. Landes and Posner, 'Market Power in Antitrust', 938; Bishop and Walker, *Economics of EC Competition Law*, p. 85; Werden, 'Demand Elasticities in Antitrust', 384 ff; Baker, 'Market Definition', 130–31.

constitutes a distinct legal element with its own substantive significance in the analysis of non-discrimination.

Moving from these broad considerations to the mechanism of the specific principles, it becomes apparent that the circumstances of the market definition exercise vary considerably.

Merger control: The critical issue for merger control is – in simplified terms – whether post-merger the firm will have the power to increase prices or otherwise restrain competition either in coordination with its competitors (coordinated effects) or unilaterally (unilateral effects). For the purpose of market definition, the question thus becomes whether in the *future* market, consumers have the possibility to switch to an alternative product if the merged entity increases prices for its products. Hence, the focus of the market definition analysis clearly lies on the structure of the market in the future and the merged firm's position in that market.[56]

Single firm conduct: The analysis of single firm conduct follows a two-step approach, consisting of assessing (i) the company's market power; and (ii) whether the behaviour in which it is engaging is illegal.[57] Unlike merger control, the question of market power is not directed at a future post-merger market situation, but at past and present behaviour and market structures, with a very limited view to future developments.[58] Moreover, in merger control the market analysis is based on a functioning market situation, whereas in a unilateral conduct case the market may already be distorted by monopoly or dominant-position behaviour.

These conceptual differences strongly affect the legal analysis of market power. In the case of merger control, market power is primarily determined on the basis of the merged entity's market share in the future relevant market as well as barriers to entry and potential competition. In contrast, in cases of unilateral conduct, additional elements are available for the analysis of market or monopoly power, in particular price

[56] See e.g. Sullivan and Harrison, *Antitrust and Economic Implications*, p. 327; Neveling, *Marktabgrenzung bei der Fusionskontrolle*, pp. 37–38.

[57] The concept regarding single firm conduct differs between US and EU law, in that the Sherman Act outlaws conduct aimed at monopolizing the market, whereas Art. 102 TFEU only prohibits the abuse of – but not the conduct aimed at – gaining market power, see above, 14.I.

[58] For US law see *US* v. *Microsoft Corp.*, 253 F 3d 34 (D.C.Cir. 2001), pp. 53 f: 'The test of reasonable interchangeability, however, required the District Court to consider only substitutes that constrain pricing in the reasonably foreseeable future, and only products that can enter the market in a relatively short time can perform this function'; for EC law see Market Definition Notice, para.12; further Behrens, 'Marktbeherrschungsbegriff in EGV 82', pp. 39–42.

and profit margins, anticompetitive effects as well as conduct of the firm in question. In particular under the US approach to section 2 Sherman Act, the question of the relevant market is strongly influenced not only by the structure of the market, but also by the behaviour of the firm under scrutiny. In other words, if a certain behaviour only makes sense from the perspective of a firm that has market power (for instance if it is pricing at a monopoly level), then it is likely that the firm actually does have monopoly power in the relevant market.[59] Accordingly, the analysis of the relevant market may to a certain extent be biased by the conduct under scrutiny,[60] or market power may be established on the basis of direct evidence without defining a relevant market in the first place.[61] With regard to Article 102 TFEU, the ECJ in general insists on a determination of the dominant position independently from the conduct; however, even in EU law there is a tendency to infer the relevant market from the abusive conduct.[62]

Trade non-discrimination: Contrasting this reasoning with international trade and non-discrimination, it becomes apparent that there are a number of similarities and differences. Unlike merger control, but similar to single-firm behaviour, the market in non-discrimination cases is already distorted by the putative trade barrier which affords a competitive advantage to the domestic product or service. In competition law, the products of the merging entities or the monopoly are

[59] *US* v. *Microsoft Corp.*, 253 F 3d 34 (D.C.Cir. 2001), pp. 57 f: 'More telling, the District Court found that some aspects of Microsoft's behavior are difficult to explain unless Windows is a monopoly product. For instance, according to the District Court, the company set the price of Windows without considering rivals' prices, something a firm without a monopoly would have been unable to do. The District Court also found that Microsoft's pattern of exclusionary conduct could only be rational "if the firm knew that it possessed monopoly power"'; see further Fisher, 'Detecting Market Power', pp. 364–71.

[60] In *Eastman Kodak Co.* v. *Image Technical Services*, 504 US 451 (1992) the decision defining 'servicing and repair of Kodak copying equipment' as the relevant market seems strongly influenced by the behaviour of Kodak thwarting independent service companies. Similarly, defining 'Skiing in Aspen' as a relevant market in *Aspen Skiing Co.* v. *Aspen Highlands Skiing Corp.*, 472 US 585 (1985) irrespective of competing neighbouring resorts seems strongly influenced by the anticompetitive behaviour of the Aspen Skiing Company.

[61] See e.g. *Re/Max Int'l* v. *Realty One*, 173 F 3d 995 (6th Cir. 1999), p. 1016: 'There are two ways to establish the first element, that is, that the defendant holds monopoly power. The first is by presenting direct evidence "showing the exercise of actual control over prices or the actual exclusion of competitors" [reference omitted]. The second is by presenting circumstantial evidence of monopoly power by showing a high market share within a defined market [reference omitted]'; see also Competition and Monopoly Report, pp. 27 ff; Merger Guidelines Commentary, p. 10.

[62] Behrens, 'Marktbeherrschungsbegriff in EGV 82', pp. 41–42; Mestmäcker and Schweitzer, *Europäisches Wettbewerbsrecht*, § 16, paras. 3–4.

competing in the relevant market with possible substitutes. In trade, the products or services may not yet be competing at all (e.g. in case of an import or sales ban) or, in a more similar way to monopoly cases, they may be competing on unequal competitive terms (e.g. higher taxes or technical regulations).

Moreover, market definition in competition law primarily serves as a prerequisite for the assessment of market power.[63] In merger control, the relevant market allows the market share of the merged entity in the future to be determined, and in single-firm behaviour the relevant market allows an assessment of whether the firm had or has monopoly power or a dominant position. In contrast, trade non-discrimination is not concerned with market power at all. In fact, it is irrelevant whether the imported product or service accounts for 1 or 70 per cent of the domestic market. Similarly, while the conduct of the alleged monopoly may indicate the scope of the relevant market for purposes of section 2 of the Sherman Act and Article 102 of the TFEU, the conduct of any producer or supplier is irrelevant for purposes of trade non-discrimination. Accordingly, the methodology for market definition in cases on unilateral conduct may be less suitable for a comparative analysis with 'likeness' in trade.

Finally, considering that the focus of trade is not on consumer welfare, it is important to stress that the relevant test is not – as one might expect in analogy to the question for merger control asking whether prices will rise post-merger – whether as a result of lifting the trade barrier, prices of domestic products and services will go down. For instance, lifting a trade barrier for imported bananas may ultimately lead to a decrease in prices of locally produced apples. However, since international trade primarily protects competitive opportunities of foreign producers and suppliers, the only relevant question is whether any of the domestic consumers are likely to switch to the imported product or service if its price is reduced due to the disappearance of the trade barrier. Similarly again to merger control, the analysis in trade looks at present and future markets, but not so much at markets in the past.[64]

[63] Cárdenas Tomažič, *Marktabgrenzung*, pp. 23–25.

[64] This is the ECJ approach with regard to Art. 110 TFEU (ex Art. 90 TEC), see Case 170/78 *Commission* v. *United Kingdom* [1980] ECR 417, para.6: 'it is necessary to consider not only the present state of the market but also the possibilities for development within the context of free movement of goods at the community level and the future potential for the substitution of products for one another which may be revealed by the intensification of trade'.

C Broad 'likeness' in trade vs. narrow markets in competition law

In *Korea – Alcoholic Beverages*, the Panel inferred from the different policy objectives that the market must be defined more broadly in international trade law than in competition law:

> 'Trade law generally, and Article III in particular, focuses on the promotion of economic opportunities for importers through the elimination of discriminatory governmental measures which impair fair international trade. Thus, trade law addresses the issue of the potentiality to compete. Antitrust law generally focuses on firms' practices or structural modifications which may prevent or restrain or eliminate competition. It is not illogical that markets be defined more broadly when implementing laws primarily designed to protect competitive opportunities than when implementing laws designed to protect the actual mechanisms of competition. In our view, it can thus be appropriate to utilize a broader concept of markets with respect to Article III:2, second sentence, than is used in antitrust law.'[65]

The Panel undermined its point with various examples from EU jurisprudence. The TFEU is particularly useful for a direct comparison between trade and competition policy, considering that it contains both trade non-discrimination as well as competition law provisions that are applied and interpreted by the same institutions and courts. At the same time, Article 110 TFEU (ex Art. 90 of the TEC) is very similar to the language, purpose and structure of Article III:2 GATT.[66] One Panel explicitly affirmed the value of ECJ jurisprudence pertaining to Article 110 of the TFEU on tax discrimination (ex Art. 90 TEC, formerly Art. 95 TEC) and Article 102 of the TFEU on abusive conduct (ex Art. 82 of the TEC, formerly Art. 86 of the TEC) for better understanding of the relationship between non-discrimination provisions and competition law.[67] The following overview of various cases illustrates the different approaches within the EU:

> *Alcoholic Beverages*: In a number of tax non-discrimination cases on Article 90 of the TEC, the ECJ defined the relevant market broadly so

[65] Para 10.81 (fns omitted); confirmed in Panel Report, *Chile – Alcoholic Beverages*, para.7.87.

[66] See e.g. Slotboom, 'Different Treaty Purposes', 558–76; Kuyper, 'Tax Discrimination', 143–44.

[67] Panel Report, *Korea – Alcoholic Beverages*, para.10.81: 'We are mindful that the Treaty of Rome is different in scope and purpose from the General Agreement, the similarity of Article 95 and Article III, notwithstanding. Nonetheless, we observe that there is relevance in examining how the ECJ has defined markets in similar situations to assist in understanding the relationship between the analysis of non-discrimination provisions and competition law'.

as to include all alcoholic beverages.[68] In a first case, France taxed spirits made from cereals (whisky) higher than spirits distilled from wine and fruit (cognac); the ECJ found that these beverages are in the same market for purposes of TEC 90, para.2,[69] and that the French tax scheme thus is discriminatory. Moreover, in other cases the ECJ specified that a strong consumer preference for a certain local beverage (e.g. Ouzo in Greece) is not determinative for the question of substitutability under Art. 90 of the TEC.[70] It is interesting to contrast these findings on markets under Art. 90 of the TEC with the definition of the relevant market in the merger case *Guiness/Grand Metropolitan*, where the Commission found that '[t]he importance of branding, and its application to individual spirit types, is a key characteristic of competition in the spirits industry and is not consistent with a product market wider than that for each main spirit type'.[71] It concluded that at least in some Member States, Scotch whisky and domestic whisky constitute two distinct markets.[72] Nonetheless, the merger was found to be in compliance with the common market, subject to certain conditions. In comparison, WTO jurisprudence suggests that alcoholic beverages are 'like' and/or 'directly competitive or substitutable' products.[73]

Bananas and other fruits: Another case on tax discrimination concerned the bananas and fruit market.[74] In this case, Italy taxed imported bananas at a higher level than locally produced table fruit; the ECJ found bananas and other fruit to be in a competitive relationship for purposes of Article 90, para.2 TEC[75] and struck down the Italian tax scheme. In contrast, in a competition law case pertaining to the fruit market, the ECJ examined whether United Brands abused a dominant position by importing Chiquita bananas into the EU and, *inter alia*, imposing on the

68 For an overview of early cases see Swanson, 'Alcohol Cases', 288 ff.

69 Case 168/78 *Commission* v. *French Republic* [1980] ECR 347, para.40: 'spirits obtained from cereals … have, as products obtained from distillation, sufficient characteristics in common with other spirits to constitute at least in certain circumstances an alternative choice for consumers'; also Case 171/78 *Commission* v. *Kingdom of Denmark* [1980] ECR 447, para.34: 'it is impossible reasonably to contest that all those beverages are without exception in at least partial competition with the product benefited by the Danish legislation'; Case 319/81 *Commission* v. *Italian Republic* [1983] ECR 601, para.16.

70 Case 230/89 *Commission* v. *Hellenic Republic* [1991] ECR I-1909, para.9; Case 170/78 *Commission* v. *United Kingdom* [1980] ECR 417, para.14.

71 Case IV/M.938 *Guinness/Grand Metropolitan* OJ 1998 L288/24, para.14.

72 Ibid., paras. 123, 147.

73 Panel Reports, *Japan – Alcoholic Beverages II*; *Korea – Alcoholic Beverages*; *Chile – Alcoholic Beverages*.

74 On this issue also Lonbay, 'Tax Cases', 48–49.

75 Case 184/85 *Commission* v. *Italian Republic* [1987] ECR 2013, para.12: 'Although bananas and table fruit typically produced in Italy are not similar products within the meaning of the first paragraph of Article 95, bananas do afford an alternative choice to consumers of fruit. As a result, bananas must be regarded in partial competition with such fruit'.

ripeners and distributors in the EU a prohibition to resell the bananas to dealers from other countries. The analysis under Article 82 of the TEC required determining whether United Brands had a dominant position in the relevant market. The ECJ found that bananas have certain 'characteristics, appearance, taste, softness, seedlessness, easy handling, a constant level of production which enable it to satisfy the constant needs of an important section of the population consisting of the very young, the old and the sick'.[76] Bananas were found to be sufficiently distinct from other fresh fruit so as to constitute its own product market which, in consequence, led to a finding of dominant position and ultimately abusive conduct.

Automobiles: In the automobile sector, the discrepancy between markets for purposes of non-discrimination and competition law is somewhat less pronounced. For purposes of Article 90 para.1 TEC, the ECJ found that 'cars are similar ... if their characteristics and the needs which they serve place them in a competitive relationship ... [T]he degree of competition between two models depends on the extent to which they meet various requirements regarding price, size, comfort, performance, fuel consumption, durability, reliability and other matters'.[77] This finding suggests that more than one relevant market exists in the automobile sector, which is similar to the approach generally adopted by the Commission in competition law.[78]

Against the background of this overview it becomes apparent that the interpretation of the market by the ECJ and the Commission is indeed broader for purposes of non-discrimination and narrower in the case of competition law.[79] At least in two cases, the parties even proposed that the criteria applied by the ECJ with regard to competition rules contained in the same treaty, in particular cross-elasticity, should also be relevant for purposes of Article 110, para.2 of the TFEU (ex Art. 90, para.2

[76] Case 27/76 *United Brands* v. *Commission* [1978] ECR 207, para.31; criticized by Bishop and Walker, *Economics of EC Competition Law*, p. 92 ('toothless fallacy').

[77] Case C-421/97 *Tarantik* v. *Direction des services fiscaux de Seine-et-Marne* [1999] ECR I-3633, para.28; Case C-265/99 *Commission* v. *French Republic* [2001] ECR I-2305, para.43.

[78] Case COMP/36.264 *Mercedes-Benz* OJ 2002 L257/1, paras. 144 ff: 'The broadest relevant product market might be deemed to be the market for all cars. The relevant market would then extend from very small cars through luxury cars to sports cars. However, this cannot be accepted. It is obvious that, from the point of view of the buyer, very small cars are, for example, not interchangeable with medium-sized or luxury cars: a buyer (private customer, commercial user of passenger vehicles) will not regard the various segments to be interchangeable if the focus is on the characteristics relevant to the selection of a certain vehicle'; see also Case COMP/36.653 *Opel*, OJ 2001 L059/1, para.183; question left open in Case COMP/36.623 *SEP/Automobiles Peugeot SA*, OJ 2006 L173/20, para.4.

[79] Demaret, 'Non-Discrimination Principle', p. 178; but see Englisch, *Wettbewerbsgleichheit*, p. 296.

of the TEC).[80] Somewhat surprisingly, the ECJ did not incorporate these arguments in its reasoning and non-discrimination cases never refer to market definition of Article 102 of the TFEU (ex Art. 82 of the TEC).

More illustrative examples on different scopes of product markets in trade and competition can be found in US antitrust and merger law.

> *Sugar*: In the section 7 *Archer-Daniels-Midland* case, the court of appeals reversed the lower court's finding on the relevant market, essentially separating high fructose corn syrup (HFCS) from the sugar market for reasons of significant price differences.[81] In contrast, the Panel in *Mexico – Taxes on Soft Drinks* found that HFCS and cane sugar are directly competitive or substitutable for purposes of Article III:4 GATT (para 8.78).

A policy reason explaining why the breadth of markets differs between non-discrimination and competition, as identified by the Panel in *Korea – Alcoholic Beverages*, is that trade protects potential competition and competitive opportunities for foreign competitors, whereas competition law is more aimed at the protection of domestic consumers.[82] However, it appears that the true reason for defining smaller and narrower markets in competition law as compared to international trade is more of a pragmatic legal than of a policy nature. In competition law, a narrow definition of the relevant market is more likely to bring about a finding that the single firm conduct or the merger is illegal. In a narrowly defined market, a merger between two firms is more likely to be anticompetitive and thus prohibited. Similarly, a firm is more likely in a dominant or monopoly position in a narrowly defined market than in a broad market. In trade law, however, the result of a narrow market or 'likeness' analysis is exactly reverse. A narrow definition of the market leads to unlikeness between the products or the services in question, and thus to the result that the measure in question cannot be discriminatory. In contrast, a violation of the non-discrimination obligation is more likely to occur if 'likeness' is defined

[80] Case 171/78 *Commission* v. *Kingdom of Denmark* [1980] ECR 447, para.28; Opinion of the Advocate General Vilaça, Case 356/85 *Commission* v. *Kingdom of Belgium* [1987] ECR 3299, para.122.

[81] *US* v. *Archer-Daniels-Midland*, 695 F Supp 1000 (S.D. Iowa 1987), rev'd 866 F 2d 242 (8th Cir. 1988), p. 246.

[82] But see Horn and Mavroidis, 'Interpretation of National Treatment', 66–67: 'we do not see that the differences between purposes of the two types of law are as important as claimed. The oft-maintained purpose of Article III – to protect expectations of "competitive relationships" – seems very similar to the main purposes of competition law – to protect "fair" competition, or competition in general'. However, as noted here, modern competition law is more about consumer welfare than fair competition.

broadly.[83] Considering that both domains pursue a procompetitive goal, it is understandable that markets in similar industries are defined differently in the respective legal domains.[84] These considerations reaffirm that markets need not be identically defined for each legal principle; however, it is difficult to see why the courts and WTO adjudicating bodies do not apply similar methods in the analysis of markets.

D *Direct comparison in trade vs. relevant market in competition*

Competition law is first and foremost concerned with market power. In merger control as well as unilateral conduct, market power constitutes one of the legal elements in the analysis. While there are different methodologies that can be used to measure market power, the most important factor is the firm's market share in comparison to its competitors. Since market share cannot be determined in the abstract, it is necessary to define a relevant market, consisting of three components: the product or service market, the geographical market and the temporal market. The product or service market consists of all products or services which are in a competitive relationship, thereby imposing competitive constraints on a particular firm. For instance, in the case of a merger between two beer producers, the evaluation of market share requires determining all beverages that are in a competitive relationship, such as other beer brands, other alcoholic beverages or even non-alcoholic beverages. The more beverages included in the product market, the lower the market share of the firms in question. The geographical market requires evaluating the physical area on which the products or services compete, such as local, regional, national or even international markets. Finally, some markets require determining a temporal delimitation. The temporal market may be relevant if a certain product or service is only offered on the market over a limited period of time or if market power is only temporal, for instance in case of expositions or sports events.[85]

International trade law, in contrast, does not apply to behaviour of private companies, but to measures adopted by sovereign states.

[83] Against this background it is not surprising that in *Korea – Alcoholic Beverages* the respondent Korea invoked EC competition law jurisprudence defining narrow markets for cola-flavoured soft drinks, Panel Report, para.6.236.

[84] Goco, '"Likeness", and Market Definition', 332.

[85] See e.g. a temporal delimitation regarding entry tickets for the Soccer World Cup, Commission Case IV/33.384 and IV/33.378 *Distribution of Package Tours 1990 World Cup*, OJ 1992 L326/31, paras. 79 ff.

Market power and market shares are thus irrelevant for the analysis of non-discrimination obligations. Accordingly, the WTO adjudicating bodies refrained from defining a market that includes all competitive products or services for purposes of non-discrimination; they limited the comparison to the two or very few products or services which are subject to the trade measure under scrutiny and an allegedly 'like' domestic product or service. Consequently, since trade non-discrimination does not require the definition of a relevant market, the geographical and temporal components have not received much attention; the relevant geographical market may be defined as the area where the measure under scrutiny applies, which generally corresponds with the respondent's entire jurisdiction.[86] It follows from these considerations that the exercise of market definition has so far been more complex than the question of 'likeness'. The former requires a comparison of many not pre-defined products or services in terms of their competitive relationship, resulting in a conclusion on the relevant market. The analysis of 'likeness', in contrast, has been limited to a comparison between two or few pre-defined products or services, resulting in a conclusion of either being or not being in a competitive relationship.

Such a limited market analysis under non-discrimination may no longer be sufficient to meet the new requirements arising from an implementation of the asymmetric impact test under the element of 'less favourable treatment'.[87] Following such a test, the impact of a measure must be assessed in light of all foreign products or services – including those which are not affected by the measure under scrutiny – which compete with domestic products or services. Consequently, the legal analysis

[86] Englisch, *Wettbewerbsgleichheit*, p. 296: 'Der räumlich relevante Markt ist im Übrigen durch den Zweck des Diskriminierungsverbotes vorgegeben: Es handelt sich um den jeweiligen nationalen Teilmarkt im Zielland oder im Herkunftsland'; Choi, '*Like Products*', pp. 198–99, n 143; but see Marchetti and Mavroidis, 'Challenges for GATS', 533: 'In the case of trade in services, in our view, any analysis of competition should take into account both the product and the geographic market'.

[87] Ehring, 'De Facto Discrimination', 972, arguing for a determination of the entire market in order to assess asymmetric or symmetric impact under 'less favourable treatment'; the Appellate Body recognized the identification of 'product categories' as an 'analytical tool' for likeness, see Appellate Body Report, *Korea – Alcoholic Beverages*, para.142, and referred to a relevant market at least in one instance, see Appellate Body Report, *Korea – Various Measures on Beef*, para.137: 'Whether or not imported products are treated "less favourably" than like domestic products should be assessed ... by examining whether a measure modifies the *conditions of competition* in the *relevant market* to the detriment of imported products' (first emphasis original, second added); see also Panel Report, *Chile – Alcoholic Beverages*, paras. 7.26 ff.

of non-discrimination needs to approach competition law reasoning in that it requires a fully fledged definition of the relevant market.

III Market definition

The European Commission adopted the Market Definition Notice in 1997 in order to improve the transparency and predictability for legal practitioners and businesses in regard to the market analysis of competition law.[88] It was developed on the basis of previous ECJ jurisprudence and 'tries to set out in coherent, readable fashion the economic principles on which the Commission bases its approach to the definition of relevant markets'.[89] The EU Merger Guidelines specifically refer to and incorporate the Market Definition Notice.[90] Yet, as set out in para.1 of the Notice, it provides guidance not only for the definition of the relevant market in the context of merger control, but for EU competition law in general, including the examination of dominant positions of Article 102 TFEU (ex Art. 82 TEC) and of the impact of cartels pursuant to Article 101 TFEU (ex Art. 81 TEC). Moreover, the Commission adopted more specific guidelines on the application of competition rules and the definition of relevant markets in specific sectors, such as telecommunications.[91]

Unlike the European Commission, the federal antitrust agencies in the US – namely the Antitrust Division of the Department of Justice and the Federal Trade Commission – did not adopt specific guidelines on market definition, but incorporated the concept in the respective guidelines and publications on merger control and unilateral conduct.[92] While these guidelines constitute an important element in the interpretation of US antitrust law, the only authoritative source remains to be case law.

[88] Commission Notice on the definition of relevant market for the purposes of Community competition law, OJ 1997 C372/5.

[89] European Commission, *XXVIIth Report on competition policy* (1997), para.44, available at http://ec.europa.eu/comm/competition/annual_reports/rap97_en.html.

[90] Guidelines on the assessment of horizontal mergers under the Council Regulation on the control of concentrations between undertakings, OJ 2004 C31/5, para.10(b): 'The main purpose of market definition is to identify in a systematic way the immediate competitive constraints facing the merged entity. Guidance on this issue can be found in the Commission's Notice on the definition of the relevant market for the purposes of Community competition law'.

[91] See e.g. Commission Recommendation of 11 February 2003 on Relevant Markets within the Electronic Communications Sector, OJ L114/45; for a comprehensive overview see Burri Nenova, *Electronic Communications and Competition*, pp. 134 ff, 212 ff.

[92] US Merger Guidelines; Merger Guidelines Commentary; Competition and Monopoly Report.

According to the US Supreme Court, a '[d]etermination of the relevant market is a necessary predicate to a finding of a violation of the Clayton Act because the threatened monopoly must be one which will substantially lessen competition "within the area of effective competition"'.[93] Similarly for section 2 of the Sherman Act cases, the analysis typically begins by looking at the firm's market share.[94] Commonly, US courts treat both Sherman Act and Clayton Act cases as authority on market definition.[95]

Both in EU and US competition law, the main approach for defining the relevant product or service market is to focus on the main sources of competitive constraints, notably demand substitutability, supply substitutability as well as potential competition.[96]

A Demand substitutability

The first and most important competitive constraint analysed in market definition is demand substitutability or 'reasonable interchangeability'.

1. Competition law

In the EU, the Market Definition Notice defines the relevant market as comprising 'all those products and/or services which are regarded

[93] *US* v. *E.I. du Pont de Nemours & Co.*, 353 US 586 (1957), p. 593 (fn omitted); see also *US* v. *Aluminum Co. of America*, 377 US 271 (1964), p. 282.

[94] *Movie 1 & 2* v. *United Artists Commc'ns*, 909 F 2d 1245 (9th Cir. 1990), p. 1254: 'although market share does not alone determine monopoly power, market share is perhaps the most important factor to consider in determining the presence or absence of monopoly power'.

[95] See e.g. *US* v. *Grinnell Corp.*, 384 US 563 (1966), p. 573: 'We see no reason to differentiate between "line" of commerce in the context of the Clayton Act and "part" of commerce for purposes of the Sherman Act'; but see above, n 45; for an overview of cases see ABA Section of Antitrust Law, *Antitrust Law Developments*, p. 553.

[96] See e.g. Market Definition Notice, para.13; Bishop and Walker, *Economics of EC Competition Law*, p. 90. To be recalled, the relevant market is only one of many tools in competition law to measure market power. To the extent market power is assessed on the basis of other elements – such as monopoly pricing, profit margins or conduct – these elements at least indirectly affect the scope of the relevant market. For instance, if pricing policy and profit margin clearly show that a firm has monopoly power, then the relevant market is determined indirectly on the basis of this conduct, and not on the basis of a traditional market definition exercise of substitutability. Considering that market power and unilateral conduct is irrelevant for the purpose of trade non-discrimination, the comparative approach between the two domains must be limited to 'likeness' and market definition in a narrow sense.

as interchangeable or substitutable by the consumer, by reason of the products' characteristics, their prices and their intended use'.[97] Interestingly, the criteria of 'characteristics' and 'use' are very similar to the first three criteria of the *Border Tax Adjustments* framework of WTO rules on non-discrimination. Market definition is thus clearly about determining the competitive relationship between products or services, which is assessed on the basis of interchangeability and substitutability from a consumer's perspective. This approach has been consistently applied by the EU courts.[98] The Market Definition Notice establishes a hierarchy between different factors of the relevant market, giving demand substitutability a clear priority:

> 'From an economic point of view, for the definition of the relevant market, demand substitution constitutes the most immediate and effective disciplinary force on the suppliers of a given product, in particular in relation to their pricing decisions. A firm or a group of firms cannot have a significant impact on the prevailing conditions of sale, such as prices, if its customers are in a position to switch easily to available substitute

[97] Market Definition Notice, para.7; for a comprehensive overview of demand substitutability see e.g. Monopolkommission, *Ökonomische Kriterien*, pp. 198–99; Hildebrand, *Economic Analysis in EC Competition Rules*, pp. 289, 332–34; Mueller, *Abschied vom Bedarfsmarktkonzept?*, pp. 54 ff; Baur, 'Der relevante Markt', *passim*; for an economic analysis Landes and Posner, 'Market Power in Antitrust'.

[98] The test of interchangeability and substitutability from a consumer's perspective was first introduced in Case 6/72 *Europemballage and Continental Can* v. *Commission* [1973] ECR 215, para.32; confirmed in Case 27/76 *United Brands* v. *Commission* [1978] ECR 207, para.12; Case 85/76 *Hoffmann-La Roche* v. *Commission* [1979] ECR 461, para.23; Case 31/80 *L'Oréal* v. *De Nieuwe AMCK* [1980] ECR 3775, para.25; Case 322/81 *Michelin* v. *Commission* [1983] ECR 3461, para.37; Case C-62/86 *AKZO Chemie* v. *Commission* [1991] ECR I-3359, paras. 50 f; Case 66/86 *Ahmed Saeed Flugreisen and Others* v. *Zentrale zur Bekämpfung unlauteren Wettbewerbs* [1989] ECR 803, para.40; Case T-30/89 *Hilti* v. *Commission* [1991] ECR II-1439, para.64; Case C-333/94 *Tetra Pak International* v. *Commission* [1996] ECR I-5951, para.13; Case T-504/93 *Tiercé Ladbroke* v. *Commission* [1997] ECR II-923, para.81; Case T-229/94 *Deutsche Bahn* v. *Commission* [1997] ECR II-1689, para.54; Case T-65/96 *Kish Glass* v. *Commission* [2000] ECR II-1885, para.62; Case C-7/97 *Oscar Bronner* v. *Mediaprint* [1998] ECR I-7791, para.33; Case C-475/99 *Ambulanz Glöckner* v. *Landkreis Südwestpfalz* [2001] ECR I-8089, para.33; Case C-462/99 *Connect Austria Gesellschaft für Telekommunikation* v. *Telekom-Control-Kommission, and Mobilkom Austria* [2003] ECR I-5197, para.75; Case T-340/03, *France Télécom* v. *Commission* [2007] ECR II-107, para.78; most recently Case C-49/07 *Motosykletistiki Omospondia Ellados* v. *Elliniko Dimosio*, para.32: 'According to settled case-law … the relevant product or service market includes products or services which are substitutable or sufficiently interchangeable with the product or service in question, not only in terms of their objective characteristics, by virtue of which they are particularly suitable for satisfying the constant needs of consumers, but also in terms of the conditions of competition and the structure of supply and demand on the market in question'.

> products or to suppliers located elsewhere. Basically, the exercise of market definition consists in identifying the effective alternative sources of supply for the customers of the undertakings involved, in terms both of products/services and of geographic location of suppliers.'[99]

In the US, courts have long stressed that relevant product and service markets should be defined on the basis of demand substitutability.[100] The Supreme Court announced the doctrinal test in the monopolization case *Cellophane*, holding that the relevant market consists of services or products 'reasonably interchangeable by consumers for the same purposes'.[101] The same principle was adopted by the Supreme Court with regard to merger cases under the Clayton Act, finding that 'the outer boundaries of a product market are determined by the reasonable interchangeability of use or the cross-elasticity of demand between the product itself and substitutes for it'.[102] The US Merger Guidelines follow these decisions, clearly focusing on substitutability of demand.[103] Similarly, the Department of Justice most recently stated that for purposes of the Sherman and Clayton Act, the relevant product market 'Is composed of products that have reasonable interchangeability for the purposes for which they are produced – price, use and qualities considered'.[104]

99 Market Definition Notice, paras. 13 f; see also Case T-177/04 *EasyJet Airline* v. *Commission* [2006] ECR II-1931, para.99, referring to and endorsing the Market Definition Notice, para. 13.

100 For a discussion of early Supreme Court cases see Pitofsky, 'New Definitions of Relevant Market', 1813–17; Werden, 'History of Market Delineation', 139 ff; ABA Section of Antitrust Law, *Antitrust Law Developments*, p. 557, n 37, citing cases.

101 *US* v. *E. I. du Pont de Nemours & Co. (Cellophane)*, 351 US 377 (1956), p. 395; see already *Times-Picayune Publishing Co.* v. *US*, 345 US 594 (1953), p. 612, n 31; confirmed in *US* v. *Grinnell Corp.*, 384 US 563 (1966), p. 584: 'this Court has always recognized that the market must include products or services "reasonably interchangeable" with those of the alleged monopolist'; *Eastman Kodak Co.* v. *Image Technical Services*, 504 US 451 (1992), p. 469: 'The extent to which one market prevents exploitation of another market depends on the extent to which consumers will change their consumption of one product in response to a price change in another'.

102 *Brown Shoe Co.* v. *US*, 370 US 294 (1962), p. 325; see already *US* v. *E. I. du Pont de Nemours & Co.*, 353 US 586 (1957), pp. 593 f: where the court found that 'automotive finishes and fabrics have sufficient peculiar characteristics ... to make them a "line of commerce" within the meaning of the Clayton Act' without, however, referring to the concept of market definition developed in *Cellophane*; see also *US* v. *Continental Can Co.*, 378 US 441 (1964), p. 449; more recently *US* v. *Oracle Corp.*, 331 F Supp 2d 1098 (N.D.Cal. 2004), p. 1131.

103 US Merger Guidelines, p. 4: 'Market definition focuses solely on demand substitution factors – i.e., possible consumer responses.'

104 Competition and Monopoly Report, p. 25, quoting the Supreme Court from *US* v. *E. I. du Pont de Nemours & Co. (Cellophane)*, 351 US 377 (1956), p. 404.

2. Application to trade non-discrimination

Competition law directly applies the concept of demand substitutability for market definition and courts generally use a standard of 'reasonable interchangeability'. In contrast, WTO adjudicating bodies are very reluctant to apply the term 'demand substitutability' in the context of 'likeness', but instead refer to the concepts of 'competitive relationship', 'substitutability' and sometimes also 'interchangeability'. Presumably, this terminology draws from the wording in *Ad* Article III:2 GATT which refers to 'directly competitive or substitutable' products. The following finding of the Appellate Body in *EC – Asbestos* comprehensively summarizes the approach with regard to Article III:4 GATT:

> '[A] determination of "likeness" under Article III:4 is, fundamentally, a determination about the nature and extent of a competitive relationship between and among products. In saying this, we are mindful that there is a spectrum of degrees of "competitiveness" or "substitutability" of products in the marketplace, and that it is difficult, if not impossible, in the abstract, to indicate precisely where on this spectrum the word "like" in Article III:4 of the GATT 1994 falls. We are not saying that *all* products which are in *some* competitive relationship are "like products" under Article III:4.'[105]

Considering the context in which the WTO adjudicating bodies apply the terms 'competitive relationship', 'substitutability' and 'interchangeability', it can be noted that these terms simply constitute different forms of expressing the same general concept of demand substitutability. Hence, even though the WTO adjudicating bodies refrain from explicitly incorporating demand substitutability into the legal analysis of 'likeness', they still apply the concept implicitly by shaping the four factors from *Border Tax Adjustments* in accordance with the general principle of competitive relationship. This approach entails a number of disadvantages.

First, the current approach creates considerable legal uncertainty and unnecessary complications in the legal analysis. For instance, the Appellate Body in *EC – Asbestos* expressed concerns regarding the overlap of the four factors.

> '[A]lthough each criterion addresses, in principle, a different aspect of the products involved, which should be examined separately, the different criteria are interrelated. For instance, the physical properties of

[105] Appellate Body Report, *EC – Asbestos*, para.99, entire para.reproduced above 5.I.B, n 38.

a product shape and limit the end-uses to which the products can be devoted. Consumer perceptions may similarly influence – modify or even render obsolete – traditional uses of the products. Tariff classification clearly reflects the physical properties of a product.'[106]

In the same case, the Appellate Body seemed uncertain as to how it should take account of health risks in the analysis of 'likeness'.

> 'We are very much of the view that evidence relating to the health risks associated with a product may be pertinent in an examination of "likeness" under Article III:4 of the GATT 1994. We do not, however, consider that the evidence relating to the health risks associated with chrysotile asbestos fibres need be examined under a *separate* criterion, because we believe that this evidence can be evaluated under the existing criteria of physical properties, and of consumers' tastes and habits.'[107]

An explicit commitment to demand substitutability as an additional step in the 'likeness' analysis would greatly enhance the legal certainty as to which evidence and factors may be taken into account and it would render obsolete any concern of overlap between, as well as categorization of evidence among, the four *Border Tax Adjustments* factors.[108]

Second, the analysis of 'likeness' under WTO law lacks a clear commitment to competitive relationship and demand substitutability across *all* non-discrimination obligations. The WTO adjudicating bodies take the stance that WTO Agreements contain different standards of 'likeness'. Accordingly, the standard of 'like products' in GATT Article III:2, first sentence, is largely confined to a physical characteristics test, whereas 'like products' in Article III:4 and 'directly competitive and substitutable' products in Article III:2, second sentence, require a marketplace test similar to the concept of market definition.[109] However, as argued above, the relevance of these different standards is limited, as it is only plausible to distinguish between the narrow standard of GATT Article III:2, first sentence, and all other marketplace standards focusing on the competitive relationship. Moreover, different standards do not *per se* inhibit an approach similar to the concept of market definition. In fact, it would easily be possible to link these different standards to different degrees of competitive relationship or substitutability.[110] In consequence, a high

[106] Ibid., para.102. [107] Ibid., para.113.

[108] Horn and Mavroidis, 'Economic and Legal Aspects of MFN', 242: 'the Panel does not understand that cross-price elasticity reflects all the other criteria mentioned'.

[109] See above, 5.I.

[110] Same opinion Emch, 'What are "Like" Products?', 398.

degree of substitutability would be required to meet the narrow standard of GATT Article III:2, first sentence, and a lower degree for all other GATT/GATS non-discrimination provisions.

Third, WTO jurisprudence developed different theories of 'likeness', namely – as referred to in this study – a theory of 'objective or competitive likeness' and 'subjective or regulatory likeness'. The latter approach is considerably different from the concept of market definition, in that it allows for the consideration of criteria that are unrelated to determine demand substitutability. Typically, this theory allows to negate 'likeness' on the basis of criteria related to the regulatory context and PPMs. However, since the Appellate Body rejected the subjective theory, there remains nothing in the way of adopting an approach that focuses more directly on demand substitutability. Moreover, a clear commitment to the theory of competitive 'likeness' leaves sufficient leeway to account for the regulatory purpose of a measure under scrutiny. If the regulatory purpose reflects a product or service distinction that is sufficiently strong to largely negate demand substitutability, then such a measure could remain in place due to the 'unlikeness' of the products or services at issue. This could, for instance, be the case for a measure prohibiting the sale of asbestos fibres, considering that due to health concerns consumers would not see asbestos and asbestos free fibres as substitutes. In contrast, if the product or service distinction does not affect demand substitutability, the purpose of the regulation could still be considered as a justification.

In sum, the WTO adjudicating bodies implicitly take an approach of demand substitutability for the analysis of 'likeness' that is similar to the definition of markets. However, in order to enhance legal security, it would be desirable that the analysis is more explicitly focused on demand substitutability for the purpose of all WTO non-discrimination provisions.[111] This approach is not alien to the GATS. In *Mexico – Telecoms*, the Panel already conducted a market definition exercise for purposes of the Reference Paper on Basic Telecommunications, relying heavily on competition law theories and demand substitutability.[112]

[111] See also Trebilcock and Giri, 'National Treatment Principle', 61: 'it is inexplicable that international trade tribunals would not draw much more extensively on the framework of analysis and body of experience that has developed in competition law in many jurisdictions around the world in addressing precisely the same question'.

[112] Para 7.152.

3. Assessing demand substitutability: converging market definition and 'likeness'

The EU Market Definition Notice states that there 'is a range of evidence permitting an assessment of the extent to which substitution would take place' and that '[i]n most cases, a decision will have to be based on the consideration of a number of criteria and different items of evidence'.[113] In delimiting this broad approach, however, the Notice specifically identifies different categories of types of evidence that are relevant for the analysis of product markets.[114] Similarly, the US Merger Guidelines note that all relevant evidence is taken into account[115] and US courts consider a wide variety of evidence in the analysis of market definition:

> 'The boundaries of such a submarket may be determined by examining such practical indicia as industry or public recognition of the submarket as a separate economic entity, the product's peculiar characteristics and uses, unique production facilities, distinct customers, distinct prices, sensitivity to price changes, and specialized vendors.'[116]

According to WTO jurisprudence, all evidence is relevant for the analysis of 'likeness' and the *Border Tax Adjustments* framework generally requires that the available evidence is categorized and examined under the four factors of (i) properties, nature and quality; (ii) end-uses; (iii) consumers' tastes and habits; and (iv) tariff classification. Yet, the Appellate Body opened the door to take into account additional criteria in case pertinent evidence could not be categorized within the existing framework. While the *Border Tax Adjustments* framework in the context of services has been discussed in chapter 13, this chapter now turns to the question of what additional evidence typically analysed in competition law could be useful in the context of 'likeness', both in GATT and GATS, and what type of evidence WTO adjudicating bodies have already considered outside the *Border Tax Adjustments* framework.

a. Price elasticity of demand and the SSNIP test Price elasticity of demand as a measure of responsiveness is one of the most common factors referred to for the analysis of demand substitutability and for determining the boundaries of a product market. Own-price elasticity measures the effect of a change in price on the demand of a particular

113 Market Definition Notice, para.25.

114 Ibid., paras. 36 ff.

115 US Merger Guidelines, p. 6.

116 *Brown Shoe Co.* v. *US*, 370 US 294 (1962), p. 325; see also Baker, 'Market Definition', 139 ff.

product or service.[117] Cross-price elasticity measures 'the extent to which consumers will change their consumption of one product in response to a price change in another'.[118] Under a high degree of cross-price elasticity, even a small increase in price for one product causes a high number of consumers to switch to another product, indicating that both products are part of the same relevant market. In contrast, under a low degree of cross-price elasticity, only a small number of consumers change to the other product even if price increases are high, indicating that there are two separate product markets.[119]

Both the US and the EU apply the empirical 'small but significant non-transitory increase in price' (SSNIP) test as a quantitative instrument to determine price elasticity of demand.[120] According to the EU Market Definition Notice, the examination follows a 'speculative experiment' that consists of the question whether a small but significant deterioration of performance of product A would induce a high number of customers to change to product B.[121] The deterioration of performance can result either from a decrease in quality or an increase in price; both causes are equally pertinent for the question of substitutability, however, in the context of competition policy the focus usually is on price. The test is typically conducted under the assumption of a 5 to 10 per cent increase in price, depending on the industry and circumstances. If, as a direct result of this hypothetical price increase, sufficient customers would switch to product B such that the producer of A would find the price increase unprofitable, product B is included in the relevant market. The same exercise is then continued on the basis of product B in comparison to product C and so on, until a price increase does not yield any more substitutes. This methodological approach, known as the SSNIP test, was first developed in the US Merger Guidelines and was later borrowed by the European Commission for purposes of the Market Definition Notice.[122] Meanwhile, the test

[117] Lindsay and Scola, 'Market Definition', p. 265.

[118] *Eastman Kodak Co.* v. *Image Technical Services*, 504 US 451 (1992), p. 469; see also Werden, 'Demand Elasticities in Antitrust', 398 ff; Cárdenas Tomažič, *Marktabgrenzung*, pp. 41–42.

[119] See e.g. ABA Section of Antitrust Law, *Antitrust Law Developments*, pp. 562–66; ABA Section of Antitrust Law, *Market Power Handbook*, pp. 58–59; Mueller, *Abschied vom Bedarfsmarktkonzept?*, p. 114; for an economic introduction to elasticity see e.g. Sullivan and Harrison, *Antitrust and Economic Implications*, pp. 11–14.

[120] EC terminology also uses the term 'Hypothetical Monopolist Test', see e.g. Hildebrand, 'Market Research Tools', 317.

[121] Market Definition Notice, para.15; for the US see Merger Guidelines Commentary, p. 5.

[122] US Merger Guidelines, p. 6; Mestmäcker and Schweitzer, *Europäisches Wettbewerbsrecht*, § 16, para.6; Cárdenas Tomažič, *Marktabgrenzung*, pp. 44–49.

serves as a standard for market definition in many different jurisdictions throughout the world.[123]

The theory of price elasticity and the SSNIP test have been subject to various critics both practically and conceptually. The most common sceptical remarks concern the difficulty to put the theoretical test into practice, the difficulty to obtain relevant data or the difficulty to identify the price based on which the hypothetical increase is applied.[124] One particular weakness of the SSNIP test, commonly referred to as the *Cellophane* fallacy, deserves closer attention. As explained previously, market analysis for merger cases takes a forward-looking approach, meaning that the current price on which the hypothetical increase is added generally reflects a competitive price in a functioning market. Hence, the current price is close to the competitive price. In contrast, with regard to most single-firm behaviour cases, the market is already distorted by the abusive or monopolizing conduct of the dominant firm, allowing the latter to impose monopoly prices above prices that would normally prevail in a competitive market. Thus, the current price is likely to be higher than the competitive price, but even a monopolized product may reach a price high enough for a critical mass of customers to switch to alternatives which may not be close substitutes. Given that a dominant firm striving to maximize profits would usually price just below the point where a critical mass of buyers shift to alternatives, the SSNIP test with a hypothetical increase of the current price would make the relevant market appear much larger than it would be if the increase had been calculated on the basis of a competitive price. In consequence, the market share of the putative monopoly or dominant firm appears smaller than it should be, resulting in the erroneous conclusion that no market power exists.[125]

> The *Cellophane* fallacy received its name from the case *du Pont de Nemours & Co.*,[126] where the question arose whether du Pont had monopoly power, given that it produced almost 75 per cent for the US cellophane market,

[123] See Bishop and Walker, *Economics of EC Competition Law*, p. 88, identifying Australia, Brazil, Bulgaria, Canada, Israel, The Netherlands, New Zealand, UK.

[124] See e.g. O'Donoghue and Padilla, *Law and Economics of Article 82 EC*, p. 81; Werden, 'History of Market Delineation', 200 with references; Werden, 'Justice Department's Merger Guidelines', 531 ff; Mueller, *Abschied vom Bedarfsmarktkonzept?*, pp. 130–31.

[125] See e.g. Landes and Posner, 'Market Power in Antitrust', 961; Posner, *Antitrust Law*, pp. 150–511; Lindsay and Scola, 'Market Definition', pp. 257–58; Werden, 'History of Market Delineation', 135–39, with references; Bishop and Walker, *Economics of EC Competition Law*, pp. 98–104; White, 'Market Power and Market Definition', pp. 919–20; ABA Section of Antitrust Law, *Market Power Handbook*, pp. 59–60.

[126] *US* v. *E. I. du Pont de Nemours & Co. (Cellophane)*, 351 US 377 (1956).

which it sold at prices 2 to 3 times higher compared to other flexible packaging materials. The court found cellophane to be part of a broad market including all flexible packaging materials, arguing *inter alia* that du Pont could not raise its prices without losing too many customers to other flexible wrapping materials. Commentators criticized the court's analysis with the argument that du Pont was already pricing at monopoly levels.

In sum, the *Cellophane* fallacy proclaims that a certain product or service may have no substitutes at a 10 per cent increase of a competitive price, but it may receive substitutes at a 10 per cent increase of a monopoly price. The analysis should thus always be based on the hypothetical increase of a competitive price, which for purposes of merger control would usually be the current price.[127] In cases of single-firm behaviour, the competitive price is more difficult to determine if the dominant firm is already pricing at a higher level. Nonetheless, the US Department of Justice states that despite the SSNIP's limitations 'in the section 2 context, there exists no clear and widely accepted alternative to the hypothetical-monopolist methodology for defining relevant markets'.[128]

The conclusion that 'likeness' should centre on substitutability of demand triggers the follow-up question whether WTO adjudicating bodies could feasibly apply a method similar to the SSNIP test, focusing on cross-price elasticity of demand.[129] In *Japan – Alcoholic Beverages II* the Panel took the view that economic tools of market analysis, such as cross-price elasticity, may be taken into consideration for the purpose of a 'likeness' analysis.

'In the Panel's view, the decisive criterion in order to determine whether two products are directly competitive or substitutable is whether they have common end-uses, *inter alia*, as shown by elasticity of substitution' (para 6.22). On appeal, the Appellate Body agreed with the Panel

[127] US Merger Guidelines, p. 7: 'the Agency will use prevailing prices ... unless premerger circumstances are strongly suggestive of coordinated interaction, in which case the Agency will use a price more reflective of the competitive price'.

[128] Competition and Monopoly Report, p. 27.

[129] See also Neven, 'How Should "Protection" be Evaluated?', 437–39; Trebilcock and Giri, 'National Treatment Principle', 60–61; Horn and Mavroidis, 'Economic and Legal Aspects of MFN', 242: 'the Panel does not understand that cross-price elasticity reflects all the other criteria mentioned'; Marchetti and Mavroidis, 'Challenges for GATS', 534: 'A look into the relevant market, as expressed, *inter alia*, by elasticities of substitution, seems to be more appropriate'; Pillai, 'Review: Verhoosel, National Treatment', 339; Krajewski, *National Regulation*, p. 100; Matheny, '"Like Products" and Cultural Products', 265–66; but see Howse and Tuerk, 'WTO Impact on Internal Regulations', p. 297: 'what is at stake is a contextual and qualitative judgement about competitive relationships, not merely the economic analysis of cross-elasticity of demand'.

that cross-elasticity is a relevant but not decisive criterion in the 'likeness' analysis (p 26). However, neither the Panel nor the Appellate Body conducted a quantitative analysis of cross-elasticity.

In *Korea – Alcoholic Beverages*, the Panel even devoted an entire section to cross-elasticity. However, it considerably limited any relevance of a quantitative analysis because, according to the Panel, the result would be inconclusive due to the fact that consumer preference may be strongly influenced by the trade barrier in place (para 10.44). The Appellate Body held in this regard that 'we share the Panel's reluctance to rely unduly on quantitative analyses of the competitive relationship. In our view, an approach that focused solely on the quantitative overlap of competition would, in essence, make cross-price elasticity *the* decisive criterion in determining whether products are "directly competitive or substitutable"' (para 134, emphasis original).

In this case, the relevance of a quantitative analysis was rejected mainly because of concerns that the result may be flawed due to the fact that consumer behaviour is likely to be influenced by the trade barrier under scrutiny.[130] This justified concern is at the heart of the issue of potential and future competition discussed under section 14.III.C below. It may be for this reason and the lack of relevant data that the concept of price elasticity of demand did not receive much attention in trade non-discrimination outside the three alcoholic beverages cases.[131] Despite this reluctance of the WTO adjudicating bodies, the hypothesis proposed by a comparative analysis between market definition and 'likeness' is that price elasticity should be examined by virtue of a 'speculative experiment'[132] in the context of 'likeness'. An adaptation of the SSNIP test to the analysis of 'likeness' in non-discrimination requires determining three parameters, (i) namely the initial price of the products; (ii) the change in performance of one of the products; and (iii) the critical mass or threshold of consumers that substitute the products as a result of the performance change.

To be recalled, in a merger analysis the SSNIP test looks at consumer reactions under the assumption of a 5–10 per cent increase of current – at the same time deemed competitive – prices. With regard to single-firm behaviour, the *Cellophane* fallacy requires basing the price increase on the hypothetical competitive price – usually lower than current prices – as otherwise the market will appear larger than it actually is. In trade

130 The same concern was expressed again by the Panel Report, *Chile – Alcoholic Beverages*, paras. 7.68 ff, issue not appealed.

131 See also Horn and Mavroidis, 'Economic and Legal Aspects of MFN', 242; Horn and Mavroidis, 'Interpretation of National Treatment', 61–62.

132 Market Definition Notice, para.15.

cases, the market situation is comparable to the one in single-firm behaviour cases, in that the market is distorted not by the monopoly power of the firm, but by the trade obstacle. Accordingly, the imported product or service is offered on the domestic market at a higher price than it would be without the trade obstacle.

> For instance, the domestic product A is not subject to government issued constraints and is thus sold at its competitive price of 100. Assume the competitive price of the imported product B is 90, but it is subject to a trade obstacle such as an internal regulation or an internal tax of 20 per cent. Consequently, product B is sold for 108, which is above its competitive price.

Against this background, there are different ways of how the SSNIP-type test could be adjusted to fit the concept of 'likeness' in non-discrimination.

Demand substitutability at current or competitive prices without elasticity: If a quantitative analysis of demand substitutability at current market conditions and current prices – i.e. with the discriminatory trade obstacle in place and without a hypothetical change in price – demonstrates that consumers view the products as interchangeable, this would already be a very strong indication for the existence of 'likeness'. This test does not measure price elasticity as it does not evaluate how demand is affected by the *change* in price of a certain product. It essentially corresponds to the analysis the WTO adjudicating bodies are currently conducting under the *Border Tax Adjustments* framework.[133]

Elasticity on the basis of current prices: The easiest option for applying the SSNIP test to the 'likeness' analysis is to ask whether, on the basis of current prices, an increase in price of the domestic product or service A would cause an increase of demand for the imported product or service B. The same result would be achieved by measuring how the price decrease of the imported product affects demand decrease for the domestic product. If, on the one hand, a certain number of consumers are prepared to substitute one product for another as a result of the price change *despite the trade barrier*, then the two products are most certainly 'alike'. On the other hand, a low coefficient of cross-price elasticity is not an indication for 'unlikeness', considering that the imported product is not currently offered at a competitive price.[134] Due to the trade barrier in place, the test

[133] With regard to potential, latent and future competition see below, 14.III.C.

[134] See Panel Report, *Chile – Alcoholic Beverages*, para.7.70: 'A high coefficient of cross-price elasticity would of course lend more credence to a claim of direct competitiveness or

understates the consumers' willingness to switch products, reason for which the relevant market appears smaller than it may actually be. This result could be referred to as a 'reverse *Cellophane* fallacy'.[135]

Alternatively, it is possible to measure the increase in demand for the domestic product A following a hypothetical price increase of the imported product B. Considering that the imported product is already sold above competitive prices due to the trade barrier, it is likely that a very large number of consumers switch to the domestic product as a result of the additional price increase. This situation corresponds to the regular *Cellophane* fallacy where price increases are based on a monopoly price. As a result, the test overstates the consumers' willingness to substitute the two products and the market may appear broader than it actually is. The same result would be achieved by measuring how a price decrease of the domestic product affects demand decrease for the imported product. Presumptively, a large number of consumers would switch from the already overpriced imported product to the cheaper domestic product.

Elasticity on the basis of competitive prices: The *Cellophane* fallacy could be avoided by calculating the hypothetical change in price on the basis of competitive instead of current prices. In a similar way to the analysis in single-firm behaviour, this test requires determining the 'but-for' competitive price by reducing the price of the imported product B in the amount equivalent to the cost of the trade obstacle.[136] However, assessing the value or cost of the trade obstacle may be a difficult if not impossible exercise, depending on the measure under scrutiny. The easiest trade obstacles to evaluate are internal taxes. Here the cost of the trade obstacle equals the difference in taxation between the domestic and the imported product. In contrast, a monetary quantification of internal regulations is much more difficult. Measures such as technical standards or authorization and qualification requirements may create transaction costs for foreign competitors which cannot easily be evaluated in numbers. In some cases, particularly in the case of services, the regulation may even completely hinder the foreign producer or supplier

substitutability, although a low coefficient of cross-price elasticity is not necessarily fatal to a claim of direct competitiveness or substitutability. Indeed, a low coefficient of cross-price elasticity may be due to the very measures in question in the dispute'.

135 Emch, 'What are "Like" Products?', 385; on this issue see also Froeb and Werden, 'Reverse *Cellophane* Fallacy'.

136 Alternatively, the cost of the trade obstacle could be added to the domestic product or half of the cost could be added to the domestic and subtracted from the imported product, see Emch, 'What are "Like" Products?', 386.

from offering its product or service on the domestic market. The same is true for import and sales bans. In these cases, the 'but-for' competitive price could be determined by requesting information on cost structure from the exporting producers as a basis for calculating the price level at which they would be able to offer the product or service on the domestic market. Another possibility is to consider price levels that prevail in markets outside the regulatory country.[137]

Hypothetical price change and critical mass of consumer loss: The next issue that arises with an SSNIP test for 'likeness' concerns the question of how many consumers are required to switch as a result of the hypothetical change in price in order to conclude that the products are 'alike'. Not any *de minimis* degree of substitutability or price elasticity is sufficient to form a single product market.[138] In competition law, the critical mass is determined by the question of *profitability* which in turn is linked to the concept of market power. In other words, if the number of losses in sold items reaches a level at which the 5–10 per cent price increase is unprofitable for the firm under scrutiny, then the products are considered as part of the same market. The 5–10 per cent increase is justified by the fact that this is the type of price increase merger control aims to prevent.

In contrast, trade law is concerned with competitive opportunities, not with market power and profitability.[139] It is thus more difficult to economically justify a benchmark for the degree of change in price and consumer demand. One option is to borrow the profitable increase of 5–10 per cent criterion from competition law for lack of a better alternative, noting however that the breadth of markets should not be identical in competition and trade. Another option reflecting best the underlying objective of protecting competitive opportunities is to reverse the test by measuring elasticity with a 'small but significant non-transitory decrease in price' (SSNDP) instead of an SSNIP test.[140] This approach requires reducing the current price of the imported products or services to a competitive level by the value of the trade barrier. The decisive question then becomes if any and how many consumers switch from a

[137] See below, 14.III.A.3.h.

[138] Sandrock, 'Grundprobleme der sachlichen Marktabgrenzung', p. 464.

[139] For this reason rejecting an SSNIP test for 'likeness', Emch, 'What are "Like" Products?', 387–88; but see Neven, 'How Should "Protection" be Evaluated?', 438.

[140] For the proposal of an SSNDP test for market definition see O'Donoghue and Padilla, *Law and Economics of Article 82 EC*, pp. 83–84; Baker, 'Market Definition', 164; in the trade context Goco, '"Likeness", and Market Definition', 334.

specific domestic to the imported products or services. The threshold of change in demand should be linked to the profitability for the foreign company. In other words, if the lifting of the trade barrier raises profitability for the foreign company *to the direct detriment* of a domestic product or service, then the products or services are 'like' for purposes of non-discrimination. The increased profitability must be at least noticeable, such that one single consumer prepared to switch to the imported product or service is insufficient to affirm 'likeness'. The required threshold depends on the product or service in question. For instance, the threshold is expected to be lower for highly individualized and expensive services with little or no transportation costs as opposed to a mass produced low-cost product.

In sum, it may be concluded that a test for price elasticity is difficult to implement in the context of trade non-discrimination. However, elasticity still has a certain value for the 'likeness' analysis:

- The inability of domestic companies to profitably raise prices by 5–10 per cent at *current* prices – i.e. despite the trade barrier in place – should at least create a presumption of 'likeness', but has no value for a conclusion of 'unlikeness'.
- The inability of domestic companies to profitably raise prices by 5–10 per cent at *competitive* prices – i.e. without the trade barrier – is a strong indication for 'likeness', considering that the breadth of relevant markets is broader in trade than in competition law.
- The most informative way to measure price elasticity for 'likeness' is to lift the trade barrier by hypothetically reducing the price of the imported product or service and to measure the shift in consumer demand from a specific domestic to the imported product or service in the light of the foreign firm's profitability.

b. Physical characteristics and end-use (objective element) Evidence on physical characteristics and intended use of a product or service serves as a first indication limiting the field of possible substitutes.[141] These criteria are also referred to as elements of functional interchangeability.[142]

[141] See e.g. *US* v. *E. I. du Pont de Nemours & Co. (Cellophane)*, 351 US 377 (1956), p. 411 (physical characteristics of flexible wrappings); for the EC see e.g. Commission Case COMP/M.1672 *Volvo/Scania* OJ 2001 L143/74, paras. 14 ff (trucks above and below 16 tonnes).

[142] Lindsay and Scola, 'Market Definition', p. 259; Cárdenas Tomažič, *Marktabgrenzung*, p 35 (Industriekonzept) and p. 36 (funktionelle Ähnlichkeit); Neveling, *Marktabgrenzung bei der Fusionskontrolle*, p. 157.

Differences in grade or quality are also criteria to be considered under this objective category.[143] It is noteworthy that similar to the WTO adjudicating bodies' practice on 'likeness', most of the EU decisions pertaining to market definition rely more or less heavily on physical characteristics and end-use.[144] Yet, the EU Market Definition Notice clearly states the shortcomings of a purely objective–functional analysis of substitutability. Considerations other than characteristics and end-use may influence customer behaviour, reason for which an objective analysis may not accurately reflect the market situation. The Market Definition Notice states that 'differences in product characteristics are not in themselves sufficient to exclude demand substitutability, since this will depend to a large extent on how customers value different characteristics'.[145] Similarly, US courts tend to find that quality 'distinctions are economically meaningless where the differences are actually a *spectrum* of price and quality differences'.[146] The evidence related to the physical characteristics and end-use of a product or service is identical to the first two factors from *Border Tax Adjustments*: 'properties, nature and quality' as well as 'end-uses', both of which have been discussed under chapter 13 above.

c. Views of consumers, customers and competitors (subjective element) Evidence of consumer views on the interchangeability of consumer goods and services is an important subjective–functional element for the analysis of demand substitutability.[147] Since it is difficult to assess

[143] See e.g. *International Boxing Club* v. *US*, 358 US 242 (1959), p. 252, where championship boxing contests were considered as 'cream' of boxing, thus constituting a separate market.

[144] See e.g. Kauper, 'Problem of Market Definition', 1697, 1735, criticizing the qualitative approach; O'Donoghue and Padilla, *Law and Economics of Article 82 EC*, p. 86, referring to Cases 27/76 *United Brands* v. *Commission* [1978] ECR 207, paras. 12–35; C-333/94 *Tetra Pak International* v. *Commission* [1996] ECR I-5951, paras. 7–20; Case 31/80 *L'Oréal* v. *De Nieuwe AMCK* [1980] ECR 3775, para.25; Case T-7/93 *Langnese Iglo GmbH* v. *Commission* [1995] ECR II-1533, para.61; further Commission Case COMP/37.792 *Microsoft* (no OJ publication), paras. 411 ff; Case COMP/38.096 *Clearstream* (no OJ publication), para.199; Case COMP/38.233 *Wanadoo Interactive* (no OJ publication), paras. 174 ff.

[145] Market Definition Notice, para.36; also Mueller, *Abschied vom Bedarfsmarktkonzept?*, p. 60; Lindsay and Scola, 'Market Definition', p. 260; Bishop and Walker, *Economics of EC Competition Law*, p. 107.

[146] *Murrow Furniture Galleries* v. *Thomasville Furniture Industries*, 889 F 2d 524 (4th Cir. 1989), p. 528.

[147] For the EC see e.g. Market Definition Notice, para.41; Case T-7/93 *Langnese Iglo GmbH* v. *Commission* [1995] ECR II-1533, para.60; Commission Case IV/M.1524 *Airtours/First Choice* OJ 2000 L93/1, para.12: 'a somewhat narrower approach is considered to be justified in the present case in regard to distinguishing separate markets for package holidays

the views of end-consumers, the European Commission usually relies on marketing and market research studies undertaken by the parties and their competitors for the purpose of their internal price policies and marketing actions. Other evidence taken into account are consumer surveys, data from consumer purchasing patterns and retailers' views. In addition to end-consumers, the European Commission directly contacts the main competitors of the companies under scrutiny and, in case of non-consumer goods, its customers. Their view on possible market reactions in case of increased prices of the relevant product or service by 5 to 10 per cent is taken into consideration, which is basically a qualitative application of the SSNIP test.[148] Similarly, US courts take into account evidence on market views expressed by the relevant industry,[149] and views of firms on who their competitors are.[150] The Merger Guidelines Commentary even states that '[c]ustomers typically are the best source, and in some cases they may be the only source, of critical information on the factors that govern their ability and willingness to substitute in the event of a price increase'.[151] In comparison, it is interesting to note that German competition practice does not consider the views of actual, but only of the informed 'model' or 'average' consumer.[152] This approach requires developing an abstract and ideal-type consumer.

to long-haul and short-haul destinations' (rev'd on other grounds); for the US see e.g. *Fineman* v. *Armstrong World Industries*, 980 F 2d 171 (3rd Cir. 1992); in general Cárdenas Tomažič, *Marktabgrenzung*, p. 37 (Verwenderorientierte subjektive Ähnlichkeit).

148 Market Definition Notice, para.40; Lindsay and Scola, 'Market Definition', pp. 268–69; O'Donoghue and Padilla, *Law and Economics of Article 82 EC*, pp. 86–88.

149 See e.g. *Fineman* v. *Armstrong World Industries*, 980 F 2d 171 (3rd Cir. 1992), p. 199 (industry distinguishes carpeting market from market for resilient floor covering); *FTC* v. *Warner Communications*, 742 F 2d 1156 (9th Cir. 1984), p. 1163 (record industry distinguishes market for pre-recorded music from market for recorded music); *PepsiCo* v. *Coca-Cola*, 315 F 3d 101 (2nd Cir. 2002), p. 107 (former CEO of PepsiCo would '[n]ever ever ... think of or refer to a delivery method as a market').

150 See e.g. *US* v. *Continental Can Co.*, 378 US 441 (1964), pp. 454 f: 'each industry take into consideration the price of the containers of the opposing industry in formulating their own pricing policy'.

151 Merger Guidelines Commentary, p. 9.

152 BGH Beschluss vom 16.12.1976, KVR 2/76, WuW/E BGH 1445, p. 1447 (*Valium*); Wiedemann, 'Verbot Mißbrauchs marktbeherrschender Stellungen', n 8: 'Die Bezugnahme auf den "verständigen Verbraucher" bedeutet nach Rechtsprechung und Verwaltungspraxis, daß auf einen "vernünftigen durchschnittlichen Abnehmer" abzustellen ist'; Mueller, *Abschied vom Bedarfsmarktkonzept?*, p. 73; Cárdenas Tomažič, *Marktabgrenzung*, pp. 49–51; for critical comments see Sandrock, 'Grundprobleme der sachlichen Marktabgrenzung', p. 470; Bishop and Walker, *Economics of EC Competition Law*, p. 129.

Generally, this type of evidence corresponds to the third factor from *Border Tax Adjustments*.[153] In a similar way to competition law, the WTO adjudicating bodies have previously considered marketing strategies, without, however, attributing it specifically to consumers' tastes and habits.[154] The Panel in *Japan – Alcoholic Beverages II*, for instance, explicitly stated the usefulness of examining marketing strategies in the context of cross-price elasticity.[155] In *Korea – Alcoholic Beverages* the Panel also considered marketing strategies, albeit in the context of physical characteristics:

> 'Marketing strategies that highlight fundamental product distinctions or, alternatively, underlying similarities may be useful tools for analysis. However, marketing strategies sometimes aim to create distinctions that are primarily perceptual between products with very similar physical characteristics. The existence of such perceptions based on marketing strategies rather than physical similarities and potential end uses does not mean that products are not at least potentially competitive. Indeed, it is natural and logical that marketers would recognize the possibility of capitalizing on the tax differentiation to create a marketing advantage.' (para 10.65)

In essence, the Panel opines that marketing may create perceptual differences that should not be overvalued. However, the more accurate argument seems to be that if a company highlights distinctions between its own and another product, it indicates precisely that these two products are in a competitive relationship.[156] Marketing strategies were also considered in *Chile – Alcoholic Beverages*, but primarily with regard to end-uses.[157] In *Canada – Periodicals* the Panel implicitly referred to marketing strategies by stating that '[i]t is most likely that the two volumes would have been *designed* for the same readership with the same tastes and habits'.[158] In the more recent case *Mexico – Taxes on Soft Drinks* the Panel finally attributed the evidence related to marketing strategies to the criterion of consumers' tastes and habits.[159] Another type of evidence which

[153] See above, 13.III.

[154] Melloni, *National Treatment in GATT*, p. 135.

[155] Para 6.28: 'greater emphasis should be placed on elasticity of substitution. In this context, factors like marketing strategies could also prove to be relevant criteria, since what is at issue is the responsiveness of consumers to the various products offered in the market'.

[156] But see Horn and Mavroidis, 'Interpretation of National Treatment', 62–63.

[157] Para 7.46: 'The evidence of trends towards increasing overlap in end-uses is supported by the marketing strategies of the domestic Chilean companies'.

[158] Panel Report, *Canada – Periodicals*, para.5.25 (emphasis added).

[159] Para 8.134.

the Appellate Body admitted under the heading of consumers' tastes and habits relates to health risks of products. In *EC – Asbestos*, the Appellate Body explicitly reversed the Panel on its holding that all evidence related to 'risks' is excluded from the 'likeness' analysis.[160]

In order to receive a more coherent picture on consumers' tastes and habits, it would be similarly important for the panels to consider additional evidence, such as data on consumer surveys as well as opinions of competitors and retailers. However, due to differences in WTO and competition law proceedings, WTO panels neither have the duty nor the competence to obtain such evidence (see *below*, sub-section j). It must thus be up to the governments of the respective parties to the disputes to actively gather this information from its industries and consumers. Finally, it is suggested that the subjective–functional substitutability should not go as far as to take into account the subjective views of uninformed, misinformed or irrational consumers. Similar to the German practice of relevant markets, the analysis of substitutability must be based on an informed and reasonable average consumer.[161] Such a standard is particularly important with regard to the issue of PPMs (*below*, chapter 15).

d. Price differences and price trends Competition authorities and sometimes courts both in the US and the EU rely on differences in price as an indication for a relevant market.[162] Yet, high and low pricing of similar products does not prevent *per se* the definition of one single relevant

[160] Panel Report, *EC – Asbestos*, para.8.132, rev'd by the Appellate Body Report, paras. 113 and 122.

[161] Also Trebilcock and Howse, *Regulation of International Trade*, p. 105: 'the test from the perspective of consumer tastes and habits is whether the products would be substitutable and in a competitive relationship in an *idealized* marketplace, one where consumers have full information' (emphasis original); also Howse and Tuerk, 'WTO Impact on Internal Regulations', p. 301.

[162] For the US see e.g. *US* v. *Aluminum Co. of America*, 377 US 271 (1964), p. 276: 50–65 per cent price difference between aluminum and copper conductor justifies distinct markets; *US* v. *Archer-Daniels-Midland*, 866 F 2d 242 (8th Cir. 1988), p. 246; for the EC see e.g. Commission Case IV/M.619 *Gencor/Lonrho*, OJ 1997 L011/30, para.41: 'The substantial difference in the price levels of gold and platinum jewellery on the Japanese market could also be an indicator that gold and platinum in jewellery are not to any large extent substitutes for jewellery purposes'; Lindsay and Scola, 'Market Definition', pp. 263–64, referring to Commission Case COMP/37.792 *Microsoft* (no OJ publication), paras. 369–82; see also Case C-185/95 *Baustahlgewebe GmbH* v. *Commission* [1998] ECR I-8417, para.99; Mueller, *Abschied vom Bedarfsmarktkonzept?*, p. 61; Cárdenas Tomažič, *Marktabgrenzung*, p. 74.

market.[163] In fact, price differences should be considered cautiously as evidence for distinct markets, as it may well be that consumers see the high- and low-priced products or services as alternatives.[164] In addition to the difference in current prices, evidence from previous price trends may constitute an indication for demand substitutability.[165] Movements of prices for products and services in the same market are more likely to correlate than prices of those in different markets.

Price differences and previous price trends are not part of the *Border Tax Adjustments* framework and they are not usually examined by the WTO adjudicating bodies as part of the 'likeness' analysis. The few reports devoting an argument to 'prices' usually focused on cross-price issues, but not so much on price differences and trends.[166] Notable exceptions are the Panel Report on *Korea – Alcoholic Beverages*, which acknowledged that there are 'significant price differences between the imported and domestic products'. Yet, the Panel rejected the differences as not decisive and emphasized that 'behavioural changes that occur due to relative price movements are more important than absolute price differences'.[167] Similarly, the Panel in *Dominican Republic – Import and Sale of Cigarettes* found that '[t]he distinction between different price segments may be particularly important for the analysis under Article III:2 [first sentence] of the GATT, since the Selective Consumption Tax was applied on an *ad valorem* basis, i.e. was related to the price of the product'.[168] However, the argument of the Dominican Republic was more aimed at the differences in quality of cigarettes, which it found to be linked to prices. The Panel did not find the price differences to be sufficiently pertinent for a conclusion of 'unlikeness'.

In sum, small price differences may be an indication that the services or products are alike as they facilitate interchangeability by consumers. In contrast, high price differences are not necessarily an indication for

[163] See e.g. *US* v. *E. I. du Pont de Nemours & Co. (Cellophane)*, 351 US 377 (1956), p. 401: Cellophane is in the same market with other flexible wrappings despite a price difference of 200–300 per cent.

[164] For a criticism of price comparison see Baker, 'Market Definition', 152–53; Bishop and Walker, *Economics of EC Competition Law*, p. 109.

[165] See e.g. *US* v. *Aluminum Co. of America*, 377 US 271 (1964), p. 276.

[166] Panel Reports, *Korea – Alcoholic Beverages*, paras. 10.87 ff; *Chile – Alcoholic Beverages*, paras. 7.60 ff; *Indonesia – Autos*, para.14.173 (price as part of physical characteristics); but see also argument by the EC in GATT Panel Report, *EEC – Animal Feed Proteins*, para.3.4; Panel Report, *Korea – Various Measures on Beef*, para.618.

[167] Para 10.94; see also Emch, 'What are "Like" Products?', 388–90.

[168] Para 7.331.

'unlikeness' as they may simply reflect the additional transaction costs of the trade obstacle.[169]

e. Evidence of substitution in the past Evidence relating to events in the recent past offering examples of substitution between certain products or services is, to the extent available, decisive for the definition of a product market. The Market Definition Notice lists events such as shocks in the market, changes in relative prices or launches of new products or services. In case such events existed in the recent past, the consumer reactions in terms of demand will be determinant in establishing substitutability.[170] Conversely, evidence showing that demand for a specific product remained stable over an extended period of time indicates that this product constitutes its own product market.[171]

While evidence of substitution in the past is not part of the *Border Tax Adjustments* framework, it should be considered in the 'likeness' analysis as a largely decisive criterion, to the extent that relevant information is available. In *Mexico – Taxes on Soft Drinks*, for instance, the Panel considered evidence which showed that when HFCS became available in Mexico, Mexican producers of soft drinks started to use HFCS instead of cane sugar; when Mexico imposed the tax on HFCS, Mexican producers switched back to cane sugar.[172] It follows that evidence of substitution in the past is particularly relevant for purposes of 'likeness' if the imported product or service was already available on the domestic market prior to the adoption of the trade obstacle.

f. Barriers to substitution Even if evidence suggests that certain products or services are *prima facia* substitutable, the consideration of certain barriers and costs may lead to the conclusion of two distinct product markets. The Notice states that an exhaustive; list of all possible barriers to substitution is impossible to compile, however, it mentions regulatory barriers, constraints from downstream markets, investment

[169] On this issue see 'potential competition in a narrow sense', below 14.III.C.2.a; on price differences see also Horn and Mavroidis, 'Interpretation of National Treatment', 64.

[170] Market Definition Notice, para.38; Commission Case IV/M.430 *Procter & Gamble/VP Schickedanz (II)*, OJ 1994 L354/32, paras. 62–71; see also US Merger Guidelines, p. 6.

[171] C-333/94 *Tetra Pak International* v. *Commission* [1996] ECR I-5951, para.15: 'packaging materials other than carton were able to gain only a marginal share of the UHT-milk packaging market … such stability in demand is a relevant criterion for determining whether carton is interchangeable with other materials'.

[172] Panel Report, *Mexico – Taxes on Soft Drinks*, paras. 8.72 ff.

in capital, production process, learning and human capital as well as customer location and others.[173] For instance, in the *Microsoft* case the relevant market was influenced by the fact that customers could not easily switch from Windows to Mac OS due to the incurring costs of acquiring new hardware.[174]

For good reasons, barriers to substitution are not explicitly part of the WTO adjudicating bodies' analysis of 'likeness'. In competition law, it is useful to consider barriers to substitutability as they create smaller markets and indicate that market power exists. An analogous analysis for purposes of 'likeness' may play against the objective of non-discrimination, which is to protect competitive opportunities. For instance, a small number of consumers willing to make the investment for a new computer in order to switch from Microsoft Windows to Mac OS may not affect Microsoft's market power. However, from the perspective of trade law, the small number of consumers may be sufficient to create competitive opportunities for Mac OS. Consequently, barriers to substitution must be considered very cautiously in trade non-discrimination, such that a barrier only negates 'likeness' if it is sufficiently high so as to obviate the creation of competitive opportunities.

g. **Determination by national authorities** In some cases, panels considered public statements made by national authorities – in particular those of the respondent – on their view of interchangeability between the products in question. For instance, the Panel in *Mexico – Taxes on Soft Drinks* took into account a press release issued by the Mexican Ministry of Economics according to which it became apparent that the government regarded HFCS and cane sugar as interchangeable.[175] An approach that is even more pertinent in the light of the present comparative analysis is the Panel's reference to decisions by the Mexican competition authorities, according to which HFCS is a close substitute for refined sugar and cane sugar.[176] Similarly, the Panel in *Chile – Alcoholic Beverages* referred to a decision of the Chilean competition authorities regarding a merger between two pisco producers, which explicitly stated that consumers regard other alcoholic beverages as alternatives to pisco. The Panel noted that competition law generally defines narrower markets than trade law, concluding that if two products are part of the same market for purposes

[173] Market Definition Notice, para.42; see also US Merger Guidelines, p. 7.

[174] *US* v. *Microsoft Corp.*, 253 F 3d 34 (D.C.Cir.), p. 52.

[175] Paras 8.76 f.

[176] Para 8.77.

of competition law, they must necessarily be alike for purposes of Article III GATT.[177] On a final note, even the tribunal in *ADM* v. *Mexico* referred to the market analysis by Mexican competition authorities for purposes of 'like circumstances' in NAFTA chapter 11.[178]

h. Evidence from other markets Given that competition in the domestic market is distorted by the putative trade obstacle, it may be the case that no accurate and useful data can be obtained from the domestic market. For this reason, the Panel in *Korea – Alcoholic Beverages* found it appropriate to take into account the competitive relationship of soju and other alcoholic beverages in markets outside of Korea. Similarly, the Panel considered it relevant 'as to how Korean manufacturers of soju are marketing their beverages outside Korea'.[179] Korea's challenge of the Panel's approach was rejected by the Appellate Body. The latter confirmed the Panel's reasoning, at the same time setting out certain requirements which a comparative market study should meet:

> 'It seems to us that evidence from other markets may be pertinent to the examination of the market at issue, particularly when demand on that market has been influenced by regulatory barriers to trade or to competition. Clearly, not every other market will be relevant to the market at issue. But if another market displays characteristics similar to the market at issue, then evidence of consumer demand in that other market may have some relevance to the market at issue.' (para 137)

Hence, evidence from other markets with similar conditions may be relevant directly for the question of interchangeability. At the same time, a foreign market analysis could be useful for determining the competitive price of the imported product or service as a basis for the SSNDP test.

i. Channels of distribution and points of sale As in competition law, WTO jurisprudence takes into account distribution channels as evidence for determining competitive relationships.[180] The Panel in *Korea – Alcoholic Beverages* found that '[t]here is considerable evidence of overlap in channels of distribution and points of sale of these products and such evidence is supportive of a finding that the identified imported and

[177] Paras 7.86 ff. [178] Para 201.

[179] Paras 10.45 f; see also Quick and Lau, 'Environmentally Motivated Tax Distinctions', 431; Emch, 'What are "Like" Products?', 393–94.

[180] For competition law see e.g. *US* v. *Dentsply Intern.*, 399 F 3d 181 (3rd Cir. 2005), p. 188; *PepsiCo* v. *Coca-Cola*, 114 F Supp 2d 243 (S.D.N.Y. 2000), pp. 249 f, aff'd 315 F 3d 101 (2nd Cir. 2002).

domestic products are directly competitive or substitutable'.[181] The argument was confirmed by the Panel in *Chile – Alcoholic Beverages*, finding that '[i]n our view, if products have quite distinct channels of distribution that could be a negative indicator with respect to substitutability'.[182] There is some overlap between channels of distribution and end-uses, in that 'channels of distribution tend to reveal present market structure, while end-uses deals with both the current overlap, if any, and potential for future overlap'.[183] Later panels thus examined channels of distribution under the 'end-uses' factor of the *Border Tax Adjustments* framework.[184]

j. Procedural issues of obtaining evidence In antitrust and merger proceedings, the concerned firms are parties to the proceedings. Hence, national competition authorities and courts may compel the firms to make available information which is important for the determination of the relevant product or service markets. The EU Market Definition Notice provides that the Commission firstly relies on the evidence submitted by the firms concerned. Preference is given to marketing and market research studies as well as consumer surveys which have been undertaken by the firms in their normal course of business and strategic planning. Surveys conducted for purposes of a specific case are considered with more caution. The information received by the firms involved should allow a broad determination of the relevant market, noting that it is often sufficient to determine whether product A and B belong to the same market, without the need to clearly delimit the entire product market. In case additional information is needed, the Commission directly contacts the main customers and companies in the industry or service sector as well as professional associations and companies active in upstream markets. The factual evidence is obtained by addressing written requests and questionnaires to the different sources, identifying the perception about reactions to hypothetical price increases and its effect on competition. Similarly in the US, consumer surveys are relied upon as evidence and consumer witnesses are questioned in jury trials.[185]

[181] Para 10.86. [182] Para 7.59.

[183] Panel Report, *Korea – Alcoholic Beverages*, para.10.83.

[184] Panel Report, *Mexico – Taxes on Soft Drinks*, para.8.133: 'The evidence also indicates that, regardless of the caloric sweetener used, soft drinks and syrups use similar distribution channels'; see also Melloni, *National Treatment in GATT*, pp. 134–35; Horn and Mavroidis, 'Interpretation of National Treatment', 63–64.

[185] For the EC see Market Definition Notice, paras. 33, 40 f; for the US see e.g. *Fineman* v. *Armstrong World Industries*, 980 F 2d 171 (3rd Cir. 1992), p. 199 (evidence of consumer preference for floor coverings); *R.D. Imports Ryno Industries* v. *Mazda Distributors*

While this type of evidence would be extremely helpful for the analysis of demand substitutability in the context of 'likeness', the WTO adjudicating bodies are faced with procedural and practical limitations as to the means of obtaining such data and information. Most importantly, the companies concerned are not directly party to WTO dispute settlement proceedings. Their interests are represented by their respective governments. Accordingly, a panel has no authority to compel the concerned companies to make internal information available. Moreover, not even the parties – i.e. the governments – may obtain information from the adversary party by discovery or other procedural instruments. In consequence, it is much more difficult for a WTO panel to obtain evidence similar to that usually available to competition authorities and courts.

The only instrument available to a panel is Article 13 DSU, pursuant to which it has the authority to seek information from any relevant source, including any individual, body or expert which it deems appropriate.[186] Hence, in theory a panel could contact the producers or suppliers of the product or service in question, their competitors as well as their suppliers, customers and consumers. However, for practical reasons a panel is unlikely to directly contact individuals, as such surveys would be too time consuming and very laborious for the WTO secretariat to administer. For these reasons, the WTO adjudicating bodies typically rely on evidence submitted by the governments which may include studies on substitutability, cross-price elasticity and consumer views.[187] However, it is submitted that if the WTO adjudicating bodies adopt a 'likeness' test clearly focusing on demand substitutability, the parties will automatically provide more relevant evidence in order to support their arguments in a given dispute.

B Supply substitutability

In addition to demand substitutability, market definition in competition law may also require taking into account supply-side substitutability. While demand-side substitutability asks the question of whether consumers would buy a certain product as a substitute for another, supply-side substitution focuses on the issue of whether suppliers not currently producing a certain

(Gulf), 807 F 2d 1222 (5th Cir. 1987), p. 1225 (consumer views on substitutability of cars); see also above, 14.III.A.3.c.

[186] On Art. 13 DSU see Oesch, *Standards of Review*, p. 111: 'this provision endows panels with a virtually unlimited power to undertake and control the process by which they inform themselves of the relevant facts'.

[187] See e.g. consumer survey introduced by the EC in Panel Report, *Chile – Alcoholic Beverages*, para.7.60.

product could begin the production of such products. Substitutability of supply is generally defined as 'the extent to which producers of one product would be willing to shift their resources to producing another product in response to an increase in the price of the other product'.[188] In other words, product A is substitutable with product B if a demand for increased performance by consumers of product B (i.e. lower prices or higher quality) would cause producers to switch to product A for which no increased performance is demanded (i.e. possibility to sell for higher prices or lower quality).

1. Competition law

In order to avoid any confusion in the discussion of supply substitutability, it is important to note at the outset that, in theory, supply substitutability can be taken into consideration at three different stages of the market power analysis in competition law:[189]

- *Relevant product market*: A first approach consists of considering supply substitutability for the definition of the relevant product market itself. According to the EU Market Definition Notice, supply substitutability may be relevant for market definition if, in the given market, 'its effects are equivalent to those of demand substitution in terms of *effectiveness* and *immediacy*'.[190] This could be the case if suppliers are in a position to switch the production from one product to another in the short term and without incurring significant costs or risks, indicating the existence of a competitive relationship between the respective producers. The Market Definition Notice states the example of different qualities of paper that may not be considered substitutable from a consumer point of view. But since producers may easily produce all qualities of paper, there is only one relevant product market for all sorts of paper. The reasoning is similar for the most part of US antitrust law, where some US courts have taken supply substitutability into account at the stage of market definition.[191] Like in the EU, 'the relative ease of shifting production is a determinative factor'.[192]

[188] *AD/SAT* v. *Associated Press*, 181 F 3d 216 (2nd Cir. 1999), p. 227; see also Market Definition Notice, paras. 20–23; Monopolkommission, *Ökonomische Kriterien*, pp. 205–6; Hildebrand, *Economic Analysis in EC Competition Rules*, pp. 290, 334–39.

[189] Werden, 'Justice Department's Merger Guidelines', 519.

[190] Market Definition Notice, para.20 (emphasis added); comprehensively Lindsay and Scola, 'Market Definition', pp. 270 ff; Mueller, *Abschied vom Bedarfsmarktkonzept?*, p. 73; Neveling, *Marktabgrenzung bei der Fusionskontrolle*, p. 167.

[191] See e.g. *Rebel Oil Co.* v. *Atlantic Richfield Co.*, 51 F 3d 1421 (9th Cir. 1995), p. 1436: 'market definition must be based on supply elasticity as well as demand elasticity'; see also *Twin City Sportservice* v. *Charles O. Finley & Co.*, 512 F 2d 1264 (9th Cir. 1975), p. 1271.

[192] ABA Section of Antitrust Law, *Antitrust Law Developments*, p. 577, citing cases.

- *Identification of market participants and calculation of market share*: The second theory of supply substitutability is to consider production response for the identification of competitors and calculation of market shares, only *after* the relevant product market has been defined. In other words, producers which are not currently engaged in the relevant market, but could easily do so, are taken into consideration for the calculation of market shares. Referring to the paper example, high-quality paper would be regarded as a distinct product market from low-quality paper. However, the market share of producers of high-quality paper is adjusted downwards, as producers of other types of paper may at any time substitute their production with high-quality paper. In other words, *all* producers of paper are assigned a share in the narrow product market of high-quality paper.
- *Barriers to entry*: Finally, the last step at which supply substitutability may be considered is as part of *de novo* market entry, which takes place only after the market shares have been calculated. The rationale of the third approach is that low barriers to market entry may prevent a firm with high market shares from exercising market power. As an example, an undertaking with a high market share in the paper market is unlikely to abuse its position if there were low barriers for new producers to enter the paper market.

The most recent US Merger Guidelines take the approach that market definition *only* looks at demand substitutability, whereas '[s]upply substitution factors – i.e., possible production responses – are considered elsewhere in the Guidelines in the identification of firms that participate in the relevant market and the analysis of entry'.[193] Under the EU Market Definition Notice, in contrast, supply substitutability is considered at the second or third step only if it is *not* sufficiently effective and immediate to impact the relevant market itself, for instance because of the need for additional investments, strategic decisions or time delays.[194] Generally speaking, the second and third theory of supply substitutability relate to the competitive constraint of potential competition discussed under section 14.III.C below.[195] This stage of the comparative analysis is only concerned

[193] US Merger Guidelines, p. 4; supporting the Merger Guidelines approach Baker, 'Market Definition', 134 ff.

[194] EC Market Definition Notice, paras. 14 and 20; Case IV/M.1225 *Enso/Stora* OJ 1999 L254/9, paras. 37 ff; see below 14.III.C.1.

[195] On the relationship between supply substitutability and potential competition see e.g. Joined cases T-191, T-212–14/98 *Atlantic Container Line* v. *Commission* [2003] ECR II-3275, para.834; Lindsay and Scola, 'Market Definition', pp. 271–72.

with immediate and effective supply substitutability directly affecting the scope of the product market itself. The question thus is whether supply-side factors may enlarge the relevant market beyond products and services which are substitutable from a demand perspective.

2. Application to trade non-discrimination

To date, WTO adjudicating bodies have not considered supply substitutability in the 'likeness' analysis of non-discrimination.[196] One of the reasons may be that due to conceptual differences, supply substitutability is less relevant for purposes of non-discrimination and 'likeness'. In competition law, supply substitutability focuses more on the *producers* than on the products. For instance, if producers of product B can easily switch their production to product A, the *producers* of A and B are considered to be in a competitive relationship and are thus part of the same product market. The size of the market affects the respective market shares and, consequently, market power. Conversely, GATT rules on non-discrimination exclusively apply to the *product* rather than the producer.[197] The issue is not whether competition is constrained by competitors, but whether and how competition between different products is constrained by a state measure. Hence, in the context of GATT it is more difficult to make an argument of supply substitutability, as it requires extending its explicit protection of competitive opportunities for products to an implicit protection of producers.[198] In the case of GATS, however, 'likeness' is not only about the competitive relationship of the services, but also of the *suppliers*. Thus, the argument of supply substitutability may be easier to justify.

In spite of these reservations, the relevance of supply substitutability may depend on the chosen standard for 'less favourable treatment'.

[196] For marginal references to supply substitutability in the context of the SCM Agreement see Panel Reports, *Korea – Commercial Vessels*, Annex D paras. 108 f; *US – Export Restraints*, Annex B-3 para.3.

[197] See also above, 10.I.B.2.d.

[198] Emch, 'What are "Like" Products?', 373–74; also in the EC non-discrimination context Englisch, *Wettbewerbsgleichheit*, p. 296: 'Die Intensität des Wettbewerbs muss von der Nachfrageseite her beurteilt werden'; but see Choi, '*Like Products*', p. 35, who argues that 'the "practical" objective of these provisions [of GATT] is principally directed towards prohibiting governments from intervening in the flow of comparative advantage between *products* and, thus, of competitive relationships between *producers* of the products' (emphasis original); also supporting supply substitutability in trade non-discrimination Horn and Mavroidis, 'Interpretation of National Treatment', 61; Neven, 'How Should "Protection" be Evaluated?', 438; Melloni, *National Treatment in GATT*, p. 127; Krajewski, 'Review: Choi, Like Products', 201.

As argued under part I, this study endorses the asymmetric impact test according to which non-discrimination is only triggered if a higher percentage of a certain group of imports is disfavoured by the measure in comparison to the percentage of a competing group of domestic goods or services. This section thus firstly analyses the relevance of supply substitutability under the traditional approach of direct comparison between two products or services and, in a second step, turns to supply substitutability under an asymmetric impact test. At the outset it is important to recall that this comparative analysis is only concerned with *de facto* measures, given that in cases of *de jure* discriminations there is no need to prove the existence of a 'like' product or service.[199]

a. Supply substitutability and direct comparison: an issue of scope Different constellations are possible under a direct comparison of two products or two services, depending on whether or not (i) the products under scrutiny are substitutable from the demand side and (ii) both the foreign and domestic producers are able to substitute the production.

- *Effect of supply substitutability if demand substitutability is low*: If the conclusions from the demand-side analysis show that there is no interchangeability between the products, the question becomes whether supply substitutability could be important enough so as to support an overall conclusion of 'likeness'. The following fact pattern illustrates a basis on which different scenarios can arise:

> Products A and B are not considered as substitutes from a consumer's perspective; however, some suppliers may switch their production easily from one to another. Different scenarios can be played out if the importing country imposes an internal tax or regulation on product B (e.g. 10 per cent tax).

- *Substitutability by domestic and foreign suppliers*: Under the first scenario, both domestic and foreign producers have the ability and capacity to easily switch between the production of A and B.[200] In case of the 10 per cent tax on product B, the most opportunistic behaviour for producers is to switch to the production of product A. If, on the one hand, both domestic and foreign producers have the ability to do so and if demand for product A is sufficiently high to absorb the increased supply, then no competitive disadvantage – or less favourable treatment – occurs for foreign producers of product A and B. If, on the other hand, domestic producers continue to produce product B and foreign producers

[199] See above, 3.II.A, n 122. [200] See also Choi, '*Like Products*', pp. 35–49.

continue to import product B despite the 10 per cent tax, then *a priori* no question of supply substitutability arises. In fact, domestic and imported 'like products' B are treated equally. In sum, supply substitutability does not seem to have any effect on the demand-side 'likeness' analysis if supply substitutability exists for both domestic and foreign producers.[201]

– *Substitutability by domestic suppliers only*: In this setting, domestic producers of product A could effectively and immediately switch to the production of the imported product B, the latter being subject to some form of internal trade barrier. Foreign producers, in contrast, are unable to substitute the production of B with the production of A (e.g. climate conditions for agricultural products) or they cannot effectively compete with product A on the domestic market (e.g. high transportation costs for the substitute product). In consequence, domestic producers A/B will escape the 10 per cent tax by focusing on the production of product A only, whereas foreign producers B are compelled to bear the 10 per cent tax increase. In this case, the foreign producers suffer a competitive disadvantage compared to their domestic competitors. Hence, one could make the argument that products A and B are alike solely on the basis of supply substitutability.[202] Following this theory, supply substitutability has potential that could greatly extend the scope of non-discrimination.

> For instance, while consumers may regard different sorts of fruit as substitutable,[203] beef and oranges are very likely to be considered as 'unlike' under a demand-side analysis. If, for instance, Italy decided to impose a 20 per cent sales tax on oranges but not on beef, a foreign orange farmer from a country where cattle breeding is not feasible could argue that beef and milk are 'like' oranges because Italian farmers could avoid the tax by switching to the production of more profitable beef or milk.

[201] But note that the relevance of supply substitutability changes under the asymmetric impact test (below, sub-section b).

[202] Yet, trade jurisprudence shows that markets are generally defined broader for purposes of 'likeness' than for purposes of market definition, indicating that 'likeness' requires less demand-side flexibility than market definition in competition law. Accordingly, there may be less need to resort to supply substitutability in the context of the 'likeness' analysis.

[203] For an example from EC law see Case 184/85 *Commission* v. *Italian Republic* [1987] ECR 2013, para.12: 'Although bananas and table fruit typically produced in Italy are not similar products within the meaning of the first paragraph of Article 95, bananas do afford an alternative choice to consumers of fruit. As a result, bananas must be regarded in partial competition with such fruit'.

In effect, the question here is no longer whether beef and oranges are alike, but whether the farmers compete with one another or, in different terms, whether GATT rules on non-discrimination should protect foreign producers as opposed to products only. Consequently, supply substitutability in this context is more an issue of scope than of 'likeness'. Considering that the WTO adjudicating bodies decided consistently that GATT rules on non-discrimination are limited to products as such, it appears that supply-side factors may not be taken into consideration for the 'likeness' analysis.[204] Arguably, such an extended interpretation of 'likeness' in the light of supply substitutability would only be in line with the object and purpose of trade non-discrimination rules if the regulatory purpose is taken into account as a counterbalance. In other words, the complainant would be required to demonstrate – in addition to supply substitutability – that the 20 per cent tax is primarily designed to protect domestic farmers from foreign competitors.

- *Substitutability by foreign suppliers only*: Under this assumption, foreign producers of product B could effectively and immediately switch to the production of the domestically produced product A as a response to the internal measure affecting the sale of product B. Domestic producers, in contrast, are unable to substitute the production of B with the production of A. In this case, foreign producers are not truly harmed by the trade barrier as they can switch to an alternative product without incurring any transaction costs. There is thus no reason why, in circumstances like these, supply substitutability should override the conclusion of 'unlikeness' from the demand substitutability analysis.
- *Effect of supply substitutability if demand substitutability is high*: If the conclusion from the analysis of demand substitutability shows that products A and B are alike, it is highly unlikely that the absence of supply substitutability negates the overall conclusion on 'likeness'. For instance, if imported bananas are considered 'like' domestically grown apples from a consumer's perspective, then a possible absence of supply substitutability between bananas and apples does not affect the conclusion on 'likeness' in any way. In this scenario, the relevance of supply substitutability is limited to reinforce a conclusion of 'likeness' on grounds of demand substitutability.[205]

[204] On limitation to products as such see above, 10.I.B.2.d and below, 15.I; see also Emch, 'What are "Like" Products?', 373–75.

[205] Similar result Choi, '*Like Products*', pp. 37–38.

– *Supply substitutability under GATS in particular*: Under GATS, suppliers trading their services under modes 3 and 4 are direct beneficiaries of non-discrimination. Following the Appellate Body in *EC – Bananas III* and *Canada – Autos*, a proper approach requires first determining whether the measure under scrutiny falls within the scope of GATS and its non-discrimination provision and, second, analysing the substantive elements.[206] Whether or not a measure is subject to GATS non-discrimination obligations depends on whether it affects a person directly in its capacity as a service supplier in terms of Article I:1 GATS. This issue of whether a measure is subject to GATS must be separated from the question of whether a person qualifies as a service supplier in terms of the GATS and thus benefits from the non-discrimination obligations.

> In *EC – Bananas III* the WTO adjudicating bodies did not separately analyse whether the import licensing procedures affect vertically integrated companies in their capacity as wholesale suppliers. They only addressed the issue of whether vertically integrated companies capable of executing all activities related to wholesaling of bananas could be regarded as 'service suppliers'. In this regard, the Panel stated: 'Where operators form part of vertically integrated companies, they have the capability and opportunity to enter the wholesale service market. They could at any time decide to re-sell bananas which they have imported or acquired from EU producers, or cleared in customs, or ripened instead of further transferring or processing bananas within an integrated company'. (para 7.320, confirmed by Appellate Body, paras. 227 f)

This ruling has been generally interpreted by commentators to signify that trade-restrictive measures may be subject to GATS obligations even if they affect a service that is not actually, but could potentially be supplied by foreign suppliers with the necessary capabilities. If any potential service supplier is regarded as beneficiary of the GATS non-discrimination obligations, it would also include *de novo* market entrants and those suppliers who substitute the services in the long term and at high costs. This approach not only indefinitely expands the scope of the GATS rules on non-discrimination, it also frustrates the asymmetric impact test of 'less favourable treatment', which requires that foreign suppliers are, as a group, more heavily affected than the corresponding group of domestic suppliers.[207] In fact, if (non-immediate and non-effective) potential

[206] See above, 9.II.

[207] Critically also Zdouc, '(1999) Dispute Settlement Practice', 327; Zdouc, *Comparative Analysis of GATS and GATT*, pp. 133–35; Feinäugle, 'Art. XXVIII GATS', pp. 553–54; Krajewski, *National Regulation*, p. 103; Krajewski and Engelke, 'Art. XVII GATS', p. 406.

suppliers were included in the analysis, it would be impossible to circumscribe a specific group of suppliers. For this reason, it is submitted that the scope of GATS should be narrowed from potential suppliers to one of immediate and effective supply substitutability. Supply substitutability in a narrow sense limits the beneficiaries to those suppliers who can immediately and effectively – i.e. at virtually no cost – switch to the supply of the service that is subject to the trade restriction. A modified structure of the methodological test could look as follows:

- First, analyse the measure under scrutiny in the abstract and determine which service transactions could be affected by the measure.
- Second, determine (i) whether any foreign suppliers actively engage in the supply of these services, including those suppliers who could immediately and effectively switch to the supply of those services; and (ii) whether or how these suppliers and services are affected by the measure.

As this overview illustrates, supply substitutability in this context is not primarily relevant for the analysis of 'likeness', but for the determination of the beneficiaries of GATS non-discrimination in relation to a specific measure.

b. Supply substitutability and asymmetric impact: an issue of market definition To be recalled, the asymmetric impact test requires defining the entire relevant market and determining whether the group of foreign products is more negatively affected by the measure than the group of domestic products. Consequently, one could make the argument that suppliers and producers who are able to immediately and effectively switch to the production of a product which is part of the relevant market as defined by demand substitutability, should also be taken into account for the impact assessment.

> For instance, if high-quality paper is not substitutable with low-quality paper from a demand-side perspective, they could still be regarded as 'alike' in the light of supply substitutability for purposes of impact assessment. Hence, the impact of a tax on high-quality paper would require (i) defining a 'high-quality paper' market (demand substitutability) as enclosing 'all types of paper' (supply substitutability); and (ii) determining whether the group of imported 'all types paper' is affected more heavily by the tax than the group of domestic 'all types paper'.

Again, under GATT rules on non-discrimination such an approach would entail acknowledging that non-discrimination protects competitive opportunities of producers rather than of specific products only. Yet, it differs from the above situations of 'direct comparison' which would allow the claim that a tax on animal-related imports results in 'less favourable treatment' of imported beef and milk as compared to domestic fruit. The asymmetric impact test requires comparing *all* foreign substitutable products (demand and supply) with *all* domestic substitutable products (demand and supply).

In contrast to GATT, GATS non-discrimination rules even mandate such an approach by specifically referring to suppliers as part of the scope of the obligation.

> For example, different types of banking services – such as deposit and lending services – may not be regarded as substitutable from the demand side, but are perfectly substitutable from a supplier's perspective. Hence, the impact of a measure affecting a specific type of banking service would need to be assessed on the basis of a relevant market extending to *all* banking services.

A similar result could be achieved with the theory of 'cluster markets', which is particularly pertinent for the definition of relevant markets in service sectors. US courts developed this theory as an alternative to substitutability. Under this approach, the relevant market consists of a 'cluster' of distinct services which are complements rather than substitutes.[208] The cluster market theory was first adopted by the Supreme Court in *Philadelphia National Bank*, where it recognized that 'the cluster of products (various kinds of credit) and services (such as checking accounts and trust administration) denoted by the term "commercial bank" ... composes a distinct line of commerce'.[209] The rationale behind the cluster market is that all cluster services are typically offered in a group, which may be for reasons of cost savings and convenience or settled consumer preference to purchase the individual services in a group. Accordingly, the individual cluster services face no competition independently, but the supplier of an individual cluster service competes with the supplier of another cluster service. In a later case, the Supreme Court applied the cluster market theory to find that the clusters of fire protection and burglary protection services are 'a single basic service – the protection of property through use of a central service station – that must be compared with all other forms of property protection', taking into account the fact that '[c]entral station companies recognize that, to compete effectively, they

[208] On cluster markets see e.g. Ayres, 'Cluster Markets', *passim*; Baker, 'Market Definition', 157–59; Sullivan and Grimes, *Law of Antitrust*, p. 67.

[209] *US* v. *Philadelphia Nat'l Bank*, 374 US 321 (1963), p. 356.

must offer all or nearly all types of service'.[210] Other sectors where the relevant market has been defined as composed of different clusters are, for instance, hospital services[211] and educational services.[212]

In conclusion, the methodology for a GATS test as outlined in the previous section could thus continue as follows.

- If foreign services and suppliers are affected and thus GATS applies: Third, determine the relevant market on the basis of (i) services which are substitutable from the demand side (including potential and future competition on the demand side, see below, 14.III.C) as well as; (ii) suppliers who can immediately and effectively switch to the supply of a service that is part of the relevant service market (supply substitutability); and (iii) cluster services which are typically offered in a group (cluster markets);
- Fourth, determine whether the group of foreign suppliers and services is more heavily affected negatively than the group of domestic suppliers and services.

C *Potential and future competition*

The final competitive constraint relevant in competition law is potential competition.[213] For purposes of the comparative analysis, potential competition is referred to here as including future competition, *de novo* market entry as well as non-effective and non-immediate supply substitutability.[214] Moreover, it must be made clear whether potential and future

210 *US* v. *Grinnell Corp.*, 384 US 563 (1966), p. 572.

211 See e.g. *FTC* v. *University Health*, 938 F 2d 1206 (11th Cir. 1991), p. 1211: relevant market including all 'in-patient services by acute-care hospital'.

212 *Hamilton Chapter of Alpha Delta Phi* v. *Hamilton Coll.*, 106 F Supp 2d 406 (N.D.N.Y. 2000), p. 412: 'prospective students consider a cluster of services necessarily offered by nearly every college, such as academic services, health services, financial aid and residential services, as well as qualities such as size and location'.

213 Potential competition in this context must be distinguished from the 'potential competition doctrine' under § 7 Clayton Act, according to which a merger may be unlawful if the acquiring firm has the possibility to enter the market of the target by less anticompetitive means, such as *de novo* entry or acquisition of a smaller competitor, see e.g. *US* v. *Marine Bancorporation*, 418 US 602 (1974), pp. 623 f; the doctrine is particularly relevant for conglomerate mergers, see e.g. Pitofsky, 'New Definitions of Relevant Market', 1831–33; Sullivan and Grimes, *Law of Antitrust*, pp. 655–66; Baur, 'Der relevante Markt', p. 307 (Theorie des Angebotsraums); Sullivan and Harrison, *Antitrust and Economic Implications*, pp. 330–31.

214 Supply substitutability is considered at this stage of the analysis if competitors may switch to the product or service in question, but not with the required effectiveness and

competition is analysed from the demand- or the supply side. Supply-side potential competition focuses on whether a market participant is likely to face new competitors as a reaction to its own behaviour or to a change on the demand side.

> For instance, an undertaking with a high market share in a defined product market is unlikely to abuse its position if barriers to entry are low or if it faces new competitors in the near future.

Demand-side potential and future competition, in contrast, analyses whether consumers view a new product as substitutable to another due to changes on the supply side.

> For instance, consumers may not currently view two products as substitutable if one product is – due to a trade barrier – very expensive or not even available. Nonetheless, the two products may potentially compete with one another if they would be regarded as substitutable if the conditions of supply would change due to the absence of the trade barrier.

Supply-side potential competition is particularly relevant in competition law which focuses on the question of market power. In contrast, trade law is more concerned with competitive opportunities and thus focuses on potential competition on the demand side.

1. Competition law: supply-side potential and future competition

The EU Market Definition Notice identifies potential competition as a third competitive constraint, in addition to demand and supply substitutability.[215] However, this element is not considered as part of the market analysis itself, but as an instrument to assess the circumstances related to the conditions of market entry. Hence, potential competition serves as a means to correct the results of a market analysis and the analysis of a firm's position in such a market. More specifically, if the high market share of a firm or an undertaking indicates a dominant position in the relevant product market, then the consideration of potential competition may allow for the conclusion that in fact no dominance exists.[216]

immediacy that would influence the relevant market itself, see above, 14.III.B.1; also Werden, 'Justice Department's Merger Guidelines', 519.

215 Market Definition Notice, para.24; Neveling, *Marktabgrenzung bei der Fusionskontrolle*, pp. 164–65.

216 See e.g. Case C-12/03 P, *Commission* v. *Tetra Laval* [2005] ECR I-987, para.125: 'the Commission, when assessing the compatibility of a concentration with the common market, must take account of a number of factors, such as the structure of the relevant

In US antitrust law, the Merger Guidelines provide that supply response is relevant to determine whether additional competitors participate in the relevant market, thereby reducing market shares.[217] *De novo* market entry is taken into account at a later stage after market shares have been determined, analyzing whether entry into the market is easy enough so that the merged firm could not maintain a price increase above pre-merger levels.[218] Courts consider a variety of factors for ease of entry, such as the need for high investments over a long period of time with low profit margins.[219]

In general terms, ease of entry is particularly important in the context of merger control, which takes a view at whether the merged firm will be able to exercise market power in a future market. However, market entry also plays a role in Article 102 TFEU and section 2 Sherman Act cases, where the absence of barriers to entry may indicate that the firm is not in a dominant position or does not have monopoly power.

2. Application to trade non-discrimination

In competition law, potential competition is considered not to define the relevant market, but to assess market shares and allocate market power. Accordingly, potential competition is equated with future competition on the *supply side* in view of assessing the firm's market power. In contrast, since trade non-discrimination is not concerned with market shares, the WTO adjudicating bodies' approach to potential and future competition focuses on developments on the *demand side* only. For the purpose of a comparative approach, an analogous categorization of these concepts is thus not appropriate.[220] It is necessary to reorganize the categorization of these elements into demand-side potential competition in a narrow sense (*below*, (a)), demand-side future competition (b) as well as future competition on the supply side (c).

a. Demand-side potential competition in a narrow sense Potential competition in a narrow sense (or latent competition) is relevant because the analysis of 'likeness' takes place in a market which is distorted by the

markets, actual or potential competition from undertakings, the position of the undertakings concerned and their economic and financial power, possible options available to suppliers and users, any barriers to entry and trends in supply and demand'; Case T-340/03, *France Télécom* v. *Commission* [2007] ECR II-107, paras. 110 ff.

217 US Merger Guidelines, pp. 11 f; defined as 'measurement approach for supply substitutability', see Werden, 'Justice Department's Merger Guidelines', 519.

218 US Merger Guidelines, pp. 25 ff.

219 See e.g. *Monfort of Colorado* v. *Cargill*, 761 F 2d 570 (10th Cir. 1985), p. 579.

220 See also Emch, 'What are "Like" Products?', 376–79.

putative trade barrier. In the case of an import and sales ban, the imported product does not compete with its potential domestic substitutes at all; in the case of a tax or regulatory discrimination, the imported product suffers higher transaction costs and competes on unequal terms with domestic products. In consequence, consumers may not view the imported product as a suitable substitute due to its higher price, its absence from the market or any other inconvenience resulting from discriminatory regulations. An examination of the actual competition in the current market would thus inevitably result in a conclusion of 'unlikeness' between the products in question.

> The Panel in *Japan – Alcoholic Beverages II* recognized that a tax system discriminating against imports 'has the consequence of creating and even freezing preferences for domestic goods. In the Panel's view, this meant that consumer surveys in a country with such a tax system would likely understate the degree of potential competitiveness between substitutable products.'[221]

Since non-discrimination in international trade protects competitive opportunities – and not just actual export volumes –,[222] the 'likeness' analysis must be focused on the question of whether the imported and domestic products under scrutiny would potentially compete with one another if the trade barrier were lifted. This 'but-for' approach was explicitly confirmed by the Appellate Body when it stated that 'Korea agrees that this provision [i.e. GATT III:2, second sentence] is not intended to exclude products that are not directly competitive or substitutable because of the contested measure itself'.[223]

[221] Panel Report, *Japan – Alcoholic Beverages II*, para.6.28, citing GATT Panel Report, *Japan – Alcoholic Beverages I*, para.5.9; see also Appellate Body Report, *Canada – Periodicals*, p. 28: '[W]e are not impressed either by Canada's argument that the market share of imported and domestic magazines has remained remarkably constant over the last 30-plus years, and that one would have expected some variation if competitive forces had been in play to the degree necessary to meet the standard of "directly competitive" goods. This argument would have weight only if Canada had not protected the domestic production of Canadian periodicals.'

[222] Appellate Body Report, *Japan – Alcoholic Beverages II*, p. 15: 'Article III protects expectations not of any particular trade volume but rather of the equal competitive relationship between imported and domestic products'; confirmed in Panel Report, *Chile – Alcoholic Beverages*, para.7.21.

[223] Appellate Body Report, *Korea – Alcoholic Beverages*, para.112 and also paras. 6, 43, 72, 93 (arguments of parties); see also Panel Reports, *Korea – Alcoholic Beverages*, para.10.47; *Mexico – Taxes on Soft Drinks*, paras. 4.47 f. (argument of US); *Chile – Alcoholic Beverages*, paras. 4.41 ff (arguments of EC), paras. 5.6 f (arguments of Canada).

Finally, in *EC – Asbestos* the Appellate Body confirmed its approach for cases where competition between the domestic and the foreign product is completely eliminated due to an import and sales ban of the latter:

> 'In our Report in *Korea – Alcoholic Beverages*, we observed that, "[p]articularly in a market where there are regulatory barriers to trade or to competition, there may well be latent demand" for a product. We noted that, in such situations, "it may be highly relevant to examine latent demand" that is suppressed by regulatory barriers.'[224]

The Appellate Body's view on potential and latent competition with respect to the GATT deserves full support, given that any other approach would completely inhibit the objective and purpose of non-discrimination in international trade. However, the Appellate Body has been less clear with regard to its approach to potential competition in the context of GATS. In contrast to the usual GATT approach, the Appellate Body requires – prior to the analysis of a substantive GATS provision – to determine whether the measure is covered by GATS.[225] In *Canada – Autos*, it ruled that a measure only falls within the GATS scope of application (i) if there *is* trade in services in the sense of Article I:2; and (ii) if the measure *affects* such trade in services within the meaning of Article I:1.[226] Strictly speaking, GATS would thus not be applicable if the measure under scrutiny prevents *actual* trade in the respective service. For this reason, the Appellate Body's test must be understood such that it can also be met if the measure affects *potential* trade in the respective service.[227]

b. Demand-side future competition The WTO adjudicating bodies do not distinguish between potential competition in a narrow sense (i.e. 'but-for' the trade barrier) and potential competition in terms of future

[224] Appellate Body Report, *EC – Asbestos*, para.123 (fns omitted); see also Appellate Body Report, *Canada – Periodicals*, p. 23: 'as there were no imports of split-run editions of periodicals because of the import prohibition ... hypothetical imports of split-run periodicals have to be considered'.

[225] See above, 9.II; Appellate Body Report, *Canada – Autos*, paras. 151 f; under GATT it is generally not required to determine its scope before analysing a substantive obligations, see Zdouc, *Comparative Analysis of GATS and GATT*, p. 156; Zdouc, '(2004) Dispute Settlement Practice', pp. 393–94.

[226] Appellate Body Report, *Canada – Autos*, para.155.

[227] See also Zdouc, '(2004) Dispute Settlement Practice', p. 393; Leroux, 'GATS Case Law', 755.

competition. They discuss both elements under the single heading of 'potential competition'.

> The EU very accurately made the distinction in its submission in *Chile – Alcoholic Beverages*, stating that 'the notion of potential competition must be deemed to include not only competition that would exist "but for" the tax measures at issue, but also competition that could be reasonably expected to develop in the future having regard, for example, to existing trends in the market concerned or to the situation prevailing in other markets' (para 4.41, see also paras. 5.6–5.7 for arguments by Canada).

The EU based its argument for future competition exclusively on developments on the demand side. More specifically, it asserted that distilled spirits constitute an 'experience good' which must be purchased and consumed before consumers could appreciate its aptitude to satisfy their needs. Moreover, it argued that consumers would only gradually change their habits, for which reason the analysis of 'likeness' should consider future developments in consumer behaviour.[228] The Panel largely followed the EU's argument:

> 'We agree that panels should look at evidence of trends and changes in consumption patterns and make an assessment as to whether such trends and patterns lead to the conclusion that the products in question are either directly competitive or substitutable now or can reasonably be expected to become directly competitive or substitutable in the near future.' (para 7.24)

The Panel in *Korea – Alcoholic Beverages* followed a similar approach:

> 'We will not attempt to speculate on what could happen in the distant future, but we will consider evidence pertaining to what could reasonably be expected to occur in the near future based on the evidence presented ... If one is dealing with products that are experience based consumer items, then trends are particularly important and it would be unrealistic and, indeed, analytically unhelpful to attempt to separate every piece of evidence and disregard that which discusses implications for market structure in the near future.' (para 10.50)

The Appellate Body upheld the Panel's finding by stating that it declined 'to take a static view of the term "directly competitive or substitutable"'.[229]

[228] Ibid., para.4.43; on experience goods see also Panel Report, *Korea – Alcoholic Beverages*, para.10.44.

[229] Appellate Body Report, *Korea – Alcoholic Beverages*, para.120, even though it is not quite clear whether the Appellate Body made this statement in reference to potential competition in a narrow sense or indeed in reference to future competition.

This approach to future competition is in essence not much different from market definition in merger control cases, which always takes into consideration future developments in the post-merger market.

c. **Supply-side future competition** While supply-side future competition and market entry are highly relevant in competition law to correct erroneous results from market definition and share allocation, they have almost no bearing for the question of 'likeness'. There are only two situations in which market entry could at least theoretically be relevant.

Potential or future competition by domestic companies: The first constellation is similar to the example on 'substitutability by domestic suppliers only' discussed under section 14.III.B.2.a above. The imported product or service B which is subject to a trade obstacle does not face any actual, potential or future domestic substitutes from a demand side. At the same time, domestic companies do not currently produce or supply B. However, if barriers to market entry are low, one could assume that domestic companies are likely to enter the market and compete with the imported product or service. If, on the one hand, the measure is designed such that future domestic competitors will be unaffected by the trade obstacle (e.g. a sales tax), then the measure qualifies as *de jure* discrimination and the question of 'likeness' does not arise in the first place.[230] On the other hand, if the measure applies to current imports and future domestic competitors alike, then there is no 'less favourable treatment'.

Potential or future competition by importing companies: The second constellation is exactly opposite from the first. Domestic companies do not currently face competition from imported products or services, but foreign *de novo* market entrants could start the importation of competing products or services. As outlined above, the WTO adjudicating bod ies considered this possibility in the context of GATS, finding that even potential suppliers could benefit from the non-discrimination obligations. In order to avoid an over-broad application of non-discrimination and assure a proper analysis of the element 'less favourable treatment', it is argued that the scope should not expand to potential and future suppliers in general. Beneficiaries should be limited to mode 3 and 4 suppliers who meet the standard of supply substitutability in a narrow sense (above, 14.III.B.2.a).

[230] See above, 3.II.A, n 122.

IV Conclusions

Against the background of this chapter, it appears that despite the various differences in the respective approaches, the 'likeness' analysis is in effect not very far apart from the definition of a product market in competition law. The Appellate Body in various instances held that 'likeness' 'is, fundamentally, a determination about the nature and extent of a competitive relationship between and among products',[231] and it even confirmed that economic tools of market analysis, such as cross-price elasticity, may be taken into consideration.[232] In some cases, the adjudicating bodies considered findings of national competition authorities on market definition as evidence for purposes of 'likeness'.

Despite these similarities and overlaps, the methodological approaches between the legal analysis of 'likeness' and the definition of markets are considerably different. From a methodological point of view, it is necessary to distinguish between legal elements, facts and evidence, plus the frequently used expression of criteria or factors. According to the general theory of law, evidence is used to prove a certain fact, thus allowing to subsume the fact with the legal element and to draw a legal conclusion. In competition law, the relevant market and market share are factual elements for the analysis of market power as a legal element. The competitive constraints of demand and supply substitutability constitute the criteria needed to delineate the product market, with priority given to substitutability of demand. Finally, the evidence referred to above serves to determine whether or not there is demand substitutability. The legal analysis for market definition in competition law is illustrated in Figure 14.1.

In the context of WTO non-discrimination, the methodological approach is somewhat less sophisticated. In contrast to market definition, 'likeness' constitutes a direct legal element – next to less favourable treatment – in the analysis of discriminatory regulations. Under the *Border Tax Adjustments* framework, 'likeness' is analysed on the basis of the four factual criteria: (i) properties, nature and quality of the products; (ii) end-uses of the products; (iii) consumers' tastes and habits; and (iv) tariff classification of the products. However, the Appellate Body also stated that these factors are

[231] Appellate Body Report, *EC – Asbestos*, para.99, entire para.reproduced above, 5.I.B, n 38.

[232] Panel Report, *Japan – Alcoholic Beverages II*, para.6.22: 'In the Panel's view, the decisive criterion in order to determine whether two products are directly competitive or substitutable is whether they have common end-uses, *inter alia*, as shown by elasticity of substitution', confirmed in the Appellate Body Reports, *Japan – Alcoholic Beverages II*, p. 26 and *Canada – Periodicals*, pp. 27 ff.

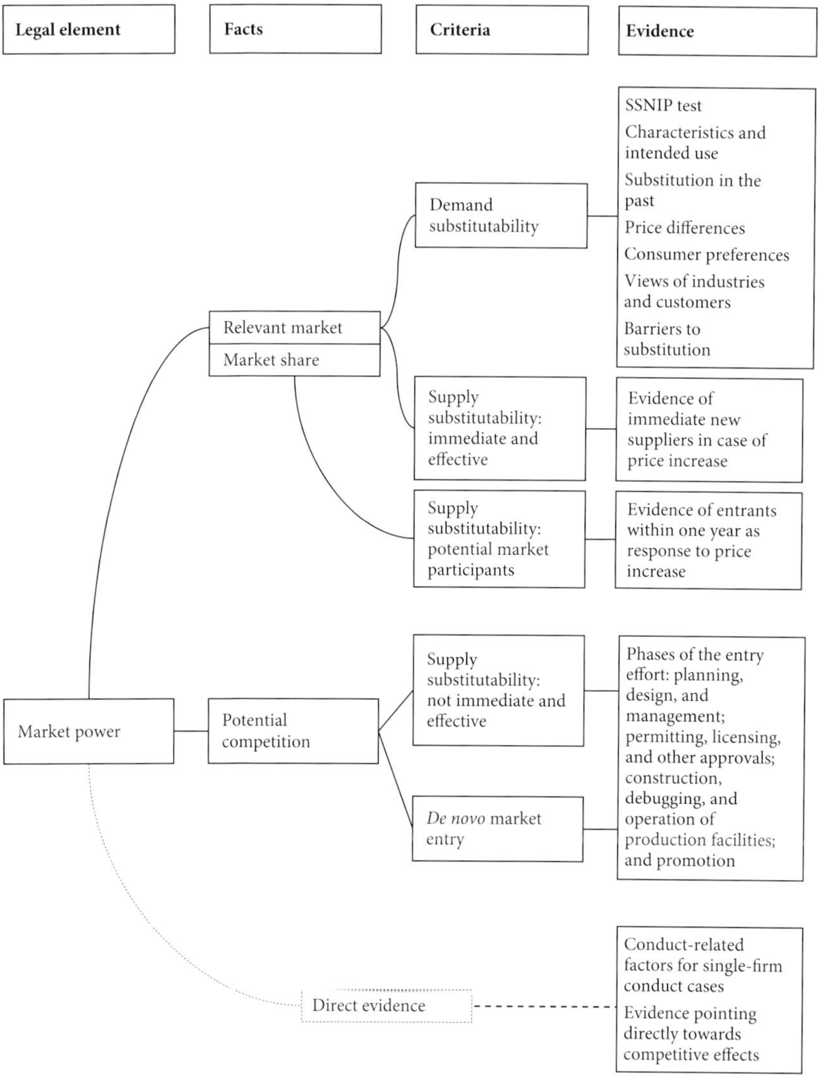

Figure 14.1 Market definition

'simply tools to assist in the task of sorting and examining the relevant evidence. They are neither a treaty-mandated nor a closed list of criteria that will determine the legal characterization of products. More important, the adoption of a particular framework to aid in the examination of evidence does not dissolve the duty or the need to examine, in each case, *all* of the

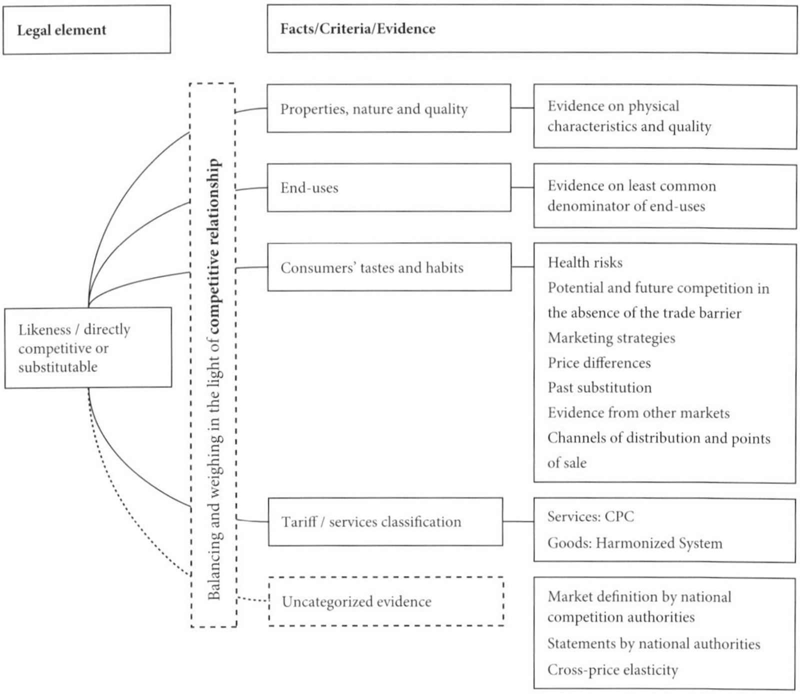

Figure 14.2 *Border Tax Adjustments* framework

pertinent evidence.'[233] The legal analysis is illustrated in Figure 14.2, clearly showing the different approach from market definition.

By focusing directly on the four factors designed to determine 'likeness', the WTO approach basically skips the step of explicitly determining a degree of substitutability. This approach is problematic with regard to the question of whether and how evidence relevant for substitutability, but not directly linked to the four factors, should be taken into account. With regard to Article III:4 GATT, the Appellate Body indicated what additional evidence could be relevant:

> 'The kind of evidence to be examined in assessing the "likeness" of products will, necessarily, depend upon the particular products and the legal provision at issue … Accordingly, whether the *Border Tax Adjustments* framework is adopted or not, it is important under Article III:4 to take account of evidence which indicates whether, and to what extent, the products involved are – or could be – in a competitive relationship in the marketplace'.[234]

[233] Appellate Body Report, *EC – Asbestos*, para.102.
[234] Ibid., para.103.

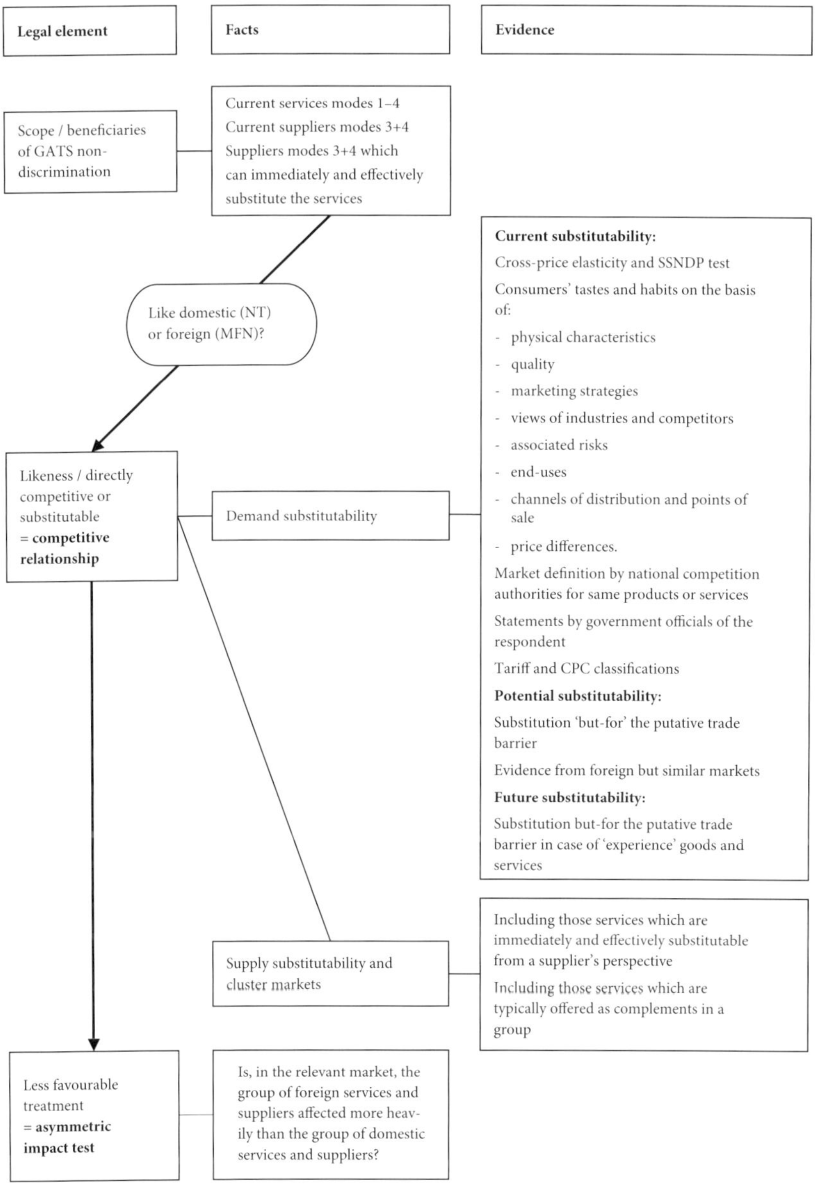

Figure 14.3 Substitutability framework

In addition to the different methodological approaches, the weighing of evidence differs considerably between trade and competition law. In WTO law on non-discrimination, the evidence related to the product's properties, nature and quality as well as its end-uses are of considerable importance for the analysis of 'likeness'. Each criteria has its own substantive value and is balanced with the criterion of consumers' tastes and habits; the latter is by itself insufficient for a conclusion of 'likeness'. Under the Market Definition Notice, in contrast, the characteristics and intended end-use are mentioned only as preliminary indicators to identify and limit the field of possible substitutes. The substantive analysis, in turn, is more based on economic considerations, such as the SSNIP test as quantitative analysis and additional qualitative evidence apt to indicate the degree of demand substitutability.

This study submits that there is no reasonable explanation for the different approach to the 'likeness' analysis. For reasons of legal certainty, it would be highly desirable that the Appellate Body develops the framework from *Border Tax Adjustments* into a more coherent test applicable for all non-discrimination provisions and focusing clearly on substitutability of demand. A refined test based on an economic interpretation of 'likeness' in WTO non-discrimination rules is illustrated in Figure 14.3.

Under such an approach, supply substitutability is not part of the 'likeness' analysis, but serves to expand the scope of GATS non-discrimination to foreign mode 3 and 4 service suppliers who are not currently offering the service subject to the trade measure, but who could immediately and effectively begin to do so. For purposes of both GATT and GATS, demand substitutability is defined as the decisive element for the assessment of 'likeness'. All evidence likely to show current, potential and future competition from the demand side must be taken into account, including a quantitative analysis in the form of a modified SSNIP test.

15

The PPM-problem in the GATS 'likeness' context

The issue of 'process and production methods' (PPM) in the context of international trade is highly nuanced and evokes a number of general policy questions about the role of the WTO in fields such as environment and human rights on the one hand, as well as many very technical legal questions in the application of WTO law on the other hand. The core issue at the centre of the product–process debate essentially relates to the question whether Members should be allowed under their WTO obligations to distinguish between products on the basis of the production method. More specifically, could a Member treat a foreign product subject to a low PPM-standard less favourably than domestic products that are processed and produced in accordance with higher standards?

A true PPM-measure pursues primarily policy goals unrelated to trade. Most of the time, the measure is aimed at subjects such as labour standards, human rights, environmental protection or animal welfare.[1] Governments pursue these objectives with different types of measures, many of which affect international trade and are potentially discriminatory. At the outset it is important to distinguish between origin-based and explicitly PPM-based differential treatment. For instance, a measure can prohibit all seal fur imports from Canada because some Canadian hunters kill seals in a cruel way (origin-based but PPM-motivated measure) or it can generally prohibit the sale of seal fur if the seals are killed cruelly (explicit PPM measure).[2] The way the measure is designed has an important impact on the legal analysis under WTO law. Origin-based *de jure* discrimination constitutes – even if it is based on PPM-considerations – a *prima facie* violation of Articles I or III GATT (non-discrimination) or Article XI GATT (elimination of quantitative restrictions) and is only WTO compliant

1 See e.g. Cottier and Oesch, *International Trade Regulation*, p. 412; Swinbank, 'Animal Welfare', 697 ff.

2 See e.g. Howse and Regan, 'Product/Process Distinction', 269; for a general critique on this distinction see Gaines, 'Processes and Production Methods', 419; for further typologies of PPMs see e.g. Charnovitz, 'Environmental "PPMs"', 67; Potts, *Legality of PPMs*, p. 8.

if it can be justified under Article XX GATT.[3] The following considerations are thus only concerned with PPM-based *de facto* discriminations. Among the most common measures are labelling requirements, surtax or border tax adjustments as well as sales or import bans for the products subject to low PPM-standards.[4] The motivations behind such measures are manifold. They could induce foreign production to apply a higher PPM-standard, avoid increasing market demand for low PPM-standard products, or simply prevent any involvement in such products.[5] Yet, a PPM-measure could also be used as an umbrella to conceal a purely protectionist trade restriction.[6] Similarly, a PPM-based surtax or border tax adjustment could aim to level the playing field by counterbalancing a competitive – deemed immoral – advantage that is unavailable to domestic producers due to stricter and higher standards for PPM.[7]

Given that many PPM and trade discussions on the policy level neglect to take into account the specific legal technicalities and also because the PPM-terminology is not always used consistently, there still remains some confusion and misunderstanding about the legality of PPM-measures under the WTO.[8] It is thus necessary to outline the legal framework within which PPM-measures have to be assessed as well as the developments in WTO jurisprudence.

I Analysis of PPM-measures in GATT

A number of GATT panels in the early' 90s established an approach which has been identified by *Hudec* and other commentators as the 'product–process doctrine', according to which PPM-measures *prima facie* violate

[3] See above, 3.I.A.1, n 12.

[4] Jackson, *World Trading System*, p. 236.

[5] Howse and Regan, 'Product/Process Distinction', 274–75.

[6] For instance, the famous 1904 German trade measure allowing tariff reductions for 'large dappled mountain cattle or brown cattle reared at a spot at least 300 meters above sea level and which have at least one month's grazing each year at a spot at least 800 meters above sea level' was obviously not adopted for reasons of cow welfare, but to favour cattle from Switzerland and the Austrian Tyrol over French, Belgian, Dutch, Danish and Russian cattle, see League of Nations, 'The Most-Favoured-Nation Clause', **22** *The American Journal of International Law* (1928) 133, 145.

[7] Economically motivated PPM-measures are more problematic under WTO law, see e.g. Charnovitz, 'Environmental "PPMs"', 106, who argues that 'the WTO should not tolerate an economic motivation for imposing a PPM on imports'.

[8] Similarly Pauwelyn, 'GATT Phantoms Still Haunt the WTO', 576; Charnovitz, 'Environmental "PPMs"', 76.

GATT obligations.[9] Such a rigid understanding is no longer appropriate, as it does not reflect further developments in WTO jurisprudence. As a general overview, PPM-measures can be accommodated under the WTO obligations either (i) by taking the regulatory purpose into consideration in the non-discrimination analysis (e.g. aim and effects test); (ii) by taking PPMs into consideration as factors in the 'like product' analysis; or (iii) by justifying the measure under the general exceptions clause. In light of these considerations, the legal questions can be summarized as follows:

- Pursuant to *Ad* Article III GATT, should a PPM-measure be analysed under Article III (national treatment) or Article XI (market access) GATT?
- In the case of Article III GATT, could PPM-factors be considered in the 'like product' analysis?
- Where PPM-factors are excluded and the products are found 'alike' despite different PPMs, could the regulatory purpose be considered under any element of the non-discrimination analysis (e.g. aim and effects test or subjective analysis of 'less favourable treatment')?[10]
- Where (i) PPM-factors and the regulatory purpose are excluded from the non-discrimination analysis and (ii) foreign products are treated less favourably, could the PPM-measure be justified under Article XX GATT?

For the purpose of this study, the Article III and XI distinction[11] as well as the question of justifiability and extraterritoriality[12] are not of primary interest. The comparative analysis is limited to the question of whether PPM considerations can lead to a finding of 'unlikeness' between products under GATT rules on non-discrimination and if or how the reasoning differs in the GATS context. In regard to the PPM and 'likeness' analysis, it is possible to distinguish three conceptually different theories. First, PPM-measures could be addressed with the aim and effects test (regulatory likeness). Second, the likeness analysis could be based directly on

[9] For a comprehensive discussion of the doctrine e.g. Puth, *Produkt-Prozess-Doktrin*, pp. 64 ff; Conrad, 'Process and Production Methods', section I.C; opposing the doctrine e.g. Hudec, 'Product-Process Doctrine', pp. 198–99; Howse and Regan, 'Product/Process Distinction', 251–52; supporting the doctrine e.g. Jackson, 'Greening the GATT', p. 44; Jackson, 'Shrimp/Turtle and Product/Process', 303 ff; Marceau and Trachtman, 'Domestic Regulations of Goods', 857.

[10] On regulatory purpose see above, 3.III.A.

[11] On this distinction and *Ad* Article III GATT see above, 10.I.B.2.d.

[12] See e.g. Appellate Body Report, *US – Shrimp*, para. 133; Bartels, 'Extraterritorial Jurisdiction', 358 ff; Diebold, 'Morals and Order Exceptions', 68 ff; Calster, 'EU, Trade, Environment and Unilateralism', 16.

PPMs and third, the competitive relationship between the products could be denied following an application of the traditional factors from the *Border Tax Adjustments* framework (competitive likeness).

The first approach consists of considering the aim and effects or the regulatory purpose of the measure; given that the PPM-measure aims at a policy objective related to, for instance, environmental protection or labour regulation, the 'aim and effects' test within the 'like product' analysis would allow for a conclusion that for the purpose of the non-discrimination obligation, the child-manufactured soccer ball or the brutally killed seal are not 'like' the 'properly' manufactured corresponding product.[13] However, since the aim and effects test has been rejected by WTO jurisprudence, this approach is no longer a valid option.

A conceptually different approach that leads to the same result is to allow PPM-factors themselves – instead of the regulatory purpose – to flow into the 'like product' analysis in addition to the traditional factors from *Border Tax Adjustments*. This method is difficult to categorize, as it falls somewhere between the strict 'competitive likeness' and the broad 'regulatory likeness' theory. In other words, two competitive products could be qualified as 'unlike' on the basis of different PPMs without directly considering the regulatory purpose of the measure. Yet, the GATT/WTO adjudicating bodies have been very reluctant to analyse the question of 'like products' directly on process–production factors,[14] noting that GATT rules only apply to the *product* and cannot be extended to the *producer*.

> In *US – Gasoline*, for instance, the US differentiated between foreign and domestic gasoline based on characteristics of refiners, blenders and importers as well as the nature of the data held by them. The Panel refused to qualify the products at issue as 'unlike', stating that 'Article III:4 of the

[13] With regard to PPM and aim/effect see e.g. Charnovitz, 'Environmental "PPMs"', 90: 'the aim-and-effect test could have provided a doctrinal basis for distinguishing two otherwise like products that differ only in conformity to the PPM'; Puth, *Produkt-Prozess-Doktrin*, pp. 240 ff; Zedalis, 'Product v. Non-Product Distinctions', 110–11.

[14] The first case where a PPM-measure was found to violate GATT non-discrimination (Article I) was the GATT Panel Report, *Belgium – Family Allowances*, para. 3; however, this case is of limited authority, given that the measure at issue qualified as *de jure* discrimination, see Howse and Regan, 'Product/Process Distinction', 262–63; Charnovitz, 'Origin-based Discrimination', 12; on the exclusion of PPM-criteria in the 'like products' analysis see e.g. Cottier and Oesch, *International Trade Regulation*, pp. 412 ff; McGovern, *International Trade Regulation*, § 8.122, issue 20; Jackson, Davey and Sykes, *International Economic Relations*, p. 578; Jackson, *World Trading System*, p. 236; Calster, *Environmental Challenge*, p. 53.

> General Agreement deals with the treatment to be accorded to like *products*; its wording does not allow less favourable treatment dependent on the characteristics of the *producer*' (para 6.11, emphasis added). The Panel went on to conclude that an opposite interpretation of Article III would mean 'that the treatment of imported and domestic goods concerned could no longer be assured on the objective basis of their likeness as products. Rather, imported goods would be exposed to a highly subjective and variable treatment according to extraneous factors. This would thereby create great instability and uncertainty in the conditions of competition as between domestic and imported goods in a manner fundamentally inconsistent with the object and purpose of Article III' (para 6.12).[15]

The Appellate Body later mitigated this rigid view on the 'like product' analysis by finding that *all evidence* must be considered in the analysis of 'likeness'.[16] This holding constitutes the basis for the third theory, according to which a 'competitive likeness' allows the consideration of PPMs under the traditional *Border Tax Adjustments* framework. Under this theory, it is firstly necessary to distinguish between the two different categories of PPMs, namely the so-called product-related and the non-product-related PPM.[17] The distinguishing criterion between these two categories is not always used consistently. One approach distinguishes the two groups on the basis of whether or not the PPM affects the *physical characteristics* of the product.[18] A second school of thought differentiates on the basis of the PPM's *policy goal*; accordingly, product-related PPMs 'are used to assure the functionality of the product' while non-product-related PPMs are 'designed to achieve a social purpose that may or may not matter to the consumer'.[19] The resulting difference between these two approaches is minor, relating only to the fact that proponents of the second approach consider that not all product-related PPMs designed to specify the functionality of the product necessarily cause a detectable modification of the product's physical characteristics. For the purpose of this study and the 'like product' analysis, the important question is whether the PPM leaves any traceable physical characteristics in the product,

[15] Similarly also GATT Panel Report, *US – Malt Beverages*, para. 5.19 (size of breweries does not affect 'likeness' of beer); see also above, 10.I.B.2.d.

[16] Appellate Body Report, *EC – Asbestos*, para. 113; see also above, 13.III.

[17] See e.g. OECD, Process and Production Methods (PPMs), Work Programme on Trade and Environment (1997), OCDE/GD(97)137, pp. 12 ff; Charnovitz, 'Environmental "PPMs"', 65; Gaines, 'Processes and Production Methods', 396.

[18] Stilwell and Bohanes, 'Trade and the Environment', p. 540.

[19] Charnovitz, 'Environmental "PPMs"', 65.

reason for which this study will follow a slightly different terminology of 'incorporated' and 'unincorporated' PPMs.[20]

In the case of incorporated PPMs, the WTO adjudicating bodies have some leeway to uphold a PPM-measure on the basis that the products are 'not like' in view of the different physical characteristics.[21] From a systemic point of view, it is not the PPM that is introduced as its own criterion in the 'like product' analysis, but the physically detectable results of the PPM are taken into account under the first criterion, that is the properties, nature and quality of the products. Yet, this solution is limited to the narrow standard of 'likeness' in Article III:2, first sentence, GATT, which cumulatively requires a competitive relationship *and* physical resemblance.[22] In the case of the broader standard of 'likeness' focusing only on a competitive relationship or if the PPMs leave no traces on the final product (unincorporated PPMs), PPM-measures are more difficult to uphold. A theory that has gained new momentum with the Appellate Body Report *EC – Asbestos* follows the argument that products should be distinguished on the basis of their PPM to the extent that they are recognized by the consumers as two different products.[23] The third factor from *Border Tax Adjustments* allows physically identical products to be distinguished based on consumers' tastes and habits. If the consumers do not consider two identical but differently produced products as substitutable, there is no competitive relationship and thus no 'likeness' between the products at issue. The new test proposed in the previous chapter 14 for a 'likeness' analysis focusing on demand substitutability is sufficiently refined to take account of many PPM-measures. More specifically, the number of fully informed consumers to substitute a domestic high PPM for an imported low PPM product in case of a small but significant

[20] See Calster, *Environmental Challenge*, p. 40.

[21] See e.g. Bronckers and McNelis, '"Like Product" Definition', pp. 374–76; Stilwell and Bohanes, 'Trade and the Environment', p. 540; Senti, *WTO*, pp. 315–16; with regard to TBT/SPS Agreements see Rege, 'Environment-Related Issues', 110–11.

[22] On the economic narrow interpretation of 'likeness' see above, 3.II.B.1.b.

[23] See e.g. Pauwelyn, 'GATT Phantoms Still Haunt the WTO', 586; Howse and Tuerk, 'WTO Impact on Internal Regulations', p. 289; Bronckers and McNelis, '"Like Product" Definition', p. 375; Schlagenhof, 'Environmental Process and Production Methods', 129; Thaggert, 'Like Products and Extrajurisdictionality', p. 72; Howse, 'Shrimp/Turtle Case', 515; Cottier, Tuerk and Panizzon, 'Handel und Umwelt', 157; Bossche, Schrijver and Faber, *Unilateral Measures*, p. 63; Potts, *Legality of PPMs*, pp. 14 ff; but see critically Puth, *Produkt-Prozess-Doktrin*, p. 248; Marceau and Trachtman, 'Domestic Regulations of Goods', 859; Verhoosel, *National Treatment*, p. 57; Quick and Lau, 'Environmentally Motivated Tax Distinctions', 432; De Búrca, 'Concept of Discrimination', p. 193; on the possibility to influence consumer choice see Kysar, 'Process/Product Distinction', 578 ff.

decrease in price (e.g. 5 per cent) of the product with low PPMs (e.g. labour exploitation, environmentally harmful) may – depending on the circumstances – not be sufficiently high to substantially increase the profitability for the foreign producer to export its products. In consequence, the suggested demand substitutability analysis allows for sufficient leeway to find products with different standards of PPM as 'unlike' for purposes of non-discrimination.

II Analysis of SSM-measures in GATS

The PPM-problem receives a new dimension in the context of services trade. First, since services are neither 'processed' nor 'produced', the GATT terminology of PPM is not suitable. This does not mean, however, that the analogous problem does not exist. While products can be produced by different methods, services can be supplied by different methods. It is thus more appropriate to speak of 'service supply methods' or SSMs. A second difference relates to the fact that a product is separable from its production methods, whereas the service is usually inseparable from the supplier and the method of supply. Third, the GATT ambiguity of whether a PPM-measure can be subject to a non-discrimination provision that is limited to the treatment of *products* does not arise under GATS, considering that Articles II and XVII specifically apply to *suppliers*. Finally, while PPMs always take place outside the jurisdiction of the importing Member, modes 3 and 4 of service supply necessarily entail that the SSM occurs on the importing Member's territory.[24]

> Assume, for instance, an Indian construction company wishes to send 14-year-old construction workers to a building site located in Switzerland under mode 4 and challenges the Swiss prohibition for child work before a WTO panel for breach of the GATS national treatment obligation.[25] Without doubt, the construction services provided by Swiss and Indian companies are considered 'like' in terms of Article XVII GATS. The remaining question hence is whether Swiss adult workers are 'like' Indian child workers.

[24] Nicolaïdis and Trachtman, 'Policed Regulation', p. 253.

[25] This example presupposes, of course, that India could establish that Swiss law on the protection of minors – which is applied to domestic and foreign service suppliers alike – discriminates *de facto* against Indian suppliers. This could be possible if Indian labour law would, for instance, set a minimum age at 14 while Switzerland would require a minimum age of 16. In this constellation, Indian companies employing suppliers between the ages of 14–15 would, *de facto*, be treated less favourably than 'like' Swiss companies; for more examples, see Diebold, 'Morals and Order Exceptions', 71 ff.

It is argued here that a Member must be able to regulate foreign suppliers operating within its own jurisdiction without automatically violating GATS non-discrimination rules. A first way to accommodate SSM-measures under GATS would be to consider the regulatory context as part of the non-discrimination analysis, either within 'likeness' or for purposes of 'less favourable treatment'. This approach is generally followed by NAFTA tribunals in the interpretation of 'like circumstances'.[26] Yet, the Appellate Body rejected the subjective theory not only with regard to 'likeness', but for Articles II and XVII GATS entirely.[27] In addition, the interpretation of non-discrimination developed in the previous chapters clearly favours a purely economic interpretation of 'likeness' in combination with the asymmetric impact test for 'less favourable treatment'. At the same time, this approach rules out a purely objective interpretation of 'likeness' that would allow to differentiate on the basis of supplier-related criteria which have no impact on the competitive relationship. In sum, an SSM-measure violates GATS national treatment if foreign suppliers and their service are, as a group, disfavoured in comparison to a competing group of domestic suppliers and services. Yet, the respondent may still be able to justify its measure under Article XIV GATS.

The first step thus requires analysing whether the services and suppliers subject to the SSM-measure are 'like' domestic services and suppliers in the light of an economic interpretation. It is submitted that regardless of whether the modified *Border Tax Adjustments* or the here-preferred substitutability framework is applied, it will in many cases be possible to find unlikeness between the different suppliers. As a prerequisite, it is necessary to depart from the panel jurisprudence according to which two suppliers are automatically alike if they supply 'like' services.[28] Quite frequently, it will be the case that an SSM-measure can only be upheld if supplier-related characteristics may be considered to conclude an overall situation of 'unlikeness' in spite of the similarities between the services. As argued under section 13.I.B above, the criterion of properties, nature and quality of the *Border Tax Adjustments* framework allows for the consideration of differences in service supply methods, which must then be

[26] See above, 7.II.B.

[27] Appellate Body Report, *EC – Bananas III*, para. 241: 'We see no specific authority either in Article II or in Article XVII of the GATS for the proposition that the "aims and effects" of a measure are in any way relevant in determining whether that measure is inconsistent with those provisions'.

[28] See above, 10.I; Krajewski, *National Regulation*, pp. 105–6; Krajewski and Engelke, 'Art. XVII GATS', p. 406.

analysed through the informed consumer's lens. For instance, a difference in methods of supply of construction services by employing child workers allows for the valid argument that child construction workers are not 'like' adult construction workers in the light of Swiss consumers' tastes and habits. Or, in terms of the proposed substitutability framework, the number of consumers to substitute a domestic company employing adult workers for a foreign company employing child workers – at current prices or in the case of a small but significant decrease in the price of the foreign service – would not be sufficiently high so as to substantially increase profitability of the foreign company or decrease profitability of the domestic company.

If under the first step the conclusion is that 'likeness' exists, then the complainant still has to show that the group of foreign suppliers and services is treated less favourably than the group of domestic services and suppliers. In many cases of SSM-measures, the respondent will not be able to fulfil this requirement easily. Finally, the respondent may still justify an SSM measure under Article XIV GATS even if there is less favourable treatment between like services or suppliers. For two reasons, a respondent in a GATS case is more likely to successfully justify an SSM-measure than he or she would in a GATT case involving a PPM-measure.

First, Article XIV(a) GATS allows measures that are necessary to protect public morals *and* public order to be justified, whereas the analogous provision in Article XX(a) GATT is limited to public morals. The reason for an additional public order exception in GATS may be due to the fact that the service supply as an 'activity' is more likely to imperil public order than trade in physical goods. Moreover, measures regulating hazardous goods do not require a public order exception as they can be justified for health reasons under Article XX(b) GATT. In contrast, a public order exception is important in the services context, as it could justify qualification or examination requirements for service suppliers (e.g. for lawyers or teachers), infrastructure regulations (e.g. phone and TV lines or train tracks) or regulations with regard to public services and access to necessities.[29] Moreover, additional exceptions apply in specific sectors, such as the 'prudential reasons' exception pertaining to trade in financial services. Article 2.1 of the GATS Annex on Financial Services allows Members to adopt measures for the protection of investors, depositors and policy holders.[30]

[29] Diebold, 'Morals and Order Exceptions', 73.

[30] See e.g. Bogdandy and Windsor, 'Annex on Financial Services', pp. 634–35; Gkoutzinis, 'Trade in Banking Services', 902.

Second, the justification of PPM-measures may fail under GATT because its policy objective is aimed at extraterritorial values. In other words, a PPM-measure is only justifiable if there is a sufficiently strong nexus between the policy objective of the measure and the territory of the respondent.

> For instance, in *US – Shrimp* the Appellate Body found that there is a sufficiently strong nexus between US territory and its measure banning the importation of certain shrimp in order to protect sea turtles (Article XX(g) GATT), considering that sea turtles may migrate to the waters subject to US jurisdiction (para 133).[31]

In the context of GATS, however, the problem of extraterritoriality is unlikely to arise with regard to SSM-measures governing the supply of services under modes 3 and 4. In this case the service supply takes place directly on the respondent's territory and hence the measures regulating the method of supply are aimed at the protection of domestic values.[32]

In sum, the non-discrimination obligations within the GATS framework allow for sufficient latitude in the regulation of service supply methods, in particular for services supplied under modes 3 and 4.

[31] See also Bartels, 'Extraterritorial Jurisdiction', 358 ff.

[32] For a discussion of public order and extraterritoriality in relation to Article XIV(a) GATS see Diebold, 'Morals and Order Exceptions', 70 ff.

16

Concluding summary: substitutability framework

Part IV seeked to develop a methodology for the analysis of 'likeness' in GATS non-discrimination rules, using the *Border Tax Adjustments* framework from GATT and WTO jurisprudence on 'like products' as a starting point. The criteria of this framework have been subject to continuous evolution and the test has been applied very inconsistently by different GATT 1947 and WTO panels. The Appellate Body in *EC – Asbestos* eventually clarified the structure of the *Border Tax Adjustments* test. It found that the framework must be applied in view of determining the competitive relationship and that each criteria has its independent and individual significance. Consequently, in spite of the Appellate Body's commitment to an economic analysis of 'likeness', competing products could still be found 'unlike' on the basis of differences in their properties, nature and quality. To the extent that future WTO jurisprudence continues to apply the *Border Tax Adjustments* criteria, it is submitted that the framework should be modified such that the criterion of consumers' tastes and habits is given a decisive role. Consequently, the other criteria of properties, nature and quality, end-uses and classification remain relevant, but only to the extent that they reveal product features which are perceived by consumers as reinforcing or weakening substitutability. Such a modified *Border Tax Adjustments* approach focusing on consumers' tastes and habits could arguably work also for assessing 'like services and service suppliers' in GATS.

However, an even better solution would be to largely abandon the classic *Border Tax Adjustments* framework in exchange for a new test designed to define the relevant product or service market on the basis of substitutability. Such a substitutability framework not only reflects the purpose of non-discrimination more accurately, it is even a prerequisite for the application of the asymmetric impact test under 'less favourable treatment'. Under this approach, it will no longer be sufficient for a claimant to show how one of its products or services is treated less favourably in comparison to a particular 'like' domestic product or service; the claimant will have to demonstrate how its foreign product or service is affected by a measure in relation to the entire relevant market. The methodologies for a relevant market test can be largely transposed from competition law practice, keeping in mind, however, that competition law applies such a test to detect market power, whereas trade non-discrimination protects competitive opportunities. This difference entails that the concepts of supply substitutability as well as potential and future competition have a different significance under market definition for purposes of trade than for competition law. In contrast, the methods used to assess demand substitutability in competition law can also be applied in the context of trade non-discrimination.

Finally, chapter 15 submits that the proposed substitutability framework is adequate to address measures which, in GATT language, differentiate on the basis of process and production methods rather than of the products themselves. The PPM problem is likely to arise also under GATS, given that suppliers use different methods to supply similar services. The issue of regulating 'service supply methods' is even more sensitive in the GATS context, considering that regulations addressing modes 3 and 4 of supply concern situations which take place on the territory of the importing Member. Under the substitutability framework, differences in methods of supply allow for a conclusion of 'unlikeness' to the extent that they are perceived by consumers as restraining or even negating substitutability. Yet, even if 'likeness' and an 'asymmetric impact' on foreign services and suppliers exists, the broad public order exception of Article XIV(a) GATS should allow most SSM-regulations to be justified.

Summary of conclusions

This study seeked to develop a theory for the 'like services and service suppliers' concept as it is embodied in the GATS non-discrimination obligations of MFN and national treatment, applying primarily a contextual and comparative methodology. As the main results developed in the course of this work have been summarized in a concluding chapter at the end of each of the four parts, this final part completes this book with a concise summary of all conclusions.

I The underlying policy choice

Part I highlighted the fact that an interpretation of 'likeness' is inevitably linked with the policy question of how permissive or intrusive the non-discrimination principle in WTO law should be construed. The creation of an intrusive form of a non-discrimination principle is a matter of policy choice rather than of legal interpretation and involves institutional and constitutional considerations. The legal interpretative tools are only of limited use for answering such fundamental questions. The text of the non-discrimination provisions does not provide much guidance and in principle allows for a wide spectrum of different forms of non-discrimination. On the very permissive side is an obligation which is limited to the prohibition of nationality-based *de jure* discrimination, where the existence of a 'like' product or service is presumed and the regulatory objectives are considered either as an element of non-discrimination or as grounds for justification. On the other side of the spectrum is the very intrusive prohibition of *de facto* non-discriminations which construes 'less favourable treatment' as an obligation to treat all foreign products or services equivalent to the 'best' treatment accorded to a 'like' domestic product or service (diagonal test), which adopts a very broad economic interpretation of 'likeness' and which allows a consideration of the regulatory purpose only as justification. This study submits that the appropriate standard for WTO non-discrimination is found in the centre of the two extremes. More precisely, parts I and II demonstrate that the 'likeness' concept in WTO rules on non-discrimination follows a broad but exclusively economic interpretation. In order to prevent an overly intrusive application, the broad standard of 'likeness' is counterbalanced with an asymmetric impact test for 'less favourable treatment'. The policy objective, finally, is not part of the non-discrimination obligation, but is considered in a second step under the general exceptions clause.

If *arguendo* a purpose-oriented approach should prevail in future WTO/GATS jurisprudence on the interpretation of non-discrimination, it would be highly desirable that the relevance of the regulatory purpose is not concealed, but that it becomes an overt part of the analysis. The jurisprudence of arbitral tribunals on the element of 'like circumstances' in NAFTA chapter 11 rules on non-discrimination could serve as a model. Following this approach, the question would have to be whether, in addition to a competitive relationship, the services and suppliers are 'in like circumstances' from a regulatory perspective. Alternatively, more recent contributions of scholarly work suggest that the non-discrimination analysis should shift from the traditionally strong focus on 'likeness' towards more attention on the element of 'less favourable treatment'. Following the rejection of the 'aim and effects' test under 'likeness', this theory maintains that 'less favourable treatment' allows for considerations of the regulatory purpose. Whichever methodology should, if at all, be chosen, it should be done consistently for reasons of legal certainty. Moreover, if purpose considerations are included in the non-discrimination analysis of WTO law, it would need to be done properly. In fact, purpose alone would give Members too much leeway to circumvent their non-discrimination obligations, reason for which it would need to be limited with some kind of necessity or proportionality test. Yet, it is to be expected that once 'purpose' and 'necessity' become a central element in the non-discrimination analysis, the focus will automatically shift away from 'likeness' and 'less favourable treatment'. If a trade-restrictive internal regulation is found to have a protectionist purpose or to apply unnecessary means in the pursuit of a legitimate purpose, it would be highly unlikely that the measure is upheld for reasons of 'unlikeness' or lack of 'less favourable treatment'. Consequently, it would be inevitable that the principle of 'non-discrimination' transforms into an obligation of 'non-restriction' along the lines of Articles 34 and 56 TFEU (ex Arts. 28 and 49 of the TEC). In other words, the incorporation of the regulatory purpose and necessity in the analysis of non-discrimination would not – as intended by most proponents of this approach – lead to a more permissive application of non-discrimination; to the contrary, this approach has potentially very constraining consequences on the regulatory autonomy of the WTO Members. Yet, it is questionable whether the current institutional framework of the WTO is appropriate to administer and apply such a far reaching instrument of trade liberalization.

II A methodology for 'likeness' in GATS

On the basis of this conceptual interpretation of non-discrimination, the study seeked to develop a methodology for the 'likeness' analysis in GATS. The main foundations for this analysis are the *Border Tax Adjustments* framework from GATT/WTO jurisprudence on 'like products' and the 'relevant market' concept from competition law.

A *The pragmatic approach:* Border Tax Adjustments *framework*

The *Border Tax Adjustments* framework allows the WTO adjudicating bodies to take a very pragmatic and flexible approach to the issue of 'likeness'. Under this framework, the criterion of 'properties, nature and quality' has an independent and equally important value in comparison to the criteria of end-uses and consumers' tastes and habits. Consequently, even though the Appellate Body acknowledged that competitive relationship is the guiding principle of the test, the framework leaves some leeway to conclude that two competing services or suppliers are 'unlike' on the basis of differences in properties, nature or quality. The adjudicating bodies thus have the flexibility to uphold measures which – for non-protectionist purposes – differentiate between natural person and company suppliers or between suppliers using different methods of supply by finding 'unlikeness', even if there is a perfect competitive relationship. On the one hand, such a flexible approach certainly has its appeal, as it allows sensitive claims directed against internal non-protectionist measures to rejected. On the other hand, this test is subject to the main criticism that the criterion of properties, nature and quality is nothing else than an umbrella hiding the fact that the regulatory purpose of the measure is taken into account. For instance, a difference in quality – as its own criterion and in disregard of its effect on the competitive relationship – may only be sufficient for a conclusion of 'unlikeness' because the measure under scrutiny is aimed at ensuring a certain standard and protecting consumers. Considering that the Appellate Body in *EC – Bananas III* discarded any relevance of a measure's 'aims' under Articles II and XVII GATS, it would be highly contradictory to introduce the purpose under the umbrella of the criterion of properties, nature and quality.

B *The doctrinal approach: substitutability framework*

The interpretation of Articles II and XVII GATS suggests that the doctrinal test should be guided by economic considerations only. The main argument in support of this conclusion is that Article XVII:3 GATS itself acknowledges 'conditions of competition' as the guiding principle of non-discrimination. Moreover, the GATS framework leaves sufficient leeway for considering the regulatory purpose under the general exceptions clause, sector-specific exceptions and the system of scheduling commitments. Finally, this approach is in line with GATS negotiating history as well as the long recognized understanding that WTO rules on non-discrimination are designed to protect competitive opportunities.

In light of the Appellate Body's jurisprudence on the scope of GATS and its substantive provisions in combination with the here-proposed test, the structure of a non-discrimination analysis would look as follows:

- First, analyse the measure under scrutiny in the abstract and determine which service transactions could be affected by the measure.
- Second, determine (i) whether any foreign suppliers actively engage in the supply of these services, including those suppliers who could immediately and effectively switch to the supply of those services; and (ii) whether these suppliers and services are affected by the measure.
- If foreign services and suppliers are affected and thus GATS applies: Third, determine the relevant market.
- Fourth, determine whether the group of foreign suppliers and services of the relevant market is more heavily negatively affected than the group of domestic suppliers and services of the relevant market (asymmetric impact test).

This study suggests that a definition of the relevant market for purposes of 'likeness' should follow *mutatis mutandis* the methodology developed in competition law practice. Hence, 'likeness' should be assessed under a framework focusing on substitutability on the basis of (i) services which are substitutable from the demand side (including potential and future competition on the demand side); as well as (ii) suppliers who can immediately and effectively switch to the supply of a service that is part of the relevant service market (supply substitutability); and (iii) cluster services which are typically offered in a group (cluster markets). This methodology entails a number of advantages for resolving the technical issues arising under the element of 'like services and service suppliers' in GATS as well as for shaping a balanced form of non-discrimination:

- *Service–supplier relationship*: The wording of the 'likeness' element in GATS non-discrimination rules is ambiguous as to the question of whether only the services, only the suppliers or both need to be 'alike'. The proposed 'merged test' in combination with the market definition approach requires that all service-related and all supplier-related factors which affect the competitive relationship are taken into consideration. This test requires weighing and balancing the different factors; while service-related factors will always be significant, supplier-related factors would presumably weigh more for measures affecting modes 3 and 4 in comparison to measures relating to modes 1 and 2.
- *Cross-mode and cross-method 'likeness'*: The market definition approach also entails that factors related to modes and methods of supply are relevant to the extent that they affect the competitive relationship between the service suppliers. Consequently, differences in modes or methods do not *per se* prevent the services or suppliers from being 'alike' for purposes of GATS non-discrimination rules.
- *Asymmetric impact test for 'less favourable treatment'*: GATS and other WTO non-discrimination provisions are not designed as an obligation to treat all foreign economic actors equivalent to the 'best' treatment accorded to a 'like' domestic economic actor. Consequently, WTO non-discrimination rules require assessing the impact of a measure in a relevant market and determining whether foreign actors are more heavily affected than domestic actors. The exercise of such an asymmetric impact test requires that the entire relevant product or service market is defined.
- *Protecting overall competitive opportunities*: The wide breadth of 'likeness' requires adopting a more restrictive interpretation of 'less favourable treatment' in order to avoid an overly intrusive form of non-discrimination. For this reason and in light of footnote 10 to Article XVII, it is submitted that GATS rules on non-discrimination protect overall and not mode- or method-specific competitive opportunities. Consequently, the effect of the measure needs to be assessed on the basis of a relevant market comprising *all* competing foreign and domestic services and suppliers, even if the measure only affects a specific mode or a specific method of supply. This approach has the advantage that

a measure restricting a specific method of supply (e.g. electronic supply) does not automatically violate GATS non-discrimination, even if electronic supply competes with on-site supply and is thus considered 'alike'. In fact, the competitive conditions remain intact if there are other means or modes available to foreign suppliers, which allow them to compete on a level playing field with domestic suppliers. Finally, such an approach does not undermine the individual commitments as they remain important in order to determine whether a measure is subject to GATS national treatment in the first place.

Next to these advantages, the submitted methodology of an asymmetric impact in the relevant market entails one drawback. In fact, the administration of such a test is very demanding for the WTO adjudicating bodies. It not only requires a certain level of economic expertise, but also that the needed economic data is made available by the parties. However, considering that competition authorities and courts applying competition law have been able to define relevant markets for decades, it may be expected that the WTO adjudicating bodies should also be able to successfully implement a market-based test of non-discrimination.

BIBLIOGRAPHY

ABA Section of Antitrust Law, *Market Power Handbook: Competition Law and Economic Foundations* (Chicago, IL: ABA Publishing, 2005).

Antitrust Law Developments, 6th edition, vol. I (Chicago, IL: ABA Publishing, 2007).

Abbott, Frederick M., Christine Breining-Kaufmann and Thomas Cottier (eds.), *International Trade and Human Rights – Foundations and Conceptual Issues* (Ann Arbor, MI: University of Michigan Press, 2006).

Abu-Akeel, Aly K., 'Definition of Trade in Services under the GATS: Legal Implications', **32** *George Washington Journal of International Law & Economics* (1999) 189–210.

'The MFN as it Applies to Service Trade – New Problems for an Old Concept', **33**(4) *Journal of World Trade* (1999) 103–29.

Adlung, Rudolf, 'Health and Social Services', in: WTO-Secretariat (ed.), *Guide to the GATS: An Overview of Issues for Further Liberalization of Trade in Services* (The Hague: Kluwer Law International, 2001), pp. 369–98.

'Economic Effects of Services Liberalization', in: WTO-Secretariat (ed.), *Guide to the GATS: An Overview of Issues for Further Liberalization of Trade in Services* (The Hague: Kluwer Law International, 2001), pp. 1–6.

'Public Services and the GATS', **9** *Journal of International Economic Law* (2006) 455–85.

Adlung, Rudolf and Martín Molinuevo, 'Bilateralism in Services Trade: Is There Fire Behind the (BIT-)Smoke?', **11** *Journal of International Economic Law* (2008) 365–409.

Ahnlid, Anders, 'Comparing GATT and GATS: Regime Creation Under and After Hegemony', **3** *Review of International Political Economy* (1996) 65–94.

Andenas, Mads and Stefan Zleptnig, 'Proportionality and Balancing in WTO Law: A Comparative Perspective', in: Kern Alexander and Mads Andenas (eds.), *The World Trade Organization and Trade in Services* (Leiden: Martinus Nijhoff Publishers, 2008), pp. 147–71.

Appleton, Arthur E., 'The Agreement on Technical Barriers to Trade', in: Patrick F. J. Macrory, Arthur E. Appleton and Michael G. Plummer (eds.), *The World Trade Organization: Legal, Economic and Political Analysis*, vol. I (New York, NY: Springer, 2005), pp. 371–409.

Aristotle, in: Trevor J. Saunders (ed.), *Politics, Books I and II* (Clarendon Press/ Oxford University Press 1995).

'Nicomachean Ethics' in: Roger Crisp (ed.), *Nicomachean Ethics* (Cambridge University Press, 2000).

Arnardóttir, Oddný Mjöll, *Equality and Non-discrimination under the European Convention on Human Rights* (The Hague: Martinus Nijhoff Publishers, 2003).

Ayres, Ian, 'Rationalizing Antitrust Cluster Markets', **95** *Yale Law Journal* (1985) 109–24.

Baker, Jonathan B., 'Market Definition: An Analytical Overview', **74** *Antitrust Law Journal* (2007) 129–73.

Baker, Stewart A., Peter Lichtenbaum, Maury D. Shenk and Matthews S. Yeo, 'E-Products and the WTO', **35** *International Lawyer* (2001) 5–21.

Bartels, Lorand, 'Article XX of GATT and the Problem of Extraterritorial Jurisdiction', **36** *Journal of World Trade* (2002) 353–403.

Baur, Jürgen F., 'Der relevante Markt – eine durchaus notwendige Figur des Rechts der Zusammenschlusskontrolle', in: Hans Merz and Walter R Schluep (eds.), *Recht und Wirtschaft heute, Festgabe Max Kummer* (Berne: Stämpfli, 1980), pp. 293–309.

Becker, Ulrich, 'EGV Artikel 28–30', in: Juergen Schwarze (ed.), *EU-Kommentar*, 2nd edition (Baden-Baden: Nomos, 2009).

Behrens, Peter, 'Der Marktbeherrschungsbegriff in Artikel 82 EG', in: Börris Ahrens, Peter Behrens and Philipp von Dietze (eds.), *Marktmacht und Missbrauch* (Baden-Baden: Nomos, 2007), pp. 37–42.

Bellis, Jean-François, 'Anti-competitive Practices and the WTO: The Elusive Search for New World Trade Rules', in: Marco Bronckers and Reinhard Quick (eds.), *New Directions in International Economic Law: Essays in Honour of John H. Jackson* (The Hague: Kluwer Law International, 2000), pp. 361–68.

Berg, Gerald C., 'An Economic Interpretation of "Like-Product"', **30**(2) *Journal of World Trade* (1996) 195–209.

Berrisch, Georg M., 'Allgemeines Zoll- und Handelsabkommen (GATT 1994)', in: Hans-Joachim Prieß and Georg M. Berrisch (eds.), *WTO-Handbuch – World Trade Organisation* (Munich: Verlag C.H. Beck, 2003).

Bhagwati, Jagdish N. and Robert E. Hudec (eds.), *Fair Trade and Harmonization – Prerequisites For Free Trade?*, vol. II: Legal analysis (Cambridge, MA: MIT Press, 1996).

Bhala, Raj, *International Trade Law: Interdisciplinary Theory and Practice*, 3rd edition (Newark, NJ: LexisNexis, 2007).

Bigdeli, Sadeq Z. and Stefan Rechsteiner, 'Commentary to Article VIII GATS (monopolies and exclusive service suppliers)', in: Rüdiger Wolfrum, Peter-Tobias Stoll and Clemens Feinäugle (eds.), *WTO – Trade in Services: Max Planck Commentaries on World Trade Law*, vol. 6 (Leiden: Martinus Nijhoff Publishers, 2008), pp. 205–19.

Bishop, Simon and Mike Walker, *The Economics of EC Competition Law: Concepts, Application and Measurement* (London: Sweet & Maxwell, 2002).

Bjorklund, Andrea K., 'National Treatment', in: August Reinisch (ed.), *Standards of Investment Protection* (Oxford University Press, 2008), pp. 29–58.

Bobjoseph, Mathew, *The WTO Agreements on Telecommunications* (Berne: Peter Lang Publishers, 2003).

Bogdandy, Armin von and Joseph Windsor, 'Commentary to Annex on Financial Services', in: Rüdiger Wolfrum, Peter-Tobias Stoll and Clemens Feinäugle (eds.), *WTO – Trade in Services: Max Planck Commentaries on World Trade Law*, vol. 6 (Leiden: Martinus Nijhoff Publishers, 2008), pp. 618–39.

Bossche, Peter Van den, Nico Schrijver and Gerrit Faber, 'Unilateral Measures Addressing Non-Trade Concerns', *The Ministry of Foreign Affairs of The Netherlands* (2007), available at SSRN: http://ssrn.com/abstract=1021946.

Bossche, Peter Van den, *The Law and Policy of the World Trade Organization – Text, Cases and Materials*, 2nd edition (Cambridge University Press, 2008).

Bronckers, Marco, 'The WTO Reference Paper on Telecommunications: A Model for WTO Competition Law?', in: Marco Bronckers and Reinhard Quick (eds.), *New Directions in International Economic Law: Essays in Honour of John H. Jackson* (The Hague: Kluwer Law International, 2000), pp. 371–89.

Bronckers, Marco and Natalie McNelis, 'Rethinking the "Like Product" Definition in GATT 1994: Anti-Dumping and Environmental Protection', in: Thomas Cottier and Petros C. Mavroidis (eds.), *Regulatory Barriers and the Principle of Non-Discrimination in World Trade Law: Past, Present, and Future* (Ann Arbor, MI: University of Michigan Press, 2000), pp. 345–85.

Bronckers, Marco and Pierre Larouche, 'Telecommunications Services', in: Patrick F. J. Macrory, Arthur E. Appleton and Michael G. Plummer (eds.), *The World Trade Organization: Legal, Economic and Political Analysis*, vol. I (New York, NY: Springer, 2005), pp. 989–1040.

'A Review of the WTO Regime for Telecommunications Services', in: Kern Alexander and Mads Andenas (eds.), *The World Trade Organization and Trade in Services* (Leiden: Martinus Nijhoff Publishers, 2008), pp 319–79.

Brown Weiss, Edith and John H. Jackson, 'The Framework for Environment and Trade Disputes', in: Edith Brown Weiss, John H. Jackson and Nathalie Bernasconi-Osterwalder (eds.), *Reconciling Environment and Trade*, 2nd edition (Leiden: Martinus Nijhoff Publishers, 2008), pp. 1–46.

Brownlie, Ian, *Principles of Public International Law*, 7th edition (Oxford University Press, 2009).

Burri Nenova, Mira, *EC Electronic Communications and Competition Law* (London: Cameron May, 2007).

Calster, Geert Van, *International & EU Trade Law: The Environmental Challenge* (London: Cameron May, 2000).

'The EU, Trade, Environment and Unilateralism: Passing the Buck', **5** *European Foreign Affairs Review* (2000) 9–34.

Cameron, James, Paul Demaret and Damien Geradin (eds.), *Trade & The Environment: The Search for Balance*, vol. I (London: Cameron May, 1994).

Cárdenas Tomažič, José Luis, *Rolle, Kriterien und Methodik der kartellrechtlichen Marktabgrenzung: eine juristische und ökonomische Analyse* (Karlsruhe: Universitätsverlag Karlsruhe, 2005).

Carter, Robert L., 'Insurance', in: Patrick A. Messerlin and Karl P. Sauvant (eds.), *The Uruguay Round: Services in the World Economy* (Washington DC: World Bank/ The United Nations Centre on Transnational Corporations, 1990), pp. 60–68.

Cass, Ronald and Eli M. Noam, 'The Economics and Politics of Trade in Services: A United States Perspective', in: Daniel Friedmann and Ernst-Joachim Mestmäcker (eds.), *Rules for Free International Trade in Services – Symposium in Tel Aviv* (Baden-Baden: Nomos, 1990), pp. 43–87.

Chanda, Rupa, 'Inter-modal Linkages in Services Trade', *OECD Trade Policy Working Papers, No. 30, OECD Publishing* (2006), available at http://ideas.repec.org/p/oec/traaab/30-en.html

Chapman, Michael J. and Paul J. Tauber, 'Liberalizing International Trade in Legal Services: A Proposal for an Annex on Legal Services under the General Agreement on Trade in Services', **16** *Michigan Journal of International Law* (1995) 941–80.

Charnovitz, Steve, 'Green Roots, Bad Pruning: GATT Rules and their Application to Environmental Trade Measures', **7** *Tulane Environmental Law Journal* (1994) 299–352.

'WTO's *Alcoholic Beverages* Decision', **6** *Review of European Community & International Environmental Law* (1997) 198–203.

'The Law of Environmental "PPMs" in the WTO: Debunking the Myth of Illegality', **27** *Yale Journal of International Law* (2002) 59–110.

'Belgian Family Allowances and the Challenge of Origin-based Discrimination', **4** *World Trade Review* (2005) 7–26.

Cho, Sungjoon, *Free Markets and Social Regulation: A Reform Agenda of the Global Trading System* (London: Kluwer Law International, 2003).

Choi, Won-Mog, 'Overcoming the "Aim and Effect" Theory: Interpretation of the "Like Product" in GATT Article III', **8** *UC Davis Journal of International Law and Policy* (2002) 107–31.

'Like Products' in International Trade Law – Towards a Consistent GATT/WTO Jurisprudence (Oxford University Press, 2003).

Cone, Sydney M., 'The Asbestos Case and Dispute Settlement in the World Trade Organization: The Uneasy Relationship between Panels and the Appellate Body', **23** *Michigan Journal of International Law* (2001) 103–42.

Conrad, Christiane R., 'The Status of Measures Linked to Non-physical Aspects and Process and Production Methods in WTO Law', *PhD thesis, University of Bern/World Trade Institute* (2009), draft on file with author.

Copeland, Bryan and Aaditya Mattoo, 'The Basic Economics of Services Trade', in: Aaditya Mattoo, Robert M. Stern and Gianni Zanini (eds.), *A Handbook of International Trade in Services* (Oxford University Press, 2008), pp. 84–129.

Cossy, Mireille, 'Determining Likeness under the GATS: Squaring the Circle?', *WTO Staff Working Paper No. ERSD-2006-08* (2006), available at SSRN http://ssrn.com/abstract=935213;.

'Some Thoughts on the Concept of "Likeness" in the GATS', in: Marion Panizzon, Nicole Pohl and Pierre Sauvé (eds.), *GATS and the Regulation of International Trade in Services* (Cambridge University Press, 2008), pp. 327–57.

Cottier, Thomas, 'The WTO and Environmental Law: Three Points for Discussion', in: Agata Fijalkowski and James Cameron (eds.), *Trade and the Environment: Bridging the Gap* (London: Cameron May, 1998), pp. 56–64.

Cottier, Thomas and Alexandra Caplazi, 'Labour Standards and World Trade Law: Interfacing Legitimate Concerns', in: Thomas Geiser, Hans Schmid and Emil Walter-Busch (eds.), *Arbeit in der Schweiz des 20. Jahrhunderts: Wirtschaftliche, rechtliche und soziale Perspektiven* (Berne: Paul Haupt, 1998), pp. 469–508.

Cottier, Thomas and Petros C. Mavroidis, 'Regulatory Barriers and the Principle of Non-Discrimination in World Trade Law: An Overview', in: Thomas Cottier and Petros C. Mavroidis (eds.), *Regulatory Barriers and the Principle of Non-Discrimination in World Trade Law: Past, Present, and Future* (Ann Arbor, MI: University of Michigan Press, 2000), pp. 1–10.

Cottier, Thomas, Elisabeth Tuerk and Marion Panizzon, 'Handel und Umwelt im Recht der WTO: Auf dem Weg zur praktischen Konkordanz', *Zeitschrift für Umweltrecht, Sonderheft* (2003) 155–66.

Cottier, Thomas and Matthias Oesch, *International Trade Regulation – Law and Policy in the WTO, the European Union and Switzerland* (London: Cameron May & Staempfli Publishers, 2005).

Cottier, Thomas, 'From Progressive Liberalization to Progressive Regulation in WTO Law', **9** *Journal of International Economic Law* (2006) 779–821.

Cottier, Thomas, Panagiotis Delimatsis and Nicolas F. Diebold, 'Commentary to Article XIV GATS (general exceptions)', in: Rüdiger Wolfrum, Peter-Tobias Stoll and Clemens Feinäugle (eds.), *WTO – Trade in Services: Max Planck Commentaries on World Trade Law*, vol. 6 (Leiden: Martinus Nijhoff Publishers, 2008), pp. 287–328.

Cottier, Thomas and Petros C. Mavroidis (eds.), *The Role of the Judge in International Trade Regulation – Experience and Lessons for the WTO* (Ann Arbor, MI: University of Michigan Press, 2003).

Cottier, Thomas, Joost Pauwelyn and Elisabeth B ürgi (eds.), *Human Rights and International Trade* (Oxford University Press, 2005).

Craig, Paul, 'The Nature of the Community: Integration, Democracy, and Legitimacy', in: Paul Craig and Gráinne De Búrca (eds.), *The Evolution of EU Law* (Oxford University Press, 1999), pp. 1–54.

Cseres, Katalin Judit, *Competition Law and Consumer Protection* (The Hague: Kluwer Law International, 2005).

Davey, William J. and Joost Pauwelyn, 'MFN Unconditionality: A Legal Analysis of the Concept in View of its Evolution in the GATT/WTO Jurisprudence with Particular Reference to the Issue of "Like Product"', in: Thomas Cottier and Petros C. Mavroidis (eds.), *Regulatory Barriers and the Principle of Non-Discrimination in World Trade Law: Past, Present, and Future* (Ann Arbor, MI: University of Michigan Press, 2000), pp. 13–50.

Davey, William J., 'Specificities of WTO Dispute Settlement in Services Cases', in: Marion Panizzon, Nicole Pohl and Pierre Sauvé (eds.), *GATS and the Regulation of International Trade in Services* (Cambridge University Press, 2008), pp. 276–95.

De Búrca, Gráinne, 'Unpacking the Concept of Discrimination in EC and International Trade Law', in: Catherine Barnard and Joanne Scott (eds.), *The Law of the Single European Market – Unpacking the Premises* (Oxford: Hart Publishing, 2002), pp. 181–95.

Deardorff, Alan V. and Robert M. Stern, 'Empirical Analysis of Barriers to International Services Transactions and the Consequences of Liberalization', in: Aaditya Mattoo, Robert M. Stern and Gianni Zanini (eds.), *A Handbook of International Trade in Services* (Oxford University Press, 2008), pp. 169–220.

Delimatsis, Panagiotis, 'Don't Gamble with GATS – The Interaction between Articles VI, XVI, XVII and XVIII GATS in the Light of the US–Gambling Case', **40** *Journal of World Trade* (2006) 1059–80.

International Trade in Services and Domestic Regulations – Necessity, Transparency, and Regulatory Diversity (Oxford University Press, 2007).

Demaret, Paul, 'The Non-Discrimination Principle and the Removal of Fiscal Barriers to Intra-Community Trade', in: Thomas Cottier and Petros C. Mavroidis (eds.), *Regulatory Barriers and the Principle of Non-Discrimination in World Trade Law: Past, Present, and Future* (Ann Arbor, MI: University of Michigan Press, 2000), pp. 171–89.

Desmedt, Axel, 'Proportionality in WTO Law', **4** *Journal of International Economic Law* (2001) 441–80.

Diebold, Nicolas F., 'The Morals and Order Exceptions in WTO Law: Balancing the Toothless Tiger and the Undermining Mole', **11** *Journal of International Economic Law* (2008) 43–74.

'Non-Discrimination and the Pillars of International Economic Law: Comparative Analysis and Building Coherency', *Society of International Economic Law (SIEL), Second Biennial Global Conference, University of Barcelona, IELPO Programme, July 8–10*, 2010, available at SSRN http://ssrn.com/abstract=1632927.

Diebold, Nicolas F. and Matthias Oesch, 'Die Durchsetzung von WTO-Recht durch Schweizer Unternehmen', *Aktuelle Juristische Praxis* (2008) 1525–52.

Dijk, Pieter van, Fried van Hoof, Arjen van Rijn and Leo Zwaak (eds.), *Theory and Practice of the European Convention on Human Rights*, 4th edition (Antwerpen: Intersentia, 2006).

DiMascio, Nicholas and Joost Pauwelyn, 'Nondiscrimination in Trade and Investment Treaties: Worlds Apart or Two Sides of the Same Coin?', **102** *American Journal of International Law* (2008) 48–89.

Doebbler, Curtis F. J., *The Principle of Non-Discrimination in International Law* (Washington DC: CD Publishing, 2007).

Dolzer, Rudolf and Christoph Schreuer, *Principles of International Investment Law* (Oxford University Press, 2008).

Drake, William J. and Kalypso Nicolaidïs, 'Global Electronic Commerce and GATS: The Millennium Round and Beyond', in: Pierre Sauvé and Robert M Stern (eds.), *GATS 2000 – New Directions in Services Trade Liberalization* (Washington DC: Bookings Institution Press, 2000), pp. 399–437.

Eeckhout, Piet, 'After Keck and Mithouard: Free Movement of Goods in the EC, Market Access, and Non-Discrimination', in: Thomas Cottier and Petros C Mavroidis (eds.), *Regulatory Barriers and the Principle of Non-Discrimination in World Trade Law: Past, Present, and Future* (Ann Arbor, MI: University of Michigan Press, 2000), pp. 191–206.

'Constitutional Concepts for Free Trade in Services', in: Gráinne De Búrca and Joanne Scott (eds.), *The EU and the WTO: Legal Constitutional Issues* (Oxford: Hart Publishing, 2001), pp. 211–36.

Ehlermann, Claus-Dieter and Lothar Ehring, 'WTO Dispute Settlement and Competition Law: Views from the Perspective of the Appellate Body's Experience', **26** *Fordham International Law Journal* (2003) 1505–61.

Ehlers, Dirk, Hans-Michael Wolffgang and Marc Lechleitner (eds.), *Rechtsfragen des internationalen Dienstleistungsverkehrs – Tagungsband zum 10. Münsteraner Außenwirtschaftsrechtstag* (Frankfurt a.M.: Verlag Recht und Wirtschaft, 2006).

Ehring, Lothar, 'De Facto Discrimination in World Trade Law; National and Most-Favoured-Nation Treatment – or Equal Treatment?', **36** *Journal of World Trade* (2002) 921–77.

Elhauge, Einer 'Defining Better Monopolization Standards', **56** *Stanford Law Review* (2003) 253–344.

Emch, Adrian, 'Same Same But Different? Fiscal Discrimination in WTO Law and EU Law: What are "Like" Products?', **32** *Legal Issues of Economic Integration* (2005) 369–415.

Englisch, Joachim, *Wettbewerbsgleichheit im grenzüberschreitenden Handel: Mit Schlussfolgerungen für indirekte Steuern* (Tuebingen: Mohr Siebeck, 2008).

Farber, Daniel A. and Robert E. Hudec, 'GATT Legal Restraints on Domestic Environmental Regulations', in: Jagdish N. Bhagwati and Robert E. Hudec (eds.), *Fair Trade and Harmonization – Prerequisites For Free Trade?*, vol. II: Legal analysis (Cambridge, MA: MIT Press, 1996), pp. 59–94.

Fauchald, Ole Kristian, *Environmental Taxes and Trade Discrimination* (London: Kluwer Law International, 1998).

'Flexibility and Predictability under the World Trade Organization's Non-Discrimination Clauses', **37** *Journal of World Trade* (2003) 443–82.

Feinäugle, Clemens, 'Commentary to Article XXVIII GATS (definitions)', in: Rüdiger Wolfrum, Peter-Tobias Stoll and Clemens Feinäugle (eds.), *WTO – Trade in Services: Max Planck Commentaries on World Trade Law*, vol. 6 (Leiden: Martinus Nijhoff Publishers, 2008), pp. 540–64.

Fischer, Thomas M., *Die Entbündelung der letzten Meile in der Schweiz im Lichte des GATS* (Berne: Peter Lang, 2004).

Fisher, Franklin M., 'Detecting Market Power', in: Wayne Dale Collins (ed.), *Issues in Competition Law and Policy*, vol. I (Chicago, IL: ABA Section of Antitrust Law, 2008), pp. 353–71.

Footer, Mary E. and Carol George, 'The General Agreement on Trade in Services', in: Patrick F. J. Macrory, Arthur E. Appleton and Michael G. Plummer (eds.), *The World Trade Organization: Legal, Economic and Political Analysis*, vol. I (New York, NY: Springer, 2005), pp. 799–953.

Forrester Q. C., Ian S. and Tashi Kaul, 'Tariff Classification', in: Patrick FJ Macrory, Arthur E. Appleton and Michael G. Plummer (eds.), *The World Trade Organization: Legal, Economic and Political Analysis*, vol. I (New York, NY: Springer, 2005), pp. 1581–99.

Fox, Eleanor M., 'Antitrust Law on a Global Scale: Races Up, Down and Sideways', in: Daniel C. Esty and Damien Geradin (eds.), *Regulatory Competition and Economic Integration* (Oxford University Press, 2001), pp. 348–63.

Franck, Susan D., 'Occidental Exploration & Production Co. v. Republic of Ecuador. Final Award. London Court of International Arbitration Administered Case No. UN 3467', **99** *The American Journal of International Law* (2005) 675–81.

Francois, Joseph and Ian Wooton, 'Market Structure, Trade Liberalization and the GATS', **17** *European Journal of Political Economy* (2001) 389–402.

Froeb, Luke M. and Gregory J. Werden, 'The Reverse *Cellophane* Fallacy in Market Delineation', **7** *Review of Industrial Organization* (1992) 241–47.

Gaines, Sanford E., 'Processes and Production Methods: How to Produce Sound Policy for Environmental PPM-Based Trade Measures?', **27** *Columbia Journal of Environmental Law* (2002) 383–432.

Gamberale, Carlo, 'Legal Services', in: WTO-Secretariat (ed.), *Guide to the GATS: An Overview of Issues for Further Liberalization of Trade in Services* (The Hague: Kluwer Law International 2001), pp. 399–427.

Gao, Henry, 'Commentary to Telecommunications Services: Reference Paper', in: Rüdiger Wolfrum, Peter-Tobias Stoll and Clemens Feinäugle (eds.), *WTO – Trade in Services: Max Planck Commentaries on World Trade Law*, vol. 6 (Leiden: Martinus Nijhoff Publishers, 2008), pp. 718–47.

Gardner, Richard N., *Sterling-Dollar Diplomacy – The Origins and the Prospects of Our International Economic Order*, New, expanded edition (New York, NY: McGraw-Hill, 1969).

Gelb, Alan H. and Silvia B. Sagari, 'Banking', in: Patrick A. Messerlin and Karl P. Sauvant (eds.), *The Uruguay Round: Services in the World Economy* (Washington DC: World Bank/The United Nations Centre on Transnational Corporations, 1990), pp. 49–59.

Gifford, Daniel J. and Mitsuo Matsushita, 'Antitrust or Competition Laws Viewed in a Trading Context: Harmony or Dissonance?', in: Jagdish N. Bhagwati and Robert E. Hudec (eds.), *Fair Trade and Harmonization – Prerequisites For Free Trade?*, vol. II: Legal analysis (Cambridge, MA: MIT Press, 1996), pp. 269–331.

Gkoutzinis, Apostolos, 'International Trade in Banking Services and the Role of the WTO: Discussing the Legal Framework and Policy Objectives of the General Agreement on Trade in Services and the Current State of Play in the Doha Round of Trade Negotiations', **39** *International Lawyer* (2005) 877–914.

Goco, Jonell B., 'Non-Discrimination, "Likeness", and Market Definition in World Trade Organization Jurisprudence', **40** *Journal of World Trade* (2006) 315–40.

Golz, Tilman, *Der sachlich relevante Markt bei Verlagserzeugnissen* (Heidelberg: C.F. Mueller, 2003).

Grierson-Weiler, Todd J. and Ian A. Laird, 'Standards of Treatment', in: Peter Muchlinski, Federico Ortino and Christoph Schreuer (eds.), *The Oxford Handbook of International Investment Law* (Oxford University Press, 2008), pp. 259–304.

Grubel, Herbert G., 'All Traded Services are Embodied in Materials or People', **10** *The World Economy* (1987) 319–30.

Guzman, Andrew T., 'International Competition Law', in: Andrew T Guzman and Alan O Sykes (eds.), *Research Handbook in International Economic Law* (Cheltenham: Edward Elgar Publishing 2007), pp. 418–43.

Hawk, Barry E., 'Article 82 and Section 2: Abuse and Monopolizing Conduct', in: Wayne Dale Collins (ed.), *Issues in Competition Law and Policy*, vol. II (Chicago, IL: ABA Section of Antitrust Law, 2008), pp. 871–94.

Heinze, Eric, *The Logic of Equality: A Formal Analysis of Non-discrimination Law* (Burlington, VT: Ashgate, 2003).

Hildebrand, Doris, *The Role of Economic Analysis in the EC Competition Rules*, 2nd edition (The Hague: Kluwer Law International, 2002).

'Using Conjoint Analysis for Market Definition: Application of Modern Market Research Tools to Implement the Hypothetical Monopolist Test', **29** *World Competition* (2006) 315–35.

Hilf, Meinhard and Sebastian Puth, 'The Principle of Proportionality on its Way into WTO/GATT Law', in: Armin von Bogdandy, Petros C. Mavroidis and Yves Mény (eds.), *European Integration and International Co-ordination – Studies in Transnational Economic Law in Honour of Claus-Dieter Ehlermann* (The Hague: Kluwer Law International, 2002), pp. 199–218.

Hindley, Brian and Alasdair Smith, 'Comparative Advantage and Trade in Services', 7 *The World Economy* (1984) 369–90.

Hindley, Brian, 'Principles in Factor-related Trade in Services', in: Patrick A. Messerlin and Karl P. Sauvant (eds.), *The Uruguay Round: Services in the World Economy* (Washington DC: World Bank/The United Nations Centre on Transnational Corporations, 1990), pp. 12–18.

Hoekman, Bernard, 'Services-Related Production, Employment, Trade, and Factor Movements', in: Patrick A. Messerlin and Karl P. Sauvant (eds.), *The Uruguay Round: Services in the World Economy* (Washington DC: World Bank/The United Nations Centre on Transnational Corporations, 1990), pp. 27–46.

Hoekman, Bernard and Carlos Primo Alberto Braga, 'Protection and Trade in Services: A Survey', *World Bank Policy Research Working Paper No. 1747* (1997), available at SSRN http://ssrn.com/abstract=569236.

Hoekman, Bernard and Aaditya Mattoo, 'Services, Economic Development and the Next Round of Negotiations on Services', **12** *Journal of International Development* (2000) 283–96.

Hoekman, Bernard and Patrick A. Messerlin, 'Liberalizing Trade in Services: Reciprocal Negotiations and Regulatory Reform', in: Pierre Sauvé and Robert M. Stern (eds.), *GATS 2000 – New Directions in Services Trade Liberalization* (Washington DC: Bookings Institution Press, 2000), pp. 487–508.

Hoekman, Bernard and Michel Kostecki, *The Political Economy of the World Trading System – The WTO and Beyond*, 2nd edition (Oxford University Press, 2001).

Hoekman, Bernard and Aaditya Mattoo, 'International Trade: Trade in Services', in: Andrew T. Guzman and Alan O. Sykes (eds.), *Research Handbook in International Economic Law* (Cheltenham: Edward Elgar Publishing, 2007), pp. 113–50.

'Services Trade and Growth', in: Juan A Marchetti and Martin Roy (eds.), *Opening Markets for Trade in Services – Countries and Sectors in Bilateral and WTO Negotiations* (Cambridge University Press, 2009), pp. 21–58.

Holoubek, Michael, 'EGV Artikel 49/50', in: Juergen Schwarze (ed.), *EU-Kommentar*, 2nd edition (Baden-Baden: Nomos, 2009).

Honeck, Dale, 'Audiovisual Services', in: WTO-Secretariat (ed.), *Guide to the GATS: An Overview of Issues for Further Liberalization of Trade in Services* (The Hague: Kluwer Law International, 2001), pp. 133–51.

Horn, Henrik and Petros C. Mavroidis, 'Economic and Legal Aspects of the Most-Favored-Nation Clause', **17** *European Journal of Political Economy* (2001) 233–79.

'Still Hazy after All These Years: The Interpretation of National Treatment in the GATT/WTO Case-law on Tax Discrimination', **15** *European Journal of International Law* (2004) 39–69.

Horn, Henrik and Joseph H. Weiler, 'European Communities – Measures Affecting Asbestos and Asbestos-Containing Products', **3** *World Trade Review* (2004) 129–51.

Howse, Robert and Donald H. Regan, 'The Product/Process Distinction – An Illusory Basis for Disciplining "Unilateralism" in Trade Policy', **11** *European Journal of International Law* (2000) 249–89.

Howse, Robert and Elisabeth Tuerk, 'The WTO Impact on Internal Regulations – A Case Study of the Canada-EC Asbestos Dispute', in: Gráinne De Búrca and Joanne Scott (eds.), *The EU and the WTO: Legal Constitutional Issues* (Oxford: Hart Publishing, 2001), pp. 283–328.

Howse, Robert, 'The Appellate Body Rulings in the Shrimp/Turtle Case: A new Legal Baseline for the Trade and Environment Debate', *Columbia Journal of Environmental Law* (2002) 491–521.

Howse, Robert and Elisabeth Tuerk, 'The WTO Negotiations on Services: The Regulatory State up for Grabs', *Canada Watch, vol. 9, nos. 1–2* (2002) 3–6, available at www.law.nyu.edu/faculty/facultyprofiles/rhowse/pubsfordownload/index.htm.

Hudec, Robert E., 'Tiger, Tiger in the House: A Critical Appraisal of the Case Against Discriminatory Trade Measures', in: Ernst-Ulrich Petersmann and Meinhard Hilf (eds.), *The New GATT Round of Multilateral Trade Negotiations: Legal and Economic Problems*, 2nd edition (Deventer: Kluwer Law and Taxation Publisher, 1991), pp. 165–212.

'GATT/WTO Constraints on National Regulation: Requiem for an "Aim and Effects" Test', **32** *International Lawyer* (1998) 619–49.

'"Like Product": The Differences in Meaning in GATT Articles I and III', in: Thomas Cottier and Petros C. Mavroidis (eds.), *Regulatory Barriers and the Principle of Non-Discrimination in World Trade Law: Past, Present, and Future* (Ann Arbor, MI: University of Michigan Press, 2000), pp. 101–23.

'The Product-Process Doctrine in GATT/WTO Jurisprudence', in: Marco Bronckers and Reinhard Quick (eds.), *New Directions in International Economic Law: Essays in Honour of John H. Jackson* (The Hague: Kluwer Law International, 2000), pp. 187–217.

Hull, Cordell, *The Memoirs of Cordell Hull*, vol. 1 (New York, NY: Macmillan Co., 1948).

Hylton, Keith N., *Antitrust Law: Economic Theory and Common Law Evolution* (Cambridge University Press, 2003).

Irwin, Douglas A., Petros C. Mavroidis and Alan O. Sykes, *The Genesis of the GATT* (New York, NY: Cambridge University Press, 2008).

Ishikawa, Yoshimichi, 'Burden of Proof in the WTO Dispute Settlement Procedure', *PhD thesis, University of Bern/World Trade Institute* (2009), draft on file with author.

Jackson, John H., *World Trade and the Law of GATT (A Legal Analysis of the General Agreement on Tariffs and Trade)* (Charlottesville, VA: The Michie Company, 1969).

'Constructing a Constitution for Trade in Services', **11** *The World Economy* (1988) 187–202.

International Competition in Services: A Constitutional Framework (Washington DC: American Enterprise Institute for Public Policy Research, 1988).

'National Treatment Obligations and Non-tariff Barriers', **10** *Michigan Journal of International Law* (1989) 207–20.

'Greening the GATT: Trade Rules and Environmental Policy', in: James Cameron, Paul Demaret and Damien Geradin (eds.), *Trade & The Environment: The Search for Balance*, vol. I (London: Cameron May, 1994), pp. 39–51.

The World Trading System: Law and Policy of International Economic Relations, 2nd edition (Cambridge, MA: MIT Press, 1997).

The Jurisprudence of GATT and the WTO: Insights on Treaty Law and Economic Relations (Cambridge University Press, 2000).

'Comments on Shrimp/Turtle and the Product/Process Distinction', **11** *European Journal of International Law* (2000) 303–7.

Jackson, John H., William J. Davey and Alan O. Sykes, *Legal Problems of International Economic Relations – Cases, Materials and Text*, 5th edition (St. Paul, MN: Thomson/West, 2008).

Janow, Merit E., 'Trade and Competition Policy', in: Patrick F. J. Macrory, Arthur E. Appleton and Michael G. Plummer (eds.), *The World Trade Organization: Legal, Economic and Political Analysis*, vol. II (New York, NY: Springer, 2005), pp. 487–510.

Jones, Geoffry, *Multinationals and Global Capitalism: From the Nineteenth to the Twenty-First Century* (Oxford University Press, 2005).

Kaufmann, Christine and Rolf H. Weber, 'Reconciling Liberalized Trade in Financial Services and Domestic Regulation', in: Kern Alexander and Mads Andenas (eds.), *The World Trade Organization and Trade in Services* (Leiden: Martinus Nijhoff Publishers, 2008), pp. 411–27.

Kauper, Thomas E., 'The Problem of Market Definition under EC Competition Law', **20** *Fordham International Law Journal* (1997) 1682–767.

Kearns, Jason, 'International Competition Policy and the GATS: A Proposal to Address Market Access Limitations in the Distribution Services Sector', in: Marco Bronckers and Gary N. Horlick (eds.), *WTO Jurisprudence and Policy: Practitioners' Perspectives* (London: Cameron May, 2004), pp. 649–86.

Kenen, Peter B., *The International Economy*, 4th edition (Cambridge University Press, 2000).

Kono, Masamichi, 'Construction and Related Service Industries', in: WTO-Secretariat (ed.), *Guide to the GATS: An Overview of Issues for Further*

Liberalization of Trade in Services (The Hague: Kluwer Law International, 2001), pp. 181–91.

'Architectural and Engineering Services', in: WTO-Secretariat (ed.), *Guide to the GATS: An Overview of Issues for Further Liberalization of Trade in Services* (The Hague: Kluwer Law International, 2001), pp. 117–32.

Krajewski, Markus, *National Regulation and Trade Liberalization in Services – The Legal Impact of the General Agreement on Trade in Services (GATS) on National Regulatory Autonomy* (The Hague: Kluwer Law International, 2003).

'Public Services and Trade Liberalization: Mapping the Legal Framework', **6** *Journal of International Economic Law* (2003) 341–67.

'Book Review: Won-Mog Choi, Like Products in International Trade Law – Towards a Consistent GATT/WTO Jurisprudence', **15** *King's College Law Journal* (2004) 198–202.

'Commentary to Article VI (domestic regulation)', in: Rüdiger Wolfrum, Peter-Tobias Stoll and Clemens Feinäugle (eds.), *WTO – Trade in Services: Max Planck Commentaries on World Trade Law*, vol. 6 (Leiden: Martinus Nijhoff Publishers, 2008), pp. 165–96.

'Comment: *Quis custodiet necessitatem?* Adjudicating Necessity in Multilateral Systems and the Importance of Judicial Dialogue', in: Marion Panizzon, Nicole Pohl and Pierre Sauvé (eds.), *GATS and the Regulation of International Trade in Services* (Cambridge University Press, 2008), pp. 397–403.

Krajewski, Markus and Maika Engelke, 'Commentary to Article XVII GATS (national treatment)', in: Rüdiger Wolfrum, Peter-Tobias Stoll and Clemens Feinäugle (eds.), *WTO – Trade in Services: Max Planck Commentaries on World Trade Law*, vol. 6 (Leiden: Martinus Nijhoff Publishers, 2008), pp. 396–420.

Kreinin, Mordeachai E. and Michael G. Plummer, 'Economic Principles of International Trade', in: Patrick F. J. Macrory, Arthur E. Appleton and Michael G. Plummer (eds.), *The World Trade Organization: Legal, Economic and Political Analysis*, vol. II (New York, NY: Springer, 2005), pp. 3–22.

Krommenacker, Raymond J., 'Multilateral Services Negotiations: From Interest Lateralism to Reasoned Multilateralism in the Context of the Servicization of the Economy', in: Ernst-Ulrich Petersmann and Meinhard Hilf (eds.), *The New GATT Round of Multilateral Trade Negotiations – Legal and Economic Problems*, 2nd edition (Deventer: Kluwer Law and Taxation Publishers,, 1991), pp. 455–74.

Kuyper, Pieter J., 'Booze and Fast Cars: Tax Discrimination under GATT and the EC', *Legal Issues of Economic Integration* (1996/1) 129–44.

Kysar, Douglas A., 'Preferences for Process: The Process/Product Distinction and the Regulation of Consumer Choice', **118** *Harvard Law Review* (2004) 525–642.

Landes, William M and Richard A Posner, 'Market Power in Antitrust Cases', **94** *Harvard Law Review* (1981) 937–96.

Lang, Andrew, 'The GATS and Regulatory Autonomy: A Case Study of Social Regulation of the Water Industry', 7 *Journal of International Economic Law* (2004) 801–38.

League of Nations, 'The Most Favoured-Nation Clause', **22** *The American Journal of International Law* (1928) 133.

Lee, James, 'Construction', in: Patrick A Messerlin and Karl P Sauvant (eds.), *The Uruguay Round: Services in the World Economy* (Washington DC: World Bank/The United Nations Centre on Transnational Corporations, 1990), pp. 69–76.

Leroux, Eric H, 'Eleven Years of GATS Case Law: What Have we Learned?', **10** *Journal of International Economic Law* (2007) 749–93.

Lindsay, Alistair and Nicholas Scola, 'Market Definition', in: Peter QC Roth and Vivien Rose (eds.), *Bellamy & Child European Community Law of Competition*, 6th edition (Oxford University Press, 2008), pp. 239–302.

Loenen, Titia and Peter R. Rodrigues (eds.), *Non-Discrimination Law: Comparative Perspectives* (The Hague: Martinus Nijhoff Publishers, 1999).

Lonbay, Julian, 'A Review of Recent Tax Cases – Wine, Gambling, Fast Cars and Bananas', **14** *European Law Review* (1989) 48–56.

Low, Patrick and Aaditya Mattoo, 'Is There a Better Way? Alternative Approaches to Liberalization under GATS', in: Pierre Sauvé and Robert M Stern (eds.), *GATS 2000 – New Directions in Services Trade Liberalization* (Washington DC: Bookings Institution Press, 2000), pp. 449–72.

Lowenfeld, Andreas F, *International Economic Law*, 2nd edition (Oxford University Press, 2008).

Macrory, Patrick FJ, Arthur E Appleton and Michael G Plummer (eds.), *The World Trade Organization: Legal, Economic and Political Analysis*, vol. I (New York, NY: Springer, 2005).

Mallampally, Padma, 'Professional Services', in: Patrick A Messerlin and Karl P Sauvant (eds.), *The Uruguay Round: Services in the World Economy* (Washington DC: World Bank/The United Nations Centre on Transnational Corporations, 1990), pp. 94–104.

Marceau, Gabrielle and Joel P Trachtman, 'The Technical Barriers to Trade Agreement, the Sanitary and Phytosanitary Measures Agreement and the General Agreement on Tariffs and Trade: A Map of the World Trade Organization Law of Domestic Regulations of Goods', **36** *Journal of World Trade* (2002) 811–81.

Marchetti, Juan A and Petros C Mavroidis, 'What Are the Main Challenges for the GATS Framework? Don't Talk About Revolution', **5** *European Business Organization Law Review* (2004) 511–62.

Marconini, Mario, 'The Uruguay Round Negotiations on Services: An Overview', in: Patrick A Messerlin and Karl P Sauvant (eds.), *The Uruguay*

Round: Services in the World Economy (Washington DC: World Bank/The United Nations Centre on Transnational Corporations, 1990), pp. 19–26.

Marsden, Philip, A. *Competition Policy for the WTO* (London: Cameron May, 2003).

Matheny, Richard L., 'In the Wake of the Flood: "Like Products" and Cultural Products after the World Trade Organization's Decision in Canada – Certain Measures Concerning Periodicals', **147** *University of Pennsylvania Law Review* (1998) 245–78.

Matsushita, Mitsuo, 'Appellate Body Jurisprudence on the GATS and TRIPS Agreement', in: Federico Ortino and Ernst-Ulrich Petersmann (eds.), *The WTO Dispute Settlement System 1995–2003* (The Hague: Kluwer Law International, 2004), pp. 455–74.

Matsushita, Mitsuo, Thomas J. Schoenbaum and Petros C. Mavroidis, *The World Trade Organization – Law, Practice, and Policy*, 2nd edition (Oxford University Press, 2006).

Mattoo, Aaditya, 'National Treatment in the GATS – Corner-Stone or Pandora's Box?', **31**(1) *Journal of World Trade* (1997) 107–35.

Mattoo, Aaditya and Arvind Subramanian, 'Regulatory Autonomy and Multilateral Disciplines: The Dilemma and a Possible Resolution', **1** *Journal of International Economic Law* (1998) 303–22.

Mattoo, Aaditya, 'MFN and the GATS', in: Thomas Cottier and Petros C. Mavroidis (eds.), *Regulatory Barriers and the Principle of Non-Discrimination in World Trade Law: Past, Present, and Future* (Ann Arbor, MI: University of Michigan Press, 2000), pp. 51–99.

'Distribution Services', in: WTO-Secretariat (ed.), *Guide to the GATS: An Overview of Issues for Further Liberalization of Trade in Services* (The Hague: Kluwer Law International, 2001), pp. 193–227.

'Shaping Future GATS Rules for Trade in Services', *World Bank Policy Research Working Paper No. 2596* (2001), available at SSRN http://ssrn.com/abstract=632665

Mattoo, Aaditya and Pierre Sauvé, 'Domestic Regulation and Trade in Services: Key Issues', in: Aaditya Mattoo and Pierre Sauvé (eds.), *Domestic Regulation and Service Trade Liberalization* (Washington DC: World Bank & Oxford University Press, 2003), pp. 1–6.

Mattoo, Aaditya and Sacha Wunsch-Vincent, 'Pre-empting Protectionism in Services: The GATS and Outsourcing', **7** *Journal of International Economic Law* (2004) 765–800.

Mattoo, Aaditya and Antonia Carzaniga (eds.), *Moving People to Deliver Services* (Washington DC: World Bank & Oxford University Press, 2003).

Mavroidis, Petros C., '"Like Products": Some Thoughts at the Positive and Normative Level', in: Thomas Cottier and Petros C. Mavroidis (eds.), *Regulatory Barriers and the Principle of Non-Discrimination in World Trade Law: Past, Present, and Future* (Ann Arbor, MI: University of Michigan Press, 2000), pp. 125–35.

Mavroidis, Petros C. and Damien J. Neven, 'The WTO Agreement on Telecommunications: It's never too late', in: Damien Géradin (ed.), *The Liberalization of State Monopolies in the European Union and Beyond* (The Hague: Kluwer Law International, 2000), pp. 307–18.

Mavroidis, Petros C., *The General Agreement on Tariffs and Trade: A Commentary* (Oxford University Press, 2005).

'Highway XVI re-visited: The Road from Non-discrimination to Market Access in GATS', **6** *World Trade Review* (2007) 1–23.

McGovern, Edmond, *International Trade Regulation* (Exeter: Globefield Press, 1995).

McLachlan, Campbell, QC Laurence Shore and Matthew Weiniger, *International Investment Arbitration – Substantive Principles* (Oxford University Press, 2007).

Melloni, Mattia, *The Principle of National Treatment in the GATT: A Survey of the Jurisprudence, Practice and Policy* (Brussels: Bruylant, 2005).

Messerlin, Patrick A. and Karl P. Sauvant (eds.), *The Uruguay Round: Services in the World Economy* (Washington DC: World Bank/The United Nations Centre on Transnational Corporations, 1990).

Mestmäcker, Ernst-Joachim, 'Free Trade in Services: Regional and Global Perspectives', in: Daniel Friedmann and Ernst-Joachim Mestmäcker (eds.), *Rules for Free International Trade in Services – Symposium in Tel Aviv* (Baden-Baden: Nomos, 1990), pp. 9–24.

Mestmäcker, Ernst-Joachim and Heike Schweitzer, *Europäisches Wettbewerbsrecht*, 2nd edition (Munich: Verlag C. H. Beck, 2004).

Michaelis, Martin, 'Dienstleistungshandel (GATS)', in: Meinhard Hilf and Stefan Oeter (eds.), *WTO-Recht* (Baden-Baden: Nomos, 2005).

Mitchell, Andrew D., 'Towards Compatibility: The Future of Electronic Commerce within the Global Trading System', **4** *Journal of International Economic Law* (2001) 683–723.

Molinuevo, Martín, 'International Disputes in Investment in Services: Access, Substantial Rights and Remedies in WTO and Investment Arbitration', *PhD thesis, University of Bern/World Trade Institute* (2009), draft on file with author.

Monopolkommission, *Ökonomische Kriterien für die Rechts-anwendung: Hauptgutachten 1982/1983* (Baden-Baden: Nomos Verlagsgesellschaft, 1984).

Morrison, Peter K., 'WTO Dispute Settlement in Services: Procedural and Substantive Aspects', in: Ernst-Ulrich Petersmann (ed.), *International Trade Law and the GATT/WTO Dispute Settlement System* (The Hague: Kluwer Law International, 1997), pp. 377–93.

Motta, Massimo, *Competition Policy – Theory and Practice* (Cambridge University Press, 2004).

Mueller, Christian, *Abschied vom Bedarfsmarktkonzept bei der Marktabgrenzung?* (Baden-Baden: Nomos, 2007).

Neveling, Kirsten, *Die sachliche Marktabgrenzung bei der Fusionskontrolle im deutschen und europäischen Recht* (Tuebingen: Medien Verlag Köhler, 2003).

Neven, Damien J., 'The Economic Evaluation of Protection under Art. III: Some Principles and Suggestions for the Definition of a Trade Relevant Market', in: Thomas Cottier and Petros C. Mavroidis (eds.), *Regulatory Barriers and the Principle of Non-Discrimination in World Trade Law: Past, Present, and Future* (Ann Arbor, MI: University of Michigan Press, 2000), pp. 331–41.

'How Should "Protection" be Evaluated in Article III GATT Disputes?', **17** *European Journal of Political Economy* (2001) 421–44.

Newcombe, Andrew and Lluís Paradell, *Law and Practice of Investment Treaties – Standards of Treatment* (Austin, TX: Wolters Kluwer Law and Business, 2009).

Nicolaïdis, Kalypso and Joel P. Trachtman, 'From Policed Regulation to Managed Recognition in GATS', in: Pierre Sauvé and Robert M. Stern (eds.), *GATS 2000 – New Directions in Services Trade Liberalization* (Washington DC: Bookings Institution Press, 2000), pp. 241–82.

Nnona, George C., 'Multidisciplinary Practice under the World Trade Organization's Services Regime', **16** *Indiana International & Comperative Law Review* (2005) 73–115.

Nolde, Boris, 'La Clause de la Nation la Plus Favorisée et les Tarifs Préférentiels', **39** *Recueil des cours – L'Academie de Droit International de la Haye* (1932) 1–130.

O ' Donoghue, Robert and A. Jorge Padilla, *The Law and Economics of Article 82 EC* (Oxford: Hart Publishing, 2006).

O' Leary, Siofra, 'The Free Movement of Persons and Services', in: Paul Craig and Gráinne De Búrca (eds.), *The Evolution of EU Law* (Oxford University Press, 1999), pp. 377–416.

Oesch, Matthias, *Standards of Review in WTO Dispute Resolution* (Oxford University Press, 2003).

Differenzierung und Typisierung – Zur Dogmatik der Rechtsgleichheit in der Rechtsetzung (Berne: Staempfli Verlag, 2008).

'Commercial Treaties', in: Rüdiger Wolfrum (ed.), *Max Planck Encyclopedia of Public International Law* (Oxford University Press, 2008), online edition www.mpepil.com.

Oppermann, Thomas, *Europarecht*, 3rd edition (Munich: Verlag C.H. Beck, 2005).

Ortino, Federico, '*WTO Jurisprudence on De Jure* and *De Facto* Discrimination', in: Federico Ortino and Ernst-Ulrich Petersmann (eds.), *The WTO Dispute Settlement System 1995–2003* (The Hague: Kluwer Law International, 2004), pp. 217–62.

Basic Legal Instruments for the Liberalisation of Trade – A Comparative Analysis of EC and WTO Law (Oxford: Hart Publishing, 2004).

'From "Non-discrimination" to "Reasonableness": A Paradigm Shift in International Economic Law?', *Jean Monnet Working Paper No. 01/05* (2005), available at SSRN http://ssrn.com/abstract=922524.

'Treaty Interpretation and the WTO Appellate Body Report in *US – Gambling*: A Critique', **9** *Journal of International Economic Law* (2006) 117–48.

'The Principle of Non-Discrimination and its Exceptions in GATS: Selected Legal Issues', in: Kern Alexander and Mads Andenas (eds.), *The World Trade Organization and Trade in Services* (Leiden: Martinus Nijhoff Publishers, 2008), pp. 173–204.

Pauletto, Christian, 'Comment: Digital Trade: Technology versus Legislators', in: Marion Panizzon, Nicole Pohl and Pierre Sauvé (eds.), *GATS and the Regulation of International Trade in Services* (Cambridge University Press, 2008), pp. 530–33.

Pauwelyn, Joost, 'Evidence, Proof and Persuasion in WTO Dispute Settlement – Who Bears the Burden?', **1** *Journal of International Economic Law* (1998) 227–58.

'The WTO Agreement on Sanitary and Phytosanitary (SPS) Measures as Applied in the First Three SPS Disputes', **2** *Journal of International Economic Law* (1999) 641–64.

'Recent Books on Trade and Environment: GATT Phantoms Still Haunt the WTO', **15** *European Journal of International Law* (2004) 575–92.

'Rien ne Va Plus? Distinguishing Domestic Regulation from Market Access in GATT and GATS', **4** *World Trade Review* (2005) 131–70.

'Comment: The Unbearable Lightness of Likeness', in: Marion Panizzon, Nicole Pohl and Pierre Sauvé (eds.), *GATS and the Regulation of International Trade in Services* (Cambridge University Press, 2008), pp. 358–69.

Peritz, Rudolph J. R., *Competition Policy in America – History, Rhetoric, Law* (Oxford University Press, 1996).

Peters, Anne, 'Die Strukturähnlichkeit der Diskriminierungsverbote im Menschenrechtsbereich und im Welthandelsrecht – Eine exemplarische Prüfung der Fragmentierungsthese', in: Stephan Breitenmoser, Bernhard Ehrenzeller, Marco Sassòli, Walter Stoffel and Beatrice Wagner Pfeifer (eds.), *Human Rights, Democracy and the Rule of Law / Menschenrechte, Demokratie und Rechtsstaat / Droits de l'homme, démocratie et état de droit: Liber Amicorum Luzius Wildhaber* (Zurich: DIKE/Nomos, 2007), pp. 551–93.

Petersmann, Ernst-Ulrich, 'Economic, Legal and Political Functions of the Principle of Non-discrimination', **9** *The World Economy* (1986) 113–21.

Pillai, Rajesh, 'Book Review: Gaëtan Verhoosel, National Treatment and WTO Dispute Settlement', **1** *World Trade Review* (2002) 321–43.

Piraino, Thomas A., 'Identifying Monopolists' Exclusionary Conduct under the Sherman Act', **75** *New York University Law Review* (2000) 809–92.

Pitofsky, Robert, 'New Definitions of Relevant Market and the Assault on Antitrust', **90** *Columbia Law Review* (1990) 1805–64.

Pitschas, Christian, 'Übereinkommen über den Handel mit Dienstleistungen (GATS)', in: Hans-Joachim Prieß and Georg M. Berrisch (eds.), *WTO-Handbuch – World Trade Organisation* (Munich: Verlag C.H. Beck, 2003).

'Subventionen, Schutzmaßnahmen und öffentliche Auftragsvergabe', in: Dirk Ehlers, Hans-Michael Wolffgang and Marc Lechleitner (eds.), *Rechtsfragen des internationalen Dienstleistungsverkehrs – Tagungsband zum 10. Münsteraner Außenwirtschaftsrechtstag* (Frankfurt a.M.: Verlag Recht und Wirtschaft, 2006), pp. 103–27.

Poretti, Pietro, 'Waiting for Godot: Subsidy Disciplines in Services Trade', in: Marion Panizzon, Nicole Pohl and Pierre Sauvé (eds.), *GATS and the Regulation of International Trade in Services* (Cambridge University Press, 2008), pp. 466–88.

Porges, Amelia and Joel P. Trachtman, 'Robert Hudec and Domestic Regulation: The Resurrection of Aim and Effects', **37** *Journal of World Trade* (2003) 783–99.

Posner, Richard A., *Antitrust Law*, 2nd edition (Chicago, IL: University of Chicago Press, 2001).

Potts, Jason, *The Legality of PPMs under the GATT: Challenges and Opportunities for Sustainable Trade Policy* (Winnipeg: International Institute for Sustainable Development 2008), available at www.iisd.org/pdf/2008/ppms_gatt.pdf.

Puth, Sebastian, *WTO und Umwelt: Die Produkt-Prozess-Doktrin* (Berlin: Duncker & Humblot, 2003).

Qin, Julia Ya, 'Defining Nondiscrimination under the Law of the World Trade Organization', **23** *Boston University International Law Journal* (2005) 215–97.

Quick, Reinhard and Christian Lau, 'Environmentally Motivated Tax Distinctions and WTO Law – The European Commission's Green Paper on Integrated Product Policy in Light of the "Like Product" and "PPM" Debates', **6** *Journal of International Economic Law* (2003) 419–58.

Qureshi, Asif H., *Interpreting WTO Agreements – Problems and Perspectives* (Cambridge University Press, 2006).

Read, Robert, 'Like Products, Health & Environmental Exceptions: The Interpretation of PPMs in Recent WTO Trade Dispute Cases', **5** *Estey Centre Journal of International Law and Trade Policy* (2004) 123–46.

Regan, Donald H., 'Regulatory Purpose and "Like Products" in Article III:4 of the GATT (With Additional Remarks on Article III:2)', **36** *Journal of World Trade* (2002) 443–78.

'Further Thoughts on the Role of Regulatory Purpose under Article III of the General Agreement on Tariffs and Trade: A Tribute to Bob Hudec', **37** *Journal of World Trade* (2003) 737–60.

Rege, Vinod, 'GATT Law and Environment-Related Issues Affecting the Trade of Developing Countries', **28**(3) *Journal of World Trade* (1994) 95–169.

Reyna, Jimmie V., 'Services', in: Terence P Stewart (ed.), *The GATT Uruguay Round – A Negotiating History (1986–1992): Commentary*, vol. II (Deventer: Kluwer Law and Taxation Publishers, 1993).

Rhoodie, Eschel M., *Discrimination in the Constitutions of the World: A Study of the Group Rights Problem* (Columbus, GA: Brentwood, 1984).

Roessler, Frieder, 'Diverging Domestic Policies and Multilateral Trade Integration', in: Jagdish N. Bhagwati and Robert E. Hudec (eds.), *Fair Trade and Harmonization – Prerequisites For Free Trade?*, vol. II: Legal analysis (Cambridge, MA: MIT Press, 1996), pp. 21–56.

'Beyond the Ostensible – A Tribute to Professor Robert Hudec's Insight on the Determination of the Likeness of Products under the National Treatment Provisions of the General Agreement on Tariffs and Trade', **37** *Journal of World Trade* (2003) 771–81.

Rose, Vivien and Peter QC Roth, 'The Treaty and its Territorial Reach', in: Peter QC Roth and Vivien Rose (eds.), *Bellamy & Child European Community Law of Competition*, 6th edition (Oxford University Press, 2008), pp. 1–90.

Rule, Charles F. and David L. Meyer, 'An Antitrust Enforcement Policy to Maximize the Economic Wealth of all Consumers', in: Thomas E. Sullivan (ed.), *The Political Economy of the Sherman Act – The First One Hundred Years* (New York, NY: Oxford University Press, 1991), pp. 210–26.

Sampson, Gary P. and Richard H. Snape, 'Identifying the Issues in Trade in Services', **8** *The World Economy* (1985) 171–82.

Sandrock, Otto, 'Grundprobleme der sachlichen Marktabgrenzung', in: Hans Merz and Walter R. Schluep (eds.), *Recht und Wirtschaft heute, Festgabe Max Kummer* (Berne: Stämpfli, 1980), pp. 449–86.

Sauvant, Karl P., 'The Tradability of Services', in: Patrick A Messerlin and Karl P. Sauvant (eds.), *The Uruguay Round: Services in the World Economy* (Washington DC: World Bank/The United Nations Centre on Transnational Corporations, 1990), pp. 114–22.

Sauvignon, Édouard, *La Clause de la Nation la Plus Favorisée* (Grenoble: Presses Universitaires de Grenoble, 1972).

Schefer, Krista N., *International Trade in Financial Services: The NAFTA Provisions* (The Hague: Kluwer Law International, 1999).

Schiek, Dagmar and Victoria Chege (eds.), *European Union Non-Discrimination Law: Comparative Perspectives on Multidimensional Equality Law* (London: Routledge-Cavendish, 2009).

Schlagenhof, Markus, 'Trade Measures Based on Environmental Process and Production Methods', **29**(6) *Journal of World Trade* (1995) 123–55.

Schwartz, Warren F. and Alan O. Sykes, 'The Economics of the Most-Favoured-Nation Clause', in: Jagdeep S. Bhandari and Alan O. Sykes (eds.), *Economic Dimensions in International Law: Comparative and Empirical Perspectives* (Cambridge University Press, 1997), pp. 43–79.

Seibert-Fohr, Anja, 'Commentary to Article 2 SPS (basic rights and obligations)', in: Rüdiger Wolfrum, Peter-Tobias Stoll and Anja Seibert-Fohr (eds.), *WTO – Technical Barriers and SPS Measures: Max Planck Commentaries on World Trade Law*, vol. 3 (Leiden: Martinus Nijhoff Publishers, 2007), pp. 392–411.

Senti, Richard, *WTO – System und Funktionsweise der Welthandelsordnung* (Zurich: Schulthess & Verlag Österreich, 2000).

Slotboom, Marco M., 'Do Different Treaty Purposes Matter for Treaty Interpretation? – The Elimination of Discriminatory Internal Taxes in EC and WTO Law', **4** *Journal of International Economic Law* (2001) 557–79.

Smith, Fiona and Lorna Woods, 'A Distinction Without a Difference: Exploring the Boundary Between Goods and Services in the World Trade Organization and the European Union', **12** *Columbia Journal of European Law* (2005) 1–51.

Snape, Richard H., 'Principles in Trade in Services', in: Patrick A. Messerlin and Karl P. Sauvant (eds.), *The Uruguay Round: Services in the World Economy* (Washington DC: World Bank/The United Nations Centre on Transnational Corporations, 1990), pp. 5–11.

Srinivasan, Thirukodikaval N., 'Nondiscrimination in GATT/WTO: Was There Anything to Begin With and Is There Anything Left?', **4** *World Trade Review* (2005) 69–95.

Stadler, Christoph, *Die Liberalisierung des Dienstleistungshandels am Beispiel der Versicherungen: Kernelemente bilateraler und multilateraler Ordnungsrahmen einschliesslich des GATS* (Berlin: Duncker & Humblot, 1992).

Stewart, Taimoon, 'The Fate of Competition Policy in Cancun: Politics or Substance?', **31** *Legal Issues of Economic Integration* (2004) 7–12.

Stewart, Terence P. and David P. Mueller, 'Commentary to Article 2 ADA (determination of dumping)', in: Rüdiger Wolfrum, Peter-Tobias Stoll and Clemens Feinäugle (eds.), *WTO – Trade Remedies: Max Planck Commentaries on World Trade Law*, vol. 4 (Leiden: Martinus Nijhoff Publishers, 2008), pp. 11–46.

Stilwell, Matthew and Jan Bohanes, 'Trade and the Environment', in: Patrick F. J. Macrory, Arthur E. Appleton and Michael G. Plummer (eds.), *The World Trade Organization: Legal, Economic and Political Analysis*, vol. II (New York, NY: Springer, 2005), pp. 511–69.

Stoll, Peter-Tobias and Frank Schorkopf, *WTO – World Economic Order, World Trade Law: Max Planck Commentaries on World Trade Law*, vol. 1 (Leiden: Martinus Nijhoff Publishers, 2006).

Sullivan, Lawrence A. and Warren S. Grimes, *The Law of Antitrust: An Integrated Handbook*, 2nd edition (St. Paul, MN: Thomson/West, 2006).

Sullivan, Thomas E. and Jeffrey L. Harrison, *Understanding Antitrust and its Economic Implications*, 4th edition (Newark, NJ: Lexisnexis, 2003).

Sullivan, Thomas E. (ed.), *The Political Economy of the Sherman Act – The First One Hundred Years* (New York, NY: Oxford University Press, 1991).

Swanson, Steven R., 'Concepts of Similarity and Indirect Protection under EEC Treaty Article 95: The Alcohol Cases', **15** *Vanderbilt Journal of Transnational Law* (1982) 277–308.

Swinbank, Alan, 'Like Products, Animal Welfare and the World Trade Organization', **40** *Journal of World Trade* (2006) 687–711.

Sykes, Alan O., 'Comparative Advantage and the Normative Economics of International Trade Policy', **1** *Journal of International Economic Law* (1998) 49–82.

'Regulatory Protectionism and the Law of International Trade', **66** *University of Chicago Law Review* (1999) 1–46.

'International Trade: Trade Remedies', in: Andrew T. Guzman and Alan O. Sykes (eds.), *Research Handbook in International Economic Law* (Cheltenham: Edward Elgar Publishing, 2007), pp. 62–150.

Tamiotti, Ludivine, 'Commentary to Article 2 TBT (preparation, adoption and application of technical regulations)', in: Rüdiger Wolfrum, Peter-Tobias Stoll and Anja Seibert-Fohr (eds.), *WTO – Technical Barriers and SPS Measures: Max Planck Commentaries on World Trade Law*, vol. 3 (Leiden: Martinus Nijhoff Publishers, 2007), pp. 210–34.

Terry, Laurel S., 'But what will the WTO Disciplines Apply to? Distinguishing Among Market Access, National Treatment and Article VI:4 Measures when Applying the GATS to Legal Services', *Professional Lawyer* (2003) 83–114.

Thagesen, Rikke and Alan Matthews, 'The EU's Common Banana Regime: An Initial Evaluation', **35** *Journal of Common Market Studies* (1997) 615–27.

Thaggert, Henry L., 'A closer look at the Tuna–Dolphin Case: "Like Products" and "Extra jurisdictionality" in the Trade and Environment Context', in: James Cameron, Paul Demaret and Damien Geradin, *Trade & The Environment: The Search for Balance*, vol. 1 (London: Cameron May, 1994), 69–95.

Tietje, Christian, *Normative Grundstrukturen der Behandlung nichttarifärer Handelshemmnisse in der WTO/GATT-Rechtsordnung* (Berlin: Duncker & Humblot, 1998).

'Stärken und Schwächen des GATS', in: Dirk Ehlers, Hans-Michael Wolffgang and Marc Lechleitner (eds.), *Rechtsfragen des internationalen Dienstleistungsverkehrs – Tagungsband zum 10. Münsteraner Außenwirtschaftsrechtstag* (Frankfurt a.M.: Verlag Recht und Wirtschaft, 2006), pp. 7–25.

Trachtman, Joel P., 'Lessons for the GATS From Existing WTO Rules on Domestic Regulation', in: Aaditya Mattoo and Pierre Sauvé (eds.), *Domestic Regulation and Service Trade Liberalization* (Washington DC: World Bank & Oxford University Press, 2003), pp. 57–81.

'The Agency Model of Judging in Economic Integration: Balancing Responsabilities', in: Thomas Cottier and Petros C Mavroidis (eds.), *The Role of the Judge in International Trade Regulation – Experience and Lessons for the WTO* (Ann Arbor, MI: University of Michigan Press, 2003), pp. 135–50.

Trebilcock, Michael, 'Competition Policy and Trade Policy – Mediating the Interface', **30**(4) *Journal of World Trade* (1996) 71–106.

Trebilcock, Michael J. and Shiva K. Giri, 'The National Treatment Principle in International Trade Law', *American Law & Economics Association Annual Meetings* (2004), available at http://law.bepress.com/cgi/viewcontent.cgi?article=1007&context=alea; reprinted in: E. Kwan Choi/James C. Hartigan (eds.), *Handbook of International Trade*, vol. II (Blackwell Publishing, 2004).

Trebilcock, Michael J. and Robert Howse, *The Regulation of International Trade*, 3rd edition (London: Routledge, 2005).

Trebilcock, Michael J. and Michael Fishbein, 'International Trade: Barriers to Trade', in: Andrew T. Guzman and Alan O. Sykes (eds.), *Research Handbook in International Economic Law* (Cheltenham: Edward Elgar Publishing, 2007), pp. 1–61.

Tsai, Edward S, '"Like" is a four-letter word-GATT Article III's "Like Product" Conundrum', **17** *Berkeley Journal of International Law* (1999) 26–60.

Verhoosel, Gaëtan, *National Treatment and WTO Dispute Settlement – Adjudicating the Boundaries of Regulatory Autonomy* (Oxford: Hart Publishing, 2002).

Vermulst, Edwin and Paul Waer, *E.C. Anti-Dumping Law and Practice* (London: Sweet & Maxwell, 1996).

Vranes, Erich, *Trade and the Environment: Fundamental Issues in International Law, WTO Law, and Legal Theory* (Oxford University Press, 2009).

Waldmann, Bernhard, *Das Diskriminierungsverbot von Art. 8 Abs. 2 BV als besonderer Gleichheitssatz – unter besonderer Berücksichtigung der völkerrechtlichen Diskriminierungsverbote einerseits und der Rechtslage in den USA, in Deutschland, Frankreich sowie dem europäischen Gemeinschaftsrecht andererseits* (Berne: Staempfli Verlag, 2003).

Wang, Yi, 'Most-Favoured-Nation Treatment under the General Agreement on Trade in Services – And its Application in Financial Services', **30**(1) *Journal of World Trade* (1996) 91–124.

Warner, Mark A., 'After Seattle: Is There a Future for Trade and Competition Policy Rule-Making?', **26** *Brooklyn Journal of International Law* (2000) 307–62.

Weber, Rolf H., 'International E-Trade', **41** *International Lawyer* (2007) 845–72.

Weiler, Joseph H., 'The Constitution of the Common Market Place: Text and Context in the Evolution of the Free Movement of Goods', in: Paul Craig and Gráinne De Búrca (eds.), *The Evolution of EU Law* (Oxford University Press 1999), pp. 349–76.

Weiler, Todd, 'Prohibitions Against Discrimination in NAFTA Chapter 11', in: Todd Weiler (ed.), *NAFTA Investment Law and Arbitration: Past Issues, Current Practice, Future Prospects* (Ardsley, NY: Transnational Publishers, 2004), pp. 27–48.

'Saving Oscar Chin: Non-Discrimination in International Investment Law', in: Todd Weiler (ed.), *International Investment Law and Arbitration: Leading Cases from the ICSID, NAFTA, Bilateral Treaties and Customary International Law* (London: Cameron May, 2005), pp. 557–96.

Weiss, Friedl, 'The General Agreement on Trade in Services 1994', **32** *Common Market Law Review* (1995) 1177–225.

Weitbrecht, Andreas, 'From Freiburg to Chicago and Beyond – The First 50 Years of European Competition Law', **29** *European Competition Law Review* (2008) 81–88.

Werden, Gregory J., 'Market Delineation and the Justice Department's Merger Guidelines', *Duke Law Journal* (1983) 514–79.

'The History of Antitrust Market Delineation', **76** *Marquette Law Review* (1992) 123–215.

'Demand Elasticities in Antitrust Analysis', *Antitrust Law Journal* (1998) 363–409.

Westen, Peter, *Speaking of Equality: An Analysis of the Rhetorical Force of Equality in Moral and Legal Discourse* (Princeton, NJ: Princeton University Press, 1990).

White, Lawrence J., 'Market Power and Market Definition in Monopolization Cases', in: Wayne Dale Collins (ed.), *Issues in Competition Law and Policy*, vol. II (Chicago, IL: ABA Section of Antitrust Law, 2008), pp. 913–24.

Wiedemann, Gerhard, 'Das Verbot des Mißbrauchs marktbeherrschender Stellungen im deutschen Kartellrecht', in: Gerhard Wiedemann (ed.), *Handbuch des Kartellrechts*, 2nd edition (Munich: C.H. Beck, 2008).

Wilsher, Daniel, 'Does Keck Discrimination Make any Sense? An Assessment of the Non-Discrimination Principle within the European Single Market', **33** *European Law Review* (2008) 3–22.

Wolfrum, Rüdiger, 'Commentary to Article II GATS (most-favoured-nation treatment)', in: Rüdiger Wolfrum, Peter-Tobias Stoll and Clemens Feinäugle (eds.), *WTO – Trade in Services: Max Planck Commentaries on World Trade Law*, vol. 6 (Leiden: Martinus Nijhoff Publishers, 2008), pp. 71–91.

Wolfrum, R üdiger, Peter-Tobias Stoll and Clemens Fein äugle (eds.), *WTO – Trade Remedies: Max Planck Commentaries on World Trade Law*, vol. 4 (Leiden: Martinus Nijhoff Publishers, 2008).

Wouters, Jan and Dominic Coppens, 'GATS and Domestic Regulation', in: Kern Alexander and Mads Andenas (eds.), *The World Trade Organization and Trade in Services* (Leiden: Martinus Nijhoff Publishers, 2008), pp. 207–63.

WTO-Secretariat, *A Handbook on the GATS Agreement* (Cambridge University Press, 2005).

Wunsch-Vincent, Sacha, *The WTO, the Internet and Trade in Digital Products: EC-US Perspectives* (Oxford: Hart Publishing, 2006).

'The Internet, Cross-Border Trade in Services, and the GATS: Lessons from US-Gambling', **5** *World Trade Review* (2006) 319–55.

'Trade Rules for the Digital Age', in: Marion Panizzon, Nicole Pohl and Pierre Sauvé (eds.), *GATS and the Regulation of International Trade in Services* (Cambridge University Press, 2008), pp. 497–529.

Wyss, David, *Bankdienstleistungen im Allgemeinen Dienstleistungsabkommen der WTO – Auswirkungen auf das schweizerische Bankenrecht* (Berne: Peter Lang, 1999).

Zacharias, Diana, 'Commentary to Article I GATS (scope and definition)', in: Rüdiger Wolfrum, Peter-Tobias Stoll and Clemens Feinäugle (eds.), *WTO – Trade in Services: Max Planck Commentaries on World Trade Law*, vol. 6 (Leiden: Martinus Nijhoff Publishers, 2008), pp. 31–69.

Zdouc, Werner, 'WTO Dispute Settlement Practice Relating to the GATS', **2** *Journal of International Economic Law* (1999) 295–346.

Legal Problems Arising under the General Agreement on Trade in Services – Comparative Analysis of GATS and GATT (Bamberg: Difo-Druck, 2002).

'WTO Dispute Settlement Practice Relating to the General Agreement on Trade in Services', in: Federico Ortino and Ernst-Ulrich Petersmann (eds.), *The WTO Dispute Settlement System 1995–2003* (The Hague: Kluwer Law International, 2004), pp. 381–420.

'Streitigkeiten über den Dienstleistungsverkehr vor dem DSB', in: Dirk Ehlers, Hans-Michael Wolffgang and Marc Lechleitner (eds.), *Rechtsfragen des internationalen Dienstleistungsverkehrs – Tagungsband zum 10. Münsteraner Außenwirtschaftsrechtstag* (Frankfurt a.M.: Verlag Recht und Wirtschaft, 2006), pp. 129–42.

Zedalis, Rex J., 'A Theory of the GATT "Like" Product Common Language Cases', **27** *Vanderbilt Journal of Transnational Law* (1994) 33–134.

'Product v. Non-Product Based Distinctions in GATT Article III Trade and Environment Jurisprudence: Recent Developments', **6** *European Environmental Law Review* (1997) 108–12.

Zleptnig, Stefan, 'The GATS and Internet-Based Services: Between Market Access and Domestic Regulation', in: Kern Alexander and Mads Andenas (eds.), *The World Trade Organization and Trade in Services* (Leiden: Martinus Nijhoff Publishers, 2008), pp. 381–410.

INDEX